ROLL THE BONES

THE

HISTORY

OF GAMBLING

ROLL THE BONES

David G. Schwartz

GOTHAM BOOKS

GOTHAM BOOKS
Published by Penguin Group (USA) Inc.
375 Hudson Street, New York, New York 10014, U.S.A.
Penguin Group (Canada), 90 Eglinton Avenue East, Suite 700, Toronto, Ontario M4P 2Y3, Canada
(a division of Pearson Penguin Canada Inc.); Penguin Books Ltd, 80 Strand, London WC2R 0RL,
England; Penguin Ireland, 25 St Stephen's Green, Dublin 2, Ireland (a division of Penguin Books Ltd);
Penguin Group (Australia), 250 Camberwell Road, Camberwell, Victoria 3124, Australia (a division of
Pearson Australia Group Pty Ltd); Penguin Books India Pvt Ltd, 11 Community Centre, Panchsheel
Park, New Delhi – 110 017, India; Penguin Group (NZ), cnr Airborne and Rosedale Roads,
Albany, Auckland 1310, New Zealand (a division of Pearson New Zealand Ltd); Penguin Books
(South Africa) (Pty) Ltd, 24 Sturdee Avenue, Rosebank, Johannesburg 2196, South Africa

Penguin Books Ltd, Registered Offices: 80 Strand, London WC2R 0RL, England

Published by Gotham Books, a division of Penguin Group (USA) Inc.

First printing, October 2006
1   3   5   7   9   10   8   6   4   2

Photo credits are listed on pages 547–549 and constitute an extension of the copyright page.

Gotham Books and the skyscraper logo are trademarks of Penguin Group (USA) Inc.

LIBRARY OF CONGRESS CATALOGING-IN-PUBLICATION DATA

Schwartz, David G., 1973–
Roll the bones : the history of gambling / David G. Schwartz.
p.   cm.
Includes bibliographical references.
ISBN 1-592-40208-9 (hardcover)
1. Gambling—History.   I. Title.
HV6710.S38 2006
795.09—dc22
2006017509

Printed in the United States of America
Set in Adobe Caslon
Designed by Elke Sigal

While the author has made every effort to provide accurate telephone numbers and Internet addresses
at the time of publication, neither the publisher nor the author assumes any responsibility for errors,
or for changes that occur after publication. Further, the publisher does not have any control over
and does not assume any responsibility for author or third-party Web sites or their content.

For Eric H. Monkkonen (1942–2005),
my dissertation advisor, mentor, and friend

CONTENTS

◆ ◆ ◆

CONTENTS

◆ ◆ ◆

CONTENTS

◆ ◆ ◆

FOREWORD

by James McManus

◆ ◆ ◆

Whoever wants to know the heart and mind of earth's citizens needs to understand gambling. In every tribe and country today, physical games represent, and often have startling price tags attached to, hunter and warrior skills. Why? Because our ancestors depended for their survival on the ability of a few elite males to run fast and wield lethal projectiles, against either wild animals or enemy tribesmen. Today's athletes mimic those feats in symbolic rituals, sometimes called games, while the rest of us make financial and emotional wagers on the outcome. At a higher symbolic level, cerebral games like poker, chess, bridge, and what we call "handicapping" mimic what scouts, hunting-party leaders, tribal chiefs and—nowadays—team captains, coaches, generals, and presidents do. While our physical and mental skill sets both continue to evolve, the competitive goal deep in our cells feels pretty much the same as it did twenty thousand years ago on the African savannah—not starving to death or getting eaten alive by hyenas, or pillaged and raped by the guys from across the river. Go, team! Who's your daddy? She's all in! He scores!

David Schwartz's comprehensive new history illuminates these feelings and behaviors as no book before it. He has marshaled evidence from hundreds of sources and deftly braided it into a five-thousand-year saga of risk and reward. From the gambler's hymn in the *Rig Veda* in the third millennium B.C. through cockfights and dice games and bullfights all the way up to Internet gambling and $2 billion casinos, Schwartz provides the telling anecdotes and clinching minutiae to help us understand the risk-taking fervor that destroys many lives but advances human civilization.

In America, the story begins rather late but it picks up steam—and big bucks—in a hurry. From Puritan whist tables, Mississippi riverboats, and Gold Rush saloons to Wall Street, Las Vegas, and Internet gambling sites, the ways we've done battle and business and explored our vast continent have echoed, and been echoed *by*, our risk-loving acumen. We now host *two* annual World Series in which the players wear sunglasses, sateen jackets, and baseball caps. In both contests luck, probability, decoys, position, and stealing are critical. One game seems to have been invented near New York just before the Civil War, the other in New Orleans during the Jefferson administration. In 2006 they continue to vie for the title of national pastime, while the older game seems poised to become the planet's main gambling contest.

In the meantime our judges and presidents gamble, Tony Soprano hosts the executive seven-card stud game, and professional athletes wager long money on whose suitcase will appear first on the airport carousel. (Michael Jordan, for one, liked to tip the baggage handlers beforehand.) Poker and football are avidly contested on Super Bowl Sunday, everyone bets on March Madness, and winners get showered with endorsements and take star turns on Leno and Letterman. In many jurisdictions, however, even low-stakes action is subject to raids by police.

More than a few folks believe that gambling isn't natural or virtuous. For a long time it went hand in hand with hard liquor, foul cigars, loose women, and concealed weapons. Even today, gamblers either lose money or take other people's—not by hard, honest toil, but by cunning and ruthlessness. This helps to explain why the two main strains of our heritage will forever be in conflict. But the risk-averse Puritan work ethic has taken the American people at least as far as the frontiersman's urge to light out and seize the main chance; in balance, they've made us who we are.

Our ambivalence about games becomes more pronounced as the possibility of cheating increases. In 1861 a British vessel bearing Confederate envoys across the Atlantic was intercepted by a Yankee captain, creating a problem that threatened to bring England into the war on the side of the South. "One war at a time" was President Lincoln's rationale as he freed the ambassadors. Lesser politicians demanded to know whether he would also apologize to the Crown. Said Lincoln: "Your question reminds me of an incident which occurred out west. Two roughs were playing cards for high stakes, when one of them, suspecting his adversary of foul play, straightway drew his bowie-knife from his belt and pinned the hand of the other player upon the table, exclaiming, 'If you haven't got the ace of spades under your palm, I'll apologize.'"

Young Dwight D. Eisenhower courted Mamie Doud with his poker winnings. As supreme allied commander, he outfoxed the Nazis on D-day, and as president he pulled off a nuclear bluff against Mao over Quemoy and Matsu. He got called, however, by Khrushchev when a U-2 "weather plane" was shot down in Soviet airspace. His vice president, Richard Nixon, had won enough playing five-card stud in the navy to finance his first congressional campaign. Atop the Republican ticket, however, both men downplayed their poker credentials, fearing they would alienate voters. Hearing this, one of Nixon's professors at Whittier College remarked, "A man who couldn't hold his own in a first-class poker game isn't fit to be president of the United States."

In November 2000, with our country's line of succession up for grabs for the first time since 1789, supreme courts in Tallahassee and Washington decreed whether chads had been dimpled or pregnant, noodged, or in some cases, eaten. In other recounts, the lead in New Mexico changed hands three times, with one count putting Al Gore ahead of George W. Bush by four votes. If the final tally had ended in a tie, New Mexico's constitution declared that its electoral votes would go to the winner of a mutually agreed-upon game of chance. No-limit Texas hold'em, anyone?

In a more recent showdown, generals commanded by President Bush deployed desert-camouflage decks to target the fifty-two most-wanted Baathists. Mr. Bush had implied he would call France's bluff in a UN Security Council vote on whether to support the invasion of Iraq. "It's time," he said, "for people to show their cards." Meanwhile, many wonder whether Mr. Bush has artfully countered the bargaining chips in Iranian and North Korean arsenals while playing "Plutonium Poker." (The term is Fred Kaplan's, in Slate.com.) Pyongyang, Tehran, Al-Qaeda, and Iraqi insurgents all may remind us of what the Texas oilman Crandall Addington said during the 1981 World Series: "Limit poker is a science, but no-limit is an art. In limit, you are shooting at a target. In no-limit, the target comes alive and shoots back at you."

Our keenest observer of all, Alexis de Tocqueville, wrote this in *Democracy in America*: "Those living in the instability of a democracy have the constant image of chance before them, and, in the end, they come to like all those projects in which chance plays a part." This was true, he deduced, "not only because of the promise of profit but because they like the emotions evoked." It remains unclear which gambling games Tocqueville had witnessed, but the perceptive Frenchman came to appreciate our allegiance to chance while traveling in 1831 aboard the steamboat *Louisville* along the Mississippi River, the original American mainstream.

In the pages that follow, David Schwartz follows through and expands upon Tocqueville's insight. And he makes clear that it's not just Americans who like rolling the bones. Mesopotamians were casting colored stones and *astragali* (the huckle bones of sheep) for edification and profit long before dice, cards, or numbers were invented. Several millenniums later, in every quadrant of the globe, games of chance continue to feature erotic, mathematical, fiduciary, and religious components. It's no exaggeration at all to say that human beings adore them.

And if Thomas Friedman is right when he argues that the world is flat, the gambling world's even flatter. My opponents this morning on Poker-Stars.com, for example, include "birdwings" from Lebanon, "boxclock" from Glenview, "dedor" from Tel Aviv and "wasp" from County Derry. As we chat and compete, they could be sitting in front of a desktop computer at home or a laptop three gates down the concourse from me. Next week, two or more of us might be sitting elbow to elbow at the live event hosted by PokerStars in the Bahamas, a tournament played mostly by people who won their $8,000 seat on the site. The prize money will be deposited in PokerStars accounts then recirculate back into—where?

A lot of folks besides federal prosecutors wonder exactly where all of this virtual action takes place. In a cable submerged 619 miles ENE of Paradise Island? Well, not exactly. The home office may be on the Isle of Man, the hardware on an Indian reservation in Canada, with most of the staff working in a call center in Hyderabad, India. The players are in twenty-four time zones across all six inhabited continents and on scores of ships at sea.

Dice and decks of cards may be illegal these days in most of modern Mesopotamia—they certainly are in Iran—but surely someone over there will snag a satellite hookup and sit down this morning to play with us.

PROLOGUE

The Rainmaker Reborn

• • •

June 5, 1637. The Puritans are on the march, and for the Pequot of the Connecticut River Valley, the world is ending.

Pequot translates as "destroyer" in the Algonquian language, and the name underscores that nation's fearsome reputation. Centuries ago, the Pequot and Mohegan had migrated together into Connecticut from the Hudson River Valley, then split into two warring tribes. When not warring with the Mohegan and Narragansett, the Pequot collect tribute from surrounding villages whose residents cringe with fear at the mention of the Pequot and their fierce sachem Sassacus. But as the "Great Migration" of Puritans overspills its original plantings at Massachusetts Bay, the encroachments of the English colonists begin to threaten Pequot dominance of the area. A showdown is inevitable.

An escalating series of kidnappings, raids, and assaults soon leads to open warfare between the Pequot and English. Years earlier, the newcomers had celebrated the first Thanksgiving by feasting on wild turkey and venison with their new Indian neighbors. Now, old friendships are forgotten in the name of expansion, and English guns are matched against the legendary ferocity of the Pequot.

Initially, the Pequot fares well. But by May 1637, English forces led by Captain John Mason had allied with the Mohegan and Narragansett, who had earlier rebuffed a Pequot overture to join a pan-Indian alliance and drive the invaders into the sea. Together, the English and their allies had launched damaging counterattacks and begun to turn the tide against the Pequot.

On that fateful June day, Mason leads 150 Englishmen and sixty Mohegan warriors under the command of the sachem Uncas against the fortified Pequot village at Mystic. After firing their muskets on the palisades, the English burst through the wall into the village itself. Crying, "We must burn them!" Mason touches a firebrand to a wigwam, then leads a retreat from the village. The English and their Indian allies form a ring around the palisades, watching as flames swiftly overrun the fort "to the extream Amazement of the Enemy, and the great Rejoycing of ourselves," according to Mason. The blaze spreads rapidly that hot and dry morning; the entire village is soon afire. The English indiscriminately shoot at Pequot fleeing the conflagration and cut down with swords those who escape the burning palisades. In less than an hour, as many as seven hundred Pequot men, women, and children perish.

Mason has obliterated a major Pequot village and snapped the will of the Pequot fighters. Over the next few months, the colonists and their Indian allies track down, capture, and kill the remaining Pequot. Captives are dispersed as slaves among surrounding tribes, in English households, and as far south as the Caribbean. The Mohegan kill the terrible Sassacus in August, sending his head to the English at Hartford as a gesture of friendship. The Pequot power is broken.

In the peace settlement of September 21, 1638, the English and their Indian allies agree that the Pequot must never threaten revenge. The victors prohibit any survivors from speaking the Pequot language or even identifying themselves as Pequot. The river that bears their name is renamed the Thames, and their eponymous central village is rechristened New London. The Connecticut countryside, which once reverberated with the sounds of Pequot warriors demanding tribute, fears them no more.

February 6, 2004. A nation has risen from the ashes.

Popular comedian Chris Rock entertains a crowd paying as much as $110 per ticket at the Fox Theater, a venue that casino icon Frank Sinatra opened in 1993. On this night, Rock is simply one attraction at Foxwoods Resort Casino, a collection of six casinos with 350 table games and 6,400 slot machines, the world's largest bingo hall, over fourteen hundred rooms and suites, twenty-four restaurants (including the aptly named Rainmaker Café), a convention center, a four-thousand-seat arena, and a championship golf course, all rising incongruously out of the once quiet woods near Ledyard, Connecticut.

While the God-fearing Puritans would be aghast at the notion that a 4.7-million-square-foot complex dedicated to pleasure and indulgence had been erected in their former dominion, they would be positively mortified that the Mashantucket Pequot, a resurgent remnant of the tribe they had attempted to wipe from history, owned it. Nearly four centuries after their supposed eradication, the descendants of Sassacus no longer send war parties to neighboring villages to collect tribute; instead, forty-thousand visitors come to Foxwoods each day, leaving somewhere in the neighborhood of $67 million in monthly slot losses as tribute. Of this, a cut of about $16.5 million is forwarded to the state of Connecticut for the privilege of operating the casino.

The Pequot had an improbable journey back from obscurity. Granted two reservations in 1683, the tribe's membership declined precipitously over the next three centuries; by 1910, only three families lived on the Ledyard reservation, which had been reduced to less than two hundred acres. But in 1983, tribal chairman Skip Hayward, assisted by Indian rights attorney Tom Tureen, won the tribe federal recognition over the initial veto of President Ronald Reagan. The sovereign tribe started offering high-stakes bingo in a hastily constructed hall in 1986. This humble start would ultimately yield the world's most profitable casino. In 1992, after striking a compact with the state of Connecticut, the tribe added table games, and in the following year, its slot machines started accepting coins. Since then, the casino has expanded regularly, clogging Route 2 with traffic that was unimaginable a scant decade earlier. Although most visitors hail from New York and New England, travelers from as far as Abu Dhabi, Taiwan, and Singapore arrive weekly for flings at fate. Foxwoods is a truly cosmopolitan island in the New England woods—even the money to build Foxwoods came from Malaysian multibillionaire Lim Goh Tong, owner of that country's monopoly casino, Genting Highlands.

As purveyors of casino entertainment and collectors of tribute, the Pequot are not alone. About ten miles away, their erstwhile mortal enemies the Mohegan operate their own gargantuan gambling/entertainment complex in Uncasville, named for the sachem who sent the head of Sassacus to the English. In a 1994 agreement, the tribes guaranteed the state of Connecticut an annual payment of $80 million or twenty-five percent of their slot revenue, whichever was greater (invariably, it is the percentage). This pact has lifted the Indian tribes out of poverty, luring millions of supplicants to chance within the palisades of the Pequot and Mohegan, and garnering nearly $2 billion in tax revenue for the state since its signing. It has brought these Connecticut Indians money and influence. For decades, "friends of the Indian" had labored to bring Indians into the mainstream of American economic life with little result. Where they failed, gambling has succeeded, reversing the course of four hundred years of Anglo-Indian relations.

The story of Connecticut's casinos is remarkable but hardly unusual. Many Americans think that "serious gambling" is confined to the well-known casino destinations of Las Vegas and Atlantic City, but it is actually nearly everywhere. With a growing assortment of casinos, racetracks, bingo halls, and lottery tickets available at convenience stores in nearly every state, Americans are never far from a chance to take a chance. Gambling is more than a pastime—it is big business. In 2004, Americans lost over $78 billion on a variety of games of chance. About half of this money went to casinos—both commercial, state-regulated facilities and Indian gambling halls—while the balance was wagered on lotteries, horse- and dog-race betting, bingo, and noncasino card rooms. Gambling's appeal to Americans is nothing if not broad based. In 2004, approximately fifty-four million Americans visited a casino, and countless more bought lottery tickets, daubed bingo cards, and bet on horses and sports. More American adults gamble than abstain.

Even before an unprecedented explosion of legal gambling in the past fifty years, the U.S. has long been a gambling nation. Poker, a game that evolved on the Mississippi River and in the American West, has become one of the world's most popular games, and with the slot machine, Americans brought gambling into the Machine Age. Bingo, an American innovation of the Depression years, has similarly crossed the oceans. The American casino hub, Las Vegas, has displaced Monte Carlo as the world's gambling capital and shows no signs of yielding the honor anytime soon.

Americans are joined by other nations in chasing fortune. Canadians have commercial and charitable casinos as well as a range of lottery and video lottery products. Australians gamble on "pokies," slots, lotteries, race and sports betting, and keno. Macao, a former Portuguese colony, has had a monopoly on casino gambling in China for nearly forty years, and it faces competition from casinos in the Philippines, South Korea, Cambodia, and Malaysia. Casinos span the African continent from Cairo to Cape Town, Latin American nations from Costa Rica to Chile have casinos and slot parlors, and Europe boasts casinos, lotteries, and bookmaking. Gambling is often as easy as buying a ticket: International lottery sales in calendar year 2001 topped $125.6 billion. In all, over two hundred and fifty jurisdictions throughout the world offer legal gambling of some kind. Casinos, pari-mutuel wagering on horses, greyhounds, and jai alai, lotteries, and other forms of betting together comprise a world betting market valued at nearly $1 trillion dollars per year. From the tundra of Siberia to the windy shores of Tierra del Fuego, from balmy Mediterranean waters to the Nevada desert, over the oceans and across each continent, gambling unites humanity.

———

So where did gambling originate, and why has it remained so popular?

The human brain does not yield its secrets easily—while scientists can tell us that gambling activity stimulates certain neuroreceptors, they cannot conclusively say why people find gambling so alluring, let alone why some prefer video poker and others blackjack. But, in the forty-thousand or so years that we have thrown sticks, drawn lots, rolled dice, tossed cards, and pulled handles, humans have left ample evidence of our gambling passion in the historical record. By piecing together these traces, we can reconstruct the evolution of gambling.

Gambling and gamblers have left imprints throughout history in curious, sometimes surprising ways. Games of chance have evolved over many centuries, changing and maturing along with civilization. As new technologies—from block printing to the Internet—have become available, people have used them to gamble. Early mathematics and statistical sciences developed in part to explain the vagaries of chance. Gambling flourished in the neighborhood of Shakespeare's Globe Theater and in the imperial courts of China. European colonial ventures, including the Virginia Company, received financing from lotteries, and the British Stamp Tax, which included levies on playing cards, helped spur the colonials into rebellion against the Crown. The consolidation of German states into Prussia forced the closure of German casinos and led to the establishment of Monte Carlo as a gaming monopoly. Leaders from Julius Caesar to Franklin Roosevelt (who offered Americans a "New Deal") have used gambling metaphors to speak to the people.

The history of gambling has many elements of a high-stakes Texas hold 'em game: cunning calculations, audacious gambits, and reversals of fortune. Always a part of human culture, its evolution never ceases, and at every juncture of history, it seems, the gambler is nearby.

ROLL THE BONES

PART ONE

The Discovery of Gambling

◆ ◆ ◆

Although the ground had been rumbling for days, the hangers-on in the Taverna Lusoria worried not a bit. Seventeen years earlier, an earthquake had leveled much of Pompeii; even the Forum had crumbled. Yet its inhabitants rebuilt the city, and only the most timid interpreted the sudden drying-up of wells and springs as an omen that the ground might again be unhappy.

Marked by a sign of a drinking vessel flanked by two phalluses, the Taverna Lusoria plainly advertised its business. The tavern was a place where men could pursue diverse paths to pleasure. The entire first floor was dedicated to drinking and gambling, while upstairs men could cavort, out of sight, with the relatively discreet ladies of the establishment.

The Taverna Lusoria was one of many places in Pompeii where gambling, though technically illegal, was openly conducted. Gambling was a regular feature of the small fast-food and drink establishments that dotted the streets of the city. Called Popinae, *these food stalls were common throughout the Roman Republic, and later Empire; in his Philippics against Marc Antony, Cicero charged his rival with wasting his life in* popinae *and brothels, gambling and drinking.*

The respectable people of Pompeii did not deign to enter the popinae *or the Taverna Lusoria: such establishments catered to thieves, professional gamesters, executioners, and bargemen—rough customers, to say the least. That's not to say that they didn't throw dice occasionally: The satirist Juvenal noted that if a man were wealthy, Romans accepted his gambling with a smile, but castigated a poor man who indulged in such a shameful hobby.*

Inured to the hard knocks of life, the customers of the Taverna Lusoria were not scared by the tremors that had been making the lamps sway for the past four days. But, the diehard gamblers noted, the shaking ground did not refuse the thrown dice. So, like their countrymen in popinae, *bars, brothels, and inns throughout the Empire, they played on, betting money, clothing, weapons, or the next round of drinks. Some played simple games that rewarded the player who threw the highest point total;*

others preferred more intricate games where the dice allowed one to move a gaming piece across a board. The taverna's owner happily accommodated all, providing dice and game boards, and even advancing customers credit, either for drinks, liaisons upstairs, or gambling. He kept a running tab of who owed what in chalk on the walls of his establishment.

Though outside the taverna, the animals of Pompeii were now desperately barking, whining, and pacing, it seemed that the dice would continue to roll forever. But suddenly, early in the afternoon on August 24, 79 A.D., Mount Vesuvius burst open, sending a cloud of ash and rock into the sky. It quickly began to rain pumice on the streets of Pompeii. Those who could took to the streets in a panic; choked by dust, stumbling in a suddenly sunless afternoon, thousands were killed. Those who remained in Pompeii perished a few hours later when a wall of volcanic rock surged over the city. The volcano, which buried Pompeii for centuries, did what the edicts of Roman law could not: It stopped gambling in the the city. Those who perished with their debts still chalked up on the wall of the Taverna Lusoria were denied a final spin of fortune's wheel, though they learned the truth of a maxim illustrated in a Pompeiian mosaic: "Death Equalizes All."

I

Thoth's Gift

◆ ◆ ◆

THE ANCIENT ORIGINS OF GAMBLING

Ancient storytellers said that gambling was part of our lives for a reason: A cunning god or hero taught people to gamble. Whether it was the coyote or spider trying to trick his fellows or a siege-bound king hoping to rally his troops, the invention of gambling was a discrete event to be cherished or cursed.

Modern historians can't give their audiences such easy, entertaining explanations of how gambling began. Their gambling stories begin without offering the credit—or blame—to an inventive Paleolithic rounder who rolled the first bones. But this is not unusual. No one can say exactly who invented prayer, music, farming, medicine, or money. The same must be said for gambling: It is simply older than history.

The gambling impulse even predates humanity: A variety of animals, from bees to primates, embrace risk for a chance at a reward. A 2005 Duke University study found that macaque monkeys preferred to follow a "riskier" target, which gave them varying amounts of juice, over a "safe" one, which always gave the same—they just like gambling. Intriguingly, the monkeys preferred the riskier target even when it gave them consistently less juice than the safe one, and continued to choose the riskier target in the face of diminishing returns when a single large one was still in memory. Chasing the jackpot is nothing new.

Whatever the secret gambling lives of our primate ancestors, humans have long been apt gamblers. The hunter-gatherer lifestyle of early cultures was, like mining or fishing today, predicated on risk: On any given day, one might find lunch or become lunch. The unknown was omnipresent yet still mysterious, something approached with mingled hope, fear, and superstition. As they discovered new technologies, protohumans gained more control over their environment, but they still retained a fascination with chance. When the ancestors of modern humans began using tools more than half a million years ago, they could also modify stone, wood, and bone to test the unknown. These were the first gambling tools.

But these early "gamblers" weren't simply playing for amusement: The first ventures into chance were usually more religious than recreational. Divination is the practice of using supernatural or intuitive means to tell the future or reveal information hidden to reason. Creative diviners have invented dozens of randomizing mechanisms. Some are downright messy: Haruspicy, a favorite of the ancient Greeks and Etruscans, involves reading the entrails—particularly the liver—of a ritually slaughtered beast. Others are more fragrant: Karydaomancers tell the future using coconut shells. Oomancers interpret the patterns made by broken eggs; their clients can presumably enjoy a glimpse into the future along with a tasty omelet. Copromancers and uromancers look for signs in feces and urine, respectively; if one finds these practices noisome, then perhaps phyllorhodomancy, using rose petals to divine, is for him. And, of course, there are the better-known forms of fortune telling involving tea leaves, palmistry, astrology, and tarot-card reading—a modern form of divination that was, ironically, once a gambling game.

The oldest and most widespread divination "game" is odds and evens. It has a long history and is found throughout the world. Evidence for odds and evens divination can be found in ancient texts, and it has survived into the modern era among some African tribes. Although details of the ritual vary across the world, the essential elements are a number of small objects, such as nuts or stones, and a container, which may be a priest or shaman's hands or a spiritually invested relic. The querent asks a question of the priest/shaman, who then pours out the objects; if the number is even, the answer is yes, and if odd, the answer is no. Some cultures always use odd for yes and even for no, but in each case the rules are established before the cast, and the answer is not subject to appeal.

Odds and evens is quick and unambiguous, but most people seek more nuanced glimpses into the future. Divination by sortilege (interpreting patterns in thrown objects) allows for many shades of meaning. Early humans threw and read virtually anything for portents, including plants, sticks, stones, and bones. Cleromancy, the casting of lots, would gradually evolve from sacred ritual to profane amusement—dice. Lots could be made from anything, but small bones became the preferred medium. The *astragalus* (plural, *astragali*), also called the hucklebone, is a bone immediately above the talus, or heel bone. In many animals—particularly domesticated sheep and goats—the astragalus can be thrown to produce a more or less random result, though modern-day craps players bear little resemblance to Sumerian priests "rolling the bones" for hopeful supplicants.

The astragalus had four unsymmetrical large sides—concave, convex, broad, and narrow (it was impossible for the bone to come to rest on either of its two rounded ends). Each side stood for a distinct outcome. From using astragali to forecast future events, it was a simple step to simply put stakes on the outcome of a throw. The line between divination and gambling is blurred. One hunter, for example, might say to another, "If the bones land short side up, we will search for game to the south; if not, we look north," thus using the astragali to plumb the future. But after the hunt, the hunters might cast bones to determine who went home with the most desirable cuts. If ascribing the roll of the bones to the will of a divine presence, that would be divination; if the hunters simply rolled and hoped for the best, they were gambling.

Several early archaeological sites throughout Europe, the Mediterranean, and the Near East include astragali and collections of small, differently colored stones—possibly counters. These could be used in the earliest form of craps, complete with primitive dice and ancient chips. The relative ubiquity of ancient astragali suggests that they must have had some everyday function— they are simply too common to have been used only by a small priestly caste. Unless people did not make day-to-day decisions without rolling the bones, the best explanation for their prevalence is that astragali were used for entertainment as well.

The invention of agriculture about ten thousand years ago triggered a revolution in human living that would ultimately lead to cities, commerce, and money—and a dramatic expansion in gambling. In his classic 1948 survey of

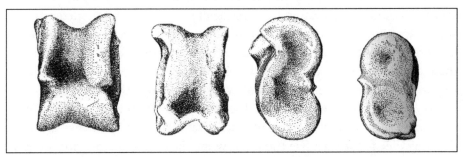

The precursors of modern dice were sheep hucklebones or astragali, known to the Romans as *tali*. At some point, people conflated hucklebone with knucklebone and began referring to astragali as knucklebones, though they are not, strictly speaking, skeletal remains of knuckles. Four sides of a single astragalus are seen here.

world cultures, anthropologist Alfred Kroeber found it more prudent to enumerate the peoples who did not gamble, rather than those who did. Those who didn't included native Australians, Pacific Islanders insulated from mainland influences, the scattered populations of subarctic North America, inhabitants of the more remote reaches of India and South America, and those of the eastern half of sub-Saharan Africa.

So, according to Kroeber, the list of gambling cultures includes most of the indigenous peoples of Europe, Asia, Africa, and the Americas. Though "puritanical religions" such as more extreme variants of Protestantism and Buddhism and mainstream Islam decried gambling, Kroeber found that gambling could not be systematically correlated with lifestyle, ideas toward wealth, or religion. Cultures with no concept of personal wealth gambled, as did those obsessed with the accumulation of it. He concluded that peoples somehow resolved to tolerate or ignore gambling and then adapted their existing ideas to it. Interestingly, he found that gambling spread across the continents not in connection to a specific game, but as an attitude. Cultures decide whether to gamble or not and then choose their games.

Anthropologists have identified Mesopotamia, the land between the Tigris and Euphrates Rivers in present-day Iraq, as the place where modern urban society originated when, seven thousand years ago, Mesopotamians began building the first cities. Archaeologists have discovered astragali in all periods of Mesopotamian history. The Mesopotamians used astragali to gamble, giving the convex narrow side a value of one, the convex broad side three, the concave broad side four, and the concave narrow side six: This would become the accepted standard throughout the Middle East and Mediterranean.

When Mesopotamian fortune-tellers filed down their knucklebones and marked them with insignia, they took the first steps toward modern dice. It is easy to imagine the evolution from astragali to dice: The four-sided astragali simply were at first transformed into cubes, most likely to make them roll more randomly. Because of variations in bone density and structure, though, these cubical astragali would have inevitably rolled unevenly; it was a logical step to carve more honest dice out of ivory, wood, and other materials.

The earliest six-sided dice yet discovered, dating from about 3000 B.C., were unearthed in what is today northern Iraq. Although humans have been shooting dice for at least five thousand years, the oldest dice are not precisely like modern ones. On any honest set of dice in use today, opposite sides will add up to seven, while Mesopotamian dice usually did not. The first known dice have one opposite six, two opposite three, and four opposite five. Other dice from other locations have different orientations. It was not until about 3,300 years ago that dice with sides arranged in the standard way begin to predominate. Nearly all dice use pips (dots) and not numerals to indicate value, probably because the form of dice was fixed around 1300 B.C., far earlier than the development of the Hindu-Arabic system of numbers, which originated around 700 A.D. and was not widely used in most of Europe until the fifteenth century. Dice are older than numbers.

Mesopotamians played a game that is likely the ancestor of backgammon. Five gaming boards dating from 3000 B.C. have been found in the royal tombs at Ur, suggesting that it was an entirely respectable diversion. This game used four-sided pyramidal dice. They also played a Parcheesi-like game. Both of these board games used dice to determine how far a game piece could be moved. These may not have been strictly gambling games, with stakes passing from losers to winners, but the line between games played only for amusement and those played for money was more permeable than it is today. In the precursors to the modern chess, dice were also essential to play, reflecting a time when chance and fortune were seen as being as essential to success in battle as strategy. Later, the development of rationalism drove this random element from the simulated battle of chess, but the ancients knew that war, like dice, was a game of chance.

While the surviving fragments of Mesopotamian literature, such as the *Epic of Gilgamesh*, do not mention gambling, the presence of so many kinds of dice and board games in archaeological sites betrays the Mesopotamians as adept gamblers. Farther to the east, in the kingdom of Persia (comprising present-day Iran), gambling was just as popular. It seems to have been a common diversion in the royal court, and a tale related by the Greek historian Plutarch shows just how seriously Persians took their wagering. Around 400 B.C., King Artaxerxes directed his trusted eunuch Mesabetes to cut off the hand and head of his younger brother Cyrus, who had fallen in battle while disputing Artaxerxes' claim to the throne. Artaxerxes' mother, Parysatis, hatched a plan to revenge herself on the king and, more directly, the eunuch who had violated the corpse of Cyrus.

Since she had gambled for amusement with her husband before his death, Parysatis was a skilled dice player. One day, she casually began shooting dice with Artaxerxes, lulling him into believing she had forgotten the small matter of her murdered youngest son. She staked and lost a considerable sum, which she promptly paid off. Feigning frustration and grumbling that she had no money left, she proposed that they instead use slaves as stakes. The ingenious Parysatis then skillfully reversed her ill fortune and found herself in possession of Mesabetes, whom she quickly had flayed alive. When Artaxerxes tried to protest, she laughingly rebuffed him with words to the effect that she had borne her losses without complaining, and he should do likewise. The ancient Persians took gambling—and gambling debts—quite seriously.

The Persians had rivals for gambling enthusiasm in one of the world's oldest enduring civilizations, that of Egypt. Five thousand years ago, scribes in the kingdoms of Upper and Lower Egypt were hard at work keeping detailed hieroglyphic records. Their wisdom was celebrated. Socrates often relied on Egyptian wisdom for backup: When introducing a certain argument, he related that, as the Egyptians knew about it, it must be old—and true. Later scholars were not above this kind of bottom dealing; when the eighteenth-century savant Antoine Court de Gébelin wanted to establish tarot cards as tools for esoteric divination, he simply announced that the game was, in fact, a product of ancient Egypt (it wasn't, but Gébelin successfully established the tarot as a hermetic discipline).

The Egyptians claimed the god Thoth (usually depicted as an ibis-headed man or dog-faced baboon) invented gambling.* He was the divine physician and the god charged with enforcing *maat,* or divine order, an arbiter whose counsel was especially treasured, and a judge of the dead. Gambling in the land of the Nile was thus linked to secret knowledge (Thoth was the inventor of writing) and divine justice.

The pictographs that adorn Egyptian tombs include scenes of gambling, which was amply documented in hieroglyphics. The severity of the laws against gambling that can be found in the records of the ancient dynasties indicate that it continued to be widespread despite its prohibition. If convicted of gambling under these laws, a man would be sent to labor in the quarries— possibly, some of the forced labor used to build the great pyramids came from oppressed dice-throwers.

Game playing was already an advanced art in Egypt as early as 3500 B.C. Many "race games" (in which players raced pieces to a finish point) used two astragali to determine the motion of the game pieces. A set from a typical race game, the "Palm Tree Game," dating from approximately 2000 B.C., has been recovered amid the ruins of Thebes. Players rolled astragali to determine how many spaces their pieces could move. Some may have been more complex;

---

*Thoth is the Greek version of his name; in Egypt, his name sounded more like Tahouty or Djeheuty.

Senet, for example, used a board with three rows of ten spaces and may have been an ancestor of backgammon. Other games included Mehen ("Game of the Coiled Snake"), Hounds and Jackals ("Game of Fifty-eight Holes"), and Tau ("Game of 20 Squares"). Wagering at board games and at odds and evens may have been common long before the appearance of cubical dice during the Ptolemaic period (circa 300 B.C.), but it was not until then that dicing became popular as a game of chance in and of itself.

The deities and demigods of ancient Egypt gambled as much as their mortal worshipers. In fact, the length of the year was attributed to a gambling match. In Plutarch's version of the tale, the powerful sun god Ra became jealous of the love between Geb, god of the earth, and Nut, goddess of the sky. He cursed Nut, decreeing that she would bear children in no month and no year. Distraught at the possibility of remaining childless, Nut turned to the erudite Thoth for assistance.

Thoth, by a stroke of luck, had been playing draughts (a game resembling checkers) with the moon, whom he had trounced. Having won from his lunar opponent one seventy-second part of every day, Thoth pooled his jackpot into five whole days, which he added to the end of the existing 360-day Egyptian calendar. Nut then gave birth to five children on each of the added days, from whom all other life ultimately developed. Thoth's gambling victory allowed for the birth of humanity itself and more practically let the Egyptians align their 360-day lunar calendar with the more accurate 365 solar one.

Gambling proliferated across the Sahara Desert and throughout the African continent. As in other parts of the world, it often developed from divination ceremonies, which placed a premium on random events. Yoruba sixteen-cowrie divination, still practiced in parts of Nigeria, is a prime example of African divination. In the ceremony, an experienced reader tosses sixteen cowrie shells; according to the figure they make upon falling, he recites a specified series of verses. If the client wishes more specific information, the reader can toss the cowries again. The reader can also toss the shells to obtain answers to a series of yes-or-no questions.

The scarcity of documentary evidence of sub-Saharan African cultures in antiquity makes it difficult to chart the development of gambling there with as much ease as in Egypt or the Mediterranean. But the wide range of gambling recorded in cultures throughout Africa by anthropologists suggests that the practice was, for millennia, as widespread as human settlement itself.

In contrast, there is a mountain of information on gambling in India. The Indian subcontinent is today home to over one billion people, dozens of language groups, and the modern nations of India, Bangladesh, and Pakistan.

Indian civilization is quite old—there is evidence of large, thriving cities beginning about 4,500 years ago. Gambling was part of Indian history from its
beginnings. Primitive dice have been discovered at one of these sites,
Mohenjo-Daro, and at later settlements throughout India, along with artistic
representations of dice and dice-playing.

Just as Mesopotamian dice evolved from astragali, Indian dice developed
from the brown nuts of the *vibhitaka* tree, which had five slightly flattened
sides. During the Vedic period of Indian history (until roughly 500 B.C.),
these were the most commonly used dice in India. In place of actual nuts,
some used wooden, ivory, silver, or golden dice, or terracotta dice colored
black and red. After the Vedic period, perhaps owing to a Greek or Persian influence, four-sided oblong dice (astragali) became popular.

Although cubical dice did not reach India until around 600 ., the literary and archaeological evidence shows that Indians were surrounded by
opportunities to gamble long before then. *Vibhitaka* dice playing was widespread. Indians proved just as adept at using animals to gamble as they were
in adapting nuts to that purpose. Indians might have originally domesticated chickens to gamble on them, and cockfighting thrived in India from
2000 B.C. onward. This sport, which would by the nineteenth century be
celebrated worldwide, allowed humans to bet on which of two fighting
birds would triumph. Other animals were both a vehicle for gambling and
the prize itself. Vedic literature speaks of chariot races with cattle as the
stakes.

Vedic-era Indians diced in an assembly hall called the *sabha*. Originally,
they may have just considered certain assembly places luckier than others
and chosen to gamble there, but as time went on some gambling places received kingly sanction, while those who gambled elsewhere were subject to a
fine. One source says that gambling halls needed a telltale archlike structure
near the door so that respectable nongamblers would not mistakenly enter.
The great Sanskrit epic *Mahabharata* (written about 1500 B.C.) relates the
story of a king who built an assembly hall with a thousand pillars and a hundred golden doors spiked with diamonds, with golden seats and lavish
beds—this was, presumably, the Vedic version of the carpet joint.

The actual method of playing *vibhitaka* is open to some conjecture. Players may have merely chosen odd or even, then counted the *vibhitaka* nuts
landing in a circle. In other games, there were several ranked throws, named
after the four ages of the world defined in Hindu literature. First one, then a
second player threw down dice, and the number of dice—not the point totals

of their sides—was then divided by four or five. An evenly divisible number meant *kirta*, the highest throw; three remaining meant *treta*, two meant *divapara*, and one, *kali*, the worst throw. Other dice games required the dice to be marked; on a four-sided die (astragalus), four represented *kirta*, three *treta*, two *divapara*, and one *kali*. There were at least twenty-five different forms of Indian gambling in ancient and classical times, some of which used money as the stakes, others of which used animals, particularly cocks and rams.

Indian dice games began as religious or divination rituals and continued to have mystical significance. Classical Indian literature describes the god Shiva playing dice with his wife, Pravati. The back-and-forth series of games between them and their two sons is commemorated today in the holiday of Diwali, or the festival of lights, which is considered a lucky day for gambling, and it is said that one who does not gamble on Diwali may be reincarnated as a donkey. Most incredibly, ritualized gambling was part of the ritual expiation used to cure a boy who had been attacked by a dog-demon (today's medical science would diagnose him with epilepsy; it is not known how effective the cure was).

Both public and private gambling houses were common, though they catered only to men. There is not much evidence to suggest that women freely entered these gambling houses, or that they gambled at all. But the houses had a clear hierarchy. Some stories reference the *askavapa*, a professional dice-player who supervised the king's play, oversaw gambling halls, and collected the king's share of the proceeds. A writer named Yajnawalkya describes the *sabhika*, an officer charged with keeping a gambling house. The *sabhika* maintained the house and its gambling equipment, collected winnings, watched for cheating, and settled all disputes. In some cases, he advanced money for losers to pay to winners. To gamblers the *sabhika's* word was the law. In one story, a *sabhika* beat an indebted gambler with sticks and, when the loser fell unconscious, directed him to be thrown down a well, an intimidating if very not effective method of debt collection. In return for executing these responsibilities, the *sabhika* received between five and ten percent of the stakes, from which he paid a fixed portion to the king—maybe the first gambling revenue tax.

Gambling abounds in Indian literature. The *Rig Veda*, a collection of over one thousand religious hymns, was composed over several hundred years, possibly as early as the fourth millennium B.C. and certainly completed between 1500 and 1200 B.C. Hymn number thirty-four in the tenth mandala is known as the gambler's hymn, and is said to have been composed by a gambling sage who had lost everything through dice. In its fourteen stanzas, the gambler's hymn expresses the sorrow of a penitent gambler. The hymn begins:

> *These dice nuts, born of a lofty tree in a windy spot, which dance on this gambling ground, make me almost mad. These wakeful dice intoxicate me like a draft of Soma from Mount Mujavant.*
>
> *Never has she said an angry word to me, nor has she ever scolded me. She has been so pleasing to me and my friends. With all this without any fault of hers I have driven my devoted wife away because of a die exceeding by one [an unlucky throw].*
>
> *My mother-in-law hates me; my wife pushes me away. In his defeat the gambler finds none to pity him. No one has use for a gambler, like an aged horse put up for sale.*

Lamenting that the "dice are like pieces of divine coal, which cause the hearts to burn, though remaining themselves cold," the gambler's hymn is a sober, plaintive plea of obsession. But one interpretation considers the hymn part of a ritual to guarantee *success* in gambling. A hopeful seeker took three dice nuts from the *vibhitaka* tree, dosed them with perfume, then recited the first stanza at night while holding the dice. After sunrise, he recited the entire hymn at the gambling hall, then touched the head of the person from whom he wanted to win and read another stanza.

Others say that the hymn is a prayer for release from the clutches of an addiction to dice, as the gambler asks in the final stanza that the dice enchant another in his place: "Let your wrath and grudge be appeased! Let another fall in the range of the brown ones." Another professor has interpreted the hymn as "an Act of Truth" recited by the gambler to signify the unification of his will with the cosmos, with the hope that this admission will purge him of the desire to gamble. Whatever its ritual function, the hymn remains a beautiful and touching work of literature. Written at least three thousand years ago, it retains an uncanny resonance even today for those who gamble more than they should.

There are numerous other examples of dicing in Indian literature, and the epic *Mahabharata* can be said to hinge on gambling. The second longest literary work in the world, the *Mahabharata* combines Hindu religon, philosophy, and mythology and is about four times longer than the Bible. The story is chiefly that of the struggle between the Kaurava and Pandava branches of the royal family for the throne of Hastinapura. The epic begins with the Pandavas at the height of their power and fortune and the Kauravas envious.

Sakuni of the Kauravas was skilled in playing with dice, particularly loaded ones. The Kauravas, led by Duryodhana, challenged the honest Yudhishthira of the Pandavas to a dice game against Sakuni; honor compelled him to accept against his will. Yudhishthira lost first a pearl, then a thousand bags with a thousand gold pieces in each, then a thousand war elephants, then all his slaves, and finally went "all in" by wagering—and losing—his entire kingdom, then his own freedom, and finally that of his wife Draupadi, though she refused to become Duryodhana's slave because, she said, her husband had first lost his own freedom and had no standing to wager anyone else. Yudhishthira continued to lose until the Padavas were banished from their own former kingdom. The Pandavas then begin their long exile and quest for revenge. In the climax of the epic, they regain at last the throne at the battle of Kurushetra.

The mythic *Mahabharata* was only one Indian source that condemned gambling. The *smirti,* a collection of poems, myths, and laws, prohibited a king from four vices: dicing, drinking, women, and hunting. According to the law of Manu, a Hindu Noah who built a boat to escape a flood, gambling was "open theft" that led to the downfall of princes, and should be violently punished. Manu urged that gamblers should be banished, along with dancers, cruel men, heretics, and liquor merchants. Others, considering that the desire to gamble could not be totally extinguished, instead recommended that the king control it tightly and, as a matter of course, take a share of the stakes— the origin of the *sabhika.* From the plaintive lament of the gambler's hymn to the role of authorities in regulating and taxing gambling, Vedic India seems to have been not so different from today's world.

East of India, the cultures of eastern Asia place as high a premium on gambling as any in the world. While the frequency of gambling activity in many parts of the world, including Europe and North America, was high in ancient times, East Asia had perhaps the greatest intensity of gambling, with higher stakes played for more regularly. From playing cards to keno, Asian cultures have made several important contributions to today's global culture of gambling.

China has a long gambling tradition. The ancient Chinese held random events in high regard; as early as the Shang period (beginning circa 1700 B.C.), they consulted oracles for guidance in making major decisions. Instead of eviscerating farm animals like the Etruscans, these diviners engraved turtle shells or animal bones with written characters, applied heated bronze pins to the opposite sides, then compared the pattern of the cracks to the characters. These oracles, or *shih*, eventually became the respected scholar gentry of China, proof that, as much as many societies have damned gambling, those who can harness and interpret random events, be it cracked bones or rolled ones, can frequently gain power and respect.

By the Chou period (circa the first millennium B.C.), Chinese culture and cities were flourishing, and gambling was entrenched as a common pastime. In addition to shops selling jewels, clothing, and food, most Chinese cities had gambling houses on their commercial streets. Betting on fighting animals, from quails and thrushes to fish and even crickets (otherwise placid crickets would have their heads tickled with a feather until they charged each other), was quite widespread. Interestingly, even in the age of mechanical and digital gambling, this ancient tradition persists. In the summer of 2004, Hong Kong police arrested 115 people after breaking up an insect-fighting ring in Kowloon, seizing nearly two hundred crickets, some of them worth as much as $20,000. Subsequent raids proved that the sport would not die easily.

The Chinese played a version of the lotto as early as the tenth century A.D., about five centuries before it appeared in Europe. In the Game of Thirty-six Animals or Hua-Hoey Lottery, one of thirty-six cards illustrated with different animals was selected at random. Betting schemes on this game varied, but it survived into the nineteenth century and emigrants from the Celestial Empire brought it with them to Europe and the Americas (it is similar to the Brazilian *jogo do bichos*, which remains popular today).

In the fourth century B.C., players bet on the board game *po*, which mingled skill and chance, as well as other diversions. The Chinese soon found new, more robust ways to gamble. By 200 B.C., betting on cockfights, horse and dog races, and other sports was common in China. The *Han Shu*, a classic Chinese history dating from 115 B.C., laments that young, wealthy government officials were throwing the common people into confusion through an overindulgence in games of chance.

But few heeded the scribe's warnings. Over the following centuries, Chinese gamblers continued to play heartily and even found new ways to gamble. They adopted Western-style dice around the seventh century A.D. and by 900 had turned them into dominoes, which they called *kwat pai*, or "bone tablets." A set of Chinese dominoes consisted of twenty-one numbers, of which eleven appeared twice, giving a total of thirty-two tiles. These tiles were made of ivory, in which case their pips were red and black, or ebony, in which case the pips were red and white. As with the modern game of *pai gow*, players attempted to pair tiles according to their values. Domino games had descriptive titles: English translations such as "to dispute for tens" and "turning heavens and nines" barely suggest their poetry. The Chinese also devised mahjong tiles, fan-tan (a game played with circular disks), and the forerunners of lotteries, bingo, and keno. Gamblers would owe their greatest debt, though, to a comparatively late Chinese invention: playing cards.

Gambling cultures in the rest of Asia varied widely. Koreans gambled on a number of board games as well as rather obscure events such as oxen fights, kite battles, and the fall of a rake. They also adopted most of the games invented by the Chinese: Korean dominoes are known as *ho hpai,* or "foreign tablets," suggesting their Chinese origin. Until relatively recent historic times, the Japanese had far less gambling than either Koreans or the Chinese. To the north of China, the Mongols were reputed to shun gambling for physical exercise. Farther to the west, the Turks adopted dice around 600 A.D., which facilitated the spread of dice gambling across Central Asia. Not to be left out, the Kazakhs also embraced gambling by casting lots, wagering on races, and betting on an indigenous rodeo-style event known as "goat wrestling." The latter was particularly inventive, as riders tried to hoist a decapitated goat onto their horse without falling off, while others tried to recapture it. If nothing else, this proves the incredible creativity of those intent on a good game of chance.

As gambling developed along with civilizations in Africa, Europe, and Asia, the isolated pre-Columbian peoples of the Americas devised their own games. As in the Old World, Native American gambling descended from divination, and sometimes the line between the two was blurred. Religious ceremonies made use of ritualized gambling throughout both North and South America.

Thousands of years before Columbus sailed, the first North Americans were already peoples of chance. The Spanish conquistadors, French Jesuits and trappers, and English colonists who arrived after 1492 described a diversity of gambling games throughout the continent. Native American games of chance fell into two general categories: guessing games and dice games. Guessing games were usually accompanied by singing and drumming, and were divided into four basic types. "Stick games" featured a bundle of sticks or arrows held in both of a player's hands; the opponent had to guess which hand held a certain stick. In the "hand game," one player held two or four sticks in his hands, and the opponent had to guess which hand held the *unmarked* stick. Those playing "four-stick games" guessed on the configuration of marked pairs of sticks. A final type of game, called the "hidden-ball" or "moccasin" game, a possible ancestor of the shell game, consisted of four hollow wooden tubes, moccasins, or holes in the earth where a stone, stick or bullet had been hidden.

Dice games were more numerous and more complicated than guessing games. In contrast to guessing games, they were usually played in silence. Stewart Culin, an anthropologist who cataloged North American Indian games in the early twentieth century, counted over one hundred traditional dice games throughout the continent. Native American dice were two sided. Indians fashioned dice from a diversity of materials. Plumstones, or plum pits (the most popular) ranged from the Atlantic Coast to the Rockies; sticks and split canes predominated in the Southwest and Pacific Coast; *patol* dice (fashioned from sticks) filtered northward into the Southwest from Mesoamerica; shells were mostly used in northern California; and beaver teeth radiated outward from the Pacific Northwest. Dice were also made from bone, antler, animal teeth, nutshells, seeds, kernels, sticks, shell, and, after their importation by Europeans, glass and metal.

Methods of playing varied tremendously, but most games followed the same general pattern, with two sides, either individual players or teams, pitted against each other. Usually, two or four people played the actual game, with dozens of spectators betting on the outcome. Players essentially bet on which side (black or white, flat or curved) the plumstones, teeth, or sticks would fall. Men and women both played dice in Native American societies, though usually separately, and men almost always "played" the ceremonial forms of the game.

Though men and women did not usually play together, gambling was often conducted in mixed company. In some instances, teams of women played against teams of men, or mixed crowds of spectators bet on all-female contests.

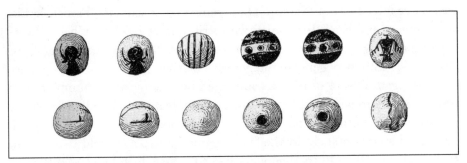

Plumstone dice of the Yankton Sioux (of present-day Minnesota and South Dakota); the top row depicts the stones' fronts, the bottom row their backs.

Among the Pawnee, an agricultural people of what is now Nebraska, crowds of women gamblers were just as boisterous as their male counterparts. There is some scholarly disagreement about the extent of female wagering—the predominant view is that they wagered mostly personal ornaments, while men gambled valuable weapons or horses (after their introduction by the Spanish). Assiniboin women were often physically beaten by their husband for their gambling losses, though the Pawnee men seem to have more forbearance. One of their maxims says, "Hungry is the man whose wife gambles," suggesting that men patiently tolerated their wives' absence from the hearth while they played. But men consistently gambled for higher stakes than women. There are several references to husbands gambling away wives in myths and stories, but no reported instances of wives staking their husbands.

Though gambling was a widespread social and even sacred activity, Native American myths betray a predominantly negative image of gambling. Many tribes conflated the mythical gambler with the trickster, a shifty, evil-hearted spirit who usually brought evil. The Paiute of the Great Basin, for example, believed that trickster Cunawabi, the bringer of night and sickness, was a gambler. Friendly gods might suggest to mortals that they stop gambling. In a Tlingit myth collected in the Pacific Northwest, Raven advised a man who loved to gamble despite his ill luck that he should stop: "Gambling is not very good. There will always be hard feelings between gamblers."

Despite these cautionary notes, gambling remained a universal activity among North American Indians, as attested to by its prevalence at the time of European contact. After that contact, European influences began to filter into indigenous Indian gaming forms. Later iterations of Native American myths speak of indigenous spirits and people playing with cards, a European introduction, showing the degree to which new types of gambling had infiltrated traditional cultures.

South of the Rio Grande, gambling took several different forms. The *patol* dice games, later played by Indians of the southwest United States, diffused northward from Mesoamerica, which roughly comprises the modern nations of Mexico, Belize, Guatemala, Honduras, and El Salvador. Aztecs wagered everything from blankets and corncobs to palaces and gardens, according to their means. Nearly everyone, from the king's household to commoners, played *patolli*. Gamblers entered gaming houses with their gambling mats and a basket with the game's dice and counters, lit incense, and made an offering to a dice god known as Macuilxochitl, whom they appealed to as they tossed the dice. Some gambled themselves into slavery and even human sacrifice.

The most infamous form of Mesoamerican gambling was wagering on ball games, which were fierce and often bloody spectacles. The inhabitants of Mesoamerica had begun playing ball games by 1500 B.C. These games utilized a technology unknown in the Old World: the production of rubber. When the Spanish first spied bouncing, noisy rubber balls, they were astonished, at first thinking that the balls were demonically possessed. But it was as familiar to Mesoamericans as astragali to a Sumerian or *vibhitaka* nuts to a Vedic-era Indian.

The ball game first developed with the coastal Olmec peoples, became highly elaborated with the Maya (200–600 A.D.) and reached its peak on the Veracruz coast of Mexico in Mayan Late Classic period (900 A.D.). It was still flourishing at the time of the Spanish conquest in the early sixteenth century and survived throughout the colonial era of Mexican history (to 1821). A form of the game lingers even today in the Mexican state of Sinaloa, over 3,500 years after its birth. Over 1,500 ball courts have been discovered from El Salvador in the south to Sinaloa in the north; there is evidence that the game was once played as far north as southern Arizona and on the Caribbean islands of Cuba, Dominica, and Puerto Rico.

Mesoamerican ball courts varied in size, but most were around 120 by 30 feet, with two parallel structures enclosing an I-shaped alley with two "end zones." The courts were painted vividly and represented enormous outlays of wealth and resources. To motivate players, possibly, life-sized friezes depicted postgame human sacrifices. There were many variations on the game, but essentially it pitted two teams against each other. Teams scored when an opposing player missed a shot at one of two stone hoops set at center court, failed to return the ball before it bounced twice, or allowed it to go out of bounds. If a player successfully shot the ball through a hoop, the game ended with his team's victory.

Throughout Mesoamerica, ball games were a mixture of ritual, drama, and athleticism. Originally, game playing may have been confined to special religious occasions, but by 1521, Spanish invaders reported mostly secular games of chance and sport taking place on the courts. Ritual human sacrifice was an integral part of "religious" games (courtside panels at the Chichen Itza courts vividly illustrate this). The victims may have been the losing team, the losing captain, a previously chosen child, or captives taken in war. Even if they were not slaughtered after a defeat, players risked serious injury and even death from the hard rubber ball whizzing mercilessly through the air. Injuries were as common as in football today, and medical treatment was considerably less sophisticated.

Spectators wagered on their favorite team and, before games, recited incantations to the waters, the trees, the animals, and the gods in an effort to gain supernatural favor. Players also gambled, presumably on themselves (ritual sacrifice of the losers would have discouraged throwgames). In the early sixteenth century, a Spanish priest described Aztec nobles punctiliously honoring their debts. Others, who gambled their homes and even themselves on the outcome of games, might be sacrificed if not ransomed as slaves.

The ball game was central to Mesoamerican religion and culture. Part II of the Mayan creation myth *Popul Vuh* begins when two brothers, Hun Hunahpu and Vucub Hunahpu, disturbed the Lords of the Underworld with their loud ball playing. The Lords then tricked the brothers into descending into the Underworld to compete with them there. The brothers were defeated through the Lords' superior skill and guile and sacrificially decapitated. The Lords buried the brothers' bodies beneath the ball court and stuck the head of Hun Hunahpu in a calabash tree; its spittle then impregnated a goddess, who fled to earth. She gave birth to the Hero Twins, who grew strong and skilled. When summoned to the Underworld for a game, the twins would defeat the Lords of the Underworld and retrieve the bodies of their father and uncle. In Mesoamerica, the tale of birth, death, and resurrection, recurrent in myth and religion throughout the world, found its expression on the ball court. This is only one reminder of how seriously the ancients took gambling.

2

The Die Is Cast

◆ ◆ ◆

Although every part of the ancient world was rich in gambling, the games that most people now play have their roots in the Mediterranean world, particularly Greece and Rome.

Like the Egyptians before them, the ancient Greeks believed gambling had divine origins. Several members of their pantheon were known to play for pleasure and profit. According to Greek mythology, a divine gambling match shaped the very cosmos. Zeus, Poseidon, and Hades cast lots to divide the universe. Zeus won the heavens, Poseidon the "gray sea," and Hades the "mists and the darkness" of the underworld. Hades hardly took his share with equanimity; he was sullen, miserable with the fate that consigned him to the lower world.

The Greek god Hermes (known to the Romans as Mercury) was identified as the god of luck and patron of gamblers. This god was also the god of divination, animal husbandry, rustic poetry, travel, trade, the home, language, thievery, athletics, and language. He could bless his favored followers with true omens, success in business, or persuasive speech. Nor was he above working both sides against the middle: As the patron of thieves, he could grant stealth and success, and as the patron of the home, protection from thieves—the original protection racket, perhaps. Hermes/Mercury was conflated with the Egyptian Thoth, a god with a similarly wide portfolio, and the Norse Woden.

According to Greek legends, the gods sometimes deigned to play with mortals. The high priest of the temple of Hercules was known to gamble with his god for unusual stakes: If the priest won, the god would grant him a special favor, and if the god won, the priest would procure a courtesan for him.

Some Greeks looked beyond the stories of Olympian high rollers and searched for more down-to-earth explanations of gambling's origin. Often, these were no less fantastic than stories of polytheistic past-posting. According to the most widely quoted legend the heroic Palamedes invented games of chance to while away the ten years spent besieging Troy. Sophocles specifically credited the enterprising Palamedes with the invention of dice. A grandson of the sea god Poseidon, the prolific Palamedes is also credited with creating counting, coinage, weights and measures, and several letters of the alphabet. But he made a mistake in tricking Odysseus into enlisting in the Trojan War, and as retribution, Odysseus framed Palamedes as a Trojan collaborator and had him stoned to death.

The historian Herodotus wrote in the fifth century B.C. that the Lydians (who lived in present-day Turkey) had invented gambling during the reign of Atys, long before. The Lydians were far from humble: They also claimed to have created the first gold and silver coins and retail shopping. The Lydian invention of gambling was a reaction not to the prosperity brought by trading, but to a terrible shortage of corn, which apparently could not be bought retail from surrounding regions. In these years, Lydians claimed, they devised ball, dice, and knucklebone games, though they refused credit for draughts, a board game. Gambling for the Lydians was an emergency measure: They would gamble one day so as to distract themselves from thoughts of food, and eat the next to distract themselves from gambling.

After eighteen years of eating one day and gambling the next, the king decided that the famine was only getting worse, so he divided his nation in two and decided by the casting of lots who would stay in Lydia and who would undertake a compulsory emigration under the leadership of his son Tyrrhenus. Thus ended the famine. The story is a brilliant allegory of the role of gambling in many societies. The Lydians reportedly also invented money, and the surpluses that also allowed them to develop retailing would have made them ideal gamblers. Embraced by governments, it can be used for definite social and economic purposes; today, many governments use gaming levies to keep other taxes low without cutting spending, but none directly substitute gambling for food.

The most basic Greek game was an adaptation of odds and evens, a ubiquitous divination ritual. As a game of chance, one player held a small number of objects—beads, nuts, stones, or even dice—in his hand, and the other player guessed whether the total was odd or even. As another variant of the either/or game, Greeks played heads or tails. In this simple game, players call heads or tails, and whichever player correctly picks the side landing faceup is the winner. A popular game throughout history, heads or tails is also known as "cross and pile," after an old French coin that had a cross on one side and a pillar on the other. The Greeks called it *Ostra Kinda,* and it began as a game played by young boys, who used seashells by blacking out one side and calling black or white while the shell was in the air.

Either/or games satisfied children and casual players, but the Greeks reserved more passion for more sophisticated forms of gambling. Cockfighting emerged as a popular Greek pastime in the fifth century B.C. According to legend, the Athenian leader Themistocles introduced it after seeing two birds fighting during the Persian War. He urged his troops to fight with as much heart as the skirmishing birds. After the Greek victory in that war, cockfights became an annual rite at Athens, originally as a patriotic display, but later for its own enjoyment. Betting added to that enjoyment. Cockfighting had radiated westward from India and China over the preceding centuries, and spread from Athens to the rest of Greece, Asia Minor, and Sicily.

The Greeks continued to closely associate gambling and divination by using astragali in their temples to assay the future. Astragali were also used for both adults' and children's games—young girls played a game similar to jacks, in which the player had to catch tossed bones on the back of her hand without dropping any already there. But before long, they were used for gambling. Usually, Greeks used four astragali to play (just as oracles used four astragali to divine the future). The game of throwing astragali depended on a player getting a higher-ranked throw than his opponent. The worst possible throw, four ones, was known as "the dog's throw," and the best, known as the "Venus throw," had each astragalus showing a different value.

Greeks also used six-sided dice, which they called *kuboi* (from the same root as our word "cube"). The earliest known dice from the Grecian mainland date from approximately the seventh century B.C. Dice have been found in the Acropolis, in sanctuaries, and tombs, suggesting that they retained some of their supernatural aura. Dice figured in several board games popular across the early Mediterranean world, but when Greeks spoke simply of "dicing," they usually meant to play for stakes.

Gods and humans are seen gambling on an assortment of surviving Greek votive reliefs, vases, and paintings. One marble relief dating from the fourth century B.C. depicts a friendly game of dice between Eros, Aphrodite, and a nude youth, and numerous other artworks of the period show both men and women playing dice, suggesting that women as well as men gambled. The heroes Ajax and Achilles were an especially popular pair of dice players.

When throwing dice, Greeks usually shook three dice in a special cup and threw them onto a board. As with astragali, the lowest throw was the dog (three ones), though the highest was three sixes, not the Venus throw. Archaeologists have found Greek dice with fourteen, eighteen, and even twenty sides, and as proof that some things never change, they have also dug up cheaters' dice from this period; some have numbers omitted or duplicated, while others have been weighted to make lucky throws a bit easier. In addition to bequeathing geometry, philosophy, and deductive science to the ages, it seems, the Greeks also passed on some tricks still used by crossroaders today.

Spectators bet on Greek contests of skill, such as the annual games at Olympus, Delphi, Corinth, and Nemea. Chariot races and horse races drew huge crowds, and athletes competed in footraces (including one in full armor), discus and javelin throwing, long jumping, and three forms of combat: wrestling, boxing, and *pankration,* a precursor to modern no-holds-barred mixed martial arts, which combined wrestling and striking. Victorious athletes might be commemorated by odes or statues, given prize money, or feted in their hometowns. Such widespread civic appreciation of an athlete's prowess was bolstered by betting on him.

Gambling grew even further with the rise of Rome. The Roman Republic and later the Roman Empire dominated the Mediterranean world from the second century B.C. to sixth century A.D. These conquerors were no strangers to chance or gambling. The Romans of the early first millennium A.D. lived without anything that we would recognize as science and, until the acceptance of Christianity in the fourth century, considered religion more a matter of civic duty than personal comfort or devotion. They breathed in a superstitious world, filled with signs and prodigies that seemed to offer the only clues to an otherwise inexplicable life. Romans neurotically consulted astrologers, read "auspices" (i.e., interpreted goat livers), and begged interpretations of dreams from soothsayers daily.

The Greek goddess of luck, Tyche, became Fortuna, or fortune, to the Romans. Romans, without much understanding of cause and effect in this world or hope for reward in the next, lived in constant awe of fickle Fortune or resigned themselves to a nonnegotiable Fate. In such a world, chance loomed large. The Roman polymath Pliny the Elder wrote in the first century A.D. that Fortune was invoked as the one cause of everything: "We are so much at the mercy of chance that Chance is our god." The Rutulian king Turnus, in Virgil's *Aeneid,* readied his troops for combat by reminding them that Fortune had sent what they had wished for, "a battle with a worthy foe," and that "fortune favors the brave."

Unsurprisingly, these fatalistic Romans gambled incessantly. Gambling was more than a pastime for the Romans—it was a metaphor for life itself. Julius Caesar, returning from Gaul in 49 B.C., faced a monumental decision:

Should he cross the Rubicon into Italy with his army and seek to take power at Rome by force? After seeing a supernatural apparition seize a trumpet, let loose a mighty call, and cross the river, Caesar decided that the gods were favorable to a bold crossing. As he ordered his men to bear their arms into Italy and thus begin a civil war, he remarked, "The die is cast."

Caesar meant that, having made his decision, he must leave the results to Fortune, who would decide the outcome as surely as she determined the fall of the dice. In the most important political and military decision of his career, Caesar's first instinct was to use the language of gambling to inspire his soldiers and explain himself to posterity. It is as if, upon issuing the final orders to storm the beaches at Normandy on June 6, 1944, General Dwight D. Eisenhower had announced, "We've gone all in." Living in a world ruled by an inscrutable Fortune, the Romans saw every day as a gamble.

Romans incorporated gambling into their lives in a variety of ways. When priests needed to fill a seat in the College of Vestal Virgins, they held a draft lottery, which all girls of eligible age had to enter. The lucky winner would spend the next thirty years tending the sacred fire of Vesta in the Roman Forum; should she let it be extinguished, the punishment was death. Similarly, Vestal Virgins had to maintain a strict oath of celibacy, under penalty of being buried alive. Noble Roman families made little pretense of their machinations to keep their daughters out of this lottery. Julius Caesar reportedly settled civil and even criminal disputes by flipping a coin. Leaving decisions of state to chance was not restricted to the whims of the despot, but was actually embraced as a "democratic" solution and even used to select leaders, including city magistrates and other high positions. The Romans combined elected offices with those chosen by lot, a unique solution to the problems of representative democracy.

The Romans adopted many of their games from the Greeks, such as odds and evens (which they called *par impar*), heads and tails, and cockfighting. They became particularly partial to the last. Though the Romans of the Republic originally professed to scorn cockfighting as an uncivilized sport, by the first century A.D. it was popular enough in Imperial Rome that one writer complained that enthusiastic gentleman bettors squandered their estates wagering on cockfights.

But it was the Greek games of astragali and dicing (or, as the Romans called them, *tali* and *tessarae*) in which the Romans truly excelled. Like the Greeks, the Romans used four *tali* or three *tessarae* when gambling, and followed similar rules for the ranking of throws. Those throwing *tessarae* strove to get three sixes, with all ones the lowest throw. Dice throwing inspired a

Roman proverb translated as "Either three aces or three sixes," or, as Frank Sinatra might sing, all or nothing at all.

Wherever the Romans went, they brought dice with them, and dice were a daily part of life for the city dwellers of the Roman Empire. Roman inns advertised both their comestibles and their gaming tables, and archaeologists have uncovered numerous gaming tables among Roman ruins, particularly military camps. More than one hundred dice boards from the classical era have been discovered in the city of Rome, and more have been found throughout Italy and as far off as England. Soldiers played dice games to consume the tedious hours spent on guard duty, and one Roman dice game was known as *ludus latrunculorum,* "the game of soldiers." Playing with dice was indisputably a popular diversion of the masses by the first century B.C. Dicing figured into some drinking games that would put today's college students to shame, in which players were forced to drink as many cups of wine as points on dice they had thrown. If one made the Venus throw during a drinking bout he was given the title of "master of revels."

Gambling at dice reigned supreme even among the elites of Rome. Many of the early Roman emperors distinguished themselves by their gambling. Augustus Caesar, the first Roman emperor, believed that Fortuna had adopted him as her favored son. As proof of his destiny, he claimed to always beat his onetime partner and later rival, Marc Antony, in dicing, lot throwing, and cockfighting. Consequently, he enjoyed relatively moderate gambling, particularly as he got older. He regularly diced with his dining companions, and gave his guests two and half gold pieces' worth of silver with which to gamble all night on simple games of odds and evens. The emperor did not play to win and enjoyed a reputation as a generous, rather than merciless, player. At his dinner parties he auctioned tickets to prizes of unequal value— an early lottery. In doing so, he injected an element of gambling in the distribution of gifts and avoided alienating guests by giving them inferior presents; the guest could only blame Fortuna if he received a less valuable gift than a rival or social inferior.

Other emperors' reckless, uncontrolled gambling was seen as evidence of their degeneracy. The emperor Caligula, unlike Augustus, did not see gambling as a pleasant diversion but instead played to win, at all costs, always cheating and lying. If he did lose, he was apt to make up for his bad luck at others' expense. Once, when on a losing streak, he reportedly left a game, went into the street where some rich citizens were passing, and had them arrested and their estates confiscated. He then returned to the game, boasting of his good luck. Caligula did not even let grief stop him from gambling; on the day of his sister's funeral, he played dice. When he himself was murdered, few mourned his passing.

Before he ascended to the office of emperor, Caligula's successor, Claudius, gained a reputation as a dissolute drinker and gambler. Being of a literary bent (he wrote a Roman history, an eight-volume autobiography, and twenty-eight books in Greek), Claudius penned a book about dice throwing, perhaps the earliest how-to gambling guide. Unfortunately, it has been lost. He even had a special board installed in his carriage that let him throw dice evenly while traveling. He was so scatterbrained, it is said, that he sent for men to gamble with him, long after he had sent them to their executions. He would then gamble against their estates. The writer Seneca, depicting Claudius in hell, condemned him to a gambler's version of the more familiar punishment of Tantalus (the glutton who, in the afterworld, had food and drink just beyond his reach). Claudius perpetually casts dice with a bottom-less box; he is always throwing but has never thrown as the dice are shaken but never leave the box.

Claudius's successor, Nero, played for even higher stakes. Nero often boasted that "true gentlemen always throw their money about" (an attitude adopted by gambling aristocrats ever since), and staked four thousand gold pieces on each pip of the winning throw of the dice; playing in this fashion, he could lose a maximum of 96,000 gold pieces on a single throw—a far cry from the two and a half pieces that lasted Augustus's guests all night. A later emperor, Vitellus, first came to the attention of Claudius and Nero because of his skill at dicing. Commodus, the son of the stoic philosopher/emperor Marcus Aurelius, reportedly turned the Imperial Palace into a casino.

Though they were devoted gamblers, Romans were not at ease with gambling. On the contrary, *aleator,* Latin for "gambler," was a mildly derogatory term, and Roman laws passed during the Republic remained on the books under the emperors, though they were often disdained (the emperors frequently being the first to ignore them). Gamblers could not sue to claim gambling debts, but losers could sue to recover losses. The *aedile* of the commons was charged with punishing gamblers who, if convicted, faced a fine of four times what they had wagered. Despite the prohibitions, the hardy weed of gambling proved impossible to stamp out; proscriptions against it seemed to have ultimately been ignored.

Despite the official prohibitions, old men were permitted to gamble without fear of arrest, and during the year-end holiday of Saturnalia gambling rules could be flouted with impunity. By tacit understanding, gamblers were not disturbed in the backrooms of *cauponae* (inns), *popinae* (food stalls), and *thermopolia* (taverns). The law did not even try to criminalize the *susceptor,* an innkeeper who fostered gambling in his establishment—it only declared that he could not sue to recover damages to his property inflicted by customers irate at their losses or elated over their victories. The walls of Pompeii, preserved by the eruption of Mount Vesuvius in 79 A.D., contain scrawled graffiti with gambling references such as "Get up! You don't know a thing about this game! Make room for better players." One can sense the angst of a modern-day serious blackjack player broiling at the clueless neophyte hitting on hard fifteens. One series of pictures at Pompeii even relates a gambling-related brawl.

In addition to playing with bones and dice, choosing odds and evens, and wagering on gamecocks, Romans enjoyed betting on their "national pastime," the games held for the enjoyment of the masses. Held throughout the empire at circuses and amphitheaters, these public amusements included chariot races (the most popular spectacle); a hunt, which pitted exotic animals against each other or humans; gory, intricate public executions; gladiator combat; and re-creations of famous battles, even maritime ones. Betting began with the morning hunt and likely intensified as the day went on. Partisans of various gladiators and circus factions (usually Reds, Whites, Blues, and Greens competed in the spectacles) backed their passion up with a wager, just like today's sports fans. The poor and unemployed bet with particular vigor. "Hence," writes one historian, "these explosions of exuberant joy, the outbursts of rage when the victor was proclaimed." The emperors were wise to provide a lavish public banquet after the day's games had finished (the first all-you-can-eat buffet for gamblers), succoring those who had lost everything. This may have been instituted to prevent rioting by impoverished bettors.

Elements of chance figured in the games themselves, as gladiators were sorted by skill and then paired by the drawing of lots. The Roman games gave even those who did not attend ample opportunity to gamble. Emperors like Agrippa, Nero, and Commodus, after the combats had finished, would further allow the crowd to "gamble" by firing tokens representing gifts into the stands. The struggles for these tokens was often bloody, as many plebians borrowed money against the value of these "gifts" or had taken money from an "investor" who demanded a maximum number of tokens.

Gambling increased in popularity as the Roman Empire declined in strength. Antigambler Andrew Steinmetz wrote in the nineteenth century that when Constantine abandoned Rome to found Constantinople as the

Empire's eastern capital (330 A.D.), "every inhabitant of that city . . . was addicted to gambling," by implication tying the two facts together. Even contemporary Roman writers thought their countrymen gambled too much. Juvenal, writing in the early second century A.D., described the "madness" of games of chance as "furious," as men no longer carried their purses to the gaming table, but rather their iron chests. Though Romans played only with cash and not for credit, they still made good work of ruining their fortunes and even infected invading barbarian nations with the "vice" that was mingled with the best features of Roman life.

But those barbarians were, in fact, already gambling on their own. The historian Tacitus described the ancient inhabitants of Germany as particularly avid gamblers. Legendary drinkers, but according to Tacitus the Germans "seriously" gambled even when sober. As in the story of the *Mahabharata*, they played for escalating stakes, wagering even their liberty on the final throw. The loser then voluntarily went into slavery, allowing himself to be bound and sold, which according to Tacitus was called an honor. Perhaps it is no coincidence that the Germans worshiped Mercury (the god of divination) above all other gods and were second to none in employing divination by lot. Like the Romans, the Germans were a people of chance.

As diehard gamblers, the Romans bequeathed to the world a legacy of official hypocrisy concerning games of chance. While, in their celebrated codices of law, gambling was to be sternly punished, emperors openly gambled to excess. The Roman tension between proscribed law and permitted fun would reverberate well into present times.

Because many Protestant denominations in England and the United States have been profoundly uneasy about gambling, some believe that Christianity and the religions of the Near East from which it developed (chief among them Judaism) are inherently opposed to gambling. One nineteenth-century writer wondered in print why Jesus and the disciples had not specifically condemned gambling; he believed that this must have been some accidental oversight, and by no means that true Christians might be permitted to gamble.

In fact, there is more than a little divinely sanctioned "gambling" recorded in the Bible. As in other religions, the hand of God worked through the lot-casting process to see the divine will manifested. Lot casting helped the Israelites bridge an important gap: Direct prophecy and revelation were rare, and they needed a form of divination not prohibited by biblical strictures against witchcraft and necromancy. The Urim and Thummin, priestly devices used to express the will of God, may have been lots. Lots most commonly took the form of dicelike bones; despite the high-sounding phrase *casting for lots,* priests were essentially rolling dice. They were used for religious rituals as when God commanded Moses to instruct his brother Aaron, the first high priest, to use lots in presenting a sin offering to God. The goat whose lot fell to the Lord was to be sacrificed, and the other was to be the scapegoat, who was sent into the desert, to carry away the sins of the Israelites.

Biblical-era Israelites also used lots for administrative purposes. Upon entering the land of Canaan, Joshua commanded the land to be surveyed, then, "in the presence of the Lord," cast lots to determine which tribe received which lands. Just as Octavian used lotteries to distribute gifts of unequal value to his dinner guests, this mechanism allowed Joshua to effectively divide the land without the appearance of giving preference to any tribe. Later, Saul was chosen king by lot, and priests determined the order of the ministering by drawing lots impartially. So lots helped both religious and political leaders remove themselves from making difficult decisions and gave the appearance of divine sanction to random selections. Furthermore, lots sometimes had quasi-judicial uses. When Jonah attempted to flee by boat from the calling of God to preach against the wicked men of Nineveh, God sent a storm to stop him. The sailors cast lots to determine on whose account the seas had been disturbed, and the lot fell on Jonah. As it is written in Proverbs 18:18, "The lot ends contention."

Lots were also a symbol of despair and conquest. When God told the prophet Ezekiel to warn the people of Israel that both righteous and wicked would be consumed by his wrath, he sent the king of Babylon to attack Jerusalem by influencing the fall of the lot: "For the king of Babylon will stop at the fork in the road, at the junction of the two roads, to seek an omen: He will cast lots with arrows, he will consult his idols, he will examine the liver. Into his right hand will come the lot for Jerusalem." Consulting with idols and reading livers were both forbidden to Israelites, yet God made it clear that he could influence the fall of the lot. Victorious armies cast lots for Jerusalem, its conquered peoples, and defeated nobles as a way to divide the spoils. The Psalmist speaks of himself in an hour of desperation, driven to the wall by wild animals and evil men: "They divide my garments among them and cast lots for my clothing." To be the subject of a biblical lot casting could only mean the worst.

The Hebrew Bible never specifically mentions gambling, leading to some flexibility in its acceptance. It is not known if ancient Israelites cast lots for nonreligious purposes, but scholars believe that they did not use dice until the era of Herod, in the first century A.D. Gambling never received explicit priestly or royal approval in biblical times, though it was sometimes useful. According to tradition, a form of gambling even helped to sustain religious learning during a dark period in Jewish history. Upon his succession to the throne of Syria in 175 B.C., Antiochus began bitterly oppressing Judea, prohibiting practice of the Jewish religion. Those who clandestinely studied Torah began playing with the dreidel, a four-sided top, which can be thought of as essentially a four-sided die that is spun instead of thrown. If asked by an Antiochan official what they were doing, the scholars would innocently claim they were gambling—a permissible pastime. Antiochus's oppression ended with a successful revolt led by the nationalist Maccabees, commemorated as the holiday of Hannukah. The dreidel game is still played, particularly among children, and may be an archaic surviving example of other dice games of antiquity.

Despite this instance of gambling aiding education, the sages who compiled and commentated on Jewish law found it somewhat undesirable. According to the Babylonian Talmud, the mammoth compilation of Jewish oral laws and traditions, habitual dice-players were not permitted to be magistrates or witnesses in court. According to one rabbinic interpretation, this was because dice players did not "occupy themselves with the welfare of the world." Only those who repented of gambling could be accepted as full citizens. Other sages, though, qualified the rejection of gamblers as witnesses, holding that only those who had no other occupation (i.e., professional gamblers) could be barred from testimony.

Later Jewish thought produced no consensus on gambling. Given the absence of specific biblical sanction or outright condemnation, both antigamblers and gambling apologists advanced scriptural justifications for their positions. The Talmudic suggestion that professional gamblers lived in ignorance of the betterment of society suggests the common view that gamblers were parasites that did not produce valuable goods or provide useful services. Like that of many other religions, Judaism's disapproval of gambling stopped well short of condemnation.

Christians felt a similar ambiguity. The unsavory image of gambling at the crucifixion of Christ is not specifically antithetical to gambling. Soldiers casting lots for the clothes of Jesus was a well-known metaphor for despair. John (19:24), specifically wrote that the lot casting fulfilled the prophecy of Psalm 22:18, that lots would be cast for the garments of one forsaken by God. But lots also figured positively in the early church. After the betrayal and death of Judas, the eleven remaining apostles needed to choose his replacement. After nominating two men, Barsabbas and Matthias, they prayed, asking God to reveal to them his chosen one. They then cast lots, which fell to Matthias, who became the new apostle.

The early church had no real restrictions on gambling and might even have condoned it at times. Some early Christians found gambling to be a matter of faith. An *alveus* (a backgammon-like game) board discovered in Rome has an inscription translated as:

> If after this manner one should play at the throws of the *alveus*, Jesus Christ gives victory, and assistance to those who wrote his name, even in such trifling matters as playing this game.

Today, most Christian churches frown upon the idea that Jesus takes an active interest in games of chance, but this inscription is the ancient equivalent of modern-day professional athletes thanking God for victory in postgame celebrations. Even later, around the year 960 A.D., Bishop Wibold of Cambrai (France) used a dice game to spread the Gospel. Wibold created a list of fifty-six virtues—one for each possible throw of three dice. In this game, the caster threw the dice, noted the result, looked up the corresponding virtue, and meditated on it for a certain time.

Despite these examples of tolerance, most church leaders considered gambling bad. The emperor Justinian, both the emperor of the Eastern Roman (Byzantine) Empire and head of the Orthodox Church, issued the *Corpus Juris Civilis,* a compendium of civil and canon law, in 529. Justinian acknowledged that gambling was ancient, but as people were "playing night and day, for silver, gold, and jewels, to the ruin of their fortune," he banned gambling in public or private houses. Not only gamblers, but even spectators could be punished. Five years later, Justinian announced an addendum to the law; having observed that several clergy, even bishops, still participated in gaming, he decreed that any cleric caught engaging in or observing gambling would be suspended and subject to canonical penance.

Later Christian authorities continued to warn against gambling, but prohibitions on it were almost always riddled with loopholes or just ignored. The first Holy Roman Emperor, Charlemagne, felt compelled to declare that any cleric or layman who resolved to be a gamester would be excommunicated. Charlemagne's son, Louis the Pious, blunted the prohibition in 818, ruling that gambling clergy would only be suspended from office for three years. When Otto I issued his own ecclesiastical statutes in 952, only bishops, presbyters, and deacons were subject to the ban on gambling, though they would be deposed from office if they "refused admonition to amend."

Some church authorities took the stance that gambling itself was not immoral but became a vice only "by circumstances." By itself, it might be an innocent, though not useful, recreation. When pursued too eagerly or excessively, though, it inevitably led to troubles. The loss of time from more serious pursuits that might better glorify God, the incidence of profane language at the gaming table, violence arising from gambling quarrels, and frauds perpetrated by cheaters made gambling scandalous.

Although Jewish and Christian religious leaders were free to tolerate gambling or fulminate against it, Islam took a less equivocal stance. Making rapid conquests after the death of its founding prophet, Muhammad, in 622, within a century Islam had pushed its boundaries to include a wide swath of the world from northwest India to the Iberian peninsula. Before the rise of Islam, the nomadic traders of Arabia, familiar with surrounding cultures, undoubtedly had acquaintance with dice playing and lot casting, activities that could be either religious divination or secular entertainment.

Islam's holy book, the Koran, speaks with great authority on the subject of gambling. In one section, the Koran tells believers that in both intoxicants and gambling there is simultaneously great utility and great sin, though the sin outweighs the utility. Those who ask whether they can play are told to spend on these only as much as they can afford to lose—sensible advice in any age and, seemingly, not an ironclad prohibition, but the same sort of cautionary admonition found in many other faiths. But another verse clarifies the Muslim stance on gambling, classing it, along with drinking, setting up idols, and arrow divination, as an abomination and the handiwork of Satan, to be strenuously avoided. Satan himself sowed enmity and hatred among Muslim brethren with drinking and gambling, distracting the faithful from worship and religious study.

With such stern pronouncements against gambling in its holy scriptures, mainstream Islam officially maintained a prohibition against it. This is not to say that no Muslims gambled; like many otherwise religious people, when it comes to gambling some Muslims chose to err on the side of temptation rather than righteousness, playing on despite the risk to the soul. Others mitigated the Koranic prohibition by donating all winnings to charity, or by playing for no stakes. As a result, gambling persisted.

Betting games are mentioned sporadically throughout historical Muslim literature, suggesting that gambling never really disappeared. The Persian mystic Rumi, writing in the thirteenth century, wrote that one should "gamble everything for love/if you're a true human being." Gambling games like chess and *nard* (an early form of blackjack) were common in Islamic regions. Horse racing for stakes, which had been common in the pre-Muslim period, continued after the spread of Islam throughout the Near East, and elephant races, camel races, and even pigeon races could be found. As in other countries, interest in these diversions was justified as aiding military preparedness and, in the case of the pigeons, communication. Cockfighting was also common.

Gambling remained widespread in Italy long after the last Roman emperor disappeared. Though the prospering trade economy faltered, along with the ready cash that boosted Roman gambling, nevertheless gambling continued throughout Europe as the empire split, then crumbled, and the Dark Ages began. Though the stakes diminished, enthusiasm did not.

Medieval Europeans continued to play with knucklebones, though they seldom cast them as dice. Instead, they used them to play games similar to modern jacks or marbles; deftness of hand, not luck of a throw, determined the outcome of the game. Dicing, however, remained popular, as did board games such as backgammon (also known as trictrac). Starting with Richard II (r. 1377–1399), English monarchs repeatedly outlawed gambling, demanding instead that subjects practice archery. Sharp archers may have combined the two by betting on archery contests. Other semiathletic games, such as lawn bowling, Italian bocce, German skittles, and quoits (horseshoes), may have involved betting and were frequently denounced by monarchs intent on their subjects preparing instead for war.

But war was seldom an excuse to stop gambling. Indeed, "mock war" sports like the "skullball" predecessors of football and rugby, as well as chivalric tournaments and jousting competitions, may have inspired betting. Soldiers, as they had in Roman times, continued to gamble, often to distraction. When Richard I of England and Philip II of France led the Third Crusade in 1190, they issued an edict that forbade all below the rank of knight from playing any kind of game for money, restricted knights, clergy, and members of royal retinues to losses of 20 shillings within any twenty-four-hour period, and sportingly allowed the kings to play for whatever stakes they wished. Still, it is likely that gambling continued unchecked. A twelfth-century account of Bernard of Clairvaux, which advertised for the glory of the Knights Templar, praised them for forswearing dice and chess, presumably in contrast to other military orders that embraced these two recreations.

Jean de Joinville, the chronicler of the Seventh Crusade (1248–1254), recounted an incident that speaks to the prevalence of gambling among soldiers and nobles at the time, particularly when idling the hours away at sea. The French king Louis IX (later canonized as Saint Louis), grieving at the death of his brother the count of Artois, was bothered by the fact that his other brother, the count of Anjou, avoided his company while they were sailing to Acre. One day, upon learning that Anjou was playing a game of chance with Gautier de Nemours, the king decided that he had had enough and, though weakened by illness, snatched the board and dice from the players and tossed it into the sea. The crafty Nemours benefited from the king's ill temper, as, according to Joinville, "he tipped all the money on the table—and there was plenty of it—into his lap and took it away with him."

So gambling was common, but not always considered appropriate. The rules of knighthood, written and unwritten, would ultimately gel into the code of chivalry. In the late thirteenth century, Ramon Llull, a Catalan philosopher, penned *The Book of the Order of Chivalry*, which stressed the religious honor of knighthood and the knight's obligation to seek and defend justice. Llull did not condemn or condone gambling, instead cautioning knights to avoid the sins of "too much" and those of "too little." This was the cardinal virtue of temperance, which he defined as a reasonable middle ground between the two extremes. Following such advice, one could expect knights to gamble moderately; indeed later aristocrats took it as their birthright to do so. Given that Llull explicitly branded knights who resorted to divination and soothsaying as both displeasing to God and chivalric failures, his failure to condemn gambling likely meant that it was tolerable if not taken to excess.

About a century later, a French knight set down his own *Book of Chivalry*, which warned against excessive greed, particularly as it manifested itself in games of dice. The knight cautioned that, "when it is engaged in through greed for gain," dice was no longer a game and could a sap a young man's finances to the point of despair. But dice were not the only cause of ruin; the game of "real tennis" (an indoor game whose players originally used gloved hands to smack the ball) had caused many to lose "their chattels and their inheritance." Women, for whom ball games used to be pastime and pleasure, suffered grievously from "real tennis." The prospective knight should instead embrace the habits of highly successful paladins, which included jousting, conversation, dancing, and singing in the company of ladies and damsels. "One should leave playing dice for money to rakes, bawds, and tavern rogues," the knight concluded, revealing that it was not unseemly to play dice merely for sport or diversion.

The English were similarly enamored of gambling. A twelfth-century English chronicler declared that clergy and bishops were fond of dicing, and the diplomat, author, and bishop John of Salisbury (1115–1180) denounced "the damnable art of dice playing." Later royal decrees criminalized dicing, and criminal records from the City of London dating as far back as 1311 show that those who were "wont to entice strangers . . . to a tavern, and there deceive them by using false dice" or otherwise made their livings from playing at dice were often imprisoned.

Geoffrey Chaucer, whose fourteenth-century writings mark the beginnings of a distinctly English literature, described gamblers and gambling in his *Canterbury Tales*. "The Cook's Tale" is a sketch of Perkin Reveler, an apprentice who loves the tavern better than his master's victual shop and is renowned as the best dice-shooting apprentice in town. Perkin energetically pursued dice, wine, song, dance, and girls of joy, to the unfortunate detriment of his victualing. After his master learned of his perfidy and discharged him from his apprenticeship, Perkin moved in with a fellow dicer whose wife supplemented his income by prostitution; surrounded by whores and thieves, this reveler was happy in his element. At that point, regrettably, the tale leaves off, but it does show that dicing was a common sport of laborers in medieval England, that one could shoot dice in the street or in a tavern, and that the game occupied the same social margins as drinking, dancing, and whoring.

In "The Pardoner's Tale," Chaucer painted the three roisterers around whom the tale revolves as thoroughly debauched by their drinking and gambling. Two of the derelicts plot to murder their companion and split his share of a found treasure so that "Then may we both our lusts all fulfill, And play at dice right at our own will." In an aside on the evils of swearing, Chaucer described "hazard" as "the very mother of all lies." Its fruit included swearing, anger, deceit, and murder. If even a noble prince gambled, Chaucer wrote, his reputation would suffer, the more so because better was expected of him. Throughout the *Tales*, gambling is depicted as a worthless obsession.

Yet gambling was widely popular in England before and after Chaucer's time. Fairs, festivals, and traveling carnivals, each of which likely had plenty of gambling, crossed and recrossed the English countryside during medieval and Renaissance times. As was true in earlier times, archery and archery contests remained important because they contributed to the national defense. Archery was celebrated as an honest, wholesome sport (before the adoption of gunpowder weapons, it was the bulwark of England's armies), and a 1545 author described the sport as a cure for "evil gaming." Still, there is no reason that competitors or spectators might not have gambled on the outcome of archery contests, or on other popular sports of the time, such as the lost game of shin kicking, in which participants literally kicked each other in the shins as a means of measuring physical endurance and athletic ability.

Some medieval monarchs issued edicts to their citizens banning gambling and other leisure activities. Others took a more balanced view of life and encouraged their subjects to have a little fun—Alphonso X of Castile was one such happy-go-lucky king. In the late thirteenth century Alphonso commissioned a ninety-eight-page, 150-illustration *Book of Games* for the benefit of "those who like to enjoy themselves in private to avoid the annoyance and unpleasantness of public places, or those who have fallen into another's power, either in prison, or slavery, or as seafarers, and in general all those who are looking for a pleasant pastime which will bring them comfort and dispel their boredom."

About two thirds of the book concerns chess, with dice and board games taking up the rest. The king contrasted games of skill, such as chess, with those of luck, like dice, and found that though table games like backgammon, which incorporated skill, were more important and popular, even they could not be played without dice. Thus, he concluded that dice were a fit topic for kingly discourse. The king further described the proper cubical shape of dice and warned that misshapen dice could be used for cheating, "and that would be trickery more than luck," though he also told readers how to use loaded dice. Most of the games illustrated in the manuscript use three dice. Alphonso expounds on several games. Some are simple, in which the highest roll wins. Others, such as *hazard* and *marlota*, were early versions of craps, in which a player first rolls a number, then has to roll it again before his or her opponent. The word *hazard* was apparently derived from the Arabic word for dice, *az-zahr*. According to one account, Europeans learned of the game following an eighth-century Saracen invasion of Corsica, from whence it filtered to the Continent. Other accounts have hazard brought back from the Crusades during the twelfth century, and it was certainly widely established by the next century. Some illustrations show women playing. Hazard was by this time played among all Europeans, not just Alphonso's Castilian subjects— Dante mentioned the game in the sixth canto of his *Paradiso,* and there are several other references to the game throughout the continent.

Francesco Petrarca, also known as Petrarch (1304–1374), the Italian poet and humanist considered a father of the Renaissance, covered gambling in his *De Remediis utriusque Fortunae,* translated as *Remedies for Fortune Fair and Foul.* He described dicing as "pernicious" and argued that just because emperors had indulged did not give free reign to lesser men to do so. Petrarch classified gambling as "an inexplicable, gaping cesspool . . . leading to abject

Detail from an illustration of the game of hazard appearing
in Alphonso X's *Book of the Games of Chance*, published in the 13th century.

desperation," something that meant only "pain and anguish." He believed
that, win or lose, gambling was unprofitable, because "he who loses suffers
and he who wins is tempted and lured into the trap." Petrarch warned that
"what you won, a thousand will wrest from you here and there; what you lose,
no one will give back to you." Even when a winner, he reasoned, the gambler
did not truly profit.

Petrarch declared that all money was unstable, whirling away "possibly due
to the roundness of the coins," further elaborating that money won by gambling was the least stable of all. Because losing became more bitter after having tasted winning, those who gambled were destined to become caught in a
vicious cycle of chasing losses; Petrarch likened the pleasure of gambling to a
sweet poison that would erupt in one's veins. Consoling a loser, Petrarch reminded him that losing was not as bad as winning, which was really usury and
not honest gain: "There is more reason for joy now than when you win and
jump in false glee," Petrarch counseled. "A bad beating is better than a fawn-
ing falsehood!" Those who lost and learned a lesson from it might "win in the
game of conduct" and remove themselves from the cesspool of gambling. If
neither loss nor shame could teach a man not to gamble, Petrarch concluded,
words were useless.

Despite Petrarch's reasoned arguments, gambling continued, and even
grew in popularity. In a panegyric to the grand marketplace of Florence, the

Mercato Vecchio, the fourteenth-century poet Antonio Pucci included gambling in the list of wonders found there. In between his praise of the tradesmen who called the Mercato home, Pucci noted that in the market "the hustlers are in their element," as it had moneylenders, ragmen, exchange dealers, and gambling houses. In those early days of entrepreneurial finance, the lines between gambling, speculation, and financial services were often blurry. Pucci further described noblemen and -women watching "the costerwomen [hawkers of goods] and the gambling hustlers come to blows" and noted that sometimes the hustlers of the market attacked each other with knives, "disturbing the beauty of the piazza."

The widespread gambling of the medieval period could inspire tragedy or farce. The *Decameron*, which Petrarch's student Boccaccio finished in 1353, has a gambling story that is more of the latter. It tells of the inveterate gambler Cecco Fortarrigo, a servant to a young nobleman, Cecco Angiolieri. While en route to the March of Ancona, where Angiolieri hopes to impress a cardinal with his wealth and gain a prominent position, the pair stop at a tavern. While Angiolieri sleeps, Fortarrigo loses all of his money and his clothes, excepting his undershirt, gambling; he then sneaks into the room and takes Angiolieri's money, which he also loses. Angiolieri refuses to help Fortarrigo reclaim his clothes (he, after all, is now penniless as well), and rides off. But Fortarrigo runs after him and convinces a band of peasants that Angiolieri has robbed him of his money and clothes. The peasants then force Angiolieri to dismount and disrobe, give his mount and clothes to the purported victim Fortarrigo, and force Angiolieri to walk back to town in shame wearing only his undershirt. Unfortunately, Boccaccio did not specify what game the crafty Fortarrigo played, but it seems a fair conclusion that gambling at taverns, probably with dice, was common enough in fourteenth-century Italy.

Playing for high stakes, playing to kill time, or playing because one simply could not stop—all were hallmarks of gambling before most of today's dominant religions were born. While these religions have often criticized gambling, they have only rarely condemned it. The roots of gambling could not be pulled up by imperial edict or religious vituperation. Over the coming centuries, human ingenuity would continue to find new ways to gamble, and moralists would continue to grapple with the consequences.

3

Knaves and Kings

◆ ◆ ◆

CARDS COME INTO PLAY

In the first half of the second millennium A.D., a revolutionary form of gambling swept across Asia and Europe. Allowing for infinitely more variation than dice games, capable of artistic embellishment and even educational lessons, playing cards would supplant dice as the favored gambling mechanism in most of the world.

Nearly every serious collector or historian of playing cards, it seems, has a pet theory about where these gambling devices first appeared. Those looking for definitive archaeological evidence of the earliest playing cards have been supremely disappointed, chiefly because of the fragility of cards. Unlike dice or coins, which can endure the millennia little the worse for wear, playing cards have short lives. Without material evidence, it is difficult to say exactly who has been playing cards the longest.

Still, people love unraveling a mystery almost as much as they adore gambling, and scores have tried to puzzle out the origin of cards. Around 1900, Stewart Culin, an anthropologist devoted to the study of Asian and American Indian games, concluded that both playing cards and chess descended from Korean divinatory arrows used in the sixth century. These symbolic arrows were actually slips of bamboo. Culin deduced that secular playing cards evolved from the original, sacred divinatory arrows because they looked similar and because the Korean term for cards, *htou-tjyen,* translated literally as "fighting tablets."

Most Korean packs had eight suits of ten cards each; the suits were man, fish, crow, pheasant, antelope, star, rabbit, and horse. The ten cards of each suit were numbers one to nine and "the general," the tenth and highest-ranking card.* The cards were made from oiled silk and were approximately eight inches long and one-half inch wide.

---

*The eighty cards of the common Korean deck correspond well with the Chinese lottery game known in America as keno.

The most popular game in Korea in the late nineteenth century closely resembled baccarat; it is not known how long this game had been played in the
country. In this game, *yet pang mang i,* or "sweetmeat pestle," two players drew
two or three cards, trying to get a total value of eight or nine. As in baccarat,
if the total exceeded nine, only the last digit of the total counted. Another
common game, *tong tang,* had between three and six players, with rules something like those of modern rummy games, in which players discard and pick
up cards with an eye toward creating melds, or matches. The melding principle is common in many Asian games, including noncard games like mahjong
and those played with dominoes or *pai gow* tiles.

Culin was unable to provide any reliable date for the introduction of Korean cards, and believed that Chinese cards evolved from Korean ones because of their similarity in design. Chinese cards do indeed bear some
resemblance to Korean cards. They are also relatively slender, though stouter
than their Korean counterparts, usually measuring between three and five
inches long and one half to one and a half inches wide. But the Chinese
were not so quick to acknowledge the influence of their neighbors. The
compiler of *Ching-tsze-tung,* a Chinese dictionary dating from 1628, cited a
legend that fixed the creation of *teen-tsze-pae,* or "dotted cards," in the early
twelfth century. According to the story, the bored occupants of the emperor's harem invented playing cards to keep themselves amused. There
were, after all, over three thousand "ladies of the palace," including the empress, wives, consorts, assistant consorts, concubines, and assistant concubines, and only one emperor to go around. The *Ching-tsze-tung* dated the
innovation to 1120 and reported playing cards to have been widespread by
1131.

Culin divided Chinese cards into four types: those based on money, those
derived from dominoes, those developed from chess, and assorted others.
Money-token cards were further divided into *kwan pai,* or "stick cards," *liut
chi,* or "wastepaper," and *chung fat,* or "hit and go." The simplest *kwan pai* pack
had thirty cards, with number cards one to nine in three suits, as well as three
court cards. The suits were *tsin,* cash, *sok,* strings, and *man,* myriads. The most
common court cards were *hung fa,* red flower, *pak fa,* white flower, and *tsin
man,* thousand myriads. Usually, four packs of thirty, joined by between two
and six special kam, or "gold" cards, formed a complete set; the gold cards
were wild, being used to take the place of any card needed to complete a set
or trick. The other money-token cards were slightly different. *Liut chi* card
games had four suits—cash, strings of cash, myriads of strings, and tens of

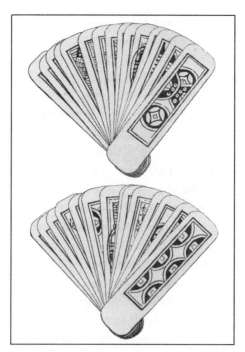

Chinese playing cards.

myriads—and were played only in South China, while *chung fat* games were only found in Chekiang and Kiangsu provinces.

In appearance, Chinese cards differed superficially from modern European playing cards, though there were some similarities. Like European cards, they were mass produced by woodblock printing on thin cardboard. Their backs were red, black, or yellow, usually plain but sometimes with a diamond pattern, and their faces had printed black pips on a white background, sometimes with red Chinese characters. Some packs had pictorial depictions of the animals representing their suits, while others merely had the name of the animal. The cards were rounded at the top and bottom and left a small unmarked space, which enabled the player to spread the cards in a familiar "fan" pattern; one Chinese word for cards, *shen,* translates as fan. Chinese players customarily fanned their cards from the top, unlike European players, who did so from the bottom. Some Chinese cards had markings at both ends, which let a player easily read them without flipping them over, an innovation that would not become widespread on European decks until the nineteenth century. Other similarities between Chinese and European cards leave open the possibility that the former inspired the latter. Red and black, the colors most prominent on Chinese card faces, became the dominant colors of not only European card suits, but even other casino games, like roulette.

A Venetian tradition holds that a native son, Marco Polo, brought playing cards back with him from China. But his father, Maffeo, and uncle Niccolò did not bring cards back with them when they returned from their first journey to the East in 1269 (though they were almost certainly present in China at the time), and there is no documentation that Marco brought them back either. Marco's published account of his travels, *Il Milone,* makes no mention of playing cards, let alone his family's introduction of them to Venice. Indeed, playing cards are first recorded in Italy nearly eighty years after he returned from Asia. Also, the earliest known European cards look remarkably different from Chinese ones. If Europe borrowed cards from the Chinese, it was by a far more circuitous route than the one the Polos traveled.

China was not the only area in Asia to boast of having invented cards. The Indian subcontinent developed its own style of playing cards and a card-creation myth similar to China's. According to Hindu legend, the highly strung wife of a maharajah was both bored and boundlessly irritated by her husband's habit of pulling at his beard. She then devised a game that would allow them both to pass the time indoors and give him something to do with his hands. This legend satisfies few historians but, like the Chinese myth, links playing cards with leisure and royalty. Most historians believe that playing cards were actually introduced to the subcontinent via Persia.

Traditional Indian playing cards were round, unlike those of virtually every other country. The first reference to the game of *ganjifa,* the dominant Indian card game, dates from the sixteenth century, though *kridapatram,* literally "painted rags for playing," are supposed to be several centuries older. *Ganjifa,* which is a borrowing of the Farsi *"ganjifeh"* or playing card, substantiates the theory that cards came to India from Persia, likely before the Mughal conquest of the sixteenth century. The Mughals were Islamic, though not strict adherents to the letter of Koranic law. In addition to allowing Hindus latitude in the practice of their religion, they apparently tolerated cardplaying. The first known Indian reference to *ganjifa,* in fact, comes from a biography of the Mughal emperor Babur. In addition to describing the cards used to play the game, it records that Babur himself delighted in playing with his daughter and made gifts of packs of cards.

A *ganjifa* deck had eight, ten, or twelve suits of twelve cards each, with ten numbered cards and two court cards, a king and his second, a vizier or minister. Early suit signs included horses, elephants, soldiers, forts, ships, women, serpents, and demons. Eventually, *ganjifa* became a vehicle for Hindu religion and folklore. The ten-suited pack of *dashavatara ganjifa* featured an incarnation of Vishnu presiding over each suit, and this game spread rapidly throughout India. Other decks took other elements of Hindu tradition, and these, too, became widespread.

Indian playing cards were fashioned out of everything from ivory and mother-of-pearl to wood, paper, cloth, and even fish scales and palm leaves. A class of craftsmen called *chitrakars* worked laboriously to produce colorful *ganjifa* cards, hand-painting, engraving, and enameling them with brightly colored backs and detailed faces. The production of *ganjifa* cards is still an active, though declining, industry in India, hailed by its partisans as an indigenous craft that must be preserved. When the author of the *Rig Veda* penned the gambler's hymn, he surely never imagined that, a few millennia later, playing cards would be championed as an essential element of Indian culture.

Playing cards were indisputably diverse throughout Asia in the early second millennium A.D. It is likely that the idea of gambling with ranked cards filtered westward from China, leaving each culture free to develop its own

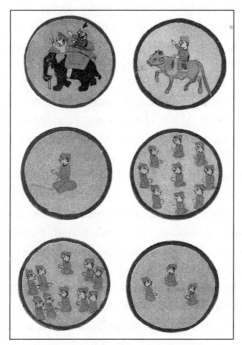

These yellow-colored, circular playing cards are typical of traditional cards found on the Indian subcontinent.

variant. Cards did more than just pass through lands under the sway of Islam; rather, they enjoyed a paradoxically prolific development there. One theory holds that Chinese expatriates in the town of Tabriz introduced playing cards into Persia in the late thirteenth century, along with paper money. From here, Persians developed their own sets of cards, which circulated throughout the Islamic world and, from Egypt and Syria, to seafaring Venetian traders, who took them back to Europe. The Mameluke set of playing cards, dated to around 1500 and discovered in Istanbul, has four suits: cup, swords, coins, and polo sticks, each with thirteen cards, one to ten and three court cards, a king *(malik),* governor *(naib),* and vice-governor *(naib thani).* Unlike European cards, these "court" or "face" cards typically did not have pictorial representations, which is an understandable result of the Muslim imperative against artistic reproductions of the human form. Though this pack is over a century younger than the oldest known reference to cards in Europe, fragments of similar cards have been dated to the thirteenth century, making them old enough to have preceded European ones.

The game of *ganjifa,* which ultimately became the national card game of India, developed first in Persia. In the early sixteenth century, the poet Ahli Shirazi wrote the *Rubaiyat-i-Ganjifa,* a poem with ninety-six quatrains, one for each card in a *ganjifa* deck. The poem has no details about the style of play but preserves the eight suit names and their rank: slave, crown, sword, gold coin, harp, document, silver coin, and stores. Other sources document the popularity of *ganjifa* at this time, and it was apparently a favorite of Ismail, the first shah of the Safavid Dynasty. It was ultimately suppressed in the seventeenth century by Shah Abbas II and survives today only in India.

The Islamic tolerance of cards allowed for their transmission to Europe. By the late fourteenth century, the Crusaders, though not successful in holding the Holy Land from the Saracens, had brought back several innovations, and the dawn of the Renaissance was beginning to break. At precisely this moment, playing cards burst onto the European scene, ready to enthrall a people eager for more gambling. The best available evidence indicates that cards were introduced to Europe by way of Italy. The suit signs on the earliest known Italian cards, *coppe* (cups), *spadi* (swords), *denari* (coins), and *bastoni* (batons or sticks), were clearly derived from the Arab suits, with one sensible alteration. Because polo was not widely known in Europe until the nineteenth century, Italians logically turned the polo sticks into batons. Further, the swords on Italian decks were curved, like Saracen blades, and the retention of a money suit recalls Chinese playing cards.

Venetians and Genoese traders commanded networks of ships and caravans that spanned from India and China, through the south of Russia, into the Sahara Desert, and as far west as England. Florentine families maintained commercial agents in cities as diverse as Seville, Majorca, Barcelona, Marseilles, Nice, Avignon, Paris, Lyon, Bruges, Cyprus, Constantinople, and Jerusalem, and it is possible that that they, too, helped disseminate playing cards. With an economic surplus and a thriving arts community (card making was then an artistic endeavor), northern Italy was uniquely disposed to capitalize on the innovation of playing cards by manufacturing them itself.

These early Italian decks had fifty-two cards, with numbered cards from one to ten and three court cards duplicated in the four suits discussed above. They hewed closely to their Saracen models; the court cards, for example, usually consisted of the king, *cavallo* ("knight"), and *fante* ("foot soldier"), though sometimes Italian card makers may have substituted a queen for the *cavallo*. The first hand-painted cards were extremely expensive. But with the application of mass-production techniques such as stenciling, wood engraving, and block printing, playing cards were produced cheaply enough to become a game of the masses, and spread like wildfire across Europe.

The Italians played several card games. *Trappola*, reportedly the oldest one, used a standard deck from which the threes, fours, fives, and sixes had been removed, leaving thirty-six cards. The object of the game was to score points by taking tricks, or combinations of cards. Two other games, basset and primero or primiera (also called *il frusso* or flush), were also popular in the fifteenth century (primero became a favorite game of peasants). Primiera was a vying game and may be described as a vague ancestor of poker in that regard. Essentially, players of vying games are dealt cards, then vie with each other by increasing their stakes. The winner is the player who holds the best combination of cards, or the one whose opponents fear is holding the best combination. Like primero, the game became extremely popular in England, and other vying games, such as English brag, French *bouilotte* and *poque,* German *poch,* and Spanish *mus,* are variations on the vying theme first seen in primiera. The vying principle filtered as far as Persia, where by the eighteenth century a twenty-card game called *as nas,* with some similarities to American poker, was being played. All of these games are ancestors of poker only to the extent that they are the best-known vying games of their own country and epoch; there is little evidence to trace poker's roots directly to any one of these games.

The highest ranks of Italian society embraced playing cards, setting very public examples for all to emulate. Lorenzo de' Medici (1449–1492) was an

Early Italian playing cards, with suits of swords, maces, coins, and cups.

archetypical Renaissance man: an astute politician, a patron of technology and the arts, sponsoring Leonardo da Vinci, Michelangelo, Botticelli, Donatello, and others. Known as *il Magnifico* ("the Magnificent") by his contemporaries in Florence, he was undoubtedly one of the leading citizens of his day. He embraced card games, mentioned *la bassetta* and *il frusso* in his poetry, gained renown as a player, and is apocryphally believed to have created a few games.

Playing cards rapidly traced the commercial routes that wily Venetians, Genoese, Florentines, and Milanese had established, spreading just as quickly as a grimmer Italian import, the Black Death. A Spanish reference to the game of *naip* in 1371 may be the first European reference to cards (the Spanish word for cards is *naipes,* and the Arab word is *naib,* reinforcing the Saracen origin theory). Within a few years, references to cards were legion. In 1377, a revision to a Paris antigambling law added cards to the list of prohibited games; in the same year, the Florentine senate passed a resolution regulating the play of "a certain game called *naibbe,* [which] has recently been introduced into these parts." A Swiss monk, Johannes von Rheinfelden of Basel, wrote that "a certain game, called the game of cards, has reached us in the present year, namely A.D. 1377." He further described the game, which was played with a fifty-two-card deck with four suits, each of which had ten numbered cards, a king, and two "marshals."

The new game spread farther: Cards were prohibited (and therefore, it stands to reason, already popular) in Regensburg, a Bavarian city, in 1379 and mentioned in the accounts of the duchess of Brabant (in today's Belgium) and her husband, Wenceslas of Luxembourg. The ducal couple, the account books noted, had been provided a sum of money to purchase playing cards. Also in that year, an Italian chronicler noted dryly: "In the year 1379, was brought into Viterbo the game of cards, which comes from the country of the Saracens." By 1380, then, chronicles and law books in Italy, Paris, Spain, Germany, and Switzerland had all noted the recent arrival of playing cards.

By 1393, cards were common enough in France that the treasurer to French king Charles VI could note in his accounts that he had paid out to a painter fifty-six sols for "three packs of cards, gilt and colored, and variously ornamented, for the amusement of the king." Playing cards might have been a royal perquisite then, but a scant six years later they had become so widespread that the provost of Paris included them in an edict forbidding working people from playing games of chance on working days.

Cards continued to be the rage in the Italian states, sometimes to the displeasure of their rulers. Amadeus VIII, duke of Savoy, issued an antigambling edict in 1430, nine years before his election as Pope Felix V. In it, he specified that playing any game for money was forbidden, though players could indulge themselves in certain approved games, provided the stakes were only food and drink. Cards were included in the list of forbidden recreations, with a curious exception: "Nevertheless, they are allowed to women, with whom men may also play, provided that they play only for pins." *Pins* is taken to mean anything of trifling value, and is the origin of the phrase *pin money*, which would be used to describe the stakes women wagered into the twentieth century.

While most Italians loved playing cards, some concluded that the new diversion was only the vice of gambling with a new face. Bernardin of Siena, an eloquent Franciscan, helped spur a religious revival starting in 1417 in Milan, as he toured Italy, preaching eloquently against whatever local vice reigned supreme. After hearing his denunciations, his followers repented of their sins by casting their "vanities" into a fire. Usury and internecine conflicts were his chief targets, but on March 5, 1423, he preached a sermon in Bologna against gambling. Standing on the steps of the church of St. Petronius, he lashed out against gambling and luxury. The assembled churchgoers were so moved by his eloquence that they immediately scrambled to find whatever dice or cards they could and cast them into the fire.

But this crusade against vice, like so many others, had its victims. As the true believers continued heaping their gambling implements into the fire, a disconsolate man began openly weeping. He protested to Bernardin that, as he was a card maker with no other livelihood, he was now condemned to starvation. The preacher—who would be canonized as St. Bernardin soon after his death—urged the man to use his skill at painting to instead make copies of a sacred monogram surrounded by the sun's rays. The erstwhile card maker did so and, reportedly, became wealthier than ever. The story may be apocryphal—Bernardin's oration against gambling might have been temporarily effective in curing the Bolognese of their gambling, but the card maker likely would have had a boom in business soon after Bernardin departed and the townspeople reconsidered. Still, it shows that by the early fifteenth century, card making was a specialized business.

Later antigambling campaigns were more sinister. A former Dominican priest named Girolamo Savonarola followed Bernardin's route but raised his bonfires of the vanities to the level of compulsion. Lorenzo de' Medici, a confirmed gambler and art lover (thus embracing two of Savonarola's bugbears), but also a devout man, personally invited Savonarola to preach in Florence. This was a decision that Lorenzo's heirs would regret, as Savonarola was not content with mere spiritual leadership. When he assumed control of Florence after agitating for the ejection of the Medicis in 1494, he established a "Christian and free" republic, in which the word of God—as interpreted by Savonarola—was law. In 1497, seeking to purge Florence of all unholy influences, he organized another bonfire of the vanities. He sent his followers door-to-door collecting mirrors, dresses, cosmetics, books, and works of art of dubious morality (including several Botticelli originals), and burned them all in Florence's Piazza della Signoria. Along with many invaluable Renaissance works of art and literature, the believers also reduced to ashes gaming tables and equipment. Within a few months the Florentines tired of virtue and, after rioting and revolt, reopened their taverns. Savonarola, after being excommunicated by Pope Alexander IV, was in 1498 simultaneously hanged and burned in the Piazza della Signoria, where both the vanities and those he had condemned as heretics had been immolated. The Medicis soon returned to power and gambling quickly resumed.

Cardplaying had become such a popular and enduring obsession in Renaissance Europe because of the variety of games it allowed and because of a new technology—block printing. Block printing allowed card makers to create

wooden engravings of the card faces that were quickly and cheaply duplicated. The earliest surviving wood-engraved prints date from the 1420s and
principally concern religious subjects, though it is interesting to note that
most of these saints' portraits are roughly the same size and design as playing
cards. As a result of mass production, the price of playing cards dropped precipitously. Hand-painted decks executed for aristocrats might cost the equivalent of several hundred dollars today, as did a pack of cards painted for a
Milanese nobleman in 1415. Forty years later, a pack made for the dauphin of
France cost about three dollars. Further standardization of the deck would ultimately drop the cost even lower.

In the fifteenth century, Europe would slowly recover from the demo-
graphic ravages of the Black Death, which, by lowering the population, raised
the value of labor, thus improving the lot of peasants and workmen who survived. This new distribution of wealth would help nurture the Renaissance,
and it also seems to have aided the proliferation of playing cards, and a general expansion of gambling.

Immediately upon the introduction of cards into Italy from the Arab world,
the most common game was *trappola*, which apparently crossed the Mediterranean along with the cards themselves. But card makers in the north of Italy
soon designed a new deck of cards (or rather several styles of a new deck)
used to play a different game: *trionfo, trarocci,* or, as it has become known in
the French, tarot. The word literally means "triumphs" or "trumps" and is derived from the twenty-two cards that "trump" (triumph over) all the others.
The game added a new dimension to the trick-taking games that already proliferated, as these cards could be played at any juncture to take a trick.

Today, the tarot pack is known in much of the world as a vehicle for divination and fortune telling, but this is a relatively late adaptation, dating to
the late eighteenth century. Tarot cards were invented as playing cards, with
all of the mystic charm of today's standard deck. Tarot cards borrowed the
standard fifty-two-card deck, which in Italy had suits of swords, coins, cups,
and batons, added an additional court card, the queen (making for a total of
four court cards), and twenty-two picture cards. These picture cards were
numbered from one to twenty-one, and depicted, in order, the *bagatto* (moun-
tebank), the Popess, the Empress, the Emperor, the Pope, Love, the Chariot,
Justice, the Hermit, the Wheel of Fortune, Fortitude, the Hanged Man
(Traitor), Death, Temperance, the Devil, the Tower (House of God), the
Star, the Moon, the Sun, the Angel (of judgment), and the World. *Il matto,* or
the Fool, was unnumbered. In some decks, cards had slightly different names,

or the order might be switched; the Popess ranked anywhere from second to fifth. But the general subjects of the numbered "triumph" or trump cards remained remarkably similar as the tarot spread throughout Italy and then Europe in the fifteenth and sixteenth centuries.

Players used the tarot deck to play a family of games. Generally, they were trick-taking games (like modern bridge) in which the *trionfi* were permanent trump cards. The player who had the best chance at scoring the first trick, or who had won the previous trick, led by playing a card of his choice. Play then rotated counterclockwise; players had to play a card of the same suit or a trump. The winning player would win the trick and gain points for the value of the individual cards in the trick.

Tarots were invented in the early fifteenth century, most likely around the year 1425, in northern Italy, possibly in Bologna, Ferrara, or Milan. These cities, together with Florence, would become the major Italian centers for tarot card manufacture. The first known reference to tarots dates from 1442, in a note in the accounts of the d'Este court of Ferrara. In 1450, Duke Francesco Sforza of Milan penned a letter to his treasurer in which he asked for a tarot pack or, if one could not be procured, a regular deck, so by this time tarot was distinct from standard playing cards.

Tarot became wildly popular in the courts of northern Italy. A 1450 Florentine edict specified *trionfo* as a game that was *not* to be prohibited, as do several similar laws from across Italy in the second half of the fifteenth century. In these codes, both tarot and chess were identified as permissible games that mixed chance with skill. Still, the game had its opponents; a sermon compiled in 1500 denounces tarot, dice, and table games as devilish devices.

The French and their Swiss men-at-arms who occupied Milan in the early sixteenth century brought tarot back to their native lands. From France and Switzerland, tarot migrated into the German states and, from there, into the vast domains of the Hapsburg Empire. As a result, tarot playing spread to nearly every European country, with the exception of Spain, Portugal, and Britain, enjoying its highest esteem from roughly 1750 to 1850. After that time, the game declined in popularity, though it is still played in some regions even today.

In the eighteenth century, those with occult leanings invested the tarot deck with a cosmic significance. Antoine Court de Gébelin, a French Protestant savant, wrote an essay for a 1781 encyclopedia averring that the tarot deck actually had ancient roots: It was a book of hermetic Egyptian wisdom (written, of course, by Thoth himself), disguised by priests as a pack of playing cards so that their lore would survive the imminent decline of their civilization.

Jean-Baptiste Aliette, a Parisian writer and print seller who styled himself "Etteilla," developed his own style of cartomancy (divination using playing cards). After the publication of Gébelin's essay, he issued a book of his own that detailed the "history" of the tarot deck and gave interpretations of its meanings.

Once the Gébelin and Etteila had "established" the secret origins of the tarot, tarot cartomancy spread throughout Europe and into Britain, its colonies in the Caribbean and elsewhere, and the newly independent United States. Since the game of tarot was unknown in most of these places, the metaphysical interpretation of the deck did not seem outlandish at all. The trumps were called the "major arcana," the cards of the standard deck the "minor arcana," coins became pentacles and batons became wands, but otherwise, the tarot deck as used by fortune tellers is virtually identical with those first played in fifteenth-century Italy. The Pope and Popess have been replaced by the Hierophant and High Priestess, successfully erasing the most obvious Christian references in it (though Renaissance players would have immediately recognized the cardinal virtues of fortitude and temperance among the trumps as well). Used by fortune tellers around the world, the tarot deck has gone full circle, returning the tools of gambling to their divinatory roots.

Standard decks spread as quickly as the tarot. Northern Italian traders likely brought cards into Spain. Playing cards soon proved to be just as popular there as they had been in Italy. By 1540 they had long been in use, and in that year a traveler recounted that he had sojourned many leagues in that country where he could not buy bread, wine, or any necessities of life, "but that in every miserable village cards were to be bought."

Spaniards slightly modified the Italian deck, and decks from Spain and Italy are sometimes called Latin decks. The Spaniards made minor changes to the Italian suits: They straightened the swords and transformed the batons into heavy clubs, which often sported knobs or leaves. On numbered cards, the suit signs were arranged in more easily readable patterns. The early Italian cards had bunched the signs together in hard-to-make-out patterns, and Spanish card makers began the tradition of simply laying the signs out in regularly spaced intervals. They kept the king and knight as the top two face cards but replaced the foot soldier with *sota*, a male infantryman or, sometimes, a maidservant. Often, Spanish players shorted the pack by omitting tens, nines, and eights, or only tens. To this day, the American casino game of Spanish twenty-one is played without tens.

Hombre, the first quintessentially Spanish game, developed in the six-teenth century. It originally featured four players using forty cards—the stan-dard deck minus the eights, nines, and tens. Play began when the dealer gave each player nine cards and placed the remaining four into a pile as "stock." The player to the right of the dealer, known as "the man" *(hombre)*, got the right to begin play and to declare the trump. Black-suited cards ranked high to low from king to two, while red-suited cards inverted the rank of num-bered cards: two was high and seven was low. Players who declared them-selves "hombre" sought to win more tricks than any of their three opponents. By the middle of the seventeenth century, Spanish players had switched to a three-player version they called *renegado,* or "traitor." This version, also known as *hombre* or, in England ombre (pronounced "umber"), spread to En-gland, France, and Italy. From the seventeenth through nineteenth centuries, it was popular game throughout Europe. A five-handed variant, *cinquillo,* also proved fashionable in Spain.

Portuguese players introduced a few small changes to the Latin deck, us-ing a forty-eight-card version that omitted the tens, or the forty-card deck that also struck the nines and eights. When Portuguese sailors began making voyages of trade and discovery to Africa and Asia, they brought these cards with them. In the sixteenth century, Portuguese cards began appearing in lo-cales as far ranging as India, Java, and Brazil. Brazilians remained relatively faithful to Portuguese designs, making few deliberate changes. Card makers in other countries, though, made some interesting modifications. Indian card makers adopted several elements of the Portuguese deck, joined them to the traditional hand-painting techniques used to make *ganjifa* cards, and cre-ated several hybrid decks that were neither entirely Indian nor Portuguese. In Indonesia, Javanese card makers produced intricately detailed cards that far outdistanced their plain European ancestors.

In the sixteenth century, the Portuguese sailed to Japan. The Japanese, though they called the strangers barbarians, evinced a fascination with their alien culture and quickly developed an appreciation for playing cards. Cards of Portuguese influence, called *Tensho-karuta,* flourished from 1573 to 1592. Japanese card makers made few changes in card design. When Shogun Iemitsu expelled the Portuguese in 1639, playing cards at first remained per-missible, though ten years later they, too, were prohibited. In general, these Japanese authorities vigorously suppressed all Western influences in the fol-lowing years, including Western gambling. When the Japanese began to pro-duce cards again, most of the obvious Portuguese influence was gone. Still, the persistence of a forty-eight-card deck long served as a subtle reminder of the Portuguese influence.

Spanish voyagers brought cards to the New World. One legend holds that the sailors on Columbus's 1492 transatlantic journey brought cards with them but, believing that divine anger at their gambling had doomed their ships in the unfamiliar waters, tossed them overboard. Upon landfall, they promptly made new cards from leaves. Cards were common among the conquistadors. The chronicler of the conquest of Florida wrote that the soldiers involved in that campaign burned their cards after an early battle but later repented of their antigambling ways and improvised new ones from parchment, "which they painted admirably, as if they had followed the business all their lives." Gambling became so popular that the soldiers were forced to pass the cards throughout the army in shifts. Though the duke of Medina commanded that all soldiers and mariners who sailed in the Spanish Armada against England in 1588 abstain from cards, this was apparently of little help, as the English sea dogs soundly defeated the Armada.

Spanish playing cards filtered northward from their colonial possessions in Mexico. Native Americans, long used to gambling, quickly took to the European idea of playing cards. Like other Spanish imports—guns, horses, and deadly pathogens such as smallpox—playing cards diffused through North America faster than the Spanish colonizers themselves. Using bark, skin, and other materials, Indians of the American Southwest made faithful copies of Spanish-suited cards and continued to use them into the late nineteenth century. A favorite Native American game, *coon can* or *conquian,* is an American original, having developed in Mexico (or in parts of the southwestern United States once part of Mexico). It was played with a forty-card deck (lacking eights, nines, and tens), and a player won by matching out cards; this may have been one of the ancestors of modern rummy games.

The "barbarian" German tribes continued tossing dice after their conquest of the Romans and conversion to Christianity. Through the dawn of the Reformation in the early sixteenth century, Germans remained committed to gambling.* Cardplaying evidently passed from Italy into Germany fairly quickly,

---

*When speaking of "German" gambling in the medieval and early modern period, it is important to remember that there was no nation-state of Germany, just as there was no "Italy." Rather, the lands that today comprise that nation were divided into dozens of small principalities, with larger political units like the Holy Roman Empire (which, historical wags love to remind us, was none of the three) sometimes exerting influence. Unlike England and France, in which kings both gambled and issued edicts regulating the practice, one must look to the cities for evidence of German gambling.

as evidenced by the 1379 Regensburg ordinance forbidding excessive card-playing. Nuremberg's shifting gambling ordinances show the increasing toleration that card playing enjoyed. In the fourteenth century, the *Rat* (municipal assembly) at first forbade playing cards, but as that provision was ignored, it then attempted to construct a regulatory regime. Playing cards, checkers, or bowling for drinks or for a pfennig was allowed. Two laws passed in 1485 permitted the playing of cards but sought to curtail money games, fining any man or woman caught playing one 5 pounds. The inn owner where the game took place was to be fined 2 pounds if the game was conducted during normal business hours in public view (and 10 pounds if it took place after hours or behind closed doors). A later ordinance specifically barred card- and dice playing from the lawn of the town hall and on workdays but permitted games on holidays.

By this time, the Germans had already stopped importing Italian cards and begun making their own. The cities of Augsburg, Nuremberg, and Ulm were the centers of German card manufacturing in the fifteenth century. The German pupils soon surpassed their Italian tutors, and the exportation of German cards triggered a small crisis in Venice. As early as 1441, the master card makers of Venice complained that inexpensive German imports were flooding the market and reducing Venetian masters to poverty: "The art and mystery of card making . . . has fallen into total decay through the great quantity of foreign playing cards, and colored printed figures which were brought into the city." The card painters successfully lobbied their senate to pass a statute banning the importation of printed and painted playing cards from elsewhere. This measure may have propped up the Venetian industry, but it did nothing to halt the flowering of the German card manufacturing.

The German art of card making flourished in part because of superior technology. By the 1430s, artisans had begun creating sheets of cards from wood or copper engravings, eventually using woodblock printing and stencils to quickly and efficiently create cheap multicolor cards. The apparently bottomless market for playing cards made card making a true growth industry; in 1414, the city of Nuremberg had a single professional card maker, but by the end of the century thirty-seven card makers worked there.

The German deck had anywhere between thirty-six and fifty-six cards. The most common deck of the sixteenth century had forty-eight cards: numbered cards from two through ten (the two was equivalent to the "one," or modern ace, and the ten usually featured a banner rather than a number), and a king, *obermann* (over-valet), and *untermann* (under-valet). Though Germans experimented with a dizzying variety of suits, including pomegranates, ducks, dogs, winepots, roses, cups, and books, the default standard became acorns, hearts, bells, and leaves. Typically, the court cards featured simple representations of their subjects, and suit signs sprouted in treelike patterns on number cards.

While artisans mass-produced cheap decks, gifted artists crafted cards for more discriminating patrons. Because of their great expense, many artistic German cards have been carefully preserved. The preeminent copper engravers of the fifteenth century included an artist working in Mainz known to history only as the Master of the Playing Cards, who was the first known engraver. Beginning in 1446 with a depiction of the flagellation of Jesus, he spent several years alternating between religious subjects and playing cards. There was a market, it seems, for both.

Many of the artist-produced cards of the sixteenth century that survive feature a variety of comic or carnivalesque themes that reverse the usual order of things: Rabbits capture and roast a hunter, peasants playfully laugh and romance, a woman attempts to milk a visibly discomfited bull, women beat their husbands, and boars play tug-of-war over soft, steamy piles of feces. Artists executed these illustrations in the bottom half of the card, and they remained distinct from the tree of numbered suit signs on the top half. Other cards had images and verses preaching moderation (even restraint in gambling).

Sometimes, artisans copied the designs of these fine art playing cards and mass-produced them in black-and-white decks, making them available for mass consumption, even export. A chronicle of Ulm written in 1474 describes how "playing cards were sent in large bales to Italy, Sicily, and other places by sea, getting in exchange spices and other merchandise." Card manufacture became a thriving German industry despite the Venetian ban on importation, and the limitless market for their wares encouraged card makers to progressively greater creativity. German decks, exquisitely detailed and carefully executed, were for a time the world's finest.

Germans played several different games with these artfully produced cards. Perhaps the oldest German game was *karnoffel,* which was mentioned in a 1426 Bavarian ordinance. *Karnoffel,* meaning "hernia," was a topsy-turvy game in which lower cards beat the higher ones. On its face, *karnoffel* was a trick-taking game, like many other early card games. It was distinguished by an unusual trumping scheme, whereby the *unter* (Jack), six, and two of the trump suit were the most powerful cards. The game spread throughout German-speaking Europe and enjoyed a vogue in the sixteenth century. It is still found in Switzerland, with some modifications, under the name *kaiserspiel,* or "the kaiser game."

Poch (also known as Pochspielen or Pochen), a German game that originated in the fifteenth century, has been described as an ancestor of poker. But
it was far more complicated than poker, as betting took place in three distinct
phases. *Poch* players used a special board with eight compartments labeled
with different cards and card combinations, such as "Marriage," which de-
noted a king and queen of the trump suit. After laying stakes on these compartments, players were dealt five cards each, with the next card determining
the trump suit. In the first phase of play, players who had the cards or combinations in the trump suit won the stakes in that compartment. In the second,
players vied to determine who had the best combination of cards, which
ranked four of a kind, three of a kind, and pair. Bettors in this phase declared,
"Ich poch" ("I bet") whatever the stakes were. In the final betting phase, cards
were played out in sequences, as progressively higher-ranked cards were
played. This game remained popular in Germany for about a century and, as
glic and *poque,* crossed over to France, eventually reaching England under the
name of brag.

Like their games, German card designs influenced other countries as well.
The Swiss borrowed the German acorns and bells while substituting shields
and roses for leaves and hearts, but otherwise retained the elements of the
German deck. Polish playing cards combined the German court cards with
the Italian suit signs of cups, batons, swords, and coins. Though German influence would collapse with the explosion of the French card industry, some
parts of Germany still use the traditional German deck, a reminder of the
early years of playing cards in Europe. The exquisitely detailed artist- and
artisan-made cards of the German Renaissance and Reformation periods still
bedazzle collectors, and many German games have proven surprisingly
durable.

Despite the creativity of German card designers, their French rivals would
create the modern card deck, and French games would dominate much of the
world. French playing-card design likely jelled sometime around 1480.
Though there has been some modification in the general appearance of the
card (particularly the invention of the corner index and reversible court
cards), French suit signs are immediately recognizable. Their *piques, trèfles,
coeurs,* and *carreaux* are, essentially, the spades, clubs, hearts, and diamonds
known throughout the English-speaking world today, though they are better
translated as pikes, clovers, hearts, and tiles. Card makers agreed on a standard that made the first two suits black and the last two red. For reasons of

gentlemanly courtesy (or simply because they were easier to distinguish), the French replaced the *cavallo* with a *dame,* or queen.

According to legend, a knight, Étienne de Vignoles, nicknamed La Hire (translated as "the hero" or "the wrathful one"), designed French cards in the early fifteenth century. A French hero of the Hundred Years' War (though he spent a few years as a freebooter wreaking havoc in the north of France for good measure), La Hire has also been credited with inventing the game of piquet, which would become a national favorite in France. La Hire's partisans have credited him with French suit signs and the introduction of the queen into the pack. Some say La Hire's support of Joan of Arc, whom he helped defeat the English at the battles of Orléans and Patay, inspired him to add the queen. Étienne Chevalier (1390–1443), a royal secretary and treasurer with a gift for design, has also been advanced as the creator of the French deck, as has Jacques Coeur (1395–1456), a merchant with a far-flung trade network. Whoever created the French deck, it was quickly adopted throughout the nation with some fleeting regional variations, and then spread throughout the world.

These early French-style playing cards discovered by card historian W. A. Chatto in England were typical in having named face cards: These are the knights Lancelot, Hogier, Roland, and Valery.

French cards ended up sweeping aside Spanish, Italian, and German ones, even in their own countries, for simple reasons of clarity and economy. Unlike the intensely detailed German suit signs, which even when executed crudely were shaded and sometimes multicolored, French suit signs were easily recognizable silhouettes that could be made efficiently—and cheaply—using monochrome stencils. The twelve court cards might have additional color and detail, but card makers found the French deck congenial to mass production. So the French pack soon dominated Europe from England to Russia.

The French made up for their simple cards by identifying the court cards with historical or allegorical characters. These often shifted with the political or social breeze, but the official cast of court characters has remained relatively durable since the late sixteenth century. In the suit of hearts, Charles or Charlemagne is king, Judith (likely the Judith of the Old Testament) the queen, and La Hire, the legendary knight and putative card designer, the valet. In the spades, King David of the Old Testament reigned with Pallas (Athena of Greek mythology) as his queen and Hogier, also known as Ogier or Hogier the Dane, a semilegendary cousin and compatriot of Charlemagne, as valet. The diamonds boasted Julius Caesar as king, the Biblical Rachel as queen, and, after pushing the heroic Roland out of the picture, Hector (not Hector of Troy, but Hector de Maris, a slightly obscure knight of the Round Table) as the valet. At the top of the clubs stood Alexander the Great as king, Argine (possibly an anagram of *regina,* queen) as queen, and Lancelot of the Round Table as the valet.

The French played a number of card games during the Renaissance, some of which strongly influenced games still played today. *Basset* originated in Italy in the fifteenth century, but the French took to it so enthusiastically in the seventeenth century that the English assumed it was a French game. It was a mercantile game, pitting a banker against players. Players placed bets on spaces for each of the thirteen card ranks. In the first phase of the game, the banker turned up a single card, winning all bets placed on that card. Then the banker placed cards into two piles and either collected money for the bank or paid it to the player, depending whose cards were dealt. The French also borrowed games from Germany. *Glic* was a French adaptation of the German *poch,* and like its Teutonic forebear the game had three phases, one of which anticipated the vying action of poker, the other the sequence building of whist.

The game of piquet emerged as the most popular in France by the sixteenth century at the latest (some evidence indicates it was played as early as the fifteenth) and became the French national game. Mentioned in the sixteenth century in François Rabelais's *Gargantua* and in the first real text on gambling odds, Cardano's *Book on the Games of Chance, piquet* traveled beyond the borders of France; in England it was known as "cent." Two players used a thirty-six-card deck to play (with no twos, threes, fours, fives, and sixes) and, like *poch,* the game had several phases. Numbered cards held their face value, court cards counted for ten, and the ace for eleven. In the first phase, players could discard up to eight cards as they attempted to build the strongest combinations. In subsequent phases, players got points for the numerical value of their cards, sequences (straights), sets (three or more high-ranking cards), and tricks (players tried to match each other's high card in a particular suit). The first player to reach one hundred total points won the game. Although elements like sets and sequences are common to poker, it also has many nonpoker-like aspects, including the keeping of points, which places it in the same category as trick-taking games like bridge, cribbage, and whist. From the design of playing cards to the games themselves, the French were already exercising a tremendous influence on world gambling in the late Renaissance period, as they continue to do.

Cardplaying, having been imported to Europe from the lands of the Islamic Saracens, easily crossed religious boundaries. Though the Talmud had declared that gambling was not in the best interests of society, dice games, odds and evens, pigeon races, and *teetotum* games had become popular forms of gambling for Jews throughout ghetto communities in Europe in the Middle Ages. At the beginning of the fifteenth century, Jews joined their Christian neighbors in adopting cards, often playing together with them in gambling houses and pubs.

At times, Jewish leaders, like their Christian counterparts, acted to stem the popularity of gambling. In Italy, where Bernardin and Savonarola repeatedly denounced gambling, Jewish communities followed suit. Throughout medieval and early modern Europe, Jewish communities enacted a series of bans against gambling, specifying fines and ostracism for violators. In 1416, the Jewish community of Forli in Italy adopted an ordinance that forbade Jews from hosting or attending gambling parties with either Jews or Christians. On fast days or if sick they were permitted to "play cards to relieve their stress," but only for limited stakes. Those who flouted this provision and remained unrepentant were to be excluded from participation in religious life until they reformed.

While this statute, which was enacted as a temporary ban rather than a perpetual decree, might not have been completely effective in halting cardplaying among the Jews of Forli, it preserves for posterity two interesting points: that Jews and Christians habitually gambled together in Italy at the time and that the act of gambling itself was not entirely antithetical to Jewish law. In Forli, as in Bologna and elsewhere, it was specifically permitted on fast days, ostensibly times of personal asceticism and reflection on one's spiritual progress.

Other attempts to control gambling included personal oaths. Because reprobate gamblers usually soon resumed gambling, such oaths were officially discountenanced, as they invariably led to the commission of two violations, gambling and the breaking of an oath. Still, most rabbis refused to void these oaths. Traditional Jewish law recognized that problem gamblers might be unable to control their desires to play but considered them morally weak and punished them severely.

Still, gambling continued to stubbornly thrive among the Jews of Europe. Rabbinical pronouncements, which had little force unless aligned with communal support, only applied to residents of their own community; visitors had no obligation to follow them. In addition, rabbis were more or less unable to restrict gambling interactions between Jews and non-Jews. Thus they had no authority in the gambling houses that sprouted throughout Europe, particularly in Italy, which accepted patrons without imposing a religious test. Most communal and rabbinical edicts banned only specific games, viewed as particularly deleterious, or were intended for only a limited time. In addition, even when gambling was banned, it was usually permitted on minor holidays, such as Purim, Hannukah, the intermediary days of weeklong festivals like Passover and Sukkot, and on new moon holidays. Hannukah developed such a reputation for the relaxation of gambling prohibitions that cynics called it "the New Year for gamblers." It is probably no coincidence that this holiday was celebrated during the same season as Christmas, when Christian authorities often lifted their own bans on gambling; this practice probably came from the Roman relaxation of antigambling laws during Saturnalia.

Nor were Christian clergy necessarily averse to gambling. The strictures against clerical gambling enacted in the Code of Justinian were almost completely unsuccessful. Complaints about it continued. The Synod of Langres in 1404, for example, specifically forbade priests and monks from playing at cards, signifying that cardplaying was widespread enough to merit its own separate denunciation by that year.

Though Protestant reformers, following in the footsteps of Martin Luther, condemned the excess of the Catholic Church, demanding a complete revision of the Christian faith, they seldom commanded the eradication

of gambling. Luther himself wrote of cards on several occasions and he celebrated the uses of satirical decks as anti-Catholic propaganda. He even declared that, if he were rich, he would commission a golden chess set and silver
playing cards as a reminder that "God's chesspieces and cards are great and
mighty princes, kings, and emperors; for He always trumps or overcomes one
through another." He spoke of the Holy Roman Emperor as king of the deck
and foresaw the coming of God, who "deals out the cards, and beats the pope
with the Luther, which is his ace."

Luther never denounced cardplaying itself. But he did, like other authorities, attack those who profited from gambling, calling them "thieves before
God," and suggested that their winnings be confiscated. Some Protestant reformers proposed that playing for small stakes on both cards and dice might
be permissible during holidays, continuing, like the Jews, the Roman tradition
of festive gambling. Secular authorities throughout Europe frequently followed these suggestions. Deploring excessive gambling, or reliance on gambling for income, Protestants, like Catholics, Jews, and even Muslims, did not
seek (or were not able) to completely suppress cardplaying.

Even the abstemious Swiss reformer John Calvin, whose spiritual descen-
dents would include the prim Puritans who settled the rocky coastline of New
England, did not completely condemn card playing. In his set of ordinances
governing churchly behavior promulgated in 1547, he proclaimed, "No one is
to play at games that are dissolute, or at games played for gold or silver or at
excessive expense. As had most other religious authorities, he gave his followers a bit of latitude in playing cards for recreation rather than for profit. That
Calvin, who demanded of his followers strict austerity, and whose predestinar-
ian preaching would inspire fear and anxiety for centuries, felt that cardplaying
was not sinful, speaks to its immense popularity in sixteenth-century Europe
on both sides of the Catholic/Protestant rift.

The English, despite an early Spanish influence, ultimately adopted the
French deck, which they would later export to their American colonies. The
English named the court cards king, queen, and knave (a word that originally
meant servant), a faithful copying of the French, but mixed Latin names into
the suits. The French *coeurs* became hearts and the *carreaux* diamonds in lit-
eral translations, but the *trèfles* were called clubs, recalling the Latin *bastoni*,
and the *piques* spades, after the Latin *spados*, or swords.

Gambling with cards received a mixed reception in England. Writers like
Thomas Elyot (1531) and John Northbrooke (1577) had fulminated against
dice playing, arguing that it was a species of "plain idleness" that did nothing

to exercise the mind or the body, but hoped that cards would not be so injurious. Northbrooke held out that cardplaying, which incorporated some mental dexterity, was not all bad, though in his *Treatise Against Dicing, Dancing, Plays, and Interludes, With Other Idle Pastimes,* he marshaled a fleet of antigambling statutes and writings from throughout history to prove that gambling was bad idleness. Citing the Bible, Suetonius's *Lives of the Caesars,* Chaucer, Elyot, and many others, he concluded that dice playing was "the mother of lies, of perjuries, of theft, of debate, of injuries, of manslaughter, of the very invention of the devils of hell; an art altogether infamous, and forbidden by the laws of all nations." Yet, he realized, gaming still flaunted itself throughout the world, as it was embraced by the common people and was even "the most accustomed pastime that kings and nobles use."

Though the English royalty and nobility enjoyed cards, they were uneasy about gambling's popularity. The discomfort manifested itself in ambiguous legislation that sought to curtail gambling while encouraging the production of cards. The first parliament that met during the reign of Edward IV, in 1461, prohibited both cardplaying and dicing, except during the twelve-day Christmas holiday. Two years later, the king issued an edict banning the importation of playing cards, not because cards were seen as a baleful influence, but rather to protect the domestic card-making industry. With French card makers flooding the markets with their inexpensive mass-printed wares, this was an understandable protectionist measure, and it served to boost the growing trade of English card makers.

Later monarchs continued Edward's policies of encouraging the development of the card-making industry while attempting to limit gambling. In 1496, Henry VII forbade members of the working class from playing cards for most of the year, but allowed that servants could legally play at cards during the Christmas holiday, though only in their master's house, presumably under his supervision. Henry VIII outdid him, declaring in 1541 that, since the practice of archery was necessary for homeland defense, several categories of gaming, including bowling, tennis, dicing, and carding, were prohibited and all able-bodied men were enjoined to instead own longbows and practice archery. Still, Henry VIII remained a resolute cardplayer himself, and public gaming houses continued to flourish throughout the realm. Throughout the second half of the sixteenth century, archdeacons regularly prosecuted their parishioners for gambling when they should have been at church, and profaning the Sabbath by cardplay; two such men were sentenced to highway labor as a punishment in 1575.

Despite churchly disapproval, gambling was considered an untouchable kingly prerogative, which may explain the never-lonely office of the groom porter. It is not known when this royal official was first appointed; the earliest description appears in a book on royal offices written between 1526 and 1530. According to this account, the groom porter ensured that the king's chambers were properly outfitted with everyday furniture (tables, chairs, etc.) and gambling equipment, namely cards and dice. He also decided disputes arising from gambling at dice, cards, bowling, and other games. Those among the royal retinue who wished to gamble always found action in the groom porter's quarters, and his lodgings became notorious as a gathering point for gamblers.

In his 1610 play *The Alchemist*, Ben Jonson spoofed the "cony catchers," or swindlers, of Elizabethan England. One of his characters, trying to establish another as a man born under a lucky star, boasted that when gambling he would win within a fortnight enough "to buy a barony. They will set him Upmost, at the Groom Porter's, all the Christmas." The groom porter became notorious as a symbol of the unrestrained gambling of the Christmas season. On Christmas Day 1661, Samuel Pepys recorded in his diary that Bishop Morley had railed against the "mistaken jollity of the Court" prevailing at the groom porter's, and enjoined his flock to forswear the "excess in plays and gaming" that had come to dominate the holiday season, when gaming was completely legal, and instead remember the true meaning of Christmas and celebrate joy and hospitality. In 1668, Pepys chronicled "deep and prodigious gaming at the groom porter's, vast heaps of gold squandered away in a vain and profuse manner." Jonson felt this was a horrid vice "unsuitable to a Christian court," but apparently few others shared his inhibitions, as the office—and the royal sanction of courtly gambling—continued until the reign of George III, who abolished the office in 1772 because, according to that year's *Annual Register*, he was not accustomed to playing at hazard. He ordered the current groom porter pensioned off and decreed that "there be no card playing amongst the servants," putting an end to the 250-year tradition of a royal official whose main job was to facilitate gambling.

The king also reached into the manufacture of playing cards. Edward IV's ban on playing-card importation was an early sop to the English card makers, but later monarchs found the foreign card trade too lucrative to suppress. A royal appointee acted as a tax farmer, collecting import duties on packs of cards, keeping some of the proceeds and kicking the rest back to the king. This arrangement allowed the king to grant a sinecure and enrich the royal coffers.

In 1628, however, Charles I granted a charter organizing the card makers of London into a corporation. Only those who belonged to the company (and paid annual dues) could legally manufacture playing cards. In addition, all importation of playing cards was forbidden and all customs officers prohibited from collecting duties on card imports; any foreign cards discovered in England were to be confiscated. Thus, the charter gave the "Worshipful Company of Makers of Playing Cards" a monopoly on the English playing-card trade. To recompense the royal revenue lost from the cessation of imports, the Company was charged with paying a duty on all cards manufactured. The Company was to appoint an officer as receiver of the duty, whose job was to collect the tax, affix the necessary duty stamp, and affirm that each pack of cards had a distinguishing printer's mark. The duty on playing cards (which, as part of the Stamp Act, did much to excite American colonists in 1765) continued to be paid until the reform of the British gaming laws in 1960.

The first games to gain prominence in England were the Spanish and Italian favorites of ombre and primero, each of which enjoyed wild popularity. Three-cornered ombre tables, found ubiquitously among the furniture of the period, bear silent witness to the popularity of the three-handed game in the seventeenth and eighteenth centuries. The game of gleek resembled the French piquet more than *glic,* as it was a game with several phases of betting. Players vied for the longest series of suited cards, played out tricks, and won stakes for gleeks (threes of a kind) and mournivals (fours of a kind).

English (and later American) card makers usually left the backs of their playing cards blank, leaving them suitable for a variety of purposes. In the eighteenth century, cards sometimes served as admission tickets for university lectures. Also, they provided a common form of communication. Visitors to the houses of the well-to-do, wishing to leave a message for their would-be host, were often handed a playing card, on the back of which they wrote their name or a short note; this was the genesis of the calling card and today's business card. But gamblers didn't like the plain backs, which, easily marked, made cheating simple. In the 1830s, London printer Thomas de la Rue devised a new process of aligning colors that enabled him to print patterned backs. These had the advantage of hiding any imperfections in the paper or stray marks that "just happened" to be made on card backs. De la Rue's card printing prospered, and patterned backs became common throughout Europe and the United States by about 1850.

Other innovations also came in the nineteenth century, and these produced the deck that, in much of the world, is still used today. In the early part of that century, double-ended, reversible cards, whose top halves are duplicated (which obviates the need to rotate court cards and thus possibly tip one's hand), became popular in Europe, though they did not spread to the United States until around 1870. Americans produced two important changes that later filtered back to Europe. Euchre players added two extra wild cards, the jokers, shortly before the Civil War, bringing the total of cards in the deck to fifty-four. Shortly after that war, Americans would add corner indices, which let players quickly read cards held in a fan pattern—something that most current poker players find indispensable. This also led to a final change, the replacement of the knave by the jack. The corner indices of "K" for king and "Kn" for knave were simply too confusing, and "jack," which had been a colloquialism for the knave (as well as the name of the trump knave in the game of all fours), became the accepted term.

Thus, by about 1870, cards that look much like those currently in use were being produced throughout the United States and Europe. Since then, there have been countless new decks created, including political propaganda, educational material, and even pornography. Yet owing perhaps to the innate conservatism or superstition of cardplayers, virtually every casino game and the great majority of home and social games are played with cards whose basic elements are over half a millennium old.

PART TWO

Gambling Becomes a Science

Elizabeth Charlotte wrote a lot of letters, and for good reason. She had been married off to a brother of the French king Louis XIV at the age of nineteen in 1671. Penning an average of forty letters a week to various relatives in her German homeland no doubt helped the new duchess of Orléans feel a little less homesick, and her correspondence might have broken up the tedium of courtly life.

As she wrote to an aunt from the French court at Versailles in 1675, gambling was an essential part of that life. On a typical day, she awoke at about half past ten, attended Mass at twelve, and spent the next several hours dining and chatting with lady friends. Around six, the men of quality graced the ladies with their presence, and the day's gambling started. Following perhaps a break for opera, gambling resumed again until past ten at night.

When the court was at Versailles, she joined the king's other retainers three times a week for his jour d'appartement. All assembled in a royal salon, where they listened to music and played an assortment of games, from billiards and chess to lansquenet, trictrac, hombre, piquet, and basset. In Paris, gambling also occupied most gentlewomen; sometimes they became so embroiled in disputes over play that the dragoons were called in to restore order.

The duchess also wrote of how her husband's overfondness for lansquenet led to interminable boredom when they lived in Paris. Though he superstitiously believed that if she shared a table with him she would bring him bad luck, he insisted that she remain in the room with him, so she had to content herself with the company of a clutch of old women who also did not play. At these gatherings, all anyone did was play lansquenet, she complained. No one danced, though she herself was now too old to dance. She refused to gamble because she lacked the money and because the stakes were inordinately high. Instead, she watched in horror as the fervid cardplaying transformed gentlemen and ladies into madmen who bawled, smashed their hands onto the tables so that the whole room shook, blasphemed with impunity, and winced with piteous despair.

The abstemious German duchess was doubly unfortunate in having an insensitive husband and in being resident at the French court during an era when gambling enjoyed its first great vogue. Though she could not appreciate it, the Sun King's court was set amid a historic juncture of gambling and government, and epitomized an age where the frontiers of gambling expanded almost beyond belief.

4

Taming Tyche

◆ ◆ ◆

THE SCIENCE OF CHANCE CREATES
PROFESSIONAL GAMBLING

The ancients lacked the mathematics to explain the parameters of chance. The dicers of the Roman Empire undoubtedly knew that they could expect the Venus throw less often than others but never developed any true theory of odds. Cicero wrote that a man who tossed a Venus throw twice in a row was the beneficiary of luck rather than the personal intervention of the goddess; he felt the need to advance this as an argument, not a generally accepted principle. With no understanding of probability, the ancients were at a loss to explain precisely what the likelihood of a certain dice-cast might be. It was a world brimming with fortune and fate, but without random chance.

The Greeks attempted to understand their luck only by appealing to Tyche, goddess of fortune. The Romans, with their supplications to Fortuna, did no better. It was not until the modern era that mathematicians began to seriously ponder the nature of chance. The fourteenth-century humanist Petrarch had an inkling that gambling was on the whole unprofitable, but for moral rather than mathematical reasons—a victory meant that someone else lost, and a winner today was sure to be a loser tomorrow. With the fuller elaboration of mathematics beginning in the sixteenth century, though, the mysteries of dice would be pierced and vague guesswork replaced by a thorough understanding of probability. Tyche would be tamed, and chance would become a science.

Armed with a better understanding of the odds and how to manipulate them, gamblers could become "professionals" and make a living from more or less honest games. Over the coming centuries, the idea of "mercantile" gambling would take root, and Europeans could gamble at casinos, take chances on lotteries, and bet on horses with odds set by professionals. Probability, by giving gamblers an appreciation of the nature of chance, made possible the rise of mercantile, as opposed to social, gambling that would achieve explosive growth in Europe in the modern era.

The ascendancy of probability began with Girolamo Cardano, one of the first figures in gambling history whose life is known in vivid detail. His birth in Pavia, near Milan, in 1501 neatly symbolized the beginning of a new age in European science and life. Cardano earned fame for writings on popular science, medicine, mathematics, and ethics, what today would be termed "self-help." Cardano claimed that 131 of his books were printed during his lifetime, 111 were unpublished, and another 170 manuscripts he destroyed himself. To impress future generations with his importance, Cardano wrote an autobiography that spares no detail. With chapters on "My Manner of Walking and Talking," "Perils, Accidents, and Manifold, Diverse, and Persistent Treacheries," and "Things of Worth Which I Have Achieved in Various Studies," Cardano's *De Vita Propria Liber (The Book of My Life)* is as complete a portrait as we have of anyone from his era. If anything, Cardano provides too much information—most readers would probably rather not be familiar with his swollen left nipple. Nevertheless, Cardano's *Vita* preserves the intellect of one of his century's leading minds and sheds light on an important figure in the history of gambling.

Cardano's early life was tempestuous. His father, Fazio, was a respected Milanese scholar who studied law, medicine, and mathematics and for much of his life earned his keep teaching geometry to underprivileged boys. Fazio and Girolamo's mother, Chiara, were probably not married when Girolamo was born at Pavia (they weren't living together, in any event), but Cardano strenuously denied that he was illegitimate. Still, he admitted that his mother had tried to abort him by various means before his birth. His birth was apparently both uninvited and unwelcome.

After a sad, sickly childhood, the young man followed his father in studying medicine at the University of Pavia, though he transferred to Padua, where he distinguished himself in scholarly disputations, winning every public intellectual duel he entered, even besting faculty members. At times, he was no doubt as insufferable as any prodigy, and his prickly demeanor alienated many potential benefactors. Consequently, he spent several years in obscure poverty. But eventually his fortunes reversed and Cardano became one of the biggest celebrity scholars of the day. He contributed to several fields: In medicine, he developed an understanding of the causes and prevention of allergies and was the first to describe typhoid fever; he was the first to publish several algebraic innovations; he invented the combination lock and a mechanical shaft still used today. His talents as a physician were widely acclaimed—he

Girolamo Cardano (1501–1576) was one of the first to turn his fascination
with gambling into a scientific study of the activity.

traveled as far as Scotland to render his expert opinion—and published pro-
lifically, thus sharing his knowledge with a wider European audience.

Despite his material successes, he had a turbulent personal life. His favorite son, Giambatista, was executed in 1560 after he poisoned his wife, and
his younger son Aldo became an unrepentant gambler and petty criminal who
caused his father no end of heartache. Accused of heresy by the Church in
1570, Cardano was briefly imprisoned and stripped of his right to lecture
publicly and to publish books. He ended his days in Rome, supplementing his
own savings with a pension granted by Pope Gregory XIII—strange, considering he had been censured by the Church only a few years earlier.

He died on September 24, 1576, leaving an uneven legacy. Though popular in their own time with readers, his books were littered with errors and
omissions, and his thorny pen bought him several detractors, whom he duti-
fully cataloged in one chapter of his autobiography. His belief in fantastic
omens and superstitions led many later writers seduced by coldly rational em-
piricism to discount all of his work.

In the end, Cardano made a contribution to gambling that is no less important than his medical and mechanical improvements. Writing in the
1560s, he was the first to begin to explore the bounds of probability theory,
the mathematics that would turn gambling into a profession and a science.

Though Cardano's manuscript remained unpublished for nearly a century, when other thinkers began to piece together a mathematical discourse on probability, his insights pointed toward the coming rationalization of chance. Even today, it gives valuable evidence of the state of Italian gambling in the sixteenth century.

This Renaissance man's theoretical contributions were driven by a keen personal interest in gambling that, at times, bordered on obsession. Cardano confessed as much in his autobiography when he said that he was so addicted to the chessboard and dicing table as to be "considered deserving of the severest censure." From his student years, Cardano gambled assiduously, stopping only when he became wealthy and famous. He played at dice for twenty-five years and at chess for more than forty, not on occasion, but every day, "with the loss at once of thought, of substance, and of time."

Cardano's reasons for gambling are frankly depressing. "It was not a love of gambling, but the odium of my estate and a desire to escape, which compelled me," Cardano wrote. In other words, he gambled because he was bored and miserable—a disheartening prospect for one of history's sharpest minds. In writing of his gambling, Cardano is deliberately ambiguous. At one point in his autobiography, he boasts of having made many friendships among the nobility through his gambling, then in the next sentence declares that his private affairs suffered because of it. It may have been regret over having instructed his sons in games of chance that drove him to later denounce gambling or, perhaps, looking back on his life after his censure by church authorities, he found it necessary to downplay his own luck in gambling for the purpose of moral correctness.

In any event, Cardano says, he gave up gambling without a second thought as soon as he gained a "respectable life," though he always maintained that for those with few other prospects, gambling was not such a bad thing. "In times of great anxiety and grief," he wrote, "it is considered to be not only allowable, but even beneficial." Those condemned to death or on a sickbed could freely gamble, Cardano emphasized, though even they should be sure to exercise moderation, not betting too much. For others, gambling was permissible, but not ideal. Reading or music would be more praiseworthy, as gambling set a bad example for one's children and servants and might excite anger or ignite a quarrel over money, "a thing which is disgraceful, dangerous, and prohibited by law." The ideal occasion of gambling took place rarely, for short periods and small stakes, such as at banquets or family gatherings. The ideal opponent was a king, prelate, distinguished character, or blood relative; Cardano discountenanced playing against professional gamblers as being both disgraceful and dangerous: "You will be the loser because of their greater experience, trickery, and skill," he cautioned.

Cardano was something of a prodigy as a gambler. Whether this was because of his innate grasp of the odds and human psychology or because he might have cheated is left for his readers to deduce; Cardano certainly implied the former. Once, his gambling and temper led Cardano into rash danger. Losing in cards at the house of a senator in Venice, he realized that the deck was marked and that he was in the house of a professional cheat. Enraged, he impetuously slashed his adversary's face ("though not deeply") with his knife; he then attacked the servants and demanded to be let out of the house. The senator allowed him to escape, though Cardano's problems were not over. Stealthily fleeing the police, he fell into a canal and was rescued by the passengers of a passing skiff, who included the senator himself, his facial wounds still bound with a dressing. The senator remained mum about their earlier confrontation and appeared eager to get Cardano out of town as quickly—and silently—as possible. He nonchalantly bought Cardano a sailor suit and escorted the scholar as far as Padua.

Cardano combined his memories of practical gambling with his natural scientific inquisitiveness in the *Liber de Ludo Aleae* or *The Book on Games of Chance*. This manuscript, published only in 1663 (almost a century after his death), is a signal document in the history of probability, despite its shortcomings. It was written haphazardly, with chapters on the philosophy of luck, the ethics of play, and cheating alternating with mathematical studies of various probabilities. Even the math has its suspect moments—the manuscript was apparently a collection of hastily jotted notes, and as Cardano elaborated his earlier ideas, sometimes revising them, he often failed to delete his earlier misleading statements.

The *Liber de Ludo Aleae* was the first text published on the theory of probability and the first attempt to formulate general mathematical principles concerning random events. In chapter fourteen, when instructing his readers on combined points, Cardano stated his general law of wagers, that before agreeing to stakes one must consider the total number of outcomes and compare the number of casts that would produce a favorable outcome to those that are unfavorable. Only in this proportion, Cardano says, "can mutual wagers be laid so that one can contend on equal terms." Cardano's book on games of chance deserves recognition for this concept alone, which was revolutionary at the time and is still a working definition of basic probability. But he went farther, computing odds on the cast of one, two, and three dice, on card games, including primero (which merited two chapters by it-self), backgammon, and "games of the ancients," including the antediluvian astragali. Cardano also examined the division between games of skill and games of chance, noting that most card games join "the art of play" to pure luck.

As a both a ground-breaking work in the mechanics of chance and a chronicle of the state of play in the sixteenth century, one telling omission in the *Liber* might strike contemporary readers as odd: Cardano, it seems, has no conception of the house advantage, the key mathematical principle of most casino games today—the very foundation of professional gambling. Indeed, the scholar wrote that the most fundamental principle in gambling is equal-ity: equal conditions for opponents, bystanders, money, and the tools of play. "To the extent to which you depart from that equality, if it is in your oppo-nent's favor, you are a fool, and if it is in your own, you are unjust." Writing in the Renaissance, Cardano had no inkling of the coming revolution in gam-bling, which would see social games played among equals pushed to the side by professionally run bank games with stakes biased in the house's favor as the cost of the game.

Although Girolamo Cardano was a pioneer in the histories of both math-ematics and gambling, he just missed out on the biggest change in gambling in its seven millennia of recorded existence. The idea that probabilities might let a professional legitimately offer all comers honest play and still make a profit would ultimately lead to the transformation of gambling from a scan-dalous social diversion to a legitimate profession.

Cardano's enunciation of the general law of probability, while the earliest documented foray into the subject, may have been only the visible tip of an iceberg of scholarly discussion respecting the calculation of probability in dice throwing. Though it is likely that both gamblers and mathematicians ea-gerly discussed the rules of probability, there are few surviving examples. Still, some of the period's greatest minds were harnessed in the effort to better de-termine the odds of various gambles. Between 1613 and 1623, for example, the path-breaking astronomer Galileo Galilei, probably at the behest of his patron, Grand Duke Cosimo II of Tuscany, wrote a fragment that revisits Cardano's consideration of the problem of the odds of three thrown dice.

Galileo, who is not known to have had any personal proclivity toward gam-bling, began "Sopra le Scoperte dei Dadi" ("Concerning an Investigation on Dice") by stating the obvious: When three dice are thrown, some numbers come up more commonly than others. To get a 3 or an 18, a gambler could only roll three aces or three sixes. While this seemed to be self-evident,

Galileo wrote that there still was some mystery: while 9 and 12 could be scored in just as many ways as 10 and 11, "long observation" made dice players consider 10 and 11 more advantageous, i.e., easier to roll, than nine and twelve.

To solve the problem, Galileo systematically expounded the rules of probability much as Cardano had. A fair six-sided die gave 6 equally likely outcomes, two dice 36 (six times six), and three dice 216 (six times six times six). But these 216 outcomes yielded only 16 combinations of points, 3 through 18. After elucidating the combinations with which various points could be thrown, Galileo drew up a table illustrating the chances of rolling points 3 through 10:

Galileo's table of probabilities for a game with three dice															
10		9		8		7		6		5		4		3	
6,3,1	6	6,2,1	6	6,1,1	3	5,1,1	3	4,1,1	3	3,1,1	3	2,1,1	3	1,1,1	1
6,2,2	3	5,3,1	6	5,2,1	6	4,2,1	6	3,2,1	6	2,2,1	3				
5,4,1	6	5,2,2	3	4,3,1	6	3,3,1	3	2,2,2	1						
5,3,2	6	4,4,1	3	4,2,2	3	3,2,2	3								
4,4,2	3	4,3,2	6	3,3,2	3										
4,4,3	3	3,3,3	1												
	27		25		21		15		10		6		3		1

In "Concerning an Investigation on Dice," Galileo drew up a table to demonstrate the probabilities combinations of three thrown dice. There were six different ways to roll the 6, 3, and 1 that total ten; three ways for 6, 2, and 2, etc. Adding up all of these probabilities, Galileo correctly surmised that there were 27 different rolls—out of 216 total possible outcomes—that would yield a result of 10. He similarly deduced that 25 rolls could produce a 9, all the way down to a single roll (1, 1, 1) that would give a 3. To figure the numbers from 11 to 18, simply flip the table for 10 to 3: there are 27 ways to make an 11, and 1 chance for an 18.

Having given the mathematical probabilities for 3 through 10, Galileo concluded his didactic foray into dicing by remarking that, as these numbers totaled 108 chances, the remaining points (11 through 18) were merely an inversion of them. Thus, Galileo wrote, one could "very accurately measure all the advantages, however small they may be," of various rules of three-die games.

The mathematics behind Galileo's demonstration of dice probabilities was apparently well known before he wrote "Sopra le Scoperte Dei Dadi," and in the decades before he wrote the fragment, the revolutionary potential of probability became clear. The full implication of Galileo's math lesson—that there was a science to gambling—would transform the activity into a full-fledged business.

Previously, professional gamblers (who by definition derived their sole income from games of chance) consistently profited either through extraordinary luck—never a good bet—or through cheating others, which could be risky.

The elaboration of probability allowed for another path: using a discrepancy between the true odds and actual payouts to carve out a statistically guaranteed profit. This was the most significant change in all of gambling history and directly led to lotteries, bookmaking, and casinos. Thanks to a better understanding of probability, professional gamblers could now offer casual players the chance to bet as much as they liked against an impersonal vendor, with the "house odds" the irreducible price of entertainment.

For example, using Galileo's table above, one could go into business with three dice, a table, and a moderately sized bankroll. Paying out two hundred to one to any customer who rolls three aces seems an attractive offer. It is—for the banker. The customer will score the three aces only once out of every 216 rolls, thus leaving, in the tidy world of probabilities, a 15-unit profit for the gambling professional for every run of 216 rolls. This principle—the divide between the actual probability of various outcomes and the payouts offered to customers—allowed for the development of honestly run professional games of chance.

With the basic contours of probability well known by the middle of the seventeenth century, mathematicians moved on to more esoteric problems. One question that had been bedeviling scholars for centuries was the "problem of points." Fra Luca Paccioli, a Franciscan priest, mathematician, and friend of Leonardo da Vinci, first published the problem in 1494, though it may have been circulating in manuscript much earlier. The problem states that A and B are playing a best lot of eleven ball game, which will end when one of them has won six rounds. But they are forced to abandon play after A has won five rounds and B three. How are the stakes to be equitably divided? Cardano and his rival Niccolo "Tartaglia" Fontana (1499–1557) had offered solutions, but neither was correct. The question was fundamentally one of probabilities, and its proper solution would pave the way not only for probability theory, but for much of advanced mathematics. This major breakthrough took place in the correspondence of a parliamentary lawyer and a mathematician turned religious philosopher, correspondence that apparently began at the urging of a curious gambler.

The gambler was one Chevalier de Méré, who was himself a dabbler in mathematics. After approaching several Parisian geometers with the problem of points, in 1654 he turned to Blaise Pascal for a solution. Pascal had already established himself as one of Europe's leading mathematicians and scientists, with his theoretical contributions to geometry and the study of fluids, as well as his invention of the hydraulic press and syringe. Later, after a near-fatal accident, he would abandon his secular brilliance for religious contemplation inspired by his Jansenist enthusiasms. Prompted by de Méré, Pascal began exchanging letters with Pierre de Fermat, a counselor with the Parliament of Toulouse today best remembered as the developer of calculus.

In a series of letters, the two mathematicians tackled the problem of points, in the process creating probability theory. First, they compared solutions concerning a die game in which a player attempted to roll a six with a single die in eight rolls. Pascal asked Fermat what the player should be given if he surrendered his fourth roll in return for a fair share of the stakes. Agreeing with Fermat's answer (one sixth of the stakes), Pascal moved to another problem: Two gamblers play until either has won three games, for stakes of 32 pistoles each. After the first player has won two games and the second one, they play a fourth game with the condition that if the first man wins, he gets all 64 pistoles. If the second triumphs, they are tied at two and each takes his original 32-pistole stake, should they balk on playing a fifth game. In such a case, the first player would gain either 64 pistoles for a game-four victory or 32 for a series-evening loss. According to Pascal, the equitable division of the stakes is 32 plus 16 (one half 32) pistoles, for a total of 48.

From here, Pascal introduces several permutations on the problem, stopping play after various combinations of games. Fermat replied with another method of solving the problem using different combinations, to which Pascal responded with a critique. In future correspondence, Fermat proved his methods undeniably sound, and together in these exchanges the two developed the groundwork for future work in probability.

Pascal also solved the problem of points in another manuscript (published in 1665, though written eleven years earlier) by using a construct known today as Pascal's triangle. Pascal did not invent this figure, which he called the arithmetical triangle and which was known in China as early as the fourteenth century. It is a method for using simple arithmetic to generate a table of binomial coefficients, something that can be very handy in calculating probabilities. Beginning with a 1 at the top, someone building the triangle has only to add the two terms above a space to get that space's value.

This table allows someone to quickly size up the odds of one out of several possibilities. What, for example, are the correct odds on coin flipping? With a fair coin, even schoolchildren know that it is an even chance, or one out of two, that a flipped coin will come up heads. This possibility is in the second line of the triangle: one divided by that line's sum of two. But what is the chance that four consecutive flips will all be heads? The fifth line of the triangle has the answer: one out of sixteen. In other words, there are sixteen total combinations of coin flips. In only one combination are all heads; in four ways,

```
                    1
                   1 1
                  1 2 1
                 1 3 3 1
                1 4 6 4 1
              1 5 10 10 5 1
            1 6 15 20 15 6 1
           1 7 21 35 35 21 7 1
         1 8 28 56 70 56 28 8 1
      1 9 36 84 126 126 84 36 9 1
```

In the arithmetical triangle, each number is the sum of the two numbers immediately above it.
Mathematician Blaise Pascal used the triangle, at the Chevalier de Méré's behest,
to calculate the probabilities of winning a dice game.

there are three heads and one tails, and in six ways heads and tails are dead
even. An absolutely square wager would pay odds of fifteen to one against all
heads, according to binomial coefficients and Pascal's handy triangle.

The successors of Pascal and Fermat developed a thorough understanding
of probabilities for more complex problems. Christiaan Huygens, a revolutionary Dutch astronomer and physicist who made several observational dis-
coveries (including Saturn's moon Titan) also had a practical side epitomized
by his invention of the pendulum clock. In this spirit, perhaps, and with the
encouragement of Pascal, Huygens in 1657 published the first book on probability theory, *De Rationciniis in Aleae Ludo (On Reasoning in Games of
Chance)*.

De Ratiociniis remained the chief work on probability until the first years
of the eighteenth century. Pierre Rémond de Montmort, in his *Essai d'analyse
sur les jeux de hazard (Analytical Essay on Games of Chance)*, written in 1708,
applied previous advances in probability to card games. In swinging scientific
scrutiny onto such trivial pastimes, he wrote to banish superstition and replace
it with a world governed by definite rules. By explaining the real math that
governed games of chance, Montmort felt he might enlighten readers about
"all those areas of life in which chance plays a role."

Montmort was not alone in advancing the frontiers of knowledge. Jakob
Bernoulli, a Swiss mathematician, wrote *Ars Conjectandi (The Art of Conjecturing)*, published in 1713, which pushed the science of probability farther, as
did a Frenchman who lived in England, Abraham de Moirve, whose work, including *The Doctrine of Chances* (first published in 1718, though the definitive
third edition was released posthumously in 1756), considered the problem of

points as well as several dice problems and problems involving multiple play-ers. Aided by developments in calculus, the mathematics of probability was clearly maturing. With these advances, both independent professional gam-blers and governments interested in issuing annuities and running lotteries to defray expenses now had a necessary theoretical foundation.

The spirit of wagers and probabilities was in the air in the seventeenth century as a gambling mania fastened itself on even the devout. Blaise Pascal used a gambling analogy after he had abandoned science for religious specu-lation. Casting about for an argument for the belief in God that could con-vince atheists left unmoved by centuries of theological speculation, Pascal hit upon the idea of deism as a calculated gamble. In short, "Pascal's wager" ar-gues that belief in God is better than disbelief for purely utilitarian reasons grounded in probability theory. If one believed in God and God existed, the payoff was heaven, or infinite good. If one believed in God but no God ex-isted, the believer gained nothing, just as an unbeliever would. But if someone professed nonbelief and God did in fact exist, the penalty was hell: infinite suffering. Thus, one who believed in God could hope for either unlimited good or nothing, while a nonbeliever might be subjected to eternal torment. In Pascal's eyes, this wager had only one logical choice: belief in God.

Not seriously intended as a theological argument for the belief in, much less existence of, God, Pascal's wager still shows how Europeans began to consider their world as a gamble with definite odds and payoffs. With a solid framework of mathematical probability and a proliferation of opportunities to gamble, this was hardly surprising.

That Cardano's manuscript on games remained mum on the principle of unequal stakes—the house edge—is even more perplexing given the fact that lotteries, a gambling form predicated on a payout incommensurate with the total stakes, were conducted in his lifetime, in his northern Italian homeland. Though his work opened the door for the later development of probability theory that would prove crucial to more sophisticated lotteries and gambling schemes, neither Cardano nor his mathematician successors talked much of lotteries. Instead, they worked diligently to solve problems of half-completed dice games and coin flips.

But lotteries were the truly revolutionary gambling form of the sixteenth and seventeenth centuries, the first genuine form of institutionalized mercan-tile gambling, or gambling as a business. The idea of lotteries was, of course, nothing new by this time. Many ancient cultures used randomizing elements, be it the casting of lots or the divining of goat entrails, to apportion land or duties. In the Roman Empire, both emperors and private citizens attempted to boost their popularity by means of drawings for prizes. Sometimes, these "lotteries" took place at lavish banquets; it was custom for the hosts at Saturnalia to give out prizes to all who attended. The *missila,* or lucky items shot (with a slingshot) into the crowd at the Circus Maximus, were another sort of lottery. Banquet prize-giving survived the fall of the Roman Empire and flourished as late as the nineteenth century among the royalty of Europe, who regularly showered their courtiers with tickets that could be redeemed for toys or trinkets.

These prize drawings, though, lacked the most important feature of modern lotteries: the payment of a price or stake for a chance. Such a gambling scheme requires a densely populated urban area from which to draw sufficient ticket-buyers and, more importantly, an economy with readily circulating money. Modern lotteries first appeared instead in the Low Countries, particularly Flanders. At the time, Flanders was the most heavily industrialized area of northern Europe, possessed a flourishing economy, extensive trade, and a vibrant culture.

The earliest recorded evidence of lotteries comes from the city of L'Écluse, which in 1444 organized a lottery for the sake of raising funds for the repair of the city's walls and fortifications. With a grand prize of 300 florins, the lottery was advertised widely throughout the region—its promoters sent over 450 letters publicizing the draw to most of the major towns from Holland to Hainault. An earlier form of the lottery existed in Bruges, where it was a long-standing practice to fill vacancies in the office of the *scrooder,* who was in charge of wine-tasting and transport, by means of a random draw (in the ancient Roman tradition). To earn a chance at the *scrooder*'s job, though, one had to pay a fee. To assuage the disappointment of *scrooder* also-rans, the organizers of the drawings began awarding cash prizes to runners-up. Throughout the early sixteenth century, lottery draws with prizes of money, gold, and jewelry became common throughout what is today Belgium, Holland, and northern France.

This kind of lottery is known today as a draw game, and its identifying characteristics are the drawing of a numbered (or personally signed, in early days) ticket from a container, variously called a wheel (though it did not spin) or box. In many countries, this remained the dominant lottery game into the twenty-first century. In Renaissance Flanders, these lotteries benefited churches and guilds, and, until their suppression by municipal authorities who wished to enter the lottery market (Bruges, for example, prohibited all "private" lotteries in 1561), spread throughout the region.

Italian merchants had been resident in the region since the end of the thirteenth century, and members of Italian colonies in Bruges were active as bankers, merchants, moneylenders, and pawnbrokers. The lottery made a quick transition to Italy: Soon, medieval northern Italian shopkeepers regularly supplemented their humdrum selling of goods with a random element. For a sum, a customer could draw from a lucky jar a ticket that entitled him to the article written on it. Before long, these shopkeepers were profiting more from their drawings than from their commerce. City authorities or the local nobles soon demanded a measure of consumer protection, attention to public welfare, and a piece of the action: They insisted that all drawings be rigorously inspected to ensure their honesty and that a portion of the profits go to either the needy poor or to the authorities themselves. With this transformation, the modern lottery was born, as here can be found two key elements of today's government-sanctioned lotteries—a supervisory commission and the redistribution of revenues for charitable purposes.

With the development of capitalist economies and an increased need for cash by governments and charitable institutions, lotteries truly began to flower in the sixteenth and seventeenth centuries, particularly in the developed urban centers of northern Italy. In 1522, a Venetian diarist wrote that a secondhand clothes dealer named Geronimo Bambarara had created "a new method of commerce" by offering a chance at carpets and money prizes for any who ventured an entry fee—at first only 20 soldi, then an entire ducat. Bambarara had created a monster. Before long, the entire Rialto district was filled with nothing but lottery hawkers and players, and the cash prizes had increased from 200 to 1,500 ducats.

City authorities soon moved to suppress these raucous draws and corner the lottery business themselves. The Venetian Republic began running its own lotteries with prizes of cash, merchandise, real estate, and even government offices, including the right to collect taxes and tolls. The proceeds went to the benefit of poor young women, assistance for the generally indigent, the redemption of hostage captives in foreign lands, and other noble endeavors. The sponsors of the new lottery also wished to offer a relatively benign form of gambling that had clear social utility, believing that if people were allowed a chance on this game, they would not play other, more pernicious games. But the lottery apparently only inflamed the gambling spirit, as nonlottery gambling merrily continued, and, by the division of expensive tickets into shares, lottery betting spread to the less affluent. Italian governments became dependent on lotteries and, wishing to maximize their revenues, forbade citizens from buying tickets in foreign lotteries, paid some salaries in part with lottery tickets, and even made ticket purchases compulsory for guilds and other associations.

Venetians were long familiar with gambling. One historian has paralleled the risky nature of maritime commerce, the city's stock in trade, with the establishment of a gambling spirit, even conjecturing that when the seagoing trade started to diminish, Venetian nobles took up gambling with cards and dice out of habit. Gambling was certainly engrained into the culture of Venice; in 1229, for example, when an election to the office of doge (duke) ended in a tie, the two candidates decided the contest by a test of chance, possibly a toss of the dice. During Carnival season, which sometimes lasted from October to March, gambling was openly tolerated, and despite laws discouraging it, it flourished through the rest of the year as well.

The Venetian lottery, though it offered bettors a chance to score huge prizes, was hardly an exercise in instant gratification. Lottery drawings were drawn out, mind-numbingly anticlimactic, and torturously efficient. Tickets were not numbered; each bettor instead wrote his or her name or personal motto on a slip of paper, which went into one urn. Into the other urn went slips of paper bearing the word *pacientia,* patience, meaning "better luck tomorrow," or *precio,* prize, and a description of the prize won. Blindfolded charity boys selected winners by simultaneously drawing slips from each urn. The draw, which did not end until all tickets had been pulled and matched, could take as long as eleven days.

The Venetian version of the lottery quickly spread throughout Italy. The Genoese, not content merely to copy the Venetians, made substantial reforms in the lottery, spurred improbably by a change in election law. Each year, five new members of the ruling colleges were chosen by lot from a pool of candidates. In 1576, the doge of Genoa, Andrea Doria, designed a new system more in spirit with the age. Doria proposed assigning each of the 120 candidates a number, then simply drawing five numbers from an urn called the *seminario.* This new system of selecting candidates proved an efficient electoral reform and, as a public, random drawing, offered an excellent opportunity for a lottery. This electoral lottery became the basis for lotto-type games, which soon competed with draw lotteries.

Although betting on these election drawings was initially conducted on the sly, Genoa's authorities ultimately took a piece of the action for the public coffers. Nor did the Genoese see any point in keeping all of the fun of the election lottery for themselves: they sent lottery agents to towns throughout Europe, particularly Germany, to sell tickets and award prizes. Other Italian

Early lottery drawings on the Venetian model were solemn affairs. Two blind orphans simultaneously drew tickets from large "wheels." One represented the prize, the other the prizewinner, who wrote a name or motto on the slip. This engraving depicts a lottery drawn in Guildhall, London, in 1739.

principalities, such as Venice, Milan, and Naples, copied the Genoese lotto model in 1665, and for a while it flourished both in Italy and Germany, without much modification, though the number of possible numbers was reduced from 120 to 90 through the years. Surviving initial papal denunciations, the lottery won a new measure of legitimacy when the papacy permitted the establishment of a Roman lottery in 1732.

The original Genoese lottery lasted until the end of the eighteenth century in Germany, when most of the German states banned it, though lotto is alive and well in Italy, where a national lottery came in 1863, fast on the heels of Italian unification, and has continued into the twenty-first century.

Organized lotteries spread rapidly across Europe. Sometimes, this meant that Italians literally exported their lotteries, as the Genoese did in Germany, but other nations took the Italian lottery concept and made it their own. French lotteries have a history that rivals that of their Italian counterparts. King

Francis I authorized a French national draw lottery on the Venetian model as early as 1520. Francis bucked several centuries' worth of churchly denunciations of gambling when he boldly declared that if his subjects played the lottery, they would be too busy to fight each other and blaspheme God—ignoring the possibility that the lottery would give them only one more cause to argue and resent divine misfavor. After Francis's gambit, lotteries were sporadically conducted over the next century and a half for a variety of purposes. In 1656, a lottery raised funds for a stone bridge over the Seine in Paris, and four years later another was held for no other reason than to celebrate the nuptials of King Louis XV. In the eighteenth century, lotteries funded the construction of churches, including the structure that eventually became the Paris Panthéon, and other public buildings.

Like most others, the French lottery had a well-deserved reputation as a game with horrible odds. Most drawings, then and now, pay out less than half their gross earnings in prizes, meaning that the "house" holds more than fifty percent of all money—far worse than most casino games. But despite the odds, the indomitable house edge was not yet absolute. It is now a truism that those who make a living—or their operating budgets—from gambling never truly gamble, but while administrators were still grappling with the new science of probability, a clever man or woman had a fighting chance at beating the lottery.

One of the eighteenth century's greatest intellects and most magnetic personalities, the philosopher and writer Voltaire, undertook this very challenge. Born in 1694, the author of *Candide* cut a swath through French society, earning acclaim, exile, and, on more than one occasion, imprisonment in the Bastille with his candor and acid pen. In between writing satiric verse, authoring a controversial philosophical dictionary, and otherwise flouting authority, Voltaire was an avid gambler who preferred the card game of faro and *biribi*, an ancestor of roulette that allowed a gambler to guess which of thirty-six numbered balls a dealer would pull from a leather sack. Of gambling, Voltaire said, its law "alone admits of neither exception, relaxation, variation, nor human tyranny."

Returning to France from an English exile in late 1728, Voltaire was advised to keep a low profile, something that ran counter to his very nature. Instead of quietly biding his time, Voltaire met up with an old friend, Charles-Marie de La Condamine. La Condamine, a former army officer, was a mathematician with a definite sense of adventure—he would later become the first European to conduct an scientific exploration of the Amazon River—and exactly the kind of man Voltaire, living in France only at the sufferance of a monarch with finite patience, should have avoided. Adding fuel to this already combustible mix was the fact that both Voltaire and La Condamine were financially pressed, and neither had a particularly strong inclination for hard work.

The pair soon found a royal opportunity to use their cunning to make a killing. On October 19, 1728, Louis XV's finance minister, Le Pelletier-Desforts, published a royal decree that outlined a new lottery projected to increase the attractiveness of Parisian municipal bonds, which were losing value daily. Under the royal lottery regulations, only holders of municipal bonds could purchase tickets; this privilege, Desforts hoped, would boost sales of bonds and retire Paris's municipal debt. On the eighth of each month, starting in January 1729, a lottery draw would be held; the lucky ticket owners would each win 1,000 francs.

All this seems relatively straightforward, but Desforts set rather strange conditions for the purchase of tickets: Bondholders could only buy them in proportion to the size of their bonds. Thus, the holder of a 100,000-franc bond paid 100 francs to buy a ticket, while the holder of a 1,000-franc bond paid just one franc. Under Desforts's lottery, both the 100-franc and 1-franc tickets had an equal chance of being drawn, and each paid off 1,000 francs. Studying the mechanics of the lottery, Voltaire and La Condamine concluded that if they could swamp the drawing with one-franc tickets, they would, according to the laws of probability, strike it rich.

Voltaire and La Condamine then organized a team of bondholders and did just that. In the February draw, La Condamine cashed in thirteen winning tickets for a total of 13,000 francs. Over the next few months, Voltaire's team dominated the lottery: In October, they won 1,004,000 out of 1,040,000 francs awarded. As Voltaire's winnings continued to mount, Minister Desforts, chagrined that his lottery was enriching the sly philosopher, attempted to curb the scheme by promulgating a decree restricting the sale of low-cost tickets. But La Condamine and Voltaire continued in their winning ways. The beleaguered finance minister then refused to pay Voltaire, but the philosopher successfully argued that he and his confederates had done nothing illegal, and that Desforts's own lack of mathematical acumen was hardly his fault. Though he was loath to do so, Desforts paid Voltaire and his team in full for all of their winnings. The lottery ended in June 1730; out of total prize money of 9,600,000 francs, Voltaire personally took home at least one million francs—enough to allow him to live comfortably for the rest of his life.

Voltaire and La Condamine's fiscal piracy slowed the government's reliance on the lottery; but as the French monarchy became increasingly strapped for capital, lotteries became more and more attractive. At first, they

continued to support charities: The Loterie des Enfants Trouvés (orphans) began in 1754, and a Loterie de la Pitié followed eight years later. In 1757, with
the help of the extraordinary Venetian adventurer, notorious lover, and inveterate gambler Giacomo Casanova, the lottery finally became a regular fixture
of French royal finance. Casanova, only lately removed from a Venetian
prison, joined forces with a fellow Italian, Giovanni Antonio Calasbigi, to
promote a Genoese-style lotto game as a funding source for the École Militaire, a new French military school. Using a solid foundation of probability
theory and his personal charm, Casanova convinced the State Council to approve the new lottery. For their troubles, Calasbigi and Casanova were rewarded handsomely—Calasbigi became superintendent of the new Loterie
de l'École Royale Militaire, and Casanova received six sales offices. Though he
sold five of them for immediate money, he ran the sixth himself with the assistance of a clerk, making a fortune for himself.

Lottery drawings began in April 1758 and were initially held every other
month, but in October they became monthly events. As in the Genoese original, drawings featured five numbered balls drawn from a "wheel" (actually a
small cage) holding ninety. At first, players could bet on only one to three
numbers, but eventually other options, including the selection of up to five
numbers to be picked and betting on specific positions of winning numbers,
became available. The lottery was immediately successful, and in 1776 King
Louis XVI, perhaps at the urging of his new finance minister Jacques Necker,
transformed it into the Loterie Royale de France and initiated twice-monthly
drawings. The lottery was incredibly lucrative for the crown, contributing no
less than 10 million francs to state coffers in 1788. Its chief attraction for
most of its subscribers was the promise of instant wealth, which, in a time
and place when equality of opportunity was nonexistent, might have been
the only way for many players to escape backbreaking work and bitter
poverty.

The Loterie survived the overthrow of the monarchy in 1789 but was outlawed in 1793, its profits already diminished by war and civil chaos. In 1797,
the ruling Directoire reestablished the Loterie Nationale (sans, of course, the
Royale). In this new incarnation, the lottery continued its previous winning
ways, garnering annual revenues as high as 24 million francs and contributing
an average of two percent of the state's budget each year. But critics argued,
with increasing strength, that the lottery, which the poor played out of the
desperate hope of a windfall, was in fact a regressive tax on those who could
least afford it. French reformers succeeded, in 1836, in finally stopping the

lottery wheels from turning. Two years later they would effect a general prohibition of gambling throughout the country.

By this time, though, it was too late. The idea that chance could be tamed and turned to the aid of governments—or individuals—was nearly universal. The French would revive their lottery in the twentieth century, and even before that, they would have rivals for the title of Europe's most devoted gamblers. None would be as resolute as their cross-Channel rivals, the British.

5

The Ridotto Revolution

◆ ◆ ◆

MERCANTILE GAMBLERS CREATE THE CASINO

Lotteries symbolized the burgeoning role of gambling in sixteenth-century Italy. Even before mathematicians had elaborated a systematic consideration of chance, wily gamblers in the Italian city of Venice were beginning to apply theories of probability in practical ways that would revolutionize the world of gambling. Just as the lottery offered citizens a chance to get rich while underwriting charities or government programs, mercantile gambling—gambling run by professionals for profit—let people play against an impersonal house for the price of the house edge.

In many ways, the invention of mercantile gambling mirrored the development of modern banking. The development of these "bank games" had as much importance for gambling as the rise of banks themselves did for finance. Banknotes had circulated in China as early as the seventh century A.D. but did not become a regular feature of European life until the eighteenth century—around the same time that mercantile gambling became widespread. As investors were experimenting with joint stock companies and speculative ventures, gamblers began, increasingly, to view gambling as a business transaction rather than a friendly game between equals.

Social gambling made sense for people who gambled only in order to relieve tedium, or to enjoy special occasions. This is why ancient societies from China to Rome permitted gambling during year-end holidays, and why writers from Augustus Caesar to Girolamo Cardano condoned recreational social gambling as a fitting diversion, if indulged infrequently and according to prescribed rules. But there were always those who saw gambling not as a rare entertainment, but as a shortcut to wealth and leisure. Those who wished to extend their gambling from occasional recreation to habitual pursuit needed to possess both an unlimited income independent of unreliable gambling winnings and more free time than responsibilities. The only way to "earn" a living from gambling was either to accept stretches of poverty as the price of the game, or to cheat regularly, without scruple or detection.

The invention of mercantile gambling provided a way to legitimately make a living from gambling by running houses where gambling was permitted. It also freed gamblers from the bonds of sociability—they could now gamble against professionals whenever they wished. At the same time, the games themselves changed, becoming far more direct as rules were simplified and game durations shortened. Social gamblers might want to while away the hours over sprawling games of *trappola* with their friends, but those looking for action in gambling houses wanted a quick fix: the turn of the card at basset or faro, the spin of the roulette wheel, or a single throw of the dice.

With the introduction of bank games and the proliferation of professional gambling houses, a gambling mania swept over much of Europe. It hit different countries at slightly different times, but it is safe to say that from 1650 to 1800 gambling occupied a place in European society far more prominent than before or since. There had always been gambling, but in these years it was common on a level never before seen. With the rise of mercantile capitalism, money circulated more freely and accumulations of wealth were greater than ever before. During the same years that governments sponsored lotteries, all social classes gambled more. The emergence of mercantile gambling provided the catalyst for an increasing government interest in gambling.

One of the earliest bank games was the German lansquenet, which derived its name from the *landsknechte,* roving German mercenary knights of the sixteenth century who apparently had a nose for favorable house odds. Lansquenet was relatively straightforward: The banker matched stakes with a player or players, then dealt one card to the right and one to the left. If they were of the same suit, the bank won automatically. If not, the dealer continued laying out cards in the middle until a match appeared: If it matched the left, the bank swept the players' stakes, and if it matched the right, the players took the bank's. The lansquenet bank wasn't held by a fixed house but could rotate from player to player. In coming years, bank games would develop much greater sophistication, nowhere with as much passion as in northern Italy.

Europe's most economically, socially, and culturally advanced region, northern Italy was the birthplace of the licensed mercantile gambling house. Venice had long been a gambling mecca: In the late fourteenth century, it was one of the first places where playing cards caught on and though the lottery wasn't invented there, it gained widespread acceptance there in the sixteenth century. Especially during the Carnival season, women and men of all Venetian social classes gambled. Less affluent Venetians enjoyed card and dice games in public places, such as street corners, bridges, grand squares, and wineshops. Though these games were occasionally disrupted by the police and convicted gamblers could face fines and imprisonment, they usually ran more or less openly. Members of the nobility offered a more refined setting for their gambling: At private parties, they presented their guests with games of chance, and as most were politically well connected, these games were rarely stopped by police.

Municipal edicts banning gambling did nothing to stop its dramatic transformation in the sixteenth century. By 1567, legislation specified a new danger: the *ridotti* of nobles, places where gambling took place. The word *ridotto* is likely derived from *ridurre,* to reduce or close, or to make private. Generally, a ridotto could be anything enclosed—a top-secret meeting of government officials, or a private suite of rooms in a larger domicile. But the word soon came to suggest a semiprivate place for gambling, dancing, eating, and gossip. These notorious houses remained the haunts of the aristocracy. For the rest, inns and other public places continued to serve as convenient gathering places.

By the turn of the seventeenth century, antigambling laws reflected a change in the status of ridotti. They were no longer merely places where nobles permitted gambling and drinking: They had become places where nobles, by taking a portion of the money staked, profited directly from gambling. The nobles apparently had specialized dealers, for the Executors against Blasphemy (Esecutori contro la Bestemmia) prosecuted both nobles who owned ridotti and their employees who actually ran the games.

Chief among the games of the ridotti was *bassetto* or basset, a Venetian game that was invented in the late sixteenth century. The game of basset, notably, was a banking game without even the pretense of equality between the dealer/banker and the bettor. In addition to its main bet, where the player tried to guess whether a card would be dealt to the player or dealer pile, basset also featured a series of long shots that, though they paid off handsomely, were extremely unlikely. If a player bet his money on the king, for example, and had the first king in the deck placed in the player's pile, he could either collect three-to-one on his money or let his bet ride and hope to get the king when it was dealt again, in which case he would win seven times his original bet. If he won a second time, this bet, and the third, could also be kept alive: If he triumphed each time, he could collect up to thirty times his initial bet. This was known as the *paroli* (the origin of the English word *parlay*). Though the laws of probability declared such an eventuality highly unlikely, the willingness of bettors to press on in hopes of a larger payout made basset an extremely profitable game—for the banker.

Ridotti flourished, and, frustrated at the inability of the Venetian Inquisition* to eliminate the gambling dens, the Great Council embarked on a novel plan—the legalization of gambling, at least during Carnival, within a single specified free zone. In 1638, the Great Council opened the Ridotto in the San Moisè Palace, a four-story building owned by Marco Dandolo. This was the first legal, state-sanctioned public gambling house in European history—from this notable edifice today's casino industry can rightfully claim descent. The opening of the Ridotto represented a historic union between mercantile gamblers, who ran games for profit, and government, who sought to legitimize the gamblers for purposes of public order and revenue enhancement.

Upon entering the Ridotto, one could visit two small rooms, one selling stimulating refreshments (coffee, tea, and chocolates), and the other offering cheese, wine, fruit, and sausage. Past this initial vestibule one entered the Long Hall, a two-story room whose ceiling was painted with Gerolamo Colonna's *The Triumph of Virtue*, perhaps a warning against cheaters. Along the sides of the Long Hall, one found basset tables at which members of an impoverished clan of noblemen known as the *barnabotti* or Barnabots dealt cards and took wagers. The Barnabots, despite having limited financial means, were, as nobles, prohibited from regular employment and lived at the public's expense in the parish of St. Barnabas. Granting them the Ridotto monopoly was a step toward minimizing the public cost of maintaining them—an early example of public-interest gambling. According to Venetian law, the Barnabots who dealt games had to wear black robes and shoulder-length wigs. As these poor nobles at first lacked the money to bank games themselves, wealthier nobles or merchants sometimes put the Barnabots on salary, bankrolling their games in exchange for the lion's share of the profits.

Off the Long Hall, about six smaller rooms offered even more tables for basset, *biribisso* (the leather-sack version of roulette that the French called *biribi*), and a now-obscure Italian card game known as *panfil*. The windowless Long Hall was lit by six-armed chandeliers that hung from the ceiling and a municipally specified two candles on each table. All gamblers, except for members of the nobility, had to wear masks while gambling, something that clearly ties the legality of the Ridotto to the permissive spirit that reigned at

---

*Unlike their Spanish counterparts, this organization apparently never quite had the benefit of surprise, fear, or ruthless efficiency.

Carnival. The Ridotto began admitting customers between eight or ten in the morning, depending on the season, and stayed open until well past midnight; its votaries often emerged only in the morning, blinking in the sudden sunlight as the rest of Venice began its workday.

Though anyone wearing proper attire (a three-cornered hat, cape, and mask for men) could enter the Ridotto, the high minimum stakes served to restrict its play to the wealthy. Men and women (especially noblemen) were expected to gamble with a phlegmatic detachment that forbade both bettors and bankers from expressing even the slightest dismay at an astounding loss or the tiniest excitement over a victory. The Ridotto was nevertheless an exciting mishmash of Venetian society, with nobles, prostitutes, pimps, usurers, police informants, and degenerate gamblers mixing with curious visitors. The anonymity of the masked Carnival atmosphere no doubt lowered inhibitions. Those seeking adventure outside the bonds of marriage were seldom disappointed at the Ridotto. Its "Chamber of Sighs" was a famously darkened room upon whose couches unlucky gamblers could moan with despair, and lovers with passion.

The profit generated by the Ridotto for the Barnabots and the Venetian government only grew over the years. At the insistence of the city authorities, the Ridotto was enlarged in 1768 using money confiscated from convents, outraging the "social conservatives" of the era. A second legal ridotto opened at the San Cassian Theater, though the Ridotto at San Moisè remained the focal point of the city's gambling. The Ridotto changed its games to keep up with the times. About midway through the eighteenth century, basset began to lose popularity at the expense of faro, a game that would remain popular in Europe and the United States for the next century and a half.

Faro was first known as pharaon, after a French deck of cards that boasted the portrait of a pharaoh. Contrary to later legend, it was not born in ancient Egypt but was rather an adaptation of basset. Working on the same general principal as basset—that players bet on a card or cards that might be in the winning pile—faro had the advantage of a common layout upon which all players could bet. (In basset, a player had to produce from her own deck the card that she wished to bet on; in faro, each card was already represented on the gaming table, and she only had to place her stakes in the appropriate space.) There were other changes as well. If the cards on a single turn formed a pair, the dealer kept half the money bet. Faro players also could bet with the bank, or losing pile, and could bet on multiple cards. A final innovation allowed players to "call the turn" and predict the correct order of the three penultimate cards to be drawn (the last card, the "hock," was an automatic discard).

Whether playing basset, faro, or other games, a parade of the rich and notorious saw the inside of the Ridotto during its golden years. Even those without a propensity for wagering visited the Ridotto at least once if they had the means. The enlightened philosopher Jean-Jacques Rousseau, perhaps looking for noble savages in an urban setting, gambled only once in his life, when he visited the Ridotto in 1744. But others found themselves trapped by fortune's temptations. Lorenzo da Ponte, a poet best remembered as the librettist of three Mozart operas *(The Marriage of Figaro, Così fan tutte,* and *Don Giovanni)*, nearly came to ruin in the Ridotto; the victim of an obsessive love for a female of the Barnabot clan, he gambled himself into desperation. After witnessing his own priest steal and sell his cloak for gambling money, da Ponte vowed "no more gambling, no more women, no more Venice," and embarked on a long and varied career that brought him to the United States, where he would ultimately die in poverty.

The infamous Giacomo Casanova haunted the Ridotto during his days in Venice. A notorious gambler, he was loath to part with money earned by other means but freely lavished his gambling winnings on himself, extravagant gifts to women, and enormous gratuities to servants because he felt that it had "cost him nothing." Casanova, despite his frequent success, said that his gambling was a great mistake, as he lacked the discipline to stop playing when luck was against him; still, he spent much of his time playing faro. He crossed paths with Lorenzo da Ponte at the Ridotto and may have collaborated with him on *Don Giovanni.*

Da Ponte and Casanova were not the only ones who found the Ridotto irresistible. The combination of the Venetian mania for gambling with the house advantage of the Ridotto led to a sad phenomenon: nobles playing themselves into bankruptcy. Fortunes accumulated over generations were lost at the Ridotto and furniture, artwork, and even palaces were pledged to moneylenders in order to secure funds for more gambling.

Perhaps alarmed by the growing impoverishment of its aristocratic families, the Great Council of Venice eventually took action. A reform-minded Barnabot named Giorgio Pisani urged his colleagues that, "to preserve the piety, sound discipline, and moderate behavior" of Venetian society, they had to close the Ridotto and end the experiment in legal public gambling. On November 27, 1774, by a vote of 720 to 21, the Council passed the measure, though, according to Casanova, its members had not intended that to be the case: Each felt that since there would naturally be a majority of votes opposed to the bill, he could support it and thus claim the moral high ground. When the vote was announced, according to Casanova, the solons blankly looked at each other, stupefied at the calamity they had just authored.

After 136 years, the Ridotto was silent. The wife of a French gambler penned an epitaph for the Ridotto when she declared that, with its closure, Venice had been gripped by a morbid depression: "Usurers look as sour as lemons, shopkeepers can't sell a thing, mask makers are starving, and the Barnabot noblemen, accustomed to dealing cards ten hours a day, find their hands are withering away. Clearly, no state can keep going without the aid of vice."

The closure of the Ridotto did not mean the end of Venetian gambling, but instead heralded a new beginning. From its former center at San Moisè, gambling spread to over a hundred illicit ridotti and *casini*. Originally, a *casino* was a small house used as a gathering place by a group of people: a clubhouse. The first references to *casini* appear in the early seventeenth century, and *casini* soon became centers for gambling and gossip. The closure of the public Ridotto increased the number of these little houses: By the end of the century, there were 136 operating in Venice.

Though it was hailed as one of the most sophisticated cities of eighteenth-century Europe, Venice's days of glory did not long outlive its public Ridotto. The city's occupation by Napoleon in 1797 and its absorption into the Austrian Empire soon afterward marked the beginning of a long decline. As the city suffered, its gambling culture waned as well, as other European principalities took the lead in legalized gambling houses or, as they became known, casinos. When the government of Italy again authorized Venetian casinos in the twentieth century, these could not bring back the wayward dissipation of the Ridotto during Carnival season, but the continuation of Venetian gambling and the very word casino serve as lasting reminders of the impressive Venetian contribution to gambling history.

Though the casino was born in Venice, most of today's popular casino games, including roulette, baccarat, and blackjack, originated in France, a testament to the Gallic eagerness for the 1650–1800 European gambling craze. In these years, gambling received the sanction of the French monarch and, for a while, became the sine qua non of courtly life at Versailles. From there, it became a national obsession.

The French turned to gambling with wild abandon in the seventeenth century but had already been playing for years. For centuries, gambling had been chiefly a pastime of nobles and soldiers, particularly during the Hundred

Years' War (1337–1453), with dicing originally the game of choice, though playing cards proliferated in the latter part of the war. During the reign of Charles VI (r. 1380–1422; sometimes known as Charles the Mad), the Hôtel de Nesle attracted many nobles (it was barred to all others) who wished to gamble. A poet of the time lamented, "How many very eminent gentlemen have there lost their arms and horses, their money and lordship—a horrible folly."

Toward the end of the sixteenth century, though, gambling became more prevalent, as did those wishing to take advantage of the unwary. Upon hearing that King Henry III (r. 1574–1589) had opened gaming rooms in the Louvre, a band of Italian gamblers gained admission and took the king for thirty thousand crowns, a tremendous sum. Yet perhaps because of the religious wars that engulfed France during his reign, gambling did not enjoy anything near the level of popularity it would find in that of his successor, Henry IV. Known as "good king Henry" to this day, Henry loved gambling. More greedy than skillful, Henry became extremely displeased when he lost. As a result, smart courtiers and nobles tripped over themselves to lose to him.

During Henry IV's reign, *académies de jeux*, or gaming academies, first appeared. These were not institutions of higher learning but gaming houses that admitted all comers, from peasants to dukes, provided they could secure funds to play. These academies seem to have been in a gray area: Though tolerated by city magistrates for a financial consideration (nearly fifty flourished in Paris alone), they do not seem to have had royal sanction. Nor is it clear if, as in the Ridotto, bank games predominated, or whether these *académies* were merely places for intense social gambling. Their first heyday was brief. With the ascension of Louis XIII to the French throne in 1610, existing laws against gambling were strengthened and the *académies* were closed. Still, clandestine private gambling among the nobility continued.

The accession of the young King Louis XIV to the throne under the tutelage of Cardinal Mazarin is best remembered as the high point of French monarchical absolutism. That period also saw the most dramatic expansion of gambling throughout France. Some claimed that Mazarin introduced gambling to the French nobility at Versailles in 1648. In fact, French monarchs had long been familiar with gambling. At first, according to one chronicler, Mazarin encouraged only games with playing cards, games that might lead to gambling or might not. Before long, though, thanks to Mazarin's skill at play, games of chance predominated and, to the woe of one commentator, brought ruin to noble families. Even worse, it stultified the nobility: Before the vogue for gambling, men and women had worked at improving the art of conversation by reading, but afterward books were neglected, as were athletic pursuits and other games of skill, until men became "weaker and more sickly, more ignorant, less polished, and more dissipated." Women lost their previous mystique by spending all night out gambling with the boys and were "very ductile and complying" to those from whom they borrowed money.

With gambling a center of the thrice-weekly Grand Appartement, a gathering of all of the king's and queen's subjects on hand at Versailles, the royal palace became known as *ce tripot* ("that gambling den"). The royal apartments began to resemble a small casino where nobles contorted themselves in agony as they lost and whooped with delight when they won, unless the king himself was close by, in which case they struggled to maintain an even deportment. Cheating was rife, and some nobles gained national acclaim for their skill or luck. The king himself preferred billiards, as sitting at a card table made him fidgety, but his queen loved cards, though she perpetually lost.

Given royal imprimatur, gambling became de rigueur for members of gentle society. Respectable hosts thought nothing of mitigating their entertainment expenses by "entertaining" guests with bank games like faro, *biribi*, and *hoca*, another roulette ancestor. Curmudgeons complained that, before inviting a guest to dinner, the party giver inquired as to whether he gambled.

According to one account, during these years cardplaying spread from the army to the court, from the court to the city, and from the city to the country towns. Gambling became a French obsession during this time: Everyone, it seemed, lived only to hope for the next big win, and gambling became a favorite topic in the period's fiction and drama. Mazarin's enemies charged that he had familiarized the court with gambling as part of a cynical plot to keep the young Sun King under his thrall and to bankrupt his enemies, but it seems obvious that gambling was avidly pursued throughout the nation. After Mazarin's death in 1661, gambling continued to increase in scale, and at the passing of Louis XIV himself in 1715, its primacy in France was undisputed. One early historian wrote that at that time three quarters of the nation thought of nothing but cards and dice.

The French had a variety of reasons for gambling. Inveterate gamesters practiced their craft in hope of scratching a living from the tables. Other men and women gambled simply because it was the currently fashionable form of social intercourse. Though vast sums were won and lost, most nobles gambled with contempt for money, rather than out of greed for it. Just as the proper Venetian gentleman was to stoically win and lose without a twitch, young French gentlemen were instructed that it was their duty to gamble heavily, lose without passion, win with indifference, and to regard a gambling debt as a nearly sacred obligation. Since these debts were not covered by any legal enforcement, and rested only upon a gentleman's word, his handling of them spoke volumes about his rectitude. Thus, a generation of French nobles, whose debts to gambling cronies took precedence over those to artisans and business partners, came of age, ready to lead France into the maw of financial chaos.

In the eighteenth century, the philosophers and scientists of France moved to understand the universe as a rational, predictable place. Voltaire's using mathematics and logic to give Minister Desforts and the French royal financiers their comeuppance made it seem that gambling, if done with reason, might be rational and even enlightened.

But the official French approach to gambling was anything but enlightened. From 1643 to 1777, thirty-two official decrees announced that gambling was a crime to be sternly punished. Yet gambling only grew. The regency of Louis XV saw the royal finances and national wealth entrusted to a gambler, the notorious John Law, and licensed gambling houses known as *maisons de jeux* became fixtures of the Paris cityscape. They commonly glided by official prohibitions by maintaining a pretense of offering only card games requiring skill, collectively known as *jeux de commerce*. Games of pure chance, or *jeux de hazard*, also flourished in the *maisons de jeux*. Popular games included basset/faro, *biribi*, and lansquenet—all of them bank games, indicating that mercantile gamblers ran the houses. Gamblers also plied their trade without even superficial fear of the police at two seasonal fairs and within foreign embassies. In addition, hundreds of ostensibly illegal gambling rooms were widely known, proclaiming their existence by telltale lights at their entrance. For a kingdom that added new laws against gambling nearly every year, France had a great deal of it, both legal and illegal.

The French embraced the games played in Italy. *Hoca* or *hocca,* an early iteration of *biribi* and precursor to roulette, enjoyed a great popularity, as did basset, faro, and the ultimate mercantile game, the lottery. Particularly among the upper classes, social gambling continued alongside the new mercantile games. One of the most popular games was brelan, which was played by two to five players with a thirty-two-card deck lacking twos through sixes. Players began by anteing into the pot and receiving three cards; they could then raise the stakes, check by matching previous raises, or fold. Once betting stopped, players revealed their cards and worked to declare a winner.

The best possible hand was called the brelan, or three-of-a-kind. If more than one player had a brelan, the highest-ranked triplet won. If no player had brelan, the one with the highest point total in a single suit triumphed. But players were not guaranteed that the cards in their hands would remain theirs. After turning the cards faceup, the player with the highest card of a suit-sign "captured" all of her opponents' same-suited cards. After this reorganization, the dealer revealed a final card, *la retourne,* which was either added to a brelan to form a four-of-a-kind or taken by the player with the highest card in that suit. Superficially similar to poker, it actually had several differences: Players could lose cards from their hands, and how cards related to others in play was more important than their position within a player's hand. Three kings, for example, could be beaten by a player holding only an ace that matched one of the kings' suit, in which case he captured the king.

Wealthy Parisians soon found even more places to play. New gambling houses, called *enfers,* or hells, opened in Paris and its environs. Their sinister name revealed the intensity of gambling that took place there. One chronicler described how in the salon of one of these hells a nobleman offered his sword as his stake, a contravention of custom that appalled both the nobility and the bankers in attendance. Others retreated to spas under the pretense of seeking healthy respite at the healing springs, while they actually wanted to congregate with gamesters. Even those who could not afford bread gambled constantly, while merchants and craftsmen heaped gold upon the tables and one farmer even gambled away his harvest.

In the 1770s, government officials made two attempts to alleviate the problems of rampant, unchecked gambling and divert some of its profits toward the public good. The first was the 1776 co-option of Casanova's lottery by the king, and the second was a scheme developed a year earlier by the Parisian lieutenant of police Antoine de Sartines to license and tax gambling establishments. He permitted twelve legal gaming houses, forwarding the resulting tax to hospitals, and required them to permit women to gamble two days a week. A reported rise in crime and financial misfortunes led to their supposed suppression three years later, but the contradictory French approach continued, as both licensed and unlicensed establishments continued to operate unabated.

As the social and economic conditions in France worsened and political tensions began to mount in the late 1780s, gambling's intensity continued to increase. One might have expected the shock of the sudden regime change in 1787 combined with the vicissitudes of war, internal and external, following the Revolution to have caused a sudden, sharp decline in gambling. But gambling continued, seemingly immune from any interruption, save the temporary hiatus of the lottery from 1793 to 1797. Perhaps the French Revolution most strongly changed gambling in Britain, where escaping émigrés brought the contagion of gambling fever with them, at least in the opinion of British moralists.

The path of revolutionary gambling is best seen at the Palais Royale, a four-story behemoth north of the Louvre. This palace was originally the hereditary home of the Orléans family. When Louis Philippe Joseph I inherited it in 1785, his sumptuous lifestyle and wild betting threatened to bankrupt him. Rather than limit his spending, the liberal Philippe Égalité (as he was known) turned it into a commercial center. He converted the upper floors into apartments for rent and installed 180 shops on the ground floor. The duke rented out basement and second-floor space for restaurants, cafés, and social clubs, which began offering games of chance. Soon over a hundred gambling rooms were found there.

In the years before the Revolution, the Palais was the scene of ardent gambling. Marie-Antoinette stayed until dawn for weeks, losing spectacularly at faro. Other nobles disgraced themselves by losing unimaginable sums there as well. The liberal Philippe also opened the Palais to the middle classes, giving them an elegant place to gamble. After the 1793 guillotining of the French monarchy (including the unfortunate Philippe), gambling only escalated within the Palais Royale. In reaction, the Directorate successfully reduced the number of gambling operations to five. Though the new government did not officially sanction these five rooms, they declined to close them, thus allowing gambling-mad Parisians an important safety valve.

Apocryphally, the French Revolution led to a singular change within the rules of cards: Aces, not kings, became the highest-ranked card. But, as can be seen by looking at the rules of the much earlier game brelan, this was already a feature of at least some French games. Perhaps it is more fitting to say that games like brelan, where a single ace could sweep aside three kings, represented the building social turmoil. The Revolution's chief impact was to briefly change the composition of the French deck. With the ascension of the Republic in the 1790s, gambling with pictures of kings, queens, and their retainers became decidedly passé, and the customary court cards were replaced with representations of abstract republican virtues like Liberty or patriarchs of the new order like Voltaire. Even this change was temporary, as gamblers proved yet again to stubbornly resist innovation in the art of the playing card, and royalty soon returned.

During the years following the Revolution a new game appeared at the Palais Royale. Roulette combined the numbers of *hoca/biribi* with an English wheel used in at least three games: roly-poly or rowlet, ace of hearts, and E/O (even and odd). The English had begun playing roly-poly in 1720, when they spun a small ball around a horizontal wheel with several slots, including two that gave the banker an automatic victory. Around the same time, ace of hearts featured a farolike layout and cards painted on the wheel. When the British Parliament outlawed roly-poly and ace of hearts in 1739, one enterprising gamester circumvented the law by creating E/O, a wheel with forty slots: twenty each marked odd or even, with one of each marked for the bank. If the ball fell into a "bank" slot, the dealer collected all losing bets but did not pay winners.

When the French first began playing roly-poly or roulette, they played the unnumbered English original. Besides changing the wheel's colors to red and black from white and black, the French made no changes until, in 1796, someone fused the numbered balls and layout of the smaller, street version of *biribi* (which had thirty-six numbers to the indoor version's seventy) with the wheel of roulette. The Palais Royale game of 1796 offered all of the features of today's game: straight-up betting, red/black and even/odd betting, column betting, and other splits and combinations. Like American roulette, it had both zero and double zero, marked in green, which were neither red, black, even, nor odd (though zero is actually an even number). Even at times of revolutionary crisis, the French remained inventive gamblers, and not even the chaos of revolution and war could stop the wheels from spinning.

Nor did the rise of Napoléon Bonaparte halt gambling. Salons, legal or not, continued, and Frenchmen and -women remained drawn to them. In 1806 Napoléon created the first unambiguously legal gambling houses in France. In that year he finally legalized the five surviving gambling rooms of the Palais Royale, six more in the vicinity of that palace, and those at health resorts like Spa and Aix-les-Bains. After Napoléon's defeat at Waterloo in 1815, ironically, the Palais Royale enjoyed its most profitable year yet, as triumphant Englishmen, Prussians, Austrians, and Russians converged on Paris and celebrated by gambling at the Palais.

The emperor himself was a noted gambler, though he was slightly ahead of his time in preferring the relatively new game of vingt-et-un, better known to English speakers as "twenty-one" or blackjack. Twenty-one's roots are obscure, but it first appeared in France in the middle of the eighteenth century, probably having developed from the earlier game of thirty-one, which had been played as early as 1464. The rules of thirty-one are unknown, but it is likely that drawing cards to its eponymous number was only one phase of the game, as it was with the games of cribbage and noddy. Twenty-one emerged as its own game when the rules were altered to permit the ace to represent one or eleven and the play was shortened by drawing only to twenty-one. The game did not have the same popular appeal as faro, though it was a favorite of Louis XV's mistress Madame du Barry, and in truth it would not be until the popularization of card counting in the 1960s that the game truly came into its own. This game, perhaps, comforted Napoléon during his years of exile, and it is interesting to speculate as to whether the great general developed any counting system of his own or meekly surrendered to fortune.

Gambling would continue in France after the 1814 Bourbon Restoration. An 1818 Paris survey reported a total of twenty tables operating throughout nine legal houses. Nearly half of the tables were dedicated to roulette, with seven for *trente-et-un*, possibly the extended version of blackjack, which apparently survived alongside its quicker version. Other games played included the American craps, its ancestor hazard, and *biribi*. These licensed games operated until December 31, 1837, when the Chamber of Deputies "permanently" banned all games of chance, an act whose greatest consequence was the eventual development of Monte Carlo as a gambling haven. Even when banning gambling, the French could not help but encourage it.

PART THREE

Gambling Takes to the Sea

◆ ◆ ◆

After midnight, it seemed that all of the West End crowded into the stately club-house at 50 St. James's Street. Known informally as Crockey's or Fishmonger's Hall, the club was as famous as its owner: William Crockford, the ill-educated Cockney who was, by 1830, the chief entertainer of Britain's wealthiest gentlemen. Though a committee of such notables ostensibly controlled the membership of the club, Crock-ford himself was the chief proprietor and real power. He was a constant presence there, overseeing the festivities until well into the morning. The gastronomic cre-ations of Crockford's chef, the legendary Ude, were praised throughout Europe, and gentlemen gladly joined Crockford's so that they might enjoy his legendary repasts. The seemingly limitless wine cellar complemented Ude's gourmet dishes. But the real attraction was the playroom, where Crockford held a nightly bank of £5,000, against which all could try their luck.

There was never any shortage of players; members could bring guests, and for-eign ambassadors and diplomats were always welcome. The club became a notable haunt for Members of Parliament; while the legislative body was in session, Crock-ford served dinner from midnight to five a.m.

Crockford's became the final stop of the evening in these years. Gentlemen left balls, parties, theaters, and even other clubs and invariably made appearances at Crockford's, washing down their suppers with an unparalleled selection of wine. With the hazard room run "on the square," bettors staked enormous sums. Owing to the inevitable house advantage, however, money could not help but end up on Crockford's side of the table.

If someone had cautioned any of the gentlemen in attendance against playing by reminding them that this sort of dice play was, in fact, thoroughly illegal, they would have responded with a shrug. With guests as distinguished as the duke of Wellington (Napoléon's conquerer himself), Crockford's had nothing to fear from the police. No constable would dare to face the wrath of the club's influential members. While other gambling halls offering play to the lower classes faced the law, Crockford's remained invulnerable. As in any society as class conscious as nineteenth-century Britain, who you were invariably trumped the laws you might be breaking.

6

All Is on the Hazard

◆ ◆ ◆

THE BRITISH COME TO PLAY

Europeans, especially the French and Italians, popularized foreign inventions like playing cards and invented the mathematics that led to the discovery of probability and the rise of mercantile gambling. The British impact on gaming is not so readily apparent. In fact, opponents of gaming frequently claimed that gambling had been imported into the isles by scheming foreigners, usually Frenchmen, and that in their natural state the British Isles were free from its taint. But the British did, in fact, invent a few games and at times outpaced even the French in their gambling enthusiasm.

From the days of Roman legionaries rolling *tessarae*, the peoples of Britain have enjoyed gambling. Yet there have also been, from the earliest days, those who wished to deny the thrill of cards, dice, and betting to others. Beginning in the medieval era, opposition periodically drove gambling underground, but the British seemed constitutionally unable to deprive themselves. From around 1660 to 1740, the British passion for gambling was almost completely unrestrained. And after a generation or two of diminished ardor, the British returned to it with a vengeance late in the eighteenth century. Public tolerance would continue to ebb and flow for the next century, until the antigamblers seemed to have at last conquered the gambling hells—only, of course, to see the devils pop up again.

The most pervasive dice game, hazard, remained popular in England until the nineteenth century. Discussed in Alphonso X's *Book of Games,* the game was once ubiquitous on the Continent, and the French *hasard* became a catchall term for all games of chance in that nation, where it was widely played. But by the time that Pierre Rémond de Montmort wrote his *Essai d'analyse sur les jeux de hasard* in 1708, the game, according to him, was now being played only in England. Later records of Parisian gambling show that hazard was present in licensed game rooms, though it lacked the popular appeal of faro and roulette and may have been played mostly by British visitors. If anything, the invisibility of hazard in early eighteenth-century France illuminates the strange fascination that the game had for their cross-Channel neighbors.

Early on, hazard developed a reputation as an addictive game in England. In his *Compleat Gamester* (1674), Charles Cotton proclaimed hazard "the most bewitching game" played with dice and described an early model of gambling addiction: "When a man begins to play he knows not when to leave off; and having since accustomed himself to play at hazard he hardly ever after minds anything else." Cotton ended his notes on hazard by saying that while the man who gave up "this time-spending-money-wasting game" would be happy, a man who had never heard of it was happier still. Harsh words, to be sure, but evidently hazard was the cause of much ruin in this era.

Hazard was so ruinous because it developed before the modern understanding of probabilities, and as a result payoffs are not commensurate with the risks. As the two-dice version of the game was played, it matched a single dice thrower or caster against a player or players who matched his stake. The caster announced his "main," or a point between five and nine, and then rolled the dice. If he threw his main, he won his bet and swept the stakes. If he didn't make his main, the number rolled became his "chance," and he now had to roll it again to win; if he threw his original main, he lost. If a player rolled a two or three, or "crabs," he lost his bet, or "crabbed out" (a phrase that betrays hazard as the ancestor of craps). As players gained a better idea of the relative probabilities of various throws, they built additional rules into the game in an attempt to harmonize its chances with the actual odds. But often these only served to throw the game even further out of whack.

Other popular dice games included inn and inn, and passage. The rules of inn and inn seem simple: Two or three players laid stakes and cast four dice each. Scoring one inn (a "doublet," or two of the same number) was, in today's terminology, a "push," as no cash was won and all money remained in play. Two inns meant the caster took all the stakes; an out (no doublets) meant the caster lost his stake. Passage also relied on doublets: Using three dice, the caster continued throwing until he threw a doublet under ten (i.e, two ones, twos, threes, or fours) and lost, or threw a doublet over ten (fives and sixes) and passed, or won. This seventeenth-century game survives today in the terminology of craps, where players bet on the "pass" line.

The most popular table games (games that needed a prepared board), included backgammon (often known simply as "tables"), trictrac (or tictac), doublets, and the fetchingly named catch-dolt. Since they involved a mixture

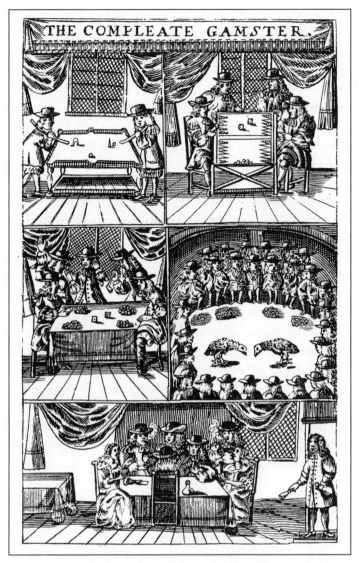

Frontispiece for Charles Cotton's Compleat Gamester *(1st edition, 1674), which shows the most popular British gambling games of the late seventeenth century. Clockwise from top left, they are billiards, backgammon, cockfighting, whist, and hazard.*

of rolling dice and moving games pieces across the board or around a circuit, they might be today classified as board games rather than gambling games. Still, for centuries the British and other Europeans gambled on these games, which combined luck with skill. Backgammon was the preeminent table game of the Middle Ages and early modern period; it is clearly illustrated and described in Alphoso X's thirteenth-century treatise on gaming and did not fall out of fashion in England until the early nineteenth century.

Chess, too, was long a betting proposition, as Cardano made clear in *The Book on Games of Chance,* but because of the natural imbalance in skill levels, most betting did not take place on full-fledged games. Rather, players usually set up a single problem—e.g., go from a set position to checkmate in five moves—and bet that an opponent could not solve it. In the end, it was likely the emergence of mercantile gambling that removed betting from table games and chess. Unlike the newly popular card and dice games, their odds were not easily quantified, and eking a profit from them was no statistical certainty.

In addition to their long-running fascination with hazard and dice games, the British adopted and invented several card games. Primero enjoyed a great vogue in the sixteenth and seventeenth centuries, though in the latter part of that century it was replaced by ombre, thanks to that game's sponsorship by Catherine of Portugal, the queen of Charles II (r. 1660–1685). Ruff was another popular game played in two variations. Ruff-and-honors, also known as slam, was so common that one author claimed its rules were intimately known by "every child of almost eight years old." French ruff was an entirely different game, though apparently a variation on the same trick-taking principle that underlay most recreational card games of the period. Other popular games of the seventeenth century included gleek (which, like primero and ombre, was best played by three), cribbage, lanterloo (later shortened to loo), bragg, and piquet, each of which contributed to the later development of poker. Leisurely whist pointed to one path of playing cards: the languid play of social gambling. But by the end of the century, gambling of all types would become a universal obsession.

By the Elizabethan era, gambling was so engrained within the English consciousness that it can be found throughout the works of William Shakespeare. He frequently uses the word *hazard,* usually in its then-understood sense of "gamble" or "risk." When the forces of the conspirators Brutus and Cassius attack Octavius and Antony in the battle of Philippi as depicted in Act V, Scene I, of *Julius Caesar,* Cassius declares that "the storm is up, and all is on the hazard." He also incorporated games into his plays. Shakespeare names specific dice games like novum (*Love's Labor's Lost*) and tray-trip (*Twelfth Night*), and the most popular card game of Elizabethan England, primero. The rakish Falstaff, one of Shakespeare's most vivid characters, declares in *The Merry Wives of Windsor* that "I never prospered since I forswore myself at primero," while lamenting his humiliation at the hands of the eponymous wives. Shakespeare's Henry VIII was fond of cards; Gardiner, when asked if he has just come from the king, announces that has just left him at primero with the Duke of Suffolk. The Bard took little artistic license here, as records of the real Henry VIII's expenses reveal frequent losses at cards.

Gambling is a central theme of *The Merchant of Venice*, fitting for a city then mad with the gambling bug. Everyone speculates: shipowners whose fleets may or may not return, moneylenders betting that their customers will default, and even a father who transforms his daughter's courtship into a lottery. The play hinges on the dilemma of Portia, a wealthy heiress who, according to the terms of her father's will, can only marry the man who correctly chooses one of three caskets. In Act III, Scene II, Portia implores Bassiano not to gamble rashly but to "pause a day or two/ Before you hazard," lest he choose wrong and lose her forever. Luckily, he chooses the right casket, which is made of lead and inscribed with the legend "Who chooseth me must give and hazard all he hath." For a people familiar with high stakes, this was an instantly understandable message.

Early in the seventeenth century, English gamblers could choose from a variety of card and dice games, in addition to the nascent sport of horse racing and other animal sports such as cockfighting and animal baiting. But the civil wars that wracked the British Isles in the 1640s disrupted gambling (as they did everything else), and the victory of Parliamentary forces and rule by Oliver Cromwell nearly destroyed it. Under Cromwell, self-denial became the law of the land. Christmas and other feast days were suppressed, replaced by monthly fasts—soldiers actually forced their way into private homes to confiscate Christmas hams. Cromwell's government banned dancing, walking anywhere except for church on Sunday, and all sports, including horse racing (even though Old Ironsides maintained his own stable) and wrestling. Adornment in clothing was outlawed. Gambling was, as a matter of course, prohibited, and Cromwell's police enforced the laws, ending bearbaiting and cockfighting by shooting the bears and wringing the necks of the fighting birds. Few gamblers were willing to court the draconian penalties, lest they follow the bears and cocks.

With the overthrow of Cromwell's Protectorate and the return of the king and his Cavalier adherents from French exile in 1660 came an outstanding explosion of libertinage. Those who had endured the enforced asceticism of the Roundheads exuberantly celebrated the end of anarchy, civil war, and despotic rule. The reign of Charles II, known as the Restoration, became infamous as one of marked depravity, as the upper classes exulted in rampant corruption, a relaxation of sexual mores, and an explosion in gambling. As such, it was the beginning of the first sustained period of English gambling enthusiasm, which lasted until the 1740s—gambling's "First Great Awakening" among the British. Hazard, cockfighting, and bearbaiting returned to prominence, alongside a host of card games imported from the court of the French king.

Those who disapproved of the newly prominent role of gambling in English society blamed the favorite English bugbear, the French. Charles II and his cronies, they alleged, picked up the gambling virus while exiled in France and, upon returning to the shores of England, infected the masses.* The expansion of gambling throughout all classes of the English, wrought by the dissolute Cavaliers, represented the moral Frenchification of the entire island. One later writer made the analogy quite explicit, writing that the English people had been susceptible to the sweeping moral laxity of the Restoration just as a human body, weakened by wounds, could not repel "the venomous attacks of alien germs."

The Restoration began the English manifestation of the pan-European gambling boom. For centuries, cultural innovations, from Christianity to coffee, had crossed the Channel, and in the late seventeenth century, gambling was the fashionable import. As in the court of Louis XV in France, gambling became customary among Charles II's retinue. Gambling frequently and freely was now a prerequisite of courtly life—it was in fact one of the only three social activities of the court (dancing and the theater joined it). As such, incessant gambling was taken to indicate high breeding. Even those formerly noted for their rectitude and probity consented to gamble once joining the elite, either for the sake of social advancement or because they had been honestly bitten by the gambling bug. Charles II himself gambled only moderately, not out of any disdain for betting, but because he simply hated to lose, which he usually did.

His subjects, far less resistant to losing, had no problem dedicating their spirits to the new fashion. Even the dignified duke of Ormonde hustled nightly into the groom porter's residence to bet wildly at cards, though his reputation was so impeccable that one of his contemporaries declared him "decent even in his vices." Even former Puritans like the famed diarist Samuel Pepys couldn't resist the occasional gamble. While Pepys disdained the high

---

*This is a sly parallel to another perceived malady foisted onto the virtuous English by the French, venereal disease, which was in popular parlance known as "the French disease." In the underworld slang of the eighteenth and nineteenth centuries, an afflicted prostitute was said to have been "Frenchified."

stakes of the groom porter's games for moderate play among friends for penny stakes, high rolling was the norm at court. One diarist described a typical night in the royal privy chamber: The king personally opened the revels by casting the dice and losing his £100, and both the gentlemen and ladies took this as their signal to play maniacally. The upright duke of Ormonde won at least £1,000 that night, and though he was more successful than most, his high betting was no exception.

Most aristocratic players gambled simply because it was the latest fashion—had the rest of the court been taken with hawking or hunting, they would have gladly exchanged their cards for outdoor gear. But for others gambling was a means of living. The chevalier de Gramont admitted that he "played high and lost but seldom," and he was typical of the cardplaying roués who earned their keep by their skill at cards. Their unlucky "victims" were sometimes habitual losers who chased after cards in a vicious cycle. The poet Sir John Denham, after regretting the time and money lost at the card table, repented of his gambling and wrote an elegant and sincere antigambling manifesto. His father, who had previously disowned him, was so impressed that he left him a hefty fortune on his death. After this coup, Denham returned to cards and soon lost his substantial inheritance.

The gambling passion in Restoration England was not confined to the wealthy and privileged. Taverns and coffeehouses spilled over with card and dice games, and gambling in one form or another could be found anywhere. As commoners and nobles bet their pence and pounds with equal ardor, gambling became an everyday diversion. A 1735 incident shows the extreme to which a gamble could be taken. In October of that year, Henry and John Trotter bet the child of James and Elizabeth Leesh against the four shillings of Robert Thomson and Thomas Ellison while playing cards "at the sign of the Salmon," one of the countless taverns where less well-off Englishmen and women gambled against each other. Thomson and Ellison won and promptly took delivery of the child. Though such stakes were exceptional enough to become news, no one apparently interfered with the child's delivery. For the gambling-mad English, a bet was a bet, no matter what the stakes.

Unlike in Venice and Paris, where mercantile gambling soon came to dominate the gambling scene, most English gamblers remained committed to social games. In 1664, Parliament passed "An Act against Deceitful, Dishonest, and Excessive Gaming" which explicitly sought to restrict gambling as a "constant trade or calling." Mercantile games remained rare until about 1677, when a croupier named Morin, apparently recently departed from France (one step ahead of the authorities), opened a basset game in the London home of the Duchess of Mazarin. Soon basset became fashionable in high society and an unavoidable amusement for those who could afford to play for high stakes. Royal mistresses, whose losses were promptly paid out of public funds—the royal treasury—lost upwards of £5,000 to the duchess on some nights.

The game apparently did not catch on with the general populace right away; as late as 1721, it retained a reputation as a courtly game properly played only by royalty and nobles. Theophilus Lucas, author of the exposé *Memoirs of the Lives, Intrigues, and Comical Adventures of the Most Famous Gamesters and Celebrated Sharpers* . . . (the full title runs on for nearly a paragraph), tellingly compared basset to the Royal Oak Lottery, in which the lottery man kept 5 parts out of 230 for his own profit. As a result, Lucas noted, the basset banker undoubtedly had "a greater opportunity of gaining, than those that play." Whoever was lucky enough to gain permission to hold the bank would inevitably "become possessor of a considerable estate" posthaste.

Though basset maintained its aristocratic reputation, because of its promise of large payouts (thirty to one if one got lucky enough), it attracted hopeful small-stakes bettors. In coffeehouses and taverns, they put up minuscule sums in hope of winning big. But, Lucas cautioned his readers, basset, like the lottery, was no way to win money. The dealer, he wrote, "if he pays you twenty pound in one night's play, only gives you opportunity in another to lose a hundred." Yet Lucas's cautionary note went virtually unheeded, as the English ultimately took to mercantile gambling with the same zeal as the Venetians and French.

The social games of the times were hardly less amenable to steady returns than basset, thanks to the cunning of certain unscrupulous players. Cheating, apparently tolerated and admired by some as "an embellishment to skillful play," was widespread, and money jumped from the pockets of willing but naïve plungers into those of slick gamesters like the chevalier de Gramont. Theophilus Lucas warned readers against sharpers who lived to cheat. "Since gaming is become a trade," he wrote, "and the adventurers thereat do not all play upon the square, my design in publishing these Memoirs is to detect the several cheats which the sharpers use." Lucas explained in great detail how sharpers used fullums (loaded dice), and topped, knapped, or slurred honest dice to get the desired cast. Though Lucas saw gaming "pursued like business, with all the eagerness of trade," this business was rarely on the up-and-up.

———

The entrepreneurs and investors who created British finance capitalism had more in common with gamblers than they would have admitted. With scant regulatory oversight and unpredictable market conditions, early stock exchanges were often similar to the Ridotto of Venice or the coffeehouses where "insurers" accepted wagers on sieges, and stock prices were far more turbulent than the relatively gentle bull and bear cycles accepted today. Early investors saw speculation as a kind of gambling, as excitement drew stock prices up without restraint and, all too often, prices collapsed. The word *bubble* soon began to denote a rush of speculation followed by a crash, and stock buyers balanced their terror of a burst bubble with their fear at being left out of a sure money-winning proposition.

The first famous bubble centered on, of all things, Dutch tulips. Brilliantly colored tulips were first imported into Europe in the middle of the sixteenth century and became an all-abiding craze among the French nobility during the rule of the Louis XIII (r. 1610–1643). This made tulips a suitably fashionable pursuit throughout all of Europe. In the United Provinces (Holland), the newly powerful class of regents—mostly businessmen and professionals—embraced the flower as a status symbol around 1620. As Dutch gentlemen with a desire to flaunt some of their newfound affluence sought out rare and beautiful tulips, prices began to escalate. Speculation in tulip bulbs became the driving force of the Dutch economy, as everyone who was able sought to convert money and property into tulips, whose price was soaring. Individual tulips were soon traded on the stock exchanges of Amsterdam, Rotterdam, and other major towns. The tulip madness reached a climax in December 1636 and January 1637, when a single bulb from the *Semper Augustus* tulip sold for 10,000 guilders, a price that could have fetched a mansion.

But the bubble burst in February 1637, and in the blink of an eye the tulip market collapsed completely. The tulipomania had simply sucked up all of the available capital, and when tulip holders could no longer command inflated prices fueled by speculation, the flowers became nearly worthless. The collapse of the Tulip Bubble in 1637 occasioned widespread financial ruin throughout Holland, as tulip dealers defaulted and those who had invested in tulip bulbs and tulip futures now found themselves penniless.

The incredible, tragic crash of the Dutch tulip market no doubt chastened some would-be speculators, but sometimes a galloping bull market seemed like such a sure thing that investors simply could not resist. To sit on the sidelines as everyone else earned double and quadruple returns on an investment seemed foolhardy and jumping on the bandwagon appeared the height of reasonability. The results, of course, were predictably catastrophic. Yet the lessons of tulipomania would nevertheless be forgotten, if they had ever been heard.

Eighty years later, another debacle unfolded in France. In 1717, John Law, a Scots economist and gambler (he had amassed a personal fortune of 100,000 livres gambling), promised a solution to France's ongoing financial crisis, escalating royal debt, and declining confidence in the government's fiscal stability: issuing banknotes. The regent, Philippe II, permitted Law to open the Banque Générale, which would offer shares to the public and issue banknotes. To create a demand for these otherwise worthless notes, the regent decreed that all payments to the crown—tax and otherwise—must be made with them. In December 1718, the scheme seemed successful, and the regent purchased the Banque from Law, reorganizing it as the Banque Royale.

Before this triumph, Law had acquired the Mississippi Company, a failing concern that had been granted the patent to trade with and sell land in France's Louisiana colony. Securing a twenty-five-year monopoly on trade with North America and the West Indies, he then bought all other trading monopolies (including those for China and the East Indies) and consolidated them as the Compagnie des Indes in 1719. Law launched an extensive publicity campaign to stir public interest in buying shares of this trading powerhouse. In January 1720, the regent placed Law in charge of all French royal finances. Law then merged the Banque Royale into the Compagnie des Indes. The Compagnie issued one stock series after another, followed by the banknotes needed to buy stock. Stock prices soon reached unthinkable heights: Shares once worth 500 livres now sold for 15,000.

Though the company successfully bought all of the government's outstanding debt (one of Law's original goals), its stock value rested solely on the confidence of investors. When two major investors demanded to immediately exchange their stock holdings for gold in the summer of 1720, panic ensued. Riots took place as investors stormed the Compagnie's office trying to redeem their shares. His system in tatters, Law hurried out of France in December 1720, bound for Venice. The government was forced to liquidate the credit instruments totaling 3 billion livres, which were now almost completely devalued. The process was painful and not always fair, but five hundred thousand investors eventually had 1.7 billion livres' worth of credit redeemed for new government bonds. "John Law's System" would long remain a byword for irrationally exuberant speculation, though Law himself was apparently none the worse for the experience and spent his last days at the Ridotto, improbably winning at basset. At his death in 1729, his son interred him in a church adjacent to the Ridotto.

Across the Channel the next major speculative frenzy, the South Sea Bubble, took London by storm slightly after John Law's scheme unraveled. This bubble scheme also involved overseas trade monopolies, which makes its course all the more unbelievable. The South Sea Company had been chartered in 1711 for the purpose of trading with the western coast of South America, then ruled by the Spanish. This occasioned a slight problem, for the Spanish, like other mercantilist powers, jealously protected their trade monopolies and refused to open the ports of Peru and Chile to the Company. Eventually Philip V of Spain assented to give the Company a patent to transport slaves to the New World and to send a trading ship once a year. Even this concession came only at the cost of a ruinous tax (one fourth of all profits, and five percent of the rest). Still, the Company put a positive spin on the arrangement, and though it only sent a single ship in 1717 before war forced a disruption of commerce, public confidence in its stock remained high.

In 1719, the South Sea Company asked Parliament to sell it the British national debt, which it claimed it could pay off by offering better terms to investors. The Company already owned over one fifth of the debt, which it had acquired for a percentage of its own stock. Over substantial opposition, the bill passed in April 1720. Shares, which had been selling for more than three-hundred pounds each, dropped in value, but the South Sea Company, spreading rumors of its planned trade exploits, successfully propped up the price. Fueled by mounting speculation, the price of stock soared, reaching £1,000 per share in August.

As the stock of the South Sea Company skyrocketed, small-scale joint stock companies (known as bubbles) sprouted everywhere. Nobles and lowly jobbers alike rushed to announce schemes and sell stock, and both men and women eagerly bought from them. Some of the bubbles had relatively straightforward aims: muslin making, lace importation, lead mining, soap making, and property insurance. Others seem chimerical notions: "trading in hair;" "for a wheel for perpetual motion"; "for insuring and increasing children's fortunes"; "for carrying on an undertaking of great advantage, but nobody to know what it is"; and several alchemical schemes, including the transmutation of quicksilver into an unnamed malleable fine metal and the extraction of silver from lead. Parliament suppressed all of these schemes when it passed, in June 1720, an act that allowed joint-stock companies to form only by royal charter—channeling all of this speculative mania into companies that had such a charter, including the South Sea Company. Stock prices continued to rise, fueling increased buying and higher prices.

After reaching its high point of £1,000 per share, though, South Sea stock began to slide in price throughout August. As with the Compagnie des Indes, public confidence in the South Sea Company evaporated, and by September the stock's value sank to £135 per share. Thousands of fortunes were lost in the crash, and the public demanded an investigation. Those responsible for the Company's rise were singled out for public censure and worse: The chancellor of the exchequer, John Aislabie, was expelled from the House of Commons and imprisoned in the Tower of London, and Company directors had varying portions of their estates confiscated.

The stock-buying public, though, learned little from all the excitement. The English gambling spirit remained irrepressible as investors sought the next "sure thing." One writer described Jonathan's, a coffeehouse near the royal exchange, as "being full of gamesters, with the same sharp, intent looks"—although these gamesters had turned in their cards and dice for stock in the Bank, East India, South Sea, and lottery tickets. Stock markets would eventually become legitimate foundations of mercantile capitalism, but as late as the nineteenth century they would be considered by the mainstream as little more than institutionalized bubbles.

Some likened stock speculation to a lottery. Indeed, by the time the British were chasing bubbles, lotteries were a national mainstay. The earliest known lottery conducted under the auspices of the English crown took place in 1569. This draw lottery, modeled closely on the Flemish/Venetian model, was organized directly on the order of Queen Elizabeth, and its promoters offered to the public four-hundred-thousand "lotts" (tickets), priced at ten shillings sterling each, which gave a chance at prizes of "ready money" and "certain sorts of merchandise." The queen had authorized this lottery for the express purpose of converting its excess revenues to "the reparations of the havens and strength of the realm, and towards other public good works." In this regard, it, like most lotteries, blended opportunities for personal enrichment (a chance at "ready money" and valuable merchandise) with civic responsibility (maintaining the kingdom's harbors and defenses).

Still, the royal lottery was not an easy sell, and it took two years to successfully complete it. Proclamations and advertisements urging public subscription to the lottery began appearing in 1567. Potential ticket buyers were urged to peruse the prizes at the sign of the Queen's Majesty's Arms, in the house of Mr. Dericke, the queen's personal jeweler. The lottery's organizers promised that it would contain "no blanks" and that each ticket buyer would win something.

According to the original plan, the organizers would sell 400,000 tickets at ten shillings each, for a total of £200,000. The grand prize was to be worth a total of £5,000 sterling total: £2,000 in cash, £600 pounds in plate, and the remainder in "good tapestry, etc." After this lucky winner, smaller prizes would be paid to the next 29,999 holders of drawn lots. The remaining 370,000 speculators would get a half a crown for their troubles. Organizers hoped to have £100,000, after expenses, dedicated to the reparations of the harbors and other good works.

In the Venetian style, purchasers wrote "posies and devises," or epigrammatic mottoes, on their tickets. Many of these "posies" implored God or Fortune to grant a lucky draw: "My pose is small/But a good lot may fall"; "We put in one lot, poor maidens we be ten/We pray God send us a good lot, and that all we may say Amen"; and this humorous couplet: "I was begotten in Calice and born in Kent/God send me a good lot to pay my rent."

Despite a massive promotional blitz, the lottery was incredibly unsuccessful: Only one twelfth of the projected £200,000 worth of tickets were actually sold, so the value of prizes was diminished accordingly. The lottery organizers decided to duplicate every entry twelve times and, similar to the Venetian style, simultaneously draw names from one wheel and winning tickets and blanks from another. The drawing, held at the west door of St. Paul's Cathedral in London, took nearly four months to complete, even though it ran "day and night," lasting from January 11 to May 6.

Nearly twenty years passed before Elizabeth's administration launched another lottery. This one was considerably less ambitious. Like its predecessor, it was to be drawn at the west gate of St. Paul's, but took "only" three days to complete. Successfully conducted in June 1586 by one John Calthorp, the chief prize in this draw was a suit of "marvelous rich and beautiful armor." There were no other major public lotteries for years, though it is likely that, as in Venice, merchants held small lotteries to dispose of otherwise slow-moving merchandise.

Kings James I and Charles I, who reigned from 1603 to 1649, moved England even farther into the lottery business, granting a variety of charters for drawings. The earliest lotteries of this period were often run by foreigners, particularly Italians. In 1606, for example, James I granted the Italian merchant Julian Miccottie a license to auction some of his wares by means of a lottery; within four months, it had become so successful that municipal authorities complained that its "great clamor and tumult" was becoming a public nuisance.

Early efforts at colonization were like a lottery: Those who sailed knew that the journey would be risky, and investors shared the risk from home. If their ship arrived laden with spices or gold, they might make fortunes, but the ship also might be lost at sea. Sir Walter Raleigh's first attempt to plant a bit of Britain in the New World in the 1580s ended in mysterious failure; a ship coming to supply the settlers at Roanoke found nothing more than a now legendary "Lost Colony."

By the time of the next major English venture, many investors considered the hazards of a colonial enterprise too risky. After James I chartered the Virginia Company of London to establish a New World colony in 1606, the venture suffered from insufficient funding, poor decision-making, and plain bad luck. The first colonists, who arrived in America in 1607, were 105 soldiers of fortune who did little more than scheme, search for gold, and squabble. They found no gold and made few attempts to grow food or build a permanent settlement. The entire enterprise almost ended in abject failure. In 1610, the colonists had just abandoned their settlement at Jamestown and were sailing to sea when they happened across the incoming new governor's ships; only his determination (and a stock of much-needed supplies) persuaded the settlers into giving frontier life another try. Still, the colony remained a money pit. The original investors had little prospect of seeing any return, and with rumors of the desperate goings-on in America spreading through London, both new recruits and new investors were scarce.

By 1612 the directors of the Virginia Company were hoping for some sort of royal bailout. King James did not grant direct assistance but gave the company the next best thing: a charter to run a public lottery. Even before the new charter granting them the lottery had been issued, those connected to the Company began to publicize this new phase of their enterprise. The lottery was duly organized, and directors offered agents one spoon, worth 20 shillings, per £3 of tickets sold.

The spoons provided little incentive to sellers and the lottery was delayed for lack of participation. Originally scheduled for May, the drawing finally began on June 29, using the cumbersome double-draw system. Sixty thousand blanks were drawn before a single prize was announced, and by July 20 the excitement was over. A London tailor named Thomas Sharplisse took away the top prize, 4,000 crowns in "fayre plate," which was ceremoniously delivered to his home. Though honestly conducted, the lottery was a failure, having sold sixty thousand fewer tickets than originally hoped. But the company still paid off all prizes at full value. Two churches, St. Mary's Colechurch and St. Mary's Woolchurch, were among the winners—evidently religious disapproval was not responsible for the lottery's poor sales.

Two years later, the Virginia Company tried again, this time offering cheaper tickets. Broadsides announced a new drawing in February 1614, though sales were so slow that the drawing was delayed until May. Even before this minilottery was completed, plans for another "Great Standing Lottery" were under way. The Company used its influence to induce livery companies (guilds), municipal authorities, and other corporate investors to buy lottery tickets. This new lottery was drawn in November 1615, but prize payments were late—four years afterward, some winners were still waiting for their rewards. Despite this, the Company continued to promote lotteries, beginning a "running" or "ring" lottery that, unlike the standing lotteries conducted in London, would be held in various towns. Owing to the increasingly poor reputation of the Virginia Company as an outfit that paid prizes only grudgingly, public agitation against the lotteries began to mount. Finally, on March 8, 1621, the king issued a proclamation that ordered the Company to cease and desist from continuing in the lottery business. Without the lottery to support it, the Virginia colony limped along, with no gold to be found, food scarce, and disease rampant. Nothing, it seemed, could produce a profit, and in 1626 the Virginia Company lost its charter and the colony fell under the direct management of the royal authorities.

In 1619, Gabriel Barber, an agent for the Virginia Company lottery, organized a lottery for the aid of Reading tradesmen. Raising the sum of £40 sterling, he transferred the money to the mayor and burgesses of Reading, who were to lend portions of it to qualified Reading freemen who provided good security and did not keep an inn or tavern and continued to live in Reading. In this way, perhaps, the lottery proceeds could provide investment capital for local tradesmen—using a lottery, in other words, to reinvest in the local community.

A series of lotteries helped finance the construction of London's waterworks. The First Royal Fishing Lottery grew out of a royal initiative to build a British fishing fleet that would compete with the state-sponsored Dutch fishermen, who were then ascendant in the waters around the British Isles. Poorly managed and inadequately financed, the undersized British fishing fleet also suffered attacks by Dutch and Spanish raiders, who sank vessels and captured and imprisoned British fishermen, holding them until a sizable ransom was paid. The Society of the Fishery of Great Britain and Ireland begged the king's permission to organize a relief lottery, similar to that of the Virginia Company, and although the king gave his permission, there is no record of a fishing lottery during his reign, nor is it known if winners were paid in seafood.

Although lotteries were scarce during the puritanical years of Oliver Cromwell's Protectorate, they returned with renewed vigor following the restoration of the British monarchy in 1660, serving a variety of purposes.

During the civil war and Cromwell's rise to power, officers who remained loyal to the monarchy had suffered severe financial setbacks. Though Parliament voted these loyalists a measure of financial relief, many felt it was not enough. Instead of requesting another handout, they asked the king's permission to run lotteries for their benefit, and Charles II granted several of these requests. The champions of British fishermen also secured title to a second Royal Fishing Lottery, as did proponents of improvements to London's water supply.

One canny bookseller proposed a series of lotteries to support his business. In 1665, noted translator and cartographer John Ogilby secured the permission of the duke of York to run a lottery to defray the costs of his bookselling business with books for prizes. In its first incarnation, Ogilby's book lottery met with calamity; first, it was delayed by a plague afflicting London; then, the Great Fire of 1666 incinerated most of Ogilby's stock of books. Ogilby's second book lottery, held in 1668, got off to a slow start but was ultimately successful. Five years later, Ogilby ran another lottery to assist him financially as he wrote a book of his own, the *Description of England*.

With the costs of maintaining its growing military and commercial empire, the English government began to reconsider granting lottery patents to private individuals. In 1694, Parliament authorized a state lottery to raise revenue to pay for a war against the French. Rather than offering prizes of plate, or books, or ready money, this lottery instead gave its winners an annuity: The big winner walked away with a £1,000 annual remittance. Other lucky adventurers could hope for lesser amounts—two thousand tickets promised their holders a £10 yearly award.

Organized by the groom porter, the king's statutory gambler in residence, this lottery was remarkably popular. Though some in Parliament had questioned the probity of permitting a known professional gambler such a prominent role in governmental finance, his knowledge of lotteries was beyond dispute (many private lotteries had been held under his auspices). He acquitted himself so well that, a year later, Parliament authorized a second lottery. Over the next seventy years, Parliament chartered over forty government-sponsored lotteries on the annuity model for a variety of purposes, such as building Westminster Bridge. These drawings provided the growing imperial government with the funds it needed to exercise its power. The government began to jealously guard its prerogative to conduct lotteries. In 1699 and again in 1739, nongovernment lotteries and other games of chance were suppressed and the purchase of foreign lottery tickets was prohibited—not, cynics said, for any moral purpose, but merely to destroy competitors.

In the reign of George III, as the escalating expenses of empire cost Britain its American colonies, royal lotteries expanded dramatically. From 1769 to 1826, the government held 126 lotteries. Though these lotteries had a diversity of prize schemes and ticket sales, they generally eschewed the earlier annuity drawings for lump-sum payments to winners. These bonanzas maintained the Venetian system, with simultaneous drawings of prize tickets from one box and subscribers from another. With two centuries of lotteries behind them, the British began to conduct more organized drawings: from 1712, drawings generally began at nine in the morning and ended by two in the afternoon, though they usually stretched over several days.

As early as the first decades of the eighteenth century, a lottery mania had fastened itself upon London. Newspapers "teemed with proposals issued by every ravenous adventurer who could collect a few valuable articles," and shopkeepers converted virtually their entire stock of goods into lottery prizes. Some lotteries almost defy description. In 1715, the owners of Sion Gardens advertised a deer lottery: three afternoons each week, they admitted the public at the cost of a shilling a head to watch the killing of the animals. Four to ten shillings bought entry into a lottery for various cuts of fresh venison; a ten-shilling man could win a filet, but the best a seven-shilling piker could hope for was a loin. This fusion of game management, gambling, and butchery demonstrates the virulent hold that the lottery had on eighteenth-century Britain.

Parliament legislated against these private lotteries, but they continued nevertheless, inspired no doubt by the excitement surrounding the state lottery. Even that draw, which contributed between £250,000 and £300,000 annually to government coffers, was not without its abuses. Corruption, the splitting of tickets, and the sale of "lottery insurance" were rampant. The "blue-coat boys," blind or simply blindfolded charity wards who drew tickets from the lottery wheels, were sometimes bribed or otherwise coerced into dishonestly influencing the outcome of the draw. In order to promote the lottery as a truly voluntary tax borne only by those with the means to afford it, Parliament set ticket prices quite high; usually the cheapest was at least £10. But a class of brokers stepped in to extend the lottery to the less well off by selling shares in individual tickets. These brokers, critics charged, exploited the poor, as did an even more insidious class of lottery hustlers: lottery insurance brokers.

In the eighteenth century, there was still a lingering moral disquiet about insurance—paying a premium against the possibility of future disaster. Some said that fire insurance was really betting against the insurer that one's house would be destroyed by a conflagration. Since the insurance buyer suffered an obvious injury and thus didn't really profit from this "gamble," though, insurance gradually became an accepted part of everyday life.

Lottery insurance brokers used tortured logic to explain that, by indemnifying their clients against loss, they were in fact providing a valuable service and not merely promoting gambling among the poorer classes. Insurance brokers allowed "clients" to ensure, for one shilling, that a particular number would not be drawn from the state lottery wheel on a particular day: These "policies" paid £10 if the number was actually drawn on that day. Policy brokers hijacked the state lottery and, using its official ticket drawings, ran cut-rate lotteries of their own. Policy, also known as the "sale of chances," therefore embodied two apparent evils: It spread lottery play to the poor, and it siphoned gambling money from the state lottery.

Some derided the whole idea of a lottery, which discouraged hard work and honest merchandising; some citizens felt justified in investing all of their money in lottery tickets and hoping for the best (rather than working for more wealth), and merchants used lies and "chimerical alarms" to dispose of their wares through lotteries rather than honest commerce.

Because of these perceived evils, and despite the fact that the state lottery continued to profitably serve the British government, public outcry against the lottery began to mount in the 1820s. Some argued that its costs—which included a troupe of paid informers (twenty-nine by 1815) and police officers who prosecuted those who profited from abusing the official lottery—when added to its social toxicity, outweighed the utility of its revenue. Britain, like other nations of the era, was stabilizing its taxation and revenue mechanisms, and the importance of the lottery in collecting money for state coffers began to diminish. In 1823, Parliament voted to end the system.

On Wednesday, October 18, 1826, the British government held its final state lottery, ending 257 years of tradition. Promoters worked at fever pitch to dispose of tickets. One advertising couplet read:

> *Run, neighbors, run, the Lottery's expiring,*
> *When Fortune's merry wheel, it will never turn more;*
> *She now supplies all numbers you're desiring,*
> *All prizes, no blanks, and twenty thousands four.*

The promotional festivities included a grand pageant with liveried banner-bearers, a full band, and various carriages representing the lottery, as well as an endless stream of broadsides and newspaper notices. Still, sales were sluggish, and the following day a newspaper printed an "epitaph" for the state lottery, which "corrupted the morals and encouraged a spirit of speculation and gambling among the lower classes of the peoples, thousands of whom fell victims" to temptations. The epitaph concluded by relating to the ages that the lottery ended "unregretted by any virtuous mind."

Though officially suppressed in England, legal drawings continued in Scotland for a time, sometimes using the same wheels formerly employed in the late English state lottery. Though Scottish authorities later officially prohibited lotteries, small-scale "draws" continued to run for the benefit of churches, clubs, and other organizations, flourishing as open secrets tolerated by the law well into the twentieth century.

Lotteries in Ireland had a more flamboyant history. In the seventeenth century, lotteries financed the restoration of the cathedral of Christ Church in Dublin, but they also had more ominous purposes. In 1653 a parliamentary decree noted that an Irish rebellion had been crushed and the lands of the insurgents were to be disposed of by means of a lottery. In the eighteenth century, lottomania seized Ireland as it had England, and lotteries, including many organized for the charity of hospitals, flourished. Lottery offices in Dublin sold tickets for both Irish and foreign lotteries, and lottery policy brokers proliferated. Despite a prohibition on state lotteries enacted in 1801, charity lotteries continued unabated throughout the nineteenth century.

Even in their heyday, lotteries hardly quenched the English proclivity for wagering. Many Englishmen and -women, worn out by the cares of daily life, chose to recuperate in health spas. A successful health resort in the eighteenth century absolutely needed one thing: a medicinal hot spring. The Ancient Romans had recognized the therapeutic value of such springs, and starting in the sixteenth century, Europeans rediscovered them.

Today hot water seems a poor reason to plan a vacation, but in the long cold years before the invention of the Jacuzzi, hot springs offered the fashionably unwell a place to gain some respite from their ailments. The springs attracted wealthy guests with plenty of money, too much spare time, and a pathological dread of boredom. Musicians, entertainers, and professional gamblers flocked to hot springs, eager to help those "seeking the cure" to ward off tedium.

There were several notable watering holes in England. One of these, Epsom, endured as a health resort long enough to give its name to "Epsom salts" (magnesium sulfate), from minerals found in its therapeutic waters. Another, Tunbridge Wells, began with the discovery of a hot spring in 1606, and it still flourishes as a resort (with golfing and horseback riding now the advertised attractions). In its early heyday in the seventeenth and eighteenth centuries, gaming rooms provided an integral part of the amusements and helped Tunbridge Wells to become a leading winter destination.

For much of the eighteenth century, Bath, located in southwest England near the Welsh border, was the most fashionable spa in England, drawing visitors from as far as the Continent. First venerated by the Celts, the town's medicinal springs became the center of a complex of baths and temples under the Roman occupation, as the hot baths were a welcome anodyne to the harsh climate. Even after the Romans abandoned Britain, the hot springs continued to flow and the town's libertine reputation was immortalized in the fourteenth century by Geoffrey Chaucer's Wife of Bath. After centuries of decline, the town began a revival in the sixteenth century, and in the next century its growth slowly continued.

With the Restoration, the royal court periodically began coming to Bath for recreation; with them they brought increased attention and prestige for the resort. By the start of Queen Anne's reign in 1702, Bath had become a regular summer destination for the royal train. Still, the resort was far from elegant. Townspeople commonly threw their refuse, including carrion from butcher shops, into the street, where they turned their pigs loose to feed and root. Rules of decorum barely contained the anarchy of the place: Those who wished danced until morning, men wearing boots and women their aprons (much to the disgrace of more genteel visitors), smoking was permitted indoors, and fervid gamblers played cards until they collapsed from exhaustion. A visitor described the town in 1702 as mean and contemptible, lacking both elegant buildings and open streets.

The chief Bath amusements were dancing and gambling. Originally held outdoors, the dances were moved inside under patronage of the duke of Beaufort, who also authorized gambling in the town hall. The supervision of both diversions fell to the office of the master of ceremonies, a figure without real authority or compensation who was, nevertheless, expected to somehow marshal the townspeople and shepherd the visitors.

Richard "Beau" Nash reigned as master of ceremonies during Bath's glory years. Nash, born to a distinguished but impecunious family, had failed to distinguish himself during a year at Oxford, as an ensign in the Guards, or as a law student. His heart lay in fashionable dressing, fast living, and persistent romancing. He claimed to support himself through his gambling winnings, but rumors persisted that he augmented this income by taking purses on the moonlit highways, until he finally revealed the truth—that he was in fact secretly receiving an allowance from a paramour. At times, Nash's need for money pressed him to accept embarrassing wagers: His friends, once, for unknown stakes, successfully goaded him into riding naked through a village astride a cow.

Despite his erratic income, Nash gained distinction in 1695 as "the master of revels," or social director, of a pageant celebrating William III's sole accession to the throne. Though a great success, it hardly relieved his financial embarrassment, and he cast about for a career that would combine his patrician instincts (his friends had nicknamed him "the Count") with his love for gambling, dancing, and extravagant living. Following the annual royal train to Bath in the summer of 1705 in search of gambling action, he soon found his calling. Over the seven-week season that attended Queen Anne's residence in town, Nash prospered at the tables, winning over £100 a week. Before the season was up Captain Webster, the reigning master of ceremonies, sensing Nash's abilities, had tapped him to serve as his chief of staff. In this capacity Nash supervised construction of a pump room, which would permit indoor appreciation of Bath's waters, kept a handle on the gaming tables, and chaperoned the nightly dances.

Webster cut quite a figure wearing a square-cut coat, a large neckerchief tied in a bow, and dark breeches stuffed into his boots, which, while dancing, he would stomp upon the floor as if crushing his enemies. A professional gambler inordinately fond of spirits, Webster had his share of enemies. One evening, a dispute over a hand of cards, fueled by liquor, escalated into hostilities. Both men wore swords, as was customary then at Bath, and honor demanded that they settle the contretemps with a duel. Meeting in the Grove, a space usually devoted to outdoor bowling (for stakes, of course), the two fatally confronted each other: Webster, run through with his adversary's sword, breathed his last on the Grove.

Chosen by the Corporation of Bath to succeed the fallen Webster, Nash immediately extended the improvements begun by his predecessor. Perhaps mindful of Captain Webster's final quarrel, he made it his first act as master of ceremonies to ban the wearing of swords, as they not only encouraged violence but also snagged and tore the ladies' overabundant dresses. With no real power to enforce his edicts, he smartly drafted a decree stating that only those *not* entitled to wear swords elsewhere could wear them at Bath. The nobility (entitled to wear swords throughout the kingdom), not wishing to appear common, immediately gave up swords, while the middle classes, wishing to emulate the true aristocrats, abandoned any pretensions toward carrying them. Slyly manipulating social pressures would become a hallmark of Nash's rule at Bath.

Bath was well served by Nash's sensibilities and his egotism. Establishing Bath as the premier resort in England became his obsession, for only in doing this could he cement his own reputation. So he began immediate reforms. Captain Webster had replaced the resident band—actually a fiddler and clarinetist—with a five-piece local ensemble, a considerable improvement. Nash fired the locals and installed a troupe of seven London musicians. The new orchestra played outdoors at the Grove and baths during the day, and indoors at the town hall at night. To pay for the upgrade, he levied a one-guinea "music subscription" on all guests.

Nash also mandated improvements in accommodations (the lodging houses were notoriously mangy and ridiculously expensive), introduced a second season from March to June, improved the roads, and got a parliamentary decree that let him institute a night watch and clean up the filthy streets. In 1708, he encouraged Thomas Harrison's construction of the Assembly House, a space in which visitors might play cards, dance, and take refreshments. He financed the building by combining its subscription charge with that of the orchestra: For two guineas, each family entering Bath got three tickets to balls held at the Assembly House. Wealthy visitors, happy to have a place where they could enjoy continuous entertainment, willingly paid Nash's subscriptions, and Bath became England's finest resort within three years of Nash's accession.

An illustration of Bath's Pump Room, where visitors enjoyed the healthy waters
before getting to the serious business of gambling.

Life at Bath revolved around the waters, gambling, and dancing. Most visitors began their day at the Pump Room, where they could watch the bathers below while slowly drinking, according to custom, three glasses of warm mineral water. In the baths, people of both sexes frolicked naked next to the truly infirm and diseased, while rambunctious onlookers sometimes flung dogs, cats, and other people into the steaming waters. At Harrison's Assembly House, visitors enjoyed elegant strolls in a tree-shaded garden, endless rounds of dancing the minuet, and light refreshments. Harrison eventually charged such high fees for the use of his Assembly House that, in 1728, Nash countenanced the construction of a rival assembly room by Humphrey Thayer. Together, Thayer's and Harrison's houses were known as the Lower Rooms (a pair of Upper Rooms opened later), where Nash invited all those in Bath to join him for daily rounds of entertainment. Additional teas and parties were held in private lodgings, and refreshments offered in coffeehouses.

Bath drew an interesting mix of the legitimately ill, bored aristocrats, upwardly mobile professionals, young girls and widows looking for husbands, handsome fortune hunters seeking moneyed women, and all manner of dealers in amusements. In between all of the parties, dances, teas, and concert breakfasts, visitors to Bath found ample time for gambling. Those interested in striking a quick fortune favored hazard and basset, while those pursuing conversation and leisurely play enjoyed whist. Gambling was everywhere, from raffles held in shops, to bets on horse racing, bowling, and prizefighting.

For decades, Bath's popularity grew, as Nash held court like a divinely appointed sovereign. He even assumed the title of master of ceremonies at the rival spa resort Tunbridge Wells and ran it as an off-season adjunct to Bath. But a growing national frustration with gambling spelled doom for the resort. In 1739, Parliament moved to abolish gambling by passing a law that forbade the most popular games, all of which were played at Bath: faro, basset, ace of hearts (a roulette precursor), and hazard. Notably, these were all mercantile games (although hazard could be played either as a social or a house-banked game). Bath's gamblers scurried to substitute other games, such as passage and the roulette ancestor roly-poly, but in the next year Parliament passed an even more stringent law, banning passage, roly-poly, and "any other instrument, engine, or device in the nature of dice having one or more figures or numbers thereon" used for betting.

Further attempts to circumvent the law included the modification of roly-poly into E/O, in which players only guessed whether a ball would fall into a slot marked even or odd, but in 1745 Parliament added this game to the codex of forbidden pleasures and declared that anyone, whether a proprietor or player, connected to a gambling house would be subject to the law. After this, public mercantile gambling ceased. Social games like whist continued to be played in the Lower Rooms, and in private rooms card and dice games, often crooked, continued, but Bath began to decline. Nash, it was discovered, had for years received a portion of the profits from gambling operators at both Bath and Tunbridge Wells, something he had deliberately concealed (in fact, he had disingenuously bemoaned his own losses at the tables). In his old age, he struggled to maintain his once-opulent lifestyle, but with the collapse of gambling he was left in dignified poverty. Behind his back, gossipers mocked him as an aging fool, and two members of White's Club in London went so far as to lay bets on who would die first, Nash or an elderly actor named Cibber (Nash had a final triumph as both bettors committed suicide before either Nash or Cibber shuffled off his mortal coil). Nash finally died on February 12, 1761, at the age of eighty-six, having presided over the glory and decline of his beloved Bath.

Gambling still continued, both in private and on horse races, in the latter part of the eighteenth century. But Bath never regained its earlier luster as a class of newly rich arrivistes disturbed the generations of habit established by the old nobility. King George IV discovered the new fashion of sea bathing and made Brighton the new popular resort. The era of pan-European tranquility augured by the Congress of Vienna in 1815 allowed the British to travel freely throughout the Continent. With the unfolding of the nineteenth century, moneyed British vacationers sought out the Alps, the Rhine, and the Riviera, all of which boasted thriving gambling and health resorts.

7

Star-Spangled Gamblers

◆ ◆ ◆

THE BIRTH OF AMERICAN GAMBLING

Gambling in America predated the republic of the United States by several thousand years, and Americans fused several traditions—European, Native American, and African—into a larger gambling culture that, with advances in transportation and communications, would spread throughout the world.

Most of the hundreds of tribes, bands, and societies of North America had well-developed gambling traditions before contact with Europeans. Native American cultures incorporated new games discovered through foreign contact into their existing ways of life. In the Southwest, gambling was a serious, even sacred, pursuit. The Navajo played certain games in the summer and others in the winter, and considered playing a summer game in January dangerously inappropriate. The *kesitce* or moccasin game was a winter game played only at night—according to local belief, any who played during the day would be instantly struck blind. To play, two sides took turns hiding a small pebble or ball in one of eight moccasins half-buried in the sand. After flipping a half-darkened chip to determine which side would hide the ball first, the winners lowered a screen over the moccasins and secreted the ball inside one. The guesser then struck a moccasin with a stick; if it contained the ball, his team took possession. If not, he was penalized a certain number of points, depending on how far off he was, and his team lost a corresponding number of counters. Special songs were sung during each round of the game, and to repeat a song in a later round was forbidden. Whichever team won all of the counters took the game and the stakes.

This game commemorated, elders said, a time when the animals of the day wished for perpetual light, while the animals of the night wanted perpetual darkness. They met at twilight to parley and decided that they should play the *kesitce* game to determine whether the sun would never rise or never set. The animals started playing, and though each side's fortunes oscillated during the long night, neither had an advantage at dawn, so the game was considered a push: Day and night continued as before. Storytellers also explained the physical characteristics of certain animals well known to the Navajo and touched on a theme common to Native American games: that of an eternal competition between opposites light and dark, winter and summer, female and male, etc.

Gamblers and tricksters are staples of Native American myths, and the Navajo told stories of a gambling god, Noquilpi. According to the Navajo, the Pueblo people had built a temple to Noquilpi at Chaco Canyon (in northern New Mexico), where they constructed a huge center of multistory buildings. Though Noquilpi's story has many variations, the best-known relates that he won all of the people of the earth and all of their possessions while playing at Chaco Canyon. Noquilpi even stole the sun's turquoise earrings, which prompted the sun to ask another god to train a Navajo man to defeat Noquilpi and return the earrings. With the help of several animals, the Navajo warrior did so. He then shot the defeated gambler god into the heavens, where he met the Carrier of the Moon, who returned him to earth, where he eventually became the god of the Mexicans.

In some versions, the gambling temple was located at Pueblo Alto, a place that many Navajo called "home of the one that wins (you) by gambling." Later archaeological investigations of Pueblo Alto have indicated that it was likely a gambling center. Sitting at the juncture of five roads that stretched for hundreds of miles, it was the crux of a huge exchange network. Goods brought there were not redistributed but instead stored in a series of great houses that were otherwise unpopulated. In most pueblos, the large central plaza was used for dancing, and its floor has been compacted by the rhythms of stamping feet. But at Pueblo Alto, the main plaza had been resurfaced with clay several times, suggesting that, whatever people were doing there, they were not dancing. It is quite possible that they were gambling.

In what is now the eastern United States, the Mound Builders, a culture that built large temples and had fairly complex societies prior to European contact, left behind *chungke* stones, flat polished disks with hollow centers that were either rolled or used as hoops through which stones were thrown. Travelers through the southeastern woodlands in the seventeenth century reported that, as a hoop and pole game, *chungke* was widespread. Even in the nineteenth century, the Creeks and Cherokees of Carolina lived in villages with large *chungke* yards, recessed spaces as large as three football fields surrounded by terraces. At the center stood a thirty-foot pole and target, at which players likely aimed spears or rocks. This was clearly a major spectator event.

Native Americans did not play games or bet on them merely for amusement. Gambling contests served as effective mechanisms to redistribute trade goods and to encourage interaction among neighbors. Men and women of all classes gambled with seeming recklessness, according to European observers, who often missed the underlying religiosity of Native American gambling. During a marathon week-long dice game, for example, the Iroquois prayed nightly for good luck, and losers often looked for supernatural explanations—offense to a good spirit or sorcery of a bad one—to explain their bad luck.

Gambling even had a role in the Spanish conquest of the Aztecs. When Hernán Cortés arrived in 1519, Montezuma believed him to be the returning god Quetzalcoatl. Montezuma brought Cortés to a ball game, and Cortés found the game interesting enough that he later sent a team to his emperor in Spain. Cortés soon imprisoned Montezuma and, to keep him occupied during his five-month captivity, played *totloque*, a game using small gold dice. The Spaniards found a passing similarity to their game of tables, or backgammon, which had been memorialized by their king Alphonso X in his thirteenth-century *Book of Games*. On one occasion, Montezuma noted that the Spaniard keeping score for Cortés was cheating; this would be the smallest injustice committed by the invaders against the Aztecs. Even the Spanish soldiers in attendance conceded that Montezuma was a generous winner who gave away everything he won. Unfortunately, Cortés was not so magnanimous, and when Montezuma surrendered his treasures to the Spanish, Cortés ordered the gold melted down. The soldiers, using playing cards improvised from parchment, immediately began gambling among themselves for their shares. Within six months, Montezuma was dead, and after finally taking his capital city of Tenochtitlán, Cortés announced his new power by promulgating a law that outlawed all gambling. Having won an empire, he was determined not to lose it back.

The Montezuma story reveals much about the fate of gambling among Native Americans. Though sacred gambling ceremonies did not stop the onslaught of the invaders, games allowed Native Americans to preserve many of their ritual observances. Tribes throughout North America continued playing traditional games into the late nineteenth century and, borrowing European imports like playing cards, incorporated them into traditional gambling practices.

With the forced pacification of most tribes in the late nineteenth century, gambling often became a vehicle for cultural regeneration and a surrogate for open aggression. Among the Pawnee, the Ghost Dance revival movement of the 1890s also saw a renewed passion for traditional games; both the hoop and pole game and a traditional hand-guessing game were incorporated into ceremonial dances. Even after defeat and subjugation, tribes continued to battle through the medium of gambling; before beginning a match, players would pantomime many old combat rituals and even declared, "We've come on the warpath for the hand game." Even as settlers took over Native American lands, they could not destroy tribal cultures or erase thousands of years of gambling tradition.

Like the Spaniards who preceded them, the first British settlers in the New World were looking for redemption, either financial or spiritual, and sometimes both. The Virginia Company, which founded a colony at Jamestown, made a series of losing gambles on its prospects in the New World. Governors railed against colonists' "bowling in the streets" while serious work remained to be done, many settlers preferred playing and gambling to work, and it was only the discovery (after the Company had lost its charter) that tobacco could be profitably marketed in Britain that the colony became a success— poetic justice for the Company's director, who had delayed awarding prizes to lottery winners.

The subsequent tobacco boom hardly made Virginia less of a gamble; prices bounced from low to high and back again with astonishing volatility, and speculators in land and tobacco sought to wring a quick profit from their holdings. In such an atmosphere, gambling was omnipresent, but it was especially cherished among the new elite of tidewater Virginia: the plantation-owning gentry who styled themselves as cavaliers and relished lives filled with hearty food, elegant clothes, bold flirtation, and relentless high-stakes gambling.

In fact, gambling, whether at cards, dice, backgammon, or billiards, became a hallmark of elite Virginian culture. As early as 1686, a visiting Frenchman reported that after dinner his Virginian hosts began gambling. By midnight, when the traveler's impatience was finally noticed by one of the absorbed card-players, he was advised to retire to his bed, as the game was just getting good. The next morning, the Frenchman awoke to find the gentlemen still intent at their game. Sometimes the urge to gamble was uncontrollable. After a particularly rough night playing dice in a coffeehouse (he lost £12) in November 1711, William Byrd II, one of the wealthiest planters in the colony, solemnly vowed in his diary never to lose more than 50 shillings and to "spend less time in gaming." Within two weeks, he reported a loss of £4 at piquet, making no comment about his earlier pledge.

But as assiduously as wealthy Virginians played cards, they reserved an even greater passion for horse racing. As in any agricultural society, horses were highly valued, and the competitive, individualistic, and materialist tidewater aristocrats considered winning a race a matter of personal honor: A man was only as good as his horse. While all those who owned horses raced along the open roads, most money changed hands on quarter-horse races—quarter-mile sprints dominated by the large plantation owners who, by insisting on high bets, kept their "inferiors" from joining the action. These races, which customarily took place on Saturday, were eventually supplanted by longer races—four miles was the usual length. No matter what the race's length, onlookers crowded around the track or course, cheered their favorite, and placed side bets among themselves, while the two competing horse owners bet between each other. By 1700 there were at least twelve well-known tracks in northern Virginia. When contestants believed they had been fouled or a loser refused to pay, the matter went before the courts, who investigated, and a jury decided the winner.

The cavaliers of Virginia weren't the only colonists to show a love for racing. Within a year of capturing the province of New Amsterdam from the Netherlands in 1664, the English governor of the newly renamed New York, Richard Nicholls, supervised the establishment of a course named Newmarket in present-day Garden City, Long Island—the first measured race course in the colonies. Another innovation took place in Charleston, South Carolina, where in 1735 wealthy horse-lovers formed a jockey club to "improve the breed" of New World horses by establishing regulations, scheduling races, and setting prizes. It was established seven years before the first surviving written notice of the British Jockey Club, a testament to the dedication of Americans to the sport.

Racing was popular throughout the colonies, but the Upper South particularly inspired horsemen. Across the Chesapeake, Marylanders felt no less passion for their horses than Virginians, and in time a rivalry flourished. Seeking the prestige bought by a fleet-footed equine, wealthy horse-lovers soon began to import prize racers, studs, and mares from England. On December 5, 1752, a race between several such imported horses was celebrated as the most important race of its time, as it matched not only horses but the two competing colonies against each other.

William Byrd III, son of the diarist who couldn't stop losing at cards, decided, upon assuming his father's estate in 1744, that he wanted to prove his own greatness by owning the fastest horse in the colonies. If he hadn't inherited a thirst for gambling from his father, he certainly picked it up when sent to study law in London, where he reportedly lost thousands of pounds in various West End clubs. In 1752, he bought Tyral, a ten-year-old chestnut horse that, though he had not had much success and was undoubtedly beyond his best racing days, he promoted as the fastest thing on four legs. Byrd offered to put up five hundred Spanish pistoles, the cost of a modest mansion, against any who would dare race against Tyral. Byrd got three takers: two Virginians, who between them brought three horses, and an Annapolis resident, militia colonel Benjamin Tasker, who entered Selima, an offspring of the renowned Godolphin Arabian.

After all of the horses were walked to the four-mile Anderson's Race Ground at Gloucester, Virginia, partisans of all five gathered and bet amongst each other. Most Virginians went for Tyral, while all of Maryland was for Selima. With the blast of a trumpet, the race started, and at the finish Selima had beaten Byrd's Tyral. Tasker returned to Maryland a hero, and Selima became an icon in the state's racing history. Indignant Virginians, upset that an imported "ringer" had beaten their own stock (which was, of course, also imported), subsequently banned all Maryland-born horses from running in Virginia. Maryland breeders, though, took pleasure in bringing their pregnant mares to foal on the Virginia side of the Potomac, thus making the offspring eligible to race in the Old Dominion. For his part, Byrd continued to buy and race Thoroughbreds (without much success) before a worldwide tobacco glut, compounded by his gambling and ostentation, drove him into massive debt and his eventual suicide in 1777.

The Puritan settlers of Massachusetts Bay, despite their sanctimonious reputations, often played cards. Puritan dogma held that gambling was bad not because of anything inherently sinful or immoral (the Bible, after all, was shot through with lot casting) but because it was an idle waste of time: Godly men and women should, instead of chatting over cards, be preparing themselves to enter heaven's kingdom. In 1646 Massachusetts passed a law that banned gambling in public houses—the first such law in the colonies—but enforcement was lax, with few church members actually fined for gambling. Still, for decades, ministers sternly reminded their flocks that to waste time at gambling was, in clergyman Increase Mather's words, "heinously sinful."

Throughout New England, colonists' ardor for fun was hardly chilled by strict Calvinist doctrine. The first Boston "ordinary" (tavern), opened in 1630, and others soon appeared throughout the region; the Connecticut government even ordered three towns to open ordinaries for the sake of travelers who were in need of entertainment. In Rhode Island, stringent regulations made ordinaries subject to strict licensure and forbade both drunkenness and card and dice play, but as the seventeenth century progressed, the number of ordinaries increased throughout New England, and government control over them waned. Ultimately, taverns became havens for all sorts of illegal gambling games, from cards to shuffleboard. They also offered a wide variety of entertainment and leisure activities: Guests ate, drank, smoked, and gambled while watching animal attractions such as trained walruses and performing pigs.

Horse racing became common in eighteenth-century New England, but it was never as popular, nor the races as regular, as in the South. Nevertheless, betting was just as common, albeit on a much smaller scale. Blood sports like bearbaiting, dogfighting, and cockfighting, long popular in England, never become widespread in New England, where colonists generally shunned physically violent sports. Officially, Puritan leaders discouraged competitive sports because they inevitably led to gambling. All five New England colonies passed early laws against gambling, though the penalties for breaking the law were usually slight.

Opposition to the perceived debauchery of the Restoration had hardened many Puritan souls against gambling in the late seventeenth century, and ministers preached sermons inveighing mightily against the sins of playing cards; but gambling refused to go away. Many towns gave out land based on lotteries, and proponents of cardplaying argued that it was an inexpensive form of recreation that encouraged the development of math skills and did not necessarily need to be bet upon. As a result, whist positively thrived, as college students, professionals, merchants, and even ministers began playing it. All fours, cribbage, and quadrille, a four-player version of the old favorite ombre, were also popular. Piquet, which combined the melding features of modern rummy with the trick taking of whist, was often condemned as a purely gambling game, though it was actually a social game played among peers. Mercantile games like faro and hazard, so popular on the other side of the Atlantic, never took root.

Pennsylvania may owe its very existence to gambling. Quaker William Penn founded the colony as a democratic, religiously tolerant haven after receiving a charter from King Charles II in 1681. Exactly why the king would grant an unpopular, socially radical religious sect a lucrative charter to prime lands in America still remains open to debate. The answer may lie in the relationship between Charles and Sir William Penn, the young Quaker's father. Although he had first sided with Parliament in the Civil War, Sir William became a favorite of Charles after the Restoration, commanding the English navy during a war with the Dutch. On his deathbed, Sir William secured a royal promise to care for his sons. It was also rumored that the inveterate gambler Charles

never paid the elder Penn for a gambling debt of £16,000 and that his granting of Pennsylvania to William Penn satisfied this debt. If true, the birthplace of American liberty was the largest marker (gambling debt) payment
ever.

In his "Great Law" of 1682, William Penn, perhaps unmindful of his father's success at cards, prohibited gambling and prescribed a fine or imprisonment for those who flouted the law. Quakers remained steadfast in their
opposition to all gambling, but, as elsewhere, prohibition was never effective,
and cardplaying, horse racing, and dicing continued. Cardplaying was so
prevalent that, by 1765, playing cards were used as admission tickets for lectures at the College of Philadelphia (today, the University of Pennsylvania).
After paying tuition, a student received a playing card on which was written
his name and the lectures he was entitled to attend.

Throughout all of the colonies, gambling was a common indoor recreation. As was the case among Native Americans, male and female British
colonists of every social standing played cards, tossed dice, and otherwise wagered. But because the taverns and clubs that permitted gambling were largely
male preserves, most heavy betting went on among men. Backgammon, often
played for high stakes, was a common game. Billiards proved a popular tavern
game and, for wealthy Americans, a showy home amusement—a man needed
great wealth to afford to dedicate an entire room to the game. Consequently,
home billiards tables were common among merchants and southern plantation owners who wanted to enjoy the pleasant company a table provided and
show off their wealth to friends, business relations, and rivals.

Some cardplaying colonists simply imitated the prevailing British fashions. Thus whist enjoyed a great popularity in eighteenth-century colonial
British North America. Many non-English games also flourished. Euchre,
which may have entered North America through French Louisiana, became a
perennial favorite. This four-player trick-based game was the first to feature
the American innovation of the joker (two wild cards included with each
deck), and it became popular throughout the United States, particularly the
North and Midwest, and Canada. Another French game, piquet, was just as
popular among less refined gamblers in all the colonies as it was in New England. Mercantile games seem to be nearly unknown in taverns, and there
were, as yet, no specialized "gambling houses," though play may have commenced at private clubs in imitation of those in the West End.

In general, thanks to wide-open play in taverns, public gambling was
available to all men regardless of background. Taverns catering to apprentices,
indentured servants, and slaves gave these men a chance for recreation, and

black Americans gambled just as did whites, though in the South they usually gambled separately. Outside of moralizing laws seeking to banish games from the colonies as idle frivolities, there was little opposition to gambling as such, although some colonies passed laws forbidding Sunday play or cheating, fighting, and other offenses related to the gaming table. Outside New England, cockfighting was just as widespread as tavern gaming, particularly in the South, and remained popular with less wealthy Americans through the eighteenth century.

With the exception of the Quakers of Pennsylvania, no colonial authorities expressed any reservations whatsoever to lotteries, at least initially. Lotteries even received scriptural justification: The Reverend William Ames, in a textbook used at Harvard and Yale, wrote that lotteries were permissible if put to a "pious use" but cautioned that ticket buyers should come in a spirit of giving rather than receiving. The acceptance of lotteries in colonial America is easy to understand when set against the positive mania for lotteries and raffles that was then endemic in the mother country. When the Crown authorized lotteries to benefit everything from bridges to booksellers, colonists turned naturally to drawings for a range of purposes.

In the colonies, where cash was scarce, lotteries also provided an excellent mechanism for selling high-cost goods and lands. Thomas Jefferson wrote that an article of property which could not be divided but had a large purchase price could often not be sold except by lottery, which was "a salutary instrument for disposing of it, where many run small risks for the chance of obtaining a high prize." One day mortgages and credit would allow Americans to buy houses and other prohibitively expensive items, but in the eighteenth century lotteries seemed as good a way as any to give the seller his asking price. Private citizens disposed of real estate, buildings, artwork, jewelry, and guns by means of lotteries, though they were not always successful. Before his untimely end, William Byrd III had vainly attempted to check his financial reverses with a land lottery.

Initially colonial authorities, preoccupied with the tasks of defense and basic organization, permitted the popular lotteries and raffles without any oversight. The British government wholeheartedly endorsed lotteries of all kinds and even voided acts of colonial legislatures intended to stop or slow lotteries. But by the middle of the eighteenth century, colonial governments had succeeded, for the most part, in assuming control of lotteries. Instead of being used by private citizens to sell property or goods, they became government instruments for the financing of public works. The first such drawing took place in Massachusetts in 1744, when the colony sought to raise £7,500 to protect the seacoast and the northern borders against the French. In what would become a familiar refrain once again in the twentieth century, the government argued that as poll and real estate taxes were already too high, a lottery was the least burdensome (and most politically popular) way to obtain the additional funds.

From the 1740s until 1776, colonial legislatures authorized 157 lotteries, most of them before the royal government decreed an end to the practice in 1769. Legislatures approved lotteries to assist their own governments, towns, churches, schools, industries, and those particularly down on their luck. In Rhode Island, for example, the legislature granted charters in 1762 for lotteries to build a poorhouse, expand a church, ransom a sailor who had fallen into the hands of the French, pave streets, and compensate a jailor whose prisoners had enlisted in the colonial army without paying for their board. Many growing colleges benefited from lotteries, including the schools that became Yale (1749), Princeton (1753, 1762), and Columbia (1746, 1748, 1753, 1754).

The prevalence of lotteries throughout the colonies underscores the ubiquity of gambling on the eve of the Revolution. Americans bought lottery tickets to benefit worthy causes and to get, for a small price, a chance at a great prize. They crowded into taverns, where drawings were tremendous public events. Though detractors lamented the numbers of the poor who bought tickets in desperate hope of gain, most American saw lotteries as sensible ways to contribute to the greater good—and get something for nothing, or next to nothing. For some, the royal restrictions placed on lotteries were yet another sign that the colonies had outgrown the imperial yoke, and one more justification for the break with Britain.

In 1765, the Stamp Act had galvanized colonial opposition to British rule and provided a flashpoint for growing proindependence sentiment. The act was not a tax on stamps but rather required the purchase of government stamps to make various documents official, from commercial contracts to newspapers. Among the items needing a stamp were playing cards, which required a 1-shilling stamp, and dice, which were to carry a 10-shilling stamp. Colonists, enraged by this intrusion on their liberty, did not care that playing cards had long carried a royal tax stamp in Britain. The Stamp Act was quickly repealed after massive public disturbances. The tax on gambling was hardly the most onerous levy in the Act (the stamp on newspapers and legal papers effectively agitated influential colonial publishers and lawyers), but it was yet another reminder of the power that the Crown held over its American subjects.

During the Revolutionary War, soldiers on both sides gambled. The orderly book of the British general Sir William Howe, who oversaw the siege of

Boston in 1775 and 1776, contained the following communication, dated July 8, 1775: "Some soldiers of the different corps have been observed gaming. The commissioned and noncommissioned officers are desired to be attentive that for the future nothing of this sort happens among the men. Such instances of idleness and depravity are always (and particularly at this time) to be prevented and suppressed." These orders, however, did not curb the gambling habits of the soldiers or officers. Instead, in cities occupied by the British, military men had a ball—literally—drinking, dancing, gambling, and flirting with sympathetic Loyalist women. Tavern owners allowed British soldiers to freely play cards, and horse races were a popular entertainment.

On the other side of the lines, General George Washington had similar concerns about gambling in his ranks. George Washington often said that gambling was "the child of avarice, the brother of iniquity, and the father of mischief." But he got himself into a fair share of mischief. From the years 1772 to 1775, he kept a detailed account of his record at the card table. Though he lost more games than he won, he knew when to fold 'em—he never lost more than six pounds in one day but took home more than £13 from an Annapolis card game in October 1772. Washington's gambling strategy carried over to the battlefield: Though he lost more battles than he won, British commander Lord Cornwallis surrendered his sword to Washington at Yorktown, and not vice versa.

Despite Washington's mild fondness for gambling (from 1772 to 1775 he recorded gambling, on average once every two weeks) he demanded that his troops put down their cards for the good of the nation. "All officers, noncommissioned officers, and soldiers," he ordered in 1776, "are positively forbid playing at cards, or other games of chance. At this time of public distress, men may find enough to do, in the service of their God and their country, without abandoning themselves to vice and immorality." But this missal was no more effective than General Howe's, and the following year he jogged his troops' memories by gravely informing them that all forms of gaming were expressly forbidden, "as being the foundation of evil, and the cause of many a brave and gallant officer's ruin." But all need not be toil: "Games of exercise, for amusement, may not only be permitted, but encouraged." Still, most officers and soldiers found ample exercise and amusement in their cards.

During the Revolution, colonial legislatures showed their new independence by authorizing lotteries with a vengeance. Since the colonies used the lotteries to pay for defense and military spending, purchasing a ticket became a mark of patriotism. Even the new Continental Congress tried to get in on the action, though gambling was, officially, against the spirit of the fledgling republic. In its Articles of Association, issued in October 1774, the First Continental Congress had declared:

> We will, in our several stations, encourage frugality, economy, and industry, and promote agriculture, arts and the manufactures of this country, especially that of wool; and will discountenance and discourage every species of extravagance and dissipation, especially all horse-racing, and all kinds of games, cockfighting, exhibitions of shews, plays, and other expensive diversions and entertainments.

The Second Continental Congress, faced with the present difficulties of organizing—and financing—an army of independence, decided that not *all* games were so extravagant, and turned to a lottery for the needed funds. On November 18, 1776, the Congress passed a law that set up a lottery in four classes. In the first-class lottery, to be held on March 1, 1777, in Philadelphia, those who bought $10 tickets would have a chance at the grand prize of $10,000. Out of the 100,000 tickets sold, 20,433 were to win some prize, though 20,000 winners would collect only $20. The $400,000 in $20 prizes would be paid in cash, the rest in loan certificates. Winners could also parlay their prizes into tickets for the second-class lottery.

There were to be 100,000 tickets each in the second-, third-, and fourth-class lotteries, priced at $20, $30, and $40, respectively, The final lottery would have a top prize of $50,000 (again, payable by loan certificate). The Congress hoped to realize $1.5 million from the lotteries, a sum that would inestimably help to underwrite the war effort. But the instability of war, galloping inflation, and difficulties in marketing the lottery throughout the colonies—combined with the interest-free loan certificate for the top prizes—made the congressional lottery a tough sell. Sales of first-class tickets were so slow that the drawing was delayed more than a year, to May 1778. Even then, barely 20,000 tickets of the original 100,000 had been sold. The drawing ended in a net loss of $72,000 for the Congress. By the time that the fourth drawing finished in 1782, the government itself had bought most of the tickets and was thus able to make a total profit of $1.2 million on the venture, although, when adjusted for inflation, the Congress's gains were actually less substantial, and hardly worth the effort taken to conduct the lottery.

When they were not debating matters of state, delegates to the Continental Congress often gambled. Thomas Jefferson, during the two June weeks he spent writing a draft of the Declaration of Independence, found time to play

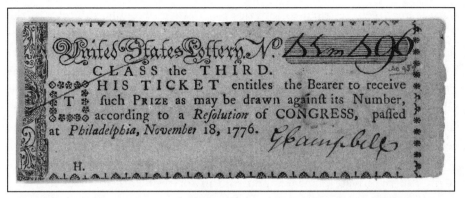

Lotteries were so popular in the British North American colonies—and the new United States—
that the Continental Congress chartered a draw to benefit the independence effort.

a little. He recorded winning and losing in moderation at backgammon, cross and pile (heads or tails), lotto, and cards during that time. Jefferson held it to be a self-evident truth that men like himself, working hard to protect the liberty of their country, deserved some time to roll dice, flip coins, and play cards. In this way, at least, he had much in common with his British brethren across the Atlantic.

The British army band may have played "The World Turned Upside Down" as General Cornwallis surrendered to the Continentals at Yorktown in 1781, but the establishment of the new United States of America did not mean quick changes in its citizens' gambling habits. Although the king's rule had been thrown off, Americans continued to use traditional cards depicting royalty in their games.

During the 1790s, neither plague nor the threat of eternal damnation could tear city-dwellers from their cards. In 1793 a yellow fever epidemic struck Philadelphia, killing five thousand people (about ten percent of the population); during the course of the decade, repeated outbreaks in Philadelphia and New York City were equally disastrous. Those who could fled for the safety of the countryside. Ministers remaining in the cities thundered from their pulpits that the yellow fever was an angry God's retribution on Sabbath-breaking, high-living sinners, and they implored the sporting masses to give up gambling and dissolution. Their pleas fell on deaf ears, as taverngoers began to bet on comparative mortality rates: Philadelphians bet that a third more New Yorkers would be carried off by the disease, while in New York bettors wagered on the opposite proposition. Even a devastating plague could become an excuse for a friendly bet in the young republic.

With gambling so common and tax structures shaky at best, the newly born states freely resorted to lotteries for a range of public projects. In the 1790s, more than two thousand state-authorized lotteries ran each year. Lottery offices in New York and Philadelphia, the biggest lottery cities, sold over $4 million worth of tickets annually. Public lotteries financed a range of improvements and took place at all levels of government: A 1793 federal lottery, which helped finance the construction of Washington, D.C., offered as its first prize an inn, Blodgett's Hotel, in the new city. George Washington himself bought the first ticket.

Though these lotteries were organized for the public benefit, they were actually run by private managers and sold in for-profit offices that charged a commission for each ticket sold. Tickets for real estate and property raffles were generally expensive, but offices divided tickets into shares, allowing poorer players a chance to participate. When honestly run, lotteries were popular alternatives to taxes, and they guaranteed tremendous profits to their organizers; the actual charity or project usually received only fifteen percent of ticket sales. Sometimes, draws verged on farce. In 1811, for example, the Massachusetts legislature chartered a lottery to raise $16,000 for improvements to Plymouth Beach. Over the next nine years, managers assiduously held regular drawings, skimmed off hefty fees for themselves, and paid out nearly $890,000 in prizes. After nearly a decade, the lottery had raised less than $10,000 for the beach project, but neither the organizers nor the public seemed to care: The former had a steady income, and the latter got the chance to win.

Despite the easy profits to be made by running lotteries honestly, some wanted more. Perfidious lottery managers and agents distinguished themselves by a range of swindles: They might leave town after selling tickets without the nicety of an actual drawing, sell worthless counterfeit tickets to real lotteries, or even sell chances to win a nonexistent lottery. Because there were so many lottery schemes throughout the states and lottery agents sold tickets for out-of-state drawings, such deceptions were simple, though they quickly became notorious. In 1823, for example, Congress sanctioned a Grand National Lottery to benefit Washington, D.C. The tickets were sold and winning numbers drawn and announced, but the manager, one Mr. Gillespie, skipped town without paying the winners. By this time, ticket buyers apparently considered such trickery a common risk, as most of the winners did not even complain. But the grand prize winner, owed $100,000, was considerably more outraged. He brought suit, and after four years of litigation, the Supreme Court ordered the city to pay him his full winning amount in 1827.

Despite the risks, citizens of the growing republic could not get enough of the lottery. Although the absolute number of chartered lotteries declined over the first thirty years of the nineteenth century, the frequency of drawing and the value of prizes increased, whipping the public into lottery frenzy. The number of lottery offices in New York City increased from 60 to 190 between 1819 and 1827, and by 1833 Philadelphia had 200 offices and even staid Boston at least 50. In 1833 a newspaper estimated that, in eight states alone, more than $67 million in tickets were sold each year, a sum said to be greater than five times the federal government's budget.

As lottery offices became ubiquitous, newspapers began carrying stories critical of them. In 1831 the Baltimore newsmagazine *Niles' Weekly Register* charged that the entire lottery business was run deceptively. But an extraordinary number of Americans remained receptive to the lottery agent's blandishments, and ticket sales continued to rise. States began investigating the lottery business, but most legislatures were clearly reluctant to bid farewell to such a lucrative revenue stream, and many simply outlawed the selling of out-of-state tickets with the hope that their own lotteries would advance.

Lotteries were also drawn to benefit private individuals. In March 1826, for example, the Virginia legislature granted the debt-ridden former president Thomas Jefferson a charter to sell off his real estate via a lottery to provide a comfortable living for his daughter after his death. The legislature appointed a committee to oversee the drawing, and the committee in turn hired Yates and McIntyre of New York, professional lottery managers, to run the operation. Yates and McIntyre printed up the tickets and prepared to distribute them, but some of Jefferson's wealthy friends tried to orchestrate the purchase of all the tickets in order to spare Jefferson the humiliation of the drawing. When Jefferson died in July, however, Yates and McIntyre went ahead with their plans and announced the lottery in a Baltimore newspaper. There were to be 11,480 tickets costing $10 each sold, each giving its owner a chance at one of three Jefferson properties: The grand prize was Monticello itself, valued at $74,000. But after few tickets sold, the lottery was abandoned and Jefferson's estate was sold off piecemeal.

Lottery winners of the day often used their prizes for personal improvement and even liberation. In 1800, Denmark Vesey, the West African–born slave of a Charleston sea captain, won a prize of $1,500 in a local lottery and purchased his freedom with it. Exceptionally industrious, he had already mastered six languages, and soon opened a carpentry shop, amassed considerable land holdings, and earned the respect of white and black Charlestonians alike. He also became an outspoken opponent of slavery, publicly denouncing the cruel system, and secretly began enlisting over nine thousand slave and free blacks in a vast insurrection. On July 14, 1822, his forces planned to seize Charleston's arsenals, murder the governor, set the city ablaze, and begin exacting retribution for years of slavery from the city's white citizens. The plot was betrayed before it was put in action, Vesey and thirty-five of his lieutenants executed, and harsh countermeasures taken by the state's slaveowners. For decades, fears of another slave rebellion haunted white South Carolinians and may have stiffened their intransigence toward abolition in the 1840s and 1850s, helping to push the state toward its fateful secession in 1861.

The Denmark Vesey story illustrates the social upheaval inherent in lotteries: The poor and powerless might, through a stroke of luck, gain a fortune. Such tumult flew in the face of the emerging Protestant capitalist ethic, which prescribed hard work and self-sacrifice as the only path to success. Working hard felt a little less satisfying when one's neighbor, or even employee, might become wealthier simply by holding a lucky ticket. Those who felt apprehensive about the lottery's leveling effects soon joined forces with others who felt that the poor who bought lottery tickets should be "protected" from scheming lottery agents. After a New York Select Committee on Lotteries, formed to investigate fraud in an 1819 Medical Science Lottery, revealed that many dishonest operators had corrupted public officials, the state required all agents to be licensed. Two years later the legislature went even farther, passing a law providing for the gradual extinction of the lottery: No new schemes were to be sanctioned, and as existing lotteries fulfilled their goals, they would not be replaced. On January 1, 1834, the final lottery ceased operations, ending legal lottery sales in one of the biggest states in the union.

The lottery was on the run worldwide. Britain had held its last drawing in 1826, France followed suit ten years later, and most of the world seemed united against the lottery. Americans, typically, split the difference: Pennsylvania, Ohio, Vermont, Maine, Massachusetts, New Jersey, New Hampshire, Illinois, Louisiana, and Vermont had all outlawed lotteries by 1840, while a few states, notably Kentucky, South Carolina, and Alabama, continued to allow them. Charleston remained a lottery center into the 1850s, and in Kentucky, draws continued, much to the chagrin of other states, who found that, despite outlawing the lottery, they could not prevent people from subscribing to its illegitimate offspring, policy.

As in Britain policy sellers were the bane of lottery managers and protectors of the poor, for slightly different reasons. Lottery organizers resented someone else profiting from their drawing, and critics charged that policy sold lottery chances to those who could least afford them. It had been only a minor annoyance until states began banning lotteries in the 1830s.

Once a state abolished its own lotteries, policy shops quickly sprouted up to take their place. These shops dropped the pretense of selling "insurance" and simply allowed people to bet on any one of several lotteries held out-of-state. Originally, New York policy sellers used the drawings of New Jersey lotteries, but when the Garden State did away with lotteries, they and operators in other states settled on a consensus choice: the Kentucky Literature Lottery, drawn in Covington. Although some policy "wheels" selected winners using illegal draws in Georgia and Missouri, the Literature Lottery was sufficiently well publicized to have the trust of the policy-buying public. It remained the leading policy option until after the Civil War, when it was replaced by the Kentucky State Lottery and Frankfort Lottery, both still drawn at Covington.

The Kentucky Literature Lottery, like all other American lotteries, was a draw game, not far removed from the earliest games of the Netherlands and Venice. But policy bosses had adapted to the times: as soon as the official numbers had been drawn, commissioners telegraphed them to cities throughout the nation, where runners quickly fanned out from telegraph offices to policy shops where anxious bettors awaited the results.

Most games involved the drawing of between eleven and fifteen numbers from a box or wheel filled with seventy-eight numbers. Players could bet on many combinations. Those picking a "day" number bet that their number would be drawn at any point, and winners were paid 5 to 1. "Station" number bettors tried to guess in which position their number would be drawn, a bet that paid 60 to 1. "Station saddle" bets called for two numbers in specified positions, and "capital saddle" bettors tried to guess the first two numbers drawn at odds of 500 to 1. The "gig" player bet on three numbers at odds of 200 to 1. "Horse" bets, in which the winner correctly guessed four of the numbers drawn, paid at 680 to 1. Needless to say, the actual odds of any of these combinations' being drawn were significantly higher than their payout, giving the operator a comfortable profitable margin.

Policy was an obsession, particularly in poor neighborhoods, and a whole industry of fortune tellers and soothsayers emerged to look into the future and interpret dreams as a way of finding winning numbers for players. Those with more self-reliance (or less cash) did not hire one of these sibyls but instead consulted a dream book. Dream books, which contained instructions on how to interpret the numerological significance of dreams, became enormously popular. Most policy sellers encouraged their clients to consult dream books; most shops maintained a copy of a well-known dream-book compendium called *The Wheel of Fortune,* some even charging customers just to look at it. Despite official disapproval and occasional efforts at suppression, policy continued to thrive into the waning years of the nineteenth century and, in many ways, laid the groundwork for the future syndicate control of illegal gambling through the "numbers rackets."

Gambling was equally difficult to contain on the frontier, which pushed steadily westward from the end of the Revolutionary War. Settlers were eager for any amusement; gambling was a common diversion, particularly cards (loo, brag, and all fours in the earliest days), dice, and horse racing. Frontier Tennessee, Kentucky, Ohio, and western New York were notorious for their gambling, which provided a rare chance for inhabitants of far-flung farms to congregate. Horse races and cockfights were held on public holidays or became an excuse for a holiday of their own. Travelers often noted the ravenous gambling appetites of westerners. Inns and taverns catering to travelers gave over most of their tables, and sometime even their floors, to card games. Gambling was so rampant that one congressman, supporting the improvement of the western transportation infrastructure, insisted that it was the only way to stem the tide of gambling. Western lands were so rich, he argued, that farmers without access to Eastern markets only worked part-time to raise enough for subsistence and spent the bulk of their time gambling. (Opening up the rivers, ironically, only increased the scope of gambling by bringing more money into the hinterlands and by permitting easier travel.)

As the market economy pushed westward, the first professional gamblers appeared. While officially reviling them as blacklegs, people never seemed to tire of playing with them. Some states passed laws that criminalized the business of gambling, but most left the activity itself intact. Thanks to young Kentucky legislator Henry Clay's intervention, an 1804 state law "to suppress the practice of gaming" condoned social games by explicitly banning only bank games "in which one player is continually opposed to all the others." This split between social and mercantile gaming was symptomatic of the fundamental ambiguity most Americans have had toward gambling: Even during the low ebb of professional mercantile games, few states dared touch the actual playing of games, something that led to the continued survival of illegal gambling organizations.

Henry Clay had good reason to keep friendly card games legal: He was one of the most renowned players of his day, winning and losing as much as $60,000 in a single night. As Clay rose to leadership as a champion of western expansion, he claimed to like playing cards more than legislating, and, through luck, boldness, or skill, won more than he lost. Many of his fellow statesmen shared his love for cards, including Massachusetts's Daniel Webster.

Clay and Webster's foil, Andrew Jackson, was no less enthusiastic a gambler. In one card game, he staked his horse against $200 and won. In 1805, he took part in one of the biggest horse races in Tennessee history when he ran his Truxton against the supposedly fastest horse in the South, Greyhound, at Hartsville. Jackson himself bet $5,000 (including $1,500 worth of his own clothes) on his horse, and throughout the Upper South men and women came to stake on either horse, betting everything from gloves to farms. Jackson's horse triumphed, and the supporters of Truxton rejoiced through the night, while many Greyhound backers had to walk home, having bet their own horses on the outcome.

Horse races like the Truxton-Greyhound contest were too infrequent for many southerners itching to gamble. Many of them preferred the easy action of faro. Faro's importance to American gambling is largely forgotten today, but in the nineteenth century it was the national game. Where London clubs of the period devoted themselves to hazard and the European resorts specialized in roulette, American professional gamblers, both itinerant and in residence at gambling houses, were infamous for faro. It was so widespread on the frontier that it was called "the game that won the West." In the 1830s, a well-traveled professional dealer kept his faro layout in a mahogany box decorated with a Bengal tiger, and his chips and layout were similarly emblazoned. The tiger became a symbol of faro, as gambling houses displayed paintings of tigers, and "bucking the tiger" became a widely known slang term for playing faro. Today, Chinese gamblers refer to slot machines as "hungry tigers" that inevitably devour the player; subconsciously, perhaps, American gamblers were saying the same thing when they bucked the tiger against a seasoned dealer.

The game had evolved from the Venetian original. Usually, a faro dealer used two assistants. One, on his right, collected bets, paid winners, and watched the players for cheating, while the other, on his left, kept track, with a small abacuslike device, of which cards had been played in the hand. Between the players and dealer stood the game layout, which had spaces for each of the thirteen value cards, usually indicated by spades. To the left, the seven occupied the farthest space, and two rows of cards—eight to king on the bottom, six through ace on the top—ran from left to right.

To play, the dealer shuffled and placed the cards faceup in a dealing box. He "burned" or discarded the top card, and then began placing cards into two piles, one for the player, the other for the bank. Each draw of two cards was called a "turn," and each game consisted of twenty-five turns: The final card in the deck was, like the first, a dead card. Players placed their bets, either on single numbers or any one of several combinations, after the deck had been shuffled and placed in the box. Players could also "go paroli" and parlay their winnings, as in basset; if the player's card won on its first appearance, he could let his winnings ride. When only three cards remained in the deck, players could "call the turn," or bet on their predicted order; if they guessed right, they were paid at four to one. On "splits" (when two cards of the same value were played), the bank took half the wager.

There were fortunes to be made by exploiting the southern love of faro. Elijah Skaggs, raised in the Kentucky backwoods amid cardplaying, cockfighting, and horse racing, made this his life's goal. By his twenty-first birthday (around 1830) he was a proficient cardsharp and could nonchalantly stack the deck, deal from the bottom, and otherwise eliminate the element of luck from the game. After winning $2,000 from his family and friends, he set out for greatness.

Skaggs made an immediate impact in Nashville, where he arrived wearing a black frock coat and broadcloth suit more suited to an itinerant minister than a gambler. New acquaintances were shocked when the solemn young man produced a faro layout from his grip instead of a Bible, and he soon acquired the sobriquet "the preaching faro dealer." People made jokes at his expense, but he had the last laugh: Skaggs became so proficient at faro trickery

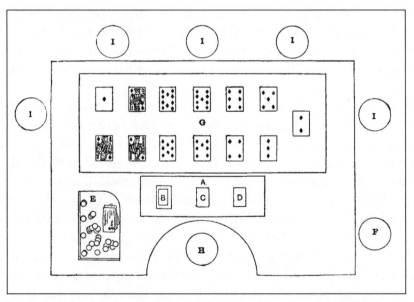

The typical faro layout, featuring *a*, the shuffling board; *b*, the faro box; *c*, the pile of dealer cards; *d*, the pile of player cards; *e*, check or chip tray; *f*, the case-keeper, who kept track of the cards in play with an abacuslike device; *g*, the layout; *h*, the dealer; *i*, the players.

that, by the 1830s, he had traveled throughout the country playing faro and made himself a wealthy man. His only regret was that he could only cheat one sucker at a time.

Skaggs soon figured a way around this obstacle. He began training a crew of faro artists whom he dispatched in pairs across the country. He sent a member of his large extended family along with each team to keep a strict accounting of its conduct. The dealers received one fourth of all profits, after expenses, and if luck ran against them and they somehow lost their bankroll, they returned to Skaggs for replenishment and reassignment. Skaggs's teams efficiently plucked pigeons for two decades, but eventually "Skaggs patent dealers" became notorious for dishonest play. In the late 1850s Skaggs retired from gambling and settled into a life of luxury on a plantation purchased with his faro profits. But his inopportune investment of most of his fortune in Confederate bonds during the Civil War impoverished him. He would die destitute in Texas in 1870, just reward, perhaps, for his decades of faro deceit.

Skaggs's organization was one of the earliest professional gambling combines, though it was not the only one. As the American economy became increasingly sophisticated, gambling houses, often modeled on the West End clubs of London, began to appear. Gambling still flourished in inns and taverns, but the new gambling houses provided the most visible places to gamble in the growing cities, though they did so while remaining legally invisible. Almost always operating in contravention of the law, they only continued to run with the acquiescence of the authorities, usually purchased outright with cash.

These houses appeared in major southern cities like New Orleans, Charleston, and Mobile by the 1810s and quickly spread northward. Within a few years, they could be found in New York and especially Washington, D.C. Though professional gamblers, newly arrived from Charleston, had filtered among the lobbyists and politicos crowding the new capital as early as 1800, the first true gambling houses did not appear until the Era of Good Feelings, those balmy years after the War of 1812 when party divisions temporarily dissolved. Congressmen were among the best customers of the dozen or so houses that by 1825 lined northern Pennsylvania Avenue and offered faro, brag, écarte, and all fours. Often, during race meets, Congress lacked the quorum to conduct its business, and when in session many legislators shamelessly bet on elections. While serving as a senator in 1826, future president Martin Van Buren wagered $10,000 and his evening clothes on one contest.

Although gambling was common in the nation's capital, it could still stir up a scandal. The alleged purchase of "gambling equipment" with public funds added fire to the first truly contentious presidential elections, those of 1828. After he moved into the White House in 1825, new president John Quincy Adams bought a secondhand billiard table to entertain guests. After he had it reupholstered, and bought a new set of balls and cues, controversy erupted. Adams had barely triumphed over Andrew Jackson, despite having received fewer popular and electoral votes: The contest was decided in the Congress, where Jacksonians charged that a "corrupt bargain" between Adams and Henry Clay had given the presidency to the New Englander. Jackson supporters formed the Democratic Party and almost immediately began campaigning again for "Old Hickory." Their eyes glittered at the prospect of a scandal in the White House.

When an inventory of expenses at the White House was published the next year, Jacksonians eagerly publicized the erroneous "fact" that public funds had been spent to buy the billiard table. A Jackson supporter in Congress decried the use of tax money to buy "gaming tables and gambling equipment" and expressed dismay at the specter of gambling in the White House, declaring that it would "shock and alarm the religious, the moral, and reflecting part of the community." Lambasting Adams for encouraging dissolute gambling was a curious tactic; the earthy Jackson was notoriously "adept at billiards, cards, dice, horse racing, cockfighting, and tavern brawls," as Adams loyalists reminded the public, and backwoods Jackson supporters had previously mocked Adams as an effete Puritan.

Adams's friends did not help the cause when they argued that, as the aristocratic diplomats of Europe enjoyed billiards, it was a virtual necessity for the nation's leader. Jackson partisans howled in response that Adams enjoyed royal extravagance at the public expense. Adams himself only clarified "billiardsgate" a year later, when he finally issued a public statement averring that he did not gamble at the table and had purchased it with his own money. Still, the matter kicked off one of the dirtiest campaigns in American history, as Adams supporters counterattacked by branding Jackson a murderer and both he and his wife adulterers. Jackson would go on to trounce Adams in the election of 1828.

Despite the furor over Adams's alleged purchase of gambling equipment, gambling remained incredibly popular, even at the highest levels. An author writing in the 1890s claimed that every president since Van Buren (who was elected in 1836), with the exception of Rutherford B. Hayes, was a known poker player. Members of Congress were similarly fond of cards, and a culture of gambling predominated in Washington. The most famous Washington gambling house was opened in 1832 by Edward Pendleton, a suave, elegant, generous Virginian who sometimes gave back in the form of a consolation loan what he had swindled at the faro table. Pendleton opened his house, which he called the Palace of Fortune, on Pennsylvania Avenue near Fourteenth Street; faro players nicknamed it the Hall of the Bleeding Heart. Like Crockford's house on St. James's Street (which was already booming when Pendleton opened his doors), Pendelton's was decorated with an eye toward lavish detail, stocked with the finest wines, and supplied with victuals by an accomplished chef. Presidents, cabinet members, senators, representatives, editors, and army officers all soon found themselves smoking, drinking, and gambling at the Hall of the Bleeding Heart.

The Hall became a haunt of lobbyists, not because they loved to gamble, but because they knew that members of Congress did. When congressmen needed a quick loan to continue playing, these lobbyists were eager to help out; favorable votes meant that the IOUs could be forgotten. Pendleton himself was a sought-after lobbyist, and many a government official who took the time to advocate a bill on his behalf was rewarded with a complimentary night at the faro table. But Pendleton's was above all else a gambling house—it employed an army of ropers who brought in prospects. Dealers were only as honest as their players were influential; presidential candidates and cabinet members were allowed to test their luck fairly, but obscure congressmen found themselves on the losing end more often than not as Pendleton instructed his dealers to "protect the house" more assiduously against them. Dozens of congressmen, particularly from the South and West, were believed to have played their salaries away at Pendleton's.

Pendleton offered only faro, though for particularly distinguished guests he allowed facilities for playing social games like brag, whist, and poker. His faro tables used white chips for one-dollar bets and red ones for five-dollar bets, a practice followed by today's casinos. Pendleton's dealers were skilled enough to bring in rolls of cash that enabled him to enjoy the high life. As tensions began to mount between northern and southern congressmen, his house remained one place where all of Washington united in pursuit of faro. Pendleton prospered, becoming one of Washington's most influential men. On his death in 1858, several Democratic congressmen served as pallbearers, and President James Buchanan even attended the funeral. The capital was divided by issues of slavery and states' rights, but nearly everyone could agree that a little gambling among gentlemen was an undisputed right.

8

Baiting John Bull

◆ ◆ ◆

Losing their American empire didn't stop the Brits from gambling. In London, a city of nearly one million in the eighteenth century, cards and dice were played on nearly every corner. Thousands of ordinaries where men gambled assiduously after dinner each night could be found throughout the city. As a consequence, ordinaries became notorious haunts for loud gossip and fraudulent gambling. Specialized gaming houses competed with ordinaries by offering no-nonsense mercantile games.

In 1731, *Gentleman's Magazine* conducted a survey of gaming "halls" specializing in faro (derided as a "cheating game") that enumerated no fewer than eighteen classes of employees, yielding the impression that the hells consistently won enough to support such specialization. The commissioner, one of the proprietors, audited the books and supervised the director, who actually ran the gaming room. Operators dealt faro, while croupiers raked in the chips. Puffs and squibs (shills) were given money to play and thus encourage others, under the watchful eye of a clerk. An army of ushers, waiters, and porters catered to the gamblers' needs. Outside, lookouts and runners helped warn against police invasion; in the event they were unsuccessful, most houses retained lawyers, bail, and affidavit men. Players clearly entered at own their risk: Many houses retained a captain, whose job was "to fight any gentleman who might be peevish about losing his money," a dunner, who recovered money lost at play, and "ruffians, bravos, and assassins," whose responsibilities can only be imagined.

These clubs offered credit and operated in constant fear of the police, necessitating several additional employees and making them even less apt to give players an honest chance—it would have been impossible to support this army of employees on the slim proceeds guaranteed by the honest house advantage. As the predations of the gaming houses grew more persistent, the public became agitated against them. The *Grub Street Journal* in 1736 printed a letter warning against puffs who induced new arrivals to London into gambling at crooked houses. Many gaming houses soon closed.

With the decline of the gaming houses, play migrated to taverns and coffeehouses, presumably more refined and intellectually stimulating establishments. In the 1740s, as reflected in the burst of antigambling legislation that had ended serious gambling at Bath, open gambling came under attack, and urban gambling survived only where it could find protective cover. Coffeehouses and chocolate houses, their close cousins, fit the bill perfectly.

Coffee- and chocolate houses of this time, unlike their modern counterparts, were more than places to grab quick refreshment or meet for a safe first date. At least two thousand of them could be found in London in the early eighteenth century, and each was the gathering place for a particular trade, profession, class, party, or nationality. Whigs and Tories, Scotsmen and Frenchmen, insurers and stockjobbers, all had their own coffeehouses. Once a coffeehouse established itself with a sufficient number of like-minded customers, it was a small step to turn the place into a club by instituting a membership charge and barring all outsiders. In addition to providing a fine place for jolly fraternization, it also provided a legitimate cover for clandestine gambling among members. The first of these, White's, opened in 1697 on St. James's Street, followed by the Cocoa-tree (just a few doors down) in 1746. In the 1760s, a host of new clubs opened nearby, leading the statesman and author Sir George Otto Trevelyan to liken St. James's Street to one vast casino.

Though no club existed solely as a gambling house, some were better known for gambling than others. In the late eighteenth century, White's, Almack's (which became Brooke's in the 1760s), Graham's, and the Cocoa-tree Club (all originally chocolate houses) were the most notorious for their gambling. In general, upper-class gambling clubs predominated in and around St. James's Street and Piccadilly in the West End. White's in particular was infamous: Faro and hazard could be played there into the late hours. Professional gamblers, provided they were not proven cheats, were happily admitted. Players who indulged in social games like chess, checkers, and backgammon had to pay a small fee to the club; such fees remained common in houses allowing social gambling. The club's members bet on more than just cards and dice: In the official betting book decades of wagers on everything from birth to death were memorialized. Because of its gambling, White's acquired something of a bad reputation and was believed to be the haunt of highwaymen, waiting patiently for the night's biggest winner to leave so that they could harvest his winnings.

According to legend, White's was the birthplace in 1765 of one of the most widely traveled of England's culinary creations, when John Montagu, the fourth earl of Sandwich, gambled for over twenty-four hours straight. Unable to tear himself from the table for dinner, he commanded a waiter to bring him a piece of meat between two slices of bread, thus letting him derive nourishment to continue playing without leaving the table or sacrificing the cards for utensils. Taking the earl's example, other players began asking for "the same as Sandwich."

Montagu's gambling is well documented—Horace Walpole wrote that, when out hunting, he brought dice so that he and his companion, the duke of Cumberland, might throw hazard. The earl himself ambiguously blamed his poor finances on "indiscretions," which certainly might include overheavy gambling. Some dispute whether the famous gambler Montagu first conceived the idea for the quick meal at the gaming table or at his desk, or if he simply emulated other gamblers in supping on bread and meat. In any case, the sandwich soon took on the name of its most famous patron.*

Club members had more to worry about than just how to best stuff their faces without soiling their cards. The rules of Almack's, a club second only to White's as a gambling roost, reveal much about the clubs. Members were not permitted to gamble in the eating room, with the exception of flipping a coin to determine who paid the bill. Players also had to keep the table minimum on the table while gambling. The club itself did not provide credit, but moneylenders always lurked nearby, eager to help plungers chase their losses. Though technically illegal, these clubs ran without fear of police intervention, largely because of the political importance of their members.

The explosion of new clubs in the late eighteenth century inspired deep suspicion. *The Times* described, in 1793, the "evil" of West End clubs in great detail. According to the account, some posh clubs existed primarily to lure and swindle young men of fortune. First, the houses plied their dupes with a fine dinner and plentiful wine, gratis. After losing all of their cash, reluctant gamblers were induced into losing even further on credit, debts that the fine young chaps usually honored rather than risk a scandal.

Even high-toned clubs offering honest games could drive their players into bankruptcy by the mere nature of mercantile gambling, which steadily leached

---

*Sandwiches remained popular with gamblers: One story claims that Reuben Kolakofsky, an Omaha grocer, invented the Reuben sandwich during a weekly poker game and that a fellow player added the item to his hotel's menu, starting this sandwich on its road to fame.

Montagu biographer N.A.M. Rodger has cast doubt on the famous story of the sandwich's origin. He believed the legend originated with a passage in a 1765 travel book that relates the story as it is known today, but claims that during that year the earl was serving as a cabinet minister and routinely worked at his desk without pause. It was here, Rodger says, that the sandwich made its debut. But two other sources insist that the sandwich has its origins at the gaming table. Edward Gibbon wrote in 1762 that a number of gentlemen supped on "a bit of cold meat, or a Sandwich" at the Cocoa-tree, and the Beef Steak Club, a gambling fraternity that met at the Shakespeare Tavern, also claimed to have invented the sandwich.

the house percentage away from players. "Low hells," meaner houses with no membership requirements and low minimums, were an even dodgier affair: If a player won fairly, he might or might not be paid. One magazine estimated that, in the early nineteenth century, about thirty hells continuously operated throughout London. These were not the elegantly furnished clubs of the West End; located in obscure corners of the city, with a sham business operated as a front, these hells accommodated up to fifty players a night, each desperately playing hazard. They required stealth and cunning to remain open, in the absence of the political influence of clubs of higher rank.

Many lower gambling houses were, like their high-toned cousins, bustout joints that lured in fresh suckers and cheated them as a matter of course. In addition, a veritable fraternity of crooked gamesters, known variously as rooks, sharps, sharpers, blacklegs, Greeks, and gripes operated throughout all levels of society. The sharpers were typically wellborn men with the benefit of a genteel education and an unctuous manner that allowed them to fleece recent acquaintances at cards, dice, billiards, or bowling with equal facility.

Curiously, many gentlemen preferred the risks of playing with sharpers. Lord Chesterfield explained that when he won from sharpers they immediately settled their debts, while gentlemen offered nothing more than genteel apologies and empty promises to pay. But according to their critics, these sharpers were hardly sporting blokes. They profited from the weakness of others and, in contrast to the insouciance of the gaming house, practiced strict sobriety: As "animal food" apparently dimmed the calculating faculties, they fed "chiefly on milk and vegetables." One contemporary writer described them in darkly Mephistophelean terms:

> As profit, not pleasure, was the aim of these knights of darkness, they lay concealed under all shapes and disguises, and followed up their game with all wariness and discretion. Like wise traders, they made it the business of their lives to excel in their calling.
>
> For this end they studied the secret mysteries of their art by night and by day; they improved on the scientific schemes of their profound master, Hoyle, and on his deep doctrines and calculations of chances. They became skillful without a rival where skill was necessary, and fraudulent without conscience where fraud was safe and advantageous; and while fortune or chance appeared to direct everything, they practiced numberless devices by which they insured [sic] her ultimate favors to themselves.

This army of darkness used numerous techniques, from altered dice and marked cards to collaborative play and deceptive dealing. Despite centuries of cautions against them and published exposés of their disguises and deceptions, there was never any shortage of gullible victims.

Gambling for profit appealed to both sexes. Well-off women with no other income sometimes allowed their houses to be turned into gambling houses. The two best known at the end of the eighteenth century, Lady Archer and Lady Buckinghamshire, were only the most prominent of a circle of "faro ladies" who owned banks in private homes. Buckinghamshire was known for sleeping with a small collection of weapons to protect her bank. Though these ladies claimed their aristocratic birth gave them license to run gambling operations as they saw fit, they were occasionally subject to police harassment and frequently the target of public ridicule—Archer apparently enjoyed makeup a little too much, and after a false report of her death had been dismissed, the *Morning Post* whimsically noted that London's makeup artists and perfumers were rejoicing.

This ridicule characterized the shift in public opinion against mercantile gambling, signaled by increasingly prominent raids on gambling houses in the late 1790s. In 1795, *The Times* reported that young women no longer played faro and did not emulate their mothers in seeking to cheat young men. But two years later, the same newspaper noted that students at leading boarding schools now learned whist and casino (like whist, a four-player social game that could, in a pinch, be played by only two or three) as a matter of course. Though mercantile gambling had apparently declined, at least among feminine society, social gambling continued unabated. As in France during the early part of the century, gambling dominated even dancing; a gentleman asking a young lady to dance at a ball was promised a terpsichorean whirl only after he had played two rubbers (best of three sets) of casino.

Even among men, faro play dwindled in early nineteenth-century England, though hazard's popularity continued unchecked. Macao, a single-card version of baccarat, enjoyed a brief surge in popularity. One Piccadilly house, Waitter's on The Street, was for a time entirely given over to it. One writer estimated that three quarters of the club's members were ruined by the game. Although it was the favored haunt of many luminaries, it lasted only twelve years before being taken over by a band of blacklegs (professional gambling cheats) and operated as a "bust-out" joint. In other clubs whist, played for high stakes, became increasingly prominent, a harbinger of the soon-to-be universal spread of that game.

Mercantile gambling, which had diminished early in the nineteenth century, surged back before mounting pressures against it drove it underground again at midcentury. According to contemporary observers, one man stood responsible for the sudden increase in gambling: William Crockford. Born to modest circumstance, Crockford started his career as a fishmonger but soon profited more from his betting at clubs and the turf. He acquired a share in Waitter's Club, then at an address near Almack's on King Street. A hazard club on Piccadilly in which he owned a share was discovered to use false dice, and Crockford hastily settled with the offended parties out of court. He incessantly quarreled with his partners and, in 1826, at the age of fifty-one, sought to build his own gambling palace on St. James's Street. Already a wealthy and infamous man about town, and despite his humble roots (he always spoke with a thick Cockney accent and mastered only the rudiments of spelling), he was both envied and feared.

Construction of the house at 50 St. James's Street caused considerable disruption along the thoroughfare, but when it opened in 1828, it was immediately acclaimed as an astonishingly lavish palace to chance. The house's decorations alone cost £100,000. Visitors entered a stately vestibule adorned with classical pillars and a domed stained-glass ceiling, from whence they could enter a dining room that rivaled "the most lordly mansion," visit the elegant drawing room, or enter the holy of holies, the handsomely furnished playroom, dominated by the oval hazard table. There, they sat in comfortable chairs and, using small hand-rakes, wagered chips valued from one to two hundred pounds.

"Who," one diarist noted during the 1830s, "that ever entered that dangerous little room can ever forget the large green table with the croupiers . . . with their suave manners, sleek appearance, stiff, white neckcloths, and the almost miraculous quickness and dexterity with which they swept away the money of the unfortunate punters?" Close by, Crockford, "snug and sly . . . watchful as the dragon that guarded the golden apples of the Hesperides," sat at a small writing table, from which he offered loans, settled markers, and resolved all disputes. For those interested in more primal sport, the basement featured a cock-fighting pit, close to the entrance of a secret passage that, in the chance of a raid, would lead bettors to a safe spot in the direction of Piccadilly.

Crockford spared no expense: He reportedly kept £70,000 worth of wine in his cellar, which ran underneath neighboring buildings. Over one thousand wealthy and fashionable members paid Crockford's annual £25 dues. Membership bought the low-cost gourmet meals prepared by Louis Eustache Ude, Crockford's virtuoso French chef, a chief attraction of the club. Visiting foreigners "of distinction" were permitted into the club as a courtesy. In the gaming room, hazard and whist prevailed, with Crockford making most of his money on the former, which he banked. Dice play was so heavy that the club reportedly

The exterior of Crockford's, the leading West End London gambling club of the 1830s.

played through £2,000 worth of the cubes a year. All the while Crockford vigilantly managed the game and scrupulously granted credit—and collected the inevitable debts. As the poshest house on St. James's, Crockford's attracted the members of neighboring clubs, who came for dinner but obligingly stayed to play hazard. Within a few years, Crockford had earned £1.2 million and inspired scores of less lavish imitators, and as his club waxed wealthy, "general gaming houses" proliferated throughout the city.

After twelve years of necessarily long hours and the stresses attendant upon the management of a gambling house, Crockford decided to retire. Though he had been able to shield himself from prosecution by exploiting the wealth and influence of his clients, he was now sixty-five years old and eager to give up the hectic life of a gaming house manager. Two former employees took over the establishment, and though Crockford avowedly surrendered all interest, it is likely that he still maintained a stake in the club that bore his name. With the change in operation came lower table limits and a noticeable decline in service.

Crockford had gotten out just in time. In the 1840s, public agitation against the club and its offspring began to mount. In 1844, a Select Committee of the Commons investigated gambling. At these hearings, members of Parliament excoriated police for allowing gaming houses to run unmolested, and the commissioner of police lamented the stealth with which operators evaded raids, making prosecutions difficult. Crockford himself testified before the committee and revealed little, carrying his secrets to the grave; he died almost immediately after his appearance, at the age of sixty-eight. As the Committee was concluding its inquiry, the suddenly vigilant police raided seventeen gaming houses in and around St. James's but did not approach Crockford's, perhaps out of respect for the departed gambler.

These raids marked the beginning of the end for Crockford's and its offspring. In August 1845 Parliament tightened sanctions against professional gaming houses. The public houses soon winked out of existence, though social gambling continued as before in private clubs. Crockford's struggled on for a few years before becoming a social club, then an art gallery, and finally the headquarters of the liberal Devonshire Club. Though mercantile gambling never truly vanished, an era had ended. A later poet wistfully invoked the forgotten good times:

> Come and once more let us greet
> The long lost pleasures of St. James's Street.

But though the hazard tables were stilled, the spirit of gambling proved to be indomitable, and play continued, though in a decidedly quieter milieu, long after the death of Crockford.

Gamblers wildly betting at clubs enjoyed quick, no-nonsense games with little subtlety or analysis. But those with a more cerebral bent desired playing cards at a more leisurely pace. For these players, there was one game that reigned supreme in the eighteenth and nineteenth centuries: whist.

Whist developed from a game based on the Italian tarot game *trionfi*. Also known as ruff or trump, this game first appeared in England in the early sixteenth century. The English almost immediately added additional advantages, or honors, to the court cards of the trump suit, transforming the game into ruff and honors. By 1621 the game had been modified and had gained a new name: whisk, which might have derived from a ruffled piece of shoulder apparel, or from a player's admonition to her partner to remain silent. By the 1660s, its name had been altered to whist, and this new appellation stuck.

At this time, whist was considered something of a low recreation. Fashionable gentlemen confined themselves to piquet, while ladies with aristocratic pretensions played ombre or its four-sided derivation, quadrille. In George Farquhar's 1707 comedy *The Beaux' Stratagem*, the city-born Mrs. Sullen sneers at "country pleasures" like smoking, drinking, and "playing at whist." Her brother, Sir Charles Freeman, likewise claims ignorance of both whist and all fours, to which the provincial Squire Sullen snorts, "Where was this man bred?" The irony was not lost on contemporary audiences. As late as 1750, whist was a widespread pastoral recreation, played during the winter break in agriculture by bored farmers and graziers. Gambling contributed considerably to the game's excitement.

By the middle of the eighteenth century, the game had coalesced into its classic form. Four players sat around a table, with those opposite each other playing as partners. The dealer dealt thirteen cards to each player and turned up his last card, whose suit became the trump, meaning that its cards would triumph over all others. The player to his left then played a card, and other players had to literally follow suit (play a card of the same suit), the origin of that expression. Whoever played the highest card, or a trump, out of the four players won the trick and got the right to lead to the next trick. Players unable to follow suit could either play a trump or play a plain suit. To win, a partnership couple had to score a specified number of tricks, ten in the original "long" form of the game, five in the later "short" version; losers might pay off winners after each game, or both sides might keep tally and settle up at the end of the session. In the 1730s, a group of gentlemen who played at the Crown coffeehouse elected to have a go at the previously disregarded country game of whist. Carefully analyzing the game, they found it to hold several complexities. After this, the game began to attract attention from urbane students of the cards.*

Whist owes its subsequent popularity to one man, whose name, if not biography, is familiar to most casual card players: Edmund Hoyle, "according to" whom generations of rulebooks were printed. For one who has achieved such fame (two hundred years after his death, he is considered the final authority, even for games not yet invented in his lifetime), his origins are obscure. It is only certain that in the 1730s he began to study whist and, in the guise of protecting the young from the deceits of sharpers, resolved to teach it professionally. To aid his instruction, Hoyle prepared notes on the rules for play. Learning to his distress that his work was circulating throughout London without his approval or remuneration, he secured copyright for it and, in 1742, issued a book with the prolix titling endemic to his age. The title begins,

---

*The ascent of whist in the eighteenth century poses a riddle: Did whist become "the unconquered lord of the board of green cloth" because, as the British gaming temper cooled, it was played for small stakes, or was it played for small stakes because it became widely played as the mania for gambling diminished? A writer of one of the hundreds of books on whist dismissed games like vingt-et-un (blackjack) as mere games "entirely of chance" not to be classed with noble whist, which he declared an essentially nongambling game owing far more to skill. Yet it has no intrinsic bar to the laying of heavy stakes.

A Short Treatise on the Game of Whist, containing the Laws of the Game, and also some Rules whereby a Beginner may, with due attention to them, attain to the Playing it well, and continues for several more sentences. Readers simply called it "Hoyle's Whist" or "Whist According to Hoyle."

The field of "how-to" gambling books was opened by Cardano, and French instruction books appeared as early as 1647, with English translations crossing the Channel in 1651. The English market for instructive gambling books exploded with the gambling boom that followed the Restoration. As early as the second edition of his *Wits Interpreter: the English Parnassus* (1662), John Cotgrave offered a chapter explaining ombre, gleek, cribbage, and picket.

The gambling boom also brought a host of lectures and pamphlets on how to avoid the wiles of sharpers. Charles Cotton subsumed some of these into his 1674 compendium of indoor and outdoor recreations, *The Compleat Gamester,* but also provided advice on billiards, an Italian variant of billiards called trucks, bowling, chess, card games (from picket to beast), backgammon, dicing, horse riding, racing, archery, and his epigone of leisure, cockfighting. Cotton's book was, in 1739, merged with Richard Seymour's *The Court Gamester.*

Hoyle's book was vital to the development of whist. With the publication of his *Short Treatise,* players at last had a handy guide to the game. Suddenly a literate, genteel pastime, whist became the latest sensation. Within a decade, it received courtly sanction as a royal amusement, and it became the favored recreation of the age. Hoyle was hailed as "a second Newton" and his dictates were universally accepted as authoritative. He then extended his empire by issuing books on backgammon, picket, brag, quadrille, and chess. After his 1769 death, publishers continued to offer "improved" editions of his books, and by the middle of the nineteenth century, his name became a generic byword for encyclopedic instructive gambling books.

Whist continued to evolve after Hoyle. One particularly avid school of players met at Bath, where in 1804 Thomas Matthews published a guide to whist that promised to educate the reader far better than Hoyle, who, according to the author, was not fit to sit with even third-rate players of the evolved game. London players also introduced innovations, including the abbreviated form known as short whist, and the game went global. Reversing the process that had attended the Restoration influx of gambling from France, the French imported whist (the first translation of Hoyle appeared in 1766), which presented at Versailles much as basset had appeared in London a century earlier. From the salons of Paris the game spread throughout Europe, finding enthusiastic players from Austria to Russia. British colonists and imperial officials transplanted the game into the farthest reaches of their empire, from Australia to Asia to Africa to the

According to the author of *The Whist Table,* the game provided a leisurely pastime that didn't require heavy stakes. He wrote that "the demon of gambling shrinks abashed before the good genius of Whist, and feels his spirit rebuked, as it is said Mark Anthony's was by Caesar."

Americas, and their former colonists in the United States took to the game enthusiastically, at least in the more settled East; George Washington was only the most preeminent citizen to enjoy the game.

From Hoyle, writers on whist had explicitly discussed the calculation of probabilities as one of the elements of skilled play. Hoyle, benefiting from the generations of mathematical interest in probability begun with Girolamo Cardano, even wrote *An Essay towards making the Doctrine of Chances easy to those who understand vulgar Arithmetic.* As whist's popularity grew, the game became a matter of serious speculation. Around 1850, a cohort of Cambridge students systematically studied whist; they continued to meet in London after they had graduated. The Little Whist School's members devoted themselves to playing, calculating, and discussing whist in all of its variations. In 1862 "Cavendish" (an unknown enthusiast's pen name) distilled these ruminations into book form as *The Principles of Whist.* Two years later, *A Treatise on Short Whist,* appended to a new edition of John Loraine Baldwin's *Laws of Whist,* extended the "philosophical" consideration of whist, taking in all elements of the game's strategy and theory. Like the game itself, intellectual analysis of it spread throughout the world. In an age besotted with scientific advance and intellectual collation, whist emerged as the thinking man's game par excellence. In the cosmopolitan Europe of the

nineteenth century, whist served as an international language that all cultured gentlefolk could speak.

Inspiring treatises, plays, and even a twelve-canto epic poem, whist reigned
without equal in the world of nineteenth-century card games and would seem to
have been a game for the ages. Yet today, it is nearly forgotten. Were it not for
references in works still read today like *Around the World in Eighty Days,* the
game might have joined costly colors, bone-ace, and Pope Joan in the discard pile
of history. But whist is really not that far gone. In the 1890s it would evolve
again, becoming bridge whist; subsequent innovations created auction whist and
then contract bridge. In this form, bridge became the supreme nongambling
card game of the twentieth century. Though it is no longer the lackadaisical
recreation of county squires or the philosophical pursuit of Cambridge scholars,
whist survives in bridge, its origins as a rustic gamble nearly unremembered.

While some English gamblers happily abandoned themselves to card play,
others craved a more primeval exhilaration, one that they could only find by
watching—and betting on—animals fighting or racing against each other.

Cockfighting is the most famous and the most storied animal sport.
Charles Cotton, who lambasted the poor odds of hazard, praised cockfighting. He declared it to be the most preferred of all games. In case his readers
had any doubts, Cotton provided a quick guide to how to best choose, breed,
train, and feed a champion fighting cock. He advised his readers on how best
to judge their birds in the four most important indicators of a battle-worthy
cock: shape, color, courage, and sharpness of heel. He gave them sage advice
on how to mate the birds to achieve suitably pugnacious progeny and implored trainers to fuss over eggs and hatchlings like a mother hen. Cocks that
crowed too young or too loudly were best consigned to the spit, as they were
born cowards sure to disappoint in battle. Exercising punctilious care over
their charges, trainers might then turn them loose in the cockpit, clipping
their feathers and moistening their heads beforehand. Cotton even gave tips
on how to cure fowl distempers and treat wounds (by sucking their blood and
washing them in warm urine, preferably in that order).

Fighting birds moved Cotton to elegiac verse: He closed *The Compleat
Gamester* with a two-page poem by one Dr. R. Wild on the raptures of gallant
fighting cocks in which a dying gamecock dictates his final testament before
giving up the ghost. Cotton was hardly the only Englishman to wax poetic
over cockfighting: Its recorded history on the island stretches back to at least
the twelfth century, when London schoolboys reportedly spent Shrove Tues-
days (the Tuesday before Lent) amusing themselves by watching birds fight,

and they were often granted allowances to purchase cocks. In addition, many schools assessed the "cockpence," a fee for staging the fights, as part of their tuition. Betting on the outcome was almost a natural progression. By 1366, cockfighting was widespread enough to occasion royal prohibition, along with other idle pastimes. Still, the sport would gain popularity and even attain royal sanction: Henry VIII installed a cockpit in the royal palace at Whitehall, and James I could not go without twice-weekly cockfights.

In the seventeenth century cockfighting continued to become more popular; at least three cockpits besides the royal range existed in London. Churchyards and even churches themselves doubled as impromptu cockpits for holidays, weddings, and funerals, though taverns and public houses were the most frequent sites. The typical cockpit measured twenty feet in diameter and was floored with a matted stage. As the bird handlers, or feeders, brought the cocks to the pit encased in the customary prefight burlap sacks, the excitement began to mount. Bets, which had begun at the prefight weigh-in, would continue to be made, as prospective bettors shouted out their wagers. Anyone who wished to match a bet yelled, "done," which sealed the deal. As the battle began, the first row of spectators leaned far over the railing, shouting encouragement to the fighters.

Cocking mains, or sets of cockfights, were elaborately staged public entertainment, conducted by a coordinating specialist, the pitmaster. Mains often pitted nearby towns or counties against each other, as residents ambled down to the cockpit to cheer on the birds owned by the local nabob. The peak of British cockfighting seems to have been the 1740s, when mains were regularly held in Bath, as good a barometer as any of the state of genteel entertainment. Gambling was clearly central to the cockfighting enterprise, which was a big-money sport, with paying audiences and substantial player-to-player betting. A set of cockfighting rules published around this time lists nineteen regulations—six related to the actual competition and seven regulated betting.

The sport was also potentially lucrative. Bird handlers, known as feeders or setters, received a regular stipend plus expenses from bird owners in return. In addition to the ego gratification of owning a champion and the prestige associated with magnanimously providing public entertainment, owners had respectable personal stakes in the outcome, wagering heavily on behalf of their bird. In addition to winning their private wagers, the owners of victorious cocks usually received a portion of the pit money, or the admissions proceeds.

Bettors and observers began to demand progressively more bloodthirsty exhibitions of "sport." Battle royals threw any number of birds into the pit and ended when only one remained standing. One single-elimination tournament named the Welsh Main paired 32 cocks who fought to the death; the survivors then paired and fought, until 31 lay dead before a single victor. Trainers began to augment their birds' sharp heels with artificial steel or silver spurs. Long after Cotton, books on how to breed and train fighting cocks remained popular, and a diversity of fighting breeds developed devoted partisans.

Though contemporary accounts of cockfights stress their broad popularity, humanitarian concerns eventually triumphed over the public's bloodlust, and Parliament officially banned cockfighting in 1835. But after its prohibition, the sport continued on the sly, its devotees balancing their zeal with the stealth needed to evade official inquiry. It remains a popular underground gambling activity in several parts of the world today.

Cockfighting was not the cruelest animal sport celebrated and wagered on in England. That honor falls to animal baiting, which involved cold-blooded torture and slaughter for sport. "Throwing at cocks," for example, proved a popular recreation for young and old; schoolboys became well practiced, as early as the sixteenth century, in hurling cudgels at scurrying birds. For twopence, older men could buy four chances at throwing clubs at a suspended clay pot holding a chicken. The man who broke the pot kept the bird and presumably ate it, if he had not mangled it already. By the early nineteenth century, throwing at cocks had been outlawed and largely suppressed.

The most commonly practiced form of animal baiting was bearbaiting, which traces its roots back to the animal entertainments of the Roman arena. Bearbaiting took place in bear gardens, whose bucolic name belied their barbaric nature. To bait a bear, organizers attached one end of a chain to a stake and the other to the bear's neck or hind leg. The organizers then let loose mastiffs to attack the bears, replacing them with others when the dogs were killed, wounded, or winded. The "sport" long enjoyed the approval of English monarchs, who maintained sloths of bears for this purpose, though it was later opposed by the Puritans—as historian Thomas Macaulay conjectured, not because it hurt the bear but because it pleased the audience.

It was a vicious spectacle. One observer of a bearbaiting in which thirteen bears were "worried by dogs" for the pleasure of Queen Elizabeth and her subjects left a vivid description:

> It was a sport very pleasant to see, to see the bear, with his pink eyes, tearing after his enemies' approach; the nimbleness and wait of the dog to take his advantage and the force and experience of the bear again to avoid his assaults: if he were bitten in one place how he would pinch in another to get free; that if he were taken

Britons bet on a number of animal sports, including bearbaiting and bullbaiting,
which pitted a large frenzied beast against smaller predators. Gamblers bet on how many dogs
it would take to overcome the bull, or how many dogs the bull would destroy.

once, then by what shift with biting, with clawing, with roaring,
with tossing and tumbling, he would work and wind himself from
them; and when he was loose to shake his ears twice or thrice with
the blood and the slaver hanging about his physiognomy.

Spectators bet money on either the bear or the dogs. Bullbaiting, which
pitched a bull against the dogs, sometimes rivaled bearbaiting's popularity,
and dogfights simply removed the bulls and bears from the equation. In a
pinch, any animal, or combination thereof, could be baited. One particularly
grisly match involved an ape tied to the back of a donkey, then matched
against fierce dogs. These spectacles continued into the nineteenth century,
declining gradually in popularity until they were outlawed with cockfighting
in 1835. Still, just as cockfighting continues to flourish underground in many
parts of the world, there are still those for whom an evening in the modern
equivalent of the bear garden is excellent entertainment.

Britons also liked to bet on themselves, wagering escalating sums on every
conceivably unpredictable outcome. A character in a period comedy of the
eighteenth century summed up the new spirit when he said, "you see the
virtue of a wager, the new, philosophical argument lately found out to decide

all questions." Englishmen and women now laid odds on anything, from the serious to the silly. This new craze might have had its roots in whimsy, but it eventually evolved into two of the most sacrosanct kinds of gambling: race and sports betting.

Wagering has been part of human life from time immemorial, but the English took the art of laying odds to a new height. By Elizabethan times, wagering had become moderately common. Shakespeare mentioned wagers in *Cymbeline* and *Hamlet,* and the intriguingly nicknamed Sir John "Lusty" Packington bet £3,000 that he could outswim three nobles from Westminster Bridge over the Thames to Greenwich. The good queen prevented him from testing his luck. But Elizabeth was not averse to a friendly wager herself; she famously lost a bet to Sir Walter Raleigh over how much smoke was in a pound of tobacco.*

Wagering became a truly British passion with the expansion of gambling that took place during and after the Restoration. Nothing was too serious to be the subject of a bet, including war. From 1688 to 1697, the Nine Years' War pitted the Grand Alliance of Spain, the Netherlands, Austria, and England against France. English merchants and "insurers" began setting odds and taking wagers on whether various cities would be the targets of military action. In 1691, insurers enjoyed a brisk March business taking bets over whether the town of Mons, near Brussels, would fall to the French siege. The holders of Mons ultimately capitulated, though not because of an actual battle: When the French threatened to fine the town 100,000 ecus for each day they had to lay siege, the inhabitants, fearing that they would soon be forced to surrender anyway, sent up the white flag. Meanwhile in England, rumors that Mons had been successfully relieved had sent anti-French bets through the roof, and the bookmakers made fortunes.

Siege betting continued throughout the war, and insurers developed a sophisticated communications network whose speed rivaled that of the government's official messengers. Insurers were not above using false heralds or circulating bogus reports to influence wagers, but when the resolution of a siege appeared imminent, Londoners raced to get their wagers down.

This macabre wagering continued on an even larger scale during the War of the Austrian Succession, 1701–1714, even involving two of the British commander's top officials. Both Major General William Cadogan, the army's quartermaster general, and James Brydges, the English forces' paymaster, used

---

*The question was settled by carefully weighing out a pound of the weed, burning it, then weighing its ashes (both agreed that the smoke represented the balance of the weight).

their access to the duke of Marlborough (hero of the battle of Blenheim, ancestor of Winston Churchill, and possibly Britain's greatest military mind) to obtain inside information to help them in their betting. It doesn't seem that Cadogan and Brydges used their influence to "throw the fight" or actively delay English military progress. Still, the image of high-ranking army officials busy arranging their bets in the middle of a war accurately captures the absolute mania for gambling that inhabited England at the time.

Newspapers and gambling club records of the era show how creatively the English found new subjects for wagers. In 1709, for example, four parliamentarians bet a crown each over whose hat would "swim" downriver fastest. The winner expressed a greater rapture "than if he had carried the most dangerous point in Parliament." Those confident in their learning bet with their brains; one young man bet another ten guineas that a certain passage was the prose of Tacitus and not some other writer, while others placed wagers on fine points of geography or history. Sir Robert Walpole lost such a bet over a quotation of Horace during a debate in the House of Commons, and he angrily surrendered the guinea wager.

Other bets had more serious stakes. In July 1774, a man bet £1,500 that, in contravention to the accepted medical knowledge and all experience, a human being could live for twelve hours underwater. He found a down-and-out guinea pig who consented to being sunk in a ship. Neither ship nor man was heard from again. This bet was outrageous but not much more morbid than others. Men bet on whose grandmother would live longer or whether a surgeon might successfully save a particular patient.

Betting could also provide an excuse to make a general ass of oneself. In 1806, Thomas Hodgson and Samuel Whitehead of York selected umpires and bet an unrecorded amount on which one could adopt the most ridiculous dress. Hodgson, whose garb was decorated with banknotes with the legend "John Bull" (the personification of England, as Uncle Sam is in the U.S.) stenciled on his back, beat Whitehead, who painted half his body black and wore half of a gaudy costume. When nature or society did not present opportunities for a bet, Englishmen invented them.

Some of the most famous wagers involved pedestrianism, or walking and running, which enjoyed a worldwide boom in the latter part of the nineteenth century. Pedestrianism began when Britons started to take long journeys simply to satisfy a bet. From the 1720s, bets over how long it would take to walk, jump, or hop a set distance became the vogue, sometimes drawing massive crowds and tremendous wagers. In 1788 and 1789, a young Irishman won a bet of £20,000 over whether he could walk to Constantinople and back in one year. Another baronet successfully wagered that he could, in a specified time, travel to Lapland and return with two women and two reindeer. With the expansion of travel and communications thanks to new technologies in the 1870s, the floodgates opened, and people from London to Philadelphia to Wellington thrilled to the exploits of marathon walkers who braved the elements—and boredom—to win a bet. These real wagers inspired the most famous literary adventure based on a bet, Jules Verne's *Around the World in Eighty Days*. In this 1872 novel, the polished, wealthy Phileas Fogg, during a whist game at the Reform Club, bets his fellow club members £20,000 that he can circumnavigate the globe in eighty days. The story inspired a successful real-life imitator, the pioneering journalist Nellie Bly—who actually made the trip in seventy-two days in the winter of 1889–1890—as well as a score of film adaptations. But to men who regularly wagered thousands of pounds on footraces and endurance challenges, Fogg's version would have been old news.

In time, betting on walking tours and classical erudition was overtaken by betting on team sports and horse racing. As in the gambling clubs, bets were recorded in books. By the middle of the nineteenth century, the idea of a betting "book" was commonplace. From there, it was a quick step to refer to the man who maintained the book as a "bookmaker," which was further shortened to "bookie" by 1885. Betting on cricket had been common since the eighteenth century, and as the game became standardized and increased in popularity in the next century, it provided much work for the newly named bookies of Britain.

Horse racing was a paragon of tenderness toward animals compared with cockfighting, bearbaiting, and dogfighting. Horse racing has been such a part of British culture for the past three hundred years that it may seem timeless. But both racing horses and betting on them has a longer history, with as many twists and hurdles as a steeplechase course.

Turf historians believe that persons of rank had raced horses in Anglo-Saxon times, even antedating the Roman occupation, but the earliest reliable written notice of horse racing in Britain dates from the twelfth century. During Henry II's reign, horses were raced at Smithfield, the leading London horse market. This makes sense: Horses could best be priced by pitting them against each other in tests of speed and endurance. During the Middle Ages, horses were primarily raced during two seasons, Easter and Whitsuntide (Pentecost, a holiday celebrated seven weeks after Easter).

Horses were raced by their owners or grooms over open terrain. Matches between two horses predominated, and the victor carried away little more than bragging rights or some trophy of nominal value. Betting was not yet an integral part of racing; on the contrary, racing, hunting, and hawking were lauded as pastimes suitable to an honorable gentleman, and their neglect in favor of cards and dice was frequently lamented. John Northbrooke, who denounced dicing, cardplaying, and other idle amusements like drama in the late sixteenth century, endorsed horse racing as providing good exercise, so presumably it was not yet a vehicle for large-scale gambling.

Racing became more organized during the reign of James I, whose love for hunting led him to an appreciation of horses and racing. During his reign, public races commenced at several places; the standard prize was a silver bell, for which reason these races were called bell courses. James I made his greatest contribution at Newmarket, then a little-known hamlet, when he began to stay there in 1605. Newmarket became the leading center for British hunting after James established a royal palace and stables there. Though he was a notoriously inept rider and did not race, himself, James encouraged racing because it allowed horsemen to test their steeds and, by encouraging competitive propagation, "improved the breed." This last justification would be cited by horse bettors for centuries to come, as they explained that their wagers were actually contributions to a fund established for that worthy purpose.

Ultimately, the British people would adopt an almost reverential attitude toward horses. King William IV later said that he considered racing to be the national sport, "the manly and noble sport of a free people," and he pledged to protect both British liberty and sports without losing sight of the enjoyment of all of his subjects. On the practical side, horses were important military assets vital to British society before the advent of mechanical transportation, and universal symbols of status and wealth. Still, something approaching the mystical clung to the four-legged creatures; a late nineteenth-century antigambler rued that "so noble an animal as the horse should be made the unconscious medium of such a degrading passion as gambling."

Gambling was not yet firmly attached to racing when James I established Newmarket as a center for royal hunting and therefore racing. Indeed, even the bells and plates given as prizes were not the victor's to enjoy: Winners frequently had to give security for the trophies for accepting them, as they would be given to the next winner of the race, much like today's Stanley Cup. Though informal matches between private gentlemen continued, bigger public races with fields as large as six horses became more common, and riders began wearing a standard jacket and cap.

When Charles I, an excellent horseman, assumed the throne in 1625, he virtually made Newmarket the center of the government; even the Lords of the Admiralty met there under Charles's aegis. Charles converted the royal hunting ground there into a racecourse, signaling the growing dominance of racing over hunting. With the accession of Cromwell, though, the prospects for Newmarket were much dimmer. In 1654, Cromwell banned horse racing not because it was an idle pastime or gambling vehicle, but because those with royalist sympathies might congregate at meets. Cromwell ordered the dispersal of the royal stables and those of several nobles, though he himself maintained several racehorses and a valued stud.

With the Restoration and reign of Charles II, racing became once again a national pastime. Charles reconstituted the Royal Stud (partially with Cromwell's prized horses) and inaugurated new racing events such as the Royal Plates and the Newmarket Town Plate. In 1666, Charles oversaw the construction of a rounded racecourse—the predecessor of modern enclosed tracks. He personally arbitrated disputes at Newmarket, which became his favorite resort, and helped to establish the town as the nexus of British racing. During this period the general rise in gambling carried over onto the turf: Betting on races became more prevalent. At this stage, horse betting was an extension of the established practice of wagering on phenomena like cockfights; there was no centralized betting business. Rather, onlookers bet among themselves on or against a particular horse, and settled accounts among themselves. Betting was a straight-up win-or-lose proposition, and favorites were penalized not by smaller payoffs, but by fixing weights to them. This was the birth of handicapping, which was originally quite literally the science of how to slow a favorite with weights to provide a more even race. Around this time professional jockeys began to displace horse owners as riders.

During the following decades racing became decidedly more regular and, perhaps not coincidentally, the subject of progressively heavier betting. William III wagered large sums on his own horses, staking 2,000 guineas in a 1698 contest against one of the duke of Somerset's mounts. William's most lasting contribution was to appoint Tregonwell Frampton, his personal horse trainer, as keeper of the running horses at Newmarket. Frampton was to serve four monarchs in the capacity. He was an able matchmaker and also a heavy gambler, though his success at the former was rumored to cloud his ability at the latter. Still, he instituted more orderly rules and procedures (regarding matchmaking and the actual conduct of races) into British racing, and when he died in 1727 he was hailed as "the father of the turf."

British racing took a step forward in the same year as Frampton's death when John Cheney began publishing his *Racing Calendar,* formally called *An Historical List of all the Horse-Matches run, and all Plates and Prizes run for in*

The St. Leger Stakes, first held in 1776, is one of the oldest continually run
horse races in the world. This illustration depicts the down-to-the-wire 1839 finish,
in which Charles XII (the favorite) nosed out Euclid.

England and Wales (of the value of ten pounds and upward). Cheney forth-
rightly published the calendar to assist in the next year's betting. He claimed
it would provide gentlemen with a pleasant diversion in the winter and, by allowing them to read trends into horse performances, permit them to better
calculate the chances of a horse winning a future meet and bet with greater
advantage. It was the ancestor of the modern racing form, and its spectacular
popularity indicates that a great many gentlemen spent time thinking about
betting on horses. Daily newspapers also began to include news about racing,
showing that sport had begun to percolate down to a wider audience. Despite
parliamentary attempts to limit racing, including restrictive legislation passed
in 1740, running horses—and betting on them—became increasingly widespread at the halfway point of the eighteenth century. As bloodier sports like
hawking, hunting, and cockfighting became less popular, racing surged ahead.

When betting on races was simply a matter of two acquaintances staking
against each other, there was little need for further oversight. But as racing expanded in sophistication, expense, and professionalization, and as betting became more of a concern, the British felt the need for a central authority to fix
regulations, set procedures, and arbitrate disputes. The Jockey Club, first mentioned in print in 1752 but likely founded at least two years earlier, grew into
such a body. It was not a social group for professional riders; rather, the word

jockey then meant horse owner. Just as London coffeehouses were being converted into official clubs reflecting the interests of their members, the Jockey Club, which began meeting at the Star and Garter in Pall Mall, soon became a formal organization with its own club. Fittingly, the Jockey Club was headquartered at Newmarket. The Club elected stewards to conduct races at Newmarket and to regulate the payment of prizes. An elite group (one could only become a member by a tightly controlled election procedure), the Jockey Club ultimately took over publication of the *Racing Calendar* and became the officially recognized national regulatory body for British horse racing.

Betting on horses was not the only sort of gambling that took place at racecourses. Before the appearance of the enclosed racecourse in 1875, collecting any sort of admission fee was out of the question. To pay for races, organizers rented a variety of concessions, including grandstands (privately run areas where wealthier patrons paid for seats), food and drink stalls, and gaming booths. These booths featured primarily E/O tables, and their presence was an essential moneymaking feature of most courses. Witnesses before Parliament in 1844 claimed that absent the revenues generated by these booths, several races would be canceled.

Despite complaints about gaming booths at courses and gaming houses in racing towns, these flourished throughout the early nineteenth century along with a new kind of gambling place: the betting house, also known as a commission office, racing bank, or betting office. These precursors of modern off-track betting shops were urban establishments where clerks took bets on all horses entered in races. By this time, oddsmaking had emerged, and bettors (known in Britain as punters) assiduously tracked the rising and falling odds of various entrants, hoping to get a lucky pick. Some betting offices were "mayfly" operations: If luck turned against them and a heavy favorite won, they simply "forgot to open" the next day. At the other end of the spectrum were large houses who, by balancing odds more carefully, took much of the chance out of accepting bets.

Along with the development of professional betting offices came a further expansion of print coverage of racing news and rumors. A new class of racing specialist appeared: the tipster, who advertised in the race papers and promised subscribers exclusive inside information to assist in their betting. Their information was often dubious at best and fraudulent at worst, but several of them carved out substantial estates by selling the illusion of advantage.*

---

*Over the next century and a half, bettors have barely become less credulous: Advertisements for myriad touts and tipsters offering "guaranteed lock picks" for football and basketball continue today.

In the eyes of the moralistic, work-driven middle class the bookmakers who ran the betting houses committed a cardinal sin: They opened the previously aristocratic preserve of betting on races to servants and workingmen who, for a small price, could hope to win big. The opponents of the lottery had made much the same argument, that betting on it unfairly took advantage of the poor, yet betting shops proliferated long after the death of the state lottery in 1826. Betting houses suffered a similar fate in 1853, when an act of Parliament made assembling in any place other than a racecourse for the purpose of betting illegal. This hardly ended lower-class betting, though—betting houses adopted the protective cover of cigar stores and poolrooms, and bookmakers fanned out into the streets and pubs.

Despite the moral protests of staid Victorians, betting on racing continued to progress, matching the rise of racing. With the development of a national railroad system, races could become truly national, as horses could travel a circuit of courses across the country. Enclosed courses, needing to attract a steady base of paying customers, actively courted both female and working-class spectators, expanding the popularity of both the sport and betting on it. Winning stakes escalated, making competition keener and horse breeding a big business. By the turn of the twentieth century, racing on enclosed courses in front of paying spectators was common, and the instant telegraphing of race odds and results to clandestine betting operations throughout the nation encouraged a boom in illicit off-track betting.

Weathering scandals, official disapproval, and the growing efforts of antigamblers (which mounted in the late nineteenth century), race betting continued to flourish into the twentieth century with the approval of the highest ranks of society. In 1886, the Prince of Wales, later to become King Edward VII, began training and racing his own Thoroughbreds, in between sessions of private gambling and trips to the French Riviera. Edward declared that horse racing might or might not produce gambling, but since it was a "manly sport which is popular with Englishmen of all classes," there was no reason to restrict it. As long as a wealthy, powerful elite continued to enjoy betting on horses, there was little that could be done to stifle it. Although praised as the "sport of kings" by its most rhapsodic devotees, in the nineteenth century horse racing became the sport of the people of Great Britain.

PART FOUR

Europeans Gamble
at Home and Abroad

♦ ♦ ♦

Journalist George Augustus Sala had a long and interesting career with London's Daily Telegraph *in the second half of the nineteenth century. As he roved about the world, penning characteristically overblown dispatches, his readers came to expect vividly rendered high adventure from him. Indeed, he wrote colorful vignettes about locales from Algeria to Russia. In his memoirs, he recalled an early adventure with his friend Dr. Strauss and a "person of gentlemanly manners" with a shadowy past and boundless optimism about his chances at the game of trente-et-quarante.*

In 1851, this mysterious stranger, whom Sala gave the apt pseudonym "Mr. Hopeful," approached Sala with a proposition: He had an unimpeachable system for beating the gaming tables. Since he only had £50 but needed £150 to put the plan into practice, he suggested that Sala could venture the additional £100 and take two thirds of the profits. With Dr. Strauss along as a disinterested observer, the trio set off for the Rhenish gambling and health resort of Aachen. Resting place of Charlemagne, it was also one of the few places in Europe where trente-et-quarante was legal.

After a long sea and rail journey, the prospectors arrived in Aachen and headed directly for the famous gaming salon. Mr. Hopeful set upon the tables immediately, placing bets with such intensity that he only paused to pass his winnings to Sala for safekeeping. When the croupiers closed the casino at midnight, Sala guessed that his pockets were bursting with far more than £150. The next day, they returned, and Hopeful's success continued. When he was ahead £800, though, hubris got the best of him, and he elected to switch to another system, equally infallible. It wasn't. Hopeful lost back most of their winnings before returning to his original system which, alas, did not turn his luck. All was soon lost. Sala, figuring he could do no worse, endeavored to try his luck at roulette, at which he quickly won, and just as quickly lost, £50. Sala had to pawn his watch, scarf pin, and rings to satisfy the trio's hotel bill and secure passage as far as Paris.

Mr. Hopeful allowed Sala to pay his hotel charges but resolutely refused to accept fare back to Paris. Allowing that his rashness in abandoning his "perfect system" had ruined them, he maintained that, with a few gold coins, he could just as quickly restore their fortunes. Sala handed him two gold coins, and after a vague letter received two weeks later asking for more money, Mr. Hopeful was heard from no more.

When writing his memoirs, Sala savored the naïveté that had left him penniless in Aachen; the town's famous hot springs reminded him of the hot water his blind faith had gotten him into. But, he wrote later, "at twenty-two years of age it does not matter much if you have been temporarily ruined at the gaming table." Sala would later return to the Rhine, drawn, like so many others, to the possibility of vacationing among the continent's elite and chasing fortune in lavish gaming salons. The hope that sprung eternal at the tables was just as sure a motivation for thousands of trips to gambling spas as the medicinal waters that bubbled forth from the earth.

9

Seeking the Cure

◆ ◆ ◆

SPA GAMBLING DEFINES EUROPE

Across Europe, the turmoil of the French Revolution marked the end of the ancien régime. Gambling faced similar tumult. The 1837 French prohibition augured a century of contraction for casino-style gambling across the continent. As other industrializing nations of Western Europe became more sensitive to the financial disorder unleashed by unlimited betting and wagering, they also moved to suppress it. But gambling survived, and even prospered, in the unlikeliest of places—health resorts.

Initially, most of those who sojourned to the spas were legitimately ill, and the therapeutic waters were plausibly the best recuperative option, given the current state of medicine. But soon, spending time at a spa became de rigueur for those with sufficient wealth to do so. After they became the Continent's chic resorts, virtually anyone of social standing summered at one of them. The bored, healthy vacationers eagerly took up gambling to pass the time. Once home to those seeking the cure for various physical afflictions, the spas—and the wild gambling that took place within them—became notorious as the cure for nothing more serious than excess wealth.

The first spa town to gain acclaim as both a health resort and an aristocratic gathering place was also the oldest. The town of Spa has since given its name generically to anyplace where healthy waters are the attraction, from aristocratic enclaves like Canyon Ranch to apartment community Jacuzzis. Spa is nestled in a green valley in the hills of the Ardennes in Liège, today a province in eastern Belgium that can rightly claim an ancient lineage: Pliny the Elder praised its bubbling waters as curative of fevers and infections in the first century A.D.

Spa's modern vogue dates to the sixteenth century. In 1559, Dr. Gilbert Lymborch wrote *Of the Acidulous Fountains of the Ardennes Forest and principally those found at Spa*. Despite its cumbersome title, this volume was quite the page turner—translated into several languages, it was widely read throughout Europe. The book gave Europeans a plausible medical justification for venturing to Spa for a convalescent vacation. Attracting visitors from throughout Europe (particularly Britons) due to the religious tolerance of the ruling prince-bishop, the principality of Liège became a haven for both Protestants and Catholics during the religious strife that marked the era.

By the beginning of the eighteenth century, Spa was well established as a health resort, thanks to the ingenuity and perseverance of the town's promoters, who even turned the decrepitude of the infamously muddy streets to their advantage. Cottage industries sprang up to make and sell oversized shoes and handmade walking sticks that allowed visitors to navigate the rubble-strewn thoroughfares. The town fathers probably kept the streets in deliberate disrepair to foster this industry. Typically, visitors awoke between five and seven in the morning, donned their shoes, grabbed their walking sticks, and trundled off to one of the three springs. Spa artisans eagerly sold them small watch-sized dials numbered one through twenty. As the visitor drank a glass of spring water, she rotated the dial to mark it, thus keeping track of her water consumption. Few were without another local item, a small box filled with orange peels, peppermint, or other spices to flavor the famous waters.

The healthy waters were the chief attraction, but a host of other amusements were easy to find. Strolling musicians serenaded visitors with melodious strains. Acrobats, jugglers, and tightrope walkers dazzled their audiences, as did ventriloquists and sleight-of-hand operators. Other attractions seem to have been taken directly from a sideshow: Armless, legless, and kneeless specimens of humanity performed various acts for the curious. Dwarves, strongmen, and prodigies rounded out the display.

The scene would not have been complete without gambling, and professional gamblers perched near the springs, offering mercantile games like faro, hazard, and *biribi*. Operating outdoors when the weather permitted, and moving indoors to private houses when it didn't, gamblers earned incredible profits during the fashionable summer season, when throngs of well-off health-seekers lounged near the springs. But others profited as well. It was reported that opportunists prowled the gambling grounds, some using wax-tipped canes to pick up dropped coins, while others trained dogs to leap forward and snatch up any loose change.

To provide visitors with more elegant—and presumably more private—gambling facilities, the reigning prince-bishop, Cardinal Jean-Théodore of Bavaria, announced in 1762 plans for a two-story casino named the Redoute, the French translation of Ridotto. Lacking perhaps in originality, the cardinal was certainly farsighted: He planned for the Redoute to host balls, concerts, and plays, as well as have elegant gambling rooms. A temporary structure opened in 1765, and four years later the permanent Redoute debuted. It was widely acclaimed as a hall fit for kings. With two gambling rooms, a reading room, and a ballroom, the Redoute offered its guests suitably lavish facilities for aristocratic entertainment.

Others began diversifying Spa's gambling. In 1773, the duke of Lauzun and Count Branicki began running horse races on a track located between Spa and Verviers. They modeled the races on those being conducted at Newmarket, the home of the British Jockey Club. This racing enterprise, the first such one on the Continent, was successful.

Another facility competed more directly with the Redoute. In 1770, the Vaux Hall opened on a rise that commanded a superior view of Spa and its surroundings. With an elegant ballroom and two gaming salons, the Vaux Hall (named after the Thames gardens in an apparent attempt to appeal to British visitors) rivaled the Redoute in its splendor. Predictably, the proprietors of the Redoute, chagrined by the loss of their monopoly, demanded satisfaction from the reigning prince-bishop, Count François de Velbrück. The count responded with an edict that combined the wisdom of Solomon with naked self-interest. He commanded that the two feuding companies unite and share the profits from the two casinos equally, minus a thirty-percent cut to be annually delivered to the prince-bishop. The casino managers combined their operations and, with heavy hearts, sent their annual tribute to Velbrück.

A group of British visitors opened the English Club in 1765. Although it did not admit the general public, the owners of the Redoute and Vauxhall resented its siphoning of gambling money away from them, and they continually petitioned the prince-bishop to suppress it. Despite the protests, the English Club persisted for about twenty years. This club emulated the gentlemen's clubs of London's West End, which were then beginning to flourish.

On August 13, 1785, a catastrophic fire destroyed an entire wing of the Redoute. This was, however, only the beginning of the disaster. Fanned by the winds, burning playing cards were blown to the southeast, where they set fire to as many as fifty thatch-roofed houses, killing three people and causing widespread destruction. Though this might have seemed to the pious to be a signal of divine disapproval of gambling, the Redoute soon continued as before, with the burned section promptly rebuilt.

The Spa casinos were renowned for their haughty croupiers and for the swarms of adventurers they attracted. One critic wrote in 1784 that the croupiers grandiosely styled themselves "captain," "gendarme," or "hussar," while they rudely dealt games with a vulgarity unbecoming such ostensibly noble gentlemen. On the opposite side of the tables, cheaters often attempted to introduce loaded dice or marked cards, though they were usually discovered before much damage could be done. In 1779, a scandal rocked the Redoute when it was discovered that one of its trusted employees had been introducing marked cards into play, allowing a confederate to make off with tremendous sums. The anger of the Redoute's managers was apparently mitigated by the fact that the offending official was a close relative of one of the casino's directors. The casino did not press charges or even fire him, but merely reprimanded the cheater and removed him from his position of responsibility.

By 1789, faro, hazard, and *biribi* had largely been replaced by roulette and trente-et-quarante. The latter, also known as *rouge et noir*, was played in France as early as 1650 but first became popular at Spa around 1780. This game, whose name means "thirty and forty," is rather simple, with only four possible bets, and it holds a razor-thin house advantage, making it one of the least unbalanced mercantile games ever offered. Even during its heyday it was rarely found outside of Europe, and it never developed any traction in American casinos, legal or illegal.

To play, the player places a bet on *rouge, noir, couleur,* or *inverse*. The croupier then lays out two rows of cards marked red and black, dealing a standard fifty-two-card deck from a six-deck shoe. Court cards count for ten, and all other cards hold their face value. When both rows total more than thirty, the game is over. The dealer then pays those who bet on the row that is closer to thirty. If the rows are tied, the money is returned to players, unless both rows equal thirty-one, in which case the house takes half of the wager, although players can buy insurance against this outcome. The *couleur* bet pays if the first card of the winning row matches that row's color (for example, a diamond or heart in *rouge*), while *inverse* is a bet for the opposite.

Most of the game's bets, then, are simple either/or propositions. The house's only advantage comes with the half loss on tied thirty-ones. Roulette, which evolved at about the same time as trente-et-quarante, offered similarly clear-cut wagers, but the addition of one or two zeroes gave the house a stronger edge. Quicker than hazard and faro, both games gave players rapid decisions, and neither required a whit of skill: Minus an unbalanced wheel, marked cards, or a crooked dealer, there was no way to use logic or reasoning to place a wager.

Though it was politically and administratively distinct from France as part of the principality of Liège, Spa was no more immune from the turmoil of the French Revolution than the neighborhoods of Paris. In Spa, the revolutionary ferment centered on a casino. In 1784, a Liège businessman named

The game of trente-et-quarante as it was played in the nineteenth century. It was, for much of the century, the second-most popular game in Europe, trailing only roulette.

Noël Levoz flouted the prince-bishop's imposition of a gaming monopoly and began building his own fashionable gambling salon. He hoped to force the managers of the existing casinos to buy him out. They refused and asked the current prince-bishop, Prince Constantine de Hoensbroek, to close Levoz's large, richly appointed gambling room.

In 1787, anticipating a move by the prince-bishop to force him out, Levoz began stockpiling weapons and ammunition in his salon. Hoensbroek then dispatched troops who, following his orders, seized the arms and occupied the casino's environs. This episode might have been written off as nothing more than a sovereign exercising his rights to enforce a monopoly, but two years later, in the summer of 1789, revolution was in the air. Hoensbroek's high-handed action against Levoz had stirred up liberal resentment against him, and on August 18, 1789, the progressive citizens of Liège finally took action. As peasants from surrounding towns stormed Spa, causing aristocratic guests to flee, rebel burghers and artisans in Liège declared a revolutionary republic. The prince-bishop abdicated before taking flight in terror.

This excitement hardly boded well for the hospitality industry of Spa. But after the Holy Roman Emperor, Joseph II of Austria, occupied the principality, refugees from France began to pour into Spa, providing a boon for the local economy. The expatriate "aristos," many of whom had escaped with fortunes in gold coins, awaited the day that they could return to France. But on September 18, 1794, the Austrian army suffered a decisive defeat at the battle of Sprimont, and the armies of the old regime abandoned Liège to the onrushing revolutionary forces. The émigrés immediately began to flee, desperate to escape the guillotine that surely awaited them should they fall into republican hands. Some nobles, unable to carry their gold-laden trunks, hid them in the surrounding forests, inspiring legends of hidden fortunes.

Liège was officially annexed to France the next year, and it never recovered from the disaster of the revolution. Those with the means left in search of better prospects, and with the tourist trade effectively ended, those left behind begged and foraged for food amid empty inns and vacant streets. Many starved to death. In 1802, the Treaty of Amiens gave momentary respite to the fighting that had disrupted Spa's trade, and visitors returned in small numbers. But when the fighting resumed again, even that trickle ceased. A catastrophic fire in 1807 destroyed nearly the entire town. Though most of the attractions, including the Redoute, were rebuilt, the town was doomed to obscurity. Even after the inauguration of peace with the Congress of Vienna in 1815, Spa held few attractions; though some visitors came and gambled perfunctorily, their numbers dwindled progressively.

For the next several decades, Spa's gambling unmistakably declined. The Redoute seemed dominated by mutual suspicion, as both croupiers and players now made no pretense of maintaining a constant vigil against cheating. A travel guide of the period declared that "the ball spins more slowly at roulette—the cards are dealt more gingerly at trente-et-quarante here than elsewhere. Nothing must be done quickly, lest somebody on one side or other should try to do [wrong to] somebody else." While the promenades and ballrooms remained pleasant enough, visitors to the gaming tables were warned to guard against the hustlers and opportunists who congregated there.

As railroads took travelers to other destinations quickly and cheaply, they bypassed Spa, and the town did not get a direct line until 1854. In the interim, a host of more fashionable mineral springs, particularly in today's Germany, had usurped Spa's place as the gathering point of polite and adventurous European society. Located along the banks of the Rhine River or in the hills of the Black Forest, these spas were eminently suited to the spirit of the Romantic era, and as the "Pearl of the Ardennes" lost its luster, they quickly outshone the original Spa.

German spa towns date to the Roman era. Most German towns with *Bad* in their names were, at one point, best known for their "baths." One such town,

Baden-Baden, on the Oos River in the western foothills of the Black Forest, was famous as a health retreat as long ago as the early third century A.D. Ruins of Roman baths, long forgotten, would be discovered in the nineteenth century, when Baden-Baden was approaching the zenith of its Romantic renown.

Though the original Roman baths had long been lost, Baden-Baden had managed to recover from the destruction of the Thirty Years' War by the middle of the eighteenth century. At that time, Baden was a small market town still encircled with walls. The chief business was the breeding and slaughter of pigs, whose carcasses were cleaned in the steaming hot spring waters, lending the village a distinctly unpleasant odor in the summer. All in all, it was an unlikely spot to take a vacation. Still, by the beginning of the next century, at Margrave Karl Friedrich's behest, a bathing commission had made serious progress toward establishing Baden as a legitimate resort.

Licensed gambling in the town was first recorded in 1748, though it may have been going on for years previously. Gambling was then authorized only in the back rooms of inns, suggesting that the town was more of a stopover than a destination resort. Later, efforts to establish more grandiose gambling facilities commenced. In 1765, a building called the Promenade House opened; in it, the town granted a Frenchman named Chevilly a gambling concession. By 1801, several local hotels had gambling rooms; commissioners of the Margrave observed the proceedings and collected a tax, which financed improvements to the baths. A second salon opened in a former Jesuit college in 1809. The operator paid a fee of 700 louis for the right to run games from May to October. These two stand-alone gambling houses, together with the gambling rooms in hotels, paid concession money into a special fund dedicated to new construction at Baden.

The resort received a boost in 1810, when author Johann Peter Hebel, one of the most popular German poets of the early nineteenth century, recuperated from his ill health at Baden-Baden. He wrote widely distributed descriptions of the attractions at the spa: gustatory extravagance, pleasant small talk with distinguished fellow health-seekers, and the exhilaration of roulette. Hebel wrote in a letter that "one lives in a completely different world" in Baden, surrounded by "glamour, high living, laziness, gambling for money, professors, along with comedians." The food and refreshments, prepared in the latest French style, were both excellent and inexpensive, and the service was impeccable. Hebel concluded that, while everything might not have been princely, it was at least "à la Paris."

Hebel's rhapsodies convinced many to take the cure at Baden. So did diplomatic exigencies. As the map of Europe was redrawn in 1814, Europe's top diplomats and kingmakers met at the Congress of Vienna. Baden-Baden stood about halfway between Vienna and Paris, Napoléon's just-conquered capital, and was a frequent stop for those shuttling between the two cities. Thanks to its central location, the resort was easily accessible to France, Scandinavia, and even Russia. The old town walls were torn down and villas and chalets sprang up across the Oos Valley. The last of the pig breeders exchanged their hogpens for hostelries. Suddenly, Baden-Baden was the most fashionable spa in Europe.

In 1824, another gambling salon, the Conversation House, replaced the Promenade House. Antoine Chabert, who had formerly owned a club in Paris's Palais Royale, received the concession in return for an annual rent of 27,000 gulden. Chabert directed both the casino and its restaurant and presided over Baden-Baden's chief gambling house until 1837, by which time he had succeeded in doubling the town's annual visitation to a still-small sixteen thousand. Chabert parlayed his limited success at Baden-Baden into the management of casinos in Wiesbaden, Ems, Schlangenbad, and Schwalbach.

Meanwhile, another wily operator had been making his mark in Paris. Born in 1778, Jacques Bénazet worked as a court clerk before becoming a lawyer and also managed a Lyons theater. Asked in 1824 to adjudicate a dispute between the two supervisors of Paris's licensed gambling, Boursault and Chalabre, Bénazet did more than simply split the difference: He slid himself into a share of the lucrative office. Three years later, he claimed the sole proprietorship of the right to oversee the legal, licensed gambling conducted in seven clubs throughout Paris. In 1835, Benazet's concession was renewed. By this time, he had acquired ownership shares in two of the city's most fashionable gaming rooms, Frascati and the Cercle des Étrangers. Nothing, it seemed, could stop him.

However, as adroit as Bénazet had proven himself in monopolizing the supervision of legal Paris gaming, he was no match for the resolve of the French Chamber of Deputies. The seven legal casinos of Paris had been incredibly profitable for Bénazet and the French government, earning between 6 and 9 million francs a year. The downside of this success was the fact that many prominent fortunes were lost on the green baize. As part of a worldwide turn away from legal gambling, whose echoes were felt even in the United States, the French deputies resolved on June 17, 1836, that the gambling clubs of France would close on December 31, 1837.

French gamblers manically plunged into the clubs during the last days of 1837, hoping to get one final shot at beating the trente-et-quarante and roulette tables. The clubs opened one last time on December 31 in near pandemonium.

Bénazet, fearing a robbery or riot, had already dispatched detachments of the police and National Guard to maintain order; he doubled the force on the final day. At 3:00 P.M., he began letting in gamblers intent on one last fling; three hours later, he had to prematurely shutter the most popular Palais Royale club after a workman committed suicide there. At ten that evening, another gambler, distraught that he would be denied the chance to win back his previous losses, shot himself outside Bénazet's Frascati, which was then closed only after the police, with great difficulty, cleared the rooms. Finally, at midnight, Bénazet ordered the police to sweep the crowds from the other clubs and, locking the doors, ended the French regime of legal gaming clubs. In the streets, assembled crowds jeered, hooted, and jubilantly screamed at the swarms of ejected gamblers, prostitutes, and adventurers. It was the end of an era.

Bézanet, however, was too clever to be left out in the cold. In October 1838, he purchased the Baden-Baden gambling concession for a 40,000-franc annual lease and an additional yearly levy of 75,000 florins for the upkeep of the surrounding grounds. Previously, Baden-Baden had been a well-regarded, if somewhat quiet, resort. No more. Owing to the sudden dearth of legal gambling in France and aided by Bézanet's astute stewardship, Baden-Baden's popularity—and revenues—exploded. By 1872, the casinos had increased their annual payments to the town to 550,000 francs, not a hard thing to do when the estimated take was 2.5 million francs a year.

Baden-Baden was so successful because Bénazet knew his market. Aware that most gamblers preferred the French language (a Frenchman, he was by no means unbiased), he ensured that, in his small corner of the Black Forest at least, French was the lingua franca, and Baden-Baden became, quite by design, a virtual suburb of Paris. The latest Parisian fashions and hairstyles were seen, restaurant menus appeared in French, and Bénazet ensured that Parisians could come to Baden without having completely left Paris behind. Masquerades, chic evening parties, and piano recitals occupied the guests when they were not gambling.

The shrewd Frenchman did quite well for himself, residing in a palatial villa, surrounded by all of the trappings of wealth. After Bénazet died in 1848 at the age of seventy, his son Edward took his place as Baden-Baden's gambling czar. Under him, a longtime dealer and supervisor known as Old Father Martin continued to oversee the day-to-day casino operations. Martin became something of an institution in French gambling. Originally a dealer at Paris's Frascati from the early years of the nineteenth century and brought along by Bénazet in 1838, Martin continued his supervisory role at Baden-Baden into the 1860s, recounting tales of past gamblers for all who would listen, unimpressed by current celebrity. In 1860, for example, all of Baden-Baden turned out for the arrival of French emperor Napoléon III, whom the Prussian prince regent William was feting in a three-day state visit. When asked why he was not hurrying to the train station to see the emperor's formal reception by an assembly of German nobles, Martin groused that he was already familiar with the leader: "Napoléon . . . Napoléon . . . Wait a minute . . . Bonaparte, isn't that right? Ah, yes, I remember him from Paris—he still owes the bank twenty-five louis."

Edward did more than preserve the venerable Martin in his role as supervisor: He actively added to the offerings at Baden-Baden. In 1855 he expanded the Conversation House, adding four elegant new rooms. Three years later, he opened a racecourse at Iffezheim, a town seven miles west of Baden-Baden. With three grandstands catering to visiting nobles, track officials and members of the local Jockey Club, and the general public, the course was an immediate success. When races began each year at the end of August, Baden-Baden was filled to capacity with eager followers of the turf, who remained throughout September.

Bénazet the younger, like his father, masterfully promoted his gambling destination. He ensured favorable press coverage of Baden-Baden and its races as far away as the United States and plied visitors with voluminous tracts that expostulated the grandeur of the small resort. Newspapers and magazines in French, German, and English spread the word that, for those who wanted healthy relaxation or the excitement of betting at trente-et-quarante or on the horses, Baden-Baden was not to be missed.

Generally speaking, the *kurzeit*, or cure season, ran from May to October. During these months, the restaurants, promenades, and gaming rooms were filled with an assortment of vacationing merchants, idling nobility, professional sharpers, and assorted hopefuls. All of Europe was equally represented, with English, Spanish, Italian, Dutch, French, German, Russian, and Scandinavian visitors outdoing other each in fashion and better in the gaming salons. A visiting Englishman described the resort in 1840 as surpassing the famous Crockford's in renown and embracing "all bearing the semblance of gentility and conducting themselves with propriety." Patrons only had to remove their hats and extinguish their pipes and cigars. Amid the dazzling chandeliers and golden pillars, players orbited the roulette and trente-et-quarante tables, laying siege to the casino's fortune with alternating moods of patient determination and passionate excitement.

From the 1830s until the 1870s, under the leadership of Jacques Bénazet and his son
Edward, Baden-Baden was perhaps Europe's most popular gambling spa.
This image of the main gambling room dates from the 1930s.

Though most players were men, several women distinguished themselves as particularly ardent gamblers. Some became celebrities. A Russian princess, for example, was noted for her large bets, though (a chronicler noted with disapproval) she had the ill-breeding to actually look anxious when luck turned against her and she lost thousands. The wife of an Italian ex-minister, however, exhibited model deportment, "smirking when she wins, and smirking when she loses." Her habiliment matched her play, and women gathered around to see what outrageous gown she would wear next. The most famous Baden-Baden female gambler, though, was Léonie Leblanc. Crowds gathered simply to watch her bet the house maximum, 6,000 francs, on each hand of trente-et-quarante.

Most of those who crowded into the Conversation House simply enjoyed the plush surroundings and took their chances at the tables as best they could. Some were not so easily satisfied. Henri Rochefort, a French politico and journalist, lost heavily at trente-et-quarante while visiting Baden-Baden in 1866, and he noted, with acid pen, that the opulence of the gaming salons indicated that the odds were stacked against the player:

> If the public were not such simpletons . . . people would make
> the mental comment that the luxury flaunted in these casinos, the

percentage paid to the political authorities who tolerate them, and the expensive theatrical performances given in them are proof positive that the player has not the slightest chance of winning a single penny.

If the proprietors of these highly ornate ogres' dens were not so certain of their clients' gullibility, they would house their croupiers in roughly whitewashed barns and appear in the gambling rooms with clothes in tatters. This would at least be an attempt to per- suade passersby that the players win so heavily as to reduce the staff at the casino to the direst poverty. But the flaunting of this daily outlay . . . can mean but one thing: "What a lot of money we must get from you, if we can spend all this and yet have ten times as much left for ourselves."

Rochefort realized that the inherent mathematical imbalance in mercantile games gave the house a formidable advantage. So did most other players, but few cared.

Perhaps some players plunged so recklessly with the odds against them because their wealth had not been particularly hard earned. Of the many for- tunes squandered at Baden-Baden, few are as famous as that of Hesse- Kassel, the northern part of the medieval German-speaking earldom of Hesse. In a less than a century, its landgraves acquired vast sums from merce- nary expeditions, then lost their prosperity and ultimately their land—chiefly because of the tables at Baden-Baden.

The tale began with Friedrich II, who became landgrave of Hesse-Kassel in 1760. Hesse-Kassel, a rocky land dominated by mountains and forests, was perpetually undeveloped. Beginning in the seventeenth century, its landgraves began to hire out their army as a way of gaining revenue that could not be wrung from the uncooperative land. Friedrich II, with no less a desire to live in style, continued the practice. Most notoriously, he rented about seventeen thousand of his soldiers to Britain's George III in the momentous year 1776. George promptly sent them to the rebellious American colonies, where, along with other German forces, they made up one third of the Crown's troops. Though despised by Patriots as mercenaries, the soldiers themselves saw little of George's lucre. Usually victims of impressment, petty criminals, or debtors forced into army service, they fought to suppress the American Revolution for little or no pay. While the Hessian troops suffered and died in America, the landgrave pocketed millions and lived in extravagance.

Wilhelm IX succeeded Friedrich as landgrave on the latter's death in

1784. If anything, he was even more despised than his father. Not content with the "blood money" garnered from his father's Hessian regiments, Wilhelm was nothing if not inventive in looking for a profit. He made thousands from cornering the grain market, but simple speculation was just a start. Despised as "hard, haughty, egotistical, tyrannical, and sordidly avaricious," he went so far as to turn his own castle at Wilhemsbad into a hotel and casino.

Wilhelm was just as narcissistic as he was greedy. Believing his grandeur to eclipse that of a garden-variety landgrave, he sought to be named a king. At an 1803 German congress, Wilhelm ridiculously achieved his ambition for advancement; though it did not make him a king, the gathering did give him a promotion, declaring him Wilhelm I, elector of Hesse; Wilhelm joined three other newly minted electors, including the margrave of Baden. Prince-electors of the Holy Roman Empire had once formed the electoral college that selected the Holy Roman Emperor. By the time that Wilhelm ascended to the office, however, it had become largely ceremonial, and the chief perquisite was that he could now style himself "Most Serene Highness," to distinguish himself from lesser princes, who were mere Serene Highnesses.

Wilhelm's triumph was short-lived. The Holy Roman Empire was abolished in 1806 after Napoléon's victories, and he never got to cast a vote. Though he didn't do any real electing, he obviously enjoyed the prestige of his title. Unable to elevate himself into a kingship, he remained "elector of Hesse" to get one over on his cousins, the landgrave of Hesse-Homburg and the grand duke of Hesse-Darmstadt. His son, Wilhelm II, succeeded him in 1821. After the excitement of the pan-European uprising of 1830, during which Wilhelm granted his subjects a constitution, he retired from his administrative duties, turning over affairs of state to his son, Friedrich Wilhelm.

In retirement, with an abundance of leisure and money and a dearth of matters to otherwise occupy him, Wilhelm turned to gambling. When Bénazet inaugurated his reign at Baden-Baden in 1838, Wilhelm quickly established himself as a regular. He gained a reputation as the most fervent gambler in residence—an honor probably more exalted than that of elector—and his only disappointment was that the gaming rooms closed in October. Not willing to wait until the start of the cure season in May, he rejoiced when, in 1843, the landgrave of Hesse-Homburg permitted a year-round casino to open in Bad Homburg, nearly in the elector's backyard. Wilhelm ultimately lost most of his fortune there. To pay back a loan graciously extended to him, he gave the casino's proprietors forty orange trees, then a rare and valuable treasure. He died in 1847, having lost at least 100,000 florins in Homburg alone.

Friedrich Wilhelm, naturally, had a jaundiced view of the Homburg casino; most of his patrimony had ended up in the pockets of its proprietors. He unsuccessfully argued for the return of the orange trees and bided his time. When the casino's owners asked permission to build a railroad to Frankfurt across Friedrich Wilhelm's land, he resolutely refused. The railroad was eventually built along a circuitous bypass route that cost considerably more than the direct line originally proposed. The elector further found his revenge by competing against Homburg. In 1849, he connected Hanau to Frankfurt by rail, then extended the track to the castle at Wilhelmsbad, which had long been a watering place and had been a casino during the reign of his grandfather.

Friedrich Wilhelm overhauled the castle, which had fallen into disrepair, and reopened the hotel casino, which had rooms for gambling, reading, and conversation on the castle's ground floor, and undersized guest-rooms on the second. Outside, visitors could take the waters, listen to public concerts, or wander about the grounds at their leisure. Despite the elector's efforts, visitation to Wilhelmsbad declined throughout the 1850s, and when the rail line from Frankfurt to Homburg finally opened in 1860, it dropped off sharply. The castle closed in 1865, with Friedrich Wilhelm's effort to regain in his own casino what had been lost in others a failure. The next year, as a consequence of choosing the wrong side (Austria) in the Austro-Prussian war, the elector lost his lands, which were annexed by victorious Prussia. Since the elector left no heir, the line of Hesse-Kassel ended with his death in 1875, less than a century after his great-grandfather had profited from the American Revolution. Though the passing of many fortunes into the coffers of the Baden-Baden casinos might be lamented, this was not one of them.

As competition from other Rhine towns mounted, Baden-Baden launched a counteroffensive. In 1862, the town opened a new theater suited for plays, ballet, and opera, and Edward Bénazet attracted the brightest stars of the musical world to better lure gamblers to the Conversation House, located conveniently near the theater. Hector Berlioz conducted the premier of his opera *Beatrice and Benedict* to open the theater, and other noted composers followed. Some, like Johannes Brahms, preferred walks in the countryside to the clangor of the Conversation House. Still, he composed some of his best-known pieces while at Baden-Baden, including the Trio for Piano, Violin, and Horn in E-flat, op. 40, Sextet no. 2 for Two Violins, Two Violas, and Two Cellos in G Major, op. 32, and parts of many others.

Other performers provided Bénazet with a double bonus; engaged at the theater to draw visitors, they also lost a considerable portion of their pay at the tables. Jacques Offenbach, composer of *Orpheus in the Underworld* and *La Vie Parisienne,* directed the Baden-Baden theater in 1868 and 1869, and he was such a successful draw—and prolific loser at roulette—that the rival town of Homburg sought to lure him away. Johann Strauss, paid 2,000 francs a performance, conducted his waltzes in the theater in 1872, and lost not only his Baden-Baden salary but most of his savings from his earlier triumphant American tour.

But the good times did not last forever. In December 1867, Edward Bénazet died while on his winter holiday at Nice. At his wife's suggestion, the Baden government appointed Bénazet's nephew and brother-in-law Jacques Dupressoir to run the gambling concession. Although Baden enjoyed a boom year in 1869 with over sixty thousand visitors, its day was passing. A profound shift in leisure travel was under way: No longer fired by the Romantic visions of Goethe or Shelley, the privileged were forsaking the Black Forest for the French Riviera. The prohibition of gambling by Prussia, effective December 31, 1872, only gave a more dramatic finale to Baden-Baden's first career as a gambling resort. The roulette tables would be stilled until 1933 when, in a quite different world, the Nazi government relegalized gambling and set the stage for Baden-Baden to reemerge as a leading German casino town. But for those seeking the cure in the Victorian age, Baden-Baden's day was done.

Russians were among the most celebrated visitors to the Rhine resorts. Countess Sophie Kissileff, who first appeared at Homburg in 1852, was long the most notorious. A common joke ran that she gambled only once a day: from eleven in the morning until eleven at night. Her husband, unwilling to brook her gambling obsession any longer, divorced her, and not even a papal edict that she cease playing could convince her to give up roulette. All told, she lost the equivalent of an estimated $4 million at Homburg, a considerable sum then and now.

Not all Russians were as gambling mad as Kissileff; many vacationers and expatriates escaped the Rhine resorts with little more than perfunctory attention to the gaming tables. Others didn't gamble at all. Nicholai Gogol, the writer best known for the novel *Dead Souls,* forswore the gambling tables for soul-searching walks through Baden-Baden's countryside. In Russia itself, the social game of whist became popular for a while. Whist gave late nineteenth-century westernizing Russians a recreation shared by the elites of Europe.

It is usually inadvisable to generalize, but even Russians felt their gambling was often distinguished by a peculiarly Slavic fatalism, and most of them tended toward the outrageous betting of Countess Kissileff rather than the quiet introspection of Gogol. Count Leo Tolstoy, on a tour of Europe in the summer of 1857, stopped at Baden-Baden, where he discovered roulette. Playing on the first evening for small sums, he spent the bulk of the next day at the Conversation House vainly trying to conquer the wheel. He lost all of his own money, plus two loans from an obliging Frenchman, and penned desperate letters to several relatives and friends, begging for backup. His countess cousin Alexandra Tolstoy sent him money, and the writer Ivan Turgenev became concerned enough to travel to Baden-Baden himself. Upon arriving, he lent Tolstoy even more money, which the count predictably lost at the tables. Shortly after Turgenev departed, Tolstoy himself left Baden-Baden in shame, cursing his inability to control his gambling.

Turgenev was more successful at taming the gaming demon. He divided most of his later life between Paris and Baden-Baden, where he lived in a well-appointed house in generous comfort. Turgenev set his novel *Smoke* in Baden-Baden. In the novel, he described the social milieu of the large Russian community and the mixture of French-, Italian-, German-, and English-speakers that gave Baden its distinctive cosmopolitan character. Turgenev assisted many of the Russian émigrés and travelers who had stayed in the Conversation House longer than they should have. Some were grateful for Turgenev's help—Tolstoy, for example, remained a friend for years, and on his deathbed Turgenev penned a final expression of affection for the count.

Turgenev did not share such warm feelings for another great Russian novelist, Fyodor Dostoyevsky, who was obsessed by gambling during what may have been his greatest creative period, 1862–1872. When he was exiled to Siberia in the 1850s, Dostoyevsky gambled often, usually losing. In 1862, he made his first trip to Wiesbaden, where he won a sizable sum. He visited Baden-Baden and Homburg in 1863, losing back all he had previously won; having lost his last gulden, he was only rescued when his onetime paramour Paulina Suslova pawned her jewelry and sent him cash. Though his bets were never that large, he played in a state of grim agitation, his creative mind exponentially magnifying every win and loss.

In 1864, back in Russia, haunted by the death of his wife and the clamoring creditors of his dead brother (whose debts he had inherited), Dostoyevsky signed a contract to deliver a novel to the publisher Selovski by November 1866. Should he miss the deadline, he would be fined substantially and forfeit the rights to all of his already published books. In early October, the situation looked dire. His masterpiece *Crime and Punishment* was as yet unfinished. The forlorn poverty of the protagonist Raskolnikov likely is rendered so well

because the author himself was keenly desperate. To satisfy Selovski, he dic-
tated, in four days, a novel to a young stenographer, Anna Grigorievna
Snitkin. Dostoyevsky beat his deadline, soon married the twenty-year-old
Snitkin, and left for the ages a classic portrait of the hope and despair of an
impetuous slave to chance, *The Gambler.*

Writing *The Gambler* did not solve Dostoyevsky's financial problems or
cathartically purge him of his gambling addiction. He fled Russia one step
ahead of his creditors and embarked on a European tour that naturally took
him along the Rhine. He was soon back at the tables again, losing steadily.
On July 4, 1867, he entered Baden-Baden, setting up house with his young
wife above a smithy, where the din of business must have been less than relaxing. His wife wrote in her diary that his appearance, red faced and with
bloodshot eyes, frightened her: His destructive passion for roulette caused her
to cry for hours, cursing gambling and Baden-Baden.

Despite his hideous appearance, the novelist enjoyed himself—at least
initially. Starting with 100 francs, he had won 4,000 in three days. Ignoring
his wife's pleas to content himself with such good fortune, Dostoyevsky held
out hope that he could continue to parlay his winnings into financial security.
His own success paled in comparison to the winnings of others, and although
he logically knew he should leave, he could not:

> Apart from my own gains, I saw every day how the other gam-
> blers won from 20,000 to 30,000 francs (one never sees anyone
> lose). Why should those others do better than I? I need the
> money more than they do. I risked again, and lost. I lost not only
> what I had won, but also my own money down to the last far-
> thing. I got feverishly excited, and lost all the time. Then I began
> to pawn my garments. Anna Grigovrievna pawned her last, her
> very last possession.

After they had lost everything, including the funds to leave Baden, the Dos-
toyevskys' landlady raised their rent. Dostoyevsky began writing frantic letters
to friends, begging more money to secure passage from the Rhineland.

With no other help forthcoming, Dostoyevsky reluctantly sought to get a
loan from his fellow novelist Turgenev, who was enjoying life in his villa,
oblivious to Dostoyevsky's suffering above the smithy. Though the pair
shared a common language and occupation, political, cultural, and artistic
differences made them enemies. Dostoyevsky had been vocal in his critique
of *Smoke,* perhaps because Turgenev might have used him as the model for

Bindasov, a boring ingrate who quadrupled a borrowed stake of 100 rubles and left the Conversation House without repaying his benefactor: He had not forgotten that a few years earlier he had lent Dostoyevsky the equivalent of $50 dollars to play roulette at Wiesbaden, and that the money had never been repaid. Dostoyevsky would later get revenge by satirizing Turgenev in *The Possessed*, but for the moment he had more a pressing need: money.

On the morning of July 10, Dostoyevsky gingerly approached Turgenev at breakfast. The heavyweights warily circled each other, trading verbal jabs and attempting to force the other into a breach of etiquette. Turgenev began to expansively declaim on his contempt for all things Russian (Dostoyevsky was a confirmed nationalist) and the merits of atheism (Dostoyevsky was devout Christian). The German-loving Turgenev declared that Russians were "bound to crawl in the dust before the Germans" and that any attempt to build a uniquely Russian culture was folly and pigheadedness. Dostoyevsky declared the Germans "swindlers and rogues," and an "evil and dishonest" nation. Turgenev, reminding his visitor that he considered himself an adoptive German, considered the last a personal affront, and the two parted company icily.[*]

Fyodor and Anna finally escaped Baden-Baden on August 23, though he continued to gamble, usually leaving his wife behind and sending her letters that cataloged and bemoaned his losses. Finally, in 1871, after his dead father appeared to him in a nightmare and warned of impending doom, Dostoyevsky repented of his gambling. Writing to his wife, he begged for forgiveness, declaring that he was "not a scoundrel, but only a gambler in the throes of his passion," and that he was now free of the chains of the gambling table: "From now on I shall think only of my work and will not dream of gambling all night as I used to do. Now my work will be better, and God will bless me!" Unlike others who have resolved to stop gambling in vain, Dostoyevsky lived up to his words and never gambled again.

At the beginning of the nineteenth century, gambling towns were relatively plentiful in German lands: There were twenty-four of them scattered across Austria, Prussia, Bavaria, Hanover, Saxony, and other principalities. But political consolidation, creeping prohibition, and simple weeding out reduced the field by about 1840 to four truly successful ones: Baden-Baden, Aachen, Wiesbaden, and Homburg.

---

[*]Dostoyevsky and Turgenev never mended their split. By the time that Dostoyevsky finally got around to repaying his $50 debt, Turgenev had forgotten how much he had originally lent, and, assuming that he had only been repaid in part, continued to believe that Dostoyevsky still owed him money.

Aachen (Aix-la-Chapelle in French), is one of the most historic cities in Europe; the Romans named it Aquis Granum for its hot sulfur springs, and it was well known for its baths in the classical period. Later, Charlemagne was buried there (his tomb is still found at the Aachen cathedral) and kings of the Holy Roman Empire were crowned there for six centuries. The westernmost city in today's Germany, it has long been a tourist destination.

By the second half of the eighteenth century, Aachen was no longer politically important, though its hot springs continued to pour water into the baths and it remained a popular resort. Consequently, it became a famous haunt for gamblers. The government leased the gambling concession to a chief banker who offered hazard; social games like billiards also saw heavy betting. By the 1860s, the place had a reputation as a place for only the most dedicated of gamblers. A traveler wrote that the town's name brought to mind "cards and dice—sharks and pigeons," and that all of Aachen was suffused with a "professional odor." The gambling was drab and mechanical, as the players moved in "deathlike silence . . . not a sound was heard but the rattle of heaped-up money, as it was passed from one side of the table to the other; nor was the smallest anxiety or emotion visible on any countenance."

Wiesbaden, a Rhine town in central Germany, had a similar history as a bath resort and was no less attractive to serious gamblers. The reigning prince of Nassau-Usingen granted a gambling concession there as early as 1771. Then, faro and basset were the dominant games, though by the time that a gaming room opened in the first Kurhaus in 1810, roulette had become the favored diversion. As elsewhere, casino profits were channeled into municipal improvements and ancillary entertainment venues like theaters and restaurants.

During the resort's nineteenth-century glory years, visitors to the more than twenty baths usually ended their day at the casino. Often, they began it there as well. An account from the 1860s describes visitors to Wiesbaden, frustrated by the Prussian government's recent edict that closed the casino in observance of the Sabbath, clamoring to begin play on Monday at 11 A.M., the customary opening hour for French and German gambling houses. Visitors of both sexes crowded forward to place their bets on roulette and trente-et-quarante. At times patronized by the wealthy and highborn, by 1868 Wiesbaden had acquired something of a down-market reputation. That year, London's *Daily Telegraph* reported that most visitors were of the lower and middle classes, with a few celebrities slumming it. With rampant gambling and opportunistic socializing, Wiesbaden was, in the author's words "naturally a Paradise . . . turned into a seventh hell by the uncontrolled rioting of human passions."

Worse yet, according to the *Daily Telegraph*, Wiesbaden had become the autumn rendezvous for "all the aged, broken-down courtesans of Paris, Vienna, and Berlin." This decrepit concert of distaff Europe painted their faces, dyed their hair, and sought relentlessly to fasten themselves onto younger and richer men in attendance. The author described them as "ghastly creatures, hideous caricatures of youth and beauty," who wheedled every meal and gambling stipend from gullible men, young and old.

In the "Countess C.," the *Daily Telegraph* reporter found a metonym for the decline of Wiesbaden. The aged countess, possessor of a huge fortune, was long a fixture in the town's gaming rooms. Even in her old age, she insisted on playing at least eight hours a day. Accompanied by eight servants, she tipped them paltry sums if she won and gave them nothing when she lost. Crying at the tables over her losses, she was more pitiable than contemptible:

> An edifying sight is this venerable dame, bearing an exalted title, as she mopes and mouths over her varying luck. . . . She is very intimate with one or two antediluvian diplomats and warriors, who are here striving to bolster themselves up for another year with the waters, and may be heard crowing out lamentations over her fatal passion for play, interspersed with bits of moss-grown scandal, disinterred from the social ruins of an age long past. . . . She has outlived all human friendships or affections, and exists only for the chink of the gold as it jingles on the gaming table. I cannot help but fancy that her last words will be *"Rien ne va plus!"* [No more bets]

The countess might have represented the decaying past, but Wiesbaden, like other German spa towns, remained fairly vibrant into the 1860s. Drawing visitors from far and wide for their baths and idyllic settings, the spa towns were preeminent locales for casinos that, as local authorities discovered, were quite lucrative. All of Europe, it seemed, mixed at the roulette tables and shared a common language of ill-fortune afterward.

One Rhine resort in particular bridged the era of gambling dominated by German spas with the coming age of Monte Carlo: Bad Homburg. Homburg did not boast an antique reputation as a Roman bath but was the very modern invention of a financially strapped landgrave and a pair of French gamblers, Louis and François Blanc.

The Blanc brothers' origins were less than auspicious. The posthumous twin sons of a penniless tax collector, they came into the world in 1806 in a small town north of Avignon, France. Receiving little formal education, they cast about France trying their hand at various enterprises, mostly in the area of finance. They won a great deal of money playing écarte (a trick-taking game similar to euchre) and baccarat and accumulated a sufficient capital reserve to open a small bank in Bordeaux in 1834.

The Blanc bank chiefly speculated in French government securities. Investors with advance notice of fluctuations in stock prices had a decided advantage, and the Blancs hit upon an idea the idea of using the French government's optical telegraph or *télégraphe aerien* to receive advance information. Rival speculators used methods ranging from carrier pigeons to windmill signaling, so they imagined that co-opting the government's system, which involved visual signals between telescope-equipped stations rather than electric transmission, was fair game.

The government, however, prohibited use of the system for such messages, so the brothers set about buying the cooperation of telegraph officials. For two years, the scheme worked perfectly; the Blancs received news of price fluctuations ahead of the curve and invested accordingly. In 1836, one of the administrators involved confessed to the scheme on his deathbed and implicated the others involved. The Blancs were tried and convicted in March 1837 of corrupting government officials. Since their crime was not seen as particularly heinous, they received no prison sentence and only minimal fines, and were thus left with the bulk of the 100,000 franc fortune they had accumulated over the previous two years. For the enterprising twins, crime apparently did pay.

Having discharged their debt to society, the Blancs were chary of remaining in Bordeaux, feeling that prospective business partners might be less forgiving than the court. So they journeyed to Paris, where they met with Jacques Bénazet. The gaming supervisor informed them of the huge profits possible in the casino business but noted that, with legal French gambling due to expire in a few short months, he was himself relocating to pursue his luck in the Rhine. The Blancs found this a wonderful idea. They settled on the Grand Duchy of Luxembourg as the best location for their gaming salon and headed north to try their luck.

The military governor was a Prussian army general who happened to be Ludwig, the reigning landgrave of Hesse-Homburg, one of the smallest principalities of the house of Hesse. Its capital, Homburg, had fewer than three thousand residents and the court was hopelessly sunk in debt. Past attempts to open a casino/spa had come to nothing; in 1830, promoters had

François Blanc, who transformed Bad Homburg into a
leading spa resort and later did the same in Monaco.

been foiled by the confusion resulting from the revolutionary ferment of that
year, and an 1836 proposal was scuttled when the Rothschild bankers refused
to lend the operators start-up capital. The next year, Ludwig himself denied
four applications from prospective concessionaires, citing the impending
French gambling prohibition and the previous failures.

But then Ludwig learned that, before the tables had been closed, the
French exchequer had raked off more than 4.5 million francs in taxes. Other
Rhine operators, including Bénazet, reinforced the landgrave's hunch that a
casino might not be so bad after all. In August 1838, the landgrave opened
the bidding for the casino and concession anew. Rejecting all the applicants as
unsuitable, he built a small pump room himself, modestly promoted the medical benefits of the local springs, and hoped for the best. Few visitors came,
though, without a casino. The Blancs, upon meeting the landgrave, seemed to
be the answer to his problems; though the resort would, at first, appeal primarily to residents of nearby Frankfurt, they envisioned bigger and better things
for themselves and the landgrave.

This happy future, however, would be denied to Ludwig. The landgrave
died on January 19, 1839, after suffering a severe chill, ironically the very

thing that might have been forestalled by a warm bath in a therapeutic spring. His heir, his brother Philip, approved of the casino enterprise and began negotiations with the Blancs. By July 1840, sufficient progress had been made for Louis Blanc to gain a personal audience with the landgrave, where he offered to build a suitable pump room in return for the annual lease on the gambling concession, which was to run until 1871. In return for the right to remain open year-round, Blanc agreed to bar all subjects of the landgrave from the casino. The contract was ratified by August, and the brothers eagerly began building their pleasure hall.

By the next May, construction of the casino formally began with the ceremonial ground-laying of the foundation stone after a procession that attracted curious spectators from as far as Frankfurt. The march ended at the site of the future casino with the performance of a specially written song. Afterward, a time capsule containing spring water, a rolled parchment declaration, coins, and wine (presumably to augur a pleasant and profitable future) was sealed by those in attendance, who took turns striking the capstone with a silver hammer. Following this ceremony was a banquet and ball, at which, for the first time, gambling began in Homburg.

Visitors, mostly from Frankfurt, played in a temporary casino. Here, the Blancs faced the reality that, all things being equal, Bad Homburg could simply not compete with established spa casinos in Baden-Baden, Ems, and Wiesbaden. The Blancs knew they could not offer the social prominence of elegant Baden-Baden, or the natural beauty of Wiesbaden. Though the springs weren't any healthier than those of any other middling spa on the Rhine or elsewhere, they engaged the services of a group of Sorbonne professors, who publicly proclaimed the superiority of the waters of Homburg.

Used to changing the rules to suit themselves, the Blancs literally did just that. While roulette tables throughout Europe had two zeros, theirs would have only one. This gave the players a noticeably better chance of winning. Since then, single-zero roulette has become standard throughout most of the world, while the only casinos to stubbornly retain the second zero are in the United States. The second Blanc innovation allowed them to shave the player's disadvantage at trente-et-quarante, already slight, even slimmer: On ties of thirty-one, the house only won if the last card in the row was black.

The Blancs knew that their profit margins would be tighter but realized that, in the long run, they couldn't lose: The house advantage inherent in their games, even though reduced, would triumph in the end. Like factories using mass production, they relied on economy of scale—more gamblers leaving less money each—for success. Still, needing security in the event of an unexpectedly lucky run by a big bettor, they secured a reserve loan from the Homburg authorities themselves.

Thus fortified, they were amply prepared for the opening of their main casino building, the Kursaal, on August 16 and 17, 1843. The Blancs feted their esteemed guests, including the landgrave himself, in an opening dinner and ball, and watched with anticipation as the guests began playing. Casino employees had been carefully instructed in the regulation of gaming: They were to quietly remove any locals, badly dressed guests, workmen, or peasants who managed to find their way into the opulent gaming salon, at the same time deferentially finding room at the tables for those deemed to be meritorious players.

The Kursaal was a stately red granite and chocolate-trim two-story building that fronted Lewis Street, Homburg's main thoroughfare. In the back was a large park laid out by the king of Prussia's own landscape gardener. Exhausted gamblers or their impatient companions could wander through its tree-lined walks and over bridges spanning a series of small lakes. Inside, the Kursaal housed a dining hall, theater, reading rooms (Blanc received all of Europe's newspapers, allowing visitors to remain in contact with their home countries), and the obligatory gaming room, which had two roulette and two trente-et-quarante tables.

Croupiers started the betting by gently intoning, *"Faites le jeu"* (Make your game), and closed it by announcing *"Rien ne va plus."* Betting went on in comparative dignity. Outward expressions of emotion were rare, as both winners and losers barely spoke above a whisper, and surrounding bystanders kept their conversations politely quiet. The dominant sounds were the calm announcements of the croupiers, the clink of gold coins, the sweeping of croupiers' rakes, and the ticking of highly ornate French clocks that decorated the gaming salon. The casino employees were renowned for their composure. An apocryphal story held that, after a disappointed loser put a gun to his head and splattered his brains across a Kursaal roulette table, the croupier merely announced, "Triple zero," before genteelly declaring the bank closed and throwing a cloth over the gore. The tale was too outrageous to be true, but it spoke to the higher truth of the imperturbable cool of Homburg dealers.

The ballroom was lavishly furnished with marble pillars and a gilded, frescoed ceiling. Red velvet couches lined the walls. Other rooms, framed by archways, were decorated various gentle colors, and smartly patterned parquet floored the entire building. Outside, a glass-enclosed colonnade with about one hundred tables provided a sweeping view of the gardens below. In the attached restaurant, famous for its fine cuisine, visitors could enjoy an elegant brunch before taking on the tables, or unwind after gambling over an uncommonly delicious dinner. Hotels in the vicinity of the Kursaal housed guests, where they lounged on porches, smoking and relaxing while attired in white sport coats and Panama hats. For the large numbers of British visitors (second to only the Russians), the Blancs provided two essential institutions: an Anglican church and a fully equipped cricket pitch.

The inducements to prospective visitors, from improved odds to the comforts of home, were fantastically successful. British writer George Augustus Sala described Homburg in the 1850s as "overflowing with life," noting the fashionably dressed men and women who flitted through the halls of the Kursaal. The gaming rooms, just short of overcrowding, overflowed with the usual suspects, "the same calculating old fogies, the same supercilious-looking young men, the same young girls and full-blown women, with a nervous quavering about the lips, the same old sinners of both sexes one has known at these places the last ten or fifteen years, busily engaged at trente-et-quarante." The roulette tables had a similar assortment, with French marquises, nervous young Englishmen, and professional gamblers, "well and ill dressed, with sharply defined Mephistophelean features, quick, restless eyes, and villainously compressed lips," and prostitutes of all nations. Circling the players were "watchful old women and Germans of hangdog look" who stood ready to pounce on any unwatched coins.

Originally, most of the upper-crust health-seekers remained at the established spas. Yet as word of Homburg's favorable odds spread, and the Blancs' press agents proved their worth, wealthier visitors became more common. By the 1850s, the Blancs' casino manager, Trittler, was writing to François that the casino had succeeded in bringing in high-end play, but only at great cost. In doing so, he might have coined a lasting term for such big spenders, noting that in order to attract the wealthy Ossokin to Homburg they had to change his Russian money at such an unfavorable rate as to lose no less than 10,000 francs. "We are throwing sprats [sardines] to catch whales," the manager wrote, "and trusting to the goddess Fortune; such proceedings can only be justified by results."*

Sometimes the results were so unfavorable that the goddess Fortune could not be held solely culpable. Beginning in the late summer of 1851, profits began to shrink, though more people were visiting the Kursaal. Specifically, the

---

Whale is still a synonym for a deep-pocketed, high-betting casino patron whose hosts labor to keep him happy and in the casino. Then as now, whales could make or break a casino's bottom line, and managers often walk on eggshells while hoping that, under a smiling Fortune, their expensive whale-baiting can be "justified by results."

trente-et-quarante tables were becoming less and less profitable, while roulette remained safely in the black. The Blanc brothers were for once at a loss. François was recovering from exhaustion and Louis was slowly dying in a convalescent home. By this point, his brother had taken over the supervision of the family business. François directed Trittler to closely analyze table performance data and investigate the croupiers—was anyone spending more money than he should have been? Blanc never identified the double-dealer(s), though the increased attention forced an end to the scheme; trente-et-quarante profits quickly regained their previous levels.

François Blanc knew quite well that, while the odds were bound to favor the house in the long run, a single, lucky, high-betting player might get the better of him in the interim. This happened most famously in 1852, when the prince of Canino methodically assaulted the bank at Homburg. Charles Lucien Bonaparte, the eldest son of Napoléon's youngest brother, Lucien, had become prince of Canino in 1840, and he already had a reputation as a gambler.

Blanc was overjoyed when the prince arrived on September 26, 1852; he wanted to attract rich and powerful visitors, and Charles Lucien was the cousin of the man who would, in a few short weeks, become the emperor of France. Arriving in the Kursaal, he immediately began playing roulette, betting nothing less than the house maximums. Playing at roulette and trente-et-quarante over the next four days, he won 180,000 francs. The Kursaal could only cover these losses because other players lost heavily that week.

After a day's break, the prince returned to the tables, this time losing most of his house maximum bets. Trittler began to relax, but by ten in the evening Bonaparte had weathered the storm, and he returned to his hotel triumphantly with 560,000 of Blanc's francs. As a committee of shareholders debated whether to lower the maximum bets and return the second zero to the roulette tables, Bonaparte packed his bags and left town. Though the Kursaal would have no chance of winning its money back from the prince, it at least did not have to face the prospect of losing any more to him. Gradually, the losses of other players compensated for the prince's plunder. Blanc even turned the situation to his advantage, instructing his press agents to emblazon news of Bonaparte's exploits across the newspapers of Europe. As a result, all the continent was soon abuzz with talk of how easy it was to win a fortune from François Blanc's Kursaal. Over the next few months, visitors flocked to the casino, which enjoyed its most successful year yet.

Blanc could bear the prince's success with equanimity because he knew that over time the house would prevail. He often said that "red sometimes wins; black sometimes wins, but white always," punning on his name. In the years after the prince's raid on Homburg, Blanc turned his attention to long-term business and personal matters. He had already scuttled attempts to legalize casinos in Turin, Savoy, Nice, and Paris, and he continued to be wary of any efforts to introduce potentially ruinous competition. Blanc also secured his own flank, turning aside German legislative proposals to ban gambling. He married Marie Hensel, the charming, though uneducated, daughter of a local cobbler, sending her to finishing school before tying the knot. She proved to be a more than capable mate and became perhaps his most trusted business advisor. By the end of the 1850s, the casino was enjoying record profits, and with the completion of the direct Frankfurt/Homburg rail line imminent, the future looked rosy.

Then, in August of 1860, he met another challenge: Thomas Garcia, a Spaniard who threatened to repeat the success of the prince of Canino. Garcia, though physically unassuming, arrived with a retinue that included his young German mistress, who remained by his side as he played. He had already developed a reputation in the illegal casinos of Paris as a bold and crafty gambler who confined himself to trente-et-quarante, with its more favorable odds. Along with his confederates he bet the absolute table maximum of 30,000 francs on play. He won over 100,000 francs several days in succession and, though he had losing spells as well, still acquitted himself admirably, once winning 260,000 francs in a single hour. Garcia then left Homburg with his pockets substantially heavier.

He returned in early September, though, and drew a crowd as he won, then lost, then won again. He finally left on September 12 with nearly 800,000 francs of the casino's reserve capital. Garcia's winnings forced a reduction of the stockholders' dividends, and some employees and shareholders began to express discontent with Blanc's administration. The asthmatic Blanc, who spent much of 1861 and 1862 trying to regain his health in Loèche-les-Bains, Switzerland, was not on hand to personally supervise the casino. The Kursaal achieved at least a symbolic victory over the intrepid Garcia when he returned in October 1861. Armed with a much smaller bankroll, he quickly lost everything, despite several emergency loans, including one from the pianist Anton Rubenstein, another confirmed gambler who had earlier borrowed money from Garcia. Garcia's partial defeat gave Blanc at least an appearance of triumph, which he was able to parlay into a consolidation of his power. Returning to Homburg late in 1862, he successfully quelled the shareholders' rebellion and staved off attempts by the landgrave's government to extract more wealth from the casino. Though victorious in his latest struggles and richer than ever, he began to feel misgivings of his own about the security of his Homburg money machine and began to consider diversification.

Blanc was right to be nervous. Even before the landgrave's government had begun grumbling for a larger cut of the profits, Blanc had stared down a full-fledged attempt to close his casino. As a consequence of the liberal revolution of February 1848, a pan-German parliament with real legislative powers was formed to bring some order to the loose German confederation. This National Assembly, headquartered in Frankfurt, began debating that the newly cohesive German central government follow the lead of France in abolishing gambling. All Germans, the ban's proponents asserted, clamored for the closure of the parasitical Rhine casinos. Certainly the landgraves and princes enriched by casinos in the principalities disagreed, but the assembly resolved in January 1849 that, effective May 1, 1849, all gambling would cease.

The reigning landgrave of Hesse-Homburg refused to accede to the closure and permitted the Kursaal to remain open after May Day had passed. The central government dispatched infantry and cavalry regiments to Homburg, where under protest the Blancs closed the Kursaal to the public. But they soon reopened as a private club, to which only card-carrying members, along with their entire families and any acquaintances they might wish to bring along, were admitted. Even this evasion was not necessary for long. Unable to enforce its edicts anywhere else, the National Assembly collapsed after Prussia withdrew its support. By the end of the summer, the casino was once again open to all.

Though it didn't last, the National Assembly's edict showed that many German people disapproved of casinos, whatever their benefits for the spa towns. It was this kind of publicity that led Dostoyevsky to declare that the press gushed over the splendor of Rhine resorts and the huge sums of money waiting to be won there. Such appeals may have been crass, but they were effective. As it became increasingly clear that much of Germany would be united during the 1860s, Blanc hoped that it would be under the aegis of Austria rather than Prussia. The Prussian government, which closed the casino at Aachen in 1854, was resolutely opposed to gambling.

The landgrave Ferdinand's death on March 24, 1866, was equally distressing. Since neither the landgrave nor any of his brothers had had any sons, the Hesse-Homburg dynasty was at an end. Luckily for Blanc, the grand duke of Hesse-Darmstadt, who absorbed the electorate, approved of the Kursaal just as much as his cousins. And for good reason: The past two decades had seen soaring visitation rates, economic development, and prosperity. But the grand duke's support proved a dead letter when he backed Austria (along with fellow gambling haven Baden) in the quick Austro-Prussian War, fought in the summer of 1866. The efficient Prussian army's crushing of the Austrians at Koniggratz on July 12 paved the way for the immediate annexation of the German states that had supported Austria.

This was bad news for Blanc, though it was cushioned by his recent acquisition of the gambling monopoly in a still-obscure Riviera principality called Monaco. In December 1867, the Prussian legislature began debating the cessation of gambling. Blanc did himself few favors by offering a large sum for disaster relief in East Prussia, which legislators correctly interpreted as a bribe. Furthermore, as a native Frenchman he was the object of dislike and suspicion during the run-up to the Franco-Prussian War of 1870. Blanc published a pamphlet stressing the tremendous prosperity of Homburg and its likely poverty without gambling, but his earlier mastery of the press deserted him; the Prussian Chamber passed, by a large majority, a law in February 1868 that ordered all gambling stopped, effective 11:00 P.M., December 31, 1872.

The law immediately changed the remaining Rhine casinos, chiefly Wiesbaden, Ems, Baden-Baden, and Homburg. They were to plow two fifths of their profits back into the development of their host towns, presumably to build tourist facilities to give the resorts a life after gambling, and they were to close the casinos on Sundays and holidays. The first Sunday without gambling in Homburg, March 29, 1868, was a dark day, as the streets were nearly deserted—a grim taste of the looming desolation.

Blanc began developing his interests in Monaco in earnest, though gamblers continued to crowd into the Rhine towns six days of the week. Most Homburg residents went on blithely entertaining visitors, imagining that, once again, Blanc would prevail. But the Prussian government was implacable. In October 1872 the gambling stopped in Wiesbaden and Ems. Homburg's Kursaal remained open, and visitors forced themselves to brave an exceptionally cold winter to enjoy its last days. Finally, in the standing-room only casino, it was five to eleven on December 31, and the croupier called out for the final bets to be placed. With a final spin of the roulette wheel (the winning number was twenty, black), François Blanc's three decades of casino ownership in Homburg were ended.

Playing at roulette and trente-et-quarante was now illegal throughout nearly all of Europe. The casino at Spa had already closed, and legal gambling in France had ended in 1837. The casino at Saxon-les-Bains, nestled amid the

Swiss Alps, remained open, but only until 1877, when it, too, was closed. The spa towns tried to encourage playing for fun at games like billiards and dominoes in the place of serious wagering on casino games, but to little avail. Visitation dropped off dramatically, and one can imagine tumbleweeds blowing through deserted streets.

The end of German gambling, though, did not leave Blanc destitute. He still enjoyed a personal fortune of more than 60 million francs. Stubborn to the last, he at first refused to surrender the Kursaal keys to the city authorities and only released them after a Prussian government commissioner compelled him to do so. Blanc quickly liquidated his remaining holdings in Homburg (chiefly a theater, restaurant, bathhouse, and offices) and looked to a brighter future along the Mediterranean coast, where he was already building his masterpiece in an impoverished Riviera principality whose name would soon become synonymous with style and sophistication, thanks to gambling.

IO

Flight of the Sparrow

◆ ◆ ◆

GAMBLING, CONQUEST, AND COLONIES

European powers took to the sea for several, sometimes contradictory, reasons: National pride, strategic influence, commerce, and religious proselytizing are only the most prominent. One of the unintended consequences of this imperial drive for military and commercial dominance was the cultural cross-pollenization of the world. The transfer of flora and fauna from the Old World to the New, known as the Columbian Exchange, was paralleled by a cultural diffusion of everything from foodstuffs to philosophy.

Gambling was part and parcel of this exchange. British colonists brought gambling with them as a reminder of home. The organizations that the British formed to conduct gambling would help forge the societies that they built in foreign lands. Whether practiced exclusively as a way of defining who was part of the ruling elite, or spread among the populace to encourage Anglicization, gambling became an integral element of the British imperial presence. Even after the sun has set on their empire, a British imprint remains on the gambling of virtually every continent.

Beginning in the middle of the eighteenth century, the British East India Company began expanding its area of influence in South Asia through treaty, trade, and conquest. By 1858, most of India had fallen under the direct rule of the British Crown, and the British would ultimately control a tremendous swath of the continent from the Afghan border into Malaysia and from the Himalayan Mountains to Sri Lanka. Later in the nineteenth century, Britain would consolidate its position in Africa, occupying Egypt and annexing or declaring sovereignty over Nigeria, Kenya, South Africa, and many areas in between. To administer these territories, Britain dispatched thousands of members of its Civil Service, now headquartered at Whitehall. They, allied with merchants and supported by members of the armed forces, would form the backbone of the British Empire. Like many other sojourners in distant lands, far from the comforts of home, they faced boredom, frustration, and anxiety. To cope, they often gambled.

Imperial gambling took two main forms: card games played in private homes and members-only clubs, and horse racing. In addition to helping Britons feel at home, horse racing had a tangible military benefit: Through competition, it encouraged the breeding of faster, stronger horses. At least that's how imperial officials justified the expense and attention lavished on the construction of racetracks and the maintenance of jockey clubs.

For generations, India was the jewel in the crown of the Empire. Gambling had long flourished in the subcontinent, from the days of gambling with *vibhitaka* nuts to the spread of *ganjifa* cards thoughout the continent. The Mogul rulers of the sixteenth and early seventeenth century, who preceded the British as the dominant power in India, were Muslims who usually granted their subjects wide latitude in how they lived and worshiped, coexisted peacefully with other religions, and neglected to literally enforce Koranic prohibitions on alcohol and gambling. It was not until the rule of Aurangzeb (1658–1707) that a Mogul endeavored to compel Islamic virtue throughout India. The son of Shah Jahan (best known today as the builder of the Taj Mahal in Agra), Aurangzeb outlawed drinking, gambling, and even music in his quest to stringently follow the Koran. By the end of Aurangzeb's reign, however, Mogul power was in the decline, and the British took control of a land that was used to at least moderate gambling.

Calcutta served as a major center for British administration, and though every British outpost of any import had its own racetrack and jockey or turf club, Calcutta was the center of racing on the subcontinent. Beginning in 1856, races for the Viceroy's Cup held at Hasting Racecourse solidified the reputation of Calcutta as a racing center. Racing was off-limits to Indians and only white civil servants, military men, and merchants were allowed into the turf clubs that controlled the sport. But with the Indianization of the British Raj in the early twentieth century, Indian elites would be admitted into the mysteries of the turf, and Indian racing would prosper through World War II.

The British racing enthusiasts at Calcutta created a unique method of gambling on horses still known around the world by the name of that city. Those participating in a "Calcutta" bid for the right to "buy" a particular horse. After the bidding is complete, each horse is awarded to the highest bidder. After the race is finished, the "owners" of the win, place, and show entries are awarded proportional shares of the total money collected. This later became a common form of gambling on golf in the United States.

Many Indians resented racecourse betting for both religious and political reasons—it violated the letter of both Islamic and Hindu law and represented the British presence. Mahatma Gandhi claimed that betting was a more pernicious evil than drinking. He would later proclaim that "the law must be against gambling" and declared that if possible he would criminalize it. But, as the father of *satyagraha* and nonviolent noncooperation, he realized that prohibitory edicts were valueless unless backed by the will of the people. He therefore urged Indians of their own volition to root out the gambling evil, which was worse than plague or earthquake, "for it destroys the soul within." After the withdrawal of British forces from India in 1949, racing survived in the major cities, but the new Republic of India declared that, after a grace period of five years, all racetrack betting would be suppressed. Perhaps mindful of Gandhi's injunction that a ban must have popular support, the government would later back away from the prohibition, and legal race betting once again became a fixture in the Republic of India.

The Indian experience provided a model for British imperial control of lands from Burma to Sierra Leone. Often, the racecourse became both a place for the agents of empire to relax and socialize and a symbol of the British intrusion. For nationalist reformers like Gandhi, betting was all the more insidious because it both represented foreign domination and appealed to locals, who eventually joined the British as enthusiastic bettors and wardens of the sport. It might be possible to read the entire history of British imperialism in the race programs and turf-club rules produced in the hundreds of imperial outposts upon which the sun never set.

Nowhere would the importance of horse racing to Britons abroad become more apparent than in Hong Kong, the British Empire's chief Asian entrepôt. From the time that the British initially occupied the small fishing village in 1841 until they relinquished the administration of a metropolis with six million residents to the People's Republic in 1997, they would create a unique culture in Hong Kong—part Chinese, part British. The civil servants and bureaucrats who represented king and country in Asia were consumed by the passion for horse racing, as were their Chinese neighbors.

In the beginning, British colonial authorities officially suppressed gambling in Hong Kong. The nearby Portuguese colony of Macau profited from this ban, serving as a welcome haven for Hong Kong gamblers, but there were other options closer to home. Before the 1898 acquisition of the New Territories across from Hong Kong Island by the British, gambling halls flourished in Kowloon City; their operators ferried gamblers from Hong Kong Island for free in order to secure their business. After 1898 the gambling halls continued to run in the Walled City, a former Chinese fort over which British administrators had ambiguous legal authority, and which would flourish as a vice district into the 1950s. But for legal, legitimate gambling, Hong Kong residents had one outlet: horse racing.

Establishing a bona fide racecourse on the mountainous terrain of Hong Kong Island took a little hustler's ingenuity. In the early 1840s, enthusiasts identified the flat, malarial swamp of Wong Nei Chong as the best site for a track, but they feared that the imperial government would not condone the undertaking. Hong Kong's governor, Sir John Davis, conveniently neglected to inform the colonial authorities in London of the true reason for the drainage of the swamp, referring vaguely in his correspondence to the effort as a health measure.

In 1845, racing began even before the completion of the new track in a lo-cale euphemistically renamed Happy Valley, opened in the following year. Both English and Chinese residents of Hong Kong shared in the excitement. A racing committee supervised the races. Betting contributed greatly to the excitement of race days, as did the fact that the racecourse was the only place where residents of all nationalities could gather together. The track was not completely democratic—with high costs of entry, early races were dominated by two rival stables belonging to the Jardine and Dent families, respectively headquartered in Hong Kong and its rival city, Shanghai. Still, Happy Valley remained a place where social barriers strictly enforced elsewhere were some-what more fluid.

In 1884, the Hong Kong Jockey Club was established to put racing on "a more stable footing." Under the leadership of its first chairman, Phineas Ryrie, the new club overcame a damaging 1885 flood and the loss of its sur-plus in 1891 due to bank failure. But the Hong Kong Jockey Club provided a stabilizing presence, performing the same functions as its British counterpart at Newmarket. By the turn of the century, men and women of all walks of life, proudly attired in their best clothes, made races the premier social event of Hong Kong.

The Jockey Club indirectly involved itself in betting as well. Bookmakers used a pari-mutuel system, in which all bets were totaled and payoffs were calculated by sharing the pool among all winning bets (minus a share for the bookmaker, naturally). This was a far more honest system than traditional bookmaking, and the Jockey Club has retained pari-mutuel betting to this day. Attempts to prohibit gambling failed: When Hong Kong governor Sir William Robinson ordered a halt to betting in 1892, attendance dropped so precipitously that he ultimately deigned to allow it again. It was a lucrative business for the Jockey Club, which auctioned off nineteen mat sheds, or structures of bamboo and fir in which betting went on, each season, and took a commission from the mat shed proprietor who ran the betting and offered other games, such as fan tan.

There was little oversight of the construction of the flimsy mat sheds, which formed an interconnected mass of bamboo, and even less regard for basic principles of fire safety. On February 26, 1918, tragedy struck when the mat sheds suddenly collapsed and an open fire in a cooking stall sparked a tremendous conflagration. Nearly seven hundred out of an estimated three thousand occupants in the mat sheds perished.

Following the tragedy of the Derby Day Massacre, the betting resumed, though the Jockey Club took safety more seriously. The races themselves became more professional, with trained jockeys rather than dilettante gentleman riders beginning to dominate. In 1930, the colonial administration began levying a two percent betting tax on Jockey Club profits. The club also became more inclusive. Following a 1925 general protest strike by the Chinese, the British began to adopt a more conciliatory tone toward the Chinese residents of Hong Kong. The next year, the Jockey Club elected to open its membership to all races, leading to a rapid influx of Chinese owners and riders. Led by Li Lan-Sang, known as "Mr. Lan," locals soon represented a majority of horse owners; within a decade, more than half of all horses raced at Happy Valley were Chinese owned.

The Japanese occupation of Hong Kong would prove the Jockey Club's biggest challenge—at one point equines were so scarce that wooden horses "racing" down wires substituted for the real thing. Following the war, the British army briefly took control of Happy Valley, but in 1946 they returned control to the Jockey Club. In the late 1940s and early 1950s, refugees from the now Communist mainland streamed into Hong Kong, straitening the city's resources. Given the prevailing antigambling mood in Britain, the Colonial Office was loath to place colonial finances in the hands of bettors. But with the ballooning profits of the Jockey Club and the increasingly desperate need for revenues, it seemed the only option.

In early 1952, Sir Arthur Morse, chairman and chief manager of the Hong Kong and Shanghai Banking Corporation (and chair of the Jockey Club's Board of Stewards), suggested that the Jockey Club voluntarily donate one third of its profits to charitable causes of the government's choosing. Three years later, the club officially resolved to give all of its excess income to community projects. In 1959, a separate company, which eventually became the Hong Kong Jockey Club Charities Trust, began to direct these projects.

Since then, the Jockey Club has directly or indirectly contributed to every facet of Hong Kong's life, with hospitals, schools, elder-care facilities, museums, and other organizations receiving funds from the club. Today the Jockey Club donates about $129 million to charity each year, making it the region's biggest charity.

In recognition of this service, Queen Elizabeth II in 1960 approved the designation of the club as a royal institution, and it officially became the Royal Hong Kong Jockey Club. This was only the first of many changes to sweep over the club that, despite its success, was still an amateur association. Night racing was inaugurated in 1973, and technological improvements allowed for the more efficient tallying of pari-mutuel bets and off-track betting. With high-rise towers now crowding the former wilderness, a much-needed expansion at Happy Valley was impossible, so in 1978 the club opened a new course, Sha Tin ("Sandy Fields"), on 250 acres of reclaimed land in the New Territories. A larger, better-designed track soon made this the track of choice for racing purists, but those charmed by the ambience of the historic course still frequent it; both tracks continued to draw huge crowds into the new millennium.

That new era is not under the stewardship of the British. Under Deng

Since its founding in 1846, in a recently drained swamp, the Happy Valley racetrack
has been a constant in Hong Kong society. Over the past 160 years the city has grown precipitously
around it. Today, with sports facilities in its infield, Happy Valley, surrounded by skyscrapers,
makes the most out of its precious real estate.

Xiaoping's "One Country, Two Systems" formula, the People's Republic of China pledged to make no major changes to Hong Kong for fifty years after it returned to Chinese sovereignty in 1997. Still, the Jockey Club respectfully dropped the "Royal" prefix in 1996, becoming once again the Hong Kong Jockey Club. Under the new regime, little else has changed. Having expanded into soccer betting and lottery operations and hosting prestigious international races, the Hong Kong Jockey Club is far more than a surviving relic of Hong Kong's colonial past: It is a living reminder of the fusion of Western and Eastern elements that has made the city one of the world's finest.

Forty miles west of Hong Kong, in the city of Macau, a different cultural synthesis took place. Macau stepped onto the world stage in the middle of the sixteenth century. Under the aegis of Prince Henry the Navigator, the Portuguese had become the outstanding mariners of the world. Seeking to confound the Mediterranean monopoly on Asian trade goods such as gold, sandalwood, silks, and spice, the intrepid Portuguese pushed southward along the coast of Africa until they had rounded the Cape of Good Hope and, ultimately, discovered an ocean route to India. From India, their trade routes continued eastward to China and Japan: Portuguese merchants first settled Macau, a slender isthmus near the mouth of the Pearl River estuary in Guangdong province, in the 1550s, chiefly as a way station between the Indian city of Goa (then the center of Portugal's Asian trade network) and China and Japan.

Chinese fishing settlements had marked the isthmus since at least the thirteenth century. Despite the initial reluctance of the Ming authorities, the Portuguese established a trading outpost there, initially paying an annual ground rent to the imperial rulers and further gaining their trust by assisting in the suppression of piracy in the surrounding waters. Macau enjoyed a golden age in the sixteenth and seventeenth centuries as the preeminent commercial and evangelical European gateway to Asia. But with Japan's closure to foreign trade in the early seventeenth century and the emergence of Great Britain as the dominant mercantile power, Macau slowly declined, a slide that could not be offset by its use as a center for trade in opium and semislave "coolie" labor. Beginning in the 1840s, British-settled Hong Kong replaced Macau as the area's primary trading center.

Faced with decline, Macau's authorities took a bold step: They legalized gambling. This happened as Macau's political status was changing. Emboldened by China's declining strength, Portugal stopped paying ground rent in

1849 and destroyed the Chinese customs post, in essence declaring its possession of the city; the Treaty of 1887 officially recognized Portugal's sovereignty over Macau. Captain Isidoro Francisco Guimarães, serving as governor of Macau from 1851 to 1863, took steps to bolster the city-state's economy by regulating and taxing vice, including both prostitution and gambling. Since at least the 1830s, the owners of illegal gambling houses had bribed officials. Guimarães, by officially licensing gambling houses, diverted this graft to the public coffers. He was immediately successful: Gambling never failed to yield revenues for the city's Portuguese masters.

Macau's gambling houses offered Chinese games, including fan-tan, *pai gow*, and, after the early twentieth century, a game called *cussec* or "big and small," also known as *sic bo*. Licensed operators also ran lotteries, with thrice-daily drawings, that inevitably attracted poor and working-class citizens.

Fan-tan was an elaboration of the ancient odd-and-even games in which a dealer covered an unknown number of white buttons with a bowl and then accepted bets on how many buttons would remain after the buttons had been divided into groups of four. Players could bet on one, two, three, or four (zero) and on combinations. *Pai gow* is played with a set of thirty-two tiles. Players receive four tiles and divide them into a high (strong) and low (weak) hand. If the player beats the dealer's high and low hands, he wins; if the dealer wins both hands, the house triumphs; a split decision is declared a push, with the player keeping his stakes.

Cussec or *sic bo* (big and small) is something of an anomaly among Chinese casino games: It is played with dice. Three dice placed in a cup, bowl, or cage are shaken, and players bet on the results; they can lay stakes on the total number of points as reckoned by the number of dots on the upturned faces of the dice, big (eleven to seventeen) or small (four to ten), or triples. Another variation popular in Macau casinos, fish-prawn-crab *cussec*, replaces the dice's pips with images of a fish, prawn, crab, coin, gourd, and rooster, each of which has an accepted numerical value. These three games were the sole offerings of licensed fan-tan houses, as no Western games were played in Macau.

Legal gambling took place either in exclusive private clubs that catered to the wealthiest and provided them a venue for player-to-player social gambling or public fan-tan houses patronized by the poorest. In the 1860s, sixteen of these houses generated respectable revenues for the government, but they did not draw wealthy travelers to Macau. These houses offered "singing girls"— often a euphemism for prostitutes—and doubled as cheap flophouses; though this satisfied some rough-and-tumble visitors, it hardly augured any future as

Fan-tan, in which players bet on how many markers remained after a group of them was divided by four, developed early in China and was ubiquitous in Chinatowns throughout the world. This 1887 illustration of a New York City fan-tan parlor shows the game as it was played in China and in the myriad lands that Chinese immigrants settled.

an international destination. Thanks in part to these gambling hells, Macau retained a reputation as a center for prostitution, slavery, gold and opium smuggling, and the domain of what one contemporary called "the flotsam of the sea, the derelicts, and more shameless, beautiful, savage women" than any other port. While this might seem a quite attractive nuisance to some, it could hardly be expected to draw the aristocratic, if not reputable, patrons of Monte Carlo.

Europeans imported horse racing into China, and the Chinese returned the favor by exporting mahjong. The game's origins are cloudy. Like those who promoted the occult tarot as the received wisdom of ancient Egypt, the early exponents of mahjong assigned it a distant, noble origin that was centuries, even millennia, in the past. Li Yu Sang, who wrote an English introduction to mahjong in 1923, reasoned that the game surely was the invention of no "ordinary" Chinese but rather an aged, distinguished scholar well versed in Confucian philosophy, mathematics, and the classics *I Ching (Book of Changes)* and *Wu Chi Ching (Book of Surprises)*. Sang assured his readers that, for those with the proper learning, the relationships between classical wisdom and the game of mahjong were manifestly obvious. According to him, the game was nothing less than "a concrete exposition of the Chinese philosophy of the universe."

Historians of mahjong believe that it actually originated as an adaptation of rummy games to tiles. The game's name yields few clues to its origin; according to Sang, "ma-ch'iau" (as he rendered the correct transliteration) meant "hemp bird" or sparrow. It may have been that the telltale clicking of tiles reminded players of twittering sparrows, or that the plucking and discarding of tiles resembled the darting flight of the bird.

The game evolved somewhere in the vicinity of the Yangtze River, possibly Nanjing or Shanghai, during or soon after the Taiping Rebellion (1851–1864). According to Sang, the game spread in the late nineteenth century from isolated scholars and retired officials seeking an indoor activity with intellectual heft to their relatives, friends, and even servants, who in turn carried the game to the broader public. In the early twentieth century, the game began to spread throughout China, and by 1920 it would be well known throughout the entire country.

To play, four players (named East, South, West, and North) use 144 tiles (136 regular pieces plus 8 bonus ones) and, through discards and pickups, try to build winning combinations. Starting with 13 tiles, the players each have a chance to pick new tiles, either those just discarded or those whose position in a central square allows their selection. Though the game had no centralized ruling body or canonical set of rules in China, a series of formulaic rituals lent it an air of solemnity and, more importantly, made it physically impossible to rig tile orders or otherwise cheat.

Because of its popularity in the booming port of Shanghai, it was perhaps inevitable that mahjong would soon find international appreciation. The game spread to Japan during the same years that it became popular throughout the Chinese mainland, but it would not be until after World War I that it was brought overseas by an enterprising American with a flair for marketing, Joseph Park Babcock.

Babcock represented the Standard Oil Company in Suzhou, a city in Jiangsu province near Nanjing and Shanghai. He discovered mahjong in the English-speaking clubs of Shanghai. He streamlined the rules to make the game more palatable to an American audience and, in 1920, started his mahjong blitz. He copyrighted the name "Mah-Jongg" and issued a small red volume modestly entitled *Babcock's Rules for Mah-Jongg, The Fascinating Chinese Game.*

In a nation rife with anti-Chinese prejudice (Chinese immigration had been officially banned since 1882), a game featuring heretofore obscure Chinese names and characters might be a tough sell, but sales of Babcock's book and "official mah-jongg" sets imported by a San Francisco merchant soared. Mahjong became the definitive craze of the early 1920s. According to historian Frederick Lewis Allen, by 1923 (when Babcock issued a second edition of his "Rules"), people around the country " 'broke the wall' and called 'pung' and 'chow' and wielded the Ming Box and talked learnedly of bamboos, flowers, seasons, South Wind, and Red Dragon." But only one year later, the new sensation of crossword puzzles replaced mahjong as the national obsession; Americans were only persuaded to drop their pencils and dictionaries with the rising popularity, later in the decade, of bridge. The game would enjoy a revival with the establishment of a National Mah Jongg League in the 1930s, but it never held the nation in quite the thrall of the early years of the Roaring Twenties. In addition to its steady popularity with immigrant and expatriate Chinese groups worldwide, mahjong spread, chiefly through the United States, to Europe. Nearly every country that adopted the game played it slightly differently. Though the game is still played worldwide, it generally has remained popular mostly in Asia.

In China, gambling at mahjong was long deplored. In 1923 the self-styled Chinese mahjong ambassador Li Yu Sang bemoaned that his countrymen had degraded the philosophical exercise into a gambling game (though it probably first developed as a gambling game) and declared that, though gambling on the Sparrow Game was both indefensible and universally condemned, it was irrepressible among all classes. Sang emphasized that although mahjong itself was faultless, betting on it had become "one of the most serious evils" facing China (this during a tumultuous period of revolution and civil war, no less). Thanks to the abuses of bettors and foreigners ignorant

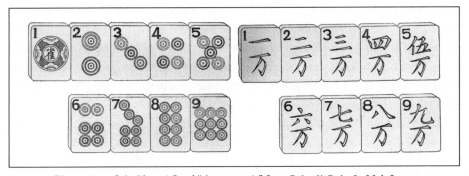

Illustrations of the "dot suit" and "character suit" from Babcock's Rules for Mah-Jongg.

of the game's true depth, "the ancient, beautiful, beneficial Chinese game has sometimes been made to assume a strange and evil appearance."

Yet those who gambled on mahjong and those outside China would become some of the game's staunchest players, particularly after the People's Republic of China officially banned the game under its general gambling prohibitions. Though the game would not be completely suppressed, it was hardly encouraged. Mahjong's decline in China was balanced by its runaway popularity in Japan, where the game remains a popular institution, with a mahjong museum near Tokyo and mahjong-themed anime and manga. The game has been superbly adapted to the computer age. Mahjong video games are incredibly popular, both in arcades and on personal computers. Though some players might be attracted to the games chiefly by the images of attractive women removing their clothing as they lose rounds, this is hardly the only reason for mahjong's endurance in Japan—on its own merits, mahjong has established itself as one of the world's most popular games.

The "sparrow" was not the only Chinese gamble to fly to distant lands. The pigeon proved equally adept at nesting wherever the Chinese established settlements in the form of a game called *pakapoo,* literally translated as "white pigeon ticket" lottery. Though often conflated with a lottery by Westerners, it was actually not a lottery, but a bank game with fixed odds.*

The game's precise origin is uncertain, but according to legend the governor of a city introduced it during the Han Dynasty (206 B.C. to 220 A.D.) as a way to generate funds for his army. In reality, it seems to have emerged in the Cantonese-speaking regions of southern China in the nineteenth century. Its unique name is apocryphally ascribed to the belief that, in the game's first days, carrier pigeons ferried tickets and winning numbers from the central office to customers.

To run a *pakapoo* "lottery," an operator printed up two sets of tickets with the first 80 characters of a well-known Chinese educational text, the *Chien Chi Mun (Book of One Thousand Characters)* volume of the *Sum Po Hung Pei Shu (The Three Red Textbooks),* which was believed to have been written in the sixth century. A player bought a ticket and crossed off ten of the characters on it. After all tickets were bought, the operators pulled twenty characters at random from a box and paid off those who properly selected five or more characters. Because the payoffs were considerably less than the true odds, pakapoo was an extraordinarily profitable mercantile game. Initially popular

---

*The mechanics of the game are virtually identical to keno, into which pakapoo evolved in the United States.

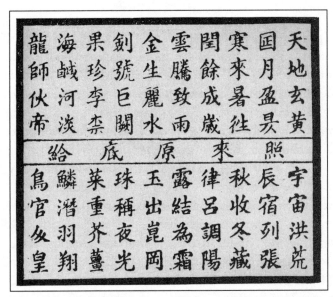

Ticket for the "White Pigeon Ticket" or *pakapoo* lottery; the first eighty characters of the *Book of One Thousand Characters* were printed on a ticket. A player selected ten or more, and hoped that his characters were drawn in the "lottery." It was a game common in China and Chinatowns throughout the world.

in China, it spread throughout areas of Chinese influence in southeast Asia and to Chinese colonies throughout the world.

Pakapoo was merely one of a family of games based on selecting characters. *Chee tam* ("eighty characters") used only the first eighty characters of the *Chien Chi Mun*. This was an expansion of the game of *chee fah*, "thirty-six numbers." To play *chee fah*, an operator chose one of thirty-six well-known names of historical Chinese characters, each of which had a corresponding number. He initialed the chosen name and number and placed it aside for safekeeping, then wrote a riddle that contained a hidden clue to the correct answer. Character number twelve, for example, was Chu Kwong Ming, a military adviser to emperor Tai Peng and a legendary strategist. Clues to his selection could include references to his career or his astrological sign. The operator, via a network of promoters, disseminated the riddle to the public, who then placed bets with agents. When the game was run in areas not exclusively inhabited by the Chinese, non-Chinese bet as well, though they merely picked numbers at random. After all bets had been collected, the operator opened the sealed box in public and paid off winners at thirty to one, odds that ensured a steady profit as long as the riddle was suitably opaque. *Chee fah* and *chee tam*, which paid off at seventy to one, were big business, and illegal numbers lottery operators in the twentieth century United States might have learned a few things from them.

When Europeans "discovered" Australia in 1522, the native inhabitants had no recognizable gambling, but the gambling spirit has found a welcome home on the continent in the years since. The settlement of the southern continent began in the late eighteenth century, a period when gambling was relatively popular in the mother country. Many convicts transported with the First Fleet to Botany Bay in 1788 had been convicted of thefts and other larcenies that frequently had their roots in gambling. In the hulks, floating prisons in which the convicts were confined before transportation to Botany Bay, gambling dice, cards, or anything else at hand was endemic.

Once arriving in Australia, some convicts gambled until they had lost all of their money and possessions, even the clothes on their backs. Cribbage and all fours were the chief games of choice. One disapproving judge wrote that swearing, profaning the Sabbath, pilfering, burglary, and murder all stemmed from cards. Even those who braved the trip to Australia by choice caught the gambling bug. These settlers habitually gambled, as farmers wagered their crops and even their farms at games like hazard. Some even wove stories of attacks by natives to excuse missing crops and provisions in order to hide the fact that they had been gambled away.

The authorities generally tolerated gambling, provided it did not become too much of a public disturbance. Officers dispatched to dissolve the crowds gathering to watch a cockfight, for example, waited until after the match had been concluded to disperse the now satisfied throng. Magistrates punished those who cheated at gambling, practiced theft in the guise (or support of) gambling, or won more than the £10 limit imposed by statute. At times they even arbitrated betting disputes.

From the beginning, Australians created their own gambling culture, distinct from Britain's. For one, in the early years there was less circulating money, so stakes were often goods or intangibles like honor. Animal blood sports survived much longer in Australia than in the mother country. In Britain, cockfighting, bearbaiting, and similar spectacles were largely suppressed by 1840. But they continued to thrive in Australia—though bullbaiting disappeared, cockfighting drew crowds of several hundred into the 1840s.

Australians raised some British betting styles to a high art. Pedestrianism remained incredibly popular in Australia long after it had been abandoned in Britain. The field even produced celebrity athletes, like "the Flying Pieman," William Francis King, a former schoolteacher who wowed Sydney with his feats of distance walking and carrying in the 1840s. He once carried a seventy-pound dog the twenty-eight-mile distance from Campbelltown to

Sydney to satisfy a wager, and to fulfill another toted a ninety-two-pound goat and twelve pounds of additional weight.

Australians bet on team and individual athletic matches with equal alacrity. Boxing and cricket were the most popular, though in a pinch Australians somehow wagered on dancing. For some, the challenge of the bet was almost more important than the game or participant. Joseph Hilton, known as Joe the Basketmaker, issued an omnibus fighting challenge that demonstrates the few parameters put on contests at the time. He offered to personally fight any man in the country of forty-four years' age and twelve-stone weight and further tendered a notice for challenges for his cock (any weight), his dog (forty-eight-pound weight class), and his wife ("any woman in the country, bar none"). The contestants in each match were to wager £5 per side. Whether Hilton had any successful challengers is not known.

Around the turn of the nineteenth century, Australian horse ownership was widespread enough that the gentry began racing each other for stakes. Though these private contests were not officially sanctioned, they were not illegal, either, and they attracted scores of spectators and bettors. In 1810, the colonial government began actively promoting racing; in that year Governor Lachlan Macquarie ordered a racecourse built at Hyde Park in Sydney, and he appointed select days for racing. As betting on the races was widespread, and cockfighting, though barred at the track, drew crowds nearby, conservative Christian groups lambasted him for encouraging gambling.

But within ten years of Governor Macquarie's sanction of horse racing at Hyde Park, the sport began a quick expansion to all areas with heavy British settlement. At first confined to large cities, racing swept forward with the frontier, and holding a race meeting became a mark of sophistication for new settlements. Originally organized by military regiments or colonial administrations and financed by subscribers, horse racing in the 1820s began to be controlled by more formal organizations. The first of these, the Sydney Turf Club, was established in 1825, and others soon followed. With the support of both colonial government and prominent citizens, they proved equal to the challenge of regularizing the rules and procedures of Australian racing.

The Australian version of the venerable sport of coursing (the duke of Norfolk drew up the first rules for coursing during the reign of Elizabeth I) first featured greyhounds chasing wallabies around a course. The sport did not catch on immediately after the formation of the first coursing club in Naracoorte, South Australia, in 1868, but after operators began substituting rabbits for wallabies five years later, coursing soon spread to Victoria, New South Wales, and Tasmania. With the helpful patronage of colonial governors, coursing was established as legitimate sport, albeit one with a small audience, by the 1880s; by the 1930s, it would evolve into the more broadly popular sport of greyhound racing.

Horse racing, though, would continue to outdistance greyhound racing and develop into an unrivaled national institution. The Melbourne Cup has become a national celebration of betting. The Victoria Turf Club ran the first Melbourne Cup in 1861. It was initially a small-scale handicap race that grew in appeal thanks to its unpredictability; with horses of greater ability weighted down, long shots had a much better chance of winning. Within five years, most of Melbourne had at least half of the day off from work on race day, which virtually guaranteed large crowds at the track and ardent betting on the outcome.

In 1895, the visiting Mark Twain declared that it was impossible to over-state the importance of Melbourne Cup Day. "Cup Day is supreme—it has no rival," Twain wrote, noting that neither in his native United States nor in any other country did a single day occasion such conversation, preparation, anticipation, and jubilation. The Cup's popularity has only grown: Today, the first Tuesday in November remains a day when nearly every Australian somehow bets. For just a few minutes, the nation's attention turns to Flem-ington Racecourse, where, in front of more than 110,000 dressed in their finest, horses handicapped for weight, age, and ability run nearly two miles in a race that, while not the favorite of horse purists, never fails to fire the excitement of Australians. That the preeminent national holiday of Aus-tralia is marked by a horse race rather than commemoration of any spiritual element or military triumph says everything about how Australians feel about gambling.

Betting on the Melbourne Cup and other Australian horse races became easier in the late nineteenth century with the invention of the totalizator, a mechanical device that automated the bookmaker's pari-mutuel balancing of race odds. South Australia moved to legalize the tote first, and though a sub-sequent antibetting law criminalized the tote in 1882, six years later it re-turned. Some states, like New South Wales and Queensland, also legalized the tote, while in others the tote opponents, which included both dyed-in-the-wool antigamblers and bookmakers chary of new competition, kept it illegal.

In Victoria, where the tote remained illegal, crafty operators still used it to tally bets. John Wren of Collingwood ran the most famous of these illegal tote parlors that masqueraded as "innocent tea shops." After a jury refused to convict him of the crime of bookmaking in 1896, he continued to run his tote, using the goodwill of the community to help him frustrate police raids.

Wren's was only the best known of these surreptitious betting shops—whether legal or illegal, tote shops throughout Australia provided working-class citizens with the same wagering opportunities afforded to those who could spend a leisurely day at the races.

Gambling with cards and dice grew in a curiously Australian manner. The law turned a blind eye to polite games of cards between gentlemen, and those with the refinement necessary to gain entrance to the pinnacle of Australian society played cards with impunity. Even the colonial governor and magistrates were known to play cards or dice. Beginning in the late 1830s, Australian gentlemen, following the example of their London counterparts at White's, Brooke's, and Crockford's, began setting up members-only clubs, though on the whole private gambling clubs were not as popular on the southern continent as in Britain.

The lower classes gambled as well. In the early nineteenth century, a Sydney district called the Rocks was particularly notorious for sheltering a number of unlicensed grog shops, which one chronicler estimated to outnumber legal public houses by two to one. Drinking potent rum, the sailors, loose women, and ruffians who inhabited the grog shops gambled voraciously. When low of funds, the resident hooligans simply found a new immigrant or tipsy naval officer to rob, either by deceptive gambling or brute force. Both grog dens and gambling houses proliferated in chancy neighborhoods, providing fortunes to their operators (who sometimes opened pawn shops nearby, both receiving stolen goods and making loans to gamblers) and material for antigambling jeremiads to opponents.

The main Australian gold rush began in Victoria in 1851, as would-be miners abandoned jobs and responsibilities and headed for the gold fields. The thousands who fled their steady work for the fickle, arduous life of gold mining were obviously taking a tremendous gamble, and they enjoyed gambling for fun as well. The second law passed by the Victorian legislature criminalized both keeping a gaming table (or a fraudulent "pretend game of chance") and obscene language; half the £5 fine was payable to the informer, and convicted gamblers or swearers could be jailed for three months.

Still, gambling proliferated on Australian mining frontiers. Most miners preferred cards, though absent them they would even toss coins, sometimes wagering as much as £100 on a single throw. The miners chiefly played social games among themselves, though a few professional gamblers worked their way through the camps; as they played dead-even social games rather than mercantile games, they remained professional only by dint of their skill in cheating.

Moralistic foes of gambling reserved some of their strongest words for those whom they considered foreigners (though, obviously, most non-Aborigines in Australia were relatively new arrivals), the Chinese. With the gold rush of the early 1850s, their numbers increased dramatically. As in their own country, the Chinese in Australia wholeheartedly embraced gambling—in the unsettled mining camps, fan-tan proved to be the most popular Chinese game. Chinese miners played incessantly, even on Sunday, when the even the least pious among the Caucasian miners deigned to listen to sermons. Christian authorities were appalled; in 1868, the Reverend William Young concluded that gambling among the Chinese in Victoria would ruin both the Chinese and the rest of Australian society. Other observers reported Chinese gamblers staking anything of value at fan-tan, living magnanimously when ahead and stealing shamelessly when losing. One could say the same of other groups, regardless of race, pursuing wealth in the diggings.

By the 1870s, Chinese immigrants were found more often in the cities, particularly Melbourne and Sidney, where curious Europeans sometimes visited the gambling houses (which frequently doubled as opium dens) of the Chinese quarter. The law prevented them from partaking in another Chinese recreation, the *pakapoo* lottery, which was apparently legal for Chinese Australians but not those of European extraction. The game was a streamlined version of its original Chinese form. For a stake of sixpence, the bettor got to strike out ten of eighty Chinese characters written on a ticket. The banker drew twenty characters at random from a bowl containing eighty. Winning tickets, with from five to ten characters matching those chosen, paid off according to the number of matching characters: Five won only one shilling and twopence, while ten brought home more than £83.

The authorities might have deemed the *pakapoo* lottery off-limits, but this did not mean that they completely suppressed the lottery spirit. Some in Australia felt that a general atmosphere of gambling pervaded the country, for better or for worse: Rampant land speculation, particularly in the 1880s and 1890s, was frequently described as gambling, and frontier land was often sold by lottery. The lures of wealth promised by gold mining made the connection even stronger. The bishop of Tasmania spoke what many felt to be an acknowledged truth when, in 1898, he declared the gambling spirit to be a "striking factor in the development of the Australian character." To prohibit lotteries in such a climate seemed, for many, hypocritical.

Starting in the 1870s, sweepstakes betting, in which bettors bought a cheap ticket for a small chance at an expensive prize, became popular. These "sweeps" were often tied to other gambling events such as the Melbourne

Cup. John James Miller pioneered the sweepstakes in New South Wales in the late 1870s with a £5,000 pound draw, but the undisputed king of the sweeps was George Adams, an English immigrant who parlayed his success as a butcher and stock dealer into ownership of Sydney's O'Brien's Hotel. From the Tattersalls Club, located in that hotel, Adams began offering public sweeps in 1881. When New South Wales criminalized sweeps operations in 1892, Adams moved to Queensland. Once there, he organized a lottery to dispose of the assets of a failed bank, but the local government proved uncooperative and he moved again, this time to Tasmania.

Adams was initially invited to Tasmania to help liquidate the assets of another bank through a lottery. But the government, needing a source of revenue, decided to put Adams to his best and highest use, which was running sweeps. In 1896, the province's curiously titled Suppression of Public Betting and Gaming Act legalized Adams's Tattersalls sweepstakes (known colloquially as "Tatt's") as a government-sponsored lottery monopoly. Using the mails, Adams sold lottery tickets throughout the continent and in other countries. Tickets initially cost £1, and though prizes were never that high, hundreds of thousands of tickets were sold for each drawing. Tasmania received a portion of the take as taxes—at one point, it got a cut of over £1.5 million a year from Tatt's. After Adams died in 1905, Tattersalls continued to offer Australians a chance at riches, remaining in Tasmania until lured back to Queensland in 1954.

Queensland, after turning Adams out in 1895, would continue to enforce its ban on lotteries, at least for a time. In 1916, the Queensland Patriotic Fund, looking for money to assist disabled veterans and the widows and children of those killed in World War I, received state approval to hold a Golden Casket lottery. The draw was not as morbid as it sounds; "caskets" in the Australian parlance are simply containers and not specifically coffins, and to skirt antilottery laws the Fund offered 723 "valuable golden caskets" as prizes. These prizes would then be bought back by the Patriotic Fund Committee for their stated cash value. Despite a slow start, the Queensland Golden Casket became a popular and efficient fund-raising mechanism, even more so in the 1930s, when it began offering less expensive tickets and started using machines to draw winners. New South Wales and West Australia soon followed Queensland's example, and by the 1950s, whether called sweeps, golden caskets, or art unions, lotteries were well enshrined in Australia.

Horse racing might be an Australian national sport, and having a go at the sweeps might be an Australian institution. But neither can boast of being an indigenous Australian game of chance like two-up, a genuine Down Under innovation. The game might have originated as early as the 1850s, and it was certainly widespread by the time of the gold fever of the late nineteenth century. Two-up was a simple game tailor-made for a rough-hewn continent. A boxer (dealer) collected a player's wager and any side bets and then gave him two coins to flip in the air. Two heads meant a victory for the player, two tails a win for the boxer, and a mixed result was a push that paid no one. The player could continue to throw as long as he kept throwing heads but could only collect his winnings after he had tossed at least three heads. To pass the coins, the player used a polished wood piece known as a kip.

Unless someone used gimmicked coins, two-up was a fair game. If not always legal, it was usually tolerated as a harmless diversion. Two-up became known worldwide during World War I and World War II, when Australian soldiers became notorious for playing it to ease the tension before an impending offensive, to pass the time while waiting for mobilization orders, and, even, according to anecdote, during the heat of battle itself. Peter Charlton, in his history of Australian gambling, writes that a Turkish pilot flying above an Australian camp during World War I, seeing "the raised eyes to heaven and the earnest bowing to the ground," mistook the excitement of a two-up school for the devotions of prayer and refused to commit the sacrilege of bombing men at worship.

Australian historian John O'Hara has written that his countrymen think of themselves as not merely a nation of gamblers, but as the greatest gamblers in the world. Today, nearly ninety percent of Australians gamble on something, and the Melbourne Cup horse race is a national holiday. According to the national folklore, Australians are so smitten with gambling that they will bet on anything, including which of two flies will reach the top of a wall first. With approximately .03 percent of the world's population, Australia has at last count twenty percent of the world's slot machines (or, as they are called there, pokies).

Across the Tasman Sea, British settlers in New Zealand created a similar gambling culture. Like those who lived in Australia and the Polynesian islands from which they originally came, the Maori who lived in New Zealand had no indigenous games of chance. As in Australia, though, British settlers proved all too eager to bring their games with them. While not exactly as gambling mad as their nearest neighbors, New Zealanders developed a distinct gaming culture of their own. When serious British settlement of the islands began in the 1830s, gambling aboard ship while en route to a new life in the Southern Hemisphere was common, and it soon developed into a class-specific institution. Working-class men passed the time playing cards, dice, and roulette, while middle-class passengers played presumably more genteel lotteries. The bounty of the sea also provided numerous opportunities, as otherwise idle crewmen and passengers caught fish and birds and raffled them off. Passengers aboard the 1879 voyage of the *Niagara* (perhaps not chastened by the Ancient Mariner's injunctions) raffled an albatross, donating the proceeds to an orphanage. Lotteries often took the form of wagering how far the ship would travel on a given day or how long it would take to reach its next destination; this turned into a lively trade, as passengers, crews, and even captains placed bets. Usually, this was done in the spirit of fun, but sometimes captains took their bets too seriously. In 1890, four ships' captains sailing from Port Chalmers entered a £50 sweepstake; the winner would be the mariner to arrive first at London. Two of the boats, perhaps driven too hard by captains intent on winning the wager and bragging rights, were lost at sea.

The rugged inhabitants of New Zealand developed an enthusiastic sporting culture, of which gambling was an essential part. In addition to gambling on the cards and dice, early New Zealanders bet on several contests more properly considered tests of skill rather than chance. Regatta days provided a chance to bet not only on the nautical races but on a host of sidelights including footraces, sack jumping, and greasy-pole climbing. In the game of lazystick, which developed on the west coast of New Zealand, opponents sat with the soles of their boots touching, each grabbing a wooden rod, and attempted to pull the other to his feet. Lazystick became a tavern fixture supervised by a promoter/bookmaker who took bets from spectators.

New Zealanders also laid stakes on a variety of more traditional sports, ranging from boxing and wrestling to cycling and pedestrianism. Sports became a commercial enterprise as promoters of competing athletes made money by booking wagers on contests. Bookmakers eagerly took action on events that they hadn't organized; New Zealand's first rifle-shooting contest, for example, was rife with bookies. Cricket in particular emerged as a sport amenable to wagers, and by the 1870s, betting on the sport was a national fascination, as newspapers printed prognostications, odds, and results for games. Though open public betting was outlawed in 1881, clandestine wagering continued. Eventually, rugby became the sport most loved by New Zealanders and bookmakers extended opportunities to wager on it.

In the New Zealand goldfields, rough-and-tumble sports like boxing, wrestling, stone tossing, and tug-of-war dominated the miners' downtime, and gambling on them was prevalent. Those lacking the physical intensity to match brawn against their fellows bet on less directly strenuous contests. Promoters pitted animals from dogs to cockroaches against each other, taking bets on the outcome. Often, groups of miners simply enjoyed playing cards, with whist, loo, twenty-one, faro, the American invention poker, and the Irish game best known as forty-fives (a trick-taking game) the most popular.

Gambling at billiards and bagatelle further enriched the wagering culture of the urban hotels that served miners. Bagatelle was a cross between billiards and bowling in which players used sticks to shoot balls at a set of pins arranged at one end of a table. Eventually, with the substitution of a spring-loaded plunger for the cuestick, a form of bagatelle would evolve into the pinball machines.

Throughout colonial New Zealand, men and women who considered themselves fairly refined gambled just as assiduously as those in the throes of gold fever. As in Australia, most cardplaying took place in private homes or in gentlemen's clubs. The first, the Wellington Club, opened in the city of that name in 1841. Though club rules ostensibly forbade gambling, most clubs had a least one room devoted to cardplay. Upper-crust women also gambled, usually at small stakes in games like bridge and whist, and in later years they frequently bought tickets for lotteries, sweepstakes, and raffles.

All of New Zealand society participated in horse racing and the betting that universally accompanied it. From 1835, when the first known horse race took place in the Bay of Islands, racing developed into a Kiwi passion. Maori bought race horses from Anglo-Australians, held races in conjunction with major meets, and eventually organized their own racing clubs. Bookmakers dominated New Zealand racing form the start; as many as sixty of them would congregate at larger races, bickering as they set odds and employing touts to drum up business. At the meet itself, bettors could choose from a number of bookmakers offering different bets, sometimes at different odds. Off-track, bookmakers also thrived, either as part-timers serving a specific neighborhood or workplace or as organized businessmen who accepted wagers in publicly accessible rooms. Bookmakers, distinguished by their loud bow-ties and bright hats, exercised a strong degree of control over betting. Even when wagering was made illegal, they advertised as "commission agents" or "turf accountants" and stayed in business. As in Britain, bookmakers, as flamboyant as they were, did not monopolize racetrack gambling; gambling booths operated with impunity, offering spectators a chance at card and carnival games.

New Zealand contributed to the world of race betting when, in 1879, a man named Ekberg invented the first mechanical totalizator. In 1865, Frenchman Pierre Oller had created a mathematical system for pooling bets and paying off winners, in proportion to the amount of money in the pool, that seemed both honest and fair, as it returned a set portion to the operator and gave the bettor fairly honest odds. But performing the myriad calculations needed to properly deduce payouts was painfully time consuming, and time was something that busy bookmakers on race day didn't have. Ekberg's mechanical invention, though a far cry from the later electronic totalizator, still allowed operators to implement a reasonably efficient pari-mutuel system. It was revolutionary, and racing clubs took to the tote almost immediately. As jockey clubs derived progressively more of their revenue from tote receipts, they became more jealously protective of their trackside gambling monopolies, and during the 1880s gaming-booth proprietors began to get the boot at tracks throughout New Zealand. In 1913, George Julius, an Australian railroad engineer and inventor, would devise a version of Ekberg's mechanical tote that combined electrical with mechanical elements. The "Julius Tote" or "Premier Tote," first installed in the Ellersie racetrack in Auckland in 1913, would become the standard pari-mutuel betting device in Europe and Asia.

Gambling throughout New Zealand evolved in the late eighteenth century, as new immigrants brought new games to the colonies with them. Among the many groups drawn to New Zealand by the Otago gold rush were Chinese miners and merchants who, much as they had in the United States and Australia, established reputations as hard workers and insatiable gamblers. After the gold rush passed, many Chinese sojourners remained in New Zealand, migrating to the large cities where they usually dwelt in Chinatowns. In the goldfields and in cities, Chinese were often subjected to selective enforcement of gambling laws, as police rushed past Western-run hotels with publicly known poker rooms to roust Chinese gambling dens. Sometimes, the Chinese gamblers, with no legal recourse, responded with pragmatic posturing. Newspaper exposés excoriated the police for allowing gambling dens to flourish in urban Chinatowns, but the law officers confronted the same problem that would face them had they tried to shutter the gentlemen's clubs or taverns that allowed Anglo-Australians to gamble freely: Virtually no one in the vicinity wanted the games to stop.

But gambling's opponents secured a victory in 1881 with the passage of the Gaming and Lotteries Act, the first New Zealand measure that sought to regulate gambling. The Act banned gaming houses, off-track tote betting, and all lotteries except those that auctioned off works of art, mechanical models, or mineral specimens. Police were empowered to forcibly enter gambling houses and billiards and bagatelle parlors and seize any gambling materials found there. But even with the letter of the law behind them, the police were reluctant to enforce the act, though over the next several decades, police regularly arrested Chinese gamblers while allowing "gentlemen" to wager in clubs and at racetracks unbothered.

The act was more successful in reducing sweepstakes. In the 1870s, sweepstakes had boomed, even as a leading newspaper denounced them as "the most evil of the gambling mania" sweeping New Zealand. At the time, between rampant land speculation, race betting, card playing, and fan-tan it seemed that all of "God's Own Country" was a giant casino. Promoters, led by Wellington's unctuous George North, organized sweepstakes on horse races, both domestic and foreign (the Melbourne Cup provided a signal opportunity), and bookmakers working out of hotels raffled off everything from exotic birds to land by lottery.

Public sentiment might have been touched by appeals that the sweeps victimized the poor, but as long as they were run fairly, wealthy New Zealanders, many of whose pockets bulged thanks to savvy land speculation, found little reason to move against them. But when the opportunist North, after organizing the biggest sweepstake to date on the Wellington Cup, absconded to San Francisco with the total receipts—having already sent his family out of the country "on holiday"—many heretofore tolerant New Zealanders demanded protection against such scoundrels.* New Zealand lotteries would not recover for decades. Only art unions were permitted to run them as directly charitable endeavors, and the government did not begin dipping its toe into the lottery pool until 1929, when it organized its own Art Union. Eventually, the Lotto would become a national obsession, but it would take generations to soften the sting of George North's perfidy. As the public outcry against gambling mounted, by 1910 bookmaking had been banned, limits had been placed on tote betting, and off-track betting driven completely underground. Ironically, the country that pioneered the use of the totalizator would for decades restrict its use.

Even while they were constructing their mercantile and military empires in Asia, the British continued to raise the stakes in North America. After the Empire had lost its lower thirteen colonies in 1783, Canada remained loyal to the Crown. Although not particularly known as ardent gamblers, Canadians have developed ways of gambling quite distinct from those of their southern neighbors.

---

*North subsequently ran a barbershop in Santa Cruz, California, and sardonically told a visiting New Zealander that he planned to lecture throughout the United States on the folly of sweepstakes betting.

Most of the First Nations (native) inhabitants of Canada gambled. The inhabitants of the Pacific Northwest, for example, played a local variant of the hand game, a guessing game in which a player picked which of two hands held a marked lot. Ring-and-pin games, in which the player tried to pass a pin or ball through a ring fastened to the end of a string, were popular from the lands of the Eskimo to Labrador. Only the scattered settlements of the far north did not indulge in gambling. The first documented European contacts with Canada took place in 1501, when the Portuguese established fisheries in the Maritimes. England followed suit, and French *voyageurs* soon began penetrating deep into the continent in search of the Northwest Passage and furs.

The French traders, trappers, soldiers, and habitants who ventured into Canada carried the gambling mania with them from France. Gambling was not nearly as frenetic as in the mother country, owing to the lower population density and the relative scarcity of ready money. But this didn't slow down the diehard gamblers of Quebec. Playing cards were readily available, even when seemingly more vital necessities were not. In fact, playing cards became an officially sanctioned substitute currency in 1685. When the annual supply ship was delayed for several months, the colony's intendant, Jacques de Nuelles, was without means to pay his troops. Lacking hard currency (which was due in the resupply), he took packs of playing cards, cut the cards into quarters, wrote a money value on each card, and notarized the scrip with his initials and seal. This improvised currency circulated until the supply ship came in carrying a stock of coin, when they were promptly exchanged for specie. Playing cards were regularly used in lieu of coin from 1700 to 1719. After a brief period of financial stability, the king himself authorized the issue of more playing-card currency in 1729. Properly notarized, government-issued playing-card money continued to circulate in French Canada until the Seven Years' War (1756–1763).

At the end of the Seven Years' War, Britain assumed control of French Canada. The influx of loyalists from the lower thirteen colonies during and after the American Revolutionary War accelerated the Anglicization of Canada, and the northern colonies closely followed Britain's gambling tastes. By 1817 gambling houses had become enough of a nuisance, both in the major cities of Montreal and Quebec and in smaller country towns, to warrant a regulatory act aimed at suppressing them, specifying the most popular forms of gambling, chiefly cards, dice, checkers, shuffleboard, and bowling. Britain's class-based approach to gambling control, which let posh West End clubs flourish unhindered while targeting the rougher gambling hells, obviously influenced this act, which specified houses that appealed to "any journeyman, apprentice, laborer, or servant" as subject to sanction. An 1860 act repeated an injunction against tavern gaming, suggesting that it still continued at that time.

It is clear that the Canadians closely followed the gambling habits of the British. Similar to the mother country, the dominant form of public gambling became betting on horse racing. Native Canadians had raced horses since the eighteenth century, and when enough Anglo- or Franco-Canadians settled in an area, they, too, began racing. Originally steeplechase racing predominated, but as society became more settled, turf and jockey clubs formed and built regular tracks. Racing grew throughout the nineteenth century; Canada's signature event, the Queen's Plate, was first run near Toronto in 1860, and by the 1880s horse racing was widespread, and bookmakers began taking bets on races.

With the promulgation of the criminal code in 1892, all gambling, with the exception of regulated on-track bookmaking, was declared illegal. Pari-mutuel betting at the racetrack soon became the only legal form of Canadian gambling, although exceptions for games run to benefit charities began to be carved out. Illegal gambling flourished as well. Chinatowns throughout Canada became notorious for their gambling dens, which, unlike the relatively open halls of Australia and New Zealand, were accessible only through alleys and built to permit the quick escape of gamblers in the event of a police raid. These clandestine dens, unlike those in Australia and New Zealand, catered exclusively to Chinese patrons.

Gambling was less well hidden in Canada's great Klondike gold rush. Starting in 1896, a flood of Argonauts, armed with the accumulated wisdom of fifty years of mineral rushes from California to Australia, poured into Alaska and the Yukon in search of gold. Like gold miners everywhere, the men searching for wealth in the Great White North freely gambled. In fact, the Klondike tended to attract those who had bounced from gold strike to gold strike, so, as the weak and irresolute had been weeded out, it tended to attract a hardened, devil-may-care fortune-seeker who did not think twice about staking everything on a turn of the cards.

The boomtown of Dawson filled with saloons seeking to capture some of the wealth of the miners, and gambling in them was rampant. The North West Mounted Police, charged with maintaining order in the region, turned a blind eye to public gambling in Dawson saloons, and NWMP superintendent Charles Constantine freely stated in the late 1890s that he would not restrict gambling. He rationalized that, out in the open, gamblers would be forced to run a "square game," while if driven underground they would resort to cheating. Since the miners would gamble anyway, it was best to give them some measure of protection. In 1901, however the federal government compelled the NWMP to observe the national gambling prohibition more literally, ending a refreshingly honest regime of tolerance for Canadians' enduring desires to gamble. It would be decades before similarly enlightened public officials, with one eye on the treasury and another on the "public good," acceded to open public gambling once more.

PART FIVE

The United States Bets Big

The Battle of Shiloh, fought in early April 1862 in southwestern Tennessee, had been, with over twenty-three thousand casualties, the bloodiest engagement in American history, a costly victory for General Grant's Union forces, and an even costlier loss for the Confederacy. In the following days, Grant's armies began preparing to capture Memphis; ultimately, his Tennessee campaign would cut the Confederacy in half.

On a moonlit night shortly after the disaster at Shiloh, Yankee and Rebel pickets held their lines a few hundred yards apart. After shooting at each other, more for sport than to advance any military strategy, the opposing sides started swapping newspapers, coffee, and tobacco. Relations became so cordial that a Yankee corporal soon sauntered over to the Confederate post, sat down, and produced a deck of cards. Beginning to play with the Rebel soldiers, he was joined by five of his compatriots. The stakes went back and forth and for a while, the soldiers forgot that they were still enemy combatants. Whether through luck or skill, the Southerners got the better of the Yankees, until only one of them remained in the game.

At that point, a Union sergeant, with four musket-toting men behind him, broke up the game, announcing that the Union soldiers were under arrest for deserting their posts. The corporal began to protest, but he was cut short by a new arrival: General Ulysses S. Grant himself, on horseback. The unfortunate Union soldiers, in hasty terror, saluted their commander and shuffled back to camp.

Before leaving, the steely-eyed general, who was himself known to play cards on occasion, removed the trademark cigar from his mouth and asked the nearest Confederate who was ahead.

"Oh, we are," replied the rebel soldier. "Those chumps you've brought down here can't play poker a little bit," another soldier piped in, "but they can fight, General."

"Have to, sometimes," the general replied before riding off into the night.

His soldiers might have been fighting for the cause of Union, but for them nothing was more American than a quick poker break.

II

Wild Cards

GAMBLING MOVES WEST

Chronicling his travels in the 1830s among the kingless peoples of the growing United States, Alexis de Tocqueville was struck by the equality of conditions there and the enterprise of the hustling Americans. For them, all of life was a gamble. "Those who live in the midst of democratic fluctuations," he wrote, "have always before their eyes the image of chance; and they end by liking all undertakings in which chance plays a part." Though his words were true for all the nation, the West (itself a moving frontier) has always been particularly attractive to gamblers.

When Thomas Jefferson bought Louisiana from Napoleon in 1803, New Orleans became the gambling capital of the United States overnight, and it would hold the title for most of the first half of the nineteenth century. The three most popular games in the United States over the next hundred and fifty years each began or were introduced to Americans in New Orleans. A century later, the city would be the birthplace of the uniquely American music, jazz; but even in the first years of the nineteenth century, New Orleans gamblers were improvising and innovating with cards and dice.

In most of the country, gambling was ostensibly illegal. Not so in New Orleans. The Crescent City was known as a gambling center from its 1718 founding. The territory itself was the centerpiece of John Law's infamous speculative scheme that almost bankrupted the French royal government in 1720, so it isn't surprising that those who actually lived in the province felt no compunctions about gambling. Under French and Spanish administration, gambling in taverns and coffeehouses was common, and despite draconian penalties for infraction, including whipping, time in the stocks, and branding, laws against gambling were usually ignored. With the American acquisition of the Louisiana Territory in 1803, New Orleans became the terminus for thousands of square miles of hinterland. Farmers and merchants from throughout the American interior swarmed into New Orleans to sell and buy goods; flush with money, many of them lost some of it at the gambling houses that soon sprouted. With such thriving trade, New Orleans quickly had more gambling per capita than any other city in the union.

In preparation for its incorporation into the United States, the Louisiana territorial legislature outlawed gambling throughout the state in 1811. But three years later, with the state safely admitted to the United States, legislators again allowed legal gambling in New Orleans under the supervision of the municipal authorities. They lacked the personnel to properly oversee the houses, and in 1820, the legislature returned to prohibition. Three years later, after concerted lobbying efforts by municipal authorities and prospective operators, the legislature approved an ambitious plan for legal gambling houses that would balance profits with philanthropy.

According to the scheme, the city would license six gambling houses that would pay $5,000 each per year. Four fifths of the $30,000 raised was earmarked for the Charity Hospital (which operated until Hurricane Katrina forced its closure in 2005) and the remainder was to subsidize the College of Orleans, an institution of higher education that would close in 1826. Within a year of their 1823 opening, the houses thrived, and their operators, demanding the police close down their unlicensed competitors, successfully forced the closure of all the illegal houses (except those in the rough river districts, where the police feared to tread). But these small houses provided no entertainment, no meals, and no refreshments other than hard liquor. Though they did a booming business among rugged merchants and river workers on a spree, these houses didn't attract the really wealthy gamblers.

John Davis, though, set a new standard when he opened a West End–style gambling palace. Born in Saint-Domingue (he relocated to New Orleans after the Haitian Revolution in the 1790s), Davis was a French-educated man of considerable wealth and social standing. In 1827 he opened his club next to his Orleans Ballroom at Orleans and Bourbon streets. Nothing like it had ever been seen before in America: Its players, who were free to help themselves to a delectable buffet, were awed by its luxury. Davis's selection of wines and liquors was renowned. Players found they didn't mind losing, so long as they found a comfortable chair in the opulent salons afterward. Davis soon opened a satellite operation on Bayou St. John to handle the weekend overflow. Within two years, his rivals realized that Davis's magnificent gambling palace was far more profitable than their humble faro dens, and they hurried to open their own high-class operations. In 1832, the legislature removed the cap on the number of licenses and raised the annual fee to $7,500. Suddenly, there were a score of legal gambling houses where high-stakes betting on faro, roulette, and, to a lesser extent, twenty-one flourished with the happy acquiescence of the law.

Davis offered the French favorite, roulette, and even a few tables for the underappreciated twenty-one, but most of his customers were intent on losing their money at one game: faro. Davis's ingenuity and cunning provided an advantage that the mathematics of the game did not. His dealers, like most others, often used perfidy to sway the odds in their favor. He also provided guests with the facilities for a number of social games, including écarte, boston, brag, and a newcomer known as poker, an American adaptation of a French game.

Those who invented the game were, unfortunately, too busy playing to keep records of its birth, but card historian David Parlett believes that poker traces its roots to earlier vying games. Some claim poker descended from an ancient Persian game known as *as nas,* but *as nas* itself is not that old and was probably inspired by the same vying games that preceded poker. As early as the sixteenth century, games like the French brelan and the Italian primero had vying elements in them. Poker's more obvious ancestor is the German game *pochen,* which consisted of three different phases: In one of them, players bet as to who had the best combination of cards. The game migrated to France in the late sixteenth century, where it became known as *poque.* By the time it reached the United States in the late eighteenth century, it was played with a twenty-card deck (A-K-Q-J-10) that allowed four players five cards each. There was only one round of betting, and no discarding or drawing of new cards.

Poque was introduced to North America via the French colony at Louisiana and became poker, thanks to casual American pronunciation of the French original, sometime between 1810 and 1825. As it was played then, the winning combinations were one pair, two pair, triplets, a full house (a triplet with a pair), and four of a kind. Two hands were absolutely unbeatable: four aces, and four kings with one ace. Between 1830 and 1850, poker players started using the full fifty-two-card deck, and both straights (a consecutive sequence of unsuited cards) and flushes (cards matching in suit) became winning combinations.

In the second half of the nineteenth century, two innovations put a decidedly American twist on the game. The introduction of the draw meant that, after the cards were dealt, players could discard those they didn't want and replace them with (hopefully) better cards. It was a fitting addition in the democratic republic, particularly out West, where many Americans went to start over. Around the same time, jackpots were added to the game: This rule prohibited players from opening unless they had paired jacks or better, while mandating that they bet if they held jacks. This rule was often unpopular, as it took away from the cherished unruliness of the game, by which someone holding no cards of value could bluff his way to victory. But, with these rule changes, poker became the American social game par exellence, and it continued to evolve into various forms to take into account changing tastes.

Craps, another New Orleans innovation, took longer to become popular but would become a leading casino game. It originated as hazard, the medieval dice game that remained a British favorite. In Europe, the game originally pitted caster against setter at fairly even odds, and most houses that featured hazard profited only by collecting a box fee; when a player hit three mains in a row, he paid the croupier his minimum bet. London gaming houses that banked hazard themselves (a variation called French hazard), turned it into a straight-up mercantile game. The game was known to French settlers in New Orleans under the name "crabs" or "craps" (from the "crabs" roll). In 1804 the wealthy planter Bernard de Marigny lost so much of his money to the game the he was forced to sell his land. He wistfully named a street carved from his property the Rue de Craps, perhaps the earliest mention of the game in America.

Sometime before 1840, anonymous Americans streamlined the game by removing from it the dice caster's "chance." Now the caster, more properly called the shooter, had to follow a simple rule: If, when coming out, he rolled seven or eleven, he automatically won, and if he got two, three, or twelve, he automatically lost, or "crapped out." Any other roll became his point, and he had to roll it before seven in order to win. African-Americans were among the first players, and likely the inventors, of American craps. Black roustabouts and other river workers up and down the Mississippi were for years the most eager players of "African dominoes," which was played as a social game. Gambling houses commercialized the game by charging a flat fee—usually between five and twenty-five cents—each time a shooter made two passes. This variation, called "take-off craps," wasn't that lucrative, so gaming operators continued to innovate, and by World War I, "bank craps," played on a layout with pass, don't pass, come, don't come, proposition, and field bets, was well known. Players spread it beyond the inner cities during World War I and World War II, when it was a common game among soldiers. By the close of World War II, it had entirely displaced faro in the legal gambling halls of Nevada and was, until the rise of blackjack in the 1960s, the preeminent American casino game.

Faro and craps were joined by chuck-a-luck, also known as sweat or sweatcloth and later birdcage (for the implement used to spin its dice). This was a game in which players bet on the outcome of a single roll of three dice. Other games were not so much gambling as they were out-and-out swindles. Thimblerig, or the shell game, involved a player trying to guess under which of three thimbles the operator had hidden a ball or pea. It was inevitably crooked. Three-card monte (not related to the Mexican card game of monte) used cards to achieve the same ends. The later variation banco, also known as bunko and bunco, was first played in San Francisco in the 1850s, and it was so notoriously dishonest that *bunco* became a synonym for any confidence game. Yet, in New Orleans and elsewhere in the growing United States, gamblers never failed to find fresh victims willing to take their chances on these swindles.

New Orleans remained the nation's gambling capital into the 1830s, though Mobile, Alabama, ran a close second. From New Orleans, professional gamblers fanned the length of the Mississippi and Ohio Rivers, and nearly every river town had a red-light district where gamblers, thieves, assassins, and prostitutes waited to entertain—and, if necessary, intimidate or even murder— gullible travelers for profit. Desperados and professional gamblers were allowed to work with impunity in underworld districts like New Orleans's Swamp, Memphis's Pinch Gut, Vicksburg's Landing, and Natchez-under-the-Hill. Local lawmen were frankly too afraid to venture into these districts.

The underground confraternity of gamblers was a loose group that never had any real organization. But in 1835, a white bandit named John A. Murrell began organizing gamblers and garden-variety ruffians in a murderous cabal known as the Clan of the Mystic Confederation. Inspired by the fears aroused by Denmark Vesey's earlier attempted insurrection, Murrell organized two thousand outlaws and began encouraging the black slaves of Louisiana and Mississippi to revolt on Christmas Day, 1835. Unlike Vesey, Murrell's men were not motivated by the injustice of slavery. Rather, they planned to use the rebellion as a cover for their brigandage: While most of the citizens hurried to quash the uprising, the Clan would attack and loot defenseless Natchez, Vicksburg (Mississippi), and New Orleans. But, as with Vesey's conspiracy, news of the plan leaked out; several black leaders of the planned uprising were executed (though Murrell remained at large), and rumors circulated that the uprising would now occur on July 4.

When the holiday rolled around, white citizens throughout Mississippi and Louisiana were understandably nervous and none too well disposed toward gamblers, whom they now saw as an enemy within even more disturbing than abolitionists. In nearly every vice district, mobs of gamblers, thugs, and prostitutes milled drunkenly about the streets. Though most of their leaders had fled, they were still restively menacing. Memphis saw some minor looting, but the hooligans became so distracted by their own carousing that the threat quickly subsided. But in Vicksburg, long a gambling center, the day began in fear and ended in murder.

The Vicksburg Volunteers, a local militia, had chosen to celebrate the nation's independence with a barbecue and speeches. In the midst of what was no doubt a particularly stirring bit of oratory, about six of the city's most notorious gamblers, boisterously intoxicated, intruded. One of them, a brawler named Francis Cabler, made his way to the rostrum, overturning tables and chairs along the way. He insulted and struck a militia officer attempting to stop him, whereupon the Volunteers bodily ejected him. Near the end of the event, word arrived that Cabler was returning, ready to kill the officer he had hit earlier and any who stood in his way. Staggering around the town's main square brandishing a pistol and knife, he was quickly disarmed and placed under arrest. The Volunteers, without resorting to the nicety of a trial, tied Cabler to a tree, administered thirty-two lashes, tarred and feathered him, and ordered him to leave town within forty-eight hours.

Outraged by this abuse of one of their number, two other gamblers, James Hoard and Henry Wyatt, drew together a band of followers and began marching on the city's hill (where most respectable citizens lived), pledging to burn down its fine houses. They were quickly repulsed, but a hastily called town meeting passed an ordinance giving all professional gamblers twenty-four hours to leave town. Most of the blacklegs melted away, but a small gang of gamblers remained. On July 6, the Volunteers made good on the town's resolve and began a search of every suspected faro house in Vicksburg, confiscating all of the gambling equipment they found. Reaching a tavern where several of the gamblers had holed up, they met with resistance. Shots fired from the second floor killed Dr. Hugh Bodley, a popular local physician. With this, the Volunteers, assisted by enraged fellow citizens, stormed the house and seized the gamblers inside. They then marched the five ruffians they had found to the grove where all of the trouble had begun at the barbecue two days earlier and, without a trial, hanged each of them. All of the faro tables and roulette wheels discovered were burned and the money found in the houses returned to citizens who could prove that they had lost it. Neither Hoard, the leader of the gamblers, nor Cabler, whose drunken antics had started the uproar, was among those hanged.

The Vicksburg lynching and lingering fears over Murrell's conspiracy forced a violent reaction against gamblers throughout the region. In cities like Lexington, Mobile, Natchez, and Cincinnati, townspeople formed antigambling societies and demanded the enforcement of laws against mercantile games. Louisiana renewed its prohibition on gambling houses, ending, at least temporarily, its experiment with legal gaming. In New Orleans, gambling houses remained strictly suppressed for about ten years, but with the 1846 mobilization for the Mexican-American War, for which the port was a major nexus, several houses opened. The houses boomed two years later with the excitement of the California Gold Rush (New Orleans was a popular port for California-bound steamers), and by 1850 it was estimated that five-hundred gambling houses were in operation. By the middle of the decade, some even rivaled Davis's in splendor, but they all would disappear—for a time—with the coming of the Civil War.

By the time that the Vicksburg Volunteers declared war on gambling in their town, it was estimated that between one thousand and fifteen hundred professionals worked the steamboats that plied the Mississippi and Ohio between New Orleans and Louisville. When the winds of reform blew down the gambling dens of their city haunts, the blacklegs there simply joined their brethren on the river, starting the golden age of the riverboat gambler.

Steamboats, which could navigate both up- and downriver, were a distinct improvement over the earlier flatboats that had previously floated goods only downriver, and after 1820, they dominated river transportation. As boats got faster, betting men began to lay stakes on which of two boats was the faster. Sometimes, captains bet as well, with frequently tragic results: Throwing safety aside, they overloaded their boat's boilers, which could win the race but might trigger a deadly explosion. In 1838 alone nearly five hundred people perished in such blasts. This major public safety issue of the day led Congress to pass its first major regulatory act when in 1852 it set standards for boiler construction and steamboat licensing.

A uniquely mixed bunch, from English lords to backwoods farmers, passed the time convivially in the upper deck's main saloon, which sported a bar at one end and tables throughout. Striking up a conversation and beginning a friendly game of cards was not difficult, and the anonymity of the riverboat gave the professional gambler a cloak of respectability. With his handsome clothes and genteel affectations, he might be anyone: a plantation owner, a merchant, a salesman—even a minister.

In the earliest days of steamboat travel, professional gamblers were rarely tolerated; if discovered, they were usually put ashore immediately. But by 1830 gamblers were such a regular presence that they were practically crew members. Some captains claimed it was bad luck to sail without a gambler and refused to leave the docks until a member of the fraternity had come on board. This new tolerance was aided by the fact that gamblers had begun cutting in the captain and crew, in effect paying a license fee for permission to operate aboard freely. Only those who perpetrated the most outrageous (or maladroit) of frauds, or those who had chosen a victim whose political or social connections demanded action, suffered any chastisement from the crew.

The archetypal riverboat gambler cut a striking figure, with his knee-length broadcloth coat, exquisitely tailored black or soft gray pants, loose-collared, ruffled white shirt, and characteristic dark hats. Even gamblers' boots were imported from Paris. They wore vests decorated with intricate designs and ornate buttons, along with a variety of ruby and gold rings, but reserved their greatest extravagance for a single signature piece: a glittering stickpin or a massive gold watch. These showboaters found their ornaments had a practical value: They were expensive, easily transportable, and quickly negotiable, and could thus be wagered when their money ran out, or pawned if in a desperate pinch.

Blacklegs happily played social games like brag, euchre, whist, boston, all fours, and poker, and mercantile ones like faro, twenty-one, and chuck-a-luck. In all games, though, they had an absolutely ironclad advantage: cheating. When, for some reason, they couldn't use gimmicked cards or slick dealing to help themselves, blacklegs used confederates who signaled their opponents' cards by a series of prearranged gestures, from hand movements to smoke puffs and cane twirls.

These professionals victimized anyone willing to play but had particularly sharp knives waiting for wealthy plantation owners and naïve young men with family fortunes to lose. They usually worked in groups of between three and six and played out a recurring social drama. Pretending to be a stranger to the dealer, a roper would steer a fresh victim to him, while a capper joined in the betting, winning big, making the dealer appear to be inexpert, and cajoling the dupe into playing for high stakes. The victim was then efficiently cleaned out.

George Devol, born in 1829, had a long career on the riverboats; in 1887 he published the autobiography *Forty Years a Gambler on the Mississippi,* which recounted a life of adventure that began when, at the age of ten, he became a cabin boy aboard the steamer *Wacousta.* He became yet another blackleg that cheated unwary travelers mercilessly, leaving a trail of empty pockets in their wake.

But Devol shows that the Mississippi gambler was not thoroughly despicable. Often, he used his dark arts to benefit those in need. Once in Natchez Devol helped a few elderly ladies trying to raise $100 for their church by raffling an embroidered lap robe. Though he had no need for such an article, Devol bought up $50 worth of chances and rigged the contest so that he won. He then returned the lap robe to the ladies, who raffled it again; after winning it a second time, he returned it again. On the third try he allowed someone else to win the lap robe, and the ladies had made $400. While he made no money from orchestrating the lottery thus, he was not being entirely altruistic: "I think that money spent did me more good than any that I ever squandered," he wrote, "for I was the recipient of the thanks as well as the prayers of the ladies." Devol also took pleasure in cheating known thieves out of stolen money, though in his memoirs he mentioned no efforts to return the money to its rightful owners. He may not have given up gambling in deference to the fire-and-brimstone-preaching ministers he met (he recounted that even men of the cloth were eager, often gullible, gamblers), but he wasn't above hedging his bets.

Cheating riverboat travelers was best accomplished through teamwork, and there was plenty of wealth to go around. But sometimes gamblers bilked their own, just for the fun of it. Devol described one such occasion when a gambler, thinking he was the captain, asked his permission to open a faro game. Devol assented, then had his partner keep the gambler occupied while Devol broke into his room, opened his suitcase, and secretly marked all of his cards. The crafty Devol then replaced the cards as they were and returned to

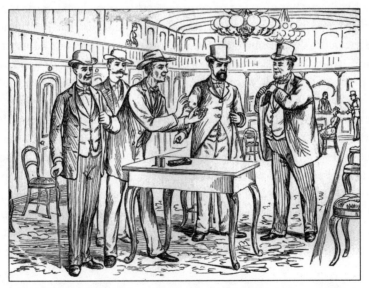

Wily riverboat gamblers dupe an unsuspecting wealthy grocer at three-card monte in an elegantly outfitted upper-deck saloon.

the deck. After supper, his new friend brought out his cards and started a game. The would-be sharper found that he had uncommonly bad luck that night, as Devol and his partner quickly broke him, even winning his gaming tools. Looking for new sport, Devol then fleeced the other passengers at three-card monte (his specialty), winning all of their money, as well as their watches and pistols. All told, the pair made $3,600 that night.

Devol lived through the golden age of the riverboat gambler, roughly 1830 to 1860. The Civil War, which lasted from 1861 to 1865, ruptured the trade between North and South that was the reason for most of the travelers to take riverboats in the first place. As war raged across the land, riverboat gamblers continued to bilk army officers and others who traveled over the rivers, and gambling continued in the cities.

When Union troops took control of New Orleans in May 1862, the city's new commander, General Benjamin F. Butler, immediately closed all gambling houses. He then began issuing licenses, allowing houses to reopen on the condition that they pay the license fee and take his brother in as a partner. George Devol, remembering the general's administration of the city, allowed that he had kept New Orleans clean but noted that his share of the gambling houses had made Butler "independently rich."*

Soldiers who took up the banner of union and fought for the North, if not already familiar with gambling, soon learned all about it. Soldiers' letters home are filled with references to the universality of gambling. One soldier wrote in his diary that nine out of ten men in his unit played cards for money and remembered that after the battle of Fredericksburg he had played in a marathon twenty-four-hour poker game. Indeed, poker was the most prevalent game, followed by twenty-one, euchre, faro, and all fours, also called seven-up or sledge. Cards were popular because they were easily portable and didn't require much level ground to play; dice were considerably less convenient, and craps was rare, though chuck-a-luck was fairly common. Soldiers also raffled items from watches to horses and bet on impromptu horse races and cockfights. Companies often maintained their ésprit de corps by adopting a fighting bird as a mascot and matching it against rival troops' champions.

Gambling was pervasive, but the stakes were paltry—not because soldiers showed much restraint, but because their pay was generally low. Some intrepid gamblers played poker during artillery bombardments, oblivious to the carnage around them. Others, remembering that many at home considered

---

*Devol was not exactly a disinterested chronicler: Butler had already thrown him in jail for bilking one of his officers and confiscated the gambler's horses.

gambling a sin, repented of it on the march to battle and cast aside their cards. If they survived the battle, they never took long to rediscover the joys of gambling, sometimes searching through the mounds of cast-off cards to pick up enough strays to build a full deck. Though some blacklegs made the rounds of army camps on payday and mercilessly stripped soldiers of their cash, for the most part Northern soldiers played social games among themselves for small stakes, a common enough phenomenon in virtually every military force since the Roman legions.

Confederates played even more than their Union enemies. Southern troops had been gambling from the war's start, but by November 1862 it had reached epidemic proportions. General Robert E. Lee issued an order in which he declared himself to be "pained to learn that the vice of gambling exists, and is becoming common in this army." Like their counterparts to the north, rebel soldiers raffled off items without limit, and betting on horse races, particularly in cavalry units, became so common that it threatened army discipline. A Texas regiment in 1863 threatened court-martial for any officer caught betting on a horse race.

Cards, particularly poker, were just as common as in the North, along with dice. In a gambling den called Devil's Half-Acre near Fredericksburg, soldiers ran chuck-a-luck games nearly nonstop during the winter of 1862–63. Officers often threatened gamblers, but players showed their Confederate patriotism by using cards adorned with Jefferson Davis or leading generals. As the South's fortunes fell, playing cards became scarcer, and gamblers could only get new decks from Union prisoners or from the haversacks of the dead. When the cards were no longer usable, the rebel soldiers continued improvising games, including paper boat races and louse fights. Despite the disapproval of leaders, including the quietly virtuous General Stonewall Jackson, Southern soldiers were, for the most part, incurable gamblers.

Some Confederates, like the Union soldiers they fought, substituted Bibles for the cards they usually carried as they marched into battle. But those tempted into discarding their "sinful" gambling tools were given pause by a cautionary tale. An inveterate rebel gambler, it was said, carried a pack of cards into combat. During the fight, a bullet hit him, but struck the cards and was deflected; he survived to play again. A soldier fighting alongside him, who carried a Bible, was also struck in the pocket, but the Bible failed to block the bullet and he died instantly. Whatever their merits as body armor, men thought twice about throwing away their cards, particularly when they knew they would be retrieving them soon after battle, anyway.

Despite the animosity between North and South, gambling sometimes brought soldiers from enemy camps together. At night, soldiers crossed the pickets and, finding a suitably neutral site, enjoyed a quick drink and game of cards together. One Southern officer, inspecting his lines late one night during the Petersburg campaign (1864–1865), found them to be nearly empty; he learned that the men charged with protecting the rebel flank were in fact playing cards in the Union trenches. Gambling was impossible to suppress on either side of the lines.

There was even a semilegendary gamblers' brigade, the Wilson Rangers, of Louisiana. A group of New Orleans gamblers, caught up in the patriotic rush to enlist at the Civil War's outbreak, formed a cavalry company of their own with George Devol as a member. They bought themselves the finest apparel, equipment, and horses to be had and made an immediate impression. "The ladies said we were the finest-looking set of men in the army," Devol wrote. They drilled strenuously: Devol recalled that they would assemble, mount their horses, and ceremoniously gallop out of the city. Upon their return, the residents cheered them, thinking that they had spent all day preparing to defend the city. But, Devol wrote, that was not exactly true:

> The first orders we would receive from our commanding officer would be: "Dismount! Hitch horses! March! Hunt shade! Begin playing!" There was not a company of cavalry in the Southern army that obeyed orders more promptly than we did; for in less than ten minutes from the time the order was given, there would not be a man in the sun. They were all in the shade, seated on the ground in little groups . . . and in each group could be seen a little book of tactics (or at least it looked something like a book from a distance). We would remain in the shade until the cool of the evening, when the orders would be given: "Cease playing! Put up books! Prepare to mount! Mount! March!"

The Wilson Rangers dreaded the possibility of actually fighting. When the Union army began marching on New Orleans, the cavalry rode out to defend the town with little heart and, at the first warning shot, promptly broke ranks and raced each other back to the city, where they removed the military insignia from their coats, buried their sabers, and tried to pass themselves off as men of peace for, as Devol wrote, "we had enough of military glory, and were tired of war." His compatriots were smart enough to know that, when the game was played with cannon shot and bullets, they were green suckers, and they had no illusions about it.

After the Civil War, railroads supplanted riverboats as the nation's transportation network. With the completion of the transcontinental railroad in 1869, the Rubicon had been crossed, and, until overtaken by the automobile, trains represented the new cutting edge. Not as picturesque as quietly gliding riverboats, they nevertheless allowed Americans to travel farther and quicker than they had before. Aboard them, gamblers worked the smoking cars with the same ingenuity they had shown on the riverboats, bilking suckers mercilessly.

With the expansion of the American economy in the postwar years, gambling houses became far more common. Soon every major city had at least one house dedicated to cards and dice, and the colorful figure of the artful blackleg gave way to the mercilessly efficient gambling syndicate, who bankrolled the major houses of the new age. In the West, though, the gambler became forever enshrined in the romantic mythology of the wild frontier. The true story of Western gambling, of course, was often just as fantastic as the tall tales it inspired, but it was, in many ways, simply an adjustment of the riverboat gambler to a new milieu: the cow towns, mining camps, and boomtowns of the Wild West.

Throughout the nineteenth century, both the law and conventional morality seemed to have a weaker hold on the Western frontier than in the more settled East. As a result, gambling flourished. While every major American city from the 1840s on had a thriving gambling underworld, in the West gambling went on full view of the public much of the time. "Wide-open" regimes, in which local law enforcement tolerated, and even supported, professional gamblers, were common. Blacklegs who had learned their craft on the riverboats followed the cowboys, prospectors, and cattle barons west; as always, they went where there was money to be made. They left in their wake a colorful legacy of anecdote, myth, and legend that remains a living part of American memory.

Anglo-Americans moving into the previously Mexican settlements of the West, found that existing Mexican towns had one or more *salas* (gambling halls). Newly settled areas also had plenty of gambling: On mining and ranching frontiers, most new arrivals were single men, freed from familial restraints, who spent most of their hard-earned cash in gambling halls, saloons, and dance halls. Gambling dominated cow towns and mining camps.

Those coming to California in the frenzied days of the Gold Rush did not wait for their arrival "in the diggings" to begin gambling. Gaming, particularly poker, ran day and night on the steamers that took men to the jumping-off points for the overland trail. As companies of men made their way to the goldfields with their wagons, they broke up the tedium of camp life with games of cards by the fire. Faro and roulette were popular for those lucky enough to spend the night in town, and who had the ready money. In Independence, Missouri, two gambling houses ran around the clock; their windows, kept permanently open, attracted scores of customers with the jingling of coin and excited chatter. Gambling was just as dangerous a diversion for those who took the isthmus route, by which Argonauts sailed from an eastern port or New Orleans, landed at Chagres on the Atlantic Coast of Panama, hacked through the jungle for two or three days to reach the Pacific port of Panama City, and caught another steamboat to San Francisco. Unfortunately, there was often a long wait for ships to California, and faro throwers, thimbleriggers, and monte dealers had a field day with unwary gold-seekers. Many a quest for gold ended at the faro tables.

Once men reached the mining camps, the lust for gambling, if anything, was even less restrained. Life in the camps was hard: All day was spent panning in rivers and picking at rocks for gold. In the evenings and on Sundays, professional gamblers were more than happy to help the weary miners relax by playing cards or roulette. One of the first businesses to open in any new settlement was invariably a gaming house in a makeshift tent. Even miners who had not gambled at home now did so without hesitation. One letter writer spoke in 1850 of a Methodist minister who spent his days mining and his nights playing monte and other games. Many miners did not wait to get back to camp to gamble, and card games in the mines themselves, with stakes of hundreds of dollars, became common.

In the boomtowns, gambling houses were, with saloons and brothels, often the most lavish structures built, and the action was intense. A visitor to Aurora, Nevada, one of these meteoric settlements, lamented the overabundance of liquor and gambling, and the miners' predilection for both: "Where men are congregated and living uncomfortably, where there are no home ties or social checks, no churches, no religions—one sees gambling and vice in all its horrible realities." The typical saloon was a one-stop shop for late-night revelers: One wall offered the bar, another a chop stand, where patrons could get fried steaks and meat, and in the rear or in a separate room stood the gambling tables, where hundreds or thousands of dollars' worth of

"Sunday amusements" in the White Pine Mining District, Nevada, 1869. The game is faro.

gold and silver was staked, joined in more upscale establishments by a billiard table.

Gambling was so common throughout the mining frontier, from California to Montana, that dogfights, bearfights, and bearbaiting were rampant. One man even proclaimed his "killer duck" an interspecies champion and pitted it against all canine challengers. It is no wonder that most who came to the goldfields in search of wealth returned home empty handed. Running a gambling house was the easiest way to mine for gold.

San Francisco stood at the center of this mining mania and, in the years after the 1848 discovery of gold at Sutter's Fort, had more gambling per capita than any other city in America. The gambling houses of San Francisco became renowned, and during the heady boom years, gambling was the chief recreation of San Franciscans.

The first gambling house was the El Dorado, which opened in the spring of 1848 in a canvas tent at Washington and Kearny Streets. The tent was soon replaced by a hastily constructed wood building whose proprietors rented out to Thomas Chambers, the El Dorado's operator, for the princely sum of $40,000 a month (at the time, a ten-room house could be built in the East for $2,000). Unlike the gambling palaces of John Davis, this resort had little luxury to it. With a monopoly, though, gamblers flocked in, hundreds each night. The El Dorado was so fantastically lucrative that, soon, a host of other gambling houses sprang up; by 1850, there were at least one thousand of them in San Francisco.

The most successful establishments were centered on Portsmouth Square, where they took up all of the eastern side, three fourths of the northern, and

much of the south. The El Dorado was king of the square, while other famous names included Dennison's Exchange, the Empire, the Mazourka, the
Arcade, the Varsouvienne, the Ward House, the Parker House, the Fontinem
House, La Souciedad, the Alhambra, and the Aguila de Oro. Fire regularly
swept through the wood shanties and ramshackle structures of San Francisco
in this era, and most gambling houses were rebuilt regularly; few, therefore,
had any luxurious furnishings, for they were more likely to be incinerated
than not. Most were built along a similar plan: a large room with a long bar
on one side, a main floor packed with tables, and an elevated stage, on which
bands performed.

There were no sumptuous complimentary buffets (food and liquor were
prohibitively expensive), but demure-looking girls selling refreshments flitted
through most houses. One of the most popular games was monte, a game invented and usually dealt by Mexicans. It was not related to the three-card version of the thimblerig swindle but rather was played with a forty-card deck
(the standard minus eights through tens). Like faro, the object of monte was
to guess the position of a drawn card. To play, the dealer accepted bets, shuffled, cut, and then drew two cards off for the bottom layout and two more for
the top layout. He then drew the "gate," and if the card matched one in the
top or bottom layout, he paid the winners accordingly.

Gambling among the Chinese immigrants in San Francisco was believed
to be inestimable. As soon as the authorities succeeded in suppressing one
gambling den, two more would sprout up elsewhere. They offered games familiar in Chinatowns around the world: fan tan, the "white pigeon ticket"
pakapoo lottery, and mahjong. As elsewhere, the Chinese disdained all Western games, not giving a whit for the charms of faro, poker, or roulette, though
whites flocked to play *pakapoo*.

San Francisco gambling houses were uniformly lucrative operations. The
El Dorado averaged profits of between $100,000 and $200,000 a month during its peak years. These establishments made their profits from hundreds of
small fry who bet between 50¢ and $10 a hand. Cumulatively, the turnover
was enormous. Initially, these profits could be enjoyed openly, as Golden State
gambling was at first completely legal. Gamblers were nevertheless linked to
political corruption, and in 1856 a series of lynchings persuaded many operators to leave for greener pastures. State laws began criminalizing specific
games, but wily operators simply renamed them and continued dealing. In
1860, an ironclad statute banned all bank games, thus ending legal mercantile
gambling. The legislature first targeted only professional gambling operators,

but in 1885 it criminalized the very act of gambling, and by 1891 the penalties for owning and playing in a game were equalized.

After vigilantes and the law pushed them out of San Francisco, professional gamblers filtered eastward. Denver, founded in 1858, became a gambling center almost immediately. In the first years, most play went on at the Denver House, a hotel made from logs that, along with its rustic charm, boasted a drinking and gambling saloon. Men bet money, real estate, and even their revolvers. Monte, faro, and three-card monte were the most common games. Though opposed by the burgeoning town's more upright citizens, professional gamblers nevertheless played, barring intermittent periods of reform closure, more or less wide open into the 1920s. The gambling in mining towns like Cripple Creek, Creede, and Leadville was similarly public. Farther to the north, with the discovery of gold in the Black Hills, Deadwood, South Dakota, became a notorious gambling center, as did Tombstone, Arizona, to the south.

The popular stereotype of the Western American gambler of this era is a rangy, mustachioed, ambling Anglo-American of southern descent, but gamblers came from every part of the United States and the world. The Chinese, Peruvians, and Australians who flooded into California with the Gold Rush (Mexicans had, of course, been there for decades already) each brought distinctive gambling habits with them. Native Americans continued their games of chance, and new arrivals, it seemed, competed with them to see who could wager the most. Wherever there was a population center, one was sure to find gamblers. In the 1870s, for example, between thirty and forty gambling houses ran in Kansas City, Missouri, though many professionals were chased across the river into Kansas City, Kansas, after the enactment of an antigambling law in 1881. Santa Fe was the unofficial gambling capital of the Southwest for much of the nineteenth century.

In the cow towns that sprouted at the juncture of railroads and cattle trails, gambling was notorious. Licentious Cheyenne, Wyoming, known as "Hell on Wheels" for most of the 1870s, saw virtually unrestricted gambling, as did a series of cow towns: Abilene, Wichita, Newton, Caldwell, Hays, Ellsworth, and the largest and westernmost, Dodge City. These towns catered to cowboys flush with money after long months on the trail, buffalo hunters, railroad workers, and soldiers. Gambling was the chief business there: Abilene had thirty gambling dens and saloons, and only three other businesses, on one of its major streets. Gambling houses helped establish the new settlements as wild hubs of mayhem.

In its heyday as a gambling nirvana, roughly 1850 to 1910, the American West produced some of the most infamous figures in the history of gambling. These fast-dealing gambling entrepreneurs of the land were cut from a different cloth than the bankers, managers, and croupiers of Baden-Baden and Monte Carlo. Some were impetuous hotheads, bluffing wildly on a hunch, while others were serenely philosophical, like Bret Harte's fictional hero John Oakhurst, who seldom lost his cool. "He was too much of a gambler not to accept Fate," Harte wrote of the black-garbed Oakhurst. "With him life was at best an uncertain game, and he recognized the usual percentage in favor of the dealer."

Real-life gamblers were no less colorful. Perhaps the best remembered is James Butler "Wild Bill" Hickok, whose death is associated to this day with a certain poker hand. Born in Illinois in 1837, Hickok was an excellent gunslinger: His fame is chiefly due to an 1868 *Harper's Magazine* article about his exploits, real and embellished, and his tour in Buffalo Bill Cody's Wild West show. His reputation helped him prevail over defter card mechanics at the gaming table. In the course of one game, a player periodically dropped cards into his hat; when satisfied with his hand, he pushed $200 into the pot. Hickok drew a pistol and declared that he was calling the hand in the hat. No one objected when he swept the pot. In another game, he was outmatched against a crew of cheaters. After going all-in and losing to a superior hand, Hickok pulled two revolvers as the winner was about to sweep the pot. Fixing his guns on the sharpers, he calmly announced that "I have a pair of sixes and they beat anything." The other gamblers made no outward protest as Hickok took the pot.

In 1876, Hickok's travels took him to Deadwood. Hickok had had a premonition that he would not leave the grimly named town alive; he was right. On August 2, 1876, he was playing poker in Saloon Number Six with his back to the door. Jack McCall, a saloon journeyman with no known quarrel or connection with Hickok, sneaked up behind the famed gunslinger and shot him in the back of the head. Hickok died instantly, clutching two black aces and two black eights. Ever since then, black aces and eights have been known as "the dead man's hand." (There has been considerable speculation about the fifth card; some say that, as the deal was in progress, Hickok hadn't yet picked it up, while others say that it was the nine, jack, or queen of diamonds, and others insist it was the queen of hearts.)

Doc Holliday was equally notorious. Born John Henry Holliday to a wealthy family in Georgia, Holliday was diagnosed with tuberculosis shortly after he completed his studies at the Dental College of Philadelphia (today part of the University of Pennsylvania) and began to practice dentistry. Like many tubercular patients of his generation, he moved to the arid West for relief from the disease. He settled in Dallas, Texas, where he opened a dental practice, though his persistent cough scared off most patients. Holliday started supplementing his income with gambling and soon abandoned his practice altogether. After killing a man in a dispute over a $500 pot, he moved, one step ahead of the law, to Jacksonborough, Texas. A magnet for trouble (and a crack shot), Holliday roamed through Denver and Wyoming, sweeping pots and finding trouble, before heading back to Texas. In Fort Griffin, he met "Big-Nosed" Kate Fisher, the dance hall girl who was to remain his chief paramour, and Wyatt Earp, the famed lawman, gambler, and saloonkeeper.

After killing a man in yet another gambling dispute and only escaping jail under the cover of a fire set by Fisher, a mean gambler herself, Holliday fled to Dodge City, where his friend Earp was marshal. Holliday further followed Earp and his brothers Jim and Virgil to Tombstone, where he supported the Earps against the McLaury and Clanton brothers in the infamous gunfight at the O.K. Corral on October 26, 1881. Acquitted of murder alongside the Earps after the gun battle, Holliday wandered to Colorado, where he spent the next few years growing progressively more ill (his tuberculosis was slowly killing him) and winning card games in mining camps throughout the state. On November 8, 1887, lying peacefully in bed with bottle of bourbon and a pack of cards, Holliday looked down at his bare feet and murmured "This is funny." He had promised Kate Fisher he would not die with his boots on, and he was right: He breathed his last shortly thereafter, a legendary gambler and gunfighter.

Another friend of Earp's, William Barclay "Bat" Masterson (whom Holliday never liked), called himself "the Genius" and related tales of his own glory to all who would listen. After a childhood in Illinois, he moved to Kansas, where he established himself as a buffalo hunter. He then tried his luck as a gambler, with little to show in Dodge but better returns in Cheyenne. Masterson was in Tombstone shortly before the legendary O.K. Corral shootout, dealing faro at the Oriental gambling house (in which Wyatt Earp owned a share and served as an enforcer). From there he returned to Denver and managed a series of gambling rooms in Colorado. He was better known for his gunplay than his dealing (though there is some confusion over exactly how many men he killed, anywhere from one to twenty-six). In 1902, Masterson surfaced in New York, where he was arrested for carrying a concealed gun and running a crooked faro game before establishing himself as a sportswriter and editor, covering boxing and baseball for the *New York Morn-ing Telegraph*. He spent the next two decades embroidering his legend and en-joying a polite infamy; President Theodore Roosevelt, who invited the gambler to the White House regularly, appointed him a United States mar-shal. He died in 1921 and would later be fictionalized by Damon Runyon as Sky Masterson in the popular musical *Guys and Dolls*.

Despite the reputation of the mining frontier as an all-male preserve, women were present in many gambling halls. Since men with money could be found in saloons and gambling halls, both were obvious places for prostitutes to cruise for customers. Saloon owners often employed women as waitresses: They found that men were far more likely to remain drinking and gambling when they could share the company of a friendly female. Beginning in San Francisco, many gambling houses hired woman dealers, on the theory that the rough miners would protest less if they lost their hard-earned gold dust to a vixenish croupier. Many women banked their own games and worked throughout the West as independent gaming entrepreneurs.

In the Mexican *salas* (gambling halls) of the Southwest, female dealers were common. The most famous was Doña María Gertrudis Barceló, better known as La Tules (a diminutive of Gertrudis). She was born south of Santa Fe (in today's New Mexico) in 1823 and began dealing in a *sala* at a young age. She was soon renowned for her beauty and grace. Men stormed the doors to lose money to her. Soon she opened her own Santa Fe *sala,* to which she at-tracted an upscale clientele, including most of the city's major figures. She outfitted it lavishly with Spanish furniture and Turkish carpets, and the cui-sine of her chefs was roundly admired. She outfitted herself extravagantly, wearing an overabundance of golden jewelry. After the American takeover of Santa Fe, she continued to prosper and died a wealthy woman in 1852.

Other women came to the West for fresh starts. Lurline Monte Verde was one of the most famous and most captivating to reinvent herself there. Born to a wealthy slaveowning Missouri family as Belle Siddons, she spent the first years of the Civil War in Missouri drawing out war secrets from Union offi-cers bedazzled by her beauty. She was arrested as a spy in 1862 but released after four months by the pliant governor. After the war, she married a doctor, who died of yellow fever, before marrying a gambler, who also soon perished, but not before teaching her the mysteries of cards. She then moved to Wi-chita and became Kansas's best twenty-one dealer, then opened her own houses in Fort Hays, Ellsworth, and Cheyenne.

Siddons next appeared in Denver in 1876 as Madame Vestal, the propri-etor of a Denver gambling establishment. She felt that her family background precluded her from hiring girls of easy virtue, so instead she offered gamblers free drinks and a (purportedly) honest game. When gold was discovered in the Black Hills, she relocated to Deadwood, where, as Lurline Monte Verde, she arrived to great fanfare: The newspaper made her debut a front-page story, trumpeting the advent of a sultry, sensuous, "flawlessly groomed beauty." Though she soon owned one of the town's leading gambling houses, she was unlucky in love. She fell for Archie McLaughlin, a stagecoach robber who was ultimately captured and hung by vigilantes. Monte Verde would survive a suicide attempt, though she spent her final years wandering around the West, a disconsolate alcoholic and lost soul.

An even more notorious female gambler had a similarly sad end. Eleanore Dumont, dressed in the latest Paris styles, appeared in the mining boomtown of Nevada City, California, one magic morning in 1854; not bad looking at all (despite a downy fuzz on her upper lip), Madame Dumont caused heads to turn from the moment of her arrival. She remained aloof from all gentleman callers but opened a club called the Vingt-et-Un, and rather appropriately dealt blackjack there. She insisted on strict decorum (no spitting or cursing) in her place, and those who defied the rules faced a disapproving stare from the proprietor and the wrath of her numerous customers, who stood in line, patiently waiting to lose to Dumont. Things went so well that she took on a partner, gambler Dave Tobin, who helped her expand into faro, chuck-a-luck, and roulette.

Their new house, called the Dumont Palace, proved a goldmine for two years, as miners continued to lose steadily to the alluring Frenchwoman. After a falling-out with Tobin, she began a peripatetic life, moving from boomtown to boomtown with the sweeping tide of ready money. She maintained a lavish house no matter where she was but outdid herself in Virginia City, Nevada, where a string orchestra gave consolation to the losers, who enjoyed gratis champagne. She traveled all the way to Montana and Idaho, but as the years went on her luck began to run out. The soft fuzz on her upper lip became more noticeable, leading one wag to nickname her "Madame Mustache," a taunt that followed her for the rest of her life. She would commit suicide near the mining camp of Bodie, California, in 1879, twenty-five years after her triumphant entrance into the Golden State.

Scores of other women earned fame and considerable wealth from gambling, including Texans Kitty "the Schemer" Leroy and Lottie Deno (born Carlotta Thompkins near Lexington, Kentucky), but few were more interesting than Alice Ivers, born in Sudbury, England, in 1851, to a respectably middle-class family. She went to school in a female seminary before her family emigrated to the United States, where they ultimately settled in Colorado.

There, Ivers married mining engineer Frank Duffield, whom she insisted on accompanying during his visits to gambling saloons. After he died in a mining accident, she decided to support herself by gambling. Though she played faro as well, someone gave her the name "Poker Alice," by which she was known for the rest of her life.

Poker Alice worked her way across the West in the 1870s and 1880s, dealing in many of the most celebrated gambling dens of the era. She considered herself more than the equal of any man and drank her liquor straight, smoked thick cigars, carried a revolver, and cursed with irreverent impunity. She had one rule, though, which she refused to relax, the residue of her seminary education: She never worked on Sunday, which was the busiest day of the week in most boomtown saloons. After marrying a fellow dealer named W. C. Tubbs, Poker Alice retired from the game and lived in an isolated cabin with her mate north of Deadwood until the winter of 1910, when Tubbs died of pneumonia. Ivers loaded his body into a wagon and drove a team of horses nearly fifty windy, snowy miles to Sturgis, where she pawned her wedding ring for $25, with which she paid for his burial.

After the funeral obsequies, she ambled into a gambling hall and asked for a job. She retrieved her wedding ring with the first twenty-five dollars she earned and continued working at the gambling hall. When Prohibition started in 1920, she ran a roadhouse catering to soldiers near Fort Meade, offering servicemen liquor, girls, and gambling six days a week (she remained steadfast in her commitment to Sabbatarianism). One night, during a disturbance, the septuagenarian shot and killed a cavalry trooper. Though she was acquitted of murder, her roadhouse days were over, and she retired to a rocking chair on her front porch, where she serenely smoked her black cigars until her death in 1930. With her death, an era in gambling ended. The past might have been the province of colorful personalities, but the future already belonged to syndicates and machines that would transform the arts of chance into a business.

12

Fools of Fortune

◆ ◆ ◆

Western gambling was the stuff of legend, but Eastern gambling was already big business by the end of the Civil War. Two kinds of gambling dens and clubs flourished then: the no-frills "low den" or "skinning house," and the posh "first-class hell." The low dens developed from taverns, while the first-class houses followed exclusive West End clubs such as Crockford's.

Houses dedicated to gambling began to emerge in the 1830s, spurred by the expansion of the American economy, the growth of cities, and the migration of professional gamblers from the South. From the colonial days, gambling had been found in taverns throughout the land, but stand-alone gambling houses were rare—when a group of New Englanders opened one in New York City in 1732, it closed almost immediately, having attracted too few customers and too much attention from the authorities. At the turn of the nineteenth century, however, professional gamblers became more numerous in the northern cities, and by the 1820s specialized gambling houses began to appear. Popular games included the old tavern favorite of backgammon and various social card games. The first successful New York gambling house, which opened in 1825 near Wall and Water Streets, was a popular gathering place for clerks, artisans, and volunteer firemen. It was a rough-hewn, democratic imitation of a London club, and it inspired several imitators.

By 1830, about a dozen gambling houses ran in New York City, where professional gamblers, armed with little more than their equipment and bankroll, offered bank games. They usually set up shop in houses that primarily offered social games—quite unlike Crockford's or the spa resorts, where a single proprietor (backed by investors), offered customers a chance to bet against the house at mercantile games. Professionals roved about the city, looked for opportunities wherever they might find them.

The "wolf trap" provided the evolutionary link between peripatetic professionals and true gambling houses. The wolf trap, also known as a snap house, deadfall, or ten-percent house, was born in Cincinnati in the late 1820s and grew to dominance after 1835, as refugees from Mississippi and Louisiana river haunts streamed into town. Any dealer could set up shop in a wolf trap with little capital, save his bankroll. A dealer who wished to "start a snap" (as banking a game was known), bought a stack of chips from the house manager; this became his bankroll for the game. Snaps ranged from $1 to $500, though most were in the $20 to $50 range. Chips could be valued at anywhere from 1 cent to 50 cents each, though they usually "cost" between 5 and 25 cents.

Wolf-trap dealers generally offered faro, though some played twenty-one or chuck-a-luck. The house provided a table for play and all necessary equipment and a surveillance officer who kept an eye on both the dealer and the players, ensuring that neither tried to defraud the house by introducing counterfeit chips. When the game ended, any players lucky enough to have won chips redeemed them from the house bank. If they broke the dealer's bank, the the house charged him nothing for use of its premises; if the dealer won, the house took ten percent of his profits as its compensation. Most wolf-trap games were honest, chiefly because most rough patrons would have thought nothing of beating a cheater senseless. But while the games themselves were usually honest, dealers frequently tried to short-change players when converting chips to cash, and players often "dropped a bet," a practice today known as "past-posting," when they surreptitiously slid a wager onto a bet that had just won. Sometimes, raucous troublemakers took the direct approach and simply "bonneted" the dealer: They threw a blanket over his head and made off with his cash while he struggled to free himself. In the wolf trap, men on both sides of the table remained constantly vigilant.

In the late 1830s, the typical Cincinnati wolf trap had a single long, narrow room, teeming with dirt, carpeted in straw mats, and amply furnished with shabby chairs, ratty tables, and spittoons improvised from sawdust-filled boxes. The only amenity (besides a series of penny pictures of various sporting scenes tacked to the walls) was a pail of water with a dipper, from which thirsty patrons were welcome to drink. Conversation ran to the topics of race-horses, steamboats, and loose women and was generously punctuated by jovial obscenities. Most wolf-trap patrons worked on steamboats as cooks, stewards, mates, pilots, and engineers, though they were often joined by the local rowdies. The professional gamblers who "opened a snap," or banked a faro game, could be easily spotted in the crowd wearing delicately embroidered shirts and bedecked in showy jewels.

Dealers liked wolf traps for the straight equipment and constant business, notwithstanding the dangers of bonneting. Players liked being able to easily find an honest game. As in other gambling rooms, segregation was common; some wolf traps catered primarily to black players (though whites frequented these as well), while most white traps were off-limits to blacks. By the 1840s, wolf traps had spread from the Queen City to St. Louis, Pittsburgh, Philadelphia, Baltimore, New York, and Boston. Still, they were largely a transitional institution.

Though the games dealt in the wolf traps were generally honest, most faro professionals needed to cheat to consistently win. When a particularly rich sucker wandered in, dealers might ask the wolf trap's owner to introduce a gaffed deck; in such a case, the owner took a twenty-five-percent share of the profit. The second-class skinning house or brace room, by contrast, was entirely dedicated to cheating. Their uniformly dishonest operators usually preyed upon new arrivals to the city. Some of them superficially resembled the first-class houses known for their fine food, flowing wines, and honest games. But most only gave players cigars and liquor and seldom allowed the player an even chance. They were open to the public and generally stayed in business by attracting casual visitors who did not know or did not care that the games were crooked. Apparently, quite a few people fell into one of these categories, because by midcentury, there were about a hundred second-class houses in New York City alone.

Other second-class houses did not even pretend to be legitimate gaming resorts; they were plainly (to all except the sucker) brace rooms, where the victim had no hope of leaving with a penny. These were more fronts for an elaborate con game than gambling rooms: They operated for the express purpose of skinning a single mark. Ropers (also known as steerers) searched the railroad stations, saloons, and hotels of the city, looking for an easy mark. Befriending the mark over a drink, the roper then extended an invitation to visit his club. The oblivious mark followed him to his doom.

Meanwhile, back at the brace room, a gaggle of cappers (shills) was lazily playing cards and swapping tales until the door bell rang. The cappers suddenly transformed themselves into bankers, merchants, and lawyers, and the owner/dealer, with the help of an assistant, started losing money to them at faro as the sucker was led to the slaughter. In some brace rooms, a table was set elaborately under the pretense that a fine dinner would be served in an hour or two; by that time, the sucker would be cleaned out and long gone, and the silverware would continue to gather dust. As the mark walked in, he heard incredible stories of the dealer's bad luck, as players spoke of winning thousands. He would join in the game enthusiastically but soon be tapped out.

When he was safely deposited back on the street by the roper, the crew divided the spoils: forty-five percent for the roper, forty-five percent for the owner, and ten percent for his assistant. From his cut, the owner paid rent and incidental expenses and the cappers, who generally got between $1 and $4 per game. Houses running only roped games became common in the 1850s, and as late as the 1870s over one hundred could be found throughout the nation: fifteen in New York, six in Philadelphia, between one and four in major cities like Boston, Baltimore, and Chicago, and at least one in burgs as small as Omaha, Leavenworth, and Providence. When Congress was in session, the District of Columbia boasted several, and in state capitals such rooms opened when the legislature sat, a sad commentary on the gullibility of the people's representatives.

Respectable marks might wander into a second-class house, mistaking it for a gentlemen's club, but no one was under any such delusions in the penny poker dens that proliferated in slum districts throughout the country, such as New York's infamous Five Points. There were no burnished chandeliers or ample sideboards here: A tallow candle jammed into a bottle provided the light, and a rough plank thrown over a pair of empty whiskey barrels the table. In 1849, a *New York Tribune* writer described "the various grades of small thieves and pickpockets" huddling over a table, dealing greasy, worn-out cards, drinking rotgut whiskey, swearing, and fighting. "At these dens men and women are indiscriminately mingled: such men! But more especially, such women!" As in the wolf traps, these rough establishments were generally as honest as the visitors were fierce.

A more refined recreation could be found at the first-class houses, which modeled themselves, with varying degrees of success, on the London clubs. Though public gambling on cards and dice was illegal, the proprietors of first-class houses smoothed over this legality with generous gifts to politicians, judges, and police. Many directly employed police as steerers. The dealers might play honestly for locally known patrons, but out-of-towners steered to a first-class house could usually expect to be cheated. When victims tried to press charges, the wheels of justice—greased by the house proprietors— quickly spun against them. A querulous mark demanding satisfaction from a judge might find himself jailed as a material witness while the offending gamblers continued to walk free. Usually his only play was to drop charges and leave town. In 1850 Horace Greeley estimated in his *New York Tribune* that more than $5 million a year was lost to professional gamblers in New York, mostly at first-class houses.

These houses were open to the general public and, like their contemporary

Rhine casinos, offered chiefly mercantile games: faro, preeminent above all, but also roulette, twenty-one, and rarely trente-et-quarante or dice games. Managers passed themselves off as gentlemen and provided a range of comforts to their guests; in every city there could be found at least one house, and often more than a dozen, that might rival Pendleton's Washington palace or John Davis's gilded New Orleans club. Free dinners were de rigueur and seldom disappointed. The finest wines were poured freely, and a man could eat and drink to his heart's content, so long as he repaired to the faro table after he was done. Just as with the second-class dives, first-class houses employed genteel-looking ropers who delivered fresh victims each evening. Sometimes, players lost merely because of the inherently unfavorable odds of mercantile games, but most houses relied on skilled dealers to cheat their way to a profit. Players seldom knew whether they were gambling or being fleeced, and many, in the excitement of the first-class house, did not initially care.

After Louisiana outlawed gambling houses in 1835, New Orleans gambling declined. At the same time, New York City's was booming. By 1850, it was apparent that the thriving commercial hub had become the nation's new gambling capital. In that year, the New York Association for the Suppression of Gambling reckoned that there were no fewer than six thousand establishments in the city that permitted gambling. About two thirds of these were primarily gambling businesses (as opposed to taverns that incidentally permitted card games), and the nearly incredible figure of 25,000 people (nearly five percent of a total population of 515,000) reportedly worked in them. Though the houses were ostensibly illegal under New York's antigambling statutes, complaisant authorities allowed them to run virtually wide open.

Most of New York's fifty or so first-class houses were owned by a small group of proprietors. Because of the inherently risky nature of honest gambling, particularly faro, syndicate ownership made sense, as it allowed owners to pool their resources and thus allow higher betting limits. Joining together also helped proprietors coordinate and pay for the corruption of the municipal, judicial, and police authorities whose forbearance was necessary for continued operation. By 1850, the syndicate structure that would dominate organized gambling (and hence organized crime) for the next century was slowly coalescing.

Though ownership of the houses was shared among limited partnerships, several operators distinguished themselves. Reuben Parsons, an enigmatic New Englander, owned shares in most of New York's poshest first-class houses. It was said that he had been a silent partner in a few New Orleans houses before he appeared in New York in the 1830s, though on his arrival he first tried to make a fortune by playing faro. After losing for about two years, he decided that the only way to make money from bucking the tiger was on the banker's side, and he bought a share in a Manhattan gambling house. He eventually parlayed this into a controlling interest in as many as ten first-class houses. He also invested successfully in the illegal lottery or "policy" games of New York and became fantastically rich man in a few years.

The wealthy Parsons was a walking contradiction. Though he banked several of the city's most flamboyant gambling houses, he dressed austerely and spoke softly. Considering himself a businessman, he seldom deigned to speak to mere gamblers and maintained a surveillance and reporting network that kept him constantly informed of his investments' progress. He put his faro and policy profits into real estate and, by the outbreak of the Civil War, had retired a millionaire from the gambling business. Not content with his ample fortune, he strayed onto Wall Street, where stock market speculation, at which he was a rank amateur, ruined him. He would die destitute in 1875.

During his years as a gambling house owner, Parsons had a number of partners, the closest of which was Henry Colton, with whom Parsons had a lifelong friendship. Together they owned one of New York's most celebrated houses, on Barclay Street. Colton had a reputation for rectitude; even his enemies admitted that if he had pursued a "respectable" business, Colton would have been a success. He schooled himself in the mathematics and procedures of games, becoming a respected solon of the table whose judgments took the force of law among the gambling fraternity. He avoided his friend Parsons's financial reverses by cunningly transferring all of his property to his wife's name in the 1870s when he was threatened by lawsuits.

Patrick Herne was as renowned for his suavity and charm as Colton was for his intelligence. Herne claimed to be an Irish aristocrat who, touring the United States in the 1830s, had been cleaned out by New Orleans faro artists and had then taken a job in a faro house. Whatever his origins, his true talents lay not in dealing but in roping new customers; he soon began receiving a cut of the profits. With the exodus of gamblers from New Orleans after 1835, Herne moved to New York, where he partnered with Parsons and Colton in several gambling houses before opening his own at 587 Broadway.

Here, Herne allowed his personality to shine, and the former roper used his exquisite charm to draw players and keep them coming back. Though most of them lost in fixed games, Herne helped them to see the bright side— even men considering suicide, it was said, could be perked up by a short chat with the genial gambler. Herne gave pikers (small-stakes bettors) and hustlers a similar treatment, greeting them affably and, during a short walk, begging them to do him the favor of not patronizing his resort for a while. It usually worked. With the authorities, he used more substantial means, sending presents and cash disbursements to his numerous friends among the police. Safe from raids, his house prospered, but Herne spent money as fast as he made it—he was indeed a terrible sucker for faro—and died nearly penniless in 1850.

There were other notable operators in midcentury New York. Sam Sudyam, a former member of the Bowery Boys gang, had gambled on a trip to the South before learning the art of the deal from Reuben Parsons. He eventually owned his own establishment with former housepainter Joe Hall, who later sold his share to Sudyam and opened houses in Philadelphia and Washington. "Shell" Burrell honestly took on all comers at roulette, while Jim Bartolf ran a refined trap on Park Place where gamblers had no chance of winning. Most of these houses opened after dark, but there was one, run by Sherlock Hillman on Liberty Street, that was open only from 11:00 A.M. to 7:00 P.M. and catered to businessmen seeking relief from the tedium of the office.

While each of these operators was famous or, at least, infamous, they would soon be eclipsed by a true heavyweight: John Morrissey.* Born in Templemore, Ireland, in 1831, Morrissey emigrated to the United States at the age of three with his parents, who settled in Troy, New York. There, Morrissey distinguished himself early on as a world-class rowdy and a ferocious brawler, becoming the unofficial no-holds-barred champion of that city. At the age of eighteen, he set off for New York City with the ambition of gaining similar prestige in the metropolis. Searching for the accomplished pugilist Dutch Charlie Duane, the young Morrissey entered the Empire Club, a gambling establishment owned by Captain Isaiah Rynders, a powerful, politically influential gambler. Upon being told that neither Duane nor any other prizefighters were in the club, Morrissey declared that he could lick any man present, whereupon he was set upon by six toughs, who attacked him with a variety of weapons, including fists, chairs, and bottles. Morrissey held his ground until dropped by a brass spittoon. Rynders was so impressed that he took the young man under his wing. Morrissey returned to Troy for a year but in 1850, found himself back in New York, where Rynders put him to work as a shoulder hitter.

---

*Morrissey partially inspired the character of Amsterdam Vallon (played by Leonardo DiCaprio) in Martin Scorsese's *Gangs of New York*, and his life was far more interesting and improbable than anything penned by a screenwriter.

Professional gamblers, gangs, and politicians of this era shared a growing affinity that ultimately led to the creation of gambling syndicates. Gambling house operators needed protection from both the law and the lawless: Zealous police could enforce antigambling ordinances and judges might impose harsh penalties for running a gambling house, while gangs of rowdies might rob or terrorize the house and its patrons. Thus, professional gamblers reached out to the law with graft and employed the outlaws as bouncers.

Criminal gangs were often more powerful than the police, whom they frequently intimidated, and, as early as the 1840s, freely ran protection rackets and engaged in arson and robbery for profit. The more astute gang leaders allied themselves with ward heelers, men who steer gang violence into political channels: By sending out groups of shoulder hitters (like young Morrissey) on election day, they ensured that voters picked the right candidates. Ward heelers emerged as political power brokers and usually controlled the elected machine politicians who in turn appointed the police. Professional gamblers like Captain Rynders, with access to large sums of money and growing influence among criminal gangs, were uniquely qualified as ward heelers. Under Rynder's tutelage, Morrissey began to rise through the ranks of Tammany Hall, New York's Democratic political machine.

Morrissey had ventured far and wide in his quest for pugilistic fame, hitting San Francisco in 1851. In that boomtown, he teamed up with a faro dealer and, becoming wealthy, gained a lasting respect for gambling profits. He had a forceful approach to customer relations. When one of his players declared he had been cheated and insulted by Morrissey, he challenged the brawler to a duel, giving the him the choice of weapons. Seeing Morrissey saunter up to the appointed spot with a butcher's cleaver tucked under each arm, he took fright and wisely ran. If Morrissey cheated anyone after this, they had the sense not to complain. After besting George Thompson in August 1852, he declared himself the Champion of America, but that title was not generally recognized until he defeated Yankee Sullivan on his return to New York the next year. He continued fighting until October 1858 when, after knocking out John C. Heenan, he announced that, as he wished to devote himself to his family and society, he was retiring from the ring.

Morrissey earned a fearsome reputation: His nickname, "Old Smoke," was inspired by a fight during which he was rolled onto a patch of burning coals but, with his flesh burning, refused to submit; he later beat his opponent senseless. He was not a huge man, standing under six feet tall and never weighing more than 180 pounds, but he was powerful and possessed of a dogged stamina; he never stopped fighting until he was the victor. One of

Morrissey's natural rivals was Butcher Bill Poole, a Whig and nativist who beat the Democratic Morrissey in an 1854 fight so intense that one onlooker, later attempting to recreate the battle for a rapt audience, mortally fractured his skull while demonstrating how strongly Poole had thrown Morrissey.* The next year, one of Morrissey's partisans shot and killed Poole, whose final words, "I die a true American," reflected the animosity between the native-born Poole and the immigrant Morrissey.

Morrissey had already begun his career as a gambling-hall operator, using his boxing purses to buy a series of houses, eventually taking over the longest-lived gambling den in New York City's history, at 8 Barclay Street, which ran continuously from 1859 to 1902 (though not under the same ownership). Morrissey established 8 Barclay as the choice destination for politicians and sporting men before selling it and opening other houses. He took on a variety of partners, and his enterprises were always successful: Thanks to his powerful Tammany connections, the police never dared to interfere with them. Morrissey even established satellite operations in the upstate health resort of Saratoga, which he would help to transform into a gambling center, and his name became synonymous with first-class gambling.

Morrissey's political stock rose along with his gambling profits. Tammany Hall chief William "Boss" Tweed recognized Morrissey as the finest vote-getter in the city, no mean feat in wards dominated by thugs, repeat voters, and outright fraud. Tweed rewarded Morrissey with the machine's support for a seat in the United States Congress, where he was elected in 1866 and 1868, becoming the first professional gambler to serve there. After an 1870 rift with Tweed, Morrissey was expelled from Tammany, and on his own captured a seat in the New York State Senate.

Successful as a businessman and politician, by 1868 Morrissey was a millionaire, though the following year, when he took the advice of Cornelius Vanderbilt and invested heavily on Wall Street, he lost much of his fortune. He never succeeded in his ambitions to be recognized as a gentleman by high society, though he remained politically potent and at least modestly wealthy until his death in 1878 from pneumonia. Still, his legacy was powerful: Because of his political might, he had been at the center of New York's gambling for more than twenty years, and his vision of Saratoga as a posh resort would eventually be realized by another famous operator, Richard Canfield.

The immigrant/nativist animus exemplified by the Morrissey/Poole feud

---

*Poole was the template for *Gangs of New York*'s Bill "the Butcher" Cutting, played by Daniel Day Lewis.

The first professional gambler elected to Congress, John Morrissey (1831–1878) parlayed
the profits from his faro houses into something close to respectability.

underscored a multicultural, polyglot city. Immigrants from around the world
poured into the United States in the nineteenth century, and in New York
City they quickly established distinctive communities with salient gambling
subcultures. Perhaps the most notorious such neighborhood was New York's
Chinatown, which, like Chinatowns throughout the world at the time, was
fairly dominated by fan-tan parlors and lottery shops. Though far from home,
it seems, the games seldom changed.

During the years that New York gamblers thronged to Morrissey's houses
and faro was "winning the West," many accomplished gamblers made names
for themselves in the Midwest. In Cincinnati, wolf traps split gamblers with
rondo houses and keno parlors. Rondo was a simplified form of billiards
that could be played as a house-banked mercantile game. To play, players
shot nine balls from one corner onto the opposite pocket. To win, a player
had to guess whether there would be an even or odd number of balls remaining. This uncomplicated game may have originated as a cross between
the numerous Native American odd/even games still played in the nineteenth
century and billiards. Rondo was found throughout the American South (including gaming centers like New Orleans and Hot Springs, Arkansas), the
Midwest, and even as far west as Arizona and California, where it appeared
as a forbidden game in the section of each state's respective penal code that

outlawed mercantile games. It was played through the early years of the twentieth century.

Keno parlors also proliferated throughout the South at this time. This game was markedly different from the keno played today. Players bought preprinted cards, with spaces divided into from three to five rows and the unique ticket number printed in the middle row in large red type. Each row had five numbers, taken from a pool of one to ninety, on it. No two cards were the same. To play, the roller placed ninety balls into a wooden sphere called a goose, shook it, and started drawing numbers. The first player to cover five numbers in a row shouted, "Keno," and won the prize. This game was also known as lotto, and it was likely descended from lotto-style lotteries. It is more recognizable as a bingo ancestor than as a forerunner of today's keno, and was popular among small-stakes gamblers wherever it appeared.

Wolf traps, rondo rooms, and keno halls kept the populace of Cincinnati enthralled until around 1850, when a growing number of first-class house operators demanded that the police, to whom they paid protection money, close these rival attractions. During the years before and after the Civil War, many riverboat gamblers would retire to Cincinnati to open gambling houses; as long as payoffs to the authorities continued, the Ohio River town was a quite friendly place to do business.

Throughout the region, just about every city of prominence sheltered at least a few members of the gambling fraternity: St. Louis, Milwaukee, Indianapolis, Cleveland, Fort Wayne, St. Paul, and Minneapolis all had significant reputations as gambling centers. Even small towns had their share of the action. In a typical burg, sporting gentlemen declared themselves a "club" and met weekly in the back of some shop where they played the popular games of the day, including the social diversions of poker and its forebears, brag, euchre, and all-fours, whist, and the mercantile games of twenty-one and faro. Layouts were crude, and the proprietor's chief sources of profit were the sale of cards and a percentage of the pot (known as a "rake") from poker and brag. In return, the housekeeper provided a clandestine meeting place (for gambling was invariably illegal), alcohol, and cigars.

When they tired of playing against each other, townspeople welcomed nattily attired professional gamblers, usually professed gentlemen from the South with languorous accents and seemingly generous dispositions. Upon blowing into town they would usually lose steadily at faro while treating fellow players to round after round of drinks, cigars, and tales from the outside. Later in the evening, as the stakes were raised, they turned the tables, taking the townspeople for all they could bear, and usually left town only a few steps ahead of the suddenly aroused simple folk. But the small town would instantly forget its anger when the next charming stranger with a real mahogany faro box strolled into town.

In larger cities, permanent gambling houses were common where proprietors could persuade the powers that be to turn a beneficially blind eye. The history of Milwaukee, a city not today renowned for its gambling, is instructive. The first faro house opened in 1843, when the city had fewer than three thousand residents. Its owner, Martin Curtis, became wealthy enough from its receipts that he invested in residential real estate and helped finance the Kirby House, the young city's most prominent hotel.

Curtis was succeeded as the city's dominant faro operator in 1848, when newcomer Tom Wicks opened a house. Wicks would reign over Milwaukee gambling for most of the next three decades. Any operator who did not work directly for him needed, at the very least, his permission to operate without interference, and his influence was so great that he ran his gambling operations from a building owned by the governor of Wisconsin. Wicks operated houses throughout the state and even opened branches in Chicago. At the height of his power, though, he made a ruinous misstep: In 1872 he sought to parlay his gambling wealth into a more "legitimate" windfall and invested heavily in the wheat market. Like most other expert gamblers who traded their cards for stocks, he soon saw his fortunes annihilated and had to sell everything he owned just to pay his debts.

Instead of rebuilding his fortune through his expert management of faro houses, Wicks turned venomously against all gambling. He publicly denounced all gamblers as frauds and promised to rid Milwaukee of them. His high-profile campaign soon faltered, but not before proving to the police that it might be just as politically expedient to close the houses as to accept their graft: They soon moved against the city's six remaining first-class houses and also instituted a crackdown on backroom gambling on rondo and poker. Predictably, gambling returned to Milwaukee soon enough, though not as openly as before.

Cities like Milwaukee might tolerate a Tom Wicks and his first-class faro houses, but they paled in comparison to the rampant illegal gambling that thrived in Chicago. Even when it was only a town, it boasted the kind of gambling subculture befitting a nineteenth-century city. The town of Chicago was incorporated in August 1833, and by December of that year a letter to the local newspaper was already complaining that authorities were lax in the enforcement of antigambling laws. Ten years later, a committee resolved to "root out" the vice of gambling and "hunt down those who gain by it an infamous subsistence." The committee urged Chicagoans to abstain from gambling with professionals and deny them social intercourse; but the games continued.

As Chicago grew in the 1840s and 1850s, it became the undisputed center of Midwestern gambling. A hustling coterie of operators ran the early gaming houses, the most exceptional of whom was John Sears. Unlike others, who took on all comers in brag, seven-up, or whist, Sears played only poker, and he was such a prodigy that it was said he had no need to ever cheat. He was also renowned for his sartorial snap and was, for years, described as Chicago's most handsome man. Where most gamblers were content to recount tales of debauchery larded with obscene oaths at the table, Sears was an oddity: Possessed of an almost mystical affection for the work of Shakespeare and Robert Burns, he sometimes burst into verse while playing. Respected by his fellows, admired by nearly all, Sears remained a scrupulously honest gambler and, as a result, died in poverty. Though other Chicago gamblers might have admired his well-groomed good looks, few emulated his candid dealing.

Sears's honest ways were quickly becoming an anachronism. In the 1850s, the old style gambling houses, which featured primarily social games, a modest ten-percent house rake, and square dealers, began to disappear. Houses now specialized in faro, whose popularity surged, and mercantile games such as roulette, chuck-a-luck, and keno, all of which were introduced by veterans of the New Orleans and New York gambling houses. Initially, these adventurers worked their magic in the existing ten-percent houses, but as they became settled in Chicago, they opened their own houses, which were unabashedly skinning operations. By the latter part of the decade, virtually every gambling house was crooked.

The more refined skinning houses were located in the heart of the city on State and Lake Streets, but the more desperate gamblers headed, almost instinctively, for a squalid quarter of town known as the Sands. Attempts to clean up this den of thieves, prostitutes, and professional gamblers were generally fruitless until the 1857 election of "Long" John Wentworth as mayor. Wentworth conceived a brilliant stratagem: He ordered the local papers to print an advertisement for a dogfight in a distant part of the city. With the most formidable rowdies thus far from the Sands, the mayor then orchestrated the organized demolition of the most ramshackle houses in the quarter. Wentworth was applauded for destroying a gamblers' vipers' nest, but the Sands' resident sharpers simply relocated. The mayor was not content with merely disrupting the gamblers and pledged to continue the fight against them wherever they might surface. After raiding a prominent house, Wentworth succeeded in forcing the closure of the public gambling houses, though gambling continued. Instead of confidently dealing out of lavishly appointed houses, faro dealers now moved furtively throughout the city, one step ahead of the police, creating an American urban institution, the floating game.

During the Civil War, Wentworth relaxed his zealous prosecution of the gambling underworld, and hundreds of desperate characters streamed into Chicago. These were not only professional gamblers, eager to rake off a portion of the city's burgeoning wealth, but also prostitutes, pickpockets, thieves, and confidence men. Preoccupied with maintaining the law in a rapidly expanding city (the population nearly tripled from 1860 to 1870), Chicago police did little to hamper the illicit trade in gambling or prostitution. Chicago gained repute as the nation's roughest city, thanks in part to the numerous saloons that boasted both free-flowing alcohol and wide-open games of chance (each of which, in its own way, contributed to violent quarrels). By 1870 the number of gambling houses was estimated in the hundreds, no mean feat in a city of fewer than three hundred thousand. Rough-and-tumble low dens were scattered throughout the city's slums, but most of the city's first-class houses—which might or might not be honest—were found in two clusters. The first was on Randolph Street between Clark and State, a stretch of the city so violent that it was known as Hair-Trigger Block. Another section, Clark Street from Randolph to Monroe, was dubbed Gamblers' Row. On these blocks, gambling houses predominated, sharing space only with a few saloons and brothels.

Initially, one of the best known houses, at 167 Randolph Street, run by "Colonel" Wat Cameron, a polite and generous southerner, was known for its honest play. Patrons, drawn in by his fair dealing, flocked to his house. The odds of the game, alas, did not guarantee Cameron enough of a profit to cover his overhead expenses (which naturally included protection payments to the police), so in 1863, Cameron took in two partners from St. Louis who quickly ran him off and converted his resort into one of the city's most infamous skinning houses.

Out of the mass of sharpers who ran gambling houses in this new era, George Trussell was one of the most dishonest and wealthiest. Trussell was a Vermont Yankee who worked as a bookkeeper in Chicago for several years before deciding that he could not maintain his extravagant lifestyle on an accountant's salary and migrated into the employ of gambling houses, first as a roper and capper but soon as an owner. By 1862 he and three partners owned several houses. His group occasioned much ill will among its rivals by its aggressive "marketing." Trussell employed groups of ropers who weren't content to trawl the train stations and hotel lobbies for suckers. Rather, they would invade the foyers of the few gambling houses known for their square dealing, snuff out its gas lamps, and inform any arrival that, while the house was unfortunately closed, there was an excellent place nearby that the house's proprietors would like the would-be gambler to visit—one of Trussell's skinning dens. Trussell became so wealthy that he was able to pay exorbitant amounts for police protection, and enjoyed both the freedom to run his houses without fear of the law and the connivance of police in raiding anyone who attempted to challenge his dominance.

Trussell also had an interest in the turf and a fascination for the horses—one in particular—that would prove tragic in 1866. Trussell had made a mistress of (and, some say, secretly married) a prostitute named Mollie, whom he set up as the madam of a luxuriant Fourth Avenue brothel. He refused to allow any woman to come between himself and Mollie, and he showered her with expensive gifts, including sparkling jewels and artfully tailored clothes. But her place in his life was challenged by Dexter, a champion trotter in which Trussell had acquired a part ownership. Suddenly, he spent all of his spare time down at the stables marveling at his great horse and boasting of him with his racetrack cronies. When Trussell neglected to ask Mollie to escort him to the festive grand opening of a new racetrack, Driving Park (at which Dexter was to race), she decided that she had had enough. The next evening, dressed in a flawless white dress whose folds concealed a pistol, she went searching for Trussell on Hair-Trigger Block. Finding him in a saloon, his glass raised in a toast to the fabulous Dexter, she accosted him. As he dragged her toward the door, she drew her gun and shot her horse-mad lover to death. She immediately screamed her regret for having killed "her George." At her trial, the jury acquitted her of murder, despite the overwhelming evidence of her guilt.

Trussell's downfall may have been a penny-opera tragedy, but the entire city endured devastation with the Great Chicago Fire, which raged from October 8 to 10, 1871. Although popular legend attributed the fire to a lantern kicked over by a cow in the DeKoven Street barn of Kate O'Leary, its actual cause remains a mystery. Daniel "Pegleg" Sullivan, shortly before his death, confessed to starting the fire with embers from a pipe, but it is more likely that dice were the cause of the blaze. Louis Cohn, who died in 1942 at the age of eighty-nine, revealed that he, Mrs. O' Leary's sons, and other local youths were busy shooting dice when one of them (most likely Sullivan) knocked over a lantern. The story has the ring of truth because one of Mrs.

O'Leary's sons, Jim, later enjoyed a career as a leading gambling-house operator in Chicago. Getting an early start in the trade, he may have contributed to one of the worst disasters in American history.

The fire did not dampen Chicagoans' enthusiasm for gambling, and in the years after the cataclysm a new boss gambler emerged: Mike McDonald, a Chicago native (b. 1839) who got his start as a professional gambler in his teens. When Mayor Wentworth closed the city's gambling houses, McDonald journeyed down to New Orleans, where he refined his skills and adopted what would become his characteristic attire of black suits with white shirts. He returned to Chicago committed to becoming the city's greatest gambler and by the time of the Civil War had largely succeeded.

McDonald furthered his ambitions in 1873 when he backed the hands-off Harvey Colvin for mayor. Colvin reversed the policies of his predecessors, who had ordered the police to conduct perfunctory raids on known gambling houses, and allowed all manner of gambling to flourish without even the shadow of a threat. One downcast reformer wrote that "the town was literally handed over to the criminal class who held high carnival by day as well as by night." McDonald thrived, opening a new gambling house, attached to a hotel and saloon, called "The Store," at Clark and Monroe Streets. This resort soon became the leading gambling house of the entire Midwest. To outward appearances, it was a square joint whose twelve faro tables, six roulette wheels, and six chuck-a-luck tables were all honestly run. But in actuality, McDonald instructed his dealers to use a sliding scale: They were to be as honest as the player was politically influential.

Monroe Heath, who succeeded Colvin as mayor in 1876, cracked down on the gambling houses, but his successor, Carter Harrison, was so lenient that the gamblers referred to him as "Our Carter." The Store remained the city's largest gambling house and would reign over the prairies into the 1890s. It had a number of Chicago rivals, among whom the Clark Street establishment of the Hankins brothers was preeminent. In 1890, it had about forty full-time employees and earned for the brothers an estimated $20,000 a month in profit. The operators refused to admit professionals, instead courting a wealthy but inexpert body of gamblers known collectively as "the dinner pail brigade." The rivalry with McDonald was a relatively friendly one, as he joined with the Hankins brothers in a bookmaking syndicate—a sign of the growing move toward cross-ownership of gambling operations that was to define the coming century.

McDonald owned a piece of, or extracted tribute from, virtually every Chicago gambling operation by 1880. By this time he had already become a millionaire and, during the 1880s, diversified into downtown real estate, ownership of the *Chicago Globe* newspaper, and large shares in several transit companies. All the while, his gambling operations reaped millions. But even he was unprepared for the rush brought by the 1893 World Columbian Exposition, which unleashed a "gambling orgy." Amid the carnival atmosphere, faro dealers, dice throwers, and bust-out artists had a field day.

But the good times did not last. Three days before the fair closed, the gamblers' euphoria was dimmed by the assassination of their beloved Carter Harrison by a disgruntled office-seeker. After his death, a Civic Federation comprised of clergy and business professionals demanded that his successor, John Patrick Hopkins, more strenuously combat the gambling element. Many of the best-known houses closed, and McDonald retired from active gambling and, until his death in 1908, could draw on his vast fortune. He came to grief when his young wife killed a man with whom she had become infatuated, though she was not imprisoned thanks to McDonald's hiring eminent legal counsel to defend her. After McDonald's retirement, many of the gambling houses reopened. In the early twentieth century, struggles over gambling houses and bookmaking monopolies would contribute to the violence of the Windy City.

Several thousand Americans made their livings from gambling, sometimes honestly but usually not. These professionals formed, by the 1840s, a distinct subculture in most cities. Writer Edgar Allan Poe, whose gambling debts complicated his already gloomy life, described the gamblers—by which he meant professional sharpers—to be found in any American city:

> They wore every variety of dress, from that of the desperate thimblerig bully, with velvet waistcoat, fancy neckerchief, gilt chains, and filigreed buttons, to that of the scrupulously inornate clergyman, than which nothing could be less liable to suspicion. Still all were distinguished by a certain sodden swarthiness of complexion, a filmy dimness of eye, and pallor and compression of lip. There were two other traits, moreover, by which I could always detect them: a guarded lowness of tone in conversation, and a more than ordinary extension of the thumb in a direction at right angles with the fingers.

These men populated the low dens and skinning houses of the cities, quick to pluck any unwary enough to play their games.

Urban professionals had country cousins as well, itinerant vagabonds known as "fakirs" who toured the nation in carnivals, running crooked games, often strolling into town to separate the yokels from their money using incredible feats of prestidigitation. Often, the fakirs cajoled the operators of legitimate county fairs, ostensibly dedicated to education and entertainment, to allow them to practice their trade on the fairgrounds. Sometimes, fair associations sold the franchise cheaply, for a bribe of as little as $50; other times, directors insisted that the fakir first submit to a show arrest and pay a fine to the local authorities. Most fakirs considered the cost of "sugaring," or bribing the local sheriff and prosecutor, a necessary business expense, and there were few local potentates whose wrath against the fakir's trickery could not be sweetened with a present of cash.

The fakirs employed a variety of crooked games. The needle wheel was one of the most ingeniously constructed and ubiquitous of attractions. This device consisted of two parts: a raised center rimmed by a sloping wheel divided into thirty-two compartments. On the wheel's table stood a box, numbered from one to thirty-two, which contained sixteen blanks and sixteen prizes. A player bought, for $1 or so, the right to place a marble in the upper wheel, which was then set into motion, just as the lower wheel was spun in the opposite direction. As the wheels slowed, the ball would drop into a slot on the lower wheel; if played fairly, the marble would have an equal chance of dropping into a winning and losing slot. But the fakir hid, beneath the wheels, an apparatus that allowed him to raise nearly invisible needles at the top of the winning slots as the wheel spun, thus blocking the marble and cheating the player.

The fakir usually employed a capper who placed a bet and won a prize. Sometimes, this capper would place his own money down and ask an onlooker to spin the wheel. Naturally eager for a free turn, the onlooker usually assented and, after losing, was convinced to go "double or nothing," multiple times, sometimes losing as much as $1,000 in this manner. Other wheel devices included the jenny wheel, a scaled-down needle wheel, and the corona or mascot, which used a pointer on a wheel numbered from one to sixty. Players bought tickets, which were placed in a box, and the wheel was then spun. The only winners were usually cappers, as the fakir could control where the needle stopped and thus ensure that no prizes were actually awarded. The squeeze spindle, a similar device, was used to defraud fairgoers for generations.

Another wheel, called the wheel of fortune, can be found today in many casinos, and its ruinous odds (it has a nearly 20% house edge, compared to 1.4% for the craps pass line) have led some to call it the "idiot wheel." Yet those who play the game in today's casinos at least have a chance of winning, whereas those who spun the wheel on the fairgrounds never had an even break. The typical wheel had numbered spaces painted on the rim, separated by tabs. A large cloth or painted table allowed players to place bets or bids for prizes won if a certain number came up. The wheel operator, by using a foot-operated lever running through the wheel, was able to stop the turn on a nonwinning number, and, as always, the only ones to win large prizes were confederates of the fakir. Another variant of the game, called "the Board of Trade Wheel," was often popular in rural districts and used, instead of numbers, representations of various commodities: pork, lard, wheat, oats, and barley.

By their nature, most fakirs slid between the cracks of history, as they hardly would have enjoyed prosperous careers if they revealed their secrets to a scribe or left detailed records of their swindles. Yet one member of this curious tribe left his story for prosperity. "Honest" John Kelly, a quintessential small-time grifter, gambler, and con artist (and one of several gamblers to share the nickname), when near his death, charged his wife with delivering his "diary" (actually little more than a set of notes) to a newspaper editor he had once taken into his confidence. The resulting biography shows a man evilly adept at fleecing others, yet naïve and unfortunate enough to be forever chasing one last big score.

Kelly, born in 1878 in sleepy Marshalltown, Iowa, was an adept pool hustler and dice mechanic by the age of fifteen. Using homemade crooked dice, he delighted in taking hard-earned money from local farmboys until, one step ahead of an unfriendly police officer, he joined up with a pair of "big-shot" gamblers—actually small-fry con artists—who, in their first adventure with Kelly, used all of their guile to evade a police dragnet and con a train conductor into taking a worthless watch in lieu of their ticket fare. Kelly and his mentors then joined a traveling carnival, where he was initiated into the "knife game," a predictably gaffed carny attraction.

The carnival was a fitting introduction to the peripatetic life that Kelly was to follow. The proprietor, one Colonel McNudder, was "a fine, bluff-looking gentleman until one got close enough to see his shifty eyes." There was not a single game of skill that did not have two modes of play: the fair game, allowed only to the cappers who stimulated yokel interest, and the crooked game, which predominated. Kelly eventually exposed the colonel's cheating in the crew's nightly poker sessions and soon lit out for greener pastures, his appetite barely whetted by what he had learned of crooked games and cheating devices.

Kelly thought that he was about to emerge into the big time, but twenty years later, he was still working the carnival circuit, supplementing his income by cheating at poker against fellow carnies and the local rubes. Throughout his life, just as he had gotten achingly close to establishing himself as a true "big shot," the cruel hand of fate snatched away his wealth. Flush with four thousand dollars from a crooked card game in which the local sheriff and his deputy were the chief victims, he barely escaped a police roust and fled to Canada without his bankroll. From Vancouver, Kelly and an accomplice took a steamer to Yokohama; while at sea, they bilked several passengers and succeeded in both fleecing and publicly humiliating a powerful Canadian industrialist. After arriving back ashore in Los Angeles with three thousand dollars, Kelly was rolled by his former partner-in-crime and was forced, hat in hand, to beg the "big-time" Angeleno gambling boss Harry Carey for a job.

After being hired as a roulette operator on Carey's offshore casino, Kelly (in the author's rendering, anyway), had a moment of self-reflection, ruing that this "was the guy that was going to come back a big shot, buy Mr. Shannon, his retired minister father-in-law, a little farm out in the country," and support his wife decently. Instead, he realized that he was nothing more than "a fifty-dollar-a-week cheater in a gambling house, living with his wife's folks and choking on every mouthful they fed him because he knew they hated him for having their daughter when he was a gambler, an outcast." Clad in a newly bought tuxedo, Kelly went to work on the boat, fleecing the wealthy gamblers aboard until one night a police raid forced him to jump overboard; though captured by the Coast Guard, he escaped when his skiff approached the shore, and sneaked off.

Since Los Angeles was now too hot for him, Kelly made his way toward Denver but was waylaid by a lonely, bearded miner who, in Kelly's account, forced him to pass counterfeit gold coins in poker games. His fraud was discovered and he spent about a year in Leavenworth federal prison. Vowing to go straight after his release, he nonetheless was ensnared by a pair of cheaters in a scam familiar to anyone who has seen *The Sting*. Kelly played his part expertly before ruining the con by cheating a boy out of five dollars with crooked dice, drawing police attention. Kelly had to skip town minus the $190,000 he had "legitimately" earned by the scam, a typical outcome for the putative big shot. Kelly then worked a legal gambling house in Agua Caliente, Mexico, and had a nice stake until it was robbed by bandits taking advantage of the confusion of Mexican Revolution. Kelly then served in the United States Army for three years and saw combat in the First World War. Returning to the states, he worked in a "boiler room" selling bogus stocks and played a small role in Arnold Rothstein's famous fixing of the 1919 World Series.

Kelly made one last try at the big time, buying an illegal casino near Canton, Ohio, but was forced to sell to a bootlegging syndicate, who had at least the courtesy to hire him back as a poker dealer at $50 a week. He spent the rest of his life working the fakir circuit and, while running a knife game (his first scam) at the 1933 Chicago World's Fair, collapsed. His dying words to his wife distilled a half century of frustration at never having made the big time: "I almost was a big shot," he told her, "I'm sorry I didn't turn out better." That was as fitting a memorial as any for the life of a small-time grifter.

Kelly wasn't the only professional to suffer regret; the confessional autobiography of the "reformed gambler" is common enough that it is virtually its own genre. Many professional gamblers, through naïveté or greed, never enjoyed the riches they fleeced from others. John Philip Quinn, an erstwhile St. Louis gambler who was brought to the side of antigambling, characterized the "downward career of a gambler" as beginning with high hopes at the prospect of a life made easy by the ruin of others, progressing to the silent villainy of a midnight prowler, and ending with the ragged garb of a tramp. Quinn felt the blackleg "enslaved by his own degraded instincts" to be as much a "fool of fortune" as those who dissipated their wealth in his crooked games.

Still, gambling remained a popular career, particularly for those who liked the world of plush houses and midnight card games. Even those with pedestrian lives jumped at the chance to profit from chance; store owners throughout the nation used a variety of tools, some straight, some crooked, but all unfavorable to the player, to perk up their bottom lines. Like the lotteries of sixteenth-century Flanders and Italy, these were essentially glorified raffles for overstocked merchandise. Tobacconists and candy-store owners used a variety of "trade stimulators," as they were politely called; each was unabashedly a gambling game. The "star pointer," for example, was a wheel of fortune fitted up to raffle off prizes.

There seemed no limit to the contraptions that could be turned into a gambling medium: One game, popular with children, involved an artificial fishpond filled with bobbing wooden fish. Paying a dime, players were allowed to use a rod to reel in a fish, from whose ventral region was pulled a slide that indicated whether the player had won a corresponding prize, whose value was usually less than one cent. The most popular trade stimulator was the cigar wheel, basically a wheel of fortune that ostensibly paid out in cigars but whose operator could choose to offer a cash equivalent. In this fashion, even the proprietor of a small tobacco shop could become a small-time gambling boss, scooping up the nickels of his patrons.

Though cigar wheels, fish ponds, and other trade stimulators were popular, a related genre of retail aids reigned supreme over late-nineteenth-century American shops, surviving even the onslaught of slot machines in the 1890s and 1900s. Game cards and punchboards allowed merchants to raffle off merchandise using an easily disposable medium: paper. The typical game card cost five cents to play and featured 255 poker hands concealed behind seals. If a player uncovered a four of a kind, he won 80 cents' worth of merchandise; full house, 50 cents; straight, 40 cents; three of a kind, 20 cents; two pair, 10 cents; jacks or better, 5 cents. If he uncovered a lower hand, he naturally received nothing. The game cards were forerunners of today's "scratchers," instant-play games authorized by many lotteries. Store proprietors could expect a profit between $2.20 and $7.00 for each card, an impressive return.

Punchboards operated on the same principle, but were larger and somewhat more substantial, and were popular in a variety of retail shops, from druggists' to dry goods emporia. Players paid a stake to punch out a slot in the board, which might reveal a prize. A very popular advertising medium, punchboards came adorned with the images of a variety of products, and

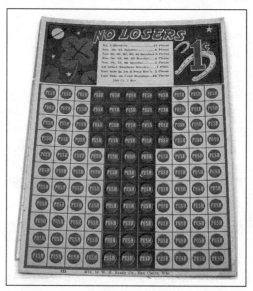

This punchboard was typical of the thousands that could be found in the tobacconists and candy stores of small-town America in the late nineteenth and early to mid-twentieth centuries. This board gave customers the chance to win a prize for a penny. Taking in $1.21, it paid out only 49 cents in prizes, leaving the store owner a respectable 72-cent profit.

themed punchboards, decorated with the colors of sports teams, were also common. Punchboards were so ubiquitous that most Americans did not consider them to be a form of gambling, and even church elders often livened up trips to the store with a quick "pick-out game."

Like all other gambling devices, punchboards had both a fair and a crooked side: One of Honest John Kelly's many adventures saw him travel across the land as a punchboard salesman who provided a confederate with the "key" to the boards. The confederate would then visit the stores Kelly had stocked with punchboards and win all of the valuable prizes. But even those who didn't enjoy this kind of inside information delighted in punchboards, which for decades was one of the most widespread gambling games in the United States. This appetite for gambling fed an extensive population of roving grifters, crooked gamblers, and con artists, each taking advantage of the suckers' hopes to get something for nothing.

PART SIX

Gambling for Fun and Profit

‎◆ ◆ ◆

The crowds thronged the casino at Monte Carlo, as usual, on the day that the cap-
tain arrived in Monaco. Not usually a gambler, he was drawn by the excitement
into the casino and, before he knew it, found himself sitting at a roulette table. A
helpful man connected with the casino in some unknown capacity had mysteriously
materialized at his elbow and without a word guided him to the table, where a seat
was immediately made available.

Out of curiosity more than anything else, he placed a small wager on black. He
watched with amusement as the croupier spun a tiny ivory ball around the rim of
the wheel, divided into thirty-seven numbered spaces. After circling for what
seemed like an eternity, the ball skipped across the numbers before settling into one
marked twenty-eight. It was black. The croupier dispassionately announced the
winning number, swept most of the bets from the green felt layout, and neatly
placed double the captain's wager before him.

On a whim, the captain took the whole amount and moved it to red. On that
spin, red came up. He was now hooked and, within a short time, found himself sev-
eral thousand francs richer. Unable to tear himself away, he was annoyed when his
officers tracked him down and remonstrated with him to leave while he was still
ahead. It was inevitable, they said, that his luck would run out and he would lose all
of his winnings back to the bank. After the officers left in frustration, the captain's
luck did turn, and he blamed them for ruining his fortune.

The next morning, the captain was the first at the casino's door when it opened
at 10:00 A.M. Winning at first, he then began losing, and soon had lost back all he
had won. It had been so easy getting the money in the first place, he temporized, that
with a sufficient capital he could easily win it back. He darted off to his ship and re-
turned with fifty thousand francs that had been entrusted to him by the Admiralty.
After he had lost that money, he saw a future with court-martial, prison, and life-
long disgrace.

After stomping throughout the casino in a barely controlled rage, he found the casino director, to whom he explained his plight. The director suavely apologized for the captain's bad luck but explained that there was nothing he could do. He had said the same to hundreds, if not thousands, of ruined gamblers before, and most had been contented with his offer of a third-class ticket back home.

The captain was not so easily dismissed. "You will give me back every penny I have lost," he haughtily declared, "or I will go back to my ship, bring it to the Bay of Monaco, and open fire upon this place."

The casino director begged a moment to reconsider. After disappearing into the casino's offices, he reemerged a short time later, apologizing profusely, and presented the captain with a stack of gold and banknotes that matched his total losses. The captain set sail, never to return to the casino again, but the story circulated among the croupiers and guests for years. Here, they said, was the only man who had ever truly been able to beat the casino at Monte Carlo.

A Sunny Place for Shady People

◆ ◆ ◆

GAMBLING ON THE FRENCH RIVIERA

François Blanc had been preparing for his departure from Homburg for more than a decade, amassing a considerable fortune and securing a new site on which to develop a gambling resort within the tiny principality of Monaco. This was a sunny but isolated spot on the Côte d'Azur (Blue Coast) or French Riviera, located midway between Nice and San Remo. Monaco had been ruled by the Grimaldi family since 1297, when Francesco Grimaldi, disguised as a monk, stealthily entered the town's fortress and, opening the doors for his Guelph followers who had fled Genoa with him, overwhelmed the fortifications and seized the enclave for himself. The family has retained control of the town ever since, with the exception of brief periods when it was under Genoese and, later, French occupation. In the fourteenth century the Grimaldis added the neighboring districts of Roquebrune and Menton to their holdings, and by the sixteenth the independence of Monaco had been recognized by France. With the masterful rule of Honoré II, the Grimaldi court of Monaco became renowned for its art collection, and Honoré gave himself the title of prince (earlier rulers had been "lord"), which is still used today. The Grimaldi family owned extensive estates in France, and coupled with the income from the agricultural produce of Menton and Roquebrune, this income subsidized a generous lifestyle.

The good times ended with the French Revolution. Prince Honoré III was deposed, the Grimaldi estates confiscated, Monaco itself annexed to France, and the royal family was imprisoned. After the fall of Napoléon, the Grimaldis were restored to their sovereign rule of Monaco. During the reign of the reactionary Honoré V (1819–1841), the first proposal to turn Monaco into a resort was floated. With its healthy climate and the addition of good lodging, fine food, and "distractions" (i.e., gambling), proponents believed it would become a popular resort. But Honoré, preoccupied with a futile struggle to return things to the way they had been in 1789, demurred.

Meanwhile, the restive districts of Menton and Roquebrune chafed under Grimaldi rule and taxation. During the revolutions of 1848, they proclaimed themselves free cities. Occupied, though not formally annexed, by Sardinia (they would be incorporated into France in 1861 with a treaty that guaranteed Monaco's continued independence), their income was lost to Monaco, which was now one twentieth of its original size. Prince Florestan I, or more accurately his able wife, Princess Caroline, began searching for any way to wring a decent income from the rocky soil they still possessed. Distilling alcohol from a local plant, lace making, and the production of perfume all failed.

Caroline refused to give up and, with the help of the Parisian lawyer A. Eynaud, began to reconsider the possibilities of a bathing and gambling resort. In 1854, they vaguely proposed forming a company that would build a bathing place, sanatorium, hotel, and casino, but could not get financing. A group of Nice investors volunteered to build the casino themselves, but they lacked money to actually start construction and were dismissed. At Caroline's urging, Eynaud journeyed to Baden-Baden to investigate the casino there, operated by Edward Bénazet. He learned that the grand duke directly earned 350,000 thousand francs a year from his share of the casino proceeds. On top of this already handsome sum, he derived an additional economic benefit from the estimated two hundred thousand wealthy visitors who thronged Baden each year in search of health and good fortune.

Inspired by Eynaud's findings, Caroline resolved to secure an effective operator who could build a resort and turn a gambling concession into a cash machine for the royal family. Caroline and Eynaud heard many proposals, but none of the operators seemed to have the savvy or finances to build and run a first-rate resort. One group was dissuaded from pursuing the franchise by their hired consultant, François Blanc, who not surprisingly told them that Monaco had few prospects as a gambling resort—he, after all, owned the casino at Homburg and had actively campaigned against any new casinos for years. He had earlier written to his manager, Trittler, that it was doubtful that anyone would be so foolish as to develop a casino at Monaco.

Blanc was dubious because the site was so isolated. Monaco could only be reached by a narrow mountain road, whose passage was dangerous, dirty, and time consuming, or a steamer that sailed irregularly from Nice. Matters were complicated by occupation of Menton and Roquebrune by Sardinia, which had opposed a casino in Nice and might preempt the rule of the Grimaldis if they flouted Sardinian morality by opening one themselves. Still, Eynaud persisted in searching for a builder. Finally, he was approached by the pair of Napoléon Langlois, a Parisian businessman, and Albert Aubert, a journalist,

▲
Mirage CEO Steve Wynn smiles as lucky winner Elmer Sherwin holds aloft a check signifying his multimillion-dollar winning Megabucks spin on the Mirage's opening night, November 22, 1989. Megabucks is typical of the wide-area progressive slots pioneered by International Game Technology that combine the instant gratification of slots with the life-changing jackpots of the lottery.

▶
Opening on April 28, 2005, the $2.7-billion Wynn Las Vegas was the world's most expensive casino resort, and allowed visionary Steve Wynn to put his signature—quite literally—on the Las Vegas Strip, by now considered the world's gambling and entertainment mecca.

Nick "the Greek" Dandolos was one of the twentieth century's most prolific gamblers. He is here in profile with legendary casino owner Benny Binion.

In 1993, Steve Wynn imploded the Dunes to make way for an entirely new resort. The Bellagio, since its 1998 opening, has been considered one of the finest hotels in the world, and has been one of the most successful resorts of the new Las Vegas Strip.

By 1986, a score of new casino resorts joined converted hotels to create jobs and revenues in Atlantic City, New Jersey. The under-construction Showboat and the project that became the Trump Taj Mahal are at the far bottom; the freshly painted Resorts International is just above them. While some of the city's classic amusement piers are still languishing in decay, the Million Dollar Pier has been transformed into the Ocean One Mall.

Opening in 1955, the Dunes was a typical Strip resort of the period, distinguished only by the oversized genie that dominated its frontage.

With the continued success of legal casinos, many Strip resorts expanded in the 1960s. The Dunes added a high-rise tower—the Diamond of the Dunes—in 1962. Supersized neon signs such as the Dunes' (which towered over the original low-slung resorts) would be given intellectual standing to match their wattage by architects Robert Venturi, Denise Scott Brown, and Steven Izenour's 1972 consideration of roadside Strip architecture, *Learning from Las Vegas*.

As can be seen from this photo of the Strip's Desert Inn casino taken on its opening night (April 24, 1950), Strip casinos of the 1950s continued to be relatively small.

In the 1950s and 1960s, Strip casinos used star entertainers to attract visitors. On March 6, 1957, Dean Martin began a solo run in the Sands Hotel's Copa Room; eventually he, Frank Sinatra, and Sammy Davis, Jr.—the Rat Pack—would become the unofficial kings of Las Vegas.

▲
In his Reno club, Bill Harrah pioneered in providing a uniformly customer-oriented gambling experience. This 1959 photo shows the inside of the club that is today Harrah's Reno.

►
Bill Harrah's name today graces the world's largest casino operating company, Harrah's Entertainment, but in his life he only owned clubs in Harrah's and Lake Tahoe. This photo was taken in the early 1970s.

Johnny Moss, left, won the first two World Series of Poker, while Jack Binion, right, is credited with deciding to use a freeze-out [n]o-limit Texas hold'em game to determine the champion. [H]ere they pose with some of Moss's winnings.

[In] the 1950s, the biggest [ca]sino action was on the [cr]aps tables, as this photo [fr]om the Sands on the [L]as Vegas Strip shows.

Gambling has continued—and even increased—during wars throughout human history. In this pen-and-ink sketch, a Civil War correspondent depicts soldiers playing the dice game chuck-a-luck in 1865.

Faro was the American national game for most of the nineteenth century. This 1867 rendering of a New York City faro bank depicts the tense moment as players await "the turn," the dealing of the last group of cards. On the right, the casekeeper tracks cards in play.

Artist's rendering of play in the Monte Carlo casino, circa 1892.

▲
A group of Native American
women from the Shoshone
tribe play cards in Utah in
this early 1870s illustration.

▶

This Henry Roth illustration
shows the outcome of a failed
attempt at cheating—the
dead man made the mistake
of dealing himself three aces
using a poorly marked deck.
Though the Wild West was
famous for similar dispute
resolution scenarios, this
drawing was the frontispiece
of David A. Curtis's *Stand
Pat, or Poker Stories from the
Mississippi.*

who lacked experience but not enthusiasm. Aubert was particularly expansive in his descriptions of the stately facilities and charming villas that they would build. All he needed was the money to start.

Despite considerable uncertainty about Langlois's capital resources, on April 26, 1856, Florestan I, in one of his final acts (he was to die and be succeeded by his son Charles III in June), granted the pair a concession to build and run a "bathing establishment." To be open year-round, the resort was to include a hotel, gardens, and regular omnibus service to and from Nice. The order specified the "amusements" that the operators could provide for bathers: "balls, concerts, fetes, games such as whist, écarte, piquet, faro, boston (a whist variant), and *reversi,* as well as roulette with either one or two zeroes, and trente-et-quarante with the *refait* or *demi-refait.*" The casino could thus compete head-to-head against Blanc's Kursaal by offering similar odds. The edict further specified government regulation: The gaming could take place only under the supervision of one or more inspectors appointed by His Serene Highness, the prince of Monaco.

Despite shaky finances, Langlois and Aubert immediately set to work, quickly acquiring land on the rocky peninsula across the harbor from Monaco proper—a section of the district known as Les Spélugues, or "the caves"—for their permanent casino. They neglected to build the actual bathhouse, hotels, or streets, or institute regular transportation from Nice, and other than issuing a wildly boastful prospectus, the operators did little else but set up tables in a temporary site, the Villa Bellevue.

Play began at the Villa Bellevue on December 14, 1856, though the villa was scarcely ready to accommodate even the least demanding of visitors. Prince Charles III's chief commissioner, Henri de Payan, had to demand of the casino's manager that they clear the building's environs of hazards that might "offend the eyes or nose." With limited table reserves, the new casino could not afford high-end play. Few gamblers made the more than four-hour land journey from Nice to Monaco.

Those who did arrive frequently were petty swindlers and rogues who passed forged banknotes and otherwise tried to cheat the house and other players. Someone tampered with the roulette wheel, either in an effort to defraud the company or to discredit it. Langlois and Aubert, unable to finance new buildings and lacking cash reserves deep enough even to put the gambling on a solid footing, were forced to sell their company in December 1857 to Pierre Auguste Daval, a landowner from Charente in central France whose finances were reputedly beyond reproach. Daval, however, proved to have no more money than his predecessors. François Blanc, sensing an opportunity, "fired" some of his most trusted employees, who then found work in Monaco, from whence they kept him well informed of the ongoing saga. Although Daval began construction of the permanent casino in May 1858, he paid no money to the prince, nor did he begin transportation improvements. Within a year, steadily losing money, he was forced to sell his ownership of the concession to a newly formed Paris company.

The new owners, whose most prominent name was that of the duc de Valmy, the wealthy and influential grandson of the French military hero François Kellerman, took possession of the concession on May 29, 1859. The company was to be run by François Lefebvre on behalf of its directors. Though they had considerably more solid finances than the previous owners, the new proprietors still found their bankroll lacking. Complicating matters, the outbreak of the Austro-Sardinian War had forced a closure of the casino. Though this war ultimately resulted in the broad international recognition of Monaco's independence and the end of the Sardinian threat, it hardly marked an auspicious beginning for the new owners.

When the war ended, Lefebvre did not reopen the previous facilities but instead commenced play in a new location in the heart of Monaco itself. Despite the complete lack of hotel facilities, the tables showed a decent average profit—a thousand francs per day. Visitors, if they could reach the casino at all, had no place to stay overnight and had to leave in the early evening. Lefebvre was not the right man to rise to the challenge of building a new gambling resort; he was afraid to even enter the gambling room, lest he be accosted by an unhappy loser. He refused to spend money to improve the facilities, and as it became clear that he could not meet the prince's deadline for completing the permanent casino by January 1, 1863, he resigned.

The duc de Valmy now openly sought to sell the resort franchise to an established Rhine operator. Wary of the political climate in Homburg, François Blanc was well disposed to listen. Eynaud's heart leapt at the chance of Blanc's duplicating his success in Homburg and had confidence in his large fortune and sagacious management. He wrote to Charles III that Blanc was a wizard, a "master in the art of dissimulating the green cloth of the gaming tables behind a veil of luxury, elegance, and pleasure."

Meanwhile, the new casino, poorly furnished and half finished, opened in February. Blanc's Homburg nemesis, Thomas Garcia, terrified the stockholders when he arrived and quickly won forty-five thousand francs at the tables. In their desperation, they hastily agreed to sell to Blanc. In March 1863, Blanc signed a contract giving him, in return for a cash payment of 1.5 million francs, complete ownership of the gaming concession until April 1, 1913.

A new day had dawned in Monaco, and Blanc promised that though he had served his apprenticeship in Homburg, he would create his masterpiece for Charles III.

Blanc formed the *Société des Bains de Mer et du Cercle des Étrangers* (Society of Sea Bathers and Circle of Foreigners) as an operating company for the casino and the related facilities. He immediately refurbished and completed the casino and adjoining Hôtel de Paris, dispatching his Homburg architect Jacobi to bring to the project the expected excellence. Blanc demanded that the hotel be among the finest in the world, and Jacobi did not disappoint. To lure serious gamblers, he immediately raised the table reserves and deposited enough money in a Nice bank to raise public confidence in the casino's solvency. Meanwhile, Blanc advanced improvements in land transport, including the establishment of a rail line, and purchased four boats to provide regular service from Nice and Genoa. He turned his army of press agents and captive journalists onto the single-minded promotion of Monaco as an elegant resort in which gold was simply waiting to be plucked from the tables. Selling a favorable building site to the owner/editor of *Le Figaro,* the populist, scandal-loving Hippolyte de Villemessant, ensured that yet another French media outlet would unabashedly promote the happiness to be found in Monaco. Blanc's efforts paid off immediately, as the number of visitors more than doubled. Blanc began to promote a scheme of "Homburg in the summer, Monaco in the winter," and, though he kept both casinos open year-round, encouraged seasonal play at both. He abolished the second zero at roulette in 1864, making sure that the change was duly promoted in the newspapers. By 1866, Blanc had spent more than two million francs improving the roads and harbor and building gardens around his casino. Yet something of a cloud still hung over the enterprise. The Italian and German cognates of *spélugues* translated loosely as "disreputable haunts," and a place named Les Spélugues was hardly a fitting site for a gambling house, no matter how elegant. Blanc campaigned with Prince Charles III to change the district's name, and on July 1, 1866, he got his wish, when the prince humbly declared that, henceforth, the area surrounding the casino was to be known as the Quartier de Monte Carlo.

After the railway opened in 1868, the casino could scarcely contain the crowds, and during the winter Monaco became Europe's chief gambling resort. The Hôtel de Paris was fully booked months in advance; tired of turning away prospective gamblers, Blanc ordered its expansion. In 1864, 70,000 people visited the casino; by 1870, the figure stood at 120,000. Yet all was not golden. Blanc wanted to improve the "quality" of visitors as well as their quantity, and an extortion attempt forced a solution. Two amateur "journalists" published a hate-filled pamphlet denouncing the casino; demanding 20,000 francs from one of Blanc's managers, they were arrested for blackmail. Learning that the pair had, in fact, patronized the casino, Blanc developed a system whereby prospective gamblers had to fill out entrance cards, and the casino reserved the right to exclude anyone it wished. Far from lowering the number of visitors, this actually helped to raise it, as entry into the casino became a mark of good bearing. Still, Monaco charged no outright visitors' tax, as did competing bathing resorts, and entry to the casino remained free. There, the newly rich could jostle those with century-old wealth, and obsessed gamblers were free to test their luck. In the words of Somerset Maugham, it was "a sunny place for shady people."

By 1872, the final year for Rhine casinos, Monte Carlo was firmly established as the jewel of the Riviera. With its new monopoly on roulette and trente-et-quarante, Monte Carlo could not help but be successful. The next year, on the close of the fashionable winter season in February, the London *Times* reported that Blanc had worked a miracle: A visitor from Nice arriving at an hour when the casino and its surrounding terrace were lit by "a thousand globes of fire" could not help but conclude that he had "left ordinary life and the countries of reality to enter into that brilliant region where all passions combine to obliterate the mind and obscure the reason." Further, the correspondent—who most likely enjoyed Blanc's largesse—declared that the casino master had created "the most luxurious, most beautiful, most enervating place in the world." Accessed by newly paved roads, surrounded by graceful gardens, the casino was the centerpiece of a wonderland where fine food could be had for a small price, perfumes wafted through the air along with charming music, and a thousand seductions awaited the unwary. For those devoted to chasing the black and the red in a refined setting, it was nothing less than an earthly paradise.

Blanc wanted to forestall any prohibition movement (and avoid a repeat of his Homburg humiliation) by accumulating political debts. He therefore made himself a friend of the French government by becoming its banker: In 1874 he gave the minister of public works a 4.8 million-franc loan to rebuild the Paris Opera House. He thereafter enjoyed rich relations with a variety of government officials, who generously facilitated the improvement of rail connections between Monaco and France. The opera house's architect, Charles Garnier, showed his appreciation by designing a theater for Blanc that adjoined the casino and provided it with its landmark two towers, which soon became an emblem of Monte Carlo.

The Monte Carlo casino's twin towers gave it a distinctive appearance.
This postcard captures the look of the casino's exterior in the late nineteenth century.

Blanc enjoyed another triumph when his daughter Louise married a poor but noble Polish aristocrat, Prince Constance Radziwill, in 1876. His rise to wealth and power was complete, though his declining health gave him little opportunity to enjoy it. Ill with bronchitis, he died at the age of seventy-one in Loèche-les-Bains on July 27, 1877, leaving a fortune of more than 88 million francs ($17.5 million in 1877 dollars) to his family. His funeral was the most extravagant that Paris had seen for years, and his charitable bequests were duly noted in his obituaries. He had outlived the farsighted Eynaud, who had served as an apt mediator between Blanc and Charles III for years, by only a few weeks. Princess Caroline, who had guided her husband and son toward her vision of a prosperous Monaco, passed away two years later.

Marie Blanc, forty-three years old at the time of Blanc's death, succeeded her husband in overseeing the Monte Carlo enterprise, and Bertora, formerly François's secretary, assumed the role of casino manager. Since 1863, Blanc had worked wonders at Monaco. Where it once had no serviceable hotels, it now had nineteen, as well as an assortment of villas and apartments to house long-term visitors. Once nearly bereft of industry, Monaco now boasted shops, restaurants, banks, and support services for the burgeoning hospitality industry that provided work for Monaco citizens, who, thanks to the tremendous sums the casino brought the government, paid no taxes.

Visitors to Monte Carlo wagered virtually any currency they wished. French five-franc coins were the most common, but lire, drachma, and even American dollars were common. Particularly large wagers were made using counters or plaques. Usually made from mother-of-pearl or ivory, the first rectangular gambling plaques were made in China in the early eighteenth century. Brought to Europe by 1720, they were generally bought by individuals for use in private games. Disc-shaped counters were used in Ancient Rome for everything from arena admissions to gambling: These are the true ancestors of today's chips. Metal "whist markers" were used to play that game in the early nineteenth century in Europe and North America.

Monte Carlo was a bit slow in adopting chips; perhaps its more sophisticated guests preferred to wager real money. Americans, who wanted money to change hands with the greatest efficiency, were among the earliest to gamble with chips. Around the middle of the nineteenth century, ivory chips became popular with poker and faro players. In the 1880s, "composition" chips, manufactured with clay and shellac, became popular. But there was a problem: Since the chips were made without designs in only in a few colors, it was easy to buy one's own chips, then surreptitiously slip them into a game. As a result, manufacturers began making engraved and inlaid litho chips, which featured hard-to-copy designs. Regular inlaid chips, featuring an inlaid color set into a differently colored chip, became common in the 1890s, and, though chips are now made of high-tech composites and sometimes embedded with radio frequency identification tags, they look similar to inlaid chips of a century ago. Monte Carlo, though, still uses the oversized plaques, continuing a tradition started generations ago.

Marie Blanc presided over the triumphant opening of the Charles Garnier–designed theater, which provided a venue for performances by Europe's finest musicians and actors. Still, she shrank from active involvement in the casino, tiring of the constant stream of letters begging for help and threatening blackmail. The croupiers were on the constant watch for cheating, and discreet detectives roamed the casino, on the lookout for pickpockets and hustlers. Sometimes the threat was more direct. At 10:00 P.M. on April 24, 1880, a bomb smuggled into one of the gaming salons exploded. Timed to go off just as the theater crowds filled the casino, the explosion was intended to create enough confusion to permit its planters to carry off the wealth on the tables.

The attackers had not counted on the stoic professionalism of the casino's guardians. Though the bomb caused considerable mayhem—windows were shattered, the gaslights extinguished, and scores of gamblers wounded by fly-ing glass—the croupiers remained coolly intent at their positions, refusing to take their eyes off the gold and banknotes heaped before them. This incident only strengthened Marie's distaste for the casino, and though she tri-umphantly saw the marriage of her second daughter to Prince Roland Bona-parte (a nephew of the prince of Canino who had nearly broken her husband at Homburg), she did not live long after that, dying quite suddenly at the age of forty-seven in 1881.

Upon her death her stepson Camille Blanc took control of the casino, af-ter having served a long apprenticeship under his father and stepmother. He encouraged his brother Edmond to pursue his love of the turf in far-off Paris, and, limiting Bertora's authority, he emerged as the managing director of the Société des Bains de Mer (SBM). He was praised as a sharp-eyed, charming figure who brought Monte Carlo into a new age by renewing its commitment to providing excellent food and lodging and by adding new at-tractions, including a seaside bathing facility and various sporting events.

In 1898, Camille Blanc renegotiated his father's original pact with Monaco's prince. SBM was charged with financing improvements to the har-bor and roads and agreed to subsidize the opera. Prince Albert also extracted the promise of a minimum payment of £50,000 a year from the casino, as well as eight percent of the gross revenues in excess of 1 million pounds. By this time, the casino's internal structure had been divided into three departments underneath the SBM umbrella. Camille Blanc, as chief director, primarily de-voted himself to the company's finances and charged the director general with overseeing the activities of the directors who headed each of the casino's departments. The Interior Department saw to purchasing, maintenance, ex-pansion, and human resources. Exterior handled legal and accounting matters as well as entertainment, utilities, and the gardens. The Games Department was composed of surveillance officers, croupiers, and their supervisors.

The croupiers were trained on-site at a six-month school that mercilessly drilled applicants in the science of dexterously handling the roulette wheel and sorting, recognizing, and paying bets. This last was no mean feat. Most casinos today have players "buy" chips of a certain color at the roulette table; matching a bet to a player is as simple as identifying whose color is whose. But as Monte Carlo roulette tables accepted all manner of gold, silver, and paper currency as live wagers, it was essential for dealers not only to remain aware of the position of bets both before and after the ball dropped but to remember which piles belonged to which hands. Generally speaking, SBM hired only those already employed with the firm in some other capacity as croupiers, and held its school at night, after their regular shift. While on duty, croupiers were watched by *chefs de parties,* who sat on high chairs overlooking the tables; they were the ancestors of today's pit bosses and floorpeople. Surveillance officials also circulated, but the croupiers enforced honor among themselves by means of a peer disciplinary council that ruled on serious allegations of fraud or stealing. For those found guilty, the penalties could be severe, including not only termination but forcible expulsion from the principality.

In the late 1860s, Blanc's casino had only four rooms. By 1910, it had been expanded countless times in a patchwork of architectural styles: Greek, Moorish, and French Second Empire. The erstwhile casino became an atrium that connected the Charles Garnier theater and the Schmit Room, the first gaming room. From the atrium, guests passed through a vestibule decorated in the Louis XVI style into the Schmit Room, which was Louis XIV. Like all the gaming salons, it had a parquet floor. The Schmit room was distinguished by its Corinthian columns and onyx pilasters, paintings inspired by the four seasons, four immense Art Nouveau chandeliers, and a ceiling vault topped with a circular skylight. The other gaming salons were a mix of styles but were similarly lavish. From the outside, two semidetached Moorish towers were the most distinctive feature of off-white Beaux Arts exterior, which was capped by green copper vaults.

Though, like his father, Camille took great pains to accommodate the press, attacks on Monte Carlo continued to circulate in the newspapers, ironically often the same ones that scant weeks before had blazoned their pages with glowing praise of the remarkable resort. (One senses that editors and/or correspondents, believing their own hyperbole, had succumbed to temptation and bet more than they should have before turning their venom against the casino.) In 1878, for example, the previously sanguine *New York Times* reported that the resort was "a sorry substitute for Baden-Baden." As most people of worth stayed at villas in Monte Carlo, hoteliers made no efforts to treat their guests with courtesy, though they charged rapacious room rates; at least the Badenites were polite. While the Baden-Baden croupiers had excelled in treating all guests with an aristocratic deference, their Monte Carlo counterparts had "the manners of cavalrymen" and rudely lectured the players, even giving them orders. The gamblers, of a lower class than those who once graced Baden-Baden, glumly suffered such abuse. Finally, petty thefts and squabbles over stakes were common, as were scenes that would be considered disgraceful in the meanest American faro bank.

Still, many wealthy and well-known visitors poured into the principality.

One son of an unnamed American railroad millionaire had quite a spree in 1882. Losing all of his ready money at trente-et-quarante, he telegraphed his mother for more, temporizing that he had lost his pocketbook. Before he could hear back, a friend loaned him some money with which he reclaimed his losses from the tables. He then telegraphed that his mother need not send anything, as his pocketbook had been found. Unwilling to quit while ahead, he returned to the tables and lost everything, whereupon he dejectedly telegraphed a third time, imploring his mother: "Do send money. Pocketbook found as stated, but with nothing in it."

This was not the only mother-son pair to make news at Monte Carlo. The Prince of Wales, who would in 1901 become King Edward VII, had long frequented the casino at Homburg and easily followed the elder Blanc to Monte Carlo. Because it was considered unseemly for the heir apparent to publicly gamble, he adopted several pseudonyms, including "Captain White" and "Baron Renfrew," which gave him a cloak of social invisibility; he flirted, gambled, and carried on his affairs in full view of the public, officially anonymous. His mother, Queen Victoria, had no more patience for the insouciance of Monaco than for her son's playboy antics. She wrote to her prime minister, William Gladstone (himself an occasional gambler), that she approved of a subscription to Thompson's anti-Monaco association, and made her hostility to the principality crystal clear in 1882 when, while passing through en route to Menton, she disdained an official presentation of flowers and spurned Charles III's offer of hospitality. This deliberate affront devastated the prince and dismayed François Blanc, who remarked that, had the queen taken up the invitation, it would have provided two million francs' worth of publicity.

Gamblers at Monte Carlo developed a set of bizarre and sometimes contradictory suspicions. Many supplicants to fortune brought religious icons with them. One woman even had a five-franc coin surreptitiously blessed by the pope (she had hidden it among a group of rosaries), and though she successfully channeled this papal benefice, she lost the amulet when a friend accidentally staked and lost the holy coin. Anglican churchgoers found similar inspiration when one of them staked heavily and won on that Sunday's hymn, numbered thirty-six. From then on, pious Englishmen and -women eagerly anticipated the selection of the hymnal, barely waiting for the service to conclude so they could rush into the casino. The pastor, suspecting something was up, loudly directed his congregants to turn to hymn number forty-seven the next Sunday. Seeing the disappointment on the faces of his flock and tired of being reduced to a roulette tipster, from then on he chose only hymns numbered above thirty-six.

By contrast, most gamblers considered priests extremely unlucky and hoped that, by curling their fingers into horns at the gaming table, they could ward off the churchly spirit. Others descended into theosophical speculation or numerological exegesis, plumbing the mystic significance of the tarot and Hebrew alphabet for lucky numbers. Some carried charms best described as pagan, including a woman who kept a bat's heart in her purse; she believed that, as a creature of the night, its sympathetic magic would bring fortune to all silver it touched. Pigs were also believed to bring luck. In the early days gamblers tried to smuggle live pigs into the gaming salons, but as the resort became more sophisticated they confined themselves to the occasional lucky pork chop. A truly bizarre superstition held that it was good luck to rub a hunchback. Other lucky charms included pieces of a hangman's rope, locks of hair, snakeskin, rat's tails, and horseshoes. The last of these, as symbols of fertility, were said to augur the collection of a large harvest. They usually did— for the casino.

By the outbreak of World War I, the casino employed more than five hundred people at the height of the winter season, which formally lasted from November to February. Croupiers were given regular salaries and pensions. Originally allowed to keep their own tips, croupiers were eventually barred from the practice. Thereafter, management permitted grateful winners to slip a few coins into "number thirty-seven," an added slot at the tables. At the end of the day, all of the tips were collected and divided among the employees.* Until 1948, managers kept half of the collection for themselves. After a sit-down strike, they consented to give the croupiers seventy percent of the takings.

The Blancs surrounded the casino with a range of other amusements. The theater, which featured in its day names as lofty as Sarah Bernhardt, Enrico Caruso, and Sergei Diaghilev, whose Russian Ballet was world renowned, provided a venue for opera, theater, and ballet. For more sporting types, pigeon shooting was a popular diversion. The harbor hosted all manner of water sports and sailing races, and bicycle races transformed Monaco streets into racetracks. With the spread of the automobile, car-racing rallies became popular, culminating in the Monte Carlo Grand Prix, first run in 1929.

No gambler, except the most willfully perverse, sits down to play with the intention of losing. In social games with some degree of strategy, players can bank on both their skill and luck to help them win. Not so for quick-decision

---

*Today's dealers will recognize the beginnings of the toke-sharing system present in most casinos today.

The Monte Carlo casino rooms were elegant, as this photo from
around the turn of the twentieth century shows.

mercantile games like roulette and trente-et-quarante. A player simply placed
her bet and hoped for the best. Controlling no element of the game's outcome, he or she could only change the size of her bet. Systems of betting, not
refinements of skill, held out the only hope that players could in fact beat the
house advantage.

Since the days of Girolamo Cardano, gamblers had tried to figure how
they could best take advantage of the odds. Subsequent innovations made the
mathematical basis of gambling clear, but did not help bettors. In fact, they
showed that no system can possibly guarantee success. While fortune can
swing in either direction over the course of an evening, because of a phenomenon mathematicians describe as "regression to the mean," given enough time
the house's statistical advantage will devour all players. Yet for centuries, players have enthusiastically embraced surefire, can't-lose systems, both borrowed
and new, that have ultimately failed.

The earliest known betting system is the Martingale progression, which
Casanova, according to his memoirs, employed in the Venice Ridotto in February 1754. The origin of the system's name is unknown, but legend links it to
a late eighteenth-century London gambling-house proprietor named Henry
Martingale. Using this uncomplicated geometric possession, Casanova simply
doubled the size of his bet after each loss. After he won, he returned his bet

to its original size. In theory, this meant that a player would win twice as much as he had lost on the previous deal, but in practice the limits of the system are clear: Unless armed with an infinite bankroll, the player has no safeguard against a bad run wiping him out. The Martingale is the quintessential negative progression system, in which players change their bets following losing hands.

Presume that a roulette player with $100 of chips places $5 bets on black. Losing her first hand, she would double her stake to $10; losing that one would require a $20 bet; and so on. If she was unlucky enough to lose four straight times (not that uncommon, as anyone who has watched roulette knows), she will not have enough in reserve for the $80 required for the fifth bet. Even if she had twice the capital, she would sooner or later butt up against the table maximum. There is more chance than science to any anecdotal successes scored with a Martingale progression. Still, some deep-thinking player found a way to elaborate the Martingale progression by devising a system where, after each losing bet, he doubled his stake and then added one betting unit. Known as the Grand Martingale, this method allows for greater returns but also bigger losses.

The opposite of the Martingale is the Paroli, or parlay; and it follows the maxim that the best defense is a good offense. Players following a Paroli progression double their stakes after winning. While this would allow a player to score a tremendous coup with a series of wins, it also means that, should he lose deep into the progression, he might be completely wiped out. Variations of the paroli include systems where the bet is increased according to a regular pattern: instead of reflexively doubling the stakes, players change the amount of units bet. A 1-3-2-6 progression, for example, has a player triple a winning bet, then stake double the original, and finally six times the base bet.

The Labouchere or cancellation system was invented by the eighteenth-century French mathematician de Cordorcet and popularized by a nineteenth-century member of the British Parliament, Henry Labouchere. In a nutshell, Labouchere devotees begin gambling by writing down a series of numbers, for example 1-2-3-4-5. The first bet is the sum of the first and last numbers, in this case 6. After losing a bet, the player writes that wager at the end of the series; after winning, she crosses out the first and last numbers in the series. Once the bettor has canceled all the numbers, she will have reached a net profit equaling the sum of the original numbers, 15 in the above example. The fatal drawback of this system is, as with the others, if the player is confronted with an unlucky run the necessary bet will soon eclipse either the player's bankroll or the table maximums.

The d'Alembert system is named for eighteenth-century mathematician Jean Le Rond d'Alembert, who edited the ground-breaking *Encyclopédie* with Denis Diderot. In mathematics, he is best known as the discoverer of d'Alembert's principle, an elaboration of the Newtonian laws of motion. The principle that bears d'Alembert's name stems from his belief that systems tend toward equilibrium: Applied to roulette, this means that the more the ball lands on black, the more likely it will be to land on red. Those seeking to use d'Alembert's idea of equilibrium to clean up at the tables add one unit to their bet when losing and subtract one when winning. In theory, at least, this would allow the average bettor to make a profit of one unit per win. In practice, though the d'Alembert system does not lead to the quick disaster possible in the classic Martingale, it is no sounder than any other system, despite the impressive intellectual achievements of its innovator.

A related system, the patience system, fuses the d'Alembert principle of equilibrium with selective betting. Patience bettors perch near the roulette wheel, waiting for a run of, for example, three straight reds. The bettor then steps in and places his money on black in the belief that black is "due" to come up. This is nonsense, as neither the ball nor the wheel feel any obligation toward maintaining the game's equilibrium: Random events are not influenced by past outcomes. While the patience system cannot guarantee winning, it does have the benefit of giving the bettor ample time sitting on the sidelines to reconsider the idea of using a system at all.

The Gagnante Marche system, known today as the streak or hot-and-cold system, turns d'Alembert on his head. According to Gagnante Marche, when you're hot, you're hot, and streaks, rather than a steady quest for equilibrium, define the game. Using this system, bettors put their money on the last side to win: If, arriving at the table, she finds black has just come up, the bettor places her money on black and leaves it there until red comes up. Thus, if one side or the other begins a streak, the bettor will be able to ride it from the beginning. This system's particular shortcoming is that, while waiting for a lucky wave, the would-be table-surfer will be pecked to death by the lurking piranha of random alternations between black and red. He is no better off than if he had simply left his money on either color and spent his energy thinking about whether to have a quick lunch in the coffee shop or wait in line at the buffet.

Though such gambling systems have existed since the mathematical advances of the eighteenth century put gambling on a surer theoretical footing, they truly blossomed in the years 1870–1914, years that also saw the greatest glory of Monte Carlo. In a sense, system gamblers were no different from the captains of industry who created business behemoths during this era: They sought to rationally exploit the resources of the casino by finding ways of taking advantage of its governing principles. This was a far cry from the noblesse oblige with which English grandees and continental bluebloods had once placed their indifferent wagers. In the late nineteenth century, as fortunes were ready to be made—or lost—in new industries, vacationing peers of the realm often found themselves rudely pushed aside by cigar-chewing industrialists, flush with new wealth. For them, roulette was not so much a leisure activity as an attempted hostile takeover of the casino. The table was a battlefield, and the player was armed only with his or her bankroll. The gambling system provided a plan of battle.

François Blanc and the casino managers remained serene in the face of system players' enthusiasm. Blanc often said that his casinos had been built on gambling systems and even circulated a story that seems more figuratively than literally true. Deciding to buy his wife a parasol that cost about one pound, he sought to test one of the most popular systems by trying to win the sum in his casino. He gave up after he found himself 1,000 pounds in the hole. Fortified by experience, he concluded that no system could possibly enable any but the richest bettor to threaten his reserves, and gave quiet encouragement to those who felt they knew better.

Still, gamblers big and small chased after the same dream of breaking the bank at Monte Carlo. Legions of small-betting gamblers thronged to Monte Carlo with the hope of parlaying a modest bankroll into a huge fortune. For the typical systems player, weeks or months of study, calculations, and dreaming culminated in a pilgrimage to the gambler's mecca, Monte Carlo. Though constantly reminded that all other systems had proved futile, each pilgrim to fortune held out the hope that his or her system could not fail.

On the face of it, "breaking the bank" would seem to indicate that the casino's reserves have been exhausted (as nearly happened at Homburg) in the face of a lucky bettor and that the house was bankrupted. But breaking the bank was actually more of a publicity stunt: It happened whenever a bettor won more than the cash reserves of a single table. The table was ceremoniously draped with black crepe and solemnly closed until a fresh infusion from the central cashier arrived. This rite began with Bénazet at his Wiesbaden casino and was copied by Blanc. When the bank was "broken," the casino was by no means insolvent, and frequently after the hiatus the player lost back all he had won. But the public spectacle of the black-garbed green cloth allowed players to believe that they had beaten Blanc at his own game, and thus encouraged even more resolute devotion to systems.

The really crafty systems figurers did not invest their own money in proving the truth of their hypotheses: They solicited backers to do so. In 1887 two Parisians developed a system that was sure to break the bank. Rather than simply heading to Monte Carlo and raking in the gold, they published a pamphlet that "demonstrated" the infallibility of the system and advertised for backers to take a share in the 1 million francs that would surely be realized from an initial bankroll of 24,000. After collecting 60,000 francs from various addle-heads foolish enough to send money through the mail, they then alighted at Blanc's casino and put their system into practice. After quickly losing 24,000 francs, they lost all faith in their system and returned to Paris, where the police promptly seized the remaining 36,000 and arrested the pair as common swindlers. Most systems of the era ended in similar frustration.

Yet there were some success stories, particularly before the science of roulette had been perfected. In 1873, an English engineer named Joseph Jaggers went on holiday at Monte Carlo. He later claimed never even to have seen a roulette wheel before. But, accustomed to exercising his intellect by designing cotton spindles, he became curious about the mechanics of roulette. The wheels, he conjectured, might have slight imperfections that would lead to certain numbers coming up more often than they should. Hiring a staff of clerks (which would seem to indicate that this was no holiday fancy; in fact the newspapers reported he had been backed by a syndicate) to record winning numbers at each of the tables, he gathered a week's worth of data. Poring through it, he noted that on a particular wheel nine numbers—7, 8, 9, 17, 18, 19, 22, 28, and 29—came up with surprising regularity. Jaggers bet accordingly and, within four days, had won £60,000.

The surveillance officers, always on the lookout for cheating, were perplexed by Jagger's success. They compared Jaggers's betting patterns with all known systems—they were already familiar with over forty of them—and found nothing, as he threw his money on the board with no discernible pattern. In actuality, Jaggers was cunning enough to place random wagers on numbers not favored by his system simply to keep his true methods obscure. Finally, in desperation they switched the roulette wheels. The next day, Jaggers stopped playing after fewer than thirty spins. Noticing suddenly that the wheel no longer had a characteristic scratch, he wandered the casino as discreetly as possible before spying "his" wheel. Sitting down, he continued his winning ways.

But the casino staff now knew Jaggers's secret. They quickly sent to Paris for spare parts and reconfigured every roulette wheel. Jaggers suspected as much, and after losing £200 in his next outing, he left the casino, packed his bags, and departed Monaco £80,000 richer, never to be seen there again. The casino directors immediately began a policy of testing with a level each table and wheel before the 10:00 A.M. start of the gambling day to guarantee that this perfectly legal method could never be used against the casino again.

Jaggers's success, of course, was not due to a betting system per se, but rather empirical application of observed inconsistencies in a single roulette wheel. As such, it did not fire the imagination as much as bona fide systems did. The public, hungry for a true system to break the bank, jumped eagerly on the bandwagon of one such claimant in 1891. The Englishman Charles Deville Wells was a poorly dressed, unremarkable flimflam artist: He once supposedly painted sparrows yellow and sold them as canaries. He took out more than two hundred patents from 1885 to 1890 on devices as varied as an automatic foghorn, a sardine-can opener, and a musical skipping rope. He so-licited investors, who generously gave him enough funds to open posh Lon-don offices and buy a yacht. With no money realized from his fanciful patents, he concluded that his best hope of satisfying his creditors would be found on the roulette tables.

Wells sailed his yacht into Monte Carlo in July 1891 and in three days had parlayed his original £400 into £40,000. He chalked his success up to his adapted Martingale system. He started with £100, doubled his bet to the maximum, and allowed it to ride for three successful bets, running his win-nings up to nearly £2,000 before returning to a £100 bet. In the course of his run he broke the bank several times. After putting in three eleven-hour days at the roulette tables, he left the casino, but not before also winning over £6,000 at trente-et-quarante.

Wells became an instant celebrity. A song written about him, prosaically titled "The Man Who Broke the Bank at Monte Carlo," caught the public fancy in Europe and the United States. All this only encouraged more tourists to test their own systems in Monte Carlo, usually unsuccessfully. Wells him-self returned in November, won an additional £10,000 in three days, and bought £2,000 worth of SBM stock before leaving. Unable to quit while he was ahead, Wells, cocksure in his own abilities, blinded by his success, or blissfully unaware of regression to the mean, returned in January aboard his new yacht.

To the surprise of no one but himself, he now lost steadily. His past soon caught up with him. His latest invention, he claimed, was a device that would increase the fuel efficiency of coal-burning engines; he was testing it on his yacht. He began to wire his investors that the machine had broken down and he needed money to effect repairs. Amid mounting suspicion, he confessed to them that he had in fact developed an unshakable betting system to which his investors were unwitting subscribers. Dissatisfied investors reported Wells's perfidy to the police. He was eventually extradited back to the United Kingdom and imprisoned for eight years after his conviction on fraud charges. He spent the rest of his life in and out of prison and on public relief, his system revealed as nothing more than blind luck and crafty salesmanship.

Debate over systems even spilled over into the newspapers. In 1903, Sir Hiram Maxim, the American inventor of the automatic machine gun (and naturalized British citizen) who had been knighted by Queen Victoria two years before, had a letter to the *New York Herald* published that refuted the "evening-up" system of one Herbert Vivian. Fitzroy Erskine, younger brother of James Francis Harry, the sitting earl of Rosslyn, joined the battle on Vivian's side, arguing that he himself had a system that could beat the bank, and that in fact anyone possessed with "fair capital, good nerve, and iron constitution" could beat the house advantage at roulette.

In 1908, Fitzroy's brother the earl arrayed himself against Maxim's dogmatic refusal to consider the possibility of a winning system. His own system was simple: Bet on a single even-money proposition, such as red, beginning with one unit, and then add one unit until the bank had been broken. Lord Rosslyn formed a syndicate of backers (including actress Lillie Langtry) and, with a team of players, put their system into operation at Monte Carlo. Rather quickly, the syndicate lost most of its money, and one of its members even collapsed from exhaustion.

This episode might have taught Rosslyn the futility of his system, but he instead goaded Maxim into a showdown. At stake was both pride and a £10 wager. The two shut themselves in a Piccadilly room with a roulette wheel and agreed that, should Rosslyn retain his theoretical £10,000 of capital (they did not use real money for the trial), at the end of two weeks he would be declared the winner. After one week, Rosslyn was ahead by £500. At this halfway point, both men hedged their bets. Rosslyn issued a written statement to the effect that while there existed no system absolutely guaranteed to break the bank, his was as close to certainty as was possible; this seemed a retreat from his earlier optimism and conceded Maxim's original thesis, that there was no such thing as a sure-win system. Maxim was more confident, saying that although the fluctuations were great, and that his bank could be wiped out by a bad run of four consecutive coups, it was his belief that "the second week will not allow such fluctuations, and that a balance in favor of the bank will be restored."

At this point, there was no guarantee that it would. Even Maxim's own wife predicted her husband's defeat. She, Maxim admitted, had invented twenty "winning systems" herself, which explains Maxim's consternation at

Rosslyn's claims. But both Mrs. Maxim and Lord Rosslyn were soon proven wrong. By the end of fourteenth day, Lord Rosslyn was £10,340 in the hole. Exhausted, he handed over to Maxim a £10 note. Maxim was victorious, though even this well-publicized failure could not dissuade systems devotees. Fresh from his annihilation of Rosslyn, Maxim received another public challenge, this one from a French "lightning calculator" named Jacques Inaudi. Weary of proving his point, Maxim suggested that Inaudi instead test his system at Monte Carlo with real money.

The enthusiasm over systems reached its peak at the turn of the twentieth century but continues to this day. The mistaken belief that previous random events somehow dictate future independent ones is known today as the *Monte Carlo Fallacy* or, more generally, *Gambler's Fallacy*. Faith in systems remained unshaken by the spectacular failures of supposed "mathematical masterminds" during the heady 1890s. Even today, books touting various surefire "betting management systems" are legion. Sometimes disguised in abstruse terminology or in the knowing talk of thousands of hours spent in real casinos, they are almost all just copies of the original systems debated in the 1890s. Even though the systems makers were rarely successful in breaking the bank at Monte Carlo, they would prove adept at breaking open the wallets of their fellow gamblers for decades to come.

The Monte Carlo monopoly on gambling was challenged, when, in 1907, the government of France authorized the public play of "games of skill," which included two games today considered more strictly games of chance: baccarat and chemin-de-fer. In actuality, the two were the same game, with the exception that the first was avowedly mercantile, banked only by the house, while the second had at least the trappings of a social game that pitted player against player.

Baccarat was born in Italy as *baccara* and was first reported in France during the long reign of Louis XIV (1643–1715). It became a favored game of the nobility but, by the Napoleonic period, could also be found in illegal gambling houses as well. After the prohibition of public gambling in 1837, it survived in private homes but did not make the jump to the Rhine along with trente-et-quarante and roulette.

Mentioned occasionally in the nineteenth century as a private game, baccarat suddenly burst into prominence in the early twentieth century in the new French Riviera casinos. It was already recognized as two games. *Chemin-de-fer* means "railroad" in French, and in "chemmy" players pass the *sabot* (shoe) across the table, perhaps in a manner reminiscent of a train. In this version of the game, the player with the shoe dealt the game and actually banked it; the privilege of holding bank was disbursed to the highest bidder, whose bid became his bet. The banker placed the amount of his winning bid on the table, and any players wishing to play *ponte* matched his bet, either in whole or in part. If several players backed *ponte*, the one with the highest bet played for all. The banker then dealt four cards facedown from the shoe: the first and third for the *ponte*, the second and fourth for himself.

To determine the winner, each player totaled his cards, which counted for face value, aces equaling one and face cards zero. If the total was more than ten, i.e., two sixes totaling twelve, the player dropped the first digit, giving him a total of two. The winner was the player with the higher point total. If the *ponte* had eight or nine, he showed his hand immediately. If dealt cards totaling zero through four, he had to ask for another card. With five, he could draw or stand, and with six and seven he had to stand. Thus, the only real strategy for *ponte* was whether to draw or stand on five. *Banco* also showed his hand immediately if dealt an eight or nine. If *ponte* did not show his hand, *banco* had to draw if his total was zero through two. If *ponte* showed his hand by asking for a new card, or if *banco* totaled three through six, *banco* had the option of drawing a fifth card. The greater freedom afforded the banker gave him an advantage over *ponte*, and those with the cash reserves to withstand the inevitable swings in fortune seemed guaranteed victory if they played long enough.

Chemin-de-fer did not pit players against the casino; rather, the casino only extracted a five percent *cagnotte* or "rake" from winning banker hands, which defrayed the costs of the dealer, equipment, and establishment. Though this game attracted swarms of rich gamblers to the Riviera casinos that sprang up in the 1910s and 1920s, the house did not profit greatly from them. Baccarat, also known as *banque à deux tableaux* (for the double-table configuration that allowed twelve players to join in) or *baccarat en banque,* was the house-banked version of chemin-de-fer, although in some clubs the right to bank the game was put out to bid, as in chemin-de-fer. The dealer dealt two player hands, one to each half of the table, and players could bet on both simultaneously. The rules were similar to those of chemin-de-fer, but with less room for player choice: Players had only the option of drawing or standing on five, and the house dealer had to scrupulously follow predetermined rules of play.

Even before its 1907 legalization, the game had spread across southern France. While still Prince of Wales, King Edward VII introduced the game to British society. It made its first American appearance in 1911 and enjoyed a brief vogue in illegal American casinos, particularly in New York City, though it never seriously challenged the dominance of craps, and was forgotten by the 1950s, when it was reintroduced in Las Vegas.

The French clubs in which baccarat had prospered prior to 1907 were formally run by a board of directors and chartered for a specific purpose, though more often than not the boards were assembled by club impresarios who, through flattery and convenient amnesia regarding gentlemanly gambling debts, were able to induce socially prominent citizens to serve as front men. The typical Paris club had a restaurant, conversation saloon, a room for small-stakes social games (poker, écarte, whist, and piquet) and a room for the major game, *baccarat en banque*. The day-to-day gambling was overseen by two gaming supervisors, working opposite shifts, who decided all disputes and ensured fair dealing, or at least the appearance thereof. They directed the activities of the other gaming employees: the croupiers, chip changers, and cashiers. Croupiers shuffled and dealt the cards, collected the house's *cagnotte*, and paid winners. In return for these responsibilities, they received a regular salary as well as one third of all tips given by players. The cashier was not a salaried employee of the casino but rather an independent contractor who lent players money in return for a share of the *cagnotte* and interest on his loans. The chip changer was a factotum of the croupier whose primary duty was to exchange chips for gold and vice versa, carrying the currency from the table to the cashier and back. As in most casinos today, the lowest-value chips were white and the next-lowest red, but larger denominations were distinguished by their size and shape rather than color.

The club also required the services of a secretary and telephone receptionist, a door porter, a bellboy, footman, a groom, and a host of restaurant employees, including a commissary steward, a headwaiter who oversaw a staff of six, a cook, a saucier, and a dishwasher. The club would stage lavish weekly banquets for its members and their guests, and at all times charged only nominal prices for its meals. Members paid annual dues of about 50 francs, of which the government extracted 20 francs as a tax. The government also placed a hundred-percent tax on cards, doubling their total cost from 2 francs 50 centimes to 5 francs, thus deriving a significant income from the clubs, as it was the custom to use a deck only once before discarding it as a safeguard against cheating.

With the new popularity of baccarat, casinos at Cannes, Antibes, Juan-les-Pins, Deauville, and Nice began to cut into Monte Carlo's profits. Since they did not have the bonanza of the lucrative mercantile game of roulette, they adopted a more balanced business plan. Instead of using entertainment and dining as loss leaders, as the Rhine resorts and Monte Carlo had, they derived substantial profits from them. Critical visitors blanched at the high prices of drinks, cigarettes, and dinners, but paid them before losing tremendous sums to each other at chemin-de-fer. Still, they paid—and played—and the Riviera casinos soon rivaled Monte Carlo itself.

But all was not cream for the new casinos. The French government extracted sixty percent of their gross profits as a tax, on top of which local authorities took another twenty percent or so. With such a heavy tax burden, the French casinos began casting envious glances at Monte Carlo. As early as 1925, they began agitating the French government to lift its ban on roulette and allow them a cut of this profitable game. Still, they had one advantage over Monte Carlo. Under a gentlemen's agreement, SBM had agreed not to allow no-limit baccarat in its public casino, and the game was generally confined to the private salons there. In the French casinos, however, well-financed players could take on virtually any bet, and one syndicate of players became so dominant that, in a few years, they assumed permanent control of most of the Blue Coast's baccarat tables.

This group, known as the Greek Syndicate, made its debut at Deauville in 1922. It was indeed composed entirely of Greeks, and led by Nicolas Zographos, one of the greatest gamblers of all time. He is one of the few people in the annals of gambling history to profit regularly from gambling, despite never owning or being employed by a casino. He died in 1953 with a personal fortune of over £5 million (after he had already given much of it away), all of it earned by playing baccarat. The other charter members included Eli Eliopulo—uncle of Zographos's wife—Yola Apolstolides, Zaret Couyoumdjian, and Athanase Vagliano, probably the least-skilled gambler of the quartet (he eventually was forced from the Syndicate for losing precipitously at chemin-de-fer).

The Syndicate coalesced in Paris, where the Greeks pooled their resources. They decided that, rather than plow their accumulated capital into purchasing a casino (in which case they would collect only the five-percent rake from winning hands), they would form a cooperative that would perpetually bank baccarat. With 50 million francs provided by Vagliano, Zographos proposed that the Syndicate announce *"tout va"* ("the sky's the limit") to the gambling world. This act of daring, Zographos prophesied, would attract every serious gambler, and a host of millionaire dabblers, each convinced that he could break the Greek bank. The group chose Deauville as the spot to take on the world.

The casino at Deauville, founded in 1912, was run by François André, a former adventurer and carnival operator, and his erstwhile rival, the elderly Eugène Cornuche. The Syndicate was immediately successful: It soon dominated baccarat play. The group triumphed because, in addition to its intimidatingly large bankroll, it had a unique asset: the near-photographic memory and unflappable cool of Nico Zographos. Baccarat was played with a shoe containing six decks of randomly shuffled cards—312 in all. Zographos was notorious for being able to remember exactly which cards had already been dealt, and could guess the last few cards with ease. He had also studied the "outs," that is, the permutations of cards that would allow him to win a hand, and knew almost instantly the odds of winning a particular hand at any point in the game.

He was more than a clever cardplayer: He was a virtuoso. Where Bénazet, Blanc, and other casino owners had relied on the steady accrual of the house edge to turn a profit, Zographos needed only his skill as a gambler and the serenity to know when to retire for the night. This was another advantage of the Syndicate: Because they did not own the casino, they could simply decide to stop banking the game when things became too heated or they were on a serious losing streak. In these cases, Zographos allowed his intellect, rather than pride, to decide whether to continue or not. Zographos professed never to feel the sway of emotions and boasted that, even as he was about to draw on a five in a move that would either win or lose him 20 million francs, he was calm. He certainly was able to stop gambling dispassionately. In 1923, for example, when the Chilean finance minister Gustavo Ross beat the Syndicate for 17 million francs and then wanted to play double or nothing, Zographos announced that he could go no farther and politely withdrew. Such occasions, though, became exceedingly rare as the Syndicate's bankroll swelled.

Zographos was more of a card technician than a gambler. Though he was willing to wager millions on the turn of a card, he had no patience for other forms of gambling and stuck strictly with baccarat, which he had analyzed so completely that, with the help of his flawless memory, playing it was hardly a gamble. He offered advice for others: "Never bet on a racehorse, the spin of a ball, or the toss of the dice." This was hardly disinterested counsel; each of these games competed with his own tables. But it is safe to say that Zographos took his own advice and never strayed from the baccarat tables that, with the world clamoring to challenge his *"tout va"* policy, gave him all the gambling he needed.

The Deauville Casino, scene of many of Zographos's triumphs, had a theater and restaurant in addition to its gaming rooms. In the atrium, boule tables swallowed the stray francs tossed on them, but the real action took place in the chemin-de-fer room, where about forty tables hosted, at peak hours, dozens of games. Unlike Rhenish casinos but similar to later Nevada casinos, it was famous for having no clocks visible. The Greek Syndicate banked the game in a private room, a holy-of-holies of baccarat. Entrance was not restricted to players, but those who wished to simply watch the games were levied an entrance fee of more than £4 by the casino. At the room's single table, Nico Zographos sat, a matador of the green felt awaiting his next challenge. The wealthiest men of Europe, the Middle East, and the Americas all tried their best, but in the end none could best him. Zographos treated his game like a business (which for him it was), never drinking, seldom smiling, and rarely speaking.

The Syndicate banked baccarat at Cannes for part of the year and eventually obtained the contract to bank baccarat at Monte Carlo itself. Zographos won money from many of the world's richest men, such as French automobile manufacturer André Citroën, who lost no less than 30 million francs to the Greek over a period of seven years. The Syndicate continued to prosper despite the hard times of the 1930s and even survived the cataclysm of World War II. Though some members were replaced, Zographos remained the group's anchor. Even after his death in 1953, the Syndicate continued to accept any bet at its baccarat games, though now none of the founding members remained. The Greek Syndicate's legacy could never be erased.

While clubs and casinos proliferated across France, Camille Blanc's luck began to run out. Somewhat infamous as a playboy, as time went on he shrank from reinvesting in Monte Carlo without outside assistance. With the coming of World War I, Blanc was placed in a bind: He had several fixed expenses, including croupier pensions, that he could not diminish, yet with war raging across Europe revenues were down. He asked the reigning prince Albert to continue a temporary reduction in his taxes. Though he agreed to concessions and extended SBM's contract to manage the casino, Albert quietly resolved to seek a wealthier lessee for his lucrative franchise.

He found a willing partner in Sir Basil Zarahoff, a Turkish-born Greek who became enormously rich in the armaments business (he was associated with Hiram Maxim, who first brought him to Monte Carlo). Zarahoff and Albert bided their time as Blanc proved increasingly unable to cope with the influx of newly rich war profiteers and other nonaristocratic arrivistes after the end of the war. Interspersed among this new crowd were confidence artists and swindlers who, in 1920 alone, cashed more than £100,000 in bad checks.

When Prince Albert died in the summer of 1922 and was succeeded by his son Louis, the stage was set for a final resolution. Louis wished to immediately undertake an upgrade to the harbor and bore a tunnel for a new road to Fontevielle, a district being reclaimed from the sea. Blanc insisted on strict economy and sought to delay the projects. With Louis's approval, Zarahoff pushed the balky Blanc aside. While Blanc was preoccupied elsewhere in May 1923, Zarahoff surreptitiously bought a controlling block of Société des Bains de Mer stock and installed himself as its new potentate. Blanc was quietly pensioned off and died in 1927.

To run the casino, Zarahoff tapped René Léon, a technically gifted university graduate in mathematics and a charming, genial host who was equally adept at handling visitors, employees, and the media. Léon, a passable tennis, golf, and polo player, had an eye on improving Monaco's sporting facilities and bettering its entertainment. In an effort to jump-start roulette, he ordered that zero be declared a dead number, with no money won or lost, for a half hour each night. While this innovation failed to catch on, he successfully raised table minimums, at Zarahoff's suggestion, and began charging casino admission fees. (Previously, only the Salons Privés, or private rooms, had such a fee.) In 1926, Léon orchestrated, at Zarahoff's request, the sale of the financier's shares of SBM to Dreyfus et Cie, a French banking company, which headed a consortium ostensibly anchored by Prince Léon Radziwill, François Blanc's grandson, though René Léon in actuality held all of the power.

Léon orchestrated several improvements, including the opening of the Summer Casino, a country club, a beach house, and the Grand Prix, which became an unrivaled automobile racing event. He hoped to give the resort appeal beyond roulette. To an extent these innovations worked, but with the onset of worldwide economic depression, Monte Carlo would face its greatest challenge yet. In 1932, SBM failed to issue a dividend for the first time in its history. Struggling to raise earnings, Leon consented to reduce entrance fees to private salons, permit chemin-de-fer in public rooms, and—to the horror of casino purists—allow the American invention of the slot machine in the atrium.

San Remo, over the Italian border, permitted roulette (after Mussolini found he was unable to suppress gambling and reopened the casino there), but the closest that French casino could come to the game that built Monte Carlo was boule, a nine-number version of roulette at which the house had a steep eleven-percent edge. Played with an awkward red rubber ball in place of the gently rolling ivory of roulette, the game was derided as a fool's gambit; that anyone played it, according to a contemporary *New York Times* correspondent, was proof of the innate human inability to resist any game of chance, no matter how ridiculous.

Responding to a decade-long campaign and the financial crisis of the Depression, in 1933 the French government bowed to their casino operators' wishes and allowed them to offer roulette and trente-et-quarante. In response, the SBM instituted no-limit baccarat and chemin-de-fer in its public rooms and testily withdrew its instructors from the dealer training school in Paris. In addition, Monte Carlo waived the five-percent commission charged on baccarat bankers in an effort that harkened back to François Blanc's elimination of roulette's second zero.

Though the baccarat giveback did not entirely erase the gains of the French competitors, Léon was able to right the foundering SBM ship before moving to Hollywood, California, in 1935 to manage the Garden of Allah nightclub. Around this time, the casino employed 404 croupiers in the summer and 620 in the winter, in addition to 46 dinner-jacketed surveillance officers who quietly walked through the salons with an eye on the gaming tables and an untold number of plainclothes detectives who kept watch over both employees and guests. Over 100 uniformed security guards stood sentry over the establishment, and an equal number of firemen remained on call at all times lest an unattended cigarette spark a conflagration. In addition, an army of gardeners, facilities maintenance employees, entertainers, cashiers, and accounts filled out the ranks of the nearly 4,000 employees directly working for SBM. Each year, the casino bought 100,000 francs' worth of new playing cards and nearly 5,000 francs in new croupiers' rakes—the old ones, hopefully, worn out by raking in players' money. The Monte Carlo casino had become a big business. World War II slowed, but did not stop, the resurgence of Monaco.

The casino kept pace with changing times. In addition to the slot machines that now lined the atrium, another American invention made its way to Monte Carlo in the 1940s: craps. According to legend, cinematic tough guy Edward G. Robinson was responsible for introducing dice to the rarefied salons of the casino. On a break from the Cannes Film Festival, he ventured into the casino and lost moderately at roulette before remarking that "what this joint needs is a real crap game." With an eye toward broadening their appeal to American tourists, the management visited Reno and imported both tables and games supervisors who instructed the croupiers in the arts of dice dealing. The presence of craps highlighted the creeping American influence on the casino, which was only natural. Moneyed German and Russian aristocrats, thanks to war and revolution, were extinct as a species, so it was natural, in the years after World War II, for SBM to increasingly cater to Americans. The marriage of Monaco's monarch, Prince Rainier III, to the American movie star Grace Kelly in 1956 may have given impetus to the trend, but it was a natural outgrowth of changes in the world's economic balance.

Perhaps the most dramatic change to Monte Carlo in the 1950s was the purchase of a controlling share of SBM stock by shipping magnate Aristotle Onassis. Holding an extensive fortune, and sharing Prince Rainier's commitment for constant improvement of Monaco, Onassis seemed the perfect savior for SBM, which was once again teetering near the brink of bankruptcy. Under his absentee ownership (he was perfectly content to leave the details of SBM's operation to others) and the guidance of the prince, Monaco continued to change with the times. This was not to everyone's liking. James Bond author Ian Fleming lamented the passing of the Russian grand dukes, English dandies, French actresses, and Indian maharajas who had once graced Monte Carlo; he found no romance in the clanging of the slot machines or vigorous dice shooting that had replaced the stately plunging at trente-et-quarante. The Onassis era ended in 1966, when Prince Rainier, who was frustrated by the shipping magnate's increasing opposition to new development, orchestrated his ouster as SBM chief.

The new management, handpicked by the prince, would pursue an ambitious program of modernization, but the casino had become but a minor part of Monaco, and with the rise of Las Vegas, Monte Carlo lost its claim to be the world's leading gambling resort. Still, more than five-hundred-thousand visitors a year, chiefly French and Italians (with healthy numbers of Americans and British), came to Monaco through the 1970s, and most of them made at least a perfunctory bet at the tables.

By the 1980s, skyscrapers crowded the whole of the principality, whose economy became increasingly dominated by financial services. Monaco's lack of income taxes and low business taxes made it a popular tax haven for both wealthy retirees and corporations. By 1988, only four percent of the government's income came directly from gambling. The principality had come far since the days of Charles III, thanks in large part to the vision of François Blanc and the insatiable appetite for gambling in the Victorian age.

Wise Guys and One-Armed Bandits

◆ ◆ ◆

BIG-CITY GAMBLING IN THE TWENTIETH CENTURY

At the turn of the twentieth century, American gambling belonged to machines. But at Saratoga Springs, the nation's most famous gambling spot, one man held sway: Richard Canfield. When his reign ended in 1907, syndicates had made gambling crime big business, and technology—from telegraphs to slots—had brought gambling into the machine age.

Settled in the late seventeenth century, Saratoga initially balanced whatever gaiety might be found at the springs with morality; in its earliest years, it had a reputation as a "moral resort" where Bible reading and hymn singing punctuated bouts of drinking the area's healthful waters. By the 1830s, though, sporty southerners had brought public dancing, billiards, and cardplaying. In Saratoga's stately hotels, like Congress Hall and the United States Hotel, private card games frequently kept guests up until dawn. Later in the decade, billiards halls began allowing faro and chuck-a-luck operators to set up shop. A professional gambler named Ben Scribner opened the first genuine gambling house in 1842 in an alley convenient to both the United States Hotel and the railroad terminal. Others soon followed, and by the late 1840s "the gamblers of Park Row" had become notorious. In addition to playing at faro houses, Saratoga's visitors could bet on trotting races, first organized in 1847.

John Morrissey, always looking to expand his Gotham faro empire, opened up a Saratoga house in 1862. Accustomed to the diverse amusements of the metropolis, he conceded that while his tables might provide ample evening recreation, there was still not much for sporting types to do during the days in Saratoga. He decided that a racecourse would fill the afternoon void well and, having no real experience running a track himself, reached out to a troika of well-known New Yorker sportsmen to build and operate the facility. John Hunter, Leonard Jerome, and William Travers bought land near an existing track and constructed a new track named the Saratoga Race Course.

The course was astonishingly successful from its 1863 opening; in the next year, its operators ran the first Travers Stakes, which is the oldest Thorough-bred stakes race still run in the United States.

The Civil War had proven a double-edged sword: Though it prevented southerners from taking their relaxation up north, it also it cut off northern-ers from the competing springs of Virginia. After the war, Saratoga became a leading summer destination. During the brief racing season, most of New York's society set filled the stands. As in his New York faro houses, Morrissey profited from these swells' wishes to gamble. He did not act as a bookmaker, setting odds and taking all comers, but instead served as stakeholder for large bets, taking a commission of between five and fifteen percent, and ran calcut-tas, from which he took a healthy consideration.

Morrissey expanded his gambling operations in 1867, opening a new red brick gambling palace called Morrissey's Club House in a reclaimed swamp on Broadway, Saratoga's main thoroughfare. Hailed as America's finest gambling club, it was the capstone of Morrissey's distinguished gambling career. Some considered it to be superior to even Bénazet's Kursaal at Baden-Baden. The handsomely decorated Club House had two rules Morrissey's staff enforced with iron resolution: No women and no Saratoga residents were permitted in the gambling rooms. Morrissey might have intended to protect Saratoga's va-cationing ladies of substance from the evils of gaming, or to ensure that, away from the prudent oversight and disapproving glances of their wives, men might be induced to gamble more freely. Women were welcome to lounge in the sa-lons and drawing rooms while their menfolk gambled, and many of them did.

Already a millionaire, Morrisey expanded the clubhouse in 1871 and the operation soon grossed over $250,000 a year. In 1872 he reportedly turned down an offer to sell the facility for a half-million dollars. By the next year, about a dozen imitators had sprung up, despite the fact that Saratoga Springs' charter specifically forbade gambling (a nicety that Morrissey overcame by unparalleled generosity to local charities and causes). Other gamblers fol-lowed suit, and the townspeople became firmly convinced that Saratoga was a far better place with gambling than without.

Others sought to emulate Morrissey's success. The North Jersey shore town of Long Branch served as the summer home of President Ulysses S. Grant (six other presidents have famously enjoyed its hospitality). Its gam-bling was energetically promoted by Johnny Chamberlain, a New York part-ner, then rival, of Morrissey's. In 1869, Chamberlain opened an ornate gambling clubhouse and then a racetrack, Monmouth Park, which drew thousands of spectators but closed its doors in 1873.* Chamberlain's Monmouth Club House cost ninety thousand dollars to build and was an exceedingly profitable investment, though Chamberlain ruined himself in the 1870s after excessive betting on his stable of Thoroughbreds.

Despite the competition, play at Saratoga remained strong. A pair of New York gambling house operators, Charles Reed and Albert Spencer, took over Morrissey's Club House, renaming it the Saratoga Club House. Spencer, who was frugal and abstemious, retired from his gambling interests to collect art and broaden his cultural horizons, while Reed took Richard Canfield on as a partner in 1893, and in the next year Canfield assumed sole possession of the Club House, as Reed sold his share to concentrate on breeding and racing horses.

Like Morrissey, Spencer, and Reed, Canfield had already become wealthy by owning New York gambling houses. Born in New Bedford, Massachusetts in 1855, Canfield traced his lineage back to the *Mayflower* and made up for his lack of formal education by becoming a voracious autodidact and patron of the arts who could converse with equal facility on the subjects of art and the Latin classics. Canfield had gotten his start in his teens with an interest in a Providence poker room and, after success at local faro houses, parlayed his winnings into a $20,000 bankroll with which he toured Europe in 1876, spending considerable time at Monte Carlo. He lost most of his money there but learned much about gambling-house management, particularly that the only way to consistently profit was to bank the game.

Canfield split the next five years between wintertime poker operations in Pawtucket and summertime work in hotels in New York and the Jersey Shore. Canfield then moved back to Providence, where he partnered in a gambling house until an unfortunate 1884 raid landed him in jail. After serving a six-month prison sentence, he decided that he would make a stab at the big-time gambling scene and relocated to New York City, where he unsuccessfully applied to deal at the famous 818 Broadway gambling house. In 1887, with the backing of a Providence gambler, he opened a Broadway poker room with 50-cent limit games and a comfortable profit of $300 a week. That was more than an average workman's annual salary then, but Canfield, still ambitious, grabbed for the brass ring: his own faro house. Partnered with David Duff, a dealer at one of Charles Reed's houses, in 1888 Canfield opened the Madison Square Club in a brownstone at 22 West Twenty-sixth Street. The club,

---

*Monmouth Park has reopened several times since, most recently in 1946 after a half-century layoff.

whose entire second floor was soon devoted to faro and roulette, was uniformly successful, and in 1890 Canfield bought out Duff, whose own gambling had become a liability, and became the Madison Square Club's sole proprietor.

Canfield transformed himself into the nation's most celebrated "prince of gamblers." His cultured mien concealed a character paradoxically shot through with steely restraint and wild impulse. Inordinately fond of good, rich foods, he struggled with his weight throughout his life, drank large amounts of wine, and smoked cigars incessantly. Yet he was also something of an ascetic, at least in the gambling underworld: Though he spent much of his time overseeing his luxury houses, he seldom entered the actual gambling rooms, and he never played himself or allowed any of his employees to gamble, though he did become wealthy through stock market speculation. He dressed conservatively, avoiding the flashy clothes and glittering jewelry that many of his fellow professionals affected. In contrast to ropers who promised their suckers sure wins, Canfield was disarmingly honest, plainly telling all who would listen that it was impossible to win against the bank and that they should never gamble more than they could afford to lose.

Canfield was even more successful in Saratoga than Manhattan, recouping his $250,000 investment in his first season there. In 1902, he added the Italian Gardens, and in the next year he built a sumptuous dining room with exquisitely detailed stained glass windows that depicted the signs of the zodiac. Owing perhaps to his own enormous appetite, Canfield placed a tremendous emphasis on the club's restaurant, which was praised as the finest in the nation and possibly one of the best in the world. Canfield hired a French chef named Columbin for $5,000 a summer and paid him to travel across Europe during the ten-month off-season in search of new gastronomic delights.

Under Canfield, as under Morrissey, the gambling room featured about ten roulette wheels and four faro tables, with private rooms for particularly heavy betting. The customary betting limits on roulette were $50 for any single number (which would pay $1,750 if it hit) and $50,000 on even-money bets (odd, even, red, black, low, and high), twice those in Monte Carlo. Faro limits were $500 for regular numbers and $1,000 for specials. Canfield used uniform chips that were transferable between his varied gambling establishments (in addition to his Saratoga and New York clubs, he briefly ran the Nautilus Club in Newport, Rhode Island), and he paid all big winners via check, though he kept as much as $1 million on hand at Saratoga to satisfy any players who demanded cash.

Canfield took on all of the leading gamblers of the day, in an era when betting was, proportionally, at its highest level in American history. Assorted princes of Wall Street and captains of industry won and lost thousands on each deal—be it cards or business. Though Canfield's New York clubs were select (there were usually only a half-dozen or so well-heeled visitors playing on any given evening), their take was enormous; players often lost $100,000 in a single night. Canfield cornered the market on high-end play.

Most of Canfield's visitors were famous for their betting, but one was absolutely infamous: John "Bet-a-Million" Gates, whose speculations in the stock market had made him a multimillionaire. He would play poker for stakes of $1 or $50,000 a hand with equal relish. When bored, he bet on coin flips. On an 1897 Chicago–Pittsburgh train trip, he won $22,000 betting on which of two raindrops would reach the bottom of a window first. He enjoyed limits as high as $5,000 per card at Canfield's, where he played for upwards of three days at a time with brief interruptions for food.

One evening in 1902, Gates played what might have been the biggest faro game ever. He lost $375,000 before dinner, after which his luck remained bad, and by 10:00 P.M. he was down $525,000. He then asked Canfield to double his limit and, betting as high as $10,000 a card, won back much of his previous losses, finishing the day out "only" $225,000. Poker games among his Chicago and New York intimates were high stakes, even by today's standards; typical pot sizes were over $50,000, and sometimes ranged as high as $1 million. Cleaned out in the Wall Street panic of 1907, Gates continued to bet heavily in private, though he no longer speculated on stocks, and in one of his final appearances, at a conference of the Southern Methodist Church, he implored his listeners never to bet on cards, dice, horses, or stocks: "once a gambler, always a gambler," he cautioned. Yet he remains notorious as perhaps the biggest big-money gambler of history.

Gates's public turn against gambling mirrored a larger reaction against the speculative excesses of the unregulated stock market and public distaste of stock-market millionaires who flaunted their wealth by losing thousands at card games. Several Progressives who championed clean government and sober work (increased regulation, prohibition of alcohol, and the passage of a national income tax were three Progressive victories) also took up the fight against gambling, and pressure forced many public gaming houses to close their doors. In 1907, Canfield closed his Saratoga resort and soon retired from gambling. The city of Saratoga Springs bought the building at a tremendous discount, turned over the top floor to a museum, and allowed card games (but not gambling), smoking, and reading in the former casino. To this day, the erstwhile casino can be rented out for weddings or other special occasions. Canfield's legacy has been no less durable. Worth more than $13 million at the turn of the century, he was, until the explosion of corporate casino ownership in the 1970s and 1980s, the richest casino promoter in American history.

With the emphasis on streamlined production and mechanization that came with the Second Industrial Revolution in the late nineteenth century, it was only a matter of time before someone invented a machine that could help people gamble faster and more efficiently. Since the early 1870s, early gambling machines—really mechanical versions of punchboards—known first as coin-in-the-slot machines and then simply slot machines, dispensed credits for cigars, candy, gum, or simply the chance to win more.

Many early slot machines mingled elements of chance and skill. A "reward-paying punching bag" let players relieve their frustrations for a nickel a punch; if they hit the bag just hard enough to drive a pointer to a designated spot on the dial, they won a prize. The "manila" required players to use a pistol to shoot a nickel into one of four slots; a successful shot won some prize, usually of dubious value. Games of chance based on dice or roulette were also common. In order to skirt restrictions on gambling, some machines gave at least token prizes, like gum or candy, for all who inserted coins, but promised bigger prizes for especially lucky players who could land a coin into the right slot. Other machines were rigged to pay off in cigars. Many slot machines, even though they clearly offered players a chance to win a prize, were fitted out with stern placards declaring, "This is not a gaming device" (losers doubtless agreed), which sometimes kept the authorities from enforcing antigambling laws.

The national poker craze of the 1880s inspired the invention of a poker-playing machine. A Brooklyn company sold the first such device in 1891, and within two years the machines were available throughout the country. On many early machines, players put in a coin, after which the machine randomly flipped through five sets of cards that displayed in a window. Lucky players won a prize in proportion to the strength of their hand: Two pair might garner only one "cigar" (or its cash equivalent, a nickel), while a full house might win four.

The machines were particularly popular in poker-infatuated San Francisco. In that city three German mechanics, Charles Fey, Gustav Schultze, and Theodore Holtz, revolutionized slot machine design. Schultze began with a machine called Horseshoes that paid a player two nickels if the game's wheel landed on one of ten horseshoes (out of twenty-five objects). Fey and Holtz opened an electrical shop that supplied parts for Schultze's slot factory, and Fey took to designing machines himself. One early try, the 4-11-44, was based on a policy combination popular among African-Americans; it allowed a player to spin three dials and paid when they hit certain combinations such as the eponymous 4-11-44. Fey then went into the slot business full-time and in 1898 built a machine called the Card Bell, which was the first poker machine that automatically paid out coins. Because Fey could not engineer an automatic payer with five reels, he reduced the number of cards to three. The reel slot machine was born.

In the next year, Fey reworked the Card Bell, renaming it the Liberty Bell.* The machine had three reels; a combination of three bells won twenty coins, and the remaining symbols, mostly card suits and horseshoes, won lesser prizes. Little could slow down San Francisco's growing slot industry, not even the catastrophic 1906 earthquake, until a 1909 law made slots unambiguously illegal. By then, city authorities had gotten nearly $200,000 each year in taxes on the city's 3,200 slots.

Even when slot machines didn't get the complete approval of the law, they often thrived in a gray zone. Machines that supposedly dispensed gum used symbols of fruit, rather than playing cards, on their reels; hence the appearance of cherries, oranges, and plums on slot reels, which supposed represented the flavors of gum a player could win. Often, even this evasion was unnecessary. A friendly payoff to the local police or judge almost always guaranteed that a slot route operator could place machines in public places with little fear of official interference. Cheating, theft, and hijacking by criminal gangs were the biggest obstacles operators faced. The first two problems were addressed by a series of mechanical improvements, as slot owners sought to keep one step ahead of ingenious tricksters who used plugged nickels or coins with strings. The third was mitigated by cutting in the gangs for a slice of the profits. As a bonus, this muscle could then be directed against competitors.

Slot machines quickly became ubiquitous throughout most American cities and grew popular with women and children. During Prohibition, when many Americans furtively sneaked off to speakeasies for forbidden pleasures, slots positively exploded, and slot routes became lucrative enterprises for Al Capone, Frank Costello, and other underworld bosses. In 1931, Costello controlled over twenty-five thousand New York slot machines that reportedly took in more than $25 million a year. Once touted as the next generation of "trade stimulators" for bars, cigar stores, and candy shops, slot machines suffered from their links with organized crime. Most states would look askance

---

*Fey was riding an upsurge in visible patriotism occasioned by the Spanish-American War—a rival slot maker, the Mills Novelty Company, named a popular machine after Admiral Dewey, a hero of the war.

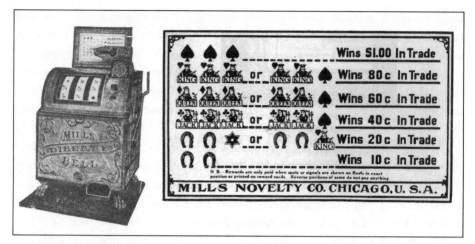

The five-cent Liberty Bell (pirated from Fey's original design) was one of many "automatic money makers" the Mills Novelty Company touted in its catalog. The accompanying pay table reveals just how small jackpots were. Slots paid off "in trade" rather than cash to skirt antigambling laws, though Mills brazenly advertised that its machines would accept—and pay off in—coin as well as tokens.

at legalizing the virally popular gambling devices in the next half-century, and they only survived with the law's blessing in a single maverick state.

Betting on races suffered a similar crisis. Racing horses had been popular in colonial America going back to the days of William Byrd III, and after the interruption caused by the Revolution racing revived. It proved especially strong in the states of Kentucky, Tennessee, Maryland, and Virginia, though many other states periodically banned racing or tried to limit betting on it. Although some southern states, particularly North Carolina, banned racing early on, generally the South proved more open to racing than the North. Though disorganized and prone to scandal, racing survived. But because of widespread concerns over cheating and an upsurge in religious intolerance for betting, the antirace lobby began to get the upper hand in the 1840s, though not without a fight. The largest crowd ever yet assembled in the nation (well over fifty thousand) gathered at the Union course in Queen's County, New York, on May 13, 1845, to see the North's champion, Fashion, lose to the pride of Tennessee, Peytona. Yet throughout the nation courses closed during the decade, including the National Race Course at Washington, D.C., whose shuttering signified the growing unease with racing.

After the Civil War, racing boomed. Most of the famous tracks and races of the twentieth century got their start in the thirty years after the end of the war. In Louisville, Kentucky, Churchill Downs opened in 1875 as the inspiration of

Meriwether Lewis Clark. Using land leased by his uncles, John and Henry Churchill, Clark built a track that eventually became known as Churchill Downs. He planned three major races: the Kentucky Derby (modeled on Britain's Epsom Derby), the Kentucky Oaks (after the Epsom Oaks), and the Clark Handicap (based on Britain's St. Leger Stakes). Clark organized a jockey club to oversee the track and the races. The Kentucky Derby would become "the most exciting two minutes in sports" and, into the twenty-first century, continue to draw crowds as the first leg of the American Triple Crown.

The second leg of the Triple Crown, the Preakness Stakes, had its origins at a dinner party. At a lavish 1868 postrace fete at Saratoga's Union Hall hotel, Maryland governor Oden Bowie volunteered his state as the site for a race to commemorate the party. He reconstituted the Maryland Jockey Club (which had been disbanded during the Civil War) and opened the Pimlico racecourse in 1870. A horse named Preakness won the first Dinner Party Stakes, and in 1873 another race was named for the victorious equine. After a fifteen-year interruption during which the race was run at New York tracks (Morris Park in the Bronx and Gravesend in Brooklyn), the race returned to Pimlico, where it has been held ever since.

The third leg of the Triple Crown (a phrase that would enter the American racing lexicon in the 1930s) is a product of the vibrant New York race scene of the 1860s. Jerome Park, which opened in the Bronx in 1866, was initially the area's leading track, and a race named for August Belmont, the Belmont Stakes, was first held there in 1866. In 1890 the Stakes moved to the Bronx's Morris Park, where it remained until 1905, when Belmont Park, just opened in Elmont, New York, claimed its namesake race.

New York led the nation in racing at the turn of the century. The Coney Island Jockey Club, formed in 1879, started racing at Prospect Park but also built a course at Gravesend that was soon praised as the finest on the East Coast. Queens's Aqueduct Race Track dates from 1894, and, though not as distinguished as Gravesend at first, survived the vicissitudes of encroaching urban growth and antibetting legislation and is the sole remaining racetrack within the five boroughs today. The initial success of these New York tracks inspired imitators across the nation, and hundreds of courses opened from New England to southern California.

Betting on horse racing changed dramatically after the Civil War. Initially, there were two types of wagering: one-on-one propositions and pool-selling or calcutta auctions. According to racing historian Roger Longrigg, the first American bookmaker to set his own odds debuted in Philadelphia in 1866.

Longrigg believes that bookmakers, though they stimulated public interest in the sport of kings, forced a decline in the quality of racing, as tracks sought foremost to create betting opportunities, not quality races between the best horses.

Bookmakers set up stands on and at tracks, posting odds on chalkboards. They did a thriving business, but in the 1880s several states responded to complaints about rigged races by banning bookmaking. Without trackside betting, racing attendance dropped off precipitously. Lower gates meant smaller purses, which meant a poorer quality of horses, who drew even smaller crowds: a vicious cycle that frequently ended in a track's closure. The boom years of the 1860s and 1870s had brought a glut of racetracks, and in the 1890s tracks began to close, while several states banned racing itself. By 1908, the number of tracks in the United States had fallen to 25 from 314 a scant eleven years earlier. New York, which outlawed betting but not racing in 1908, effectively hobbled the industry. By 1911 there was no racing at all in the state.

Banning bookmaking at tracks hardly stopped gambling, however, and the closure of racetracks barely caused a hiccup in race betting. The public now sated its racing and wagering desires far from the track. Those who merely wanted to place a casual bet used "handbooks"—bookmakers operating from a street corner or a friendly nook in a cigar store or saloon. Those who wanted more of a thrill flocked to ubiquitous urban institutions called "horse-" or "poolrooms," not because they offered customers billiards or swimming but because they offered betting pools.

Poolrooms were connected to a cross-country information network called the race wire. The wire started at the remaining racecourses in the United States, Canada, and Mexico. Runners collected information, including updates on the status of the track, horses, and jockeys, which was then transmitted via telegraph to a central headquarters and from there to poolrooms.

Inside the poolroom, a writer posted the odds on a chalkboard, while an announcer narrated the developing story in stentorian tones. Poolrooms might have free catered lunches and elegant fittings—or merely a few chairs, tables, and copies of the racing form, depending on the room's clientele. Touts fanned throughout the city (sometimes all the way into neighboring cities and even states) in search of new bettors. Poolroom patrons were a cross-section of urban citizens, male and female, old and young. They came because they wanted the excitement of betting on the horses but didn't have the time to devote a day to the races. As states began banning racing in the 1890s, many

A New York City poolroom in 1892. The writer notes the changing odds as well-to-do gamblers make their picks. Betting slips litter the floor. Thousands of these poolrooms across the nation took bets on an assortment of races, making this one of the first forms of national entertainment.

bettors found themselves living hundreds of miles from the nearest track but considered themselves devotees of the turf thanks to the poolrooms.

As race time approached, betting increased frenetically, as bettors frantically sought to get an edge by trying to overhear some critical bit of news—that the sky had clouded, a favorite was limping slightly, or a friend knew of a "sure thing." The electricity built as the the betting closed and the announcer declared that the horses were at the post, and as he narrated the race, the poolroom denizens lost themselves in a frenzy of hope. "Reformed gambler" Harry Brolaski wrote that he had seen "men and women, boys and girls, yell, call for their horses to win, scream out in their excitement, snap their fingers and jump up and down, and the race being run a thousand miles or more away. They seem to think that they are on the track."

That, of course, was the point, and the race wire was perhaps the first remote entertainment, paving the way for radio, television, and the Internet. Poolroom proprietors eagerly paid for the race wire, thus guaranteeing their patrons the most up-to-date information and allowing bettors in Pittsburgh to place informed wagers on Tijuana races. Initially, the race wire was a monopoly of Western Union: The telegraph giant considered the cross-border transmission of "racing news" a legitimate service and one that considerably helped its bottom line. For years, most of the traffic zipping over its wires was race related. But with public disapproval of race betting cresting in the 1890s, pressure on Western Union to renounce the race wire mounted. Finally, in 1904, Western Union officially stepped out of the gambling business. It was thought that without the wire, poolrooms across the nation would wither, and cities would be free from their pernicious influence. Racing opponents were overjoyed.

Those who opposed racing did not count on the ingenious maneuvering of racing information barons or the continued financial stake of the mighty Western Union in betting traffic. As soon as the company fired its "racetrack correspondents" and stopped flashing updates to poolrooms, a group of entrepreneurs leased telegraph wires from Western Union, hired their own correspondents, and jumped into the breach. Initially, several race-wire services popped up, but within a few years one—the Payne Telegraph Service, headquartered in Cincinnati—had claimed a monopoly.

Control of the wire guaranteed riches. Because every poolroom needed the wire service, each could be forced to pay astronomically high subscription charges. Since poolrooms were illegal, their operators had no legal recourse. Payne's ownership of the race-betting monopoly was short lived, however, thanks to a new player. Mont Tennes, described as the personification of Chicago's syndicated crime in the early twentieth century, was a rough customer who had begun with a series of racing handbooks, then dabbled in owning a stable of horses before deciding that bookmaking was more lucrative. Early on, Tennes had his rivals, and as disputes could hardly be settled by the courts, he grew adept at surviving beatings, assassination attempts, and even bombings. Tennes fought back and soon dominated Chicago handbooks and poolrooms, thriving despite a continued armed resistance from would-be rivals and intermittent police raids.

After watching Payne consolidate its grip on the wire service (Tennes was the Chicago franchisee of the organization), Tennes successful challenged his former partners. Always generous to obliging police officers, Tennes orchestrated raids against his competitors. He even received the blessing of the federal government, after a fashion, when in 1911 the Interstate Commerce Commission ruled that the transmission of race results was legal. Tennes survived coup attempts (several of his lieutenants attempted to supplant him) and ongoing Crime Commission and newspaper investigations into his murky gambling empire. In 1927, Tennes faced challenges anew: The state of Illinois had legalized on-track pari-mutuel betting, Al Capone and his vicious gunmen had staked a claim to the Chicago underworld that even the formidable Tennes thought twice about disputing, and one of his competitors won a legal fight to stop police raids against it. So Tennes sold his empire and retired from the business.

Tennes and his ilk, hungry to squeeze any profit they could from the sport, ruined its image. To line their own pockets, they paid off jockeys, tampered with horses, and pursued myriad other means to fix races. Scandals became commonplace, and public opinion quickly turned against the sport. The zenith of Tennes's power, the 1910s, was the low point for legal racing in the United States. Horse enthusiasts decried that such a noble beast had been degraded by human betting. Even in the Kentucky heartland of racing, things were looking grim. In 1902 the leading lights of Louisville begged Colonel Matt Winn, an energetic but otherwise undistinguished partisan of racing, to assume control of Churchill Downs. He did and, until his death in 1949 at the age of eighty-eight, tirelessly proselytized the cause of the track and the Kentucky Derby. He single-handedly established the Derby as the best-known race in the country and has been hailed as the liberator of American Thoroughbred racing from the bookmakers.

Winn saved racing from corrupting bookies and overzealous reformers by adopting the French pari-mutuel system. Before the improvements brought to the device by Australian George Julius and American Harry Straus, it was slow and often inaccurate. But, Winn reasoned, it was better than nothing and, upon finding several pari-mutuel machines in Churchill Downs's storage lockers, promptly barred all bookmakers from the track and instituted pari-mutuel betting. This quickly reversed the fortunes of Churchill Downs and the Kentucky Derby, and pointed the way to the future: In the 1920s, both track owners and state legislatures would embrace pari-mutuel betting as an honest and fiscally healthy way to let the public satisfy its betting urges.

As race betting surged forward and backward in the late nineteenth century, wagering on human sports steadily increased. The origins of what is today known as sports betting lay in the pedestrianism craze, imported from Britain in the 1860s. Since there was no money to be made by charging admission or by commercial endorsements, most pedestrians moved their feet to win wagers. As in Britain and elsewhere, major pedestrian events invariably occasioned heavy betting among the merely curious. The best-known American pedestrian, Daniel O'Leary, was hailed as a leather-shoed marvel. After beating all of his New World counterparts, he crossed the Atlantic to face Britain's famous Sir John Astley, who, according to newspapers, invented an entirely new style of walking to turn back his Yankee challenger.

Pedestrianism may seem a dubious entertainment today, but it was the first big-money sport in the United States. Soon professional trekkers (with financial backers and trainers) pushed aside amateurs. At the height of the sport's popularity, would-be champion walkers pledged to walk hundreds, even thousands, of miles to settle a bet. For some, walking was the ticket to their dreams. Arizona cowboy Daniel Newman, who accepted a wager to walk from Fort Bowie, Arizona, to San Francisco (a favorite destination for pedestrians) late in the summer of 1888, planned to average nearly forty-eight miles a day of walking in pursuit of his dream.

"If I succeed in making San Francisco in twenty-four days," he told newspaper readers, "I shall be sure that I can down any of the big walkers in the world. . . . If I win this wager, I shall try to walk on a wager to New York, and you can bet your bottom dollar that then you will hear of Dan Newman making some big stakes down there in walking. I know what I am talking about. This is the first chance I have ever had to show what I can do, and I shall show it."

By its peak in the 1880s, pedestrianism was already being outshone by the rising interest in team sports. As colleges, amateur associations, and touring professional exhibitions fielded teams, spectators enhanced their interest in the game by betting on it. Although bettors proved willing to lay wagers on virtually any sport contested by man or beast, professional baseball emerged in the 1870s as a particular favorite of the sporting crowd. Bookmakers operated in the stands, in poolrooms, and on the streets of most cities. Spectators might have been drawn to the pastime by its bucolic grace, but many of them were more hooked on the opportunities it provided for betting.

In its earliest years, baseball was regarded as almost innately corrupt. As early as 1877, a gambling scandal broke when it became known that four members of the Louisville Grays had accepted cash from a New York gambling ring to deliberately lose games. In an age when players' salaries, if they were paid at all, were pitifully low, many players happily took bribes. Since gamblers had already corrupted police and judges in most cities, doing the same in a child's game seemed no great sin. Some players cavorted with well-known gamblers and one, Hal Chase (who played in New York, Chicago, Buffalo, and Cincinnati), once attempted to bribe a relief pitcher on his way to the mound.

The most famous of the master gamblers who bribed players and made thousands as a result was Arnold Rothstein, whose name is inextricably linked with the biggest betting scandal in the history of American sports. Born in New York City in 1882, he took an early interest in "the sporting life" (gambling) and was, by the age of thirty, a prince among gamblers. Known as "the Big Bankroll," he invested in horse racing (including Maryland's Havre de Grace racetrack), gambling houses and smart (more often, crooked) betting. He was already famous for his big bets and deep pockets when his role in the fixing of the 1919 World Series etched his legacy as the mastermind of the greatest debacle in baseball, keeping his name in the public eye long after he was shot to death in November 1928, following his refusal to pay a poker debt of $320,000 (he claimed the other players were cheating).

Exactly how the infamous Black Sox scandal unfolded is still unclear. Most believe that a coterie of gamblers, led by Rothstein, offered $10,000 to eight members of the Chicago White Sox, the odds-on favorites to win that year's World Series, to throw the series to the underdog Cincinnati Reds. Cincinnati won the series five games to three, and almost immediately allegations of a fix began circulating. A series of investigatory articles in the *New York World* opened the eyes of the public, who suddenly saw evidence of fixed games everywhere. After it became clear that this was not an isolated incident (several betting scandals embroiled players in the 1920 season), the Chicago district attorney began an investigation that ultimately resulted in the trial of eight players and seven gamblers; Rothstein sweet-talked the grand jury and escaped indictment. Though the jury returned verdicts of not guilty for all of the defendants, baseball's image suffered nearly irreparable harm, and the newly powerful commissioner, Kenesaw Mountain Landis, banned all of the players for life, including "Shoeless" Joe Jackson, who played exemplary ball during the season and recanted his confession, claiming he'd never taken the money. Hal Chase, who made $40,000 by betting on the Reds, was also banned for life (though he was at the time a member of neither team). These men's exile signified the end of the gamblers' domination of America's pastime. Though betting on games continued and even expanded in the ensuing decades, the leagues kept players from associating with gamblers and cut any visible links between baseball and gambling.

Baseball bettors had company, as betting on other sports was popular as well. Nearly every sport, from collegiate sculling to amateur quoits, was wagered on in the late nineteenth and early twentieth centuries. Football was at the time a violent, low-scoring sport that lacked the wide appeal of baseball. Though there was some betting on it, the major breakthrough came in the 1930s, with the popularization of football pool cards, which allowed bettors to select several winners from a pool. More a lottery than serious sports betting, football pool cards nevertheless paved the way for increased appreciation of the gridiron. Betting on football would only truly blossom after the proliferation of point-spread betting in the 1940s.

Boxing, on the other hand, was a popular medium for gambling from its start. Most fighters were backed by one or more gamblers who hoped to recoup their investment through winning bets. As gate admission cuts were then nonexistent (to say nothing of pay-per-view revenue), betting was the only way that boxing could be profitable to its promoters. Many gamblers took every opportunity to fix fights, and public perceptions of boxing sank to new depths. States outlawed matches, and Congress even mulled banning the transmission of fight results or pictures across state lines. During the 1890s, genteel reformers sought to "rescue" the sport from gamblers by instituting the marquis of Queensbury rules, weight classes, and sanctioning bodies. Still, boxing remained a frequently barbaric spectacle, and gambling continued to generate excitement for fights.

Yet betting was not confined to violent confrontations or even organized team sports. Though pedestrianism had become a largely forgotten folly by the twentieth century, bets continued to liven up personal contests. As the sport of golf became more popular in the twentieth century, betting on it became increasingly common, whether as a gentlemanly wager or a planned hustle. Americans were not content to bet on their alma maters or pick baseball winners with thought and deliberation: They wanted, and took, the chance to bet on themselves.

As Richard Canfield stood astride New York's gambling world at the turn of the century, his contemporaries knew that he was without equal. Hailed as the last of a breed because he owned his gambling houses outright rather than as part of a syndicate, he was actually one of a kind. For decades, syndicate ownership of gambling houses had been the norm rather than the exception, both in the United States and in Europe.

Syndicated ownership made sense because of the inherently unpredictable nature of gambling. From the beginning, sharing the risk of running a faro bank made sense. Despite the romantic image of the lone-wolf gambler, gambling, whether crooked or straight, was almost always a group proposition. In addition to the help a dealer needed from ropers, shills, case keepers, and lookouts, more partners meant a deeper bankroll. So most gamblers worked in teams and shared ownership of houses.

Gambling evolved alongside mainstream American businesses. In the

1870s and 1880s, as American industrial ownership became more sophisticated, full-scale gaming syndicates became far more common. Consciously or not, these syndicates were modeled on the trusts that increasingly dominated American business. Syndicates were, in essence, small corporations that owned a house or houses. Usually, a syndicate member served as on-site manager. Members enjoyed a modicum of security in an inherently volatile business. In addition, syndicate members pooled their resources and contacts to arrange payoffs to police, judges, and politicians, buying wholesale protection for their games. Nonmembers who wished to run games were forced to take on the syndicate as a partner or face police raids.

Just as it led the nation in business, New York City had the best-developed gambling syndicate of the late nineteenth century. Though gambling was illegal, a "Gambling Commission" composed of a commissioner (head of an undisclosed city department), two state senators, and the city's leading poolroom organizer levied monthly fees on all illicit gambling operations and purportedly disbursed the riches (minus a commission) to New York's political and police elites. A 1900 *New York Times* investigation revealed that each of the city's four hundred poolrooms paid $300 a month to the Commission. Crap games, usually run in the back of taverns or billiard halls, paid $150, while each of the city's twenty luxury gaming houses paid $1,000 a month for protection. Policy writers paid a simple lump sum, and smaller gambling houses (there were two hundred of them in 1900) paid according to a sliding scale that averaged about $150 a month.

The syndicate mimicked any "legitimate" club or business organization. Prospective gaming entrepreneurs went to their police precinct captain, who forwarded membership applications to the Commission. The applicant was investigated (chiefly for his ability to pay and his "reliability") by the precinct captain, who, for his troubles, was paid a $300 initiation fee by the applicant. If the Commission, who met weekly, approved the applicant's bid to run a gaming business, they notified him and began collecting their monthly tribute; if for some reason they rejected his application, the captain was instructed to return the initiation fee. The system was an effective way to line the Commission's pockets and ensure that only "approved" operators stayed in business, as all those who defied the commission found the full fury of the police directed against them.

When confronted with evidence of the Commission's existence, the president of the Police Board and the department's commissioner both insisted that they would be the first to wipe out any vice whose existence they were informed of. Unfortunately, they explained, crap games used little more than dice and boards and therefore left little physical evidence; even poolrooms could be quickly disassembled before the police could take decisive action. When asked why no action had been taken against Canfield's Forty-fourth Street gambling palace, which was anything but clandestine, the commissioner admitted that it might exist but protested that it was a "private club" and thus "hard to get at."

Chicago also had a large syndicate. In 1890, John Philip Quinn wrote that the city's "gamblers' trust" was a "combination of sporting men" who contributed each week to a common fund whose exact purpose was known only to its superintendents but, Quinn imagined, somehow accounted for the fact that trust members enjoyed "practical immunity from police interference." The Windy City's gamblers were not alone. Minneapolis had "the combination" in the 1870s; this syndicate ran the city's two first-class houses and a host of lesser resorts. As the American business and politics became increasingly well organized in the late nineteenth century, the groups that ran that nation's gambling palaces became likewise consolidated.

Lotteries, legal or not, were another gambling business that became increasingly integrated in these years. The best known, the Louisiana Lottery, fastened itself onto the Pelican State because of the state's need for charitable contributions (to both government officials and actual good causes), an already large market for foreign lottery tickets, and an energetic group of promoters. For nearly thirty years, "the Serpent" was a notoriously aggressive monopoly that feasted off the public's desire to gamble.

In the late 1860s, the Havana Lottery sold as many tickets in New Orleans as it did in Cuba; carrier pigeons regularly ferried news of the drawings from the island to the Crescent City. A law passed in 1866, which required that all lottery brokers register with the state and pay a tax of five percent of their annual profits produced little revenue, and chagrin at seeing Louisiana dollars suctioned off to Cuba drove the mounting public support for a domestic lottery. In 1868 the legislature passed a law that chartered a lottery that could run for the next twenty-five years, provided that it gave the state $40,000 annually toward the upkeep of the city's Charity Hospital (a beneficiary of the first experiment with legal gaming in the 1820s). The lottery's stated aims were to bring in revenues for the state and to further "educational and charitable purposes." Yet in actuality the lottery's largess began with public officials, who received gifts and whose relatives found easy jobs with the company. Those who believed it represented the intrusion of a corrupt gambling monopoly—and there were many who did—could point out truthfully that the lottery had been signed into law by Governor Henry Clay Warmouth, who was ultimately impeached for malfeasance.

When it sent the bill to Warmouth's desk, the legislature did more than approve a lottery that would meet an existing demand for small-stakes betting; it unleashed a tidal wave of gambling. In 1869, the legislature voted to allow an unlimited number of gambling houses to operate in New Orleans, the only restriction being a $5,000 annual license fee. As there was no regulatory scheme enacted, crooked gambling dens soon predominated, to the extent that the forty houses that sprang up along St. Charles Avenue were popularly known as the "forty thieves." Bust-out artists from across the country flocked to New Orleans, until the local gambling fraternity cashed in a few of its political markers and succeeded in having gambling houses declared illegal once more. The city's gamblers went back to paying protection money to police and politicians, the outside sharpers returned home, and life went back to normal. Still, this revival of legal gambling houses demonstrates the atmosphere in which the lottery was born.

It was not difficult for the Louisiana Lottery's directors to remit $40,000 a year to the state; by the 1870s, its annual profits were over $1 million. Drawings were held daily, except for Sunday, and tickets to monthly super-drawings were sold throughout the United States. Louisiana, which had banned the import or sale of foreign lottery tickets to stimulate the growth of its own monopoly, happily permitted its own lottery to send tickets through the mail to states where the lottery was illegal. There, as in Louisiana itself, those who opposed the lottery decried practices they believed predatory, chiefly the selling of cheap tickets to the poor and working classes. The least expensive tickets, which cost a quarter, held out the possibility of a $3,750 win, which seemed wealth beyond imagination to those who bought them. Horror stories about impoverished households forgoing food and necessities to desperately purchase lottery tickets circulated throughout the nation.

By the late 1880s, the lottery was disturbingly successful. In New Orleans alone, 180 storefront agencies sold tickets. An 1874 *New York Times* article described the scene at one of the ticket shops in lurid detail:

> All over the city agencies of the company are established, and in the morning crowds of men and women, black and white, may be seen hurrying toward them. Twenty-five cents is the price charged for a ticket, and I am assured that at this rate a good agency sometimes takes in as much as $250 a day. At 3 o'clock each afternoon a

drawing takes place, and just before that hour, one by one, the unfortunate gamblers begin to gather around the places where "the
lucky numbers" are posted. They look anxiously at the blackboard
which tells them whether they have lost another quarter or half
dollar, then turn away to earn or borrow enough money to buy another ticket.

Though almost everyone lost, occasionally someone won, and the excitement
generated by a "big winner" only added to the throngs of lottery players.
When the Serpent won, it won, and when it lost, it won.

Growing public revulsion at such scenes added to increasing frustration
from antilottery states in which the Serpent sold its tickets. By 1890, the
Louisiana Lottery was fighting a two-front war against local opponents, who
vowed to defeat the charter when it came up for review in 1895, and agitators
in Congress, who began taking steps to deny the use of the U.S. Mail for
what was, in most states, an illegal gambling scheme. In a frenetic burst of
bribery, the lottery attempted to have the state legislature renew its charter
five years early. Despite the company's best efforts (it freely spread tens of
thousands of dollars around the legislature and offered to pay an annual tax
of $1 million if permitted to continue), the recharter bill failed.

The lottery faced even more resolute resistance from the federal government. By the 1880s, over half of the New Orleans Post Office's mail was lottery related, and it was estimated that five million Americans outside the state
bought tickets each year. In 1890, at the urging of President Benjamin Harrison, Congress passed a law that outlawed the delivery of lottery materials by
the mail. Reeling from two mortal blows, the Serpent uncoiled from its Crescent City lair and slithered southward to Honduras, where it incorporated
anew and began drawing numbers for the "Honduras Lottery." Only the
drawings took place in that country, though, as the ticket-printing and business operations of the company openly operated in Tampa, Florida. An 1892
Supreme Court decision affirmed the government's rights to ban the mailing
of lottery tickets, and an 1895 law outlawed the interstate transportation of
lottery materials, whether through the mail or otherwise. The Serpent continued to fight the government, but in 1907 it finally collapsed. Nearly seventy
years would pass from the Louisiana Lottery charter's expiration before the
next legal lottery in the United States.

The Serpent's death symbolized the decline of illegal lotteries throughout
the nation. Policy had thrived throughout much of the United States since
around 1840, with thousands of shops throughout the nation's cities dispensing

tickets to the masses. Nearly every other city allowed policy to thrive as an open secret: New York and Chicago supported over five hundred policy shops each.

Policy required large organizations—runners, bankers, and managers—and was, early on, dominated by syndicates. Reuben Parsons, "the Great American Faro Banker," made a fortune underwriting John Frink's New York policy empire in the 1850s. Though Parsons and Frink controlled the policy business of New York City, they lacked the broader vision of their successor, Zachariah Simmons, who, by cozying up to Tammany Hall and allying himself with the graft-happy Tweed Ring, soon had the city's political and police authorities in his pocket. By 1870 he had formed what he called the "Central Organization," a combine that split the city into districts. Simmons decided who would be permitted to run policy where, and received a portion of the profits for his magnanimity.

Once be became the king of New York policy, Simmons then took on America. He succeeded in gaining control of policy as far west as Wisconsin and as far south as Virginia, and each week grossed receipts of over $1 million from his twenty-city empire. He lowered the cost of entry into games from a nickel to a penny and eagerly took the bets even of schoolboys. As a mercantile lottery game, any policy operator was sure to win in the long run with an honest game. But Simmons was no slave to virtue: He was caught changing the numbers drawn in the Kentucky Lottery (which was at the time his source for daily numbers) to ones more congenial to him.

Simmons's successor as policy king, Albert J. "Al" Adams, was an even more tightfisted tycoon. After blowing into Manhattan in 1871 as a brakeman for the New Haven railroad, Adams became one of Simmons's runners. Simmons later supported Adams's opening his own policy shops, and then Adams, who followed his boss in maintaining cordial relations with Tammany Hall, took over Simmons's shops on his retirement. Adams earned a reputation as "the meanest gambler in New York"; egotistical and penurious, he was despised by nearly everyone he knew. He paid his employees the lowest salaries possible, never picked up the dinner check, and refused to even buy acquaintances a cigar or drink. His only largess came on rainy days, when he would give away his umbrella after a single use.* He boasted of the business acumen of his four sons, two of whom he had sent to law school and one of whom was imprisoned in 1904 for assaulting him.

---

*He believed that wet umbrellas were unlucky and, having the means to indulge himself, would not reuse one that had been rained on.

By the turn of the century, he presided over nearly a thousand policy shops in New York City alone. He received daily reports from each of the city's thirty policy districts and bought protection for his operations. Adams led the public to believe that the daily drawings were conducted in Frankfort and Louisville, Kentucky, by ceremoniously blindfolded boys. In fact, the winning numbers were engineered in New York (Adams's underlings invariably picked the combinations that exposed them to the smallest payout), telegraphed back to Kentucky, and from there sent out to the nation. Players gathered at his hundreds of policy shops, which were outfitted as candy or cigar stores. Adams was nothing if not inventive: He converted barbershops, bakeries, and even flower shops to policy rooms. As before, there were two games, a twelve noon draw and a five o'clock one. Thanks to his political connections, he was able to weather storm after storm of antipolicy laws.

Adams's policy operations made him a multimillionaire, and he diversified into saloon ownership (he bought more than a hundred), real estate, and shares in most of the city's gambling houses. But with the mounting Progressive opposition to urban corruption, the numbers began to run against him. In 1902, following extended agitation by the Society for the Prevention of Crime, a New York antigambling reform organization, Adams was convicted of running an illegal gambling operation and sentenced to eighteen months in prison. While he was incarcerated, his organization began to break apart. After his release from prison, he attempted to form a chain of bucket shops, penny-ante stock exchanges, but made little headway before committing suicide in the fall of 1906. His death symbolized the end of policy, and by the onset of World War I it was largely forgotten.

PART SEVEN

The Legitimization of American Gambling

The final strains of "Suspicious Minds" had barely faded away when the crowd began to spill out from the Hilton Showroom and into the casino. It was the summer of 1972 and Elvis was king, headlining the huge dinner theater in the world's largest hotel, the Las Vegas Hilton. Energized by Presley's larger-than-life performance, some excited fans milled around aimlessly, trying to preserve the moment. Others, looking at the slot machines clustered around the theater entrance, reached into their pockets for spare change. The casino had been generous enough to sign their idol for an extended engagement and price the tickets almost unbelievably cheaply: Putting a few quarters back was the least they could do to show their gratitude. With over one thousand slots standing ready, the Hilton's casino—only recently dethroned as the world's largest by the new Union Plaza downtown—was more than accommodating to those who wished to give thanks for the show.

There were a few concertgoers, though, who had found the show entertaining enough, but only now were getting a real adrenaline rush. For them, the real action was just beginning, and it would last until they became too tired to gamble any longer or they had lost their last dollar. The serious gamblers walked past the Big Six wheels with a barely a shrug: This was a sure sucker's game. A few filtered over to the baccarat tables; the game, popular in Europe since the days of Monte Carlo, had first been introduced into Las Vegas in the late 1950s at the Sands to little success; it was only recently catching on at the Hilton and Caesars Palace. Others headed over to the craps tables, opting for a longtime casino favorite.

The players walking to the blackjack tables—there were over thirty of them, by far the most of any game—vacillated between confidence and anxiety. They were resolute in the knowledge that, with their computer-tested systems, they could beat the house, but fearful of both failure and success. Should they make a mental error or forget their rules for strategy, they would quickly lose any advantage they had. On the other hand, should they play flawlessly and begin to win thousands, the casino's managers might order dealers to start shuffling midway through the shoe or simply ask them to leave. Stories circulated about players who had been "taken upstairs" and given a thorough working over after winning too much. Of course, such things only happened in the old days; this casino was run by one of the world's most respected hotel chains, and something so unseemly could never happen. Still, this was Vegas, and you never knew.

When dawn broke, there were still a few stragglers at the tables, but most had returned to their rooms. A few had won, most had lost. Even those who left Las Vegas a bit poorer after a weekend vacation, though, would return home with wild tales of nonstop gambling, limitless food, and a star-struck evening with the King. Others would brag about supplementing a convention stay with a profitable spin or two at the slots, then return to their lives in Cleveland, Bakersfield, or Peoria with no sense of shame. Casinos had become a solidly American institution.

15

Hard to Resist

◆ ◆ ◆

NEVADA BECOMES AMERICA'S GAMBLING OASIS

When the first California miners spilled eastward over the Sierra Nevadas in search of gold in the late 1850s, they brought their gambling with them. California had only banned mercantile bank games four years earlier, and social gambling was still legal there. But Nevada's territorial governor, James Nye, a New Yorker appointed by the Lincoln Administration to oversee the transition to statehood, inveighed mightily against gambling in his message to the newly assembled territorial legislature in 1861. Reminding the gathered solons of their duty to legislate against vice (including carrying concealed weapons, drinking, and Sabbath breaking), he paused before exhorting them to be particularly vigilant against gambling: "Of all the seductive vices extant, I regard that of gambling as the worst," he declared. "It holds out allurements hard to resist."

The legislators heeded Nye's admonitions and later that year prescribed stiff penalties for running a game of chance: a maximum $5,000 fine and two-year prison sentence. Even playing a game of chance was a misdemeanor with penalties of six months in jail and a $500 fine. Enforcement was left to local authorities, who balked at enforcing an unpopular law. To stimulate prosecutions, the legislature offered a $100 bounty—to be paid by defendants—for every conviction. Still, this measure was not much of a success and when Nevada became a state in 1864 members of its new legislature attempted to legalize and regulate gambling. They failed. At the urging of new governor Henry Blasdel, who was even more staunchly opposed to gambling than Nye, the legislature passed in 1865 a new law that was less harsh than the original—gaming operators were punished more mildly and players not at all—but still made gambling illegal and garnered no revenues for the state.

Governor Blasdel continued to fight ferociously against any tolerance of gambling, which he declared an "intolerable and inexcusable vice." In 1867 he

turned aside a proposal to legalize it, but in 1869 gambling supporters succeeded in passing—over the governor's veto—an act to decriminalize gambling in the Silver State. To legally offer games of chance, a proprietor had to
pay a quarterly license fee of $400 in Storey County (then the state's most
populous county and home of its biggest town, Virginia City) and $250 in all
other counties. The county sheriff collected the fee, half of which went to the
county and half to the state. There were few regulations: The gambling age
was set at seventeen, and conducting a game in the front room of a building's
bottom story was forbidden.*

Nevada's gaming laws would change over the next forty years with little
rhyme or reason. In 1871, the legislature lowered license fees but, in the next
legislative session, debated a bill to adopt California's ban on gambling.
Though that ban was defeated, the legislature began to take a harder line on
gambling. In 1875 it raised the minimum age to twenty-one, demanded a
$400 quarterly fee—paid in advance—for all operations, and prohibited gam-
bling parlors from advertising. It also passed an act to "prohibit cheating and
unlawful games," which outlawed three-card monte and similar hustles and
made cheating a felony. This measure was not designed to protect gambling
halls, as Nevada's later anticheating laws would be, but rather to safeguard the
public from con artists like Honest John Kelly who duped gullible travelers.
The law specifically empowered railroads to arrest suspected offenders.

This law protected the public from sharpers but did nothing for those
who gambled too much at honest games. The 1877 legislature came to the
rescue of these unfortunates with an "act to prohibit the winning of money
from persons who have no right to gamble it away." Under this law, any family or creditor could give a gambling proprietor notice that a particular father
or debtor should not be permitted to gamble. Anyone who accepted a wager
from someone thus identified was guilty of a misdemeanor. Men were hardly
thrilled at the prospect of being forbidden from gambling by their wives, but
the law was rarely invoked.

Throughout the remainder of the century, Nevada continued to tinker
with legal gaming, changing the provisions for first-floor gaming, hours of
operations, and permitted games. The new mechanical slot machines became
legal in 1905 with the proviso that they not be visible from the street and
their owner paid a $20 per machine quarterly license fee. Swimming against

---

*Proponents of the front-room ban reasoned that if a man or woman went through the trouble of climbing a set of stairs
or venturing into a backroom, he or she must already be committed to gambling, whereas innocent passersby might be seduced by the lure of easily available faro tables.

the antibookmaking tide, Nevada in 1903 legalized bookmaking on horse racing.

The legalization of bookmaking suggested that Nevada could profit by permitting what other states forbade. Yet this sentiment was hardly universal, and many citizens of Reno, now the state's leading city, felt that legal vice was more an embarrassment than an opportunity. Athough attempts to outlaw gambling in Reno failed in the first years of the twentieth century, legislators statewide became increasingly attuned to the small but vocal antigambling minority, most of whom were swept up in the self-improvement and antivice principles of the burgeoning Progressive movement. In 1909 the antigamblers triumphed at last when they succeeded in gaining the support of enough lawmakers to pass a law (subsequently signed by Governor Denver Dickerson) that made it illegal to deal or play a range of social (poker, bridge, whist) and mercantile (fan-tan, faro, craps) games, to maintain a slot machine, or to make book on horse races. Those who violated the law could be sentenced to as many as five years in prison. Nevada's days as a wide-open gambling haven were, it seemed, over.

But gamblers kept at least a foot in the door. Two years later, the legislature relaxed the prohibition on social games such as whist and bridge (keeping poker on the forbidden list), though it kept the ban on bank games, slots, and bookmaking. In 1913 the state's lawmakers went even farther and allowed all social games and "nickel-in-the-slot machines" played for drinks, cigars, or sums less than $2. In 1915 pari-mutuel betting was legalized, though only at tracks where races were being run. By 1919, cities and counties throughout the state were licensing card rooms that permitted social games.

While mercantile games were prohibited, another "outlaw" diversion, boxing, remained. Though other states refused to sanction prizefights, Nevada often did, and promoters staged the bouts more for the betting action than the gate receipts. Tex Rickard (who had parlayed a share in a Goldfield, Nevada, gambling hall into a career as a boxing promoter, builder of Madison Square Garden, and first owner of the New York Rangers) and others staged bouts in Goldfield and other towns in the early twentieth century, but the most famous fight he promoted—the July 4, 1910, contest between the black heavyweight champion Jack Johnson and his white challenger, Jim Jeffries—almost didn't take place in Nevada. It was only after the governor of California strenuously objected to the fight being held in his state that its location was moved to Reno. While training for the fight, Johnson got into the Nevada spirit by politely inviting in fans who came to watch him work out at a resort near Reno to have a few drinks, play some poker, and listen to a jazz band he had hired. This generosity did not offset the white public's largely hostile view of Johnson, and when the rugged fighter demolished the "Great White Hope" Jeffries at his leisure, the Reno crowd sat in stunned silence (though the news of the fight sparked race riots in other cities).

In 1920s, Reno was home to numerous legal card rooms. Clubs that allowed forbidden games flourished, often with the knowledge of the police. The leaders of Reno's gambling underworld were James McKay and William Graham, who also controlled much of the illegal trade in liquor and narcotics and prostitution (Reno's infamous Stockade, a sort of Wal-Mart for the sex trade, was theirs). Under the aegis of George Wingfield, a former cowboy and gambler who had parlayed his steely resolve into a Nevada banking and commercial empire, McKay, Graham, and their associates dominated Reno. As speakeasies and houses of prostitution already abounded in certain areas of Reno, adding a faro table or roulette wheel in a bar that already had slot machines and poker games was hardly a capital offense. Though the official licenses did not reflect it, Reno's gaming industry was booming.

In the roaring 1920s, as Americans drank bootlegged liquor in defiance of prohibition, pro- and antigambling forces fought for the soul of Nevada. No one, it seemed, was satisfied with the halfway covenant that allowed gambling but deprived legitimate business the opportunity to profit from it. Reform groups, chambers of commerce, and politicians with their ears to the electoral ground debated the merits of expanding the state's approval of social games into "wide-open" gambling and embracing protective legislation that would ban gambling entirely. At first, the antis had the upper hand; wide-open proposals died on the legislature floor in 1925 and 1927 and backers didn't even bother to introduce one in 1929. With the smaller operators of existing card rooms, moral reformers, and many business elements opposed to wide-open gaming, the chances for further progress seemed slim.

In the end, money talked. The economic malaise brought on by the Great Depression led prominent Nevadans, including big gambling operators, businesspeople, and business groups, to increasingly embrace wide-open gambling. Las Vegas real estate developer Tom Carroll bought newspaper advertisements that touted wide-open gambling and horse racing as the center of a strategy to make Nevada the nation's playground. Many found the idea laughable, but others listened. By the time that freshman assemblyman Phil Tobin, a Humboldt County rancher with no known gambling connections, introduced Assembly Bill 98 on February 13, 1931, it was clear that this year, there would be a real fight for wide-open gambling.

After extensive debate, the gaming interests carried the day: The bill passed the House and Senate. Governor Fred Balzar signed it into law on March 19, 1931. Nevadans were now free to gamble at a number of games: faro, monte, roulette, keno, fan-tan, twenty-one, blackjack (listed as separate games), seven-and-a-half, big injun, klondike, craps, stud poker, draw poker, "or any banking or percentage game" played with cards, dice, or a machine, provided they did so at a licensed establishment. Licenses for social games (poker, bridge, and whist) cost $25 per table per month, mercantile games $50 each, and slot machines $10 each. Licenses were to be approved by city commissioners and issued by county auditors, and the county sheriff was to collect all license fees. Their disposition reflects the scattered nature of the licensing and taxing process: One half of all fees went to the city or town, one quarter to the county, and one quarter to the state.

This law placed a few restrictions on gambling: It prohibited "thieving games" and cheating with marked cards or other devices, and it set the legal gaming age at twenty-one. In addition, it barred aliens from even applying for licenses, no doubt a reflection of the anti-immigrant (more particularly, anti-Asian) sentiment that was still strong in the 1930s. But, fitting its promotion as a wide-open gambling law, it gave cities tremendous latitude in licensing new gambling establishments. Along with a successful bill to cut the state's three-month residency requirement for "quickie" divorces to six weeks, the wide-open gambling act created the possibility that Nevada might indeed prosper by permitting what others forbade.

Right away, Reno profited more than any other Nevada town from the liberalization of divorce and gambling laws. Reno's "wide-open" gambling got its coming out with the Max Baer–Paolino Uzcudun fight on July 4, 1931 (promoted by Graham and McKay). It was an economic awakening. McKay and Graham had moved quickly to take advantage of legal gaming: They installed slot machines at the venue of the Baer-Uzcudun fight and built a temporary casino at the racetrack they controlled. With the passage of the six-week divorce bill, dude ranches catering to hopeful divorcees rapidly proliferated, and gambling halls were just as quick to sprout up. They offered a variety of games, including faro, panguingue, roulette, twenty-one, craps, monte, fan-tan, klondike, chuck-a-luck, hazard, rouge et noir, and several kinds of poker. As the industry became more established, though, the selection of games narrowed appreciably.

Monte, hazard, and klondike (a now-obscure dice game unrelated to the solitaire game of the same name) began appearing less frequently on license applications, and even the once-great faro was rarely found after the 1930s, either because it was too open to cheating or too even a game. Popular wisdom holds that both reasons contributed to its downfall, though mathematicians have pointed out that honest faro, as usually dealt, has a house edge comparable to that in craps, which in the 1930s became the preeminent Nevada casino game. Another game, panguingue, was occasionally found in Nevada casinos throughout much of the twentieth century. Pan was a rummylike game that came to the United States from the Philippines, where it is said to have originated among the Tagalog peoples in the early twentieth century. It proved popular on the West Coast, and many early gambling halls and even later casinos offered it.

In Reno, gambling halls were not formally restricted to any single part of town—at first—but the stretch of Center Street between Commercial Row and Second Street soon became the town's de facto casino district. McKay and Graham owned several gambling properties (including the out-of-the-way Willows, which had a reputation as a posh retreat as early as the 1920s) at various times, but the jewel of their holdings was Reno's most prominent casino of the 1930s, the Bank Club. The property began as a second-story room in which the pair ran illegal games, including a race book. When open gambling was legalized, they moved to the ground floor of the building next door. With as many as twenty table games running at peak hours and about sixty employees, it was the biggest club in town. McKay and Graham were not above using strong-arm tactics against promising rivals; they were believed to have sent confederates to sabotage the Monte Carlo, an elegant resort that closed soon after its 1931 opening. They also used their possession of the local race-wire franchise to intimidate and punish those who would not meet their demands. It was widely rumored that McKay and Graham laundered money for several notorious bank robbers and criminals. Despite its unsavory reputation, the Bank Club weathered several scandals, including Graham's fatal shooting of a professional gambler in another club (as Graham had been shot at first, it was later ruled to be self-defense).

Another murder, that of bank cashier Roy Frisch, was not so easily shrugged off. Frisch had been scheduled to testify against McKay and Graham at one of their fraud trials before he mysteriously disappeared. It was alleged, but never proved, that notorious gangster Baby Face Nelson, who was a friend of the pair, had killed Frisch. Finally, the law caught up with the Bank Club when its principals, McKay and Graham, were convicted of mail fraud (on their third trial) in 1938. Though the pair continued to operate the Bank Club through managers, it began to fade, and eventually closed.

Their first serious rival was the Palace Club, begun by a former partner of McKay and Graham, John Petricianni. Petricianni successfully raised a legal challenge to McKay and Graham's monopoly of the race wire by threatening to ask the federal authorities to more closely examine the business's legality. The Palace never quite eclipsed the Bank Club in popularity but ran a strong second for much of the 1930s. The club was regarded as the best place for gamblers to indulge in high-stakes play, and famous gamblers like Nick "the Greek" Dandolos played at the club while in town.

The Palace Club, like most other major clubs of Commercial Street, did not hire women dealers, and nonwhites, though not legally barred, were usually not welcome. But several clubs off the main drag welcomed blacks, Native Americans, and Asians. Smaller clubs usually opened their doors to anyone with money; many of these were found on Lake Street, which had been the site of Reno's Chinatown (before municipal authorities burned it to the ground in 1908). Some of them, like the New Star Club and Henry's Club, were operated by Chinese-Americans. Freddie Aoyama, a Japanese-American, managed the Reno Club, a gambling/bingo hall, in the 1930s, though he left when anti-Japanese sentiment after Pearl Harbor forced the Reno Club's Japanese-American owners to sell. Although there were not many African-Americans in Reno, the city eventually had a black-owned gambling club, the Peavine, a nightclub to which owner Harry Wright added several table games in the early 1940s. Though most major clubs adopted segregationist policies, there remained possibilities for minority players and owners in Reno.

Reno gamblers of all backgrounds shared a love for bingo and its many variations. Bingo took America by storm in the gloomy 1930s. In Reno, the game was often called tango. The gambling district boasted several tango parlors in the early 1930s, and many gambling halls had two rooms, one reserved for tango and the other for casino games. Unlike today's bingo, tango had an apparent element of skill; instead of drawing numbers from a hopper, operators had players toss balls at a target. Tango had two competitors: the game of keno, which was still played in its original form, and the Chinese lottery, easily recognizable as the *pakapoo* or White Pigeon Ticket lottery. The former was so similar to bingo that it soon lost its identity, and the latter had two disadvantages: It was traditionally drawn twice a day, far too rarely to generate action in the bustling gambling district, and it was held by authorities to be a lottery and therefore illegal in Nevada.

John Petricianni of the Palace Club introduced a variant of the *pakapoo* lottery that became an enduring casino game. He found a version of the game being legally run in Montana (where it may have been brought by peripatetic Chinese laborers) that used a punchboard with hidden capsules containing numbers rather than an urn from which slips of paper were drawn. Petricianni hired Warren Nelson to run the game in his Palace Club. Before taking bets, he convinced Nevada governor Richard Kirman that the game was not a lottery but actually "racehorse keno," where players bet on horse names, not numbers. All winners were to be paid off at the end of a game, and winners were paid by the house at fixed odds rather than out of a pool of bets; this made it a bank game and, therefore, not a lottery. Racehorse keno debuted at the Palace in June 1936 and was wildly successful, with several draws scheduled each hour. Nelson soon substituted numbered balls for the punchboard, and the modern game of keno achieved its present form. The game was so successful that it forced the New Star, which still offered the traditional twice-a-day *pakapoo* game, out of business.

A Reno icon that would soon be nationally famous debuted a year earlier when Harolds Club opened its doors. The club was owned by Harold Smith (though it was spelled without the apostrophe), whose father, Raymond I. "Pappy" Smith, had begun roving the country running carnival games in his teens. Pappy ultimately settled in northern California, where he ran games of chance at an amusement park near San Francisco and bingo games at Rio Nido in Sonoma County. With a local crackdown on bingo and related games, Pappy decided that he'd best move his operation to Reno, where his son Harold bought a floundering Virginia Street bingo parlor.

The Smiths put their carnival background to good use and introduced many innovations that eventually became standard. They started humbly, with only a roulette wheel they had salvaged from a broken-up Modesto operation and some slot machines, but soon had a variety of games. As there were already several bingo parlors in the vicinity, the Smiths did not open a bingo parlor. Still, they used their knowledge of gambling to their benefit. While most clubs had dark and forbidding interiors, Harolds was brightly lit and its employees were deliberately friendly. The Smiths also offered free lessons on how to play, something that successfully lured many novices.

Observing potential female players balking at braving the aggressively masculine gambling hall, Pappy decided to hire women dealers after the club opened. Pappy got the idea when a prospective woman gambler, after a few tentative steps inside the club, looked around, exclaimed, "There are no women here!" and ran out. Other club owners at first laughed at the idea (seemingly, they had no knowledge that women had been expert dealers for years throughout the Old West), but when they saw how female dealers brought in new customers, they soon emulated the practice. Harolds was also the first club to remain open twenty-four hours a day and the first to enjoy the luxury of air conditioning. Some of Pappy's ideas, such as a roulette game that used a live mouse, fizzled, but even when he failed, the patriarch was not defeated. The mouse game was a disaster that only lasted a week, but got the upstart club plenty of free publicity. The slogan "Harolds Club or Bust" became known worldwide as it was posted by American servicemen abroad who had appreciated Pappy's hospitality while in Reno. Domestically, the Smiths placed 2,300 signs on the nation's busiest roadways. The club was a smashing success, drawing on smaller bettors, curious tourists, and women. Though Harolds had its roots in the shady carnival past, it pointed the way toward the future of Nevada gaming: brightly lit, loudly promoted, and customer friendly. Once an outcast (the Smiths were blocked from purchasing a location on the city's main casino street, Center), Harolds helped shift the center of gravity to Virginia Street, which soon boasted most of the city's successful casinos.

Another Virginia Street upstart founded a gambling empire that would become the world's largest casino corporation. William Fisk Harrah started in the business in 1933 by taking over a Venice, California, bingolike game from his father. Harrah stood conventional wisdom on its head by firing the shills, reasoning that players would find a smaller game more attractive, since they would actually have a greater chance to win. He was right. He also insisted on giving the customer comfortable surroundings (in this case, more amply padded stools). When Harrah found himself on the wrong side of a local reform fight, he elected to try his luck in Reno.

Arriving in town in May 1937, Harrah bought a failing Center Street bingo parlor, the Silver Tango, and renamed it Harrah's Club Bingo. A marginal location, combined with keen competition, drove Harrah out of business within a matter of weeks. Harrah doggedly resolved to try again, leasing a new location on Commercial Row in July 1938 as Harrah's Plaza Tango. Harrah soon abandoned the location when he bought out a failing Virginia Street parlor, Howe's Heart Tango, renaming it Harrah's Heart Tango. This new location proved a lucky one, and Harrah quickly gained traction in the competitive bingo wars of the late 1930s. He then branched out by buying a bar in which he and a partner ran twenty-one, roulette, and slot machines, and eventually built Harrah's Club—later Harrah's Casino—on Virginia Street.

Harrah built his reputation on an attention to detail and tireless customer service. The classic story, that he demanded an immediate explanation for any burned-out light bulb, illustrates the emphasis that Harrah's managers placed on consistently presenting the best image possible. Working at Harrah's Reno gambling hall (or, starting in 1955, his Reno property) meant that an employee was thoroughly indoctrinated in the Harrah's way. In fact, those who learned their trade in Las Vegas were often told to look elsewhere when they applied for jobs at Harrah's: Managers complained that they brought bad habits—shortcuts and shoddy work—with them.

Harrah had a simple philosophy: Provide a pleasant atmosphere for middle-income gamblers and let the house advantage take care of the rest. He was among the first to begin a bus marketing program, bringing Greyhounds with visitors from San Francisco to his Tahoe property. To draw players he also engaged top-quality entertainers. An intensely introverted man, he only felt comfortable speaking with celebrities, who were often just as shy as he, or "car guys" with whom he could share his love of classic automobiles. Despite his aloofness (he seldom walked through the public areas of his own casino), Harrah brought the idea of mass production to the casino floor by creating a uniformly satisfying experience for all patrons.

While Harolds and Harrah's pursued the everyman (and everywoman) bettor, other Reno clubs harked back to the elegantly appointed casinos of

In 1937, Bill Harrah opened his first bingo parlor in bustling downtown Reno, not far from friendly rival Raymond Smith's Harolds Club.

Europe. The Deauville, which opened in 1931, catered to the wealthy set and styled itself as one of the world's most luxurious gambling houses. Unable to meet its high overhead, however, it lasted only two years. Yet others jumped to fill its meticulously shined shoes—Club Fortune, which opened in 1937, was the most successful of these. It was a combination casino-nightclub-restaurant that was aggressively promoted as the city's finest "palatial new gambling and dining spot." Though the image of patrons tossing baseballs into a moving cart to determine tango winners hardly suggests sophistication to today's readers, the club nevertheless developed a reputation as a leading nightspot. In addition to the tango salon, the Club Fortune also had a carpeted gaming room with twenty-one, craps, and roulette, the trio of games that were fast becoming the standard throughout Nevada. Touted as the ultimate Reno luxury nightspot, it suggested an alternative to the Harolds and Harrah's path, though it would be southern Nevada operators who ultimately continued on this course.

Renoites did not have to go to the large gambling houses to indulge their desires for games of chance. Virtually every public place, from bars and restaurants to hotels, bowling alleys, cigar stores, hotel lobbies, and drugstores, had slot machines. Soon after the legalization of slots in 1931, a Nevada tradition started when four Reno-area Piggly Wigglys installed slot machines. Slots in convenience stores and supermarkets remain a peculiar institution of Nevada today. Eventually slots disappeared from some of the more outrageous sites, such as soda fountains, but they remained part of many establishments, and a cadre of slot route operators, who owned small clusters of machines in several locations, soon sprang up.

As World War II approached, the Reno city council drew a red line around what had become its casino district in midtown and refused to license any gambling halls (excepting "luxury" hotels with at least one hundred rooms) outside of it. This decision pleased Renoites still opposed to gambling, existing gambling interests who had less competition to fear, and business owners in the surrounding areas who were now safe from losing their leases to lucrative casinos. Though the red line ultimately fell, it would slow the development of Reno's casino business in the crucial 1940s and 1950s.

Other areas of Nevada had a diversity of gambling clubs. At Lake Tahoe, where South Shore and North Shore clubs soon began entertaining travelers on the California-Nevada state line, gambling houses were largely seasonal, closing for the snowbound winter months until the area became a popular ski attraction. For years the preeminent Tahoe club was the Cal-Neva Lodge, which had first operated during the 1920s by straddling the border; when

Nevada authorities raided, all gambling equipment was moved to the California side of the property, and when California troopers threatened, it was shifted back to Nevada. Because it was owned by the infamous partnership of McKay and Graham, though, it was seldom disturbed. In the 1930s, the Lodge attracted a range of guests, including socialites in evening dresses, wealthy gambling habitués, and notorious gangsters like Baby Face Nelson and Pretty Boy Floyd. Though it burned to the ground in May 1937, it was quickly rebuilt and reopened in July of that year. In the 1960s, it was for a time partially owned by Frank Sinatra, who surrendered his Nevada gaming license and sold his interest after allegations that he had hosted mobster Sam Giancana at the casino.

Elsewhere, small communities, usually along important highways or at state borders, had a few gambling operations. They typically offered none of the frills of Reno clubs, but sometimes they pushed ahead of their big-city brethren. Ely-area gambling clubs competed more intensely than those in Reno and few smaller cities lacked their own gambling houses. Elko, a chief town in northeastern Nevada, boasted the Commercial Hotel, the most prominent of several bars, clubs, and hotels. Not letting their remote location or small size deter them, Elko's gambling proprietors sought to promote their town. In 1941 the Commercial's manager, Newton Crumley, Jr., scored a coup when he brought in Ted Lewis, then a popular bandleader, to star in the hotel's new showroom; this was the first major headliner to play an American casino. Lewis was followed by a parade of notables, including Ray Noble, Chico Marx, Paul Whiteman, and Sophie Tucker. Crumley set a trend in Nevada gaming; over the next several decades, casino entertainment would develop into a multimillion-dollar business in its own right.

Though many of these small-town gambling halls had enterprising owners and enthusiastic patrons, they would soon be outshone by a bright neon glare coming from the state's southern reaches. Though it was initially as obscure as Yerington, Pioche, Eureka, or Winnemucca, Las Vegas would grow to challenge and then supplant mighty Reno as the state's gaming center. Within a half century of gaming legalization, it would be considered the *world's* premiere gambling destination.

The future "gambling and entertainment capital of the world" had an inauspicious origin. Begun by the Salt Lake, Los Angeles, and San Pedro Railroad with a land auction in 1905, the town was still confused with Las Vegas, New

Mexico, a generation after its founding. Even though Las Vegas grew rapidly in the 1920s, it still had barely five thousand residents by 1930. But at the time of the 1931 gambling decriminalization, Las Vegas residents were already giddy with anticipation over a completely unrelated development: the federal government's construction of Hoover Dam southeast of the town on the Colorado River. The dam brought federal dollars and a modicum of publicity to the formerly sleepy railroad stopover. The gambling dam, however, was just about to burst, because within fifteen years legal gaming would transform the area far more than the massive engineering project to the south.

Like Reno, Las Vegas was no stranger to gambling. In the town's original master plan, the notorious Block 16 (First and Second Street between Stewart and Ogden) was designated a red light district in which saloons and brothels could operate without interference.* Fremont Street, the town's original main thoroughfare (it radiated eastward from the foot of the rail depot) was dotted with legal card rooms where prohibited games could often be found after the 1909 gambling ban.

When the state legalized gaming, cities and counties split the authority to issue licenses; their powers were mutually exclusive, so that if an establishment was in the city of Las Vegas, its owner went to the five-member City Commission, but if it was outside the city, its owner petitioned the then three-member County Commission. This would have tremendous ramifications for the future of Clark County gaming.

The City Commission acted quickly, first discussing potential Fremont Street clubs on March 25, 1931, less than a week after the legislature had approved legal gaming. Two weeks later, the Commission issued the first four licenses, and legal gambling began. This quick action was a far cry from today's ponderous licensing process, though: Licenses were screened by the commissioners and, if no one objected and everything seemed in order, they were promptly approved. There was no background investigation, environmental impact statement, or vetting of project finances.

The first licenses went to a cluster of downtown clubs: the Boulder Club, at 118 Fremont; the Las Vegas Club, at 21 and 23 Fremont (across the street from its present location); the Exchange Club, at 123 S. First Street; and the Northern Club, at 15 Fremont Street. After granting these licenses, the Commission resolved not to grant any licenses to new establishments until after it

---

*Today the former Block 16 is a parking garage for Binion's Casino.

had established a gambling zone—a formality it never pursued. Within a month, it had granted two more licenses and issued several slot-machine permits, both in established clubs and for restaurants and retail establishments. The Vegas Sweet Shoppe, for example, got seventeen machines on June 29, by far the largest number (more than double the runner-up, the Boulder Drugstore). Given that gambling was restricted to those over twenty-one, it was curious that a candy store would receive so many slots. By the next year, the Commission would issue more than a dozen licenses.

Las Vegas clubs, like those in Reno, were mostly owned by limited partnerships, in which a small group of owners, one of whom was usually an on-site manager, pooled their capital and split the profits, a pattern long established in illegal casinos throughout the nation. Proprietors had diverse backgrounds: Some had long careers in vice, while others did not. J. Kell Houssels, principal owner of the Las Vegas Club, was a trained mining engineer who found gambling more lucrative than metallurgy. He began running the Las Vegas Club as a card room and parlayed his role as a full gaming operator into interests in several downtown casinos, a successful stable of racehorses, and ownership of the Strip's Tropicana. His son, J. Kell Houssels, Jr., followed him into the business.

Women played key roles in a few of the early clubs, and a woman was among those granted the first four licenses. Mayme Stocker, along with manager Joe Morgan, received the license for the Northern Club. Her husband and sons all worked for the railroad and maintained an interest in the club, though as railroad employees they were officially barred from owning it. It had initially been a legal card room, but within two years of its becoming a full-fledged gambling hall, the Stocker family sold the operation. But she was not the only woman in Las Vegas's nascent gambling industry. The wife of Thomas Rowan, an owner of the Rainbow Club, bought out her husband's partner after his death and remained a proprietor for several years. Joe Morgan went on to open the Silver Club, an establishment that he operated with his wife, Helen, who also dealt cards and ran the roulette wheel—an early exception to the city's de facto ban on woman dealers.

These women represented the growing trend of female involvement in gambling. Although Las Vegas clubs at first did not make any special efforts to attract women, they began to admit them. By the end of the 1930s they actively sought to become more hospitable to women, adding new features, particularly dance floors and entertainment. Several specifically bought advertisements that read "Ladies welcome." But one prejudice remained: Though Reno clubs hired so many women to deal that, by the 1940s, the idea of a woman dealer was cliché, Las Vegas casinos, for the most part, refused to do so and confined women to a small circle of jobs: shill, waitress, change girl, housekeeper, and entertainer.

The early downtown gambling halls had virtually identical features: a bar, a few table games (usually twenty-one and craps, with roulette and faro often mixed in), a score of slot machines, and sometimes a room for "Tango Derby" (bingo). Mayme Stocker's 1931 application for a keno license was denied, though she received one the next year after she sued the city. After much back and forth, the city finally permitted keno, though it continued to disallow applications for racehorse keno. Soon, several clubs boasted keno parlors with more than a hundred seats.

In their advertisements, Las Vegas clubs shouted, "Come one, come all," but from the start, like Reno's establishments, they frequently barred African-Americans. Jim Crow was not, at first, absolute, though race was enough of an issue that in April 1931 the City Commission specifically stated that, despite limiting licenses, they would still consider applications by "a person of the Ethiopian Race for the conduct of a game or games in a place catering exclusively to persons of the same race only." The Commission ultimately granted such a license to a club on Stewart Street, then the site of several black-owned businesses. In the next decade, segregation in Las Vegas would

Gambling inside the Boulder Club, a typical Fremont Street gambling hall of the 1930s and 1940s. Early Las Vegas clubs featured craps, roulette, blackjack, slots, and occasionally older games like faro.

become more rigid, and clubs geared toward a black clientele—though they accepted whites as patrons without prejudice—appeared on the Westside. Some were owned by blacks and others by whites, and clubs like the Alabam, Harlem Club, Brown Derby, and Cotton Club provided virtually the only outlet for black Las Vegas residents or visitors who wished to gamble until the city's unofficial but brutally present policy of segregation crumbled in 1961.

Some club owners spoke of the need to exclude "undesirable elements" from their clubs, but they were blind to a very real danger: affiliates of organized crime who came to Las Vegas in the 1940s. Initially, legal Nevada gaming had little attraction for bootleggers and those who ran organized gambling outfits in the cities of California and the East. With money rolling in already, they had no reason to invest in the comparatively small stakes of Nevada. But a sequence of events forced a change. After the end of Prohibition in 1933, many organized crime groups replaced bootlegging with illegal gambling, which meant new entrants into the business. Next, in the mid- and late-1930s, California authorities began cracking down on illegal games, driving many illegal operators to Nevada, including the relatively clean William Harrah and Raymond Smith, but also convicted criminals and those suspected of links to organized crime.

The influx began in earnest in 1941, when the Nevada legislature passed a law that legitimized poolrooms, though they called the facilities race books. The race wire, whose domination by underworld figures could not be contested, powered illegal poolrooms throughout the nation, and through it criminal elements would find a foothold in Nevada. Even before the law, race books had been tolerated, and their history was hardly stellar; Graham and McKay had used their race-wire franchise in northern Nevada to pry their way into the management of several clubs. But with the apparent acquiescence of Nevada authorities to a gambling form universally condemned throughout the nation, even more notorious criminal elements saw opportunities for plunder.

A national war over control of the race wire had been raging. After Mont Tennes's retirement, Moses Annenberg had consolidated the racing information business under his Nationwide News Service. This made the race wire even more lucrative than it had been: His monopoly served an estimated fifteen thousand bookmakers nationwide, and estimates of its annual profits ran as high as $2 million. Facing a federal legal onslaught that eventually sent him to prison for income tax evasion, he sold off Nationwide in 1939. Two rival factions, the Continental Press Service and Trans-American Publishing, feuded for dominion of the profitable franchise. The Los Angeles representative of Trans-American, Benjamin "Bugsy" Siegel (a reputed member of Murder, Inc.), sought to expand his area of influence to Arizona and Nevada. Before long, he had acquired interests in several downtown race books, and he and his associates began planning to buy or build a casino of their own.

Siegel was not the only outlaw to search for riches in the neon oasis of Las Vegas. Guy McAfee had abandoned a career as a Los Angeles Police Department vice-squad commander for one openly dedicated to gaming after he chose to resign from the department rather than face corruption charges (he owned several illegal casinos while supposedly directing the LAPD's war against vice). With the crackdown on illegal Los Angeles gambling in the late 1930s, McAfee set up shop near Las Vegas, where he bought the 91 Club, a small roadhouse-type establishment on the then-neglected Los Angeles Highway. He and his associates bought the downtown Frontier Club in 1939, marking his debut as one of the most influential operators in the city. McAfee subsequently owned shares in several establishments and in 1946 opened the Golden Nugget, a downtown gambling hall that would prove pivotal in the career of the city's most innovative casino developer, Steve Wynn.

Another veteran of Los Angeles's gambling underworld had taken a shot in Las Vegas even earlier. Antonio Cornero Stralla, better known as Tony Cornero, had been a bootlegger during Prohibition but, like many others, diversified into gambling, running casino boats off the southern California coast in the 1930s. In 1931, he jumped at the chance to run games legally in Nevada and opened the Meadows just outside Las Vegas city limits, the first attempt at a "gambling resort" away from downtown. Though the club was officially owned by Cornero's brothers Louis and Frank (Cornero's felony conviction disqualified him), it was primarily Tony's inspiration. Located just over the city limits, where Fremont Street becomes the Boulder Highway, the gambling casino/cabaret/nightclub was designed to be the finest resort in the entire Southwest. It opened with great fanfare, but Cornero soon lost interest, leasing the property to a series of operators, and the resort struggled before closing in 1937. Cornero would return to Las Vegas in 1945 after the California authorities forced his offshore gambling boat, the S.S. *Rex,* to close. He would run a gambling hall named the S.S. *Rex* on the first floor of the Apache Hotel, which had opened in 1932 as an elegant three-story hotel and bar. It still operates today as part of Binion's casino.

The clubs of downtown Reno, Las Vegas, and small-town Nevada catered chiefly to serious gamblers. They contributed their share to county treasuries but were not viewed as essential to the state's general economy. Attempts to open more lavish resorts, such as Cornero's Meadows, were typically short lived. Yet with the arrival of World War II—and the tremendous changes in American life and culture that would follow it—gambling resorts geared to the casual gambler and leisure traveler would transform the Las Vegas Valley. Though these hotels were inspired by European spa resorts, they still owed quite a bit to the original gambling clubs of Nevada, north and south.

16

The Salvation of Sin

◆ ◆ ◆

IS GAMBLING A CRIME OR A VIRTUE?

Even before Nevada showed that gambling could be the cornerstone of an entire state's economy, Americans had begun exploring ways to channel the public's seemingly insatiable desire to gamble toward the public good. In the aftermath of the tremendous antigambling swing of the 1910s, it became apparent that, just as liquor prohibition had been largely ineffective in stopping American drinking (and, indeed, created a whole new class of outlaws), gambling prohibition served only the illegal operators and the corrupt politicians and police who gave them protection.

So beginning in the 1920s, but truly accelerating in the 1960s, state governments began to embrace gambling. At first looking merely to replace existing illegal gambling, states soon moved into the business of promoting betting and wagering. Once unthinkable, this merely signified what astute observers had known for some time: that gambling was the true American pastime.

Most states first sidled up to a relatively friendly form of gambling: horse racing. Raising, selling, and racing horses was a major economic activity that employed thousands and made millions. Legal betting, then, could be rationalized as a way to stimulate the growth of a racing industry that would return money to its investors, its employees, and the state. When Matt Winn pulled the Churchill Downs pari-mutuel machines from a forgotten storage locker, he began a process that would lead to the national revival of horse racing. Justly celebrated for making the Kentucky Derby one of the sports calendar's most anticipated events, he deserves equal credit for freeing race betting from the clutches of bookmakers. With human meddling removed from the business of setting odds and payouts for race betting, the sport received a new legitimacy. But as existing mechanical systems were unwieldy, they were used only sparingly. For pari-mutuel betting to truly catch on, it needed to be streamlined and sped up.

Engineer Harry Straus learned firsthand the frustrations of pari-mutuels on the afternoon of April 26, 1927. Though it was a Thursday, Straus decided that the day would be better spent at Maryland's Havre de Grace racetrack than at work. Receiving a hot tip that Cockney, a thoroughly mediocre runner, was a guaranteed lock, Straus checked the odds board, which had Cockney at nine to one. Straus bet $10 and returned to the window to collect his $90. To his disappointment, he learned that the actual odds at the time of his placing the bet had been close to three to one (evidently word of the fix had gotten out). Getting only $36 for his trouble, Straus began to think after a similarly disgruntled bettor remarked that, as an engineer, he should be able to design a better pari-mutuel machine.

Unlike tracks in Europe and Asia, which had adopted the "Julius Tote," an improved electrical/mechanical version of Pierre Oller's pari-mutuel contraption, American racecourses still used strictly mechanical, manually operated totalizator machines. As Straus experienced firsthand, these totes left much to be desired. He resolved to design a system that could accept thousands of bets within a few moments, keep an accurate tabulation of the odds, display the correct odds instantly, and print tickets. In conjunction with electrical engineer Johnny Johnson, he spent much of 1928 building such a machine. Invited to display his new totalizator by Britain's Betting Control Board (Parliament had just legalized pari-mutuel betting at all British tracks), he proved the worth of his invention but received only $50,000 for the sale of the British rights to his system.

In the fall of 1930, Pimlico racetrack installed part of Straus's system, the electronic display board. Several other tracks followed suit, though none took a flyer on buying the complete Straus tote system until Florida's Hialeah track did so in 1932. The machine was incredibly successful there, as it was at Chicago's Arlington Park, the second track to install it. In 1933, ten states legalized horse racing, vastly increasing Straus's market. As the Depression continued, states scrambling for financial relief, mindful of the reputable, accurate new tote system, jumped on the Straus bandwagon. Joe Hirsch, an eminent racing writer, later wrote that Straus's invention "did for racing what Babe Ruth did for baseball. Plagued by bookmakers, inaccuracies, dwindling attendance, and suspicious state legislatures, racing needed help badly, and the tote filled the bill."

Straus's improved tote accelerated a trend that had already begun. Throughout the 1920s, the racing industry had begun to recover from the ravages of reform. Pressed to the wall by antigambling reformers, horse advocates began to put their house in order. In addition to eliminating the need for bookmakers, they instituted drug testing and used technology, including improved starting gates and photo-finish cameras, to make races fairer. At least fifteen major new tracks opened and purses became much larger. The first horse to surpass the $100,000 mark in a season's earnings had done so in 1889; since then, purse sizes had stagnated and even shrunk, but in the 1930 season one horse set a new record with over $300,000 in winnings.

Despite the economic gloom of the Depression, the American public flocked to the racetracks that were opening across the land. As the economy improved, racing expanded even more, as larger purses brought keener competition. Horses became popular heroes; one, Seabiscuit, was reputed to rival President Franklin Delano Roosevelt in news coverage received. The horse was the perfect symbol for Depression and the resurgent racing industry: Tabbed as too small and too lazy to win, he was sold by his original owners to West Coast automobile entrepreneur Charles Howard, who teamed Seabiscuit with a trainer and jockey who believed in him. The horse racked up an impressive record, primarily on California's new tracks, and after a winning a 1938 special match against the mighty War Admiral (dubbed "the match of the century" in the press, and in which War Admiral was a one-to-four favorite), Seasbiscuit was declared the horse of the year. Accessible to a new generation thanks to a 2001 book by Laura Hillenbrand and its 2003 film adaptation, Seabiscuit still inspires underdogs everywhere.

World War II caused a lull in racing, not the least in California, where tracks were converted to military use (most infamously, internment camps for

Electronic tote boards changed the look of racetracks, such as Churchill Downs. The totes sparked a 1930s resurgence of horse racing and represented an early manifestation of public-interest gambling.

Americans of Japanese descent). In 1944 the government banned racing as a wartime measure, but with Allied victory in the next year the sport resumed. But racing failed to adapt to the new medium of television and lost ground to team sports, particularly baseball and football, in the 1950s and 1960s. Still, racing expanded, with more tracks and more racing days added, as state governments continued to turn to pari-mutuel betting for revenue. By 1967, however, racing attendance began to decline, a sign that the sport was in serious trouble.

As racing languished, sports betting surged ahead. During racing's 1930 heyday, it had been far better suited for gambling than team sports. Straus's tote automatically computed the pari-mutuel odds, removing the need for bookmakers to set the line. Thanks to the race wire, bettors didn't need to go to the racetrack to get action down: They could simply stop by their local poolroom, where they could bet at the latest odds and learn race results immediately. Bookmakers no longer needed to be scholars of horseflesh in order to set up shop; they needed only a subscription to the race wire, which delivered the tote-computed odds instantaneously. Racing was sanctioned by state commissions that policed the sport and guaranteed its probity to the public. Those who bet on the races took advantage of the day's most technologically sophisticated, well-organized gambling system.

Sports betting, on the other hand, was positively crude and almost completely disorganized. Betting with pool cards, in which players had to correctly guess several winning teams in order to win, was truly a gamble; bettors just played their hunches and bookmakers hoped that more would be wrong than right. Taking straight-up bets on single contests proved more problematic, since the mass of bettors inevitably favored one team or another. With bets heavily on one side, the bookmaker became, in essence, a gambler. And gambling professionals wanted to remove the gambling from their end: They preferred betting scenarios that let them rake off a respectable percentage regardless of the outcome.

Point-spread betting revolutionized sports betting, particularly for football and basketball, by letting bookmakers handicap teams. If a bookmaker felt that a team would likely win, he would tell bettors that, in order to win the bet, the team would have to win by a certain number of points. On the other hand, bettors could pick a loser that, if it lost by less than the point spread, would still pay off. This system allowed bookmakers to adjust the "line," or point handicap, as bets poured in. For example: A bookmaker starts taking bets for a game between Philadelphia and New York. Philadelphia, the stronger team, starts as a six-point favorite. Deluged by bets on Philadelphia, the bookie adjusts his line, making Philadelphia a seven-point favorite, in an effort to attract more action for New York. If successful, he will have a balanced book, or nearly equal bets on both sides. Keeping the money wagered by losers and paying winners $10 for every $11 bet, the bookmaker will generate a profit of 4.545 percent—not as lucrative as the numbers but, given a large enough volume, sufficient for a comfortable living.

The actual origins of point-spread setting and betting are somewhat murky. The general concept was used by eastern gamblers by the early twentieth century, though it did not achieve its current form until the 1940s. There is still uncertainty over who "invented" the point spread. Charles McNeil, a math teacher and securities analyst who at one time taught future president John F. Kennedy at Choate, has been given the honor, though he did not originally set out to create a new betting form. He began devising a point-handicapping system to help him better pick winners at existing odds betting. He later explained his system to bookmakers, who began using it to accept wagers on handicapped teams. But others tabbed Minnesota bookmaker Bill Hecht as the man who "evolved" the "point system of betting," and Hecht's associate Leo Hirschfeld would go on to become the nation's preeminent line-setter.

Hirschfeld developed a system that, together with the growing public preference for team sports, would help push the race wire and poolrooms toward obscurity. With the widespread availability of games on radio and later television, sports bookmakers didn't need a special wire service; they only needed someone to help them intelligently set the line. Hirschfeld's Athletic Publications, Inc., produced the weekly *Green Sheet*, a publication that offered lines on each of the week's matchups, scouting reports, and betting tips. Bookmakers could get even quicker service: For $15, the odds were telegraphed to them and for $20 a week, they were delivered by phone. By 1950, Hirschfeld had over eight thousand subscribers. Some of them were legitimate news agencies, but most were illegal bookmakers.

Thanks to Hirschfeld, bookies around the country had a safe, reliable method of setting the line. In the 1950s, betting on college and professional sports positively exploded, displacing horse-race betting for many. Because nearly all sports betting was illegal, its true extent can only be guessed. To counter its success (and bolster state revenues), New York authorized the 1970 creation of legal off-track betting facilities in New York City. OTB was a resounding success; in 1974, New York City OTB was the city's largest retailer, with over a hundred branch offices that served between 100,000 and 150,000 people a day and a telephone service that let players bet over the phone. The

OTB tail soon began to wag the racetrack dog, and in 1977 OTB revenue outpaced that of money bet at tracks.

OTB soon spread to other states (it had existed for decades in Nevada's legal race books), as most states eagerly sought to pump life into their racing industries. The racing industry did more than simply offer the convenience of off-track betting: New "exotic" wagers spiced up races. Exotics ranged from the "daily double," in which a bettor had to successfully guess the winners of two races, to the "superfecta," which she won only after guessing the top six finishers, in order. Serious bettors who made a life's study of the turf rightfully considered such exotics foolhardy bets, but casual players, accustomed to jackpot payoffs from the lottery, were often eager to accept the astronomical odds.

Pari-mutuel betting spread beyond just Thoroughbreds. Harness racing, in some parts of the country, offered more racing dates, though it consistently trailed Thoroughbred racing in betting volume. Quarter-horse racing, though it never seriously challenged Thoroughbred racing, emerged as another popular pari-mutuel sport. Nor did the betting have to be on horses. Greyhound racing has aristocratic origins as coursing, but in the twentieth century it evolved into a popular sport. In 1904, a coursing event held in South Dakota inspired its sponsor, Owen Patrick Smith, to develop a more humane alternative. He spent the next fifteen years designing and perfecting a replacement for the live rabbits still used in coursing events—he eventually developed the perfect artificial rabbit. Modern greyhound racing began in 1919, when a public dog-racing track opened at Emeryville, California, using Smith's innovation. Though the track was a failure, the idea eventually caught on, and Smith's mechanical lure aided the acceptance of the sport. Greyhound racing, distinct from coursing, had been born.

Greyhound racing spread throughout the United States during the 1920s and was introduced into Great Britain—the original home of coursing—during that decade as well. Pari-mutuel betting drew many spectators to the sport, which was routinely criticized as cruel to animals. Still, it proved popular in the United States, where it eventually spread to fifteen states, and the rest of the world. It remains particularly popular in Europe, Asia, and the Middle East.

Most American team sports were bet on with the point spread, the money line (a variant of the odds system typically used in baseball), and old-fashioned odds betting. But a traditional Basque game imported into Florida became a popular vehicle for pari-mutuel wagering. Jai alai, Basque for "merry festival," was originally played at the end of week-long religious carnivals. Teams representing rival towns took the court for three or four hours at a stretch, and partisans backed their team with wagers. The game spread throughout Spain and France and, by the twentieth century, could be found in Italy, the Philippines, South America, and Mexico, where a jai alai court, or fronton, was a popular attraction in 1930s Tijuana. Jai alai was even found in China, where it still survives in Macau.

Jai alai—without betting—was introduced to the United States at the 1904 World's Fair in St. Louis; subsequent exhibitions received lukewarm receptions. A fronton built in Hialeah, Florida, in 1924 was destroyed soon after by a hurricane, but jai alai gained popularity during the 1920s in that state. It was an exciting game: Two teams of two players each used a basketlike glove called a cesta to catch and throw a rubber ball called a pelota; a team unable to rebound the ball lost the point, which was scored to the opponent. Games were played for seven to nine points, and with many teams playing in sequence, bettors could wager on many of the same options as in horse racing, such as whether a team would win, place, or show.

When Florida legalized pari-mutuel betting in 1937, jai alai boomed, with frontons built throughout the state. By the 1970s, jai alai had spread to Nevada (where the original MGM Grand in Las Vegas and its Reno counterpart sported jai alai frontons), Connecticut, and Rhode Island. This was the golden decade for American jai alai. In the 1980s, the MGM Grand frontons closed, and by the next decade the game was no longer played in New England, as frontons were converted to other uses: Rhode Island embraced video lottery terminals to replace the revenues lost by the disappearance of jai alai. Even in Florida, jai alai fell on hard times, and the industry has survived only by turning to forms of gambling.

Horse-racing industry leaders adjusted to shrinking track attendance by legalizing poolrooms. With the 1978 Interstate Horseracing Act, Congress legalized the transmission of racing odds and results between states where racing was legal. Casino race books, tracks, and OTB locations were now free to accept wagers on races throughout the nation and around the world. With the spread of simulcast throughout the 1990s, dollars bet on racing increased, even as track attendance continued to fall. The annual off-track betting total, including simulcast, was, by the twenty-first century, more than $13 billion a year; only $2 billion was bet on live races at tracks. Simulcast made race wagering a growth industry during the otherwise moribund 1980s and 1990s.

Many tracks, though, needed even more help. With the spread of casino-style gambling throughout the nation in the 1990s, they decided that, if they couldn't beat casinos, they would join them. At their urging, several states authorized them to install slot machines or video lottery terminals, slot machines in all but name. Tracks that combined racing with casinos, soon dubbed "racinos," saw their revenues soar. They were able to offer larger purses, which led to better racing and bigger gates. West Virginia, which became the first racino state in 1990, saw a complete revival of its racetracks, which later expanded into full-fledged resorts (like Las Vegas Strip casinos) with hotels, entertainment, and shopping.

In the early twenty-first century, horse racing remained popular. The Triple Crown races—Kentucky Derby, Preakness, and Belmont Stakes—and the Breeders' Cup continue to fascinate the public, though they are not national holidays on the scale of Australia's Melbourne Cup. With simulcasting, telephone account wagering, and Internet wagering, race betting is a multibillion-dollar-a-year business. Though pari-mutuel wagering and state oversight has largely given the sport legitimacy, cheating and betting scandals still occur. In 2002, three former fraternity brothers from Drexel University in Philadelphia electronically altered a wager for the Breeders' Cup Pick Six; when the incredible longshot Volponi won the race, they stood to collect over $3 million. The statistical unlikelihood of such a wager being made legitimately triggered an investigation, and the three confessed to their fraud without collecting. The scandal showed that, no matter how technologically advanced race betting is, there are still those who will stop at nothing for a shot at a "sure thing."

As states rushed to cash in on the pari-mutuel bounty, private charitable organizations felt that they, too, were entitled to gambling-related relief. Charitable gambling juggled questions of gambling's morality: Certain religious authorities had always maintained that gambling was a sin, but, if directed toward a higher purpose, was it still sinful? In the twentieth century, many churches would politely sidestep the question of gambling's sinfulness while moving into a gambling growth industry: bingo.

Bingo took America by storm in the 1930s, but it was merely the latest twist on the sixteenth-century Genoese lottery game, lotto. Substituting cards randomly numbered from one to ninety for printed tickets, lotto operators drew wooden tokens from a bag and announced them. The first player to fill a horizontal row of five squares won the game. In this form, lotto spread throughout Europe and to the American colonies, where it further mutated into keno, a popular game in mid-nineteenth-century New Orleans and Mississippi River ports. The game was almost always illegal (though New Orleans periodically gave sanction to keno dens) but, like most other illicit games, bought protection from police and politicians.

Despite the worldwide turn against lotteries in the nineteenth century, lotto-type games survived. They were even used to educate children: Lotto games that taught spelling, math, and history were common in Europe and filtered over into the United States. (There has never been any incompatibility between gambling games and education: Some of the most exquisitely made playing cards were intended for use as teaching aids.) In the twentieth century, lotto was apparently a common game in Germany, for while touring that country in 1928, a carnival pitchman (whose name has been unfortunately forgotten) said he saw it and decided it would make an excellent carnival game.

The pitchman brought the game back to the United States and made a few changes. He gave players beans, which they placed on their cards as he called numbers he pulled from a cigar box. Calling the game Beano, he instructed players to shout, "Beano!" when they had filled a row: The winner received a kewpie doll. This rather scanty jackpot brought high excitement, as players crowded to the game, which became the most popular booth at the carnival.

In December 1929, a struggling toy salesman named Edwin Lowe visited the pitchman's booth late one night near Jacksonville, Florida. Impressed by the fact that he couldn't buy a seat at the table and that the patrons insisted on playing until 3:00 A.M., Lowe brought the game back to his hometown of New York City. He tried the game out on a group of friends using a home-made set, and it proved just as popular in Manhattan as it had been in Florida. One night, a woman, overcome with excitement at having had her final number called, jumped up and sputtered, "B-b-bingo!" Lowe decided that this was more euphonious than "beano" and began producing home versions of the game under the name Bingo.

Bingo had been used as the name of several gambling games: Consulting forgotten editions of Hoyle's and other rulebooks, one can find bingo as a card, dice, and domino game. But Lowe's name for his game became nearly universal in the 1930s. Because, in truth, the game could not be trademarked, Lowe asked his competitors to pay him the token sum of $1 a year for the use of the bingo name. Though Lowe was on shaky legal ground (he freely admitted that the game was a copy of a copy of a centuries-old European diversion), he was successful in promoting "Bingo." The name became universal in the East (in California and Nevada, the game was called "Tango" for a time), and bingo-mania ran wild through the hard-luck cities and towns of Depression America.

Gambling of all sorts boomed during the Depression, perhaps a sardonic response to the collapse of the financial system in 1929. If the nation's financial security was just a house of cards, cynics argued, common gambling was no worse than stock market speculation. Movie theaters, eager to boost attendance as discretionary spending money dried up, used raffles to draw crowds. Whether called bank night, lucky night, lucky screen, bango, or banko, such games were popular—though technically a violation of antilottery statutes.

With Lowe's bingo an immediate success, a Wilkes-Barre, Pennsylvania, church bought several of Lowe's home bingo sets and found that the game was completely unworkable: Because of the limited number of cards, each game produced several winners. Still, Lowe realized that, as a fund-raising tool, his game would be far more lucrative than as a home game, and he hired Columbia University's Carl Leffler, a mathematics professor, to develop six-thousand nonrepeating cards.

Armed with the cards, the Wilkes-Barre priest returned to his flock and began running incredibly popular bingo games. Churches and charitable organizations across the country quickly emulated the Wilkes-Barre church. Lowe moved deftly to capitalize on the trend, publishing an official bingo instructional manual and a monthly newsletter that soon boasted thirty-seven-thousand subscribers. By 1934, there had been a massive sixty-thousand-player game (reportedly the biggest ever) in Teaneck, New Jersey, and throughout the nation as many as ten-thousand bingo games were played each week.

Since bingo resembled the dreaded lottery, it was often illegal or, at best, barely legal. Even where illegal, because games were conducted by churches, they were often tolerated; even the most doggedly enthusiastic district attorney blanched at locking up a parish priest for running wildly popular games. In its classic form, bingo was a mindless game that required more patience than skill. In church basements, fraternal lodges, or specially built halls, players gathered for a night of low-stakes gambling. Church bingo games started at eight and seldom let out before eleven; players arrived with a variety of good-luck trinkets and packs of cigarettes, which they often chain-smoked as the tension built. Waitresses filtered among the tables, selling soft drinks, popcorn, and hot dogs, and players murmured words of encouragement to each other even as they hoped for their own number to be called. Though most games paid only $35, special sweepstakes could earn a player as much as $1,500.

The mechanics of play were simple. Players bought one or more cards and, as numbers were called, placed chips on them. Each card contained five

Bingo players in a Sarasota, Florida, trailer park in 1941.

rows with five numbered spaces each. The column under "B" had five num-bers from one to fifteen, "I" five from sixteen to thirty, and so on. The bingo caller announced numbers taken from a rotating cage or a blower. In its sim-plest form, the first to fill a horizontal row literally got bingo, and she shouted, "Bingo!" to end the game (after her card was verified). To break up the te-dium, operators varied the sessions by deviating from the straight and narrow: Instead of a line, players might have to fill each corner or make a geometric pattern. On a typical night, as many as a hundred games could be played.

Bingo became an integral part of the American lifestyle. By the 1950s, it had been exported abroad. It even could be found in the heart of the commu-nist Union of Soviet Socialist Republics. The American House, a Moscow club catering to American diplomats, hosted nightly games. Cards cost ten rubles, about $2.50. Originally played exclusively by Americans, the games soon attracted a host of others. "You can't keep bingo down," an American said. "The British love it, the French play, and so do Indians, Argentines, Dutch, and practically everyone else in town." Hunched over their cards, the players were a United Nations of gamblers intent on hitting the jackpot in the capital of Marxism-Leninism.

Back in the United States, bingo continued to spread. In 1974, bingo was legal in thirty-four states, and authorities estimated that close to $2 billion was spent each year on legal and illegal bingo games. People in lower income groups tended to play bingo, spending an average of less than $6 per session for the thrill of the games. Most played just to have a good time, and bingo

parlors were famously sociable places where winners basked in praise and losers comforted each other. Though bingo seemed to be small stakes, police
warned several unscrupulous bingo operators who, like casino skimmers,
failed to report their revenues to state or local regulators, or cheated players by
paying the high jackpots to confederates. Though taken far from its carnival
roots, bingo never quite escaped them. Still, along with charity casino nights
(known as "Las Vegas Nights" or "Monte Carlo Nights"), bingo laid a solid
foundation for the public acceptance of gambling as a tolerable fund-raising
tool.

While some sought to channel gambling for the public good, others continued to use it to line their own pockets. The biggest illegal game was the
numbers introduced to New York City by a group of enterprising immigrants in the 1920s. José Enrique Miró of Puerto Rico, William Brudner of
the West Indies, Alexander Pompez of Cuba, and Stephanie St. Clair of
France (known as the Madam Queen of Policy), organized illegal numbers
games in Harlem. From its base in Harlem the numbers spread to other
cities; it pushed policy out of Philadelphia but failed to displace it in
Chicago. Originally controlled by black and Hispanic immigrants, most
Harlem numbers banks eventually fell under the control of bootlegger
Dutch Schultz, though often the original owners remained as managing
partners. After Schultz was killed in 1935, other criminal syndicates assumed
command of his numbers empire and expanded it. This pattern was repeated
across the country.

This was a streamlined game that eschewed fanciful drawings by blindfolded boys for publicly known numbers published by legitimate business institutions, such as stock exchanges, pari-mutuel pools, attendance at major
sporting events, and even the United States Treasury. In the typical numbers
operation, a collector or runner accepted wagers from the public from news-
stands or street corners; many runners made regular rounds of local shops and
worksites. To play, the bettor wrote a number from 0 to 999 on a slip and gave
it to the collector. A "pickup man" collected the slips and wagers from the
runner and brought them to the central bank where the receipts were tallied
and collections, payments, and matters of police protection coordinated.
Large numbers operations had several small banks reporting to a single, larger
bank. It was a business that grew, by the late 1940s, to an estimated $2 billion
a year nationally.

Though popular wisdom held that the game was played primarily by poor
blacks, it was considerably popular among other ethnic groups, particularly

Italians and Hispanics. It was a big-city game that offered players cheap, convenient gambling fun and entrepreneurs a chance to develop a respectable, though illegal, business. Numbers was incredibly profitable: Though the true odds of a hit (correct numbers) were a thousand to one, most operators paid off at six hundred to one or even less, and players were expected to tip runners at least ten percent of their winnings. Even after administrative expenses, which included police and political payoffs, numbers operators generally received a profit of seven to ten percent of gross wagers.

Though critics charged that the numbers was a regressive gambling scheme that impoverished the inner cities, some felt otherwise. Poet Langston Hughes called the numbers "the salvation of Harlem," and it remained an institution in many neighborhoods for decades. In the early 1970s, as New York City got off-track betting, several lawmakers floated proposals to legalize the numbers "under community control." At the time, estimates of money bet on the numbers annually ranged as high as $2 billion in New York City alone. Ultimately, states would move into the business themselves, eventually supplanting urban entrepreneurs by offering daily "numbers" games as part of state-run lotteries.

In the South, a Latin-tinged lottery game emerged at about the same time as the numbers when Cuban immigrants brought *bolita* to the States. In its original incarnation the game required players to toss a sack filled with numbered balls back and forth until, at a signal, the receiver removed a ball, which was declared the winner. In the early 1930s the game, which originally required players to guess which of several numbered balls would be picked, became popular in the Cuban enclave of Ybor City, near Tampa, Florida, from whence it spread throughout the state.

During the Great Depression, *bolita* became popular with Floridians of all races, and in 1938, Tampa's 125 *bolita* operations grossed as much as $20,000 a day. State authorities appeared powerless to stop the games, and not even the intervention of the Federal Bureau of Investigation could break the power of *bolita* operators. The game eventually spread as far north as New York City, where "Spanish Raymond" Marquez presided over a vast, lucrative *bolita* empire from the 1960s until the 1990s.

Most cities also sported several other illicit games of chance: Slot machines, dice rooms, and bookmakers were common in even the smallest cities. San Bernardino, for example, was dubbed "California's Casbah" and, in the late 1940s, was a serious rival to growing Las Vegas. When reform shuttered many of the gambling dens there, southern Californians flocked to Bobby Garcia's

Double O Ranch, a Morongo Valley resort that aspired to country-club elegance. Even after a police raid forced Garcia to substitute bridge and bingo tables for craps and roulette, selected guests continued to play casino games in a back room.

A range of other cities, from Galveston, Texas, to Buffalo, New York, had thriving illegal casinos. In San Francisco, the illegal "Chinese Lottery" was just as popular as Nevada's keno, its legal counterpart. No section of the country was without its secret gambling: Butte, Montana, had action just as wild as that in Wheeling, Oklahoma City, Chicago, Boston, or Miami. But some illegal clubs were recognized as the truly elite. After Mayor Fiorello La Guardia's 1934 crackdown on illegal gambling, gambling bosses moved to the suburbs. Across the Hudson River, New Jersey's Bergen County soon boasted a string of "gambling resorts" that earned as much as $10 million a year for their proprietors, members of illegal gambling syndicates. The first such resort opened in a back room of Ben Marden's Riviera, a popular nightclub whose lavish floor shows rivaled anything that would later be found on the Las Vegas Strip.

During the late 1930s, a host of illegal casinos opened throughout the county. Typically, gambling operators secured police protection before converting former warehouses into lavishly decorated gambling and entertainment resorts. Guests were ferried from New York via Cadillac, wined, and dined before being escorted to the gaming tables. Towns such as Clifton, Leonia, Linden, Lodi, East Paterson, Little Ferry, Cliffside Park and Caldwell had, at different times, elegant illegal resorts. With public attention suddenly directed against illegal gambling by the Kefauver Committee hearings in 1950, the Bergen County casinos closed. Many of the dealers and patrons, though, moved on to Las Vegas, where they could play legally.

Longer-lived gambling dens could be found to the south, where America's Playground, Atlantic City, was for decades a "shore bet" for illicit gambling. Though it was promoted as a family resort, as early as the 1860s those who knew where to look could have some very adult fun gambling. Under the de facto rule of Enoch "Nucky" Johnson, who rose to power as the sheriff of Atlantic County in 1908, wide-open gambling was viewed as a boon to the tourist trade. Reportedly, Johnson struck a bargain with underworld eminence Charles "Lucky" Luciano in 1923 such that, in exchange for a modest ten-percent cut of the proceeds, he would permit bootlegged liquor to be landed on "his beach" and gambling operations to be run by Luciano and his friends—who included gangsters Frank Costello and Joe Adonis. A federal investigation of Johnson's vice empire revealed that there were at least twenty-five casinos and poolrooms that flourished under his protection in

Atlantic City, along with nine numbers banks; all of these conducted business openly, safe from prosecution, and earned combined profits of well over $10 million a year.

After Johnson was finally sent to prison in 1941, gambling continued, albeit in a less public fashion. Most of the city's world famous nightclubs fronted secret backroom casinos: Skinny D'Amato's famous 500 Club, where Frank Sinatra played some of his most famous shows and the comedy team of Dean Martin and Jerry Lewis was born, had a full-service casino that featured every table game found in Las Vegas, but no slot machines. The world-famous Boardwalk was a gambling mecca of another sort: Bingo and other carnival games of chance were common along the boards, and big-money poker games were common in the private rooms of its ritzy hotels. Those who wanted more casual action could play the numbers or bet on horses. Atlantic City remained a gambler's paradise until the early 1950s, when the exposure brought by the Kefauver Committee's 1951 hearings there forced an end to the wide-open days.

To the south, the Sunshine State had a similar wide-open streak. Miami and Miami Beach were both renowned for their gambling dens, but for years Edward Riley Bradley's Beach Club made Palm Beach the toniest gambling spot in the state. The club had opened in 1898 as a members-only, men-only club with few games. The following year, Bradley liberalized the entrance policy and watched the cash begin to pour in. Though housed in a simple white frame house that hardly rivaled Canfield's sumptuous clubs, Bradley insisted in providing only the finest food for his guests, who soon included many of the nation's wealthiest men and women.

Bradley put his profits from the Beach Club to good use: He bought a horse farm near Lexington, Kentucky, and became renowned as a "turfman." Between dodging sporadic antigambling drives in Palm Beach, he found the time to own four Kentucky Derby winners. He also gave back to the community—apparently a believer in Andrew Carnegie's Social Gospel, he sincerely tried to give away his fortune before he died. When a 1928 hurricane cut a swath of destruction through Palm Beach, he reportedly financed the rebuilding of all the area's churches. He also donated huge sums to Florida and Kentucky orphanages. Though he profited well from gambling, he came to believe it was a sin; before he died in 1946, he left instructions in his will that the Beach Club be donated to the city for use as a park and its gambling equipment be sent to sleep with the fishes. This hardly stopped gambling in Palm Beach, though the Beach Club's closing marked the end of a lustrous era.

On Florida's West Coast, Tampa was a thriving gambling center. American *bolita* originated in the city's Ybor City district, and the city was a gambling hotspot into the 1960s. The southern climate remained hospitable to gamblers long after the last riverboats had cruised the Mississippi. In Biloxi, Mississippi, which flourished as a tourist town before and after the Civil War, gambling never passed from the scene. As in Atlantic City, it took on a new vigor during Prohibition; an elegant but small casino opened on the Isle of Caprice, a tiny barrier island that, before its development, was known as Dog Key. Though beach erosion caused the Isle to vanish by 1932, no force of nature could stop the gambling that continued on the mainland. In both Biloxi and neighboring Gulfport, slot machines, high-stakes poker, and casino games were a natural part of life.

Though Biloxi's gambling flourished in the 1950s, a group of local reformers, following the lead of the Kefauver Committee, forced authorities to clamp down on the most blatant gambling offenders. Gambling continued in the back rooms for a while longer but increased pressure, combined with declining numbers of tourists and the destruction caused by 1969's Hurricane Camille, eventually choked Biloxi's once-thriving gambling subculture into submission.

Beaches weren't a prerequisite for a gambling haven. Hot Springs, Arkansas, developed as a health resort in the early nineteenth century but, much like Saratoga, became famous for its gambling. This was a thriving business by the 1880s, and eventually fell under the sway of "Big" Jim O'Leary, the former Chicago gambling kingpin whose name is inextricably linked with that city's disastrous 1871 fire. Hot Springs became a major gambling center and rest haven for gangsters, and remained so until it fell victim to a national drive against illegal gambling led by Attorney General Robert F. Kennedy in the early 1960s.

Some of the most notorious illegal casinos in the nation were to be found in northern Kentucky. Covington and Newport were, in the middle of the twentieth century, major gambling centers. In the state of Kentucky, casino gambling was avowedly illegal but was, for years, a de facto local option. Though gambling had been a part of Kentucky culture since its frontier days, illegal casinos dated only to Prohibition, when, it is alleged, Cleveland syndicate members "organized" the gambling action. In Newport, clubs like the Alibi, Sportsman's 316, and Tin Shack had varying degrees of squareness. Though some ran honest games, others were bust-out joints where unfortunate visitors had no chance of winning. These illegal casinos ran virtually without interference until 1961, when a local vigilance effort rode the coattails of Kennedy's national antigambling campaign and drove out gambling. This hardly meant a public renunciation of gambling as a fun pastime: The winds of reform, as in Arkansas, New Jersey, and elsewhere, blew gambling operators and their patrons straight to Las Vegas.

American-style gaming was not confined to the United States. Cuba was the preeminent Caribbean casino destination. On April 15, 1951, a full-page advertisement in *The New York Times* welcomed Americans to holiday in Cuba. It offered them "a never to-be-forgotten chapter" in their lives, and the "gayest, most glamorous, most glorious vacation ever!" The advertisement extolled the glories of Havana: "Modern hotels . . . delightful restaurants . . . fabulous nightclubs . . . racetrack thrills and other sports . . . beach bathing and pleasure . . . all these and more will fill your stay with pleasure." In addition to sparkling beaches and carefree shopping, the advertisement also highlighted "Cuba's glorious temple of the Goddess of Chance—the Grand National Casino." In the middle of the decade, tourism boosters consciously promoted Cuba as "the Las Vegas of the Caribbean," aware that the combination of vacation sunshine and gambling offered there was markedly similar to Las Vegas's action. It seemed that Cuba would become a new international gambling center.

But the best hopes of Cuban casino operators were dashed on New Year's Eve 1958/1959 when rebels led by Fidel Castro chased Fulgencio Batista, the country's ruler, into exile. As Batista fled to the Dominican Republic, Castro's forces consolidated their hold over major cities like Santiago and Santa Clara. Batista's flight inspired rioting in Havana, as hated symbols of the Batista regime, from parking meters to hotels, were targeted by looters and vandals. Casinos, connected in the public mind with foreign gangsters and Batista's proclivities for American business, were also branded as antirevolutionary. Mobs looted casinos, though the venerable Hotel Nacional was not damaged. The Plaza Hotel's recently completed casino, however, was completely destroyed, and others' gaming rooms suffered damages. Although Fidel Castro initially seemed willing to regulate rather than prohibit casino gambling, smart operators realized that casinos had no real future in Cuba. On September 29, 1961, Fidel Castro announced that casino gambling would henceforth be illegal in Havana and the last remaining casino was unceremoniously closed.

Agua Caliente, a golf course and hotel complex near Tijuana, Mexico, opened in 1928 with a luxurious casino and several restaurants. Two years later, a racetrack opened, and the resort drew Hollywood stars and wealthy Americans until President Lázaro Cárdenas ordered an end to all gambling in

1935. The racetrack reopened two years later but never recaptured its former popularity. North of the border, Montreal was a center for horse racing, thanks to modern technology. Though the local track was only open one month each year, poolrooms carried races from around the United States and Mexico. Illegal casinos featured games like roulette and craps but also barbotte, a dice game unique to Montreal that was far and away the local favorite.

Urban gambling, from bookmakers to slot machines, became so widespread that, by the 1940s, it could no longer be hidden. The voting public demanded that their elected officials do something about "syndicate crime," seemingly oblivious to the fact that, if they themselves stopped gambling illegally, the syndicates would crumble. Nevertheless, public animosity towards "boss gamblers" became a potent political issue in the late 1940s. In 1950 the ambitious Tennessee senator Estes Kefauver capitalized on the antigambling furor by chairing a special Senate committee that investigated "organized crime in interstate commerce." The Kefauver Committee's televised hearings (in which reputed gangsters invoked their Fifth Amendment rights when asked even the most basic questions) introduced a shocked public to the idea that local gambling was a big business controlled by murderous national crime syndicates.

Though Kefauver's investigations often missed the mark, the wave of reform he provoked succeeded in closing many illegal gambling centers. This time, though, state governments didn't just force gamblers to lie low until the reform impulse had passed; by and large, they moved into the lucrative gambling business themselves, under the guise of public-interest gaming. Outrage at the profits secured by gambling racketeers had given way to unabashed envy. When Attorney General Robert F. Kennedy mounted an even more concerted federal drive against "organized gambling" in 1961, he legitimately wished to purge the nation of corrupt "boss gamblers." Cynics, though, might say that he only cleared the field for a massive government takeover of the most lucrative gambling racket of them all: the numbers.

The death rattle of the Serpent echoed through the early decades of the twentieth century, as the lottery continued to have a bad reputation. When, in the 1930s, other nations began to revive their own dormant lotteries, the United States remained devoutly out of the lottery business, even though foreign lottery tickets were often available: Results of the Irish Sweepstakes and various Latin American lotteries were commonly published in newspapers. In addition, the millions of dollars wagered each year on the numbers gave the lie to the claim that Americans had rejected lotteries. But organized antigambling elements, invoking the ghost of the Serpent, were successful in blocking proposals for state-run lotteries into the 1960s.

Numbers rackets were the most common illegal game in America's cities, but those who lived in more isolated stretches of North America were not denied access to lotteries. True to the maxim that those with an abundance of lemons should best make lemonade, a group of surveyors in Nenana, Alaska (then merely an American territory), added some excitement to their jobs when, in 1917, they bet each other exactly when the ice on the Tanana River would break. Since then, the Nenana Ice Classic has become an Alaskan institution, with tickets sold statewide. Those who can predict exactly when a special tripod set on the frozen surface of the river will move a hundred feet and stop a specially designed clock win the jackpot. The Ice Classic sells fewer than 300,000 tickets a year, far fewer than other lotteries, but considering tickets are sold only in a state with a total population of about 550,000, the lottery is a testament to the enduring American fascination with gambling. And, true to form, the Ice Classic has developed into a classic example of public-interest gaming: All proceeds remaining after the winners are paid go to the local library and school.

Lotteries returned to the lower forty-eight in a state as far removed from Louisiana as can be imagined: New Hampshire. The state legislature had considered lottery proposals as early as 1937 but did not pass a lottery bill until 1963. Even then, the game was a far cry from the daily numbers: Drawings were held twice a year and tickets were a relatively expensive three dollars. New Hampshire openly went into the lottery business to dredge up additional tax revenue. With no sales or income tax, the state was dependent on real-estate and sin taxes (on alcohol and tobacco) to maintain its roads and fund its schools. When backers of the lottery declared that the state would produce over $10 million a year, the legislature and the governor listened: The lottery bill became law.

In 1964, the New Hampshire Sweepstakes began the modern era of American lotteries less than auspiciously. The Internal Revenue Service, citing a law passed in 1950 at the height of the Kefauver antigambling campaign, demanded that the state pay a ten-percent wagering excise and that each ticket vendor receive a federal tax stamp. The commission that ran the Sweepstakes paid over $500,000 to satisfy the IRS's ruling, putting a major dent into the lottery's profits. Congress later exempted state lotteries from the wagering excise tax, but this was little help to New Hampshire at the time. Ticket buyers had to register to buy tickets and provide their name and address, hardly an inducement to buy a chance in this traditional draw game. With limited distribution, expensive tickets, small prizes, and infrequent drawings, the lottery was a failure, earning only $5.7 million in its first year, and only $2 million by 1970.

Where New Hampshire had failed, New York thought it could succeed. In 1970, as it was legalizing OTB, the state also started a monthly lottery whose tickets only cost one dollar, though games were still relatively infrequent. Money only trickled in, and it seemed that perhaps legal lotteries were not such a sterling idea. But New Jersey unlocked the key to lottery prosperity: cheap tickets and frequent games. In December 1970, the Garden State unveiled a weekly lottery with 50-cent tickets and no registration requirement: a lottery for the convenience era. It was stupendously successful, raking in over $30 million in its first six months of operation. New York and New Hampshire both instituted weekly games, and within four years a range of states, including Connecticut, Pennsylvania, Massachusetts, Michigan, Illinois, Maine, and Ohio had leapt onto the lottery bandwagon, eager to tap into the suddenly rapid rush of lotto-dollars. In 1970, New York awarded the first million-dollar lottery jackpot, firing the imaginations of lottery players everywhere.

The first lotteries in New York and New Hampshire had been predicated on meeting an "unstimulated demand": The states would sell tickets, but they would not go out of their way to encourage citizens to buy them. These schemes were marginally successful at bringing in revenues and failed to cut into the play of illegal numbers. But now that states had tasted the possibilities of a well-run lottery, they soon moved to take on the numbers runners. In 1972 New Jersey began a daily lottery, and in 1975 it set up a legal three-digit daily game: a numbers racket for the computer age. By the middle of the decade, American lotteries were a billion-dollar business, and illegal numbers, though they survived (largely because winnings were tax free), were driven almost completely underground.

The growth spurt of the early 1970s was only a beginning. By the end of the decade nearly the entire northeastern United States was open to lotteries. In the 1980s the lottery moved west, as states from Iowa to California legalized games. The South, which had held out against lotteries until 1988, when Florida got into the business, joined the rest of the nation in the 1990s. By 2003, only eleven states in the Union lacked legal lotteries: Utah and Hawaii, alone among all the states, still barred all games of chance; Alaska had the

Nenana Ice Classic but no regular state lottery; Arkansas, Alabama, and North Carolina represented the last southern holdouts, and Nevada and Mississippi both had large, influential commercial casino industries that successfully scuttled lottery plans.

Critics charged that lotteries, though a voluntary tax, were a regressive levy on those who could least afford it. In many ways, they were right—during the antigambling hubbub of the early 1950s, antigamblers attacked numbers games as a cruel racket that returned barely half of its receipts to winners. State lotteries proportionally paid back even less, and winners also had to pay income tax on their jackpots. Lottery supporters rationalized that, despite worse odds, players benefited from larger jackpots (the multimillion-dollar payouts that became common to the lottery were unthinkable for numbers bankers) and the knowledge that their gambling dollars were supporting good works, ranging from school construction to programs for senior citizens.

Eager to avoid the political minefield of outright tax increases, states devised several new gambling schemes that they billed as lotteries. In 1974, the Massachusetts lottery introduced a latex-covered, scratch-off instant game. The first "scratcher" revolutionized lotteries. Even as critics charged that these "paper slot machines" could lead to dangerously uncontrolled gambling, scratchers, which allowed players the convenience of twenty-four-hour play and a measure of instant gratification (or disappointment) became ubiquitous.

Before rolling out scratchers, Massachusetts had experimented unsuccessfully with another lottery game: lotto. This was a variation of the game originally introduced by Andrea Doria in sixteenth-century Genoa and had remained popular in Europe. Instead of buying previously numbered tickets, players picked a series of numbers. At the drawing, numbered balls were drawn from a container, and players who matched all or some of the numbers could win varying amounts. Though the game sputtered in the Bay State, it was relaunched by New York in 1978. Players there quickly took to the game, which let them pick six numbers out of forty. The game went online with a network of computers in 1980, and soon awarded a $5 million jackpot. The lotto soon displaced draw games across the country as the top lottery pick, and many states just legalizing lotteries did not bother to start draw games: They simply rolled out lotto and instant games.

Other attempts to add to the lottery selection were not as successful. Attempts by Oregon and Delaware to incorporate sports betting into lottery games failed. Keno, the Nevada casino favorite, was launched in New York and Michigan in the mid-1980s, but failed to win over many players, as draws were infrequent and prizes relatively small. But lottery sales soared throughout the 1980s and 1990s, and lotto jackpots escalated. New York's $5 million payout had seemed astronomical in 1980; in 1982 New Jersey awarded a single $11.1 million jackpot. Less than a decade later, California set the bar even higher with a $118 million payoff.

Bigger jackpots enticed more players, which meant that lotteries could offer even larger jackpots, which drew in even more hopeful players. States realized that, along with spiffy marketing (most repackaged their lotto games periodically), sky-high jackpots were the best guarantee of continued sales. Combining their resources, states might be able to offer far bigger prizes than they could alone. In 1985, Maine, New Hampshire, and Vermont formed the Tri-State Lottery, which soon offered Tri-State Megabucks, a lotto game. Two years later, five states formed the Multistate Lottery Corporation, a body that eventually had twenty-three members. These states pooled their resources to offer a game called Lotto America, which at first required players to pick seven numbers from forty. Although tickets sold, the game barely covered the higher overhead of an interstate game.

In 1992, the Multistate Lottery Corporation put an end to Lotto America as the group introduced a new game, Powerball, which began as a "pick 5 out of 45, plus 1 out of 45" game with odds of more than 55 million to 1 against hitting the jackpot. Changes to the game's structure drove the odds up to 120 million to 1 against, but when the jackpots skyrocketed, players seemingly didn't mind. Multistate games lured players with jackpots that equaled the gross national income of smaller nations. In 2002, two winners (from Illinois and Michigan) split a $363 million Big Game jackpot. Had a single winner materialized, she would have earned more with that single ticket than the entire nation of Liberia did in all of 2003.

Winning the lottery was, for some, a pleasurable experience. For others, it proved to be more a burden than a windfall. After the IRS had taken a disappointing portion of the jackpot in taxes, many winners found themselves besieged by scam artists and a variety of petitioners in search of money for everything from medical care to cars. As prizes escalated to ridiculous levels, winning became an almost terrifying experience.

But for many lottery players winning is almost secondary to the ritual of buying tickets. Lottery merchants are in the business of selling hope—that hope rarely turns to wealth has done little to slow the rush of buyers, or stem the enthusiasm of public officials for this "painless" tax substitute.

17

A Place in the Sun

◆ ◆ ◆

THE STRIP IS BORN

In the 1930s, Las Vegas, Nevada, achieved national prominence. The construction and opening of nearby Hoover Dam early in the decade brought tourists and a must-see attraction. As war clouds darkened the horizon later in the decade, prospects for the city began to look up. The war would bring a jump in the city's population, as the nearby Basic Magnesium plant and Army Air Corps Gunnery School brought jobs and paychecks to the city. But even before the United States had entered World War II, the Las Vegas gambling landscape had been altered.

Though at the time it seemed like the opening of just another gambling hall, the debut of the El Rancho Vegas on April 3, 1941, signified the birth of the Las Vegas Strip and began the transition from smoky downtown gambling halls to verdant, luxurious suburban resorts. The El Rancho Vegas opened on the Los Angeles Highway (also known as Highway 91), which angled out of Las Vegas and meandered approximately three hundred miles, two lane and unpaved much of the way, southwest toward Los Angeles. Before the El Rancho Vegas, there had been a few roadhouses and nightclubs along the highway. One, Frank and Angela Detra's Pair-a-Dice, opened in 1930 and later became the 91 Club, while another, the Red Rooster, went through a series of owners. Similarly, there had been a range of roadhouses along the Boulder Highway (which, true to its name, led to Boulder City and Hoover Dam) during the 1930s. These rough nightspots catered mostly to dam workers, and when construction was complete, most of them folded. Had more visitors driven to Las Vegas from Arizona than California, the burst of development that took place on the Los Angeles Highway would probably have taken place on Boulder Highway, and Tony Cornero's Meadows would be remembered as a pioneering resort rather than the El Rancho Vegas.

The El Rancho Vegas was built after years of effort by local boosters to attract a genuine resort hotel for the city's downtown. Thomas Hull, a Californian who owned a small chain of El Rancho hotels, built one, but chose a parcel of land on Highway 91 just outside of city limits (San Francisco Street, today's Sahara Avenue), about three miles from downtown—to better attract the Angeleno tourist trade. Hull's complex had little in common with the city's previous hotels, like the Hotel Nevada/Sal Sagev (now the Golden Gate) and the Apache. Instead of bunching its rooms in a two- or three-story building whose ground floor housed a bar and casino—a steadfastly urban design—he built a sprawling complex: sixty-three rooms arranged in a series of separate bungalows surrounding a central building that had a casino, restaurant, and dinner theater. The casino resort—an isolated vacation palace in which gambling was only one of the attractions—was born.

Visitors to the El Rancho Vegas were not expected to just drop by for a shot of whiskey and a roll of the dice. Instead, the property was promoted as a full-service resort in which all of a guest's needs could be met effortlessly. During the day, guests might lounge by the pool or visit the health club for a massage or steam bath; at night, they could enjoy a fine meal and top-notch entertainment, all at a minimal cost. After the show, of course, they would gamble, and their losses would more than equal the casino's outlay on food,

The first casino resort built on Las Vegas's Highway 91, the El Rancho Vegas pioneered the integrated design that would become the hallmark of casinos along the Las Vegas Strip.

drink, and entertainment. The El Rancho Vegas began a Las Vegas tradition with its Chuck Wagon buffet (originally little more than cold cuts, but eventually to evolve into gourmet fare). As traditional urban gambling halls, be they illegal or legal, came to be regarded as hopelessly seedy, the idea of a casino as the centerpiece of a finely manicured vacation resort would dramatically change American attitudes toward gambling.

Almost immediately, Hull had competition. Later in 1941 a local partnership opened the El Cortez at 600 East Fremont Street, several blocks east of the train station and other gambling halls. Like the El Rancho Vegas, the El Cortez had a restaurant, and though it lacked a full-blown showroom it sported a cocktail lounge that became a popular entertainment venue. Its ninety hotel rooms made it one of the town's larger operations.* Another try at a downtown resort, the Nevada Biltmore, was less successful; opening in 1942 about six blocks north of the train station, like the Meadows it had a successful launch but ultimately sank; no other casino or hotel development took place near the Biltmore, and the resort closed in 1949.

After the Biltmore's failure, there were no other attempts to build big resorts downtown until the 1950s, when the resorts along the Los Angeles Highway had already shifted the center of the city's tourist economy south. Even in 1942, it was becoming apparent that the future lay there, as the El Rancho Vegas was doing tremendous business. That year it got a neighbor: the Hotel Last Frontier. It opened October 30 on the previous site of the 91 Club, which R.E. Griffith had bought from Guy McAfee. Built by Griffith and his nephew, Bill Moore (the family owned a string of movie theaters and hotels in the Southwest), this was a "luxury" casino resort similar to the El Rancho Vegas, but with a twist: It was a themed resort, Las Vegas's first.

Earlier gambling halls didn't have themes—they were simply bars with a few table games added. The El Rancho Vegas was decorated in a Western style but made little attempt to follow through on the idea, short of throwing a few cowboy hats on the walls. The Last Frontier was an entirely different creature: according to Moore, the architect, it was consciously designed to replicate the Old West, down to antiqued wood ceilings and sandstone patios. Moore transformed the existing 91 Club into the Carrillo Room lounge (named for Western movie actor Leo Carrillo) and installed the erstwhile bar of the old Arizona Club—one of Block 16's pioneering saloons from earlier in the century—as the centerpiece of the Gay Nineties Bar. But this genuine

---

*Today, the original structure is virtually intact and, minus two later high-rise tower additions, looks much the same as it did in the 1940s, when it was one of Las Vegas's most elegant attractions.

piece of saloon history wasn't authentic enough, so Moore added saddle-shaped barstools: Guests could not mistake that they had reentered the Old West.

The resort had the usual fixings (casino, bar, dinner theater, rooms, pool) but Moore felt it was incomplete. In 1947, he added the Last Frontier Village, a "genuine replica" of an old Western town with a drugstore, general store, post office, schoolhouse, and jail, a gambling hall (the Silver Slipper, which in 1951 opened as a separate casino within the village), and an assortment of artifacts collected by Robert "Doby Doc" Caudill, a gambler, collector of Western antiques, and Las Vegas institution.

Such a thoroughly themed casino was far ahead of its time, but Moore's choice of a theme left him in the past. In the 1930s and 1940s the city had promoted itself as the "Last Frontier" of the West, often using "The Old West in Modern Splendor" as a marketing catchphrase. Moore made that the resort's motto, though it became apparent, as new resorts pursued luxe rather than lassos, that the public was more interested in a sunny vacation in a lavish setting than reliving the Old West. In 1955 the Last Frontier made way for the New Frontier, a space-age hotel, and the Village eventually closed, though the Little Church of the West, once part of it, was transplanted to the southern end of the Strip, where it is still a wedding chapel today.

With the end of World War II, the floodgates opened. Tourists began discovering the pleasures of vacations in the resorts just outside Las Vegas, and developers hurried to grab a piece of this lucrative market. The next casino to open, the fabulous Flamingo, is notorious for its supposed founder, Ben Siegel. Some consider Siegel a brilliant visionary who saw limitless potential in a wasteland and successfully built and operated the city's first real casino. But there were already two flourishing casino resorts on the Los Angeles Highway when the Flamingo opened, and the idea for the resort did not come from Siegel, an unabashedly bloodthirsty gangster, but Billy Wilkerson, the suave, well-traveled publisher of the *Hollywood Reporter* and owner of several Los Angeles nightspots, including Ciro's and LaRue. Yet Wilkerson was a tragic genius: A brilliant publicist and tireless promoter, he was also, unfortunately, a self-described "degenerate pathological gambler." Urged by his friends, including 20th Century Fox cofounder Joe Schenck, to cure himself by building his own casino, Wilkerson eventually began building the "Flamingo Club" on a piece of land south of the Hotel Last Frontier.

As should have been expected from a man with severe gambling problems, Wilkerson soon ran out of money. Desperate to finish his project, he accepted an emergency infusion of capital from a group of "Eastern investors" who included

Siegel. Siegel, though he had little love for Las Vegas and no real experience in actually running a casino, much less building one, demanded a role in the decision-making process. At first deferring to Wilkerson, then merely tolerating him, Siegel eventually tired of the Flamingo's founder and, as the project's completion neared, delivered a chilling ultimatum: Wilkerson must surrender his share of the casino or suffer the consequences. Wilkerson was sufficiently awed by Siegel's reputation for violence that he hurried to the airport, flew to New York and then Paris, and checked into a room at the Hôtel George V under a pseudonym. Still apprehensive, he spent the next few weeks reading newspapers and listening nervously to each footstep outside his door.

Back in Las Vegas, Siegel seized total control of the project. He had already moved up Wilkerson's planned March 1, 1947, opening date to December 26, 1946. Though the hotel was not ready for guests, Siegel, desperate to begin generating a return on his investment, forged ahead with plans to throw open the doors of the casino and hope for the best. He capriciously changed the opening date to December 28, a Saturday, and mailed out formal invitations to an opening gala. Changing his mind again, he moved the date back to the twenty-sixth and ordered his staff to notify guests by phone. The opening was a disaster. A smattering of Hollywood B-listers showed up, but bad weather, poor timing, and Siegel's noisome reputation kept most of the stars in Los Angeles. Locals dressed in cowboy hats and boots made a mockery of Siegel's claims to have opened a chic cosmopolitan resort, and guests who won money from the tables, with no rooms at the Flamingo, returned to the accommodations at the El Rancho Vegas and Last Frontier, where they lost back money that should have stayed at the Flamingo. After less than a month, with the casino hemorrhaging cash, Siegel was forced to close the Flamingo's doors.

More concerned with prolonging his life than recouping the hundreds of thousands of dollars he'd invested in the Flamingo, Wilkerson sold his remaining interest in the property for pennies on the dollar. He returned to Hollywood, driving a bulletproof Cadillac that had once belonged to Tony Cornero. Receiving a tip that his life was still in danger, Wilkerson hastily returned to Paris to wait out the storm. Yet it was Siegel whose days were numbered. On June 20, 1947, while sitting in the living room of his mistress Virginia Hill, he was gunned down. According to popular lore, before the dust had even settled, Moe Sedway and Gus Greenbaum, representing the "syndicate" interests, confidently strode through the front doors of the Flamingo and assumed control of the operation.

The Siegel murder was never solved, triggering rampant speculation about who killed him, and why he was killed. The struggle over control of the racing wire had by then erupted into more or less open warfare in several cities, and at the time this was the most popular theory. Others have suggested that his involvement in a Mexican heroin-smuggling ring led to his murder. The possibility that his partners executed him for skimming construction money from the Flamingo only became more widespread after the growth of Las Vegas, and the gangster was enshrined as the mythic godfather of the city, even though he'd had no vision for the future of the business and was a washout as a casino operator.

Yet the Flamingo was, in the end, a success story. Purged of Siegel's vicious temper and mismanagement, it became a popular resort and one of the mainstays of the 1950s Las Vegas Strip. Underworld influence continued; in 1973 it was proved in federal court that operators had concealed alleged mob kingpin Meyer Lansky's part ownership of the casino and had been clandestinely funneling profits to him for years. Eventually, Hilton Hotels would buy the property and renovate it beyond recognition into a 3,500-room, six-tower colossus.* Though Wilkerson has been all but forgotten, the Hollywood operator ultimately found peace; after the birth of a son in 1951, he forswore gambling and, with few regrets, enjoyed a measure of happiness.

In a few years the Flamingo would be surpassed by an even swankier resort, the Desert Inn, a casino that proved to be a true pioneer. Its founder was Wilbur Clark, an affable gambling operator who had worked the national circuit of illegal casinos from Saratoga to San Diego. He had dreams of greatness (and chafed at the newfound intolerance in California for gambling) and moved to Las Vegas, where he bought into a score of gambling clubs, including the small Player's Club on the Los Angeles Highway. In 1945 he opened the downtown Monte Carlo Club on the site of the original Northern Club and bought a majority share of the El Rancho Vegas. In 1946 he sold both to begin building a predictably luxurious resort on the Los Angeles Highway.

Clark started with high hopes but soon ran out of funds. Midway through the project in 1949, desperate for capital and denied loans from traditional avenues, he turned to a group of Cleveland businessmen and gambling operators headed by Moe Dalitz. The group, which grew out of Cleveland's Mayfield Road Gang, also included Ruby Kolod, Morris Kleinman, and Sam

---

*In an attempt to cash in on its past, the modern Flamingo has adopted Siegel as its creator and has plastered his name on a theater, a deli, and most of its promotional material, with no mention of Wilkerson.

Tucker. All of these men had made livings as bootleggers or illegal gambling operators and were rumored to have ties to the criminal underworld. In return for over $1.3 million in capital, the Cleveland group received a seventy-four-percent interest in the casino. Now decades removed from the lawless Prohibition years, the members of the Dalitz syndicate hoped to find in Las Vegas one thing that their various enterprises could not give them in the East: respectability.

When the casino finally opened in 1950, Moe Dalitz was clearly in charge, though Clark's name remained on the marquee. All-star entertainers graced the Painted Desert room and gamblers filled the casino. With its three hundred guest rooms, a lavish casino, and the third-floor Skyroom lounge, the casino was an immediate hit. Clark proved an affable host and become the goodwill ambassador not just of the Desert Inn but of Las Vegas itself. Meanwhile, Dalitz and his associates, particularly his manager, Allard Roen, a sharp, college-educated star on the rise, planned to make Las Vegas more than a gambling haunt: They wanted to transform it into one of America's leading vacation resorts. The addition of the Desert Inn golf course in 1952 gave the Strip its first eighteen-hole golf course, drawing an entirely new class of wealthy vacationers to Las Vegas. The construction of the Desert Inn Estates, country club homes around the course, was an early attempt at residential living on the Strip. The Desert Inn lit the way for the development of a stretch of roadway that would, in a few short years, become truly world famous.

By the time that the Desert Inn Golf Course opened, the Los Angeles Highway was no longer merely a conduit to downtown but a destination in and of itself. Its name was hardly appropriate, and in the early 1950s civic boosters threw around several alternatives. Highway 91, the road's official designation, was even less alluring than "Los Angeles Highway." Others proposed the "Great White Way" or "Gay White Way," referencing the neon signs that now lit the desert sky in abundance. In the mid-1940s, Guy McAfee, nostalgic perhaps for Los Angeles, began facetiously calling the empty stretch of roadway between his 91 Club and downtown the Strip, after the famous Sunset Strip. The name caught on, and as resorts and their brightly lit signs filled in the once-desolate length of road, people forgot that it was originally a joke. By 1952, "Las Vegas Strip" had become the accepted name for the street. When Highway 91 officially became Las Vegas Boulevard on January 1, 1959, the transformation of the Los Angeles Highway into the Las Vegas Strip was complete.

The Strip would become a constantly changing landscape as, over the next several decades, casino operators competed to build the biggest, most expensive, and flashiest of everything. Swimming pool wars were followed by competition for star headliners. The Las Vegas Strip became famous as a place where average vacationers could holiday in supreme leisure, enjoying bountiful food and drink, abundant sunshine, and premium entertainment at minimum cost, so long as they gambled for a while. Gambling became a fun and, thanks to a nostalgia for the Wild West, even all-American activity, a far cry from its image elsewhere as a vice-ridden, crooked racket.

The new palatability of gaming was evident as early as 1955, when five new resorts debuted. The Royal Nevada opened on April 19, followed by the Riviera the very next day. The Royal Nevada struggled from the start and failed spectacularly; accused of cheating, it closed permanently in 1958.* The Riviera, the Strip's first high-rise at nine stories, also ran into immediate money problems (it had vastly overpaid opening headliner Liberace) but weathered the storm, becoming one of the Strip's most enduring properties after being taken over the by the group that owned the Flamingo. Despite fears that the Strip was overcrowded, the openings continued, with the New Frontier, a space-age themed resort, opening on the site of the Last Frontier. The Dunes rose from the desert near the Flamingo, its unimposing structure festooned with a mammoth papier-mâché sultan that beckoned ominously. The Dunes collapsed early and was soon taken over by the managers of the Sands, one of the bedrock properties of the growing Strip.

While the Riviera and Dunes ultimately survived, the real groundbreaking resort of 1955 did not. Following what had become a Las Vegas custom so entrenched that many believed it to be the law, Strip resorts did not admit African-Americans as guests and permitted them to work in only a narrow range of low-paying jobs. (This gave the lie to the promotion of the Strip as a playground for "everyone" and was unfortunately common in a nation then plagued by racial segregation.) Even superstar black entertainers who packed the Strip's showrooms were starkly informed that they could not stay at the hotel or walk through the public areas. Some, like Sammy Davis, Jr., and Lena Horne, challenged this affront, but, steadfast in the belief that it was what their white customers wanted, Strip resorts uniformly refused to accommodate black would-be patrons.

The Moulin Rouge sought to break the Las Vegas color line. Opening in

---

*After it closed, the Royal Nevada was incorporated into the neighboring Stardust.

1955 on West Bonanza Road (far from the Strip and downtown), the Moulin Rouge was primarily owned by whites (though boxer Joe Louis had a nominal share and served as a host) but advertised itself as a "cosmopolitan" resort—a well-known code-word for integrated. A full-service, Strip-style resort, it quickly became one of the city's most popular destinations, and musicians, black and white, famously patronized the lounge after finishing their shows on the Strip. Despite its popularity, it was undercapitalized and it closed within a year, and, though it periodically reopened, never again became a signature Las Vegas destination. Despite the Moulin Rouge's popularity, other resorts would not end segregation until 1960, when integration was clearly becoming the law of the land throughout the nation. It was an opportunity missed.

The 1955 financial problems—and the possibility of organized-crime control over casinos—caused real anxiety for Nevadans. In 1952, commercial gambling had eclipsed both mining and agriculture to become Nevada's biggest revenue producer. Not only casino owners and employees, but the entire state was tied to the economic well-being of the casinos. Should the industry lose public confidence or trigger federal prohibitory regulation—a very real concern in the 1950s—all would be lost. As early as 1945, the legislature had signaled the increasing importance of gaming by passing for the first time a direct levy on gaming revenue: The state was to receive one percent of gross winnings. The state Tax Commission, rather than local sheriffs, was placed in charge of collecting the new tariff.

The two challenges facing Nevada were to guarantee the fiscal strength of the gaming industry and to promote its image as a clean, honest business. In 1955, the legislature created the Gaming Control Board, a division of the Tax Commission, which would "eliminate the undesirables in Nevada gaming" and oversee the licensing and operation of casinos. This new board had three full-time members appointed by the governor and a staff of auditors, investigators, and office workers. The legislature hiked state license fees to pay for the work of this body, which was to research applicants for licenses and ensure that casinos followed all industry regulations and otherwise upheld the good name of the state. In 1959, the legislature moved the Gaming Control Board from the Tax Commission. Under the aegis of a new body, the Gaming Commission (a five-member governor-appointed body that adopted regulations governing the gaming industry), the Control Board issued and revoked licenses, imposed fines and penalties for infractions of gaming regulations, and collected all state gaming fees. The Control Board continued to serve as the state's investigatory and auditing arm.

With the establishment of stronger regulatory oversight, the casino industry was placed on a much more solid political footing. Yet if the crisis of 1955 proved to be permanent, there would be little development. With fewer than ten thousand guest rooms in resorts, hotels, and motels throughout the region, naysayers began to lament that Las Vegas had been overbuilt. In a sense they were right: The resorts had just about tapped the limits of the available vacation market. The hotels were filled over the weekend, but during the week they were frightfully destitute of guests. It seemed that the growth was at a standstill.

But casino operators realized that the Strip could be more than just a weekend playground, and they worked together to pursue another breed of traveler: the conventioneer. Starting in the late 1950s, resorts began adding convention facilities to attract meetings of professional and fraternal organizations, which were burgeoning with the expanding economy. In 1959, the Las Vegas Convention Center opened. This collaboration between the casinos was funded by taxes on guest rooms. Its location, just off the Strip on then-vacant Paradise Road, was the final proof of the shift away from downtown. One of the area's biggest visitor attractions, the Las Vegas Convention Center, was not even in the city of Las Vegas but was, like the rest of the Strip resorts, comfortably perched on county land.

Casinos outdid each other in promoting Las Vegas as a place where visitors could "get more done, then have more fun" (the convention center's official slogan). When legal gambling began in the state, few thought that gambling halls would, within thirty years, happily cater to automobile dealers, insurance professionals, Rotarians, or any of the other groups that chose to meet at Strip casinos. But, thanks to the changing perceptions of gambling, the broadening commercial availability of jet travel, and the effervescent promotion of Las Vegas as a safe, fun adult adventure land, the Strip became solidly Middle America. Casinos sponsored bridge tournaments, golf games, and other recreational activities more suited to suburban tract homes than smoky gambling halls.

The successful addition of business travelers allowed resorts to remain filled during the week. As their bottom lines improved, casinos expanded, adding at first new low-rise wings and, by the 1960s, hotel towers. They also pursued star entertainers with greater gusto. Though virtually every casino was famous as the haunt of one celebrity or another, one casino raced to the head of the pack, as it were, and made itself the undisputed cool capital of Las Vegas, if not the world: the Sands.

The Sands, which opened in 1952, was owned by a group of investors who included Texas gambler Jake Freedman and New Yorkers Carl Cohen and Jack Entratter. Entratter, who served as entertainment director of the resort, had owned the Manhattan's Copacabana lounge and used his show business connections to help put the Sands, known as "A Place in the Sun," on the map. The resort owed much of its eminence to its most famous entertainer, Frank Sinatra, who caroused onstage and off with his friends—the press dubbed the group the Rat Pack—and drew throngs of admirers to the casino. Sinatra had long since reestablished himself as one of the music world's top talents, and though his records didn't sell nearly as well as those of Elvis Presley or, later, the Beatles, Entratter was interested in more than the box office receipts. Sinatra drew a relatively affluent, middle-aged crowd with money to spend and a sense of fun—the ideal casino patron.

Together with Dean Martin and Sammy Davis, Jr., Sinatra epitomized cool for legions of fans. Supplemented with Joey Bishop, Peter Lawford, and whoever happened to show up, the big three held court at the Sands's Copa Room for much of the early to mid-1960s. While filming the quintessential casino heist movie, *Ocean's Eleven,* in 1960, the Rat Packers worked on the film in the afternoon and performed two shows each evening before drinking, gambling, and carousing all night. They defined the Las Vegas Strip for a generation.

The Las Vegas Strip of the Copa Era, the years of the Rat Pack's greatest prominence (all would continue individually as top casino showroom draws for the rest of their careers) was a far different place than it had been just a few years earlier. In 1960, after threatened public protests by the local black leaders, the Strip resort operators agreed to abandon segregationist policies; almost immediately they began organizing events to cater to black visitors. Dr. James McMillan, who as president of the local NAACP had, more than anyone else, spearheaded the integration effort, later recalled that the hotels settled for business reasons: Fearful that the bad publicity would scare off convention bookings, they quickly gave in. "Money moves the world," McMillan said. "When these fellows realized that they weren't going to lose money, that they might even make more, they were suddenly colorblind." The civil rights leader was right: The Strip casinos prospered in the 1960s by creating a gambling scene where everyone felt welcome and where everyone's money was as good as everyone else's.

Casino operators on the Las Vegas Strip excelled at promoting their resorts to casual gamblers and neophytes more interested in the dinner theater than the craps odds. But as vacationing receptionists and clerks stepped up to the tables, another breed of visitor often blended with them: the serious gambler.

These players could be professionals who made their living by winning games of chance and skill (fairly or not), or they might be amateurs who believed they had found a winning system. Since François Blanc, casino managers had scoffed at and even encouraged systems players, knowing that games like roulette and craps, in which each decision was independent of all previous decisions, were ultimately impregnable. But as the Rat Pack was wowing audiences at the Sands, genius gamblers (and those who imitated them) proved a growing concern for casino bosses.

John Scarne was the most celebrated expert gambler of the twentieth century. Born to Maria and Fiorangelo Scarnecchia in Niles, Ohio, in 1903, he grew up in Fairview, New Jersey. Coming of age during the 1920s, he decided early on that he would use his incredible skills in service of the public good rather than for illicit private gain. So while Tony Cornero and Ben Siegel were bootlegging whiskey and sponsoring illegal casinos, Scarne was perfecting card manipulation. Practicing all of the dark arts of bottom dealing, false shuffling, and card crimping, from the age of fourteen Scarne worked six hours a day on improving his game.

Had he wished, he could have been a master cheat. Instead, he worked as a professional magician before finding his true calling: educating the public about crooked gambling. He first became famous during World War II, when he served as a consultant to the American armed forces and lectured GIs on the wiles of fraudulent gamblers. He started by sending letters of advice to friends and neighbors who had been drafted and was soon hired by Special Services to educate servicemen. Scarne's message was one perfect for a nation that was becoming increasingly tolerant of gambling: The activity itself was not bad, but one had to be careful not to be made a sucker. This was the same approach that the state of Nevada adopted toward gambling by regulating it to ensure an honest reputation.

After the war, Scarne's star shone even brighter. He traveled the world, speaking before rapt audiences and helping train casino staffs from Las Vegas to Cuba (he unwillingly witnessed the Cuban Revolution while advising the Habana Hilton about card cheats). His expertise in trickery and sleight of hand helped him become a master debunker, exposing not only card and dice mechanics but all manner of frauds, including those who duped the public with tales of extrasensory perception and mind reading (he famously exposed "Lady Wonder," a reputed mind-reading horse). He was proudest of his own feats of mental ingenuity: He invented several games (though none became popular). With a reputation as the "Einstein of games," his books on cards, dice, tricks, and gambling sold well, and by educating the public about crooked games, he did a great deal to increase their comfort with square ones.

Scarne was famous for his gambling expertise, but he was not renowned as a gambler. Those famous for gambling in the early part of the century, though they styled themselves as "sportsmen," were still viewed as unsavory; given master gambler Arnold Rothstein's reported fixing of the World Series, one can understand why. But with the legitimatization of gambling, famous gamblers became almost heroic figures. Perhaps the most celebrated, and possibly the most tragic, gambling legend was Nick "the Greek" Dandolos. Born in 1883 in Crete to a wealthy family, he came to the United States at the age of eighteen, though he soon moved to Montreal and began to bet on horse races. He later transferred his play to gaming tables and by the 1920s was famous for his betting; it was said that he had broken the bank at Monte Carlo and was the only man who could consistently beat Arnold Rothstein.

Rothstein liked betting, but as his 1919 World Series fix showed, he preferred a sure thing. Dandolos, on the other hand, emerged as a champion of gambling for gambling's sake, often stating that the next best thing to playing and winning was playing and losing. "The play's the thing," he would say, a perfect message as gambling became less of a vice than a diversion. If measured by sheer dollar amount, Dandolos might have been the biggest gambler in history: He claimed to have had more than $500 million pass through his hands as he won and lost money at the tables and tracks, and estimated he had gone from wealthy to busted no fewer than seventy-three times. He lived for years in a $10 Las Vegas hotel room, becoming something of a local landmark; tourists would point and gawk at the Greek, who gambled for days on end, subsisting on little more than orange juice, chicken sandwiches, and cigars. Though he remained an institution to the end, dazzling fellow players by quoting Plato and Aristotle (he had majored in philosophy), Dandolos eventually found himself losing more than he won, and by his final days he was reduced to playing penny-ante games in southern California card rooms. Yet at his death in 1966 newspapers recounted his glory years, when he sent suits to the cleaner's with tens of thousands of dollars still hidden in them and was as much of a star at Las Vegas casinos as their headline entertainers.

Dandolos, like another Nick the Greek, the European baccarat-playing Greek Syndicate's Zographos (there have been countless Nick the Greeks, just as there have been innumerable Honest John Kellys), was celebrated mostly for his endurance and bankroll. He did not claim to have any mathematical knowledge greater than an appreciation for the game odds; he simply bet when the odds against him were at their least and hoped for the best. Unlike Scarne, he was not an "expert gambler" but a notorious one. Scarne, knowing enough of the odds to realize that the percentage always lay with the house, excelled as an ambassador for honest play but was not particularly celebrated as a gambler. Expert opinion and serious gambling, it seemed, did not quite mix.

The mathematical study of blackjack would merge deep thought with high action. Using computer simulations and mathematical theory to unlock the secrets of blackjack—the one casino game uniquely open to system play—a new generation of expert gamblers in the 1960s would elevate it into the most widely played table game in the nation.

Blackjack skill play is feasible because the game is played with a finite series of cards. In craps, the previous throw of the dice has absolutely no bearing on the next one, but in blackjack, previous hands have a direct bearing on future draws. If all the aces have been played, for example, the player has no chance of getting a "natural" blackjack (an ace and a ten-value card), which usually pays three to two. For more than a century, blackjack flew under the casino radar. While enthusiasts and dilettantes tried to break the bank at Monte Carlo with roulette betting systems, blackjack remained a relatively unimportant game.

As blackjack became more popular in Nevada gambling halls in the 1930s, bettors started to develop systems to help them track which cards had been played. They were the first card counters. Since the conventional wisdom held that betting systems were doomed to fail, given the inexorable house advantage, most casino managers laughed off claims that blackjack could be beaten. The mathematics behind early card-counting systems often being shaky, the casino bosses were usually right. Through the 1950s, card counting remained something of an occult science, known only to a few initiates and not particularly reliable.

But card counting became a very real threat to casino revenues thanks to the work of a University of California, Los Angeles, mathematics Ph.D., Edward O. Thorp. Thorp became a blackjack expert by chance: Though he was not a gambler, during a break from his teaching duties at UCLA in the late 1950s he and his wife chose to spend a few days in Las Vegas to enjoy the shows, inexpensive food, and swimming pools. They were like millions of Americans who were increasingly drawn to Las Vegas for more than gambling. Before the trip, a fellow professor directed him to a 1956 article on card counting from the *Journal of the American Statistical Association*. Titled "Optimum Strategy in Blackjack," it claimed to offer a way to limit the house edge, usually assumed to be over 2 percent, to .62 percent. Thorp tested their system "under fire" with lukewarm results (he lost $8.50).

Still, Thorp was intrigued and, upon returning home, used an IBM 704 computer to help him devise a better strategy, one that he christened "basic strategy." Simply by using this guide on when to hit and stand, Thorp found that the house's edge could be shaved to .21 percent. But he went even farther: Players who could successfully keep track of cards already played could take advantage of "favorable conditions" and actually gain an advantage over the dealer. At last, it seemed, the house would not always win.

Theoretically, Thorp's system was sound: The more high-value cards that remained in the shoe, the higher probability that the dealer, forced to draw to seventeen, would bust. By keeping a running count of high-value cards, Thorp estimated that he could gain an advantage of up to 15 percent. And he was no armchair strategist: Backed by investors, he took $10,000 to Las Vegas and put his system into action. He successfully doubled his bankroll, though casinos, suddenly wary of his winning ways, inaugurated disruptive tactics, including constant reshuffling and possibly, in one instance, a cheating dealer.

When Thorp published his system and an account of his winning field test in *Beat the Dealer* (1962), card counting became an instant phenomenon. A variety of systems soon emerged; everyone with access to a computer claimed to have developed a new, improved, guaranteed method for beating casino blackjack. Most of these were variations on Thorp's basic premise, tracking high- and low-value cards. The simplest system requires the player to give low cards (2, 3, 4, 5, 6) a value of +1, ten-value cards and aces a value of −1, and 7s, 8s, and 9s zero value. When the count is high, a player is more likely to win and should bet accordingly.

Though feasible, card counting was not foolproof. Many who tried to master counting simply lacked the concentration and quick recall necessary. In addition, casinos could easily thwart counters by arbitrarily reshuffling the cards or simply barring suspected "skill" players. Though, as places of public accommodation, casinos are forbidden to discriminate based on race, gender, handicap, or nationality, as private businesses they are allowed to refuse service at will. Thus, even though they might have a foolproof system, the deck was usually stacked against counters.

Despite the unfavorable odds, many would-be casino beaters were entranced by the mathematical certainty of winning that the card counting, if done correctly, promised. In order to frustrate casino countermeasures and to allow bigger bets by starting with a larger bankroll, team play emerged in the early 1970s. Its most famous exponent was Ken Uston, a math prodigy, Harvard MBA, and former vice president of the Pacific Stock Exchange, who, like many others, became interested in blackjack after reading *Beat the Dealer*.

In March 1974, Al Francesco, leader of a San Francisco–based blackjack team, recruited Uston. The team made money by a simple division of labor. On a typical night, it sent several card counters into a casino; each of them bet the table minimum and, using an "advanced point count" system, quietly kept track of the table's favorability. When the player's edge was strong enough, using a series of prearranged signals the counter would call over the B.P. (Big Player), who would then bet the table limit. The system worked until casino surveillance started to recognize the players' teamwork. Then, players adopted disguises and otherwise attempted to outwit casino managers, surveillance teams, and independent consultants hired to combat skill play. When he went public with his role as a "Big Player," Uston became a blackjack celebrity. Claiming to have made millions from blackjack tables in Nevada and Atlantic City, he was ultimately barred from nearly every casino in the country. He fought unsuccessfully to challenge his banishment before his death in 1987 at the age of fifty-two.

Though blackjack lost a true original with the passing of the flamboyant Uston, the idea of team play remained. The most famous blackjack team since Uston's group is the MIT card-counting team. There have actually been several counting groups affiliated with that prestigious university, but they remained relatively obscure until the 2002 book *Bringing Down the House,* in which Ben Mezrich told the story of "Kevin Lewis," a member of the early to mid-1990s edition of the team who spoke of millions of dollars in profits. Though the story was hardly revolutionary, it introduced a new generation of young players to the thrill of team play, and may have contributed to a boom in blackjack play among younger casino patrons.

As the popularity of Las Vegas soared, casinos became paradoxically both more extravagant and more egalitarian. As the booming postwar prosperity gave Americans more free time and discretionary spending, many of them chose to vacation or meet for business at the sunny suburban casino resorts of the Strip. Yet competition for customers remained fierce, and casinos pursued two strategies to lure them in: they spent lavishly on headline entertainers like Frank Sinatra, Liberace, and Nat "King" Cole, and they staged a series of increasingly outrageous publicity stunts.

Despite their reputations as pleasure palaces, the casinos of the 1950s and 1960s were, for the most part, bland, nondescript hotels with nightclubs and casinos simply tacked on: They were comfortable but hardly breathtaking. But something more grandiose was on the horizon. Jay Sarno, an accomplished developer, emerged as a visionary who brought to Las Vegas a resort where every man and woman was a Caesar, surrounded by luxury.

Sarno was already a successful motel operator: His Palo Alto Cabana had been named the most outstanding motel in the United States, and the entire chain of Cabana motels won awards for its design and service. Throughout the 1950s, he refined his architectural ideas, so much so that the Palo Alto Cabana was a scaled-down version of the eventual Caesars Palace. Stopping frequently in Las Vegas to gamble, Sarno was appalled by the blandness of the Strip resorts and, borrowing amply from the Teamsters Central States Pension Fund, started building a hotel and casino that lived up to his standards.* He placed water features and statues abundantly throughout the property and revived the idea of the themed casino, bringing back to life Ancient Rome. Even the stationery had the appearance of slightly burnt parchment. Traversing the long driveway, passing Greco-Roman-inspired fountains, guests left behind the ordinary world of mortgages and punch clocks and entered a fantasy world where they could be Caesar, Cleopatra, or whoever they wished. Despite his focus on luxury, Sarno built a solidly business-friendly resort. Caesars Palace opened in 1966 as a full-service convention resort, and its managers were just as enthused to sign the National Milk Producers as convention guests as they were to land Frank Sinatra in their showroom, the aptly named Circus Maximus.

Having built the quintessential high-end resort, Sarno was not content. His next project was an attempt to bring the excitement of a circus to the Las Vegas Strip. Circus Circus rejected the well-established model of the integrated casino resort. Sarno hoped that as a stand-alone casino, Circus Circus would be innovative enough to thrive, at least until he had the finances to add hotel rooms. Most other resorts were so unimpressive, Sarno thought, that patrons would be naturally drawn to the unique casino, which was arrayed under a permanent pink-and-white big top.

Other casinos suggested exotic locales with names like Tropicana and Riviera and let their guests' imaginations do the rest; not so for Sarno, who insisted that Circus Circus in fact be a working circus. He scoured big tops for acts and turned the casino's second floor into a carnival midway, with games and prizes galore. Honest John Kelly would have felt right at home pitching his knife game to passersby. Circus acts performed above the gaming pits,

---

*The Teamsters, under the leadership of Jimmy Hoffa, had recently become a prime source for casino capital, and they financed expansions at many Strip casinos. They had previously lent Sarno the capital for his Dallas and Atlanta Cabanas.

When it opened in 1966, Jay Sarno's Caesars Palace took lavish casino theming to an entirely new level. It quickly became one of the world's most famous casinos, and one that certain gambling-obsessed Roman emperors would have been glad to visit.

much to the consternation—and distraction—of players. Tanya, an elephant who could pull slot-machine handles and play keno, entertained visitors but was an operational liability; for years she stank up the employee dining room, located uncomfortably near her quarters.

Like many other visionaries, Sarno was not successful in all his inspirations. Opening in 1968 without a hotel, Circus Circus struggled. It did not help that Sarno actually charged admission to the casino, a common practice in Europe but anathema along the come-as-you-are Strip. Circus Circus was undeniably innovative but often unbalanced, much like Sarno. He gambled away millions in the late 1960s and early 1970s and was renowned as a lover of women, much to the chagrin of his wife, Joyce, who divorced him in 1974. Despite a rotund physique, he was an avid golfer, though not much of a health nut: His idea of a diet was to breakfast on filet mignon instead of salami.

Sarno was more successful as a casino designer than an operator. He sold Caesars Palace to the Florida-based eatery chain Lum's in 1969; Lum's would eventually discard its restaurant business and rename itself Caesars World. Over the next two decades, Caesars would become one of the most instantly recognizable names in gaming. In 1974, Sarno finally abandoned Circus Circus, selling it to William Bennett (no relation to the future secretary of education) and William Pennington. Bennett and Pennington retained Sarno's general idea of a circus casino but made it more manageable, confining the circus acts to the Midway level (out of sight of the serious gamblers) and eschewing high rollers for middle-market gamblers. Adding several hotel towers and an RV park, they made Circus Circus a top destination for budget-minded family vacationers. Though Sarno's final vision—the Grandissimo, a six-thousand-room resort replete with waterfalls and roller coasters—was never built, it would brilliantly foreshadow the super-resorts of the 1990s. Sarno was simply ahead of his time.

As Sarno was building Circus Circus, an unlikely benefactor was buying up much of the Las Vegas Strip. Howard Robard Hughes had parlayed his inheritance from a father who invented an essential oil drill bit into careers as an aviator, a Hollywood producer, and speculative businessman. By the fall of 1966, Hughes was flush with $566 million that he had received for selling his TWA stock as part of a court-ordered settlement and looking for a home that would afford him both privacy and shelter from taxes. Nevada fit the bill well; he already owned property there but decided (possibly in order to avoid process servers; he was still heavily embroiled in litigation) that he needed less permanent digs.

Following a cross-country ride in a sealed rail car, Hughes arrived in Las Vegas in the predawn hours of November 27, 1966. Stopping the train outside of town, he was taken by van to the Desert Inn, where he had reserved the entire ninth floor of the St. Andrews Tower. Once there, he comfortably took up residence, running his empire through his right hand, Robert Maheu, with whom he communicated only by memo or telephone. By the time New Year's Eve was approaching, Moe Dalitz and the Desert Inn's managers were anxious to see the Hughes party leave; they were by this time taking up two floors that should, by rights, be reserved for gamblers. With plenty of excess cash from the TWA settlement, Hughes instructed Maheu to negotiate for the purchase of the resort. On March 22, 1967, Maheu sealed the deal; at a cost of $13.2 million, Howard Hughes owned one of the Strip's most storied resorts and could stay put.

Seeing an easy way to convert his taxable TWA settlement cash into nontaxable income-earning properties, Hughes instructed Maheu to buy indiscriminately: The tally of Strip purchases included the Sands (which Frank Sinatra soon quit because of personal animosity with Hughes, to take up residence at Caesars Palace), the Frontier (a Western-themed resort that replaced the New Frontier in 1967), the Silver Slipper (part of the old Last Frontier Village), and the Castaways. He also bought the unopened Landmark, which would consistently struggle from its ill-timed 1969 opening to its 1995 implosion. Hughes also bought Harolds Club in Reno, Las Vegas's CBS affiliate KLAS-TV, vast Nevada mining claims that proved to be worthless, and much of the available real estate in and around the Las Vegas Strip. He eventually employed over eight thousand, making him the state's biggest employer.

Hughes has been hailed by some as "the man who saved Nevada" and brought reputability to the gaming industry by buying out the "mobbed-up" syndicates, but in fact he did little to alter the trajectory of the casino business. None of his acquisitions became particularly successful after his purchase. In fact, in 1969 Hughes's Nevada portfolio produced a net loss of $8.4 million. Although he spent much of 1967 and 1968 planning to build a supersonic jet airport that, he believed, would make Nevada the transportation hub of the American West, the terminal was never built. Much of his energy seems to have been wasted on ultimately unachievable goals. The Landmark, for example, which he bought against the advice of Moe Dalitz, was never profitable. In an age when the boundaries of the casino resort were pushed beyond imagination, he built nothing and changed little in the way his casinos were run. When, on Thanksgiving 1970, he was bundled down the Desert Inn fire escape and into a plane bound for the Bahamas, his Nevada empire continued running on autopilot. His Las Vegas real estate empire, which has yielded the master-planned community of Summerlin, much of Green Valley, and several other prominent areas of the growing city, has become his enduring legacy

At the time, the public was largely unaware of his growing personal eccentricities, and he was hailed as one of the most powerful forces in American business; he was still thought of as the dashing aviator of the 1930s. Yet he stood against most of the trends that would soon transform the Strip: He opposed corporate ownership and wrote a letter to Robert Maheu discountenancing the degeneration of Las Vegas into "a freak, or amusement-park category, like Coney Island." He wished to retain an image of the Las Vegas of the 1940s: a small, somewhat exclusive resort town that catered chiefly to gambling habitués and wealthy leisure-seekers. The onrushing democratization of the casino landscape simply disgusted him. And for all his millions, not even Howard Hughes could change the growing accessibility of Las Vegas casinos or the American public's burgeoning love affair with gambling. Las Vegas resorts were now more circus than cocktail party, and people couldn't get enough of them.

As the Strip opened up into America's adult playland, downtown Las Vegas grew as well, though in a profoundly different direction. Home to gambling clubs since the city's founding in 1905, it soon hosted a few full-blown casino hotels as well. The 1932 Apache and 1941 El Cortez had hotel rooms, but they were hardly palatial. With downtown already crowded, if there were to be resorts that could compete with the Strip, they would have to build up. In 1956, the Fremont, a fifteen-story hotel and casino, did just that. The Mint, which had opened in 1957 as a small gambling club, added a twenty-six-story tower in 1965 and became famous for sponsoring the Mint 400, an epic desert off-road race.* The Union Plaza, which opened in 1971 on the former site of the train depot, was even larger, and it made history when in 1975 it inaugurated the first modern casino sports book. Despite these advances, though, downtown would become famous as a throwback to a time when the stakes were high and gambling, not showrooms or pools, was the center of action.

This back-to-basics approach of downtown found its purest expression in the World Series of Poker. It was based on a simple concept: Get the best poker players in the world, offer them a gigantic purse, and let them ante and fold until only the champion remained. The World Series was hosted by gambling legend Benny Binion. Born in Pilot Grove, Texas, in 1904, Binion grew up during Prohibition and developed an early love for gambling. He moved from numbers and policy operations (dabbling along the way in bootlegging) to illegal dice games in the 1930s. Suspected of several murders, Binion backed the wrong side in a 1946 Dallas election and, with his political protection gone, moved to Las Vegas.

Once there, Binion bought an interest in J. Kell Houssels's Las Vegas Club. After Houssels moved the Las Vegas Club across Fremont Street to its current location, Binion opened the Westerner. In 1951 he acquired the Eldorado, which was on the ground floor of the Apache Hotel. He renamed it the Horseshoe, installed a carpet, and set a policy designed to attract diehard gamblers: The Horseshoe would have the highest limits in town. Where most casinos had an upper threshold of $50 on craps bets, Binion accepted wagers as high as $500 and would usually waive even this, declaring that a customer's first bet was his limit. This ran entirely against the grain. Generally speaking, casinos prefer lower betting limits; forcing patrons to spread out their bets gives the inherent house edge more chances to work. Binion, a gambler at heart, brooked little talk of percentages and instead reasoned that, as a gambling-hall owner, he was in the business of taking wagers.

With Benny's policy firmly established, the Horseshoe saw some of the largest bets ever recorded. In 1980, William Lee Bergstrom, nicknamed "the

---

*Hunter S. Thompson, assigned by *Rolling Stone* to write photo captions for the 1971 Mint 400, was inspired by his experiences to write *Fear and Loathing in Las Vegas*.

Phantom Gambler," staked $777,000 on the "don't pass" line and won. He gathered his winnings and returned to Austin, where he owned an apartment building. Early in 1984, he won $538,000 at a similar bet, and in November of that year he placed $1 million on the "don't pass" line—the biggest single bet in Nevada history—and lost. After a breakup with his male lover in February 1985, he committed suicide, and was eulogized by Benny Binion's son Ted as "the biggest bettor of all time."

Binion's fame as a casino owner did not shield him from ongoing troubles with the law. He was forced to sell Binion's in 1953 to finance his legal battles. After serving three years in Leavenworth federal prison for tax evasion, Binion returned to Las Vegas in 1957 and reacquired the Horseshoe, though he could not get his license back. Instead, his sons Jack and Ted officially owned and operated the casino, while Binion the Elder was merely listed as a consultant. But with a booth in the basement coffee shop for an office and a handshake for a guarantee, the Horseshoe remained Benny's house.

The inspiration for a poker tournament at Binion's dates back to 1949. Super-gambler Nick "the Greek" Dandolos couldn't find a poker game rich enough for his blood (he wanted a no-limit game against a single opponent), and Binion offered to get him suitable competition on one condition: that the game be played in public. Binion called his old friend Johnny Moss, a well-traveled Texas road gambler (some of his peers included Doyle Brunson, Sailor Roberts, and "Amarillo Slim" Preston). Moss was a tough customer and usually carried a revolver and a shotgun to deter would-be thieves; hijacking was an occupational peril for road gamblers of the era. He quickly caught a flight to Las Vegas. Binion placed a table near the entrance to his casino, anticipating hundreds of spectators.

On a Sunday afternoon in January, Moss (a no-limit specialist) and Dandolos greeted each other with a handshake and sat down to play. For the next five months, Binion had an attraction that put all others to shame. The pair played four or five days nonstop, pausing only then for sleep, though Dandolos spent most of his off-time at the craps tables; he was then at the peak of his powers. They started by playing five-card stud and later switched to lowball deuce to seven (in which the player with the lowest hand wins) and high-draw poker. At one point, the crowd gaped with awe when Dandolos won a half-million-dollar pot by calling Moss's bluff and winning with a jack in the hole—possibly the largest documented single hand of poker ever played in a public game to that point. During five months of marathon play, the irascible Texan gradually wore the cool Greek down. Watching Moss sweep in his last chips, Dandolos politely said, "Mr. Moss, I have to let you go," and rose from the table, an estimated $2 million poorer.

In 1969, Benny, Jack, and Ted were invited by Tom Moore, owner of Reno's Holiday casino, to an event called the Second Annual Gaming Fraternity Convention: It was the country's first major poker tournament. After buying the casino, Moore and his wife Lafayne had decided to invite fifty or so of the country's biggest gamblers to a tournament featuring table games; they hoped to draw attention to their new casino. This is, today, a common marketing tool, but it didn't quite give the Moores the push they wanted, so in the following year when they held the "convention" a second time, they switched it to high-stakes poker and invited between twenty and thirty professional poker players and bookmakers. The games included Texas hold 'em, Kansas City lowball draw, razz, stud, and ace-to-five lowball draw. Players knocked out of games could buy fresh chips and continuing playing. At the end of a week of games, legendary San Antonio poker player Crandell Addington won a silver trophy designating him as "Mr. Outside," a moniker reflecting on his status as a road, or outside player, as opposed to a casino or race book owner.

Though the Horseshoe did not even have a poker room at the time (like most other casinos, it devoted valuable floor space to profit-earning mercantile games), the family decided to adopt the tournament when Moore retired, renaming it the World Series of Poker. Moss triumphed at the first Binion's World Series of Poker in 1970. When, in 1971, Jack Binion scrapped the unwieldy election system, a freeze-out, nonlimit Texas hold 'em game determined the champion (Moss won again). Players could win bracelets in a number of different games, but to be world champion, they had to beat the best at a game that had become the Cadillac of poker.

Texas hold 'em is a community-card poker game that is related to Omaha, a game in which each player received four cards of his own ("hole cards") and five community cards were dealt to the center of the table—the flop. A player then had to use two of his own cards and three of the community cards to make the best hand. Texas hold 'em is similar, but players receive only two cards, which they must use. Some believe that Texas hold 'em split from Omaha in the 1920s, but there is no consensus.* Still, most agree that Texas hold 'em emerged in the 1920s and 1930s in the Dallas region, and spread

---

*Since the poker games of this period were woefully undocumented, it is difficult to arrive at a definitive picture of the evolution of various games played by Texas road gamblers and their fellow players. As late as 1972, *Playboy's Book of Games*, which devoted more than seventy pages to poker, listed only draw, stud, lowball, high-low, and variations of them (five-card stud, seven-card stud high-low) as commonly played forms of "the great American card game."

throughout the South after World War II. In Texas hold 'em, players bet once when they view their hole cards—the preflop—or fold. After the flop, another round of betting occurs, as after the fourth and fifth community cards are dealt. Typically, most card games have set betting limits, but World Series of Poker championship was no-limit, meaning that any player, at any stage in the game, could go "all in" and bet all of his chips.

For a $10,000 entry fee, anyone who wished could join to vie for a championship bracelet. The WSOP merged the growing popular appeal of gambling with the idea of an ultimate gambling championship. Since the game was intended primarily to publicize the casino, the Binions structured it to yield a relatively quick winner. After losing all his or her chips, a player was out for good. To keep players from playing too conservatively, antes and blinds escalated periodically. Within a few years, the World Series of Poker had become a downtown institution and gave the Horseshoe more publicity than anything, excepting perhaps its horseshoe-shaped display of $1 million in $100 bills.

While Binion's countered the glamour-soaked Strip resorts by putting the emphasis on gambling, across the street a young newcomer had his own ideas about how to run a better casino. Stephen A. Wynn was the son of Maryland bingo operator Mike Wynn. In 1963, when his father died shortly after Wynn graduated from the University of Pennsylvania with a degree in

In the 1979 World Series of Poker, the dealer gathers chips while Doyle Brunson and Hal Fowler await the next card. Fowler won the tournament that year (the first nonpro to do so) and took home $270,000.

English Literature, the young man took over his father's business. Four years later, he jumped at a chance to get into the Las Vegas gambling scene and, with $45,000 saved from his bingo profits, bought a share in the Frontier, where he learned the casino business as a slot manager and assistant credit manager.

Wynn might have remained just one of many ambitious young men if he had not made the acquaintance of E. Parry Thomas, one of the most influential figures in the history of Las Vegas gambling. Thomas was not a casino operator, a slot machine supplier, or a politician. He was a banker, and for years, his Valley Bank was the only legitimate source of capital for Las Vegas casinos. One of the most powerful men in town, he was in a position to help a young man with an eye toward advancement. He guided Wynn into ownership of a liquor distributorship and then, in 1971, helped him score a coup: Wynn bought a small sliver of land adjacent to Caesars Palace from Howard Hughes—the only parcel of land that Hughes sold during his lifetime—and sold it to Caesars for a respectable profit.

Wynn had already begun buying stock in the Golden Nugget, a rather bland downtown gambling hall that had no hotel. Wynn soon accelerated his stock purchase and, in 1973, became president and chairman of the board of the Golden Nugget. Wynn embarked on a massive housecleaning, firing thieving or dishonest employees, and commenced to dramatically remodel the casino. Within a year, Wynn had quadrupled the Golden Nugget's profits. As remarkable as Wynn's transformation of the Golden Nugget seemed, it was just a hint of things to come.

Wynn's recasting of the Golden Nugget may be one of the most dramatic stories of downtown Las Vegas, but he was not the only innovator. Jackie Gaughan pioneered many elements of casino marketing that are common today. Gaughan had learned the trade young while his family operated an illegal gambling house near Omaha, Nebraska. Stationed in Tonopah, Nevada, during World War II, Gaughan was convinced that his future lay in the Silver State. In 1946 he bought a share in the Boulder Club, which he followed in 1951 with a three-percent stake in the Flamingo. Despite this Strip venture, his destiny lay downtown. He bought the Las Vegas Club in 1959 and the El Cortez in 1963. These acquisitions formed the cornerstones of a downtown empire.

In these casinos, along with the Gold Spike, the Western, and the Plaza, Gaughan unleashed a slew of innovations. He invented the casino funbook, a book of coupons for free bets, match play (the casino in effect doubles the player's bet by matching it), two-for-one specials, and the like. Funbooks are now ubiquitous in budget-oriented casinos throughout the nation. Gaughan also started casino giveaways, which he used to perk up otherwise sluggish holidays;

by giving away boxes of candy, he was able to fill his casinos. With these promotions, Gaughan pioneered the mass-marketing of casino gaming—with the increasing popularity of American gambling, it was long overdue.

One of Gaughan's partners in the Plaza built his own casino empire that would ultimately evolve into one of the industry's most successful corporations. Sam Boyd grew up in Depression-era Oklahoma and, when his family moved to southern California, started running carnival games of chance on the Long Beach boardwalk. Boyd later ran bingo games throughout Los Angeles and on gambling ships. From 1935 to 1940 he spread the bingo gospel in Hawaii, where he ran games in Honolulu and Hilo and made several lasting relationships. Moving back to Nevada, Boyd dealt in various casinos before being drafted in 1944. On his 1946 return to Las Vegas, he worked his way up the career ladder at the El Rancho Vegas and then the Flamingo and the Thunderbird.

In 1952, Boyd borrowed and saved enough to buy a stake in the Sahara, becoming a shift manager at the new casino. When, in 1957, the Sahara's owners built downtown's Mint, Boyd bought a share and was appointed general manager. There he harked back to his carnival roots with promotions that never failed to excite patrons. Annual birthday parties for the casino featured an oversized cake, and free meal giveaways were common. Boyd's generosity made good business sense, but it also revealed a truly charitable nature—he and his family would become renowned for their deep philanthropic efforts within Las Vegas over the ensuing decades. Boyd purchased his own casino, a Henderson, Nevada, club that he renamed the Eldorado, in 1962, and left the Mint after Del Webb consolidated its control of the casino in 1966.

Boyd returned to downtown with the Union Plaza, a project whose shareholders included Jackie Gaughan and J. Kell Houssels, Jr. Boyd, as the biggest investor, ran the casino. He was the first to hire female dealers in downtown Las Vegas; though the practice had long been commonplace in Reno, Las Vegas dealer's lounges remained men's only clubs until Boyd's 1971 experiment at the Union Plaza, which he opened with a dealing staff composed exclusively of women. After making the Union Plaza a success, Boyd and his son, William, who had followed him into the business after practicing law, sold their shares to Gaughan and moved to their next development, the California. Opening in 1974, the California has become a Las Vegas landmark not for its unique architecture but for its clientele—Boyd used his Hawaiian connections to promote the hotel energetically there, and visitors from the islands soon made the California a winner.

Boyd would add Main Street Station and the Fremont to his stable of downtown gambling halls, but he would solidify his reputation in 1979 with a resort that he put his name on: Sam's Town, which, at Boulder Highway and Nellis Boulevard, catered almost entirely to locals, a market that was then untapped. Over the next two decades, a sufficient number of competitors opened that the area became known as the Boulder Strip, a down-market version of the glittering Las Vegas Strip. Leadership of the Boyd casinos soon passed to his son William Boyd, who took the company public and expanded it astoundingly, opening casinos in six states and buying the Strip landmark Stardust resort in 1985.

Though developments throughout the rest of Nevada were outshone by the stellar growth of the Strip, gambling continued to grow and thrive elsewhere as well. In Reno, Bill Harrah developed his flagship property into a full-service casino-hotel that featured some of the top entertainment stars of the day; his Tahoe casino was equally lustrous. Ernest Primm successfully challenged the city council's red line, which had kept casinos confined to a few blocks in downtown Reno, and in the 1970s a host of new casino-hotels opened. Though the south grabbed much of the glory, Reno and towns along the state line, like Jackpot, Mesquite, and, later, Primm and Laughlin, rode the gambling wave and soon had casino-hotels of their own.

The growing size of casino resorts in the 1960s forced a crisis in casino finance. In the 1940s and 1950s, casino developers, denied the usual lines of credit, were not particularly discriminating about their pool of investors. Most American companies and individuals found investing in a casino simply too risky, and for good reason: Many resorts perpetually teetered on the brink of ruin despite their popularity. Those with a background in illegal gambling (who were by definition criminals) knew that a well-run operation could not help but yield solid profits and eagerly invested, often moving to Las Vegas to work in the industry.

Since 1945, those who wished to own a share in a Nevada casino needed a state license; with the creation of the Gaming Control Board in 1955, licensing procedures were strengthened. Nevada regulatory authorities frequently granted licenses to those who had been convicted of gambling offenses, but drew the line there. Convictions for more serious crimes, ranging from extortion to murder, could disqualify an applicant from ownership. Notorious figures linked to organized crime who wanted to invest in Nevada casinos were barred. Even those who were not convicted of a crime, but merely suspected of connections with organized crime, could not be openly involved. Rather, they had to work through dummy shareholders or just give investment capital to the casino's managing principals. In the early boom years of the Strip, this practice was more common than not.

Like any other investor, someone who had illicitly invested in a Strip resort expected a dividend. Aboveboard investors could receive a share in the profits openly, but the clandestine backers, whose links to organized crime meant a great deal of subterfuge in any business dealing, received their cut of the profits by means of a process known as skimming. Skimming was possible because of loose controls over currency on the casino floor: With thousands of dollars washing through the casino every night, there was ample opportunity for money to disappear. Some skimmed funds were given to employees in a crude attempt at profit sharing; it was considered a mark of a good manager to give his employees "something extra" in return for good work (and to prevent outright theft). But most of it was sent to illicit investors.

For casino managers, skimming was a rational solution to the question of how to capitalize casinos without access to mainstream financial outlets. Yet the public was not so coolheaded about the practice—for good reason. Opponents of Nevada gaming decried a system that let money legally gambled by honest Americans be funneled to organized crime. Skimming scandals persistently dogged Strip resorts, from the Thunderbird and Tropicana in the 1950s to the Flamingo in the 1960s and the Stardust and Aladdin in the 1970s and 1980s. Through skimming, according to the industry's critics, organized crime had become entrenched in Nevada gaming.

But by the time the Stardust skimming scandal broke in 1983, mob ties were becoming a thing of the past, and in 1999 the National Gambling Impact Study Commission found that organized crime had no significant presence in Nevada gaming (or legal gaming elsewhere). There were two reasons for the turnaround: a profound generational shift within organized crime itself and the increasing professionalization of the casino business. The generation of gamblers who came of age during Prohibition had, as a matter of course, business dealings with criminal elements. When, in their forties and fifties, they wanted to "go straight," many of them moved to Las Vegas and opened casino resorts. By the 1960s, these men were in their sixties and looking to retire. They had sent their children to college, and when their progeny followed them into gaming, it was armed with business degrees rather than tommy guns. At the same time, organized crime, which once derived much of its profits from illegal gambling, had moved into narcotics and labor racketeering. Gangsters no longer had any specialized business knowledge that would help them better run or invest in casinos. So those raised in legal gaming lacked experience in "the rackets," while those who remained in organized crime soon knew little about the casino business.

At the same time, the resorts of the Strip were making gambling a more mainstream activity. Thanks to the energetic promotion of Las Vegas as a vacation and convention paradise, millions of Americans found nothing particularly unseemly about casinos. Corporate involvement on the Strip began in 1951, when principals of the Del E. Webb Corporation, one of the nation's leading builders and the owner of the New York Yankees (a team fittingly started by gamblers), helped Milton Prell secure financing for his Sahara casino. Del Webb worked with Milton Prell to build the Mint in 1957 and, four years later, bought both casinos outright.

This seems like a fairly unremarkable business transaction, but it was fraught with difficulty because of Nevada's gaming regulations. According to the law, all investors in casinos had to be investigated before being granted a license. This was a workable procedure for the few dozen shareholders in most casinos but a patent impossibility for a publicly traded corporation with thousands of constantly shifting stock owners. Del Webb was only able to buy the Sahara and Mint by skirting the letter of the law: A wholly owned subsidiary actually owned the properties and hired the Consolidated Casino Corporation, owned by Del Webb and his partners, to run the casino. Its rental fee was set to match the casino's annual revenues. Webb owned casinos for years, only selling them in the 1980s, but the convoluted administrative acrobatics needed to legally operate Nevada casinos kept other corporations out of the state.

In 1967 and 1969, thanks to the advocacy of Governor Paul Laxalt, the legislature amended the gaming laws to permit full-fledged corporate ownership of gaming properties. Publicly traded corporations were now permitted to enter the gaming business, provided that they adhered to strict licensing guidelines: All shareholders, directors, and officers of the corporate subsidiary that directly ran the casino had to be licensed. In the publicly traded company itself, only shareholders with ownership of more than five percent of the corporation's stock needed to be licensed. These changes, combined with the public perception of the Hughes purchases as a step toward legitimacy, made Nevada gaming far more palatable to mainstream investors.

Kirk Kerkorian was one of the first to capitalize on gaming's new legitimacy. Growing up in hardscrabble Depression-era central California, he parlayed a love for flying into a charter air service; Las Vegas was one of his most frequent stops. He bought a parcel of Strip land that he later sold to Jay Sarno, demurring on a lucrative rental agreement because, reportedly, he thought the resort had dim prospects.

By 1966, Kerkorian wanted to be more than a landlord: He wanted to own a resort himself. Buying land adjacent to the Las Vegas Convention Center, he hired architect Martin Stern, Jr. (who had previously built high-rise towers at the Sahara and Sands) to construct the world's biggest resort hotel. To ensure that he had a staff worthy of the facility, he hired one of the city's best managers, the Sahara's Alex Shoofey, as his casino's president. Kerkorian bought the underperforming Flamingo in 1967 (it had been notorious for its massive skimming), and Shoofey, bringing over much of his loyal staff from the Sahara, ran the resort in preparation for the opening of his new casino.

Shoofey turned the Flamingo around—bringing in over $3 million in profits in his first year in charge and $7 million in his second—but this was just a prelude for the debut of Kerkorian's juggernaut resort, the International. Opening on July 2, 1969, the International represented a gigantic leap forward in casino design. With fifteen hundred rooms, it was the world's largest hotel. It had a golf course across the street but also a full complement of swimming pools, tennis and badminton courts, Ping-Pong tables, and a health spa for the athletically inclined, seven restaurants for the hungry, the world's largest casino (at twenty-nine thousand square feet, claustrophobic by today's standards), three entertainment venues, including the International Showroom, and spacious convention facilities. A "Youth Hotel" day-care center entertained juvenile guests whose parents were having fun in the casino.

The International, which was the first Y-shaped resort on the Strip (this would be the most popular design of the 1990s), marked the start of a new generation of casino design. The first-generation Strip resorts were essentially dressed-up motels with nightclubs and restaurants attached. The second-generation International featured a massive hotel tower, sizable casino, and ample recreation, entertainment, dining, and convention facilities, all in a single integrated structure. The massive showroom (with two thousand seats, it was larger than anything yet built on the Strip) was the perfect venue for superstars like Elvis Presley.

Though the International was mightily successful, Kerkorian, stretched thin by his purchase of MGM Studios and Western Air, sold the casino to Hilton Hotels, who in 1971 acquired a majority stake in Tracinda, Kerkorian's operating company that owned the International and Flamingo. The International became the Las Vegas Hilton; Elvis stayed, and the resort became one of Las Vegas's most recognizable icons. The storied Flamingo became the Flamingo Hilton, a name that it kept until, in 2001, it became simply the Flamingo again. Despite selling his casinos, Kerkorian wasn't done with Las Vegas; in 1973 he built the even bigger MGM Grand (when it opened it was, with 2,100 rooms, the world's largest hotel). This behemoth stood tall at Flamingo Road and Las Vegas Strip and instantly became one of the Strip's top properties. But

Kerkorian was destined for even greater things; he would, in the next phase of the Strip's development, become an increasingly more important player.

Hilton's entrance into Las Vegas brought an internationally recognized hospitality chain to town, but most gaming corporations had developed out of existing partnerships. The owners of casinos as diverse as Harrah's, Showboat, and Circus Circus took their companies public to finance new acquisitions and expansion. As new capital poured in, high-rise towers blossomed along the Strip; as annual Nevada gaming revenues surpassed the $1 billion mark, the corporate era was dawning. Yet the casino that would one day be the flagship of the world's biggest gaming company had distinctly noncorporate origins. In 1973 Claudine and Shelby Williams opened the Holiday Casino, a small, expertly run casino in front of a north Strip Holiday Inn. The casino was soon one of the Strip's best. It was, in 1983, completely acquired by Holiday Inns (who three years earlier had bought a forty-percent stake in it) and, in 1992, became Harrah's Las Vegas.

Though the sky seemed the limit with the opening of the MGM Grand, the 1970s and early 1980s were difficult years for the Strip. Oil shocks and economic malaise translated into stagnation. The November 21, 1980, fire at the MGM Grand, which claimed more than eighty lives, was a tragic symbol of the Strip's new vulnerability: That the newest, most modern casino was the scene of such a disaster only intensified anxieties over the future of the Strip. With competition looming from Atlantic City's new casinos, it seemed that Las Vegas's days as a gaming mecca might be soon over.

PART EIGHT

Gambling's New Prominence

Lines began forming outside the doors of Resorts International early on the morning of Friday, May 26, 1978. This was a day that all of Atlantic City had eagerly anticipated since the passage of a pro-casino referendum in 1976: the arrival of legal casino gambling on the Boardwalk. The setting could not have been more unlikely: The casino was set to open in the former Chalfonte-Haddon Hall, whose Quaker owners had once refused to even serve alcohol to guests. Resorts, which owned a Bahamas casino, had bought the aging hotel in anticipation of the legalization of casino gambling. Now, $20 million in renovations and two years later, the company was ready to roll the dice.

For months, city officials had been nervously planning for the sudden influx of visitors to this dilapidated New Jersey shore resort: 150,000 cars a day were anticipated in a city that had only 50,000 parking spaces. The city's eight thousand hotel and motel rooms were already booked solid. Days earlier, seven hundred eager guests had filled the casino for a trial run. Nervous dealers, most of them just trained in the arts of gambling, dealt craps, blackjack, and baccarat to players who wagered fake money.

Inside, tension rose as the staff anticipated the coming deluge. Outside, the sky was overcast, but the boisterous crowd, eager to begin playing, seemed not to mind as they stood in a line that stretched six blocks. At 10:00 A.M., New Jersey governor Brendan Byrne cut a red ribbon strung across the casino's Boardwalk entrance, and a few moments later, play began. Five thousand hopeful gamblers pressed into the casino, often waiting for a space at a slot machine or craps game. Outside, a pair of models reenacted an Atlantic City tradition, the annual "unlocking of the sea." But outside of a corps of photographers, few noticed the ceremony; they were more intent on getting some action down.

Legal casino gaming had been a Nevada monopoly since 1931; in that state casinos had anchored a tourist economy and spurred the development of Las Vegas. But could that magic be recaptured? It quickly became apparent that the answer was yes. Casino staff found themselves choking on money: There was so much cash pouring into the casino, they lacked the means to accurately count it. The casino won, on average, more than $600,000 a day, a nearly unthinkable sum in 1978. Suddenly, the rush was on. By the middle of the next decade, Atlantic City's casino profits would rival those of the fabled Las Vegas Strip.

The success of Atlantic City casinos illustrated a larger trend in American gambling. Casinos had been sold to New Jersey voters as a "unique tool for urban redevelopment" that would restore Atlantic City to its former luster and provide funding for statewide programs. Increasingly, gambling was promoted as a positive social good. Upright citizens who played church bingo, bought lottery tickets that helped fund schools, and gambled on Indian reservations could feel that they were having fun but also contributing to the public good. With state and tribal governments as active promoters, legal gambling would, by the end of the twentieth century, become a bigger American pastime than baseball.

Runaway American Dream

◆ ◆ ◆

GAMBLING IN THE PUBLIC INTEREST

By the 1970s, states that embraced horse racing and lotteries found gambling tolerable and even desirable. Yet despite several states' attempts to legalize slot machines—Maryland most prominently—Nevada remained the only state to sanction casino gambling. As the nation's economic picture darkened, however, casino proposals floated in a number of states, and the most serious surfaced in New Jersey.

Citizens of Atlantic City had urged the state to legalize casino gaming there since the 1950s. Atlantic City, born as a vacation resort for Philadelphia, emerged during the Gilded Age as a national destination, one of the country's preeminent convention and exposition spots. Majestic hotels flanked the world-famous Boardwalk, whose piers hosted concerts, conventions, and product displays for companies from Heinz to General Motors, and its streets were immortalized in the Depression-era board game Monopoly. The city's nightclubs drew crowds with headline entertainers—and, until the winds of reform picked up in the early 1950s, barely concealed backroom casinos.

The reform effort, coincidentally or not, succeeded in driving out these illegal casinos just as the city was beginning to decline. The availability of cheap air travel, which facilitated the development of mass-market tourism in Florida and Las Vegas, meant that many who might have spent their vacations "down the shore" now flew to more exotic destinations. When Atlantic City hosted the Democratic National Convention in the summer of 1964, news media from around the country filed stories on the city's alarming decline. With little new investment in hotels or tourist facilities, the once-opulent resort rightfully touted as "America's Playground" became a punch line.

But some far-thinking residents, mindful of Las Vegas's success, reasoned that legal casinos might be the answer. As early as 1956, Paul "Skinny" D'Amato, owner of the fabled 500 Club, publicly urged state legislators to permit him and other nightclub and hotel owners to legally operate casinos. Two years later, Mildred Fox, owner of the Fox Manor Hotel, prompted the Women's Chamber of Commerce to promote an unsuccessful procasino drive.

As unemployment skyrocketed and the city decayed even further, locals began to organize more seriously. A December 1968 testimonial dinner thrown in D'Amato's honor at the Shelburne Hotel, according to some, began the concerted effort to bring gambling to Atlantic City. With an assortment of the area's power brokers in attendance, talk soon turned to the prospects for legal gaming: All agreed that it was essential to the city's revitalization. In the early 1970s, debate over casinos raged throughout the state, and in 1974, casino backers succeeded in placing a statewide referendum on the November ballot.

This measure, though almost unanimously supported in Atlantic City, went down in defeat. Voters in other parts of the state, leery that the referendum's wording permitted casinos "statewide" (though government officials insisted that, in practice, they would only be permitted in Atlantic City) seemingly shut the door to New Jersey casinos forever. Astute political analysts concluded that, with both religious leaders and law enforcement officials stridently urging the populace to reject gambling in the name of morality and law, it had no chance of even returning to the ballot, much less winning.

These pundits ignored the growing national move toward gaming liberalization. New Jersey had already embraced horse racing and a lottery, and with Nevada's booming success, it seemed inevitable that some state would consider legalizing casinos. Thanks to adroit political maneuvering and skillful log-rolling, the measure reappeared two years later. This time, Catholic leaders roundly supported the measure, which was rewritten to authorize casinos in Atlantic City only. Dedicating a portion of casino taxes to fund programs for senior citizens was a masterstroke that added the support of a politically potent group. With strict regulation promised, even law enforcement warmed to Atlantic City casinos. Still, the procasino lobby wanted to take no chances, and hired political consultant Sanford Weiner to assist the unfortunately named CRAC (Committee to Rebuild Atlantic City). Couching the referendum in terms of help for Atlantic City (and money for statewide programs), Weiner marshaled a then-astronomical $1 million war chest and doggedly pushed the issue throughout the state. Anticasino forces, who raised only $21,000, watched helplessly as, on November 2, 1976, the Atlantic City casino referendum passed.

The dice started rolling on May 26, 1978, when Resorts International opened in the erstwhile Haddon Hall, a converted golden-era Boardwalk hotel. Over the previous months, the state legislature had created the regulatory framework for the new industry: A Casino Control Commission would issue licenses and set policies, while the Division of Gaming Enforcement would be the investigatory and enforcement arm of the government. Government officials were particularly concerned with keeping organized crime out of the industry. During the opening festivities at Resorts, New Jersey Governor Brendan Byrne—a supporter of legal casinos—channeled Charlton Heston, warning organized crime: "Keep your filthy hands off Atlantic City! Keep the hell out of our state!" Many chuckled at the notion that the mob might only now be moving into the Garden State.

Resorts saw incredible crowds on its opening weekend, which coincided with the Memorial Day holiday. Lines to get in stretched blocks down the Boardwalk. Steve Lawrence, who along with Eydie Gormé was Resorts' opening headliner, officially placed the first legal bet in Atlantic City when he ceremoniously put $10 on pass. After rolling a five, he sevened out. This didn't dampen the ardor of the thousands of gamblers who filled the casino, standing five deep at tables and even slot machines. In its first six days of operation, Resorts made $2.9 million—a world record. In its first full year, the casino pulled in nearly $225 million. By comparison, Nevada's most lucrative casino at the time, Las Vegas's MGM Grand, brought in about $84 million a year. Suddenly, Las Vegas had a serious rival.

The next several years were noisy ones in Atlantic City, as the sound of old hotels crashing down alternated with the din of pile drivers and new construction. Caesars Boardwalk Regency opened in a hastily converted Howard Johnson's in 1979, followed by Bally's Park Place, a combination of old and new that exemplified the city's growing pains. It opened on a historic site. The Marlborough Hotel had been built in 1901 by noted architect William Lightfoot Price, and when land in front of it became available, the hotel's owners retained Price to build the Blenheim. This Boardwalk hotel was artistically and architecturally groundbreaking: Thomas Edison helped design the hotel's reinforced concrete, and it was the Boardwalk's first "fireproof" hotel and the first to feature a private bath in each room. The Blenheim's Moorish style presented Boardwalk strollers with a breathtaking display of domes and chimneys, and it stood for decades as the city's architectural centerpiece. When gaming was legalized, locals were cheered when Reese Palley, an active booster of casino gaming, bought the hotels in 1977 and announced plans to preserve the Blenheim half of the hotel and to replace the Marlborough with a modern 750-room casino hotel.

On May 26, 1978, Resorts International, Atlantic City's first casino hotel, opened in a renovated Haddon Hall. This is the Haddon Hall–Chalfonte complex in 1976, shortly before the casino referendum passed. Resorts demolished the Chalfonte (the smaller building on the left) for a hotel expansion that was never built (as of early 2006, the land is still a parking lot).

Palley succeeded in having the Blenheim placed on the National Register of Historic Buildings, but he soon stepped aside as Bally Manufacturing bought a controlling interest in the project. Bally then switched architects and announced plans to raze the Marlborough, Blenheim, and the adjacent Dennis Hotel to build a sprawling, modern casino hotel with an octagonal 385-foot hotel tower. Preservationists were aghast, but Bally cited the difficulties of bringing the old structures up to code. Ultimately, Bally chose to keep the less architecturally significant Dennis while imploding the Marlborough and Blenheim. In December 1979, Bally's Park Place opened as a 51,000-square-foot-casino complex tacked onto the renovated Dennis Hotel. Bally's eventually erected a unabashedly modern pink tower on top of the casino addition, and later added the Wild Wild West–themed casino and bought the neighboring Claridge casino (which had opened in a converted hotel), making Bally's Atlantic City (as the casino was renamed) the island's biggest casino.

The Brighton hotel-casino, soon renamed the Sands, signified another disturbing trend. Atlantic City had over a century's experience as a world-famous destination resort. Yet, aside from the first wave of casino operators who preserved the past out of expediency (they wanted to get open as quickly as possible, and renovation was faster than new construction), the city's casino resorts paid little mind to the city's rich past, its urban framework, or its pedestrian-friendly Boardwalk. Instead, they sought to scoop the casino resort up from the Nevada desert and transplant it on the Jersey Shore.

In fact, the Casino Control Act (the Atlantic City industry's enabling legislation) specified that casinos had to have at least "five-hundred first class hotel rooms," convention space, live entertainment, twenty-four-hour restaurants, and a host of other conveniences. Even advertising had to be regulated "to insure that it is truthful, in good taste, and that gambling is not the dominant theme," because New Jersey legislators were intent on using casinos to springboard Atlantic City into the destination stratosphere of the Las Vegas Strip. Yet these requirements virtually guaranteed that visitors to Atlantic City casinos wouldn't venture far from the garishly carpeted casino: All of their needs were already met there.

The renaming of the Brighton symbolized the growing "Las Vegasization" of Atlantic City: Its historic hotels would be razed and replaced with second-rate versions of Las Vegas Strip casinos. Atlantic City versions of the MGM Grand, Dunes, and Sahara were proposed but never opened, while the Sands, Caesars, and Harrah's (then only in Reno and Tahoe) Showboat, and Tropicana planted flags of Nevada icons on the dunes of Atlantic City.

The Nevada casino operator to make the biggest impact on Atlantic City wasn't a large hotel operator like Holiday Inns, Inc. (who had bought Bill Harrah's Reno and Tahoe casinos in 1980) or a big name like Caesars. It was Steve Wynn, the forward-thinking owner of downtown Las Vegas's Golden Nugget. Wynn had transformed the Golden Nugget into a full-service casino hotel that was the finest downtown. Seeing true possibility with the opening of Resorts, Wynn unobtrusively flew into Atlantic City in June 1978. Jim Crosby, chairman of Resorts International, obligingly steered Wynn to an available parcel—at the opposite end of the Boardwalk. Wynn, wearing a Willie Nelson T-shirt and drawstring pants, strolled into the Strand Motel, offered owner Manny Solomon $8.5 million, and, twenty minutes later, owned a piece of Atlantic City.

Wynn successfully courted Wall Street lenders who, charmed by the casino developer's natural charisma and ambitious vision, financed the construction of a classy white-and-gold casino hotel. Wynn's magnetic leadership made the Golden Nugget the first choice of virtually every casino employee, and his hands-on approach to player development—like Benny Binion, his downtown neighbor and mentor, he was sure to walk the casino floor—helped the casino become the city's most popular. Signing Frank Sinatra to a then-unprecedented three-year, $10 million deal as the casino's star headliner in 1983 was only icing on the cake.

In the early 1980s, Atlantic City became, arguably, the world's leading casino destination. In 1984, it had more than double the visitors of Las Vegas (28.5 million to 12.8), and, though it had one sixth the hotel rooms, half the gaming tables, one fourth the slot machines, and limited hours of operation, it nearly matched Las Vegas's $2 billion annual casino revenue. Almost all of these visitors came by car or bus; nearly one thousand buses daily brought casino patrons, chiefly from New York, Pennsylvania, and New Jersey. Supplemented by a regular parade of international high rollers chauffered in from Philadelphia and New York airports, bus people provided a stable, unspectacular customer base.

But all was not roses: Many operators chafed at overly strict regulations that involved state bureaucrats in every aspect of casino design, staffing, and operation. Caesars, Hilton, and Playboy's Hugh Hefner sank millions into casino resorts only to be told that they had been denied permanent casino licenses. The Perlman brothers, chief stockholders in Caesars World, were forced to sell their interest before the corporation could be licensed. The Playboy was the hottest property in town before being sold and renamed the Atlantis, which fittingly sank. Steve Wynn's selling his Golden Nugget to Bally Gaming in 1987 should have been a wake-up call, but regulation continued to slow development. As a result, the city was ill equipped to handle the explosive growth of casino gaming throughout the nation in the 1990s.

Some, however, found Atlantic City to be the promised land. Caesars, Tropicana, and Harrah's found that their Atlantic City branches far outperformed their original Nevada casinos: The cash flow from Harrah's Marina enabled the company to dramatically expand during the 1990s. New York developer Donald Trump was equally grateful to Atlantic City: After an unsuccessful partnership with Harrah's ended with his acquisition of Trump Plaza, he became a major figure in the city. He bought Hilton's unopened marina casino, which became Trump's Castle (later Trump Marina) and, in 1990, opened the Trump Taj Mahal. Ground for this casino had been broken in 1983 by Resorts International, but it was finally completed by Trump and opened to a fanfare of publicity. It was, for a time, the world's largest and most lucrative casino, and it would be the last new casino to open in Atlantic City for more than a decade.

Looking back, it is clear that the myopia of both regulators and casino operators was responsible for the city's failure to transform itself into a truly world-class destination. In addition to burdensome regulation, the state also limited the types of games casinos could offer: It was not until the early 1990s, when competition had already eroded the city's dominant position on the East Coast, that poker, keno, and race books were allowed in Atlantic City casinos. In addition, casinos were slow to invest in nongaming attractions. Because players drove to Atlantic City merely for convenience, they inevitably chose closer casinos as they became available.

A wave of recent development, though, may bring the time-honored vision of reestablishing Atlantic City as a world-famous vacation and business resort closer to reality. The Borgata, the city's first new casino resort since the Trump Taj Mahal, opened in 2003 to nearly universal acclaim. Operated by Boyd Gaming, joint owners with MGM Mirage, the Borgata would not be out of place on the Las Vegas Strip: It is chic, classy, and, like its Strip counterparts, very profitable. Though its golden glass façade is far removed from the graceful concrete spires of the Marlborough-Blenheim, the Borgata is a sign that Atlantic City might be returned to its original fame as a complete destination resort—a World's Playground for the twenty-first century.

Atlantic City, with its crumbling hotels and depressing spiral of unemployment, crime, and poverty, was in dire need of help, but even that resort was well off when compared to many Indian reservations. Since the beginnings of European settlement of the Americas in the sixteenth century, the native inhabitants of the New World had found themselves systematically driven onto marginal lands. In the United States, the federal government's policy toward Indians, which at one point embraced the wholesale destruction of Indian polities and culture, had softened by the 1930s. The "Indian New Deal" sought to revitalize tribes as communities and had as its goal tribal self-sufficiency rather than assimilation.

The subsequent decades of well-intentioned government aid did little to improve life on Indian reservations: They still remained remote settlements wracked with poverty and a host of social problems. With the gambling becoming an increasingly alluring revenue option for many states, it is perfectly understandable that a few tribal leaders started to look at gambling as a solution for their own problems. The federal government had actually approved tribal government supervision of gaming as early as 1924, when the Bureau of Indian Affairs officially recognized tribal gaming laws, but no tribes opened facilities catering to non-Indians.

In the late 1970s, the Penobscot Indians of Maine moved to offer bingo, followed by the Seminoles of Florida. After all, thirty-four states allowed charitable organizations to run bingo games, and Indian tribes, sorely in need of money and jobs and not run for profit, certainly qualified as charities. But Indian bingo operators soon argued that they were not subject to state oversight: Because they are sovereign political entities, tribes are not answerable to the civil laws of the states that surround them. Indian bingo operators reasoned that if bingo was not absolutely prohibited as an illegal game—was not in violation of the state's criminal code—then the state had no authority to police tribal bingo games. Tribes began offering bingo games with superjackpots, sometimes as high as $50,000. Suddenly, bingo players were finding their way to reservations, where bingo nights were much more exciting.

Rival bingo operators were understandably upset at this exercise of tribal sovereignty, as were county officials. Raids against tribal high-stakes bingo operations in California and Florida triggered legal battles that reached the Supreme Court in 1987. The Florida raid, which sparked a successful lawsuit by the Seminole tribe, was a touchstone for shifting American views toward Native Americans. While state authorities argued that the tribe should be kept from violating state laws, many outside observers vocally defended the Indians. After centuries of broken promises and unfair treaties, they argued, allowing tribes to run bingo—at which attendance was not compulsory—seemed like a small concession. Seminole chairman James Billie believed that the bingo hall gave his people a chance at turning the tables. "It's more than beads for Manhattan," he stated, referencing the story that Dutch colonists had purchased Manhattan in 1626 from its native inhabitants for $24 in beads.

Echoing Billie's sentiments, many tribes did not wait for the matter to be resolved by the courts. With unemployment as high as seventy percent and sharp cuts in federal assistance, many tribes embraced bingo. In 1983, for example, the Yaqui, an Arizona tribe, opened a $1 million, 1,300-seat bingo parlor hailed as the biggest in the West. Able to offer $12,000 jackpots that were three times as large as those presented by church and other nonprofit bingo games, the Yaqui bingo hall drew players from nearby Tucson. The two hundred nonprofit bingo halls in that city reported an immediate ten-percent fall-off in business. At the time, between forty and sixty tribes nationwide had, like the Yaqui, turned to bingo.

Later that year, 2,400 people flocked to North Carolina's remote Cherokee reservation, paying $500 each for a chance at a $200,000 jackpot. In 1984, the Otoe Missouria Indians of north-central Oklahoma opened what they claimed was the world's largest bingo hall, a 6,000-seat acre of bingo called the Red Rock Bingo Palace. Players for hundreds of miles around took buses to the remote reservation and stayed overnight in a nearby hotel, playing from noon to midnight Saturday and Sunday on alternate weekends. Some weekends, they won as much as $400,000 in prizes. The games bordered on the festive; when one of the many Texans in attendance won a game, "Deep in the Heart of Texas" played over the sound system. Yet amid the merriment, some felt lingering apprehension: One player told a reporter that she hadn't used her real name when playing because she was a Baptist. Still, they came. Whatever the concerns of existing charitable gaming operations, bingo clearly had the support of players. Nevertheless, with the laws regarding Indian gaming still ambiguous, the legal foundations of this potential goldmine remained shaky.

The Supreme Court soon swept away all doubt of the legality of tribal-run gaming operations. In February 1987, the nation's highest court issued a landmark ruling in *California v. Cabazon Band of Mission Indians:* If a state legalized a form of gambling (in California's case bingo and poker), tribes could offer that kind of gambling without any interference from—or regulation by—state, county, or municipal authorities. High-stakes bingo and no-limit card rooms on Indian reservations were now unambiguously legal; tribes could also offer lotteries and perhaps even casino gaming in states that regulated those games. In his decision, Justice Byron White declared that Indian gaming was actually a welcome opportunity for tribes to develop economically: Gambling, a proven winner in Nevada, New Jersey, and most other states, would now be tapped to end centuries of tribal misfortune.

Even before the *Cabazon* decision, the federal government had been encouraging the development of Indian gaming. As part of his mission to shrink the federal government, President Ronald Reagan had declared the reduction of tribal dependence on government funding to be a priority of his administration; he cut appropriations to tribes, forcing them to find alternate sources of funding, which could only be accomplished by developing tribal industries. Bingo fit the bill, and the Department of the Interior and Bureau of Indian Affairs approved tribal ordinances that set up high-stakes bingo games. The federal government even helped to finance tribal bingo start-ups through grants and loans.

Dispassionately, the development of tribal government gaming was about tribal sovereignty and economic development. Many states, though, viewed the growth of high-stakes bingo and the *Cabazon* decision with alarm. They were fearful that full-blown casinos might open within their boundaries and drain money from competing state gambling enterprises. Since the states were clearly powerless to control tribal-government-sanctioned gaming, a growing chorus of state governors sought help from the federal government.

In 1988 Congress passed the Indian Gaming Regulatory Act. This measure did not "legalize" or "authorize" Indian gaming, which had been flourishing for years, but rather provided rules for its continuing development.

The Act established three classes of Indian gaming. Class I games were traditional games played among tribal members and were to be regulated solely by tribes. Class II games included bingo, lotteries, and nonbank games (poker, etc). Class II operations were to be overseen by the National Indian Gaming Commission, though after a period of successful operation tribes could construct their own regulatory bodies. Class III gaming was, basically, casino gaming: slot machines and mercantile card and dice games.

Congress, wishing to give states some say in the process, declared that to run full-blown casinos, tribes first needed to ink compacts with states. These were essentially treaties between the two sovereign polities that set forth the type and number of games to be played. Though states had no power to tax tribal casinos, most compacts required tribes to pay a fixed sum or a portion of revenues each year to states. The casinos were usually regulated by tribal governments, though some states retained the right and responsibility to conduct background checks on casino employee applicants. In the IGRA, Congress pointedly echoed the sentiments of Justice White, finding that gaming was consonant with the federal goal of promoting tribal self-sufficiency and economic independence.

Even before the *Cabazon* decision or IGRA, some Indian tribes started full-fledged casinos. With the legal status of tribal gaming in doubt, many opened facilities that were primitive in comparison to the sprawling resorts of the Strip. In 1984, Frederick Dakota opened the nation's first Indian casino in his brother-in-law's converted garage on the L'Anse Indian reservation off Keweenaw Bay in northern Michigan. The erstwhile garage, insulated against the winter with chipboard walls, featured two blackjack games: a $2 table and, for high rollers, a $5 one, whose dealer's chief experience was having once run a church bingo game. Those tired of playing could relax at the three-seat bar, where well drinks cost 70 cents and high-end libations (Canadian Club whiskey) 90 cents. Both state and federal authorities refused to close down Dakota's game. In that two-car garage, the modern Indian casino was born.

Detractors scoffed at the first Indian casinos, arguing that they would never be more than glorified bingo halls. Yet within barely a decade of the passage of the Indian Gaming Regulatory Act, an Indian reservation would host the world's largest casino. Foxwoods Resort Casino in Ledyard, Connecticut, has enabled the Mashantucket Pequot reservation, which had at one point dwindled to only one member, to become one of New England's economic powerhouses.

In the 1970s, new tribal chairman Richard "Skip" Hayward convinced several of his relatives to move onto the two-hundred-acre reservation; had they abandoned it, it would have become property of the state. Hayward and the other members of the reestablished Mashantucket Pequots experimented with a few enterprises, including collecting maple syrup, cutting wood, a gravel business, and owning Mr. Pizza, a restaurant on nearby Route 2.

After securing federal recognition in 1983, the tribe tried several more enterprises before turning to bingo. Most lenders were skeptical of Pequot bingo: Straitlaced New England was, allegedly, no place to build a high-stakes bingo parlor. Yet New England had led the nation in reviving lotteries two decades earlier, and bingo has proven popular nearly everywhere in the United States. With a loan from the United Arab-American Bank, Hayward built a $4 million brick bingo parlor on Pequot land near Ledyard.

When the bingo hall opened on July 5, 1986, there were over a hundred Indian gaming operations nationwide. The Pequot bingo hall was among the most sophisticated in the country, with electronic boards that displayed the drawn numbers and computers to verify winning tickets. Helped by the Penobscots of Maine, whose own high-stakes bingo game had been curtailed by an unfavorable court ruling in 1984 (a ruling that would be effectively reversed with *Cabazon*), the Pequots found bingo exceeded all expectations, as players came by car and bus. At times, more than seventeen hundred of them crowded into the hall, vying for big jackpots and, along the way, helping the Pequots gain financial self-sufficiency.

The next step for the Pequots was opening a true casino. Because Connecticut allowed nonprofit charities to run casino games as part of "Las Vegas Nights," the tribe negotiated a compact under which it was able to open a casino. With financing from Malaysian billionaire Lim Goh Tong, who owned Malaysia's Genting Highlands casino resort, and a team of former New Jersey regulators and casino executives, the Pequots opened the Foxwoods casino on February 15, 1992.

Foxwoods was not the first Indian casino to open under the IGRA; the Flandreau Santee Sioux of North Dakota had opened one in 1990. But it quickly became the most profitable. Accessible by car from New York, Boston, and all points in between, it gave Atlantic City its first casino competition on the East Coast. Foxwoods even had a host of games that Atlantic City didn't: red dog, *pai gow* poker, horse-race simulcasting, and poker. The tribe's forty-five-table poker room was the first legal one on the East Coast. Foxwoods never closed, unlike Atlantic City casinos, which had been forced by statute to close at 4:00 A.M., or 6:00 A.M. on weekends. (Within five years, New Jersey permitted every game allowed at Foxwoods and had begun twenty-four-hour gambling.)

Foxwoods opened with few amenities: It had gift shops, eateries, and a small entertainment venue. Yet it was so profitable that it almost immediately began expanding. Frank Sinatra, the gold standard of casino entertainers since the 1950s, opened the Fox Theater in 1993; he was followed by a string of casino favorites. This gave Foxwoods a new measure of legitimacy, but the casino had already secured something more important: slot machines. Since Connecticut's charity gaming nights were free of slots, the tribe had been prohibited from installing them. In hopes that a compromise might be reached, the original casino was ringed with video poker and reel slots set for free play—though no money went in, no money came out.

In 1992, the tribe reached an agreement with Connecticut governor Lowell Weicker that authorized slot machines in return for a quarter of gross slot revenue or $100 million, whichever was greater. Foxwoods immediately installed new machines and continued to expand; by 1994 it had nearly 4,000 machines that grossed at least $800 million a year. It was by then the largest casino in the United States. Further expansions would give it over 7,400 slot machines and 388 table games by 2004, making it without question the largest casino in the entire world. With nearly fifteen hundred hotel rooms, restaurants, shopping, and convention facilities, it was a megasized Strip-style casino resort, nestled in the backwoods of Connecticut.

Foxwoods' business was so good that not even the 1996 opening of Mohegan Sun twelve miles away in Uncasville slowed its profits. The Mohegan people, once rivals of the Pequots, joined them as casino operators thanks to a three-way 1994 compact between the tribes and the state. Initially managed by South African gaming magnate Sol Kerzner's Sun International, Mohegan Sun grew to be nearly as large as Foxwoods and just as successful.

Other states had similar experiences with the "new buffalo" of Indian casinos. California had, since Gold Rush days, been a state of gamblers, and a good portion of the visitors to Las Vegas and Reno drove up from the Golden State. California Indian tribes argued that since the state's lottery used electronic devices, they were permitted to install electronic gambling devices in their card rooms and bingo halls, which were unambiguously legal under the *Cabazon* decision. By 1995 twenty tribes across the state were operating eight-thousand slot machines; one of the largest, the Barona Big Top casino in San Diego County, had over a thousand of the machines.

These machines were not quite legal, and though they were undoubtedly lucrative for tribes, most wanted to place their casinos on a more solid regulatory footing: Compacts with the state that would permit them to operate Class III casinos with table games and slots. Governor Pete Wilson negotiated such a pact with the Pala Band of Mission Indians of San Diego County, but most tribes felt it was too restrictive and in 1998 pushed for a statewide referendum, Proposition 5, that would force the governor to accept tribal casinos. Termed "The Tribal Government Gaming and Economic Self-Sufficiency Act," the referendum passed handily despite the opposition of Nevada commercial casino interests (all told, over $200 million was spent on both sides of the fight). Though it had passed convincingly, Governor Wilson challenged Proposition 5's legality and the California Supreme Court struck the measure down in 1999. A repackaged measure, Proposition 1A, was approved by voters in 2000. This time, commercial casino companies, sensing that California Indian gaming was inevitable and that there was money to be made by signing management contracts with tribal casinos, backed the proposition.

A new, friendlier governor, Gray Davis, had already begun negotiating compacts with California tribes. Agreements with over sixty tribes brought Nevada-style casino gaming to California, with blackjack and slot machines. Many existing bingo halls added slots and began planning new casinos. Within the next few years, dozens of reservations boasted glittering new casinos. The typical California Indian casino had between thirty and fifty table games, a poker room, and two thousand slot machines, the state maximum. As the state entered a financial and political crisis in 2003 culminating in the election of Arnold Schwarzenegger as governor, the restraints and financial obligations placed on tribal government casinos became a political football that, it seemed, would be in play for years.

Whatever the ultimate fiscal and political settlement reached between the governments of California and its Indian tribes, casinos soon changed the face of California gambling. Card rooms and racetracks, which had long enjoyed monopolies on live-action gambling, felt the pinch almost immediately. California citizens, suddenly presented with casino gambling closer to home, turned out in record numbers; though none of the casinos were as large as the Pequot's Foxwoods, they may have been, machine for machine, just as lucrative. Dotting the California countryside, they were further proof, if any was needed, that Californians still loved to gamble.

With the proliferation of lotteries, the sudden reality of Indian casinos, and the success of Atlantic City, many states began to reconsider their traditional prohibitions against casinos. With visitation to Las Vegas and Atlantic City breaking new records each year and no major scandals related to the operation of their casinos, allowing legal gambling seemed like anything but a gamble. Yet the inhabitants of many states still felt some compunctions about legalizing casinos: While they might be fine for vacation destinations like Las Vegas or Atlantic City or isolated Indian reservations, they were hardly appropriate for the hardworking, God-fearing communities of the heartland. Still, the potential revenue from gambling halls remained a tantalizing lure, particularly as many states suffered economically in the late 1980s. If only there were some way to legalize casino gambling without the casinos, some thought, all of their problems could be solved.

Iowa did just that when, in 1989, the state approved gambling on board riverboats. By the late 1980s, a recession had gripped the Quad Cities area of the state, as manufacturing and food processing plants closed. Searching for a way to spark local development, Art Ollie, a Democratic state legislator from Clinton, Iowa, hit upon the idea of riverboat excursions featuring gambling. Vaguely citing the heritage of Mark Twain and the legendary exploits of Mississippi riverboat gamblers, Ollie and others began seriously pushing the idea of riverboat casinos, which, they hoped, would draw tourists to the otherwise moribund region.

Bob Arnould, the speaker of the Iowa House, picked up Ollie's idea and ran with it. In the fall of 1988, Bernard Goldstein, the former owner of the Alter Company—a Quad Cities–based concern that started as a scrap-metal yard and diversified into the grain business, barge fleets, and real estate— articulated plans to build a hotel/entertainment complex with a dock that would provide access to an excursion boat outfitted with slot machines and gambling tables. Goldstein's lobbying and public-speaking efforts contributed to the August 1989 passage of a riverboat gaming act by the Iowa legislature. According to the new law, gambling was legal in licensed boats on the Mississippi, Missouri, and other rivers, if approved by the adjacent county. Riverboat gambling was about to become a reality.

The bill that the legislature passed mandated that gambling could take place only during scheduled cruises, and players were limited to bets of $5 and losses of $200 per trip. The gaming area could take up only one third of the vessel's floor space. Even with these restrictions, boosters projected that the gambling boats would draw eight million tourists to Iowa a year. Goldstein commissioned the construction of the *Emerald Lady* and *Diamond Lady,* specially designed gambling ships, and eagerly anticipated April 1, 1991, the first day that the boats could legally operate.

In the meantime, residents of Illinois, particularly Moline and Rock Island, began clamoring for a piece of the coming gambling bonanza. The state accordingly legalized riverboat gambling without the onerous bet and loss restrictions of Iowa. Even before the first boat had sailed, Iowans knew this was bad news. Goldstein scaled back plans for his gambling boats, and most of the ancillary hospitality developments never happened, as developers feared that gamblers, primarily drawn from Illinois and Missouri, would simply play at the more convenient and less restrictive Illinois boats.

Marred by competition or not, riverboat gambling still promised to transform the towns that permitted it. On April 1, 1991, a Mark Twain look-alike and a hoop-skirted southern belle welcomed visitors on board the *Diamond Lady;* owner Bernard Goldstein smashed a champagne bottle across its bow and, live on *Good Morning America,* officially launched the boat. Howard Kiel, a Quad Cities native, placed the ceremonial first bet at a craps table (he rolled a seven and won), while Vanna White gave the boat's wheel of fortune its first spin. Outfitted in mahogany, marble, and chrome, the *Diamond Lady* evoked Victorian elegance on the Mississippi.

Illinois, which passed a riverboat gaming act in January 1990, also launched its first gambling boats in 1991. Casinos in Alton and East St. Louis siphoned off gamblers from St. Louis, while boats in Elgin, Aurora, and Joliet captured most of the Chicago gamblers. Several of the earliest Iowa riverboats sailed out of state, heading for more lenient jurisdictions. In 1994, the state eased many of its restrictions, but much of the damage had already been done. Since the 1980s, Iowa has legalized bingo, lotteries, horse racing, and riverboat gaming. Yet the failure to stave off competition from Illinois has prevented Iowa from establishing itself as a true gambling destination.

Mississippi did not make the same mistake. In 1990, it had promulgated the nation's most liberal riverboat gambling law, approving an unlimited number of floating casinos on local option on the Mississippi, Gulf Coast, and virtually every other body of water in the state. The casinos did not need to cruise or even be able to sail. Although several working boats relocated from Iowa when gambling started, eventually Mississippi "riverboat casinos" became barges connected to hotel/entertainment complexes.

By a quirk of fate, the same boat that opened Iowa gaming also commenced gambling in Mississippi. Bernard Goldstein, frustrated with mounting losses on his Iowa boats, moved his flagship *Diamond Lady* and *Emerald*

Lady to Cadet Point, Biloxi. While conducting his due diligence in Biloxi, he learned of the long-gone Isle of Caprice offshore gambling resort. Wanting to make a fresh start, Goldstein redecorated his boats with palm trees and luminous colors and named his new casino, which comprised the boats and a barge to which they docked, the Isle of Capri: Both boats opened on August 1, 1993. Other boats soon followed, and Mississippi casinos were an immediate success.

Though they were legal throughout the state, only two areas became casino clusters: Tunica, close to Memphis in the north of the state, and the Gulf Coast (Biloxi, Gulfport, and Bay St. Louis) in the south. Tunica County, previously most famous for its Sugar Ditch, a slum replete with shacks, outhouses, and open sewers, became renowned as a boom town. The opening of the Splash Casino in October 1992 cut the county's unemployment rate in half. Casinos worked a similar miracle on the Gulf Coast, reviving the hopelessly stagnant tourist industry.

These casinos catered primarily to drive-in players and were not much different from completely landlocked casinos in downtown Las Vegas or Atlantic City. Casino barges were large and frequently multistory. In some, it was difficult to tell exactly when a patron had left the terra firma of the grounded hotel portion for the barge. Steve Wynn's $675 million Beau Rivage, which opened in 1999, featured a barge so spacious and a stabilization system so sophisticated that one might as well be on land. In the aftermath of Hurricane Katrina in late 2005, the Mississippi legislature approved land-based casinos near former riverboat sites on the Gulf Coast, and casinos were lauded as a major tool for the rebirth of the region's economy.

Other states followed Iowa, Mississippi, and Illinois. Louisiana became the fourth riverboat casino state in 1991 when it authorized fifteen riverboats; a year later, a land-based casino was approved for New Orleans. Despite the history of legal gaming in New Orleans, which hosted the nation's first legal casinos, casinos in Louisiana have not been the unmitigated success that they were in Mississippi. Like Iowa, Louisiana quickly became a one-stop gambling shop, with racinos, riverboat casinos, Harrah's New Orleans casino on land, and video gambling devices at bars and truckstops.

In 1998, scandal rocked the state when former governor Edwin Edwards was indicted along with six others for racketeering and extortion. Edwards was notoriously corrupt—he had already been the subject of twenty-two grand jury investigations—but seemed bulletproof, once boasting that the only way he could lose an election was to get caught "with a live boy or a dead girl." He was charged with blackmailing prospective casino licensees to the tune of $3 million. Former San Francisco 49ers chairman Eddie DeBartolo was also enmeshed in the scandal: He later testified that he had given Edwards $400,000 after Edwards had threatened to use his influence to block DeBartolo's license application. Edwards was convicted, and casinos continued to operate in Louisiana without interruption.

Missouri followed in 1992 and Indiana in 1993, bringing the number of riverboat casino states to six. Missouri attempted to limit losses, something that had been tried—and would soon be rejected—in Iowa. Boats were initially required to cruise for two hours, and patrons were limited to a $500 loss limit on each tour. Using player cards, the casino tracked purchases of gaming chips or slot machine credits. When the $500 limit was reached, the player was barred from playing any further. Though the state eventually dropped the cruise requirement and permitted patrons to come and go as they pleased, the $500 loss limit remained in force.

As riverboat gaming became a fixture of the Midwest and central South United States, a score of casino chains soon appeared, some lasting longer than others. Grand Casinos opened three Mississippi properties and invested in Bob Stupak's Stratosphere in Las Vegas before being acquired by Park Place Entertainment and ultimately folded into casino giant Harrah's. Argosy grew to become the nation's fifth-largest casino operator before being bought by racetrack and racino operator Penn National. Isle of Capri opened or bought casinos in five states and a Florida racetrack and even expanded internationally with a Bahamas location. Ameristar, a company that began as Cactus Pete's casino in Jackpot, Nevada, grew to own seven casinos. Countless other groups owned one or two casinos.

Even before the first riverboat casino had been launched, South Dakota experimented with a different model of limited gambling. A 1988 referendum permitted legal gambling in Deadwood, South Dakota, the notorious Wild West town. This was not a sweeping enactment of wide-open gambling: Only blackjack, poker, and slot machines were permitted, and bet limits were capped at $5. South Dakotans were more interested in historic preservation than recreating the Las Vegas Strip, so they limited each establishment to a maximum of thirty slot machines. To prevent monopolization of the market, all licensees had to be state residents, and none could own more than three gambling halls.

Gambling started on November 1, 1989. Operators proved ingenious in combating the restrictions on casino size, combining their properties within a single building to present the appearance of a single large gambling hall. Cadillac Jack's, for example, boasted over 170 slots and nine table games. This was no MGM Grand, but it was certainly a departure from the spirit of the

Although some states, like Illinois, initially required riverboat casinos to actually cruise, others permitted nonsailing barges that were "boats" in name only. Harrah's first riverboat property opened in 1993 in Joliet, Illinois, where the *Southern Star* and *Northern Star* sailed six three-hour tours a day. Harrah's Vicksburg (which later became the Horizon Vicksburg) was, from the start, an integrated casino-hotel complex whose gaming floor just happened to be floating on the water.

law. The state raised the betting limit to $100 in 2000, which led to a dramatic increase in blackjack play. With the popularity of the HBO series *Deadwood*, a record numbers of visitors flocked to the town to soak up the period replica atmosphere and recapture the spirit of the Old West by gambling a bit.

Limited gaming began in Colorado in 1991, when the first gambling halls opened in the historic mining towns of Cripple Creek, Blackhawk, and Central City. Gambling was limited to slot machines, poker, and blackjack and bets capped at $5. Since the state hoped to advance historic preservation and tourism though casino development, it required that all gambling halls conform to pre–World War I architectural design standards. Still, some of the larger casinos of Blackhawk, in particular, seem to be merely scaled-down versions of Las Vegas casino resorts.

But Colorado limited gaming has also created a unique gambling center. Bennett Avenue, Cripple Creek's main thoroughfare, was soon dotted with dozens of storefront gambling halls whose facades are reasonably faithful reproductions of turn-of-the-century designs. Colorful names like Creeker's, Midnight Rose, Brass Ass, and Virgin Mule adorn a row of unpretentious gambling halls that cling to the spirit of old Colorado. In some, players receive complimentary popcorn and hot dogs, a far cry from the gourmet offerings of the Vegas Strip's celebrity chef eateries, but the right fit for Bennett Avenue. Cripple Creek casinos offered something strikingly different from the Strip and Strip imitators: small, informal gambling halls set within a genuinely historic milieu.

Where Colorado and South Dakota embraced gambling, at least in part, to preserve the past, the city of Detroit courted casinos to help build its future. The city had suffered grievously since the 1970s, its industrial base decimated, many of its businesses closed, and much of its population in flight. When the neighboring province of Ontario opened the government-owned Casino Windsor on the opposite side of the Detroit River in 1994, the Motor City had a new problem: state residents spending their discretionary income in Canada. The state's legislators concluded that three casinos within the city of Detroit would recapture these gamblers and anchor future tourist development.

But the road to casino nirvana wasn't easy. Originally, planners envisioned a waterfront strip of casino hotels that would become a tourist destination. While the city attempted, unsuccessfully, to buy the land, the state allowed the three winning bidders—the Greektown Casino, owned by a local group of investors, the MGM Grand, the Detroit branch of the Las Vegas gaming giant, and the MotorCity Casino, partly owned by the Mandalay Resort Group—to operate "temporary" casinos. By 2001 these casinos were grossing over $1 billion a year, and it was becoming increasingly clear that the original development plan was not feasible. The next year, the state allowed its casinos to open permanent locations away from the waterfront.

The Greektown opened with only one restaurant but, as the only casino owned completely by Michigan residents, pointedly advertised that it wished its guests to patronize a range of local eateries. This was the exact antithesis of the Las Vegas Strip/Atlantic City model of the self-contained casino resort. The MGM Grand Detroit opened in a former Internal Revenue Service building, perhaps the most creative repurposing of a government office in a long while. The MotorCity, not to be one-upped, was housed in an extensively remodeled Wonder Bread factory, newly decorated with automobile-inspired murals.

Detroit casinos offered the usual array of games—blackjack, craps, baccarat, roulette, and slot machines—and showcased the new prominence of gambling in American life. Once, elected officials professed to consider gambling halls a disgrace. Now, they celebrated the conversion of government buildings and shuttered factories into lucrative casinos, hungry for both jobs and tax revenues. No oration about the changed place of gambling in American society could be more eloquent.

19

All In

◆ ◆ ◆

Legal gambling, on the decline worldwide at the beginning of the twentieth century, was flourishing with unprecedented vigor by its end. It is too early to judge the bigger sweep of history, but it seems that the world is entering a sustained period of gambling's growth not seen since the European gambling boom of 1650–1800.

Japan is as enthusiastic a nation of gamblers as can be found. A lottery game named *hobiki* was popular as early as the fourteenth century. Like American lotteries and bingo, this was considered "not really gambling," and paved the way for pachinko, a machine game that, in sheer volume, may be the most popular form of gambling in the world.

Pachinko has its roots in the 1920s with the "Corinthian game," an imported American pinball game styled "Korinto Gemu" by the Japanese. As an adaptation to the space-conscious island, an enterprising game maker in Osaka or Kanazawa flipped the machine upright. With a flipper shooting a small steel ball into a vertical maze of pins and holes, the player hoped that his ball landed in a special hole that would entitle him to bonus balls. Known as *pachi-pachi* and *gachanko* after the sound of the careening steel ball, the game became popular at street fairs throughout Japan in the 1930s.

During World War II the Japanese government prohibited *pachi-pachi*, but after hostilities ended it grew in popularity. Improvements to the game, which soon became known as pachinko (a combination of its previous names), made it more appealing to a wider range of players. The introduction of the "machine gun" model made playing far easier: Instead of manually inserting balls, players simply had to pull a lever to shoot them onto the board in rapid succession. Even novices could fire as many as a hundred balls per minute. Because balls could be redeemed for prizes and, indirectly, cash, the game was for many a way of gambling, even though, officially, it was not a gambling game. Whatever its legal status, the game was sweepingly popular: By 1953, there were nearly forty-five thousand pachinko parlors in Japan.

After the government outlawed the continuous-shooting machine-gun version, the pachinko industry went into a decline that was reversed only by a relaxation of the ban. The 1980 introduction of the "Fever Model," which combined elements of pachinko with slot machines, sparked another pachinko renaissance. In the 1990s *pachisuro* machines, thinly disguised Western slot machines, began appearing in many parlors, and many operators renovated their halls in an effort to attract a more diverse clientele.

Today, an estimated twenty million Japanese men and women (the game is forbidden to minors) regularly play pachinko. The elite players, professional *pachipuro*, actually earn their living from pachinko. This is possible because the game is a mixture of chance and skill. Parlor owners periodically adjust the pins on nonelectronic pachinko machines to vary the payouts, and habitual players work to identify high-paying machines and mercilessly exploit this advantage. Even electronic machines are periodically altered to boost the odds, so professionals continued to work the system in the digital age.

Though millions of Japanese play pachinko for cash every day, the game is not officially considered gambling because it is technically not played for money. Players pay a fee to "lease balls," and winners accrue buckets of the glittering globes, which they redeem at a parlor booth for prizes ranging from pickled plums and sausages to home electronics and gold nuggets. To receive cash, players take their prizes to nearby *keihin kokanjo* (prize-exchange facilities), which are not owned by the pachinko parlors but work closely with them. Literally exchanging the prize for cash through a hole in the wall, players walk away with a return on their pachinko investment, while the exchange agent will sell the prizes back to the parlor, retaining a commission.

Simply considering money wagered, pachinko is the world's biggest gambling industry. Throughout Japan, seventeen thousand parlors with five million machines take in ball rental fees of $300 billion a year, far outstripping total American casino totals: The United States has approximately six hundred casinos with five hundred thousand slot machines. Together, all American casinos make less than $50 billion per year; total American gaming revenues are about $74 billion.

The Japanese are equally enthusiastic about other gambling. Horse racing traces its roots back to the eighth century, when equine contests were a semireligious rite common at festivals. In 1862, the redoubtable British introduced modern racing into Japan at Yokohama. Modern racing dates from 1948, when the government dissolved the semiprivate Japan Racing Society and assumed all responsibility for national racing itself, channeling much of the ensuing revenues into rebuilding efforts. Japanese racing was split into "national racing," overseen by the new Japan Racing Association, and "local racing," the responsibility of local governments. National races took place on weekends and holidays, while local races became weekday events. In both national and local racing, pari-mutuel betting helped to stir fan interest, which was considerable: Racing became a popular spectator sport in Japan.

Known as *keirin,* Japanese bicycle races began in 1898, and are today a thriving form of relatively cheap entertainment: Admission to a *keirin* track is generally less than $1, and betting on the outcome gives spectators the chance to win—or lose—as much as they can risk. Races combine loud music, garish lighting, and costumes seemingly inspired by the Mighty Morphin Power Rangers. *Keirin* enthusiasts study racing forms and tabulate the potential impacts of a number of salient factors just as intently as their horse-racing brethren. At present, there are nearly fifty *keirin* tracks in Japan, including two domed circuits that allow racing no matter what the weather. Races are telecast throughout Japan, though betting is only legal when tickets are bought from machines—there is no off-course bookmaking. The government directly regulates and taxes *keirin* betting, which features seven types of bets that are similar to popular horse-racing bets. About four thousand professional *keirin* racers live in Japan, and the sport became an Olympic event in 2000.

Betting on motorboat races began in 1951. Bettors get seventy-five percent of the pari-mutuel pool returned to them as winnings, with the remaining twenty-five percent divided between sponsoring governments and organizations and the Nippon Foundation, a body dedicated to global peace and progress. Today, betting takes place at twenty-four racecourses throughout the country where, on a typical race day, twelve six-boat races take place. Betting on auto races and soccer, though not as unique as the motorboat betting, are also healthy gaming industries in Japan.

Mahjong, introduced to Japan after its first appearance in China during the late nineteenth century, proved just as popular there. Japanese mahjong developed its own idiosyncratic rule twists. Starting in the 1980s, video mahjong swept over Japan and became popular in video arcades and home computers. Though in many countries mahjong betting is almost symbolic, in Japan large sums are frequently at stake.

In the twentieth century, lotteries also returned. Popular from the fourteenth century, they were banned in 1842 but, as part of the drive to fund postwar reconstruction, returned as Takara-kuji or treasure lotteries. The national government abandoned its lottery in 1954, leaving the field open to forty-seven prefectures and twelve cities that together held a legal lottery monopoly. Together, these entities ran seven major lotteries whose popularity exceeded even that of pachinko; weekly tickets usually sold out soon after their issue. When, in 1977, tickets sold out more quickly than expected, disappointed would-be players started a riot that claimed several lives.

The Otoshi-dama Kuji, or New Year's Gift Lottery, lets senders buy postcards preprinted with numbers for less than a dime each, add a personal greeting via woodblock design at home, and mail them out to friends. When, in January, the post office announces the winning numbers, winners rush to redeem their cards for everything from sheets of stamps to consumer electronics. By the 1990s, Japan ranked fourth internationally in gross lottery sales, behind only the United States, Germany, and Spain.

Though Japan has accounted for about two thirds of Asian lottery sales, several other nations in the region also adopted lotteries throughout the twentieth century. The Hong Kong Jockey Club inaugurated a lotto-type game in that British protectorate, and Taiwan, South Korea, Malaysia, Singapore, Thailand, and the Philippines all boasted lotteries by the 1970s. In some nations, lottery and draw games were initiated to fill the consumer need and to supply additional government revenues, but in others they had more specific purposes. South Korea, for example, began a Housing Lottery in 1969 for the sole intention of raising funds to house families still displaced by the war of 1950–1953, though in the 1980s it also helped raise money for the 1988 Seoul Olympic Games.

Neighboring China is even more dedicated to gambling. Despite the Communist regime's official antigambling stance, it has a thriving legal lottery and an abudance of illegal gambling. In recent years, Macau's growth has been particularly astounding. Early in the twentieth century, the city's gambling was stagnating. Lottery tickets sold in Hong Kong and surrounding areas allowed Macau to extract a few million dollars a year from its neighbors (much to the chagrin of British and Chinese authorities), but the scheme of licensed gambling as practiced through the early 1930s produced few economic gains for Macau, which had no real agricultural, commercial, or industrial development. If gambling were to serve as the linchpin of a tourist economy—seemingly the only option remaining—Macau's rulers would have to clean it up.

At about the same time that the Nevada legislature rolled the dice on "wide-open" gambling, the Macau government undertook a complete over-haul of its legal gambling. It swept away the rabble of the fan-tan houses, re-placing the proletarian gambling havens with more refined casinos in upscale hotels. Thus, the Portuguese governor argued, Macau would attract wealthy inhabitants of surrounding Chinese cities and perhaps even the sporting gen-tlemen of Europe. Instead of licensing any operators who applied, the gover-nor granted a monopoly franchise to a single syndicate, the Tai Xing Company, run by Kening Gao and Laorong Fu. Starting in 1937 this com-pany opened casinos along the Rua da Felicidade and Rua 5 de Outubro. De-spite the governor's original plan that the casinos appeal to Europeans, these houses offered only the traditional Chinese games of chance, something that precluded their appeal to all but the most receptive of occidental visitors.

In the decades after the first casino opened in the Central Hotel, the Tai Xing Company successfully maintained its monopoly, working diligently to exclude potential rivals from the bidding process. Because Laorong Fu be-lieved (as do many Chinese), that red is lucky and white and green unlucky, he insisted that all Tai Xing employees never wear red, and that all its casinos (and even his own house) be adorned in white and green. His customers were willing to buck the superstition and continued to gamble on traditional Chi-nese games in Tai Xing casinos.

The Tai Xing monopoly survived World War II and the turmoil of the Chinese Revolution, both of which left Macau relatively unscathed. In the postwar period, Tak Iam Fu ran the company. He controlled all gambling and lotteries in Macau and had diversified into real estate (with four apartment blocks) and transportation (he owned several trade vessels). He also owned a Macau–Hong Kong ferry, which shuttled his casino customers back and forth. An absolute prohibition on gambling enacted by the People's Republic of China in 1949 gave Macau, and hence the Tai Xing Company, a regional monopoly on casinos, but China's restrictive border controls cut off the flow of visitors from the mainland, although British prohibitions on casino gam-ing kept Hong Kong a captive market.

As Macau adjusted to the postwar world, its government decided that gambling-related tourism was the colony's best hope for economic develop-ment. Law 18267, promulgated by the Portuguese colonial authority, desig-nated Macau a "tourism and gaming region," signaling the increased emphasis to be placed on gambling as an economic driver. The government opened the gaming monopoly to bidding in 1961 and awarded it to the So-ciedade de Turismo e Diversões de Macau (STDM, "the Macau Tourism and

Amusement Company"). Founded by Stanley Ho with Yin-dong Huo, De-li Ye, and Han Ye, STDM would extend its control of Macau's gambling monopoly to a near domination of the enclave, and make its managing director, Dr. Stanley Ho, wealthy and powerful.

According to his official biography, Ho started life with the proverbial silver spoon in his mouth; born November 25, 1921, into a wealthy Hong Kong family (his granduncle Sir Robert Hotung was knighted by King George V and his grandfather was a well-connected businessman), Ho lived the typical life of a rich scion, until, in 1934, his father suffered devastating financial reverses and fled to Vietnam, leaving his wife to raise her children alone. Young Stanley suddenly felt the press of poverty, and from here, his life becomes a true Horatio Alger story, as only his hard work and dedication stood between him and hunger. Ho applied himself anew to his studies, earning a scholarship to Queen's College (Hong Kong), from which he graduated with top grades, and then a place at the University of Hong Kong, where his studies were interrupted by the vicissitudes of the World War II.

Ho fled to neutral Macau before Japanese forces occupied Hong Kong, arriving with ten Hong Kong dollars in his pocket and an unquenchable ambition. He took a job as a secretary at the Companhia Leun Chong, a trading concern that acted as a middleman between Chinese, Japanese, and Portuguese interests. Ho later said he had acted as a "semi–government official," obtaining much-needed rice, sugar, and beans from the Japanese for the Macau government. He learned Japanese and Portuguese (he was already fluent in English and Chinese) and parlayed his knowledge and skill into a partnership in the firm. After the war, he pursued shipping, finance, and trade, and returned to Hong Kong in 1953 as a young millionaire.

When the Macau administration opened the gambling monopoly, Ho jumped at the chance to extend his fortune, despite his personal distaste for gambling. One of his oft-repeated aphorisms, that "success is not by luck," refutes the gambler's trust in fortune, and though called "the king of casinos" and even "the god of gambling," he has never been known to gamble himself. Nevertheless, Ho applied himself to the administration of STDM with the same fire he showed in school and with Leun Chong.

STDM started with a single casino in the Estoril Hotel and a floating casino moored in the Inner Harbor, the immodestly named Macau Palace. By 1975, STDM operated three other casinos: the Casino Kam Pek, the Jai Alai Casino, and the STDM flagship, the Casino Lisboa. STDM continued to expand its selection of betting vehicles, offering greyhound racing, jai alai (from 1972 to 1990), horse racing, instant lotteries, and eventually soccer betting.

Betting on horses in Macau is centuries old. As early as the seventeenth century, Portuguese colonists imported Iberian tests of equestrian skill, snatching rings with lances and conducting mock battles. By the early nineteenth century, a racecourse built near the barrier gate crossing into China hosted regular races. Portuguese and Chinese crowds representing a cross-section of Macau's society boisterously cheered their favorites, betting heavily on the outcome.

In 1963, STDM absorbed greyhound racing at the Macau Canidrome sponsored by the Yat Yuen Canidrome Club. The only greyhound racing track in Asia, the Canidrome still hosts sixteen races four night a week, and the public (as of early 2005) could watch and bet on the races online. The syndicate built a large modern track on Taipa Island for trotting in 1980, but it struggled and in 1989 STDM acquired the Macau Jockey Club and reconfigured the track for Thoroughbred racing.

Following a new franchise contract in 1983, casinos become more than a major source of revenue for Macau's government: They became its majority revenue producer. Rising from around thirty percent of the public revenue to nearly two thirds of it, STDM's gaming taxes kept Macau's administration afloat throughout the 1980s and 1990s, when Stanley Ho's enterprises contributed around eighty percent of Macau's tax revenue.

Still, with Macau's 1999 reversion to China came the possibility that the communist Chinese authorities might suppress Macau's casinos. But with an eye on both prosperous Hong Kong (which returned to Chinese control in 1997) and Taiwan (which Chinese authorities still wanted to reunite with the mainland), the People's Republic guaranteed no interference in Macau's economy for the next fifty years.

Stanley Ho's casinos represent a unique mélange of Eastern and Western gambling. Casino Lisboa, his flagship, has expanded over the decades to include one thousand rooms. Though STDM introduced Western games in 1962, many Asian favorites remain, including *sic bo*, fish-prawn-crab *sic bo*, *pai gow*, mahjong *pai gow*, *pacapio* (the original keno), and the venerable fan-tan. Though these games, particularly *sic bo*, have their devotees, they all bow to baccarat, now the most popular game in Macau. Other Western games, like blackjack, roulette, and boule, can be found in Macau, along with newer imports like three-card baccarat and three-card poker, though the American signature game of craps is nowhere to be found.

The Lisboa hosts weekend bingo games, and scattered around the main casino's perimeter are slot machines, another American gaming innovation that has yet to truly catch on with Macau gamblers. Slots are called tigers,

Stanley Ho's Casino Lisboa became the hub of his Macau casino,
transportation, and real estate empire.

with the intimation that they will inevitably prey upon their players. Still
Macau's operators—Chinese and Western alike—have attempted to widen
the appeal of slots. New casinos have modern slot machines, and several slots-
only halls owned by Melco, a company chaired by one of Stanley Ho's sons,
have opened throughout the city. One machine plays on the reputation of
slots as "hungry tigers" by incorporating a traditional legend about a hero who
defeated a ravenous tiger. When a player hits a jackpot, he is treated to a video
reenactment of the hero's triumph.

Chinese gamblers subscribe to a set of superstitions that seem bizarre and
perhaps even silly to Westerners, who often forget that their own superstitions are no less arbitrary or foolish. Crossing under ladders, black cats, the
number thirteen, broken mirrors, and spilled saltshakers elicit little response
in China, reminding Westerners that there is nothing universal about luck.
Instead, the visitor to a Macau casino would do well to avoid the unlucky
number of four and exult in the supremely lucky eight. She should not carry a
book into the casino, because, owing to the sound of the Cantonese word for
"book," it is considered unlucky.

To those familiar with American casinos, with their uniformly spaced slot machines and orderly assortments of table games, the Lisboa and other STDM casinos might seem downright unruly. Gamblers crowd the tables, staking wagers while stacked two or three deep, shrouded by thick clouds of cigarette smoke. Away from the hullabaloo of the main floor at the Lisboa, American visitors might be perplexed at another Macau institution—private gaming clubs. Subleased by the gaming operator to a string of junket operators and concessionaries, these rooms host high-stakes gambling in relative privacy. Regularly allowing maximum bets of up to a half-million patacas ($65,000 U.S.), these rooms attract the cream of China's gamblers, who chiefly play baccarat. With their play, STDM revenues soared, and the city administration, collecting over one third of all casino earnings as taxes, enjoyed one bumper budget surplus after another.

By the time of the reversion, Stanley Ho had become a Macau colossus: not only the most powerful man in the city, but *the* powerful man in the city. Under his leadership, STDM became a tourism giant and the biggest employer in Macau. In addition to its gaming enterprises, STDM owned or invested in several hotels, Macau's largest department store, the Macau Tower Convention and Entertainment Center (opened in 2001 and featuring the world's tenth tallest tower), the TurboJet Macau–Hong Kong ferry service, Macau International Airport, and a host of other projects. Ho was also the group executive chairman of Shun Tak Holdings, chairman of Seng Heng Bank, and a member of numerous community and philanthropic groups. Ho, the nongambler, has parlayed his Macau casino franchise into riches, influence, and (despite whispers of connections to organized crime triads), respect. For years, when Chinese gamblers planned a trip to Macau, they said that they were "going to visit Uncle Stanley."

Yet Ho's domination of Macau's casino market did not long outlast the enclave's return to Chinese rule. His monopoly franchise expired in 2001, and the new government of the Macau Special Administration Region (SAR) reopened the bidding and awarded the right to operate casinos to three entities: a subsidiary of Dr. Ho's STDM called Sociedade de Jogos de Macau (SJM); a joint venture of Las Vegas Sands, Inc. (owners of the Las Vegas Strip's Venetian); and Galaxy, a Chinese company, and Steve Wynn's Wynn Resorts. Macau's extension of casino privileges to these three groups struck a balance between preserving its history and identity and allowing new entrepreneurs to bring fresh ideas to the city, and inspired a wave of new construction.

At the same time, as the Chinese government liberalized border restrictions, a flood of new visitors descended upon Macau. Chinese authorities gradually expanded the number of cities allowed to issue tourist visas to

Macau, thus virtually guaranteeing a steady rise in that city's guests. Macau's annual visitation nearly doubled to fifteen million, and with the prospect of continued liberalization, its boosters nervously anticipated infrastructure improvements that would let the city cope with a doubling of that number.

The new entrants into Macau promised to transform the city into a true international tourist attraction. Though they combined to bid for a casino license, the Venetian group and Galaxy chose to operate separate casinos. The Venetian group opened its Sands Macau first, in May 2004, a stone's throw from the Macau ferry terminal, the point of debarkation for most arrivals from Hong Kong. The opening was not without drama; when someone spread a rumor that the casino would give away free chips on its first day, a near riot enveloped the casinos and eager crowds literally broke down the doors to get inside and begin playing. Since then, the action has settled into more consistent frenzy, and the success of the Sands Macau has demonstrated that Western operators can profitably run casinos in Macau. The Sands has already begun construction on an ambitious "Cotai Strip," an eastern version of the Las Vegas Strip built on reclaimed land. In twenty years, it is likely that Macau will be much like Las Vegas: one city featuring legal gambling among many in the region, with superior entertainment and retail offerings that give it continued luster.

A few other Asian countries permitted casinos, often with the caveat that their own citizens were forbidden from entering them. South Korea's casinos date from 1967. Located in hotels, they cater primarily to Japanese and Taiwanese visitors. Cheju Island, billed as "Korea's Hawaii," developed as South Korea's honeymoon resort of choice, though for foreign visitors, the island's eight casinos became a major attraction. As foreign casino visitation dropped in the late 1990s, the South Korean government allowed Koreans to visit a single casino, Kangwon Land, opened in 2000 in a depressed area. Though isolated, the casino proved successful, as more than two thousand Koreans passed through its doors each day, sometimes sleeping on the floor while waiting for a spot at a table.

By the 1990s, Nepal, Cambodia, and Myanmar had casinos, but the largest casino industry in the region belonged to the Philippines, whose Philippine Amusement and Gaming Corporation or PAGCOR opened nearly twenty casinos throughout the country and became a chief source of government revenue. Even North Korea, one of the world's most isolated nations, opened foreigner-only casinos in Pyongyang in the late 1990s. Supplementing its usual income streams (chiefly the sale of arms and counterfeit currency), the government in 1999 opened the Emperor Casino in isolated Raijin. It struck gold catering to Communist Chinese, at least until the Chinese government, discovering that officials were carting embezzled funds to the casino, forbade its citizens from traveling there.

Malaysia's casino monopoly has been parlayed into an empire by Tan Sri Lim Goh Tong. Lim, born in Fukien province, China, moved to Singapore in his teens and found work in construction. He gradually established himself as one of Malaysia's most influential developers. Lim was seized in 1964 by a vision for a Malaysian resort "above the clouds" that would offer a cool respite from its tropical climate. He personally oversaw the construction of a hotel, utility services, and an access road for his Genting Highlands, perched six thousand feet above sea level about forty-five miles from Kuala Lumpur. The project received a boost when, in 1969, Malaysian prime minister Tunku Abdul Rahman awarded Genting the nation's only casino license, with the caveat that Malaysian Muslims were barred from gambling at the casino, though Muslims from other nations were free to play without interference and non-Muslim Malaysians also were welcome. Despite Muslims making up about half the nation's population, the enthusiasm of ethnic Chinese in Malaysia and Singapore represented a tremendous gambling market, and Lim enjoyed a monopoly

Over the next quarter century, Lim developed Genting Highlands into one of the world's major resorts. Six hotels, including three five-star operations, offered guests over eight thousand rooms. With its convention center, entertainment venues, and restaurants, it was a supersized Las Vegas Strip casino set "on top of the clouds" (the Chinese translation of *Genting*) in a predominantly Muslim nation. The Casino de Genting offered a range of Western games from blackjack to Caribbean stud poker, and Asian favorites like *sic bo* (called *tai sai*) and *pai gow*. The casino had five separate themed gaming areas, and in 2004 a neighboring StarWorld casino, geared toward the "young at heart," offered patrons the chance to watch MTV and sip coffee while playing.

Under Lim's leadership the Genting Group became Malaysia's leading corporation, developing casinos worldwide and diversifying into noncasino hotel resorts and cruise lines, as well as seemingly unrelated areas: power generation, paper and box manufacturing, palm oil plantations, and information technology. Lim's investment in the Foxwoods casino enabled the Pequots to start a casino giant of their own in the 1990s. Though Lim had already established himself as an important Malaysian developer before he gained the nation's casino franchise, it is unlikely that he would have become so fabulously wealthy without it (with a personal net worth of over $2 billion, he regularly made *Forbes* magazine's list of the world's richest people). Worth more than even Stanley Ho, he was the world's wealthiest casino operator. In 2003, at the age of eighty-five, Tan Sri Lim Goh Tong stepped down as chairman of the Genting Group and was succeeded by his son, Tan Sri Lim Kok Thay, who had been with the company since 1976. The elder Lim's career is a testament to the powerful attraction of a casino, particularly where it is marginally forbidden.

In contrast to Malaysia's partial ban, the prohibition of gambling was almost absolute in the predominantly Muslim countries of the Middle East and northern Africa. But as oil-rich sheikhs became legendary high rollers in Monte Carlo, Las Vegas, and Atlantic City, several Islamic nations experimented with casinos open to foreigners. In cosmopolitan Lebanon, Beirut's Casino du Liban opened in 1959. Routinely profitable until it was forced to close in 1975 due to the ongoing civil war, it reopened in 1996, admitting all foreigners and even those Lebanese who were not government or military employees, cashiers, or earners of less than $20,000 a year.

Egypt has for decades encouraged a small casino industry, chiefly to generate revenues and acquire foreign currency: Egyptian nationals are barred from entering, though anyone else with a passport is welcome. In the small casinos, games include blackjack, baccarat, and even poker, and bets are often made with American dollars. Saudis are the most common visitors to Egypt's casinos, though they are joined by a healthy sprinkling of American and European tourists. Morocco and Tunisia have similar casinos, and Turkey has, since 1969, alternated between permitting and prohibiting casinos—as of 2006, they are forbidden.

Israel, laboring under no significant doctrinal objections to gambling, failed to develop land-based casinos, though casino cruise ships operated out of the Red Sea port of Eilat. In 1998, the Oasis Casino opened in Jericho under the Palestinian Authority; it was the single largest private investment in the Authority's territory. By permitting a casino that would cater to Israelis, who are esteemed as serious gamblers, the Palestinian Authority was emulating American Indian nations who used their sovereignty to offer gambling in hopes of economic development. Amid political turmoil, the casino closed in 2001. Subsequently reopened, the casino became a political football in both Israel and Palestine.

In many of the nations of the British Commonwealth, where gambling had long been an integral part of the national culture, it enjoyed unprecedented state sanction in the twentieth century. In Australia, lotteries became a regular part of life as states began to use them to raise funds. Tattersalls had been running "sweeps" in Tasmania—and selling sweepstakes tickets in other states—since 1896. Queensland's Golden Casket lottery began in 1916 as a matter of wartime expediency: It funded several war-related projects. New South Wales legalized its own lottery in 1931, and in 1954 Tattersalls relocated to Melbourne following Victoria's legitimatization of the lottery. Lotteries became an increasingly common source for government and charitable revenues, and even funded the construction of the famous Sydney Opera House, an instructive case: The original charitable appeal drew in less than $1 million toward the construction of what has become one of Australia's national treasures, but the lottery garnered more than $100 million.

Legal betting on horses similarly expanded during the twentieth century. Starting in 1960, Australian provinces began creating Totalizator Agency Boards (TABs) to oversee on- and off-course betting. In the 1940s, American soldiers stationed in Australia brought with them the gambling craze that was then sweeping their homeland: bingo. Several states licensed the game as a charitable entertainment, as most organizers used profits to assist soldiers' organizations. After the war the game, which became better known as housie-housie or simply housie, was restricted by some states but never suppressed. Dominated by female players and with most of its profits dedicated to charities, the game was viewed as a relatively innocuous form of gambling.

The same cannot be said for pokies, or poker machines, which have been widely played in Australia since the early twentieth century. These are not necessarily video poker machines; early on Australians began calling American slot machines "poker machines," because many of them retained the original card-based symbols on their reels. (The British, on the other hand, adopted "fruit machine" for the same device, focusing on the symbols that appeared on most machines.) Through the 1920s and 1930s, pokies appeared intermittently in clubs and hotels, sometimes supported by the law but illegal at other times. In 1956, New South Wales sanctioned pokie gambling in clubs, provided that they adhered to state licensing requirements. It was an auspicious decision; by 1980 the state had more than twice as many pokies as the gambling mecca of Las Vegas. By the 1990s, every state, save Tasmania, had legalized pokies in clubs, and Australia had nearly 185,000 gambling machines.

These clubs were not the gilded aristocratic hells of London's West End, or even the gentleman's retreats of nineteenth-century Australia. They were open to anyone interested in spending time with those who share common interests, including sports like bowling and golf. Revenue from the slot machines enables club members to enjoy discounted meals, drinks, and entertainment. In addition, clubs sponsor a variety of community activities and charitable projects. Sports betting, particularly on soccer and rugby, became another popular democratic gamble in the late twentieth century. But pokies continued to account for almost two thirds of all Australian gambling in 2004.

The Wrest Point Hotel Casino in Hobart, Tasmania, opened in 1973 as Australia's first legal casino, becoming Australia's largest hotel and a popular convention destination. The MGM Grand Darwin, opened in 1979 in a temporary facility, was Australia's second casino; it was sold in 2004 to New Zealand–based Sky City and became the Sky City Darwin. A host of other casinos opened in the 1980s. Lasseters, in Alice Springs, was a relatively small resort, deep within Northern Territory. Casinos opened in Adelaide, Gold Coast, Perth, and Townsville, then, in the 1990s, Canberra, Brisbane, Melbourne, and Sydney. Australian casinos are, in general, slightly scaled-down versions of their Las Vegas Strip counterparts, with lounges, restaurants, showrooms, swimming pools, and all the accoutrements expected of vacation resorts.

Given their reputations as fierce gamblers, Australians are well represented in the ranks of gambling celebrities. The winner of the 2005 World Series of Poker, for example, was Australian pro Joseph Hachem. While winning a WSOP bracelet is no mean feat, no Australian could match media baron Kerry Packer as the nation's biggest gambler. Majority shareholder in Publishing and Broadcast Limited, an Australian multimedia combine, Packer also owned an interest in Melbourne's Crown Casino and Perth's Burswood Casino, making him a rarity: the casino owner who is also a dedicated gambler. One of the world's most notorious high rollers, Packer was known to win or lose millions of dollars in a single weekend. It was said that Packer beat several Las Vegas casinos so consistently, winning tens of millions of dollars over two years, that they refused to allow him to play anymore. At the time of his death late in 2005, whether because of lucky gambling or not, his net worth was estimated at $4.7 billion.

Gambling in nearby New Zealand often overlapped Australia's. Horse racing, for example, was wildly popular in both countries, and New Zealanders frequently bet on Australian races and vice versa, though prohibitions against much gambling remained in force. In the earliest decades, bookmakers ran off-track betting illegally, using the same wire networks that worked so well for Americans. They were tacitly accepted by police; their organization, the

Dominion Sportsmen Association, even supplied official race results to government-owned radio stations.

Since 1881, pari-mutuel betting by totalizator had been legal at New Zealand's racetracks. Illegal bookmakers working away from the track thrived, however, and both racetracks and the government grew concerned. In 1951 the first off-course betting offices opened under the aegis of the Total-izator Agency Board (TAB). They were an immediate hit: Lines ran around the block, and operating hours were soon expanded to meet the demand. Though some bookmakers chose to retire, and police pressure on those who flouted the law intensified, illegal betting on races continued. By the 1980s, TAB officials demanded that the police more vigorously enforce the gambling laws and pleaded for a relaxation of their rules that would let them open branches in stores, tearooms, taverns, and hotels, much as American lotteries do. In 1983, the first subagencies opened and, along with the introduction of telephone betting, televised races, and exotic new bets, revived slumping TAB revenues.

Horse racing had competition for the New Zealand gambling dollar. Housie swept across the islands in the 1940s, and in 1959 the national government legalized it, provided that housie operators received licensing from the Department of Internal Affairs. As elsewhere, working-class women formed the core of housie enthusiasts. Most games took place in hotels in working-class areas. Concerns over the housie "epidemic" prompted more restrictive legislation in 1976 and 1982; hours of operation were cut back and prize amounts restricted. Illegal games began to proliferate, and the government responded in 1989 by authorizing "super housie," or high jackpot games, and liberalized license requirements. This move opened the door for the proliferation of smaller operators, particularly among seniors' groups. Housie has become as much an institution in New Zealand as bingo in the United States. Lotteries, poker machines, and legal casinos (in Christchurch, Auckland, Dunedin, Hamilton, and Queenstown) followed in the 1990s.

Canadians had a similarly restrictive relationship with gambling until relatively recently. Canada's 1892 Criminal Code had made all gambling illegal, with three exceptions: raffles for charitable or religious organizations, which eventually included bingo, carnival games of chance at agricultural fairs, and betting at racetracks. Bingo was particularly popular. Private bets and social card games were also common, and many other forms of gambling flourished under the radar of the police. At the racetracks, pari-mutuel systems replaced traditional bookmakers thanks to a 1920 amendment that authorized racing associations to use the machines. Though charitable and carnival games were widely varied, none of them were permitted to use dice, as a 1922 amendment to the 1893 law had specified that dice games were indisputably illegal.

In 1969, the Canadian legislature amended the Criminal Code to permit provinces to operate lotteries and slot machines, and to license charities, fairs, and social clubs to do the same, though slots were only permitted if the provincial governments themselves owned them. Lotteries helped to defray the costs of the Montreal Olympics in 1976 and the 1988 Calgary Winter Olympics. Charity bingo also soared in popularity in the 1970s, becoming a billion-dollar industry.

Canadian lotteries (offered by several provinces) developed much like those of other nations, following a unique track: They are either owned by provincial governments or dedicated to charitable organizations. This system took shape slowly. First, in 1975 an Alberta children's summer camp received permission to operate a casinos for four days to raise funds. The casino was such a success that hundreds of groups followed suit, and British Columbia, Saskatchewan, and Manitoba joined Alberta in promoting a system of permanent casinos that allowed different charity groups to participate.

From the outside, these charity casinos looked much like privately owned gambling halls. Indeed, private companies own the casinos themselves and rent out their facilities to charities, who operate the table games and keep the lion's share of profits—minus government taxes and fees. Charity casinos often turn up in unlikely places. The West Edmonton Mall, billed as the world's biggest entertainment and shopping center, has a charity casino of its own, the Palace Casino. Games offered include all of the Las Vegas favorites. Even dice were legalized in 1999 and are used to play craps and *sic bo*.

Eastern Canadian provinces took a different tack, figuring that, if casinos were to be run for the public benefit, there were no more deserving charities than the provinces themselves. In 1993, Quebec's Casino de Montréal, one of the largest in the world, opened to immediate success. The following year, the province of Ontario opened the Casino Windsor, a gambling hall a mere mile from downtown Detroit. Government-owned casinos opened in Nova Scotia in 1995, making it the sole Atlantic province with casinos. Even though these casinos are owned by the provinces, private management companies, sometimes American, often managed them, taking a share of the profits. The lucrative Casino Windsor was managed by an affiliate of Park Place Entertainment and, after 2005, Harrah's Entertainment. This has caused some consternation in Canada, as economic nationalists chafe at the flow of "public money" south of the border.

There is also controversy over government ownership of video lottery terminals (VLTs), which are essentially slot machines run by provincial lottery commissions. These machines first appeared in Atlantic provinces in 1990 and spread rapidly throughout the nation. Because they are easy to play and accessible in the course of everyday life (Nova Scotia initially permitted VLTs in convenience stores and gas stations), VLTs have drawn fire from those concerned about problem gambling. Critics wonder how a provincial government can balance its desire for higher revenues with a need to "protect" its citizens from the ravages of gambling. Though this quandary is more obvious because the provinces actually own the machines, governments around the world increasingly face these difficult questions, as their interest in gambling has shifted from control to regulation to, in many cases, active promotion.

Nations colonized by the Spanish and Portuguese had just as varied a history of gambling as those settled by the British and French. In Mexico cockfighting is a major attraction, running openly near the American border. The nation has experimented with using gambling to lure Americans south: For a time in the 1920s and 1930s, a casino at the Agua Caliente racetrack catered to Californians who were forbidden from gambling at home, but casinos were first restricted in 1935, and in 1947 the Federal Gambling and Raffles law declared casinos illegal, banning all gambling except for betting on horse racing and sports, lotteries, and raffles.

Brazil boasts an illegal game that flourishes alongside a legitimate lottery. The *jogo do bicho*, or animal lottery, despite its fanciful name, is a simple numbers game common in poorer neighborhoods. But its origins are unique. In 1888, Baron João Batista Viana Drummond, seeking to raise funds for the Rio Zoo, created a lottery that paired twenty-five animals with four numbers each; to select a winner, the lottery organizers picked a number from one to a hundred (represented by # 00). Bettors on the ostrich, for example, would win if the number picked was from one to four. The game soon spread throughout Rio and then all of Brazil. Most other gambling is illegal: Casinos have been since 1946, and bingo, which became incredibly popular in the 1990s, was outlawed in early 2004 by presidential decree, though later in that year the Senate repealed the ban. A majority of Brazilians, nevertheless, favored the closing of the bingo halls.

Latin American nations from Costa Rica to Chile have encouraged the growth of casino industries of various sizes, usually to encourage tourism and the importation of foreign currency. In general, they have alternated between state and private ownership. Panama, Uruguay, and Chile and Argentina (with the biggest industry) have all had legal casinos for decades. Until 1944, all Argentine casinos were privately owned. In that year, a presidential decree closed all private casinos; some were nationalized, while others were simply forced to close. The government placed responsibility for running the casinos in the hands of the National Lottery Administration, which had been running draw games since 1893.

In the 1940s and 1950s, the national government opened new casinos and reopened old ones. National casinos had dress codes, high betting limits, and no slot machines. This was supposed to encourage a ritzy atmosphere, but from a practical point of view, it limited revenues. In the 1960s, the national government began transferring control of casinos to provinces and authorized provinces to build their own casinos. These gambling halls usually scrapped the dress code, permitted smaller-scale betting, and installed slot machines. Predictably, they became popular with locals, and several national casinos were forced to close. In the 1980s, support for the privatization of the casino industry grew, and in the following decades many of the casinos were sold. By 2004, there were more than seventy casinos throughout the country, and casino advocates were hopeful that one would finally open in Buenos Aires itself.

In the Caribbean, a diversity of casinos sprouted near the glittering beaches, all intent on enticing the lucrative tourist trade. They had varying degrees of success. Puerto Rico, a United States commonwealth, had small casinos in several hotels by the 1960s. The Caribe Hilton, Sheraton, and San Juan casinos were the largest and most popular. The remote El Conquistador, located in Fajardo, was one of the best known, but though it was filled to capacity with gamblers during the four-month winter season, players were scarce in the off-season. Others of Puerto Rico's resorts faced this problem, to a lesser extent, complicated by the government's mandating lower betting limits and barring locals. Elsewhere the casino business proved more lucrative. The Bahamas, which first allowed casinos in the 1960s, hosted first Resorts International, then the Atlantis, on Paradise Island; by 2005 four casinos had opened. Other island nations, particularly Aruba, Curaçao, and the Dutch Antilles, have small casinos catering to foreign tourists that, tacitly or explicitly, discourage locals from playing.

Although gambling was common among the indigenous peoples of southern Africa and the first waves of European sailors, soldiers, and settlers to inhabit the area in the seventeenth and eighteenth centuries, it was outlawed in 1889 in areas under British control, as it already was in the Boer Republics. The gambling ban (which excepted horse bookmaking) continued after the consolidation of British and Boer governments into the Union of South Africa in 1910. A 1933 law stiffened antigambling penalties, and six years later the ban was extended to pin-table machines and other mechanical gambling contrivances, though totalizators were specifically excluded, as they were an integral part of the conduct of legal pari-mutuel gambling. As many other nations looked to legalize gambling in the 1960s, South Africa turned in the other direction, passing a comprehensive Gambling Act in 1965 that forbade all lotteries, sports betting, and games of chance.

Despite the ironclad prohibition against gambling, many South Africans still wanted to play. In 1976, the creation of "independent" black homelands within South Africa (though they were ostensibly separate nations, only the South African government recognized them as such) allowed for the legalization of casino gambling in the four nominally independent states of Bophuthatswana, the Ciskei, the Transkei, and Venda; Bophuthatswana and the Transkei became famous for their casino resorts built on the Las Vegas model, offering guests gambling and entertainment.

Southern Sun, the biggest casino owner, started in 1977 with a single casino in Mmabatho, the capital of Bophuthatswana, in the north of South Africa. Its chief executive, Sol Kerzner, had, in 1964, built his first hotel in Durban with borrowed money, using pictures of Miami hotels he'd clipped from travel brochures for inspiration. Kerzner followed the Mmabatho casino with a resort that was to become South Africa's most famous, Sun City. Located in a section of Bophuthatswana only about a hundred miles from Johannesburg, the Sun City resort opened in 1979 with many of the amenities usually associated with the Las Vegas Strip (and lacking in South Africa): roulette, slot machines, an eighteen-hole golf course, discos, restaurants, softcore pornographic movies, and a multiracial buffet of sequined showgirls. Half of the profits went to the government of Bophuthatswana, and though few blacks had the money to register at the hotel, many patronized the discos, restaurants, and slot machines, taking their places amid a multicultural mix of South Africans of Indian, Chinese, Afrikaner, and English descent. In a 1981 *New York Times* interview, Kerzner tactfully expressed a hope that, having learned to live together while on vacation, South Africans might be able to coexist someday at home.

Sun City triggered controversy. Kerzner, eager to establish it as an international destination, opened his checkbook to entertainers and athletes: Frank Sinatra inaugurated the seven-thousand-seat Sun City Superbowl with a nine-night stand in 1981 for a reported $1.6 million, and Sun City hosted several boxing matches. Opponents of apartheid charged that the resort legitimated the system and called on travelers and entertainers to boycott Sun City.*

Yet Sun International continued to expand, ultimately owning over a dozen homeland casinos and a string of resort hotels. In 1992 Kerzner opened the Lost City, a $300 million casino resort complex at Sun City, complete with a three-story water slide, massive wave pool, artificial volcano, and a giant casino. This audacious resort opened when homeland casinos were already in transition. The process of creating majority rule in South Africa had already begun and it was clear that the days of the homelands were numbered. Perhaps the new government might outlaw all casinos; perhaps it might allow casinos closer to Johannesburg. Neither possibility boded well for homeland casinos. In addition, a recession and the international stigma of its associations with apartheid rule had dimmed the luster of Sun City.

Kerzner, dogged by charges that he had bribed several homeland government officials, divested himself of his South African interests and moved to London. Sun International South Africa continued to operate casinos and hotels in that country, while Kerzner, with his Sun International Hotels (later renamed Kerzner International), relocated to the Bahamas. In 1994 Kerzner bought the former Resorts International casino in the Bahamas from Merv Griffin, who had owned it since 1988. He opened Atlantis on Paradise Island, an aquatic casino-hotel that he billed as the world's first amphibious resort, and bankrolled Connecticut's Mohegan Sun casino. Two years later he acquired Merv Griffin's Resorts, once Resorts International, Atlantic City's first casino. Sun International's originally announced plan to embark on a $500 million transformation of the resort into an Atlantic City Atlantis were later scaled back, and in 2001, after more than $300 million in losses, the company sold Resorts.

By the time Sol Kerzner had passed the reins of Kerzner International to his son Butch in 2004, the company had emerged as an international casino and hotel powerhouse. Meanwhile, South Africa's casino industry had seen a decade of turmoil. Even before the dissolution of the homelands, their casinos faced competition from scores of unlicensed casinos that sprang up throughout South Africa. Before they were suppressed, as many as three thousand of them were in operation; some had as many as eight hundred slot machines.

---

*In 1985, Artists United Against Apartheid, a group of "rockers and rappers united and strong," recorded a musical protest against the resort that popularized the phrase "I ain't gonna play Sun City." Several well-known entertainers, however, did play Sun City, at least until the attention drawn by the AUAA song made it an impolitic tour stop.

In 1996, South Africa's new government passed the National Gaming Act, which provided for the inauguration of a national lottery and set out the rules for the opening of as many as forty casinos. Sun International was forced to divest itself of half of its homeland casinos but remained the country's dominant casino operator. Foreign companies invested in the new South African casino industry; in 2001, Park Place Entertainment opened Caesars Gauteng on the former site of the World Trade Centre, where the multiparty negotiations that led to South Africa's first multiparty elections were held in 1992, a sure commentary on the place of gambling in the new South Africa.

Casinos in the rest of sub-Saharan Africa were small and scattered, usually found in hotels catering to foreigners. The first African casino of note, Ghana's Casino Africa, opened in Accra in 1960. Before the development of homeland casinos, gambling resorts in Swaziland and Lesotho catered to South Africans. Kenya developed a relatively large casino industry, with nine casinos catering to tourists (though winnings could not be converted into foreign currency) as well as horse racing. Oil-rich Nigeria likewise supported many casinos. Elsewhere, casinos were less common. Nations like Uganda, Benin, and Congo sported a single casino. Throughout the continent, lotteries and horse racing proved to be the most popular forms of gambling. Here, as elsewhere, twentieth-century governments invariably turned to gambling for help when facing problems of underdevelopment and revenue shortfalls.

In Europe, most of the nations that had, in the late nineteenth century, prohibited gambling brought it back, mostly to raise money. The most common were lotteries. By the 1980s, state lotteries based on the traditional draw method (numbered tickets were sold and distributed, with winners picked in a public drawing) could be found in every Western European nation save Luxembourg, whose citizens had to content themselves with Belgian lotteries. Lotto games, in which players picked up to seven numbers from a pool of up to forty-nine, spread throughout Western Europe during the 1970s. With its ease of play and higher prizes, lotto soon was more popular than classic draw lotteries, although both continued to coexist.

Horse racing, supported by both pari-mutuel betting and, in some countries, bookmakers, was present throughout Western Europe, though nowhere was it as popular as in Great Britain (in the 1980s, almost two thirds of all money bet on horses in Europe was wagered in that island nation). Football (soccer) became a pan-European obsession, and Europeans organized their football betting in a singularly efficient fashion. Toto, which grew in popularity during the 1950s, particularly in Germany, Switzerland, and Italy (where toto betting reached manic proportions), was essentially the American pool or parlay card game, where bettors picked the winners of up to twelve games. As such, it was more akin to the lotto than serious sports betting.

Toto took off, and several national lotteries banded together to form Intertoto, an early European cooperative organization, that promoted the game and football. With the success of toto, many lottery directors' only regret was that there were not enough games in the summer off-season to continue the lucrative game in those months. So in 1961 European lotteries banded together as the European Football Pool and established the International Football Cup, a tournament stocked with teams that did not qualify for the more prestigious UEFA Champions League and UEFA Cup. Everyone won: Football fans got year-round action, lotteries the same, and less successful teams a chance to compete on an international stage. To Americans, such a close partnership between gambling interests and team sports is unthinkable, but Europeans consider it as natural as a casino's sponsoring a championship boxing match.

European casinos grew dramatically during the twentieth century. The casino revival had started in 1907, when France legalized baccarat. Casinos at Cannes, Antibes, Juan-les-Pins, Deauville, and Nice really prospered after 1933, when the government permitted them to try roulette and trente-et-quarante.* Slot machines were permitted only after 1987. Though this provision was modified in 1988, when casinos were permitted in larger cities, France retained many of its smaller casinos; there were over 180 throughout the country by 2004. French casinos have sponsored many cultural events; the International Film Festival at Cannes is underwritten by the Groupe Lucien Barrière, a syndicate that owns casinos in every corner of France.

This was an arrangement followed elsewhere; the famous Montreux Jazz Festival, for example, began in the Montreux casino (also owned by the Group Lucien Barrière) in 1967 and became an internationally celebrated music event.** French casinos adhered to stricter rules than their come-as-you-are American cousins, with formal dress codes and entrance fees. Many casinos around the world adopted these policies, while others favored more lax "Las Vegas–style" rules. A dozen or so large casinos account for much of

---

*The government promulgated the 1907 law with the recent history of spa resorts in mind. As a result, French casinos had to be located in seaside resorts, thermal spas, or health retreats.

**The casino entered heavy-metal lore forever thanks to Deep Purple's "Smoke on the Water," a song that describes how, during a 1971 concert by Frank Zappa and the Mothers of Invention in the casino's showroom, a fan fired a flare gun, starting a conflagration that claimed the entire casino. Members of Deep Purple watched the building burn from across Lake Geneva and later set a narrative of the incident to music.

the country's casino business. Baccarat, blackjack, and roulette remain the most popular games, though American poker and craps have made inroads, particularly in the larger casinos. Boule and trente-et-quarante are still found, and some smaller casinos have only boule and slot machines. Despite their sophistication, with the coming of slots, they have become considerably more open than in years past and often appeal to the mass market: By the late 1900s, slots accounted for ninety percent of French casino profits. Still, the image of tuxedoed chemin-de-fer players remains a powerful draw.

In the twentieth century, no single political system had a monopoly on gambling: Fascist, socialist, and even Communist governments chartered lotteries, and Germany's National Socialist party, in 1933, reopened the casino at Baden-Baden. Though German chancellor Adolf Hitler himself approved the opening of the casino, some Nazis were distressed to learn that the French lessee designated to actually run the casino (the Brownshirts knew nothing about roulette), Paul Salles, was actually a front for other financiers, the most influential of whom were Jewish. Gambling continued at Baden-Baden until August 1944. Until the collapse of the Third Reich was imminent, a single casino operated in German-occupied Austria and another in Poland.

In the immediate postwar period, when Baden-Baden was the headquarters for French military forces in Germany, locals planned to reopen the casino as soon as possible—no matter what the political system (monarchy, dictatorship, or democracy), they were sure that a casino was the best bet for their prosperity. Elsewhere, German casinos were returning. In 1948, Bad Durkheim and Bad Neuenahr, two municipalities in the state of Rhineland-Palatinate, opened legal gambling houses, the first outside of Baden in the twentieth century. On April 1, 1950, Badeners rejoiced as the gambling rooms originally built by Bénazet nearly a century earlier reopened. Other German states licensed casinos, despite the disapproval of the federal government, and, though taxes on revenue are sometimes higher than eighty percent (Nevada casinos, by contrast, pay taxes of about 7% on gaming revenue), the industry expanded; by the time that East and West Germany reunified in 1990, West Germany had thirty-five casinos; by 1992, six casinos had already opened in the formerly Communist east.

In Austria, private gambling rooms had been the norm since the 1920s, and in 1933 the national government got in on the action by licensing casinos at several resorts. The company chosen to operate the monopoly concession, Austrian Casinos AG/Laxenburg, was, curiously, dominated by Canadians. When Hitler's Germany annexed Austria in 1938, all casinos, save the one at

Baden bei Wien, were closed. In 1944, that casino closed as well. Almost immediately after the war, Austrian casinos reopened in the western, Allied-controlled regions of the country. After Soviet withdrawal from the east in 1955, casinos reappeared there as well. Following a turbulent decade, the Austrian government stripped Austrian Casinos AG/Laxenburg of its casino concession and formed a new group, Casinos Austria, owned by a combination of government bodies, and travel, banking, and utility companies.

Under the leadership of Leo Wallner, Casinos Austria came to operate twelve casinos in Austria. Prevented from opening more casinos in its native land by the terms of its government concession, Casinos Austria grew internationally. By 2005, the company operated—and often held ownership stakes in—fifty-one casinos in thirty-five different countries, including Egypt, South Africa, Argentina, Greece, Australia, and Switzerland. It also operated over a dozen casino cruise ships—a bit of an irony for a casino monopoly in a landlocked European nation with no known nautical heritage.

Elsewhere in Europe, restrictive casino licenses became the norm in the years after World War II. Casinos from Ireland to Greece catered to both tourists and visitors; some were state owned, others privately held. But none had the bizarre history of Belgian gambling halls. Casinos had been legal in that small nation (it was home of the original Spa) until 1902, when, reportedly, the prime minister (disturbed by his son's gambling problem) prompted Parliament to ban all gambling, and the nation's casinos were closed.

But there was a complication: Nearly a decade later, King Albert I, seeking to amuse a few visiting royal guests, was told by his councillors that gambling was now illegal. It was good to be the king; he used his influence to convince the nation's procurators, or prosecuting attorneys, to tolerate a few casinos that catered to "the right people." These opened in 1911 and, though the law clearly said that gambling was illegal, continued to operate without any further supervision until 1952. In that year, procurators, still acting beyond the law, placed several restrictions on the casinos: They were to be private clubs owned by their host cities and had to verify the identities and collect membership fees from all gamblers. Over one third of Belgium's population, including those under twenty-one, lawyers, public officials, soldiers, and public employees, were excluded from gambling. Any sort of external advertising or promotion was banned, and the number of casinos limited to eight. The benign underenforcement of Belgium's gaming laws ended in 1999, when its Parliament finally declared casinos legal and permitted them to install slot machines, which had been forbidden under the old regime. The number of casinos was still restricted, and they remained relatively small, with a few table games and slots each.

Great Britain had, in 1853, suppressed legal gambling almost entirely. Still, illegal betting, particularly on horses, continued. In 1960, Parliament relegalized bookmaking, with great success. The legislation led to an unintended explosion in unregulated "social clubs" that were actually gambling casinos. Over twelve hundred of them were in operation when, in 1968, Parliament changed the law and drastically curtailed the growth of casinos. Gambling could now take place only in private clubs; a prospective visitor had to wait at least forty-eight hours after applying for admission to enter the premises, something that put a damper on catering to spontaneous tourist drop-ins. The law also limited the number of slots—increasingly the most lucrative game—to two per casino.

There were further limitations. Advertising and even overly elaborate signage was banned, and hours of operation were limited. Clubs strictly enforced their own codes of conduct, permanently barring players who flouted them. One London casino tore up the membership cards of 167 patrons who committed the offense of parking within three blocks of the casino in violation of the club's agreement with surrounding residents. This was clearly not the freewheeling "Last Frontier" of Las Vegas or Reno.

While their casino gambling took place under straitened circumstances, Britons enjoyed betting on horses and sports with unparalleled freedom. The United Kingdom is the last major holdout against pari-mutuel betting, as fixed-odds wagering with bookmakers continued to dominate that country's betting. British betting was dominated by a few major betting chains: Ladbrokes, William Hill, Coral Eurobet, and Stanley Leisure. In the late 1990s, casinos began to catch up to bookmakers: In 1997, Parliament loosened restrictions a bit, and slot machines were allowed in more locations

In the postwar years, Josip Broz Tito's Yugoslavia boasted the largest casino industry of any Communist nation, and after the dissolution of that country, casinos in many of its former provinces, particularly Croatia and Slovenia, became reasonably successful. Throughout Eastern Europe, the fall of the Iron Curtain brought an explosion in casino development. Bulgaria, Hungary, and the former Yugoslav republics saw the many new casinos, but the former Soviet Union was perhaps the state where the mushrooming of gambling halls was the most astounding. By 2005, there were sixty casinos in Moscow alone, though many of them were small and operating on the margins. Still, Russian casinos brought in $5 billion in the previous year, more than Atlantic City, New Jersey.

As casinos spread throughout Europe, any semblance of exclusivity that Monte Carlo may have retained vanished. Its casinos were now distinguished only by their history, never a quality held in high esteem by those eager to get the best odds and the highest action. Now outfitted with slot machines and featuring punto banco (American baccarat), craps, and even double-zero roulette, the four casinos of Monte Carlo still sought to cater to elite customers in the age of mass marketing. Though the name continued to inspire visions of elegance, the resort had clearly been surpassed: The four hotels of venerable Société des Bains de Mer, for example, had about one sixth as many rooms among them as Las Vegas's Monte Carlo casino resort—the Nevada theme park version was bigger than the original.

European lotteries expanded along with the continent's casinos. In 1933, the fascist government of Benito Mussolini introduced a lottery connected to an automobile race held in Tripoli, which was then a colonial possession of Italy. Other lotteries introduced after the end of World War II culminated with horse races or domestic auto races. Still, the dominant Italian lottery game is a Genoese-style lotto game, with five balls drawn out of ninety. At the dawn of the new millennium, Italians chose from ten separate wheels, and therefore ten different "lotteries," in various cities throughout the peninsula.

France joined Italy in resuming its lottery in 1933 when the Loterie Nationale (National Lottery) was reestablished under the auspices of the Société Française de Jeux, the French government's gaming monopoly. The Loterie's flagship game, the Nationale, was drawn weekly, with seven additional games run on holidays and in conjunction with major horse races. The Nationale was a simple draw game, like the traditional lotteries, where participants only had to buy a ticket and hope for the best. In 1976 the Société inaugurated Loto, a weekly game in which, as in Casanova's lottery, players picked numbers to win, in this case six out of forty-nine. Both games continued to return healthy profits to the government for decades.

To the north, in the nation of Belgium, the game also made a twentieth-century comeback. Following the decline of its colonial interests in the Congo, the government began casting about for any way to fill its budget deficits and decided to inaugurate a national lottery. Beginning in 1934, the Colonial Lottery benefited both the government and a variety of charities, foremost among them the National Charity for Disabled Ex-Servicemen. After the disruption of World War II, the Colonial Lottery resumed, though with Congo's independence in 1960 it was renamed the African Lottery before becoming in 1962 the National Lottery. Over the next forty years, the

National Lottery introduced a variety of new games, including lotto and scratch cards and became, in 2002, a completely public company. The enterprising burghers of Renaissance Bruges and Ghent would, no doubt, be proud.

In the 1930s, a decade of gambling expansion worldwide, the Parliament of the newly independent Republic of Ireland revived the state lottery with the Public Charitable Hospitals Act. This act permitted hospitals to conduct sweepstakes drawings under the watch of government auditors in order to improve their buildings and to offer free medical treatment to the needy. These drawings, which often used the results of English horse races for their random element, proved remarkably successful, with booming ticket sales in the British Isles, Europe, and throughout the world. Brokers throughout the United States, for example, offered tickets to the "Sweeps" during years of American lottery prohibition. Over the next fifty years, the Irish Sweepstakes awarded nearly a half-billion dollars' worth of prizes and, thanks to a joint program with the International Red Cross, provided benefits to hospitals throughout the world.

The British state lottery rose from the dead in the 1990s, another decade that saw a worldwide expansion in gambling. In 1994, Parliament introduced the National Lottery, a charity lottery operated by a company named Camelot, the winner of the competitive bid process. The National Lottery's flagship game is a classic lotto, with six numbers drawn from a pool of forty-nine. Britons avidly took to the lottery, and by 2004 they were betting about £90 million a week ($168 million) on the lotto and other games, including "instant win" scratch-cards.

The lottery has steadily grown. In 1997, the National Lottery began twice-weekly drawings (Wednesdays and Saturdays), and in 2002, Camelot won the right to continue to administer the lottery. The National Lottery pays less than half of its revenues back to winners as prizes and splits its profits after administrative costs between Good Causes, a fund that distributes money to a variety of charities, and the British government. After a decade of operation, Dianne Thompson, the CEO of Camelot, boasted that the National Lottery had made seventeen hundred new millionaires and contributed over £16 billion to over 180,000 charities. The people of Great Britain have come a long way from their earliest lotteries on gold plate, suits of armor, and books, and in that nation as elsewhere, the lottery has become an fundamental part of charitable and governmental funding.

Even Communists jumped on the lottery bandwagon. In 1958, the Soviet Union began offering lotteries that featured both prizes of both cash and merchandise—the latter probably the more coveted reward, given the notoriously short supply of Soviet consumer goods. On the eve of the Soviet Union's implosion, each of its fifteen constituent republics had lotteries, and national games benefiting the sports, arts, and other areas were popular: Soviet citizens spent over $700 million on draw, lotto, and instant-win tickets in 1989. After the collapse of Communism, lotteries continued to flourish in both the former Soviet Union and its erstwhile empire in Eastern Europe. The humble lottery had outlived Communism and was a sign of the worldwide popularity of gambling at the start of the twenty-first century.

PART NINE

Into the Twenty-First Century

♦ ♦ ♦

A carnival atmosphere spread over the aging Binion's Horseshoe in May 2003. Since the first satellite games had begun in early April, excitement over that year's World Series of Poker—the thirty-fourth edition of the tournament at the Horseshoe—had steadily mounted. While most tourists and conventioneers—and even high-stakes gamblers—were drawn to the glitter of the Las Vegas Strip, the casinos of downtown's Fremont Street were, for the moment, the center of the gambling universe, thanks to the increasingly intense spotlight shone on the world's most famous poker tournament.

That year, the tournament had 839 players—a substantial increase from the 450 drawn a scant three years before. Thanks to burgeoning television coverage and the proliferation of online poker, the game was returning to prominence as a quintessential American pastime. The tournament, of course, drew players from all over the world. Once, the tournament, with its $10,000 buy-in, was hallowed ground. Seasoned road gamblers like Johnny Moss, Doyle Brunson, Jack Strauss, Puggy Pearson, Crandall Addington, "Amarillo Slim" Preston, and "Cadillac Jack" Grimm, most of them from Texas, jousted with young guns like Chip Reese, nonpros like Hal Fowler, and the game's tragic wunderkind Stu Ungar, who, when he won his first gold bracelet in 1980, was the youngest player ever to do so. Now, it seemed, with poker on television and Internet tournaments providing nonthreatening proving grounds, the Series was anyone's to win.

Despite the increased attention, Binion's was still Binion's, and the game remained unmistakably old Vegas: Weathered gamblers surfaced to recount old war stories as hawkers pitched books, cigarette lighters, and jewelry outside "Benny's Bullpen," a converted multipurpose room that, for a few weeks in April and May each year, was the most important piece of real estate in the poker-playing world. Outside the bullpen, paintings of earlier tournaments hung, somberly reminding players of the glories of the past.

By the end of the fourth day of the tournament's main event—no-limit Texas *hold 'em—the field was down to nine, who took their places at the final table. Esteemed pros like Scotty Nguyen, Phil Ivey, Howard Lederer, Men Nguyen, and Annie Duke had finished in the money but out of the main table, while countless other pros did not even recoup their $10,000 entrance fee in the tournament game, though they doubtless had better luck at side games in poker rooms throughout town.*

When the smoke had cleared and the final hand was played, poker history saw a turning point. Chris Moneymaker, a Tennessee accountant who had never played a live poker tournament before and had gotten into the WSOP through an online tournament, bested Sam Farha, a cagey veteran, and took home a then-record $2.5 million jackpot. It will never be as infamous as Bill Hickok's aces and eights, but Moneymaker's full house (fives over fours) signified a dramatic change in gambling: In an increasingly borderless world, the future was online.

20

A Clockwork Volcano

• • •

TECHNOLOGY AND TRIUMPH

In the 1990s, the Las Vegas Strip reinvented itself as an adult playland that borrowed elements from around the world. Recreations of Venice, Paris, and New York shared the skyline with oversized medieval castles, exploding volcanoes, and dueling pirates. The three-mile stretch of erstwhile desert highway promised to whisk visitors to worlds of adventure, little more than a cab ride away. But the exotic atmosphere belied the serious business that gambling had become. High-tech cameras followed every throw of the dice, and random-number generators determined slot jackpots. Meanwhile, gamblers around the world logged on to the Internet to bet. Gambling may have seemed edgy and spontaneous, but it was increasingly by the numbers. Just as they tamed the fire that had destroyed Pompeii, making it punctually erupt for the delight of their guests, casino operators channeled the primal force of gambling.

By the end of the twentieth century, casino floors had changed remarkably from the days of sawdust and spittoons. Closed-circuit television cameras had replaced direct observation via catwalks, making casino surveillance much more sophisticated. Slot machines, which were once a toylike diversion on the casino's perimeter, emerged to become the casino's primary money-maker. Slots first outearned table games in 1981, and twenty years later, they accounted for two thirds of gaming revenue throughout Nevada, and even higher portions in other states.

The mechanical reel machines of the 1890s, in which customer pulled a handle to set reels into motion, had become electromechanical hybrids by the 1960s. Even though they incorporated electronics to illuminate display panels and eventually to make game-play smoother (and less susceptible to cheating), old-style slot machines were simply not that exciting: Play was slow and payouts excruciatingly low. But with advances in electronics came a new generation of slot machines. In 1963, Bally Manufacturing, a longtime slot and amusement builder, introduced a machine called Money Honey, regarded as the first modern slot. With a 2,500-coin hopper it could offer large payouts, and its electronic innards paved the way for future refinements. By the end of the decade, Bally had created five-coin multipliers—machines that let patrons play extra coins in return for higher payouts—and multiline machines, on which players had several chances to win.

As computer and television technology evolved, video slots appeared. In 1963, Nevada Electronics produced the first game that combined electronics with a video display, a blackjack game called Automatic Blackjack. It was refined by electronic engineer Richard Raven, who renamed it Dealer 21. His Raven Electronics also produced a keno-based game and video versions of reel slot machines. Video slots were initially a tough sell: Players, conditioned to the reassuring sound of spinning wheels and buzzing bells, were leery of the newfangled machines. But slot players eventually overcame their skittishness and embraced video gambling, and by the turn of the century, video slots accounted for nearly half of American gaming machines.

Video poker became one of the most popular slot games. In 1978, a former Bally distributor named William "Si" Redd purchased a fledgling video slot manufacturer named Fortune Coin. Redd, who in 1981 renamed his company International Game Technology, introduced draw poker the next year. It was not the first attempt at a video poker machine, but it was the most successful. Under Redd, IGT capitalized on its poker machines and a stream of new games made possible by more sophisticated microprocessors, soon supplanting Bally as the world's leading slot maker. In 1986, IGT's Megabucks, a progressive slot-machine system that pooled bets from machines throughout the state of Nevada, debuted. Several spin-offs followed, and Megabucks became enshrined as one of the casino floor's most exciting slots. The largest single slot jackpot to date, $39,710,826.36, was won in 2003 on a dollar Megabucks machine at Las Vegas's Excalibur by a twenty-five-year-old Los Angeles software engineer.* IGT's wide-area progressives combine the instant gratification of slots with the life-changing jackpots of lotteries—a heady combination unimaginable when the first slots were crafted.

Technology also allowed casinos to more accurately track play and better evaluate complimentaries or "comps." Traditionally, players got comps based

---

*The winner declined to have his name publicized, but soon became the subject of an urban legend claiming that he was the victim of a tragic accident or overdose, becoming the latest victim of the supposed "Megabucks curse." IGT spokespeople have strenuously denied the rumor, insisting that he is still alive and well, and that nearly all winners enjoy happiness after their life-changing jackpots.

on what casino bosses surmised about their betting: If they seemed to be playing big (or have the potential to do so) casinos gave them up to one half of their expected losses in free food, drink, entertainment, and even transportation. Seeking to routinize this rather vague process, casinos started harnessing technology to better award comps. Beginning in the 1980s and intensifying in the next decade, casinos began to issue player loyalty cards that allowed them to track exactly how much slot players put into the machines. This would take comping decisions out of the hands of casino managers, instead relying on computer software. By 2005, casinos would begin experimenting with radio frequency identification (RFID) chips that would let them track table play with similar sophistication. Though traditionalists decried computer comp systems as yet another sign of the growing impersonalization of casinos, they were simply another adjustment casinos made to their exploding popularity.

The increasing technological sophistication of Strip casinos was, for a time, obscured by their stagnation. In the 1980s, the Las Vegas Strip's luster was undeniably dimmed. Competition from Atlantic City, while it had not appreciably cut into Nevada's bottom line, presented the possibility that another city might overtake Las Vegas as America's gambling mecca.* The 1980 MGM Grand fire had signalled a crisis of confidence on the Strip: While several casinos built major expansions and off-Strip locals casinos like Sam's Town and the Bingo Palace (later Palace Station) had opened, the Strip, despite the opening of a few smaller properties, had stagnated. Increasingly considered tacky, the Las Vegas Strip was aging in place.

As casino gambling became increasingly common, Las Vegas casino operators were forced to offer more than just gambling, lest they fade away like the Monte Carlo casino in the 1930s. This had been the clarion call of casino promoters since the 1940s, but the travelers of the 1990s were more sophisticated than their earlier counterparts, demanding luxury and scoffing at the "cheap eats" and inexpensive entertainment that had long been the defining feature of the Las Vegas Strip. To survive, the Strip would have to change.

Steve Wynn, owner of downtown's Golden Nugget, initiated that change. Wynn had announced plans to build a major casino resort on the Las Vegas Strip as early as 1981. Though that original project never saw fruition, Wynn did not give up. In January 1987, when he announced the sale of the Atlantic

---

*In several statistical categories, Atlantic City actually outpaced Las Vegas in the 1980s, the leading gaming destination in the nation.

City Golden Nugget to Bally's, he revealed that he had bought a parcel of land next to Caesars Palace on which he would build a luxury resort called the Bombay.

This project ultimately evolved into the Mirage, a resort that pulled the Strip into a new realm. The Mirage fused the titanic integrated resort pioneered by Kirk Kerkorian's International with the dreamy, dramatic opulence of Caesars Palace. Yet Wynn built the Mirage to be more than a glitzier version of its predecessors. Earlier Strip resorts were casinos first and entertainment resorts second. The Mirage, by contrast, was planned to be a general vacation attraction that incidentally had a casino.

Other casinos had lustrous neon signs or sweeping porte cocheres to greet visitors; the Mirage had a 4.5-acre South Seas–styled lagoon and an artificial volcano that erupted on cue every fifteen minutes. Inside, a white tiger habitat showcased the animals of Siegfried and Roy, the illusionists who would define Las Vegas entertainment for over a decade as the Mirage's resident headliners. Guests could walk though a rain forest nestled between the entrance and the casino and check into their rooms while watching the luxuriant lobby's twenty-thousand-gallon aquarium, whose calmly gliding fish provided a counterpoint to the frenetic excitement of the casino floor.

As work progressed on the Mirage, pessimists predicted that the resort, which needed to gross $1 million per day to break even, would surely fail, a victim of its heavy debt load. When the casino opened its doors on November 22, 1989, one hundred thousand guests had been optimistically projected. But twice that number turned out, a portent of the resort's success. Caesars Palace, the reigning money king of the Las Vegas Strip, earned $300 million in 1990, the Mirage's first year. The Mirage pulled in $420 million, vivid proof that it had taken the Palace's crown. Wynn's belief that the casino with the highest overhead would enjoy the highest profits was vindicated.

Wynn's overachieving Mirage had a sequel, the adventure-themed Treasure Island, which opened in 1993 as a lower-budget version of the original— it was distinguished by the pirate battle staged hourly on its Strip frontage. Five years later, Wynn debuted the Bellagio, an even more upscale rendition of the Mirage. When it opened, the Bellagio's $1.6-billion price tag made it the most expensive hotel, casino or otherwise, yet constructed. The Mirage's volcano was outdone by an eight-acre artificial lake that, every fifteen minutes, erupted into a terpsichorean tangle of lights and towering jets of water.

Inside the Bellagio, guests were wowed by the lobby ceiling, where artist Dale Chihuly created an unmatched aerial garden of two thousand handblown glass flowers. From there, visitors could walk into the casino's botanical

When it opened in November 1989, Steve Wynn's Mirage brought a new sense of luxury to the Las Vegas Strip. In the 1990s, other operators—and Wynn himself—continued to build upscale resorts focused on more than just their casinos.

gardens, which were regularly updated to keep pace with the seasons. The Bellagio eschewed the over-the-top theming that had come to dominate the Strip: There would be no re-creation of Venice's gondolas or Paris's street sweepers. Instead, the casino's more understated décor implied the luxury of its namesake resort on Lake Como. The Bellagio gave Wynn three Strip showstoppers along with his original downtown Golden Nugget, a Laughlin Golden Nugget, and Biloxi's Beau Rivage, a Gulf Coast version of the Mirage. Each of these was, in its own way, a casino design triumph, yet there was more to Wynn's empire than attention to architectural detail. A uniquely charismatic leader in an industry that was becoming increasingly impersonal, he inspired rare loyalty in his employees.

Wynn's model, a high-end property that combined the various functions of a casino resort with a dramatic theme, became the blueprint for the 1990s expansion of the Strip. Gourmet restaurants named for celebrity chefs replaced bargain-basement buffets as the Strip's culinary signature. Previously, casino operators had intended their guest rooms to be less than welcoming: More time upstairs meant less time at the tables. Consequently, the rooms of the Strip were cheap and unspectacular. The Mirage's plush rooms and suites were part of its attraction, and subsequent properties vied to have the Strip's softest beds, biggest TVs, and most appealing room décor. Casino entertainment had been dominated by feather-and-sequin extravaganzas that, while innovative in the 1950s and 1960s, offered few surprises by the 1990s, and their lounge acts and showroom headliners were generally past their primes. Wynn brought the surreal French-Canadian Cirque du Soleil troupe to Las Vegas (eventually, they would have four shows running simultaneously on the Strip).

The Excalibur (which opened months later) by contrast, was, behind the timbered chandeliers and papier-mâché dragons, a plainly mass-market casino hotel. This four-thousand-room casino resort styled as a medieval castle was the last major Strip resort designed before the opening of the Mirage and is in many ways the anti-Mirage. Called "the granddaddy of all miniature golf castles" by architect Alan Hess, the Excalibur cost less than half to build than the Mirage. Its "Shopping Courtyard" had a string of carnival-like attractions and chintzy stores. While expansions of existing casinos, like the Stardust, Tropicana, Sahara, and Riviera guaranteed a continuing home for the "cheap room/cheap eats" visitor, all subsequent developments on the Strip hewed more closely to Wynn's vision.

Circus Circus Enterprises, the company that built Excalibur, embraced luxe as enthusiastically as anyone. Circus's next project, Luxor, was a dividing point for the company, which had changed significantly since Bennett and Pennington had mastered the low-roller family market in the 1970s. The property was designed as a "class resort" and, despite some errors in execution, marked a new direction under the growing leadership of Glenn Schaeffer. In 1984, soon after Circus Circus went public, Schaeffer, whose background included both public relations and finance, joined the company as senior vice president for casino development; he was chiefly responsible for selling Circus Circus and casino gambling to Wall Street. After the successful launch of Excalibur, Schaeffer became Circus Circus's president and heir apparent, but left the company in early 1993 after a split with company chairman Bill Bennett. Schaeffer would return, however, when, in 1995, following Bennett's ouster, Circus Circus acquired Gold Strike Resorts, a company that he had joined. With Schaeffer as president once again, the company began planning a new flagship property, Mandalay Bay. Built along the lines of Mirage rather than Excalibur, it opened in 1999 and was so successful that Circus Circus Enterprises changed its name to Mandalay Resort Group. The company that once championed budget accommodations and coffee-shop fare now had as its flagship a luxurious casino resort with a Four Seasons hotel-within-a-hotel, a fitting commentary on the transformation of the Las Vegas Strip.

It had been a remarkable change, as gambling casinos, once considered dangerously seedy or, at best, comfortably tacky, turned into hip vacation spots. Schaeffer and his Circus Circus team were not the only ones to evolve the casino environment. The openings of Mirage and Excalibur signaled the start of an incredible decade of growth along the Strip. The international economy picked up in the early 1990s, and, later in the decade, the dot-com boom produced scores of newly rich young vacationers who thought nothing of playing thousands of dollars over a weekend. As it became clear that, if presented with alluring attractions, visitors would continue to fly to Las Vegas even after casinos had been legalized closer to home, the boom began in earnest.

By the early 1990s, Kirk Kerkorian had built the world's largest hotel twice and bought Metro-Goldwyn-Mayer film studios as many times. In 1969, he had opened the International, which he sold to Hilton, and in 1973 he had debuted the MGM Grand, which he sold in 1985 to Bally Manufacturing following the lawsuits stemming from the tragic 1980 fire. Since then, he had bought and sold the Sands and Desert Inn before purchasing the Marina, a small casino hotel across from the Tropicana, in 1989. In 1991, work began on a second, grander MGM, with more than five thousand guest rooms, a vast casino, and an attached theme park.

This new MGM Grand not only recaptured the title of the world's largest hotel but was also the first $1 billion Strip resort. When it opened in December 1993, it was roughly twice the size of the average Strip casino. The MGM's green glass exterior, originally intended to evoke the Emerald City of *The Wizard of Oz,* was a clever piece of cross promotion (Kerkorian also owned the MGM movie library, which included that 1939 film classic). But the Oz theme proved uncongenial to gamblers, who wanted less of the Yellow Brick Road and more of sophisticated gambling; in retrospect, a James Bond theme (another MGM franchise) might have been more appropriate. Still, the resort was a success: repositioned as "The City of Entertainment," it formed the genesis for what would become one of the gaming industry's leaders.

MGM Grand, in partnership with Primmadonna Resorts, a company that owned three casinos at Primm on the California state line, built a neighboring casino, the Gotham-themed New York–New York, which brought a reproduction of the Manhattan skyline to the Strip in 1997. MGM subsequently acquired Primmadonna and then set its sights on a larger prize: Mirage Resorts. The board of directors of Mirage Resorts, led by Steve

Wynn, agreed in March 2000 to a $6.4-billion buyout offer from MGM Grand, Inc. The deal created MGM Mirage, a company that owned fourteen casino resorts in Nevada, Detroit, Mississippi, and Australia. At the time, some speculated that Wynn might be content to channel the $400 million in after-tax profit he made from the sale of Mirage Resorts into his art collection, while others noted that the aging Desert Inn was on the market and might present a challenge for the industry's top developer.

Wynn actually already had his eye on the Desert Inn site. He later claimed that, having built at every price point on the Las Vegas Strip, he was bored, and he accepted the buyout offer as a way for his friendly rival, Kerkorian, to help bankroll his next project, which would debut in 2005 as Wynn Las Vegas and again set the bar for casino design on the Strip. (Kerkorian and Wynn present an interesting contrast: The former opened the world's largest hotel three times, while the latter built its most expensive one three times.)

The merger highlighted the consolidation that had come to define the American casino industry. At the turn of the twenty-first century, American gaming was dominated by five large Las Vegas–based firms and a host of smaller competitors.* MGM Mirage led the way with five Strip properties, half-ownership of the Monte Carlo, a Strip resort that fittingly had more hotel rooms than the actual Monte Carlo, and assorted other properties across the world. The Mandalay Resort Group owned the other half of the Monte Carlo and its four Strip properties, with interests elsewhere.

Park Place Entertainment, the spin-off of Hilton Hotel's gaming division and Bally's Entertainment, had an even larger national presence; after its 1999 acquisition of the Caesars empire from ITT, it owned three of the "Four Corners" (the Flamingo, Bally's, and Caesars Palace), a brand-new French-themed resort, Paris, the storied Las Vegas Hilton, and casinos in Reno, Mississippi, Atlantic City, and elsewhere. It would soon rename itself Caesars Entertainment. Boyd Gaming, founded by Sam Boyd, had continued to prosper under his son, Bill Boyd, and had a similarly far-flung portfolio, with several casinos in and around Las Vegas (including the legendary Stardust) and other states. In 2003, the company opened the Borgata, the billion-dollar Atlantic City resort that rivaled anything recently built on the Strip. And Harrah's Entertainment, though it had only a single casino on the Strip itself, had become a national powerhouse, with franchises in most major markets and an

---

*This is a trend that is apparent in other areas of American business: Domestic automobile production has long been dominated by Detroit's "Big Three," and six conglomerates own ninety percent of the nation's media markets.

innovative commitment to customer service and information technology that made it consistently profitable.

Casino ownership would become even further concentrated in 2005 with another merger wave. First, MGM Mirage acquired the Mandalay Resort Group for $7.9 billion, making it the world's largest casino company. At the age of eighty-seven, Kirk Kerkorian controlled a company that owned much of the Strip and, thanks to its talented management team, was well poised for future growth. But MGM Mirage was soon dethroned by Harrah's Entertainment. Bill Harrah's name graced a company that, under Phil Satre, had grown into a byword for consistent gambling entertainment. Harrah's capped six years of acquisitions by buying Caesars Entertainment for close to $9 billion: The resulting company had over a hundred thousand employees worldwide and expected annual revenues of nearly $9 billion. Less than sixty years after Bill Harrah had struggled to establish a bingo parlor in Depression-era Reno, his company was the world's casino king.

The growing concentration of ownership on the Strip followed an unprecedented building boom. Twelve new resorts opened along Las Vegas Boulevard from 1989 to 1999, from the Stratosphere, with its namesake observation tower several blocks past the traditional boundary of the Strip at the Sahara, to Mandalay Bay, which brought a slice of the South Seas to the neighborhood of McCarran International Airport. The average new resort was suited for the age of mass market tourism: with 3,000 hotel rooms, 80 table games, and 2,500 slot machines, convention space, and numerous restaurants, shops, and entertainment venues, it could serve equally well as the backdrop for a bachelorette party, regional sales meeting, second honeymoon, or gambling jaunt.

During the early years of the boom, "family-friendly" resorts received a great deal of media attention. With the MGM Grand Adventures theme park, Circus Circus's indoor Adventure Dome, and the pirate-themed Treasure Island, some were predicting that Las Vegas would soon upstage Orlando as a family vacation destination. But after the dot-com bust Las Vegas was more successful in promoting itself as an "adult Disneyland" (a phrase uttered so often it has become cliché), and a wave of more sophisticated attractions, particularly nightclubs and "ultra lounges," became de rigueur after 2002. New resorts like the Palms and Hard Rock actively catered to twenty-somethings, a real innovation in an industry where Tom Jones had long been considered an edgy entertainer that attracted a youthful crowd.

Despite lines of clubbers winding through its casinos after midnight, the

Strip was still about more than nightlife: Conventioneers represented an increasing percentage of visitors, and people continued to bring their families for a weekend in Las Vegas.* As the city's annual visitation climbed toward forty million, Las Vegas casino operators relished their success in transcending the stigma formerly attached to gambling, and had successfully established Las Vegas as a destination for all seasons and temperaments.

But beneath all of the pirate battles and family-friendly attractions, Las Vegas remained, at heart, a gamblers' paradise. Casinos staged pitched battles to attract high rollers, known in the local parlance as whales. Executives built lavish private suites, promised copious compass, and generally catered to all of their wishes. In the late 1990s, about 250 top-echelon whales, players with credit lines of $20 million or more, were the prized bounty for casino hosts. While package-tour patrons with fanny packs, waiting in line for the buffet, fretted about blowing $20, managers warily anticipated the next move of the highest of the high rollers, knowing that a lucky weekend for them could mean the difference between the casino's showing a profit or a loss.

In the six decades since the birth of the casino resort on the Las Vegas Strip, operators have had ample time to create a science of casino design. The science—which is sometimes held to be an arcane art—starts at the floor and ends at the ceiling. The carpet is carefully selected: Loud colors convey a sense of excitement, while not distracting players (who don't stare at their feet while playing), and tight, multicolored patterns neatly hide stains. Cushioned chairs at slot machines allow a player to comfortably sit while gambling. Above the player, low ceilings and dimmed lights can create a sense of intimacy, which leads to more gambling. The sounds of fun—clanking coins, shouts of triumph, and excited conversation—also stimulate play. Some casinos, hip to aromatherapy, circulate scented air to make their patrons' stay more pleasant.**

In the mid-1990s, millions discovered the Internet, a communications medium that promised to accelerate scientific study, speed business, and allow instantaneous communication. Many users, though, logged on chiefly to download pornography, chat online, and gamble. The first "gambling" Web site appeared in 1995, but these were primarily "free" sites that offered only simulated games. Playing with valueless credits, players might as well have

---

*The continuing family appeal of the Strip is plain to anyone who walks through the lobby of Excalibur.
**But contrary to a persistent urban myth, casinos do not pump extra oxygen to stimulate gambling. This is impossible, as no casino is airtight, and is unwise, as pure oxygen is highly flammable. In casinos, cigarettes and other open flames are common, so enriching the air with oxygen would be a recipe for disaster—and a legion of lawsuits.

been mindlessly clicking on Freecell. Though this wasn't really gambling, some predicted at the time that, should live wagering be introduced, online gambling revenues could surpass $10 billion a year.

These projections bore out what many gambling operators knew: That, given the convenience of gambling over the computer, an online gaming site could be phenomenally lucrative. Later in 1995 and 1996, sites that let players deposit money via credit cards or wire transfers appeared. Many governments, not wishing to jeopardize the millions they annually took in by licensing other gambling schemes, declared Internet gambling illegal (the United States relied on an interpretation of a 1961 antibookmaking statute), but others legalized the new betting medium, frankly to create revenues and business development.

The small Caribbean nation of Antigua was one of the first to take the initiative. Antigua already had casinos catering to foreigners and, in the mid-1990s, created a free trade zone that let American bookmakers (using toll-free numbers to accept bets from the mainland) operate. Immune from American gambling prohibitions, they paid licensing fees and agreed to submit to Antiguan regulation. In a sense, Antigua treated online gaming like any other business: The island was already a minor haven for other offshore shelter businesses like ship registries and banking. With their advertisements airing on American radio stations and appearing in popular sports magazines, the Antiguan-regulated betting businesses claimed to be completely legitimate.

In 1995, these offshore sports books began to take advantage of the Internet: several posted odds and other information as well as a toll-free number that visitors could call to place bets. In the United States, some licensed gambling operators did the same. New York's Capital OTB horse-racing monopoly began posting its odds on a "virtual tote board" in 1996. Within a few years, Capital OTB used the Internet to transmit betting information and even broadcast races, though bettors still needed to use their phone to wager from home. In 1997, Idaho's Coeur d'Alene Indian tribe posted digital lottery games that it argued were Class II games permitted under the National Indian Regulatory Act. Wisconsin's attorney general begged to differ, and as a result of a court action the site was closed.

As online commerce became more sophisticated and consumers became more comfortable with transmitting financial data over the Internet, Antiguan sports books made the natural transition to complete online wagering. The World Sports Exchange pioneered when it went online in early 1997 as a full-service Internet sports book that let players actually "bet with the click of a mouse." Based in Antigua, the World Sports Exchange was the creation of Jay Cohen and Steve Schillinger, two former traders on the Pacific Stock Exchange.* For years, Schillinger had run office pools, letting fellow traders swap sports "futures" and bet on the outcome of the O.J. Simpson trial and other public events. Cohen persuaded Schillinger to move the operation online. Researching the field, they concluded that a sports book based in Antigua using the Capital OTB model was legal and, potentially, very lucrative.

Soon, others followed, and by early 1998 there were more than two dozen fully operational online sports books accepting bets from Antigua. Most looked quite similar, with pages featuring the latest odds, site rules, information about payment, and links to both sports news and problem gambling sites. Some let players bet illusory credits for fun, while most ran aggressive promotions, offering bonus cash to new sign-ups and those who referred them. Sports betting had come a long way from the street-corner bookie, though the operators of poolrooms at the turn of the previous century would not have been surprised by the marriage of high technology and gambling.

Sports books were best suited to the Internet because they were really just another medium for an age-old pastime. Whether one places his bet in person, or by telegraph, telephone, or wireless connection doesn't influence the outcome of the game or the odds offered. Provided one knows that the bookmaker will promptly pay off winners, the method of placing the bet is immaterial. (The speed with which sports books paid their winners, though, was another story.) Online casinos were different. Players anted up real money on virtual games. No real roulette dealer spun the wheel, dropped the ball, and announced the winner—a digital random-number generator simply spat out data for software to translate into a player win or loss. Slot machines had been using random-number generators for years, but playing online was still a big leap of faith. Slot machines in Atlantic City were certified by the state of New Jersey to be fair, and if one felt otherwise, he could easily prompt regulators to investigate. Should a disgruntled bettor suspect an online gaming site of cheating, he had no recourse save an appeal to a distant government. When several fly-by-night operators bilked players before disappearing, unproven online casinos faced a credibility problem.

Millions of players quickly found sites they trusted. In 1996, about 15 sites accepted real money. A year, later, over 200 sites existed. In 1999, that number more than tripled to 650, and by 2002 it had leveled off at about

---

*Where, coincidentally, blackjack's "big player" Ken Uston once worked.

1,800 gaming sites. These sites included sports books, casinos, lotteries, and horse-racing sites. The reaction of land-based gaming operators was, originally, dismissal, followed by opposition. But many soon reasoned that, with their established names and reputations for both gaming action and probity, they could become leaders in the field. Governments, too, watched the steadily rising revenue of online gambling sites and saw a potential cash cow. In many nations, though, technological and moral conservatives prevented the quick jump of governments and private gaming concerns into cyberspace.

Several European lotteries experimented with online games, and in 1999 Alice Springs, Northern Territory (Australia), made gambling history when its sole casino, Lasseters, became the first terrestrial casino to go online. The Australian federal government had permitted state and territorial legislators to set parameters for the extension of land-based operations online. Several TABs went online, but in the next year the Australian government placed a moratorium on all new online gaming sites, and in 2001 the Interactive Gaming Act, though it maintained horse and sports wagering sites, criminalized the act of offering virtual card, dice, or slot-based games to Australians. Australians wagered money with legal betting sites in ever-growing numbers but they could not enjoy the protection of betting with an Australian-regulated online casino—though foreigners did.

Larger brick-and-mortar casinos in the United Kingdom and United States cautiously explored going online. They were leery of jeopardizing their land-based licenses and thus could not accept bets with the same impunity as Caribbean-based sites that only existed in cyberspace. Britain's Aspinalls, a casino operator since 1962, launched an online casino in 2002, as did Kerzner International, which attracted a half-ownership investment from Las Vegas's Station Casinos. Las Vegas giant MGM Mirage operated a site based in the Isle of Man. Because of the unresolved legal status of online gaming, MGM Mirage Online accepted bets from citizens of only six countries. It was unprofitable and soon closed, as did the Kerzner venture, though both held out the promise that, in a less tenuous regulatory environment, well-known casinos would successfully make the transition to cyberspace.

Other nations followed Antigua, Australia, and the Isle of Man and quickly tried to maximize revenues from online betting. In March 2005, for example, the Philippine casino monopoly PAGCOR announced plans to implement TeleSabong, the world's first Internet-based cockfighting system. TeleSabong would allow online bettors to wager on a series of fights from the nation's 1,700 cockpits. Even before creating this system, PAGCOR had 312 betting stations that, linked by the Internet, let Filipinos bet online from designated locations. One of the world's oldest sports had made the transition to the twenty-first century.

Despite federal intransigence in the United States—the Justice Department under both the Clinton and Bush Administrations insisted that, according to the Wire Act, any kind of Internet gaming was illegal—several foreign governments and even American states began exploring regulation rather than prohibition. In April 2001, the Nevada legislature passed Assembly Bill 578, which created a theoretical framework for the eventual licensing and regulation of online gaming operations within the state—contingent, of course, on federal approval.

But the federal government still insisted the Internet could not be used for gambling. In March 1998, the Justice Department charged fourteen online sports-book operators from Costa Rica and Antigua with violating the Wire Act. Three of the fourteen were in the United States at the time and surrendered to authorities; most pled guilty to lesser crimes. Those still abroad, though, were in the Caribbean, and the United States could not extradite them. Should they wish to return to the United States, though, they might be arrested and put on trial.

Some returned, pled guilty, and put the charges behind them, while others elected to remain abroad, technically fugitives from American justice. Though his associates in the World Sports Exchange took this option, company president Jay Cohen chose to clear his name by returning to New York to face trial. But Cohen was found guilty in 2000 and, after exhausting his appeals, served nearly two years at Nellis Federal Prison Camp, about twenty miles from the Las Vegas Strip.

Antigua soon challenged American enforcement of the Wire Act. Along with U.S. government threats to disallow the use of credit cards for online payment, the specter of prosecution for running legal businesses hurt the Antiguan Internet betting industry. In 1999 the country boasted 119 operators that employed 3,000 Antiguans; four years later, the number had fallen to nearly one sixth of that. Antigua blamed American "aggression" for the loss and pursued a settlement under the General Agreement on Trade in Services. The GATS, which dates from 1995, bound all member bodies (which included both Antigua and the United States) to give each other equal access. Antigua argued that the United States was compelled to accept its "cross-border gaming services," an assertion that the United States denied, claiming the matter was one of criminal enforcement rather than trade in services. A World Trade Organization dispute resolution panel ruled in favor of Antigua in 2004.

The United States appealed, and though the panel affirmed its original decision, the powers of the World Trade Organization to prevent the federal government from enforcing its laws against gambling were spurious at best, and the case was far from over.

Besides sports betting, which was a natural for the Internet, the biggest expansion in online gaming has been the American classic: poker. Despite trust issues similar to that of online casino games—one doesn't know for sure whether virtual cards are randomly chosen, if other players at a virtual table are in collusion or, indeed, are a single user logged in under multiple accounts—online poker swiftly became one of the most popular games of the new millennium.

Online poker combined with an older medium, television, to spur the old game to unforeseeable levels of popularity, both in the United States and worldwide. Televised poker, in particular, expanded dramatically after 2002. The use of innovative camera techniques that allowed viewers to see players' hole cards (dealt facedown) made watching games online almost hypnotic. Soon, both the World Series of Poker (which aired on ESPN), the World Poker Tour, and a host of celebrity games were common.

The new visibility of poker sent many players online, where they found a place to learn the game in an anonymous, nonthreatening place. Instead of having to venture into a casino poker room and play against professionals, or compete against one's own friends at home, a player could gradually gain confidence (and skill) playing against people she never met, winning or losing money without embarrassment. Online poker burst into prominence when, in 2003, Chris Moneymaker, an online player who had never sat in a live tournament before, won the World Series of Poker in Las Vegas. He had earned his spot by winning a online satellite tournament held by PokerStars.com, parlaying a $40 investment into a $2.5 million payday. Suddenly, online poker had a face, and many who watched him go all in against seasoned pro Sam Farha had the dream of parlaying skill and luck into careers as professional poker players. Attendance—and jackpots—at the World Series of Poker soared, and after casino giant Harrah's purchased the tournament from Binion's in 2004, it became the center of a year-long series of satellite tournaments and sponsored poker events.

Harrah's maintained a "don't ask, don't tell" policy, refusing to acknowledge that many of the tournament's players were primarily online players. Wary of crossing Nevada regulators or Justice Department prosecutors, they and other American casino companies left the online poker field to a variety of international sites. Visitors to these sites played poker against each other, while the site, in return for providing an online betting forum, charged a rake. This was exactly what casino poker rooms did and, in fact, what ten-percent houses had done as far back as the 1830s.

One company, thanks to skillful promotion, soon came to dominate the field. Founded in 2001, Party Gaming was a model for the international Internet economy. With offices in London, the company was headquartered in Gibraltar (taking advantage of liberal tax and Internet gaming laws), while most of its employees lived and worked in India. The company's chief venture, Party Poker, grabbed over half of the world's online poker market by 2004. Taking no direct risk in the games, the site's owners earned an estimated $100,000 an hour. Poker had come a long way from cigar-store back rooms and dingy basements. It was part of a global Internet gaming market that was estimated to have pulled in revenues of over $7 billion in 2004. Little had changed since the earliest humans wagered over coin flips and the roll of bones: The gambling lure was just as potent.

21

The Dream

✦ ✦ ✦

HISTORY IN PERSPECTIVE

April 28, 2005, 12:02 A.M. The doors open at the $2.7 billion Wynn Las Vegas, the most expensive casino yet built and the self-proclaimed masterwork of visionary Steve Wynn. As the seconds tick down before the opening, he has little time to reflect on the significance of the hour: This is the third time he has opened the world's most expensive resort, and after having sold his Mirage Resorts to MGM in 2000, is a leap back into the casino world for him. When the doors open and the first guests hurry through, his mind is on the million technical problems that can be revealed under the strain of the opening. There is not much of a chance to enjoy the sight of patrons finally inside his casino, and, though he is confident his masterpiece will speak for itself, at the moment his best hope is to not be embarrassed by an errant glitch.

Thousands pour through the entrances, excited to be part of the most eagerly anticipated casino opening in years. Drawn by an urban legend (unfortunately false) which says that slots on opening night are set to pay back over a hundred percent, locals crowd the floor, as tuxedoed VIPs fresh from an earlier charity dinner enjoy the ambience, and guests from around the world snap pictures and hurry to the tables. A perceptive visitor, walking through the property, could see the resort as the culmination of seven thousand years of gambling history.

Wynn's latest manipulation of the environment is an artificial mountain whose Lake of Dreams faces inward to the casino, ensuring that its wonders are seen only by resort guests. Under the chandeliered valet porte cochere, a pair of cast-bronze guardian lions imported from China welcome visitors. They exactly match the pair sitting in front of the Bank of China and are said to prevent bad luck and negative energy from entering the building. In the casino atmosphere, they symbolize both the past of gambling (the playing cards and numerous games invented in Asia, and that region's intrepid gamblers) and this resort's present: Many of its international high rollers will hail from the Far East.

Inside the doors, a bas-relief inspired by eighteenth-century French design but calling to mind the classical era suggests the ancient Greeks and Romans casting lots and rolling bones. A visitor might linger in the glass-ceilinged atrium, with its balls of color fashioned from flowers. This indoor garden recalls the famous gardens of the German spa resorts, and its flower patterns are echoed in the ceiling all the way into the adjacent retail promenade. Stepping into the casino, the visitor moves along a marble pathway inlaid with exquisite mosaics that pick up patterns from the casino's carpet—even this typically garish feature of the gambling hall has been elevated to high art, and "carpet joint" operators from William Crockford to Jay Sarno would have approved.

Inside the casino, hundreds of slot machines—those quintessentially American gambling devices—blend with the sophisticated luxury that surrounds them, and even the penny slots are crowned by vivid plasma screen displays. Near the casino's center, a row of blackjack tables reveals the first overtly Gallic influence: Most of the games were created or nurtured in French casinos in the seventeenth and eighteenth century. Farther down are the roulette tables: This game reached its present form during the tumultuous 1790s in France.

Visitors might notice that each gaming table is topped by its own chandelier, a touch the casino's designers have borrowed from European casinos with an ingenious American twist: Thanks to technological innovation, each chandelier conceals a surveillance camera. This is a far cry from the tables in Venice's Ridotto, which were lit by two candles, and recalls instead the opulent François Blanc casinos of the Rhine and Riviera.

The elegantly appointed VIP Host Lounge, where hosts greet high rollers and, in private booths, arrange the details of their casino credit, lies a short walk from the gaming tables. Farther ahead is the buffet, though this casino favorite has clearly evolved far beyond the "chuck wagon specials" of the 1940s. No cold cuts and potato salad here: Wynn's gourmands instead feast on tandoori chicken, pesto-infused mashed potatoes, and cocktail glasses filed with ahi poke, among other delights. For dessert, custom-built sundaes, bananas Foster, and other treats are the dish of the day. Even the room is a far cry from the accommodating cafeterias found in most casinos; divided into nooks, it seems intimate and immaculately clean, a common thread running through the resort.

Past the buffet is the mirrored, wood-paneled keno lounge. This game, first developed in China, still bears a resemblance to the original *pakapoo* lottery after over a hundred years of evolution in the American West and Chinese settlements throughout the world. Farther down is another casino universal—the twenty-four-hour coffee shop—about halfway along the corridor that leads to the golf course and country club.* Both it and the golf course have been updated for the twenty-first century, but they reflect two mainstays of Las Vegas resorts: informal dining and upscale recreation. Along the way, eclectic art hangs on the walls, while uptempo Afro-Asian worldbeat music plays over the sound system.

Back in the casino, to the right of the VIP lounge, lies the heart of the casino: the baccarat room. Though blackjack and other games could be found there, the most prominent game is, of course, baccarat, which even in its streamlined American version recalls the chemin-de-fer heroics of Nick Zographos and the Greek Syndicate. Here, table minimums often start at $500, and maximum bets can range as high as $250,000 per hand; action that might have pleased Cornelius Vanderbilt, "Bet-a-Million" Gates, and the other dissolute plungers of the Gilded Age.

To the left lie the craps tables—a game with roots in New Orleans via France, England, and Crusader Spain. Though it has lost popularity since the transcendence of blackjack, slots, and poker, craps still remains the quintessential gambler's gamble, and the most rambunctious game in the casino. A nearby Big Six game—the oversized wheel of fortune—recalls the carnival attractions of grifters like Honest John Kelly. This casino, like all others, was equal parts honky tonk and dress ball.

Past the VIP lounge is the Wynn Theater, a nightly showplace for Le Rêve, the resort's signature production show, far evolved beyond the crude fiddlers and banjo players that once serenaded gamblers, though not so far removed from the extravaganzas hosted by John Davis, the gambling tycoon of 1830s New Orleans. To the left, the Corsa Cucina is both an informal Italian café and a reminder of the substantial debt the casino owes to Italy. The Ridotto, the first licensed casino, premiered in seventeenth-century Venice, a milieu that saw the birth of mercantile gambling during the late Renaissance, along with early lotteries.

Stopping short of the Ferrari showroom and to the right is the poker room, a far more luxurious space than the rough-and-tumble frontier saloons

---

*The coffee shop, named the Terrace Point Café, borrows its name from the old Desert Inn, which Wynn demolished to build the new resort. It is only one of many sly historical references to be found there.

where the game etched itself into American mythology. The walls, festooned with oversize playing cards featuring portraits of eighteenth-century French nobility, betray the game's Gallic origins. Outside the poker room, farther left and back through the casino are the race and sports books, where the sport of kings is presented for a modern audience: Thanks to simulcast, bettors can watch and wager on races from around the world. Sports bettors wager on team sports with the same enthusiasm that their nineteenth-century counterparts reserved for pedestrianism and personal tests of strength. Despite all of the plasma screen televisions and other innovations, the spirit of betting is the same as it's always been, and the men and women who once thronged telegraph-linked horse rooms or bet with street-corner bookies might feel quite at home.

As the casino completes its first hour in operation, its visitors have now settled into their groove: The excitement of gambling, rather then the novelty of the resort, now fills them. For Steve Wynn, it is still too close to the opening to savor just how strongly the guests respond to the resort. Over the coming days and weeks, visitors will discover for themselves favorite spots and unexpected surprises. Right now, Wynn is still finding out what's wrong, but as the resort adjusts to visitors, he will be able to walk around his namesake resort and enjoy the accomplishment.

Drawn to Las Vegas from around the world, the men and women who sit calculating at the blackjack tables and watching slot reels spin have witnessed a historic moment, reliving a history written by their ancestors, whatever their native land. This casino, at this moment, is the culmination of that story. In their lives, they are sure to see that history continue, as they pursue the fall of the dice, spin of the wheel, and turn of the card—above all, the ghost of luck—just as avidly as the last three hundred generations. Wherever humanity ventures, it is sure that they will bring a fascination with gambling along for the ride, and they will continue to dream about their next tryst with fortune.

ACKNOWLEDGMENTS

◆ ◆ ◆

Many people helped bring this book along. It never would have happened without a call from Gotham's Brendan Cahill, who persuaded me that a comprehensive history of world gambling could be written, and that I could do it. He did a great job of convincing me to attempt the book, and of shepherding me through the editorial process. He and Patrick Mulligan provided excellent suggestions for revisions, additions, and other changes. Others who were particularly helpful include copy editor Craig Schneider, layout editor Elke Sigal, and Lisa Johnson in publicity. Gotham's president William Shinker's support, along with everyone else at the press, was crucial as well.

At the University of Nevada–Las Vegas, where I'm the director of the Center for Gaming Research in Lied Library, I'd like to thank everyone in Special Collections, including Peter Michel, Su Kim Chung, Toby Murray, Kathy War, Jonnie Kennedy, Joyce Moore, Michael Frazier, and Dana Miller, and the staff of Document Delivery, who answered my interlibrary loan requests with incredible speed. Thanks also go to Dean of Libraries Patricia Iannuzzi, UNLV President Carol Harter, and Provost Ray Alden. At the Nevada State Museum and Historical Society, David Millman generously helped me find the only extant picture of Nick "the Greek" Dandolos that I've ever seen.

I also had help at the University of Nevada–Reno from Bill Eadington, Judy Cornelius at the Institute for the Study of Gambling and Commercial Gaming, and visiting professor Ricardo Siu. Dr. Eadington's offer of a guest lecture in his class let me try out some of the material from the first few chapters on a captive audience. The staff of UNR Special Collections, particularly Jacquelyn Sundstrand, was very accommodating, particularly in facilitating my access to the papers of Russell T. Barnhart.

A host of academic experts from around the world contributed their thoughts and, sometimes, bibliographies, including Larry Gragg at the

University of Missouri, Rolla; Annie Chan, Jason Gao, Davis Fong, and Carmen Cheng at the University of Macau; Raymond Chan and Claudia Mendes Khan at the Macau Tourism and Career Center; Kai Cheong Fok at the Macau Millennium College; Il-Yong Yang at Cheju Tourism College; Mark Balestra and Sue Schneider at the River City Group; and Stephen M. Stigler at the University of Chicago.

In the gaming industry, several people granted me access to current operations and helped me track down information about the past, including Nick Spencer at the Hong Kong Jockey Club, George Tanasijevich and Lisa Cheong at Venetian/Sands Macau, Grant Bowie at Wynn Macau, Rich Westfall at Isle of Capri, Bruce Mac Donald at Foxwoods, Denise Randazzo, Roger Thomas, Steve and Elaine Wynn at Wynn Resorts, Tex Whitson (a font of information about Binion's, poker, and the World Series of Poker), Crandall Addington, Debbie Munch of Harrah's (formerly Caesars) Entertainment, Yvette Monet and Alan Feldman of MGM Mirage, and Mando Rueda.

My family and friends were all supportive while I researched, wrote, and revised, particularly my mother, Connie, sister Pauline, my family in and around Atlantic City, and all my friends in Las Vegas, particularly my girlfriend Suni Erdelyi, who luckily met me after I'd finished most of the writing, and only had to suffer through the revisions.

I'd like to offer a thank-you to all of the enthusiasts, scholars, and gamblers who left behind the collections of stories, legends, and facts that I pored over while putting this book together.

Finally, I'd like to thank you, the reader, for having an interest in learning a little more about gambling's long history. If you'd like to learn more, please check out my Web site, www.dieiscast.com.

NOTES

◆ ◆ ◆

Prologue: Rainmaker Reborn

xv   Information on the Mystic Massacre and its consequences: Herbert Milton Sylvester, *Indian Wars of New England,* vol. 1 (Cleveland: The Arthur H. Clark Company, 1910), Chapter 3, "The Pequod War"; William Hubbard, *A Narrative of the Troubles with the Indians from the first planting thereof in the year 1607 to this present year 1677 . . . to which is added a Discourse about the warre with the Pequod* (Boston: John Foster, 1677), 127, 131; John Mason, *A Brief History of the Pequod War* (Boston: S. Kneeland and T. Green, 1736), 8–9.

Steven T. Katz, "The Pequot War Reconsidered," in Alden T. Vaughan, *New England Encounters: Indians and EuroAmericans ca. 1600–1850* (Boston: Northeastern University Press, 1999), 121–2.

xvii   On the Pequot resurgence: Kim Isaac Eisler, *Revenge of the Pequots: How a Small American Tribe Created the World's Most Profitable Casino* (New York: Simon and Schuster, 2001), 52, 87.

xviii   Statistics from American Gaming Association. "Gaming Revenue: Current Year Data." Accessed online at: *http://www.americangaming.org/ Industry/factsheets/statistics_detail.cfv?id=7.* American Gaming Association, *State of the States 2005.* Accessed online at: *http://www.americangaming.org/assets/files/uploads/2005_State_of_the_ States.pdf.*

Lottery Insider, "Preliminary Summary of Findings." Accessed at: *http://www.lotteryinsider.com.au/stats/survey.htm.*

xviii   Lottery statistics: Teresa La Fleur, ed. *La Fleur's 2002 World Lottery Almanac* (Boyds, Maryland: TLF Publications, 2002), 2.

xviii   Annual global gaming revenue estimate: *http://www.betting consultants.com/*

Part I: The Discovery of Gambling

3–4   Information about the eruption of Vesuvius and Pompeiian life: Marcel
        Biron, *Pompeii and Herculaneum: The Glory and the Grief* (New York:
        Crown Publishers, 1960), 126; Ray Laurence, *Roman Pompeii: Space and
        Society* (New York: Routledge, 1994), 70–87; Colin Armey and Brian
        Curran, Jr., *The Lost World of Pompeii* (Los Angeles: Getty Publications,
        2002), 10–14.

Chapter One: Thoth's Gift

5   Macaque gambling: Allison N. McCoy and Michael L. Platt, "Risk-
        sensitive neurons in macaque posterior cingulate cortex," *Nature Neuro-
        science* 8 (2005), 1220–7.

6   Divination: Florence N. David, *Games, Gods, and Gambling: The Origins
        and History of Probability and Statistical Ideas from the Earliest Times to
        the Newtonian Era* (New York: Hafner Publishing Company, 1962), 15;
        Clifford A Pickover, *Dreaming the Future: The Fantastic Story of Predic-
        tion* (Amherst, New York: Prometheus Books, 2001), particularly
        133–7.

7   Early astragalus finds: László Bartosiewicz, "A Systematic Review of
        Astralagus Finds From Archaeological Sites." *Antaeus* 24 (1997/1998),
        37–44, 594.

8   Distribution of gambling cultures: Alfred Kroeber, *Anthropology: Race,
        Language, Culture, Psychology, Prehistory* (New York: Harcourt, Brace &
        World, Inc., 1948), 552–3.

8–9   Evolution of dice: David, 10.

9   Mesopotamian dice games: R. C. Bell, *Board and Table Games from Many
        Civilizations* (London: Oxford University Press, 1960), 23; James Chri-
        stie, *An Inquiry into the Antient Greek Game Supposed to Have Been In-
        vented by Palamedes, Antecedent to the Siege of Troy* (London: W. Bulmer
        and Co., 1801).

9–10   The story of Parysatis: Plutarch, *Lives,* trans. John Dryden. Accessed at:
        *http://whitewolf.newcastle.edu.au/words/authors/P/Plutarch/prose/
        plutachslives/artaxerxes.html;* John Philip Quinn, *Fools of Fortune* (Chicago:
        The Anti-Gambling Association, 1890), 74–5.

10   Egyptian civilization: J. M. Roberts, *A Short History of the World* (New
        York: Oxford University Press, 1997), 51.

10   The tarot's alleged origins: Ronald Decker, Thierry DePaulis, and
        Michael Dummett, *A Wicked Pack of Cards: The Origins of the Occult Tarot*
        (New York: St. Martin's Press, 1996), 58.

10 Thoth: Robert A. Armour, *Gods and Myths of Ancient Egypt,* Second Edition (Cairo: The American University in Cairo Press, 2001), 209.

10 Egyptian antigambling laws: Andrew Steinmetz, *The Gaming Table: Its Votaries and Victims, in All Times and Countries, Especially in England and in France,* vol. 1 (Montclair, New Jersey: Patterson Smith, 1969), 56.

10 Egyptian games: Bell, 21; Spartaco Albertarelli, "Senet: a different 'gaming concept,'" in Jean Retschitzki and Rosita Haddad-Zubel, eds., *Step by Step: Proceedings of the 4th Colloquium Board Games in Academia* (Fribourg, Switzerland: Editions Universitaires, 2001), 15.

11 Thoth's wager: Armour, 9.

11 Cowrie divination: William Cascom, *Sixteen Cowries: Yoruba Divination from Africa to the New World* (Bloomington: Indiana University Press, 1980), 5–8.

11–2 Age of Indian civilization: Roberts, 62.

12–4 Indian gambling: C. Panduranga Bhatta. *Dice-Play in Sanskrit Literature: A Study* (Delhi: Amar Prakashan, 1985), vii, 8–11, 13–4, 66–7, 81, 87, 91, 107–8, 111–3, 140–3; Desh-Videsh: *http://www.deshvidesh.com/issues/desh408/diwali.htm*

15 Mahabharata: Steinmetz, 42.

15 Manu: Laws of Manu, 221–5. *http://www.sacred-texts.com/hin/manu/manu09.htm*

15 Licensing of Indian gambling: Panduranga Bhatta, 30–3.

15 Asian gambling propensity: John A. Price, "Gambling in Traditional Asia," (*Anthropologica 14* [2], 1972), 162–3.

15–6 Chinese gambling: Roberts, 69, 74.

16 Ancient cricket fighting: Price, 171.

16 Modern cricket fighting: "HK Police Smash Illegal Insect-Fighting Ring," *Channel News Asia,* September 21, 2004.

16 Hua-Hoey lottery: Stephen M. Stigler, "Casanova, 'Bonaparte,' and the Loterie de France," 7 (unpublished paper).

16 *Han Shu*: Price, 174.

16–7 Chinese dominoes: Stewart Culin, *Korean Games with Notes on the Corresponding Games of China and Japan* (Philadelphia: University of Pennsylvania, 1895), 102–3, 114.

17 Additional Chinese games: Price, 176.

17 Other Asian gambling: Price, 169–170.

17–8 Types of Indian games: Stewart Culin, *Games of the North American Indians* (New York: Dover Publications, 1975), 44.

18	Description of Indian games: Warren R. DeBoer, "Of Dice and Women: Gambling and Exchange in Native North America." *Journal of Archaeological Method and Theory,* vol. 8, no. 3 (September 2001), 218, 222–4; Culin, 44.
18	Methods of playing Indian games: Culin, 45–7.
18	Social nature of games: Culin, 45–7.
18–9	Gender and gambling: DeBoer, 227.
19	Story of Cunawabi: *http://www.pantheon.org/articles/c/cunawabi.html*
19	Raven: *http://www.sacred-texts.com/nam/nw/tmt/tmt046.htm*
19	Aztec gambling: Kathryn Gabriel, *Gambler Way: Indian Gaming in Mythology, History, and Archaeology in North America* (Boulder, Colorado: Johnson Books, 1996), 128.
20–1	Mesoamerican ballgame: Ted J. J. Leyenaar, "The Modern Ballgames of Sinaloa: A Survival of the Aztec Ullamaliztli," and E. Michael Whittington, "Introduction," in E. Michael Whittington, ed., *The Sport of Life and Death: The Mesoamerican Ballgame* (New York: Thames and Hudson, 2001), 123, 17–19; Jane Stevenson Day, "Performing on the Court," in Whittington, 65–7, 76, 84–5.

Chapter Two: The Die is Cast

22	Attributes of Hermes: Theoi Project, "Hermes." *http://www.theoi.com/Summary/Hermes.html*
22	Gambling at Hercules' temple: Andrew Steinmetz, *The Gaming Table: Its Votaries and Victims, in All Times and Countries, Especially in England and in France,* vol. 1 (Montclair, New Jersey: Patterson Smith, 1969), 4–5.
23	Palamedes inventing gambling: Quinn, 87; Christie, 14.
23	The famine of Lydia and the invention of gambling: Herodotus, *The History,* trans. Henry Cary. (Buffalo: Prometheus Books, 1992), 43.
23	Cross and pile (heads and tails): Andrew Steinmetz, *The Gaming Table: Its Votaries and Victims, in All Times and Countries, Especially in England and in France,* vol. 2 (Montclair, New Jersey: Patterson Smith, 1969), 129.
24	Invention of cockfighting: "Cock-Fighting" in *Encyclopaedia Britannica,* Eleventh Edition.
24	Greek astragalus play: Robert Garland, *The Daily Life of the Ancient Greeks* (Westport, Connecticut: Greenwood Press, 1998), 62.
24	Ranking of astragalus throws: Alice Zimmern *The Home Life of the Ancient Greeks,* trans. H. Blumner (New York: Cooper Square Publishers, 1966), 225.

24　　　Greek cubical dice: Elpis Mitropoulou, *Five Contributions to the Problems of Greek Reliefs* (Athens: Pyli Editions, 1976), 67–8, 70–5.

24　　　Ranked dice throws: Zimmern, 224–5.

24–5　　Gaffed dice: David, 11–12.

25　　　"We are so much at the mercy of chance . . .": quoted in Michael Grant, *The World of Rome* (Cleveland: The World Publishing Company, 1960), 129.

25　　　Quote from the *Aeneid*: Virgil, *Aeneid,* Book 10, line 284. *http://classics.mit.edu/Virgil/aeneid.10.×.html*

25–6　　Caesar's use of gambling imagery: Gaius Suetonius Tranquillus. Robert Graves, trans. *The Twelve Caesars* (New York: Penguin Books, 1989), 28.

26　　　The Vestal Virgin "lottery": Suetonius, 70–1.

26　　　Caesar's coin-flipping: Russell R.Esposito, *The Golden Milestone: Over 2,500 Years of Italian Contributions to Civilization,* Third Edition (New York: The New York Learning Library, 2003), 144.

26　　　Complaints about gambling's spread: "Cock-Fighting" in *Encyclopaedia Britannica,* Eleventh Edition.

26–7　　Roman dice rankings: Harry Thurston Peck, ed., *Harper's Dictionary of Classical Literature and Antiquities* (New York: Cooper Square Publishers, Inc., 1962), 1522, 1543.

27　　　Ludis Latrundulorum: Mitropoulou, 68.

27　　　Roman drinking games: Pliny the Elder, *The Natural History* (eds. John Bostock, M.D., F.R.S., H. T. Riley, Esq., B.A.) (London: Henry G. Bohu, 1855), 14, 28. *http://www.perseus.tufts.edu/cgi-bin/ptext?doc=Perseus%3-Atext%3A1999.02.0137;query=chapter%3D%23856;layout=;loc=14.29*

27　　　Octavian's gambling: Norwood Young, *Fortuna or Chance and Design* (New York: E. P. Dutton & Co., 1929), 7; Suetonius, 94–6. Jerome Carcopino. E. O. Lormier, trans., *Daily Life in Ancient Rome: The People and the City at the Height of the Empire* (New Haven: Yale University Press, 1960), 251; Nicholas Purcell, "Literate Games: Urban Society and the Game of Alea," *Past and Present,* no. 147 (May 1995), 15.

27–8　　Caligula: Suetonius, 175; Steinmetz, 66.

28　　　Claudius: Suetonius, 189, 206, 209; Quinn, 89.

28　　　Nero: Suetonius, 229.

28　　　Vitellus: Suetonius, 269.

28　　　Commodus: Bell, 31.

28　　　Peck, 53; John Disney, *A View of the Ancient Laws against Immorality and Profaneness* (Cambridge, 1729), 275.

28 Saturnalia: Peck, 53; Disney, 275.

28–9 Roman gambling laws: Carcopino, 253.

29 Pompeiian depictions of gambling: Lawrence James Ludovici, *The Itch For Play: Gamblers and Gambling in High Life and Low Life* (London: Jarrolds, 1962), 29–30.

29 Betting on circus entertainments/games: Alan Baker, *The Gladiator: The Secret History of Rome's Warrior Slaves* (New York: St. Martin's Press, 2001), 159; Carcopino, 221.

29 Gambling at the games: Baker, 183–4, 194.

29–30 Prevalence of Roman gambling: Steinmetz, 67–8.

30 German gambling: Alfred John Church, William Jackson Brodribb, Lisa Cerrato, eds., *Complete Works of Tacitus,* Perseus edition (New York: Random House, Inc., 1942), 9, 11, 24. URL: *http://www.perseus.tufts.edu/ cgi–bin/ptext?lookup=Tac.+Ger.+*

30 Christian confusion about the lack of scriptural condemnation: See *The Ruinous Consequences of Gambling* (New York: American Tract Society, 185?).

30 Lots and the scapegoat: Leviticus 16:6–10.

30–1 Lots and the division of Israel: Joshua 18:6–9.

31 Lots and selection of Saul and priests: 1 Chronicles 24:5; Nehemiah 10:34.

31 Judicial lot use by Jonah's shipmates: Jonah 1:7.

31 God influencing lots: Ezekiel 21:21–22.

31 Lot casting for plunder and captives: Obadiah 1:11; Joel 3:3; Nahum 3:10.

31 Casting lots for a forsaken one: Psalm 22:18.

31 Dice in Judea: Israel Abrahams, *Jewish Life in the Middle Ages* (Philadelphia: The Jewish Publication Society of America, 1919), 390.

32 The Chanukah story: "Chanukkah." Judaism 101. *http://www.jewfaq.org/holiday7.htm*

32 Talmudic restrictions on gamblers: *The Babylonian Talmud: Tract Sanhedrin. Section Jurisprudence (Damages)* trans. Michael L. Rodkinson (Boston: The Talmud Society, 1918), 72. *http://www.sacredtexts.com/jud/t08/t0806.htm*

32–3 Apostolic lot-casting: Acts 1:21–25

33 Alveus prayer: Christie, 29.

33 Wibold's devout dice game: David, 31–3.

33 Justinian's antigambling edicts: Disney, 277.

33 Charlemagne and Louis's antigambling edicts: Disney, 281.

34   Gambling as vice "by circumstances": Disney, 263.

34   Islamic scriptural reference to gambling: Koran 2:219, English translations cited at *http://www.usc.edu/dept/MSA/quran/002.qmt.html#002.219*
Koran 5:090-091, English translations cited at
http://www.usc.edu/dept/MSA/quran/002.qmt.html#002.590

34–5   Gambling tolerated in Islam: Coleman Barks, trans., *The Essential Rumi*
(San Francisco: HarperSanFrancisco, 1995), 193; Franz Rosenthal, *Gambling in Islam* (Leiden: E. J. Brill, 1975), 26–57.

35   European prohibitions against dicing: Paul B. Newman. *Daily Life in the
Middle Ages* (Jefferson, North Carolina: McFarland & Company, 2001),
164–171.

35   Crusader gambling: John Ashton, *The History of Gambling in England*
(London: Duckworth and Company, 1899), 13; St. Bernard of
Clairvaux, *In Praise of the New Knighthood*, trans. Conrad Greenia. Accessed at: *http://www.ordotempli.org/st__bernard_praises_the_
ordo_templi.htm*

35–6   Louis IX's anger at his brother's gambling: M. R. B. Shaw, trans., *Joinville
and Villehardouin: Chroniclers of the Crusades* (New York: Dorset Press,
1985), 265.

36   Gambling and chivalry: Ramon Lull, *The Book of the Order of Chivalry*,
trans. Robert Adams (Huntsville: Sam Houston State University Press,
1991), 92–94; Judith Herrin, ed., *A Medieval Miscellany* (New York:
Viking Studio Facsimile Editions, 1999), 158.

36–7   British gambling: Ashton, 13–14.

37   Geoffrey Chaucer, *Canterbury Tales: The Cook's Tale*, 1380. Accessed at:
http://www.pinkmonkey.com/dl/library1/chau02.pdf

37   Geoffrey Chaucer. *Canterbury Tales: The Pardoner Tale*, 1380. Accessed at:
http://www.online-literature.com/chaucer/canterbury/23/

37   Popularity of English gambling: Lilly C. Stone, "Amusements and
Sports," in Allan Mitchell and Istvan Deak, eds., *Everyman in Europe:
Essays in Social History*, Vol. 1: *The Preindustrial Millennia* (Englewood
Cliffs: Prentice Hall, 1990), 218–9.

38   Alphonso X's gaming guide: *Book of Games*, English translation accessed on *http://games.rengeekcentral.com/F01Rintro.html*,
http://games.rengeekcentral.com/F65R.html.

38   Hazard history: Alan Wykes, *Gambling* (Garden City, N.Y.: Doubleday &
Company, 1964), 137; *http://games.rengeekcentral.com/tc4.html*;
Florence N. David, *Games, Gods, and Gambling: The Origins and History of*

Probability and Statistical Ideas from the Earliest Times to the Newtonian Era (New York: Hafner Publishing Company, 1962), 35.

38–9 Petrarch and gambling: Conrad Rawski, *Petrarch's Remedies for Fortune Fair and Foul: A Modern English Translation with a Commentary,* vol. 1 (Bloomington: Indiana University Press, 1991), 60–1, 81–2.

39–40 Gambling in Florence: Antonio Pucci, "Proprietà di Mercato Vecchio," quoted in Trevor Dean, trans., *The Towns of Italy in the Later Middle Ages* (Manchester: Manchester University Press, 2000), 122–4.

40 Boccaccio, *Decameron,* Ninth Day, Novel IV. Accessed at: *http://www.stg.brown.edu/projects/decameron/engDecShowText.php?myID= nov0904&expand=day09.* Based on *The Decameron of Giovanni Boccaccio,* trans. J. M. Rigg, London, 1921.

Chapter Three: Knaves and Kings

41 Culin's theory of card evolution: Roger Tilley, *The History of Playing Cards* (New York: Clarkson N. Potter, 1973), 10–11.

42 Korean cards: Stewart Culin, *Korean Games* (Philadelphia: University of Pennsylvania, 1895), 123–126,128; David Parlett, *The Oxford Guide to Card Games* (Oxford: Oxford University Press, 1990), 143.

42–3 Chinese cards: Tilley, 7, 10; Mrs. John King Van Rensselaer, *The Devil's Picture Books: A History of Playing Cards* (New York: Dodd, Mead, and Company, 1893), 65–6.

43 Chinese card types: Culin, 135; Van Rensselaer, 67–9; Tilley, 9.

44 Legend of Marco Polo's role in introduction of cards: Van Rensselaer, 69.

44 Indian legend of card genesis: Tilley, 7–8.

44–6 *Ganjifah* and playing cards: Rudolf Von Leyden, *Ganjifa: The Playing Cards of India* (London: Victoria and Albert Museum, 1982), 4–6, 22–5, 29–30.

46 Italian adoption of Persian cards: Ronald Decker, Thierry Depaulis, and Michael Dummett, *A Wicked Pack of Cards: The Origins of the Occult Tarot* (New York: St. Martin's Press, 1996), 30.

47 Suitability of northern Italy for playing-card import/export: Sir Peter Hall, *Cities in Civilization* (New York: Fromm International, 1988), 80.

47 The Italian deck: William Andrew Chatto, *Facts and Speculations on the Origin and History of Playing Cards* (London: John Russell Smith, 1848), 229.

47 Italian card games: Tilley, 50–1; Parlett, 86.

47–8 Lorenzo de' Medici's patronage of cards: Van Rensselaer, 81.

48–9 Early mentions of cards: Parlett, 36; Chatto, 73, 76, 78.

49 Amadeus VIII's prohibition against women playing: Chatto, 81.

49–50   Bernardin's efforts to suppress cardplaying: "St. Bernardine of Siena,"
         New Advent Catholic Encyclopedia. Accessed at
         http://www.newadvent.org/cathen/02505b.htm; Chatto, 90;

50   Savonarola's denunciation of cards: "Girolamo Savonarola," *Wikipedia*.
         Accessed at *http://en.wikipedia.org/wiki/Girolamo_Savonarola*.

50–1   Impact of mass production on cards: Van Rensselaer, 34–5.
         Decker et al., 25–32.

51–2   The development of tarot games: Decker et al., 27–32, 40.

52–3   The tarot's rebirth as a tool for occult divination: Decker et al., 65, 80–90.

53   The Spanish deck: Van Rensselaer, 89; Tilley, 53. Parlett, 321.

54   Hombre: Parlett, 197–199.

54   The Portuguese deck: Tilley, 184–5.

54–5   The Portuguese deck in Asia: Tilley, 185.

55   Legendary cards on Columbus's voyage: Van Rensselaer, 112.

55   Cards in Florida and the Spanish Armada: Chatto, 106–7.

55   Conquian and Spanish cards in the New World: Tilley, 56. Parlett,
         142–143.

55–6   German gambling (and prohibitions of it): Van Rensselaer, 84;
         Laura A. Smoller, "Playing Cards and Popular Culture in Sixteenth-
         Century Nuremburg," *Sixteenth Century Journal*, vol. 17, no. 2 (Summer
         1986), 190.

56   German card-making industry: Chatto, 82; Smoller, 185.

56–7   The German deck: Smoller, 186, 192–3.

57   The Master of the Playing Cards: Tilley, 59.

57   German artist playing cards: Smoller, 194–200.

57   German artisan card-makers: Tilley, 59.

57   Karnoffel: Parlett, 165–7.

58   Poch: Parlett, 87–88.

58   German influence on other countries' card designs: Tilley, 80–5.

58–9   The French deck: Parlett, 43, 321.

59   Origins of French deck: Tilley, 67.

60   Spread of French deck: Parlett, 43.

60   Historical characters on court cards: W. Gurney Benham, *Playing Cards:
         History of the Pack and Explanations of Its Many Secrets* (London: Spring
         Books, 1957), Chapters 12–26.

60   Basset and glic: Parlett, 77, 93.

60–1   Piquet: Parlett 175–9.

61–2   Medieval Jewish gambling (and prohibitions against it): Leo Landman,
         "Jewish Attitudes Toward Gambling 2," *The Jewish Quarterly Review*, vol.

58, no. 1 (1967), 35, 41–2, 47; Israel Abrahams, *Jewish Life in the Middle Ages* (Philadelphia: The Jewish Publication Society of America, 1919), 390–4.

62   The Synod of Langres condemns gambling: Chatto, 80.

62–3   Protestants, cardplaying, and gambling: Smoller, 188–90.

63   English adoption of French deck: Tilley, 66.

63–4   British denunciations of gambling: Lilly C. Stone, "Amusements and Sports," in Allan Mitchell and Istvan Deak, eds., *Everyman in Europe: Essays in Social History,* vol. 1: *The Preindustrial Millennia* (Englewood Cliffs: Prentice Hall, 1990), 226; John Northbrooke, *A Treatise Against Dicing, Dancing, Plays, and Interludes. With Other Idle Pastimes* (London: Reprinted for the Shakespeare Society, 1843; reprinted in New York: AMS Edition, 1971), 132–3.

64   English prohibitions of gambling: Parlett, 46; Stone, 225.

64   Henry VIII bans gambling: Stone, 220.

65   Elizabethan prosecutions of gamblers: Benham, 27.

65   The groom porter: Ashton, 47–9; Ben Jonson, *The Alchemist* (Berkeley: University of California Press, 1968), 77.

65   Royal sanction of card making and the Worshipful Company of Makers of Playing Cards: Benham, 56–8.

65   Playing cards as business cards; development of de la Rue's patterned backs: Tilley, 130–1, 155–6.

66–7   Appearance of modern playing cards: Tilley, 158; *http://www.cs.man.ac.uk/playing-cards/jack+knave.html*

Part II: Gambling Becomes a Science

71–2   Elizabeth Charlotte's letters: Elisabeth Charlotte, *A Woman's Life in the Court of the Sun King: Letters of Liselotte von der Pfalz, 1652–1722* trans. Elborg Forster (Baltimore: Johns Hopkins Press, 1948), ix, 12, 38–9, 74, 86, 88.

Chapter Four: Taming Tyche

73   Cicero's thoughts on chance: Cicero, *De Divinatore,* Book II, in C. D. Onge, trans., *The Nature of the Gods and On Divination* (Amherst, NY: Prometheus Books, 1997), 251.

74   For a complete treatment of Cardano's life, see Oystein Ore, *Cardano: The Gambling Scholar* (Princeton: Princeton University Press, 1953). This book also features an English translation of the *Liber de Ludo Aleae.* For Cardano's life in his own inimitable words (in English translation), see Jerome Cardan, *The Book of My Life,* trans. Jean Stoner (New York: Dover Publications, Inc., 1962).

76–7   Cardano's gambling: Cardano, 73, 105: Ore 185–7.

77   Cardano's general law of wagers: Ore, 149.

78   Cardano on the equality of play: Ore, 189.

78–9   Gallileo and gambling: Florence N. David, *Games, Gods, and Gambling: The Origins and History of Probability and Statistical Ideas from the Earliest Times to the Newtonian Era* (New York: Hafner Publishing Company, 1962), 192. David reprints E. H. Thorne's translation of the dice fragment in her second appendix, pp. 192–5.

81   The problem of points: David, 81–8, 231–2; I. Todhunter, *A History of the Mathematical Theory of Probability, from the Time of Pascal to That of La Place* (Bronx: Chelsea Publishing Company, 1865, reprinted 1965), 15–16.

82   Pierre Rémond de Montmort: Thomas M. Kavanagh, *Enlightenment and the Shadows of Chance: The Novel and the Culture of Gambling in Eighteenth-Century France* (Baltimore: Johns Hopkins University Press, 1999), 12.

82–3   Jakob Bernoulli and Abraham de Moirve: Todhunter, 135–140.

83–4   Early lotteries: William Hone, *The Every-Day Book, or Everlasting Calendar of Popular Amusements, Sports, Pastimes, Ceremonies, Manners, Customs, and Events, Incident to Each of the Three Hundred and Sixty-five Days, in Past and Present Times* (London: William Hone, 1827), 1529.

84   Flemish origin of lotteries: C. L'Estrange Ewen, *Lotteries and Sweepstakes: An Historical, Legal, and Ethical Survey of Their Introduction, Suppression, and Re-Establishment in the British Isles* (New York: Benjamin Bloom, 1972), 24–8.

85   Italians in Bruges: Raymond de Roover, *Money, Banking, and Credit in Medieval Bruges: Italian Merchant-Bankers Lombards and Money-Changers, A Study in the Origins of Banking* (Cambridge, Mass.: The Medieval Academy of America, 1948).

85   Lotteries in Italy: Hone, 1531.

85–6   Venetian lotteries: Adrian Seville, "The Italian Roots of the Lottery," *History Today* (March 1999), 17–18; Hone, 1531; Maurice Andrieux, *Daily Life in Venice in the Time of Casanova* (London: Allen and Unwin, 1972), 130.

86–7   Genoese lotto: Seville, 18–9; Hone, 1534–5.

87–8   Early French lotteries: Elwood and Tennant, *The Whole World Lottery Guide* (Toronto: Millions Publications, 1981), 104.

88–9 Voltaire's lottery scam: Russell T. Barnhart, "How Voltaire Beat the Lottery," in Russell T. Barnhart Papers, University of Nevada Reno Special Collections. Box 12. 3–7, 10–2.

90 Other French lotteries: Kavanagh, 58–9; Stephen M. Stigler, "Casanova, 'Bonaparte,' and the Loterie de France," 1–5, 8, 11, 24.

Chapter Five: The Ridotto Revolution

93 Lansquenet: Parlett, 76–7.

93–4 Venetian gambling: Russell T. Barnhart, "Gambling with Giacomo Casanova and Lorenzo da Ponte in Eighteenth Century Venice—The Ridotto: 1638–1774," in Russell T. Barnhart Papers, University of Nevada Reno Special Collections. Box 14. 2. Cited as Barnhart (Casanova); Jonathan Walker, "Gambling and Venetian Noblemen," *Past and Present,* no. 162. (February 1999), 32–33, 77.

94 Basset: Parlett, 77.

95 The Ridotto: Barnhart (Casanova), 4–5, 13, 16; Maurice Rowdon, *The Fall of Venice* (London: Weidenfeld and Nicolson, 1970), 45.

96–7 The genesis of faro: Parlett, 78.

97 Lorenzo da Ponte at the Ridotto: Barnhart (Casanova), 9, 19–20.

97 Casanova at the Ridotto: Barnhart (Casanova), 10, 12.

97–8 Closure of the Ridotto: Maurice Andrieux, *Daily Life in London in Times of Casanova* (London: Allen and Unwin, 1972), 131; Barnhart (Casanova), 20.

98 Spread of casini: Barnhart (Casanova), 4.
Andrew Steinmetz, *The Gaming Table: Its Votaries and Victims, in All Times and Countries, Especially in England and in France,* vol. 1. Originally published 1870. Reprint published in Montclair, New Jersey: Patterson Smith, 1969, 70–2.

99 French gambling through Louis XIII: Steinmetz, 75, 84–5.

99–100 Louis XIV, Mazarin, and gambling: Steinmetz, 87–8; Nancy Mitford, *The Sun King* (New York: Penguin Books, 1994), 64–5.

100 Spread of French gambling: Kavanagh, 32; Steinmetz, 88, 99.

100–1 French rationales for gambling: Kavanagh, 42, 46.

101 *jeux de commerce* and *jeux de hazard*: Kavanagh, 30–31.

101–2 French games: Russell T. Barnhart, "The Invention of Roulette" (New York: Russell T. Barnhart, 1987), 11. Cited as Barnhart (1987), Thomas M. Kavanagh, "The Libertine's Bluff: Cards and Culture in Eighteenth-Century France," in *Eighteenth-Century Studies,* vol. 33, no. 4 (2000), 509. Cited afterward as Kavanagh (2000).

102	French gaming hells and spas: Steinmetz, 103–5.
102	French attempts to legalize gambling: Steinmetz, 105–7.
102–3	The Palais Royale: Russell T. Barnhart, "Gambling in Revolutionary Paris—The Palais Royale: 1789–1838" (New York: Russell T. Barnhart, 1990), 2–11. Cited as Barnhart (1990).
103–4	The origin of roulette: Barnhart (1987), 5–8, 14–20.
104	Napoléon legalizes gambling: Barnhart (1990), 12–16.
104–5	Blackjack: Parlett, 78–81.
105	Continuation of French legal gaming: Steinmetz, 108.

Part III: Gambling Takes to the Sea
Chapter Six: All Is on the Hazard

111–2	Hazard: David, 148; Charles Cotton, "The Compleat Gamester," in *Games and Gamesters of the Restoration* (London: George Routledge and Sons, 1930), 84; Alan Wykes, *The Complete Illustrated Guide to Gambling* (Garden City: Doubleday, 1964), 137.
112	Inn and Inn, Passage: Cotton, 80–82.
112–3	Table games: John Ashton, *The History of Gambling in England* (London: Duckworth and Company, 1899), 21.
114	Other British games: Cotton, 55; Joseph Strutt, *The Sports and Pastimes of the People of England from the Earliest Period, Including the Rural and Domestic Recreations, May Games, Mummeries, Pageants, Processions and Pompous Spectacles, Illustrated by Reproductions from Ancient Paintings in Which Are Represented Most of the Popular Diversions* (London: Methuen and Company, 1801), 262.
114–5	Gambling in Shakespeare: William Shakespeare, *Julius Caesar*. Accessed at: *http://www.languid.org/cgibin/shakespeare?st=show&show=03064*; William Shakespeare, *The Merry Wives of Windsor*. Accessed at: *http://www.languid.org/cgi-bin/shakespeare?st=show&show=02867*; William Shakespeare, *Henry VIII*. Accessed at: *http://www.languid.org/cgi-bin/shakespeare?st=show&show=03814*; William Shakespeare, *The Merchant of Venice*. Accessed at: *http://www.languid.org/cgi-bin/shakespeare?stshow&show=02614*.
115	Henry VIII's gambling: Strutt, 260.
115	Cromwell's antigambling action: Henry Steele Commager, ed., *Churchill's History of the English-Speaking Peoples* (New York: Barnes and Noble Books, 1995), 201.
115–7	Restoration gambling: Cyril Hughes Hartmann, "Introduction," in *Games and Gamesters of the Restoration* (London: George Routledge and Sons, 1930), ix–xii.

117   Betting of a child: Hone, 1344.

118   Basset becomes fashionable: Hartmann, xiv; Theophilus Lucas, *Memoirs of the Lives, Intrigues, and Comical Adventures of the Most Famous Gamesters and Celebrated Sharpers in the Reigns of Charles II, James II, William II, and Queen Anne*, in *Games and Gamesters of the Revolution* (London: George Routledge and Sons, 1930), 271.

118   Warnings against professional gamblers: Lucas, 119, 136–7, 277.

119   The Tulip Bubble: Mike Dash, *TulipoMania: The Story of the World's Most Coveted Flower and the Extraordinary Passions It Aroused* (New York: Crown Publishers, 1999), 61, 66; Charles Mackay, *Memoirs of Extraordinary Popular Delusions and the Madness of Crowds* (London: Office of the National Illustrated Library, 1852), 3.7–3.8. Accessed at: *http://www.econlib.org/library/Mackay/macExContents.html*; Dash, 109–119, 162–9.

120   John Law's scheme: Kavanagh, 67–82

121–2   The South Sea Bubble: Mackay, Chapter 2: "The South Sea Bubble," 1–2, 4–7, 9–13, 20–5.

122   Jonathan's coffeehouse: Ralph Nevill, *London Clubs: Their History & Treasures* (London: Chatto & Windus, 1911), 12.

122–3   First English lottery: Hone, 1410–1; Ewen, 6, 40, 57–63.

123   Julian Miccottie's lottery: Ewen, 69.

124   Early Virginia colony woes: Walter McDougall, *Freedom Just Around the Corner: A New American History 1585–1828* (New York: HarperCollins, 2004), 42–3.

124   Virginia Company lottery: Ewen, 71–4, 80–7; John Samuel Ezell, *Fortune's Merry Wheel: The Lottery in America* (Cambridge: Harvard University Press, 1960), 4–9.

125   Gabriel Barber's lottery: Hone, 1412.

125–6   More private lotteries: Ewen, 92, 94–106, 111, 119.

126   Parliamentary lotteries: Ewen, 127–163, 199, 232–3.

127   Continuing private lotteries: Hone, 1435, 1446.

127   Lottery corruption: Hone, 1463.

128   Lottery "insurance" and play by the poor: Ewen, 246, 255; Hone, 1454–5.

128–9   End of the British lottery: Hone, 1505, 1526.

129   Scottish lotteries: Ewen, 324.

129   Irish lotteries: Ewen, 324–345.

130   Early years of Bath: Russell T. Barnhart, *Gamblers of Yesteryear* (Las Vegas: GBC Press, 1983), 10–11; Willard Connely, *Beau Nash: Monarch of Bath and Tunbridge Wells* (London: Werner Laurie, 1955), 22–3.

130–1   Beau Nash's early years: Barnhart, 7–8; Connely, 24.

131   Captain Webster: Connely, 22–23, 27.

131–2   Nash's redevelopment of Bath: Connely, 28–34; Barnhart, 13–15; Trevor Fawcett, *Bath Entertain'd: Amusements, Recreations, & Gambling at the 18th Century Spa* (Bath: Ruton, 1998), 45–9, 69.

133   Parliamentary acts against gambling: Barnhart, 31.

133–4   Decline of Beau Nash: Barnhart, 43–7.

134   Decline of Bath: Barnhart, 49–50.

Chapter Seven: Star-Spangled Gamblers

135–6   Native American games: Culin, 346–9.

136   Noquilpi and his temple: Kathryn Gabriel, *Gambler Way: Indian Gaming in Mythology, History, and Archeology in North America* (Boulder: Johnson Books, 1996), 88–9, 100–1.

136   Chungke: Gabriel, 51.

137   Persistence of Native American gambling: Gabriel, 8–9.

137   Montezuma, Cortez, and gambling: Gabriel, 129–31.

137–8   Gambling and the Ghost Dance: Gabriel, 72–3.

138   Colonial Virginia: McDougall, 42–3, 149.

138   Early Virginia gambling: T. H. Breen, "Horses and Gentlemen: The Cultural Significance of Gambling Among the Gentry of Virginia," *The William and Mary Quarterly,* 3rd Series, vol. 34, no. 2 (April, 1977), 239, 248; Louis B. Wright and Marion Tinling, eds., *The Secret Diary of William Byrd of Westover, 1709–1712* (Richmond, Virginia: The Dietz Press, 1941), 442.

138–9   Colonial horse racing: Breen, 249–254; George DeWan, "Legacy: America's First Racecourse," in *Newsday.* Accessed at: *http://www.newsday.com/community/guide/lihistory/ ny-history-hs312b,0,5912509.story?coll=ny-lihistory-navigation*; Henry Chafetz, *Play the Devil: A History of Gambling in the United States from 1492 to 1955* (New York: Bonanza Books, 1960), 188.

139–40   Tyral/Selima race: John Eisenberg, "Off to the Races," *Smithsonian,* vol. 35, no. 5 (August 2004), 98–101.

140–1   Puritan/New England gambling: Emil Oberholzer, Jr., *Delinquent Saints: Disciplinary Action in the Early Congregational Churches of Massachusetts* (New York: Columbia University Press, 1956), 230; Larry Gragg, "Gambling," in James Ciment, ed., *Colonial America: An Encyclopedia of Social, Political, Cultural, and Economic History* (New York: M. E. Sharpe, 2006); Bruce C. Daniels, *Puritans at Play: Leisure and Recreation in Colonial New England* (New York: St. Martin's Press, 1995), 144, 152, 158, 176–81.

141–2   Penn's charter and the elder Penn's gambling: McDougall, 83–4.

142   Colonial gambling prevalence: "Gambling (1600–1754)" in *American Eras,* 8 vols. (Gale Research, 1997–1998). Reproduced in *Public History Resource Center* (Farmington Hills, Michigan: Gale Group); Chafetz, 16.

143   Reverend Ames's thoughts on the lottery: John Ezell, "The Lottery in Colonial America," *The William and Mary Quarterly,* 3rd series, vol. 5, no. 2 (April 1948), 188.

143–4   Prevalence of colonial lotteries: Ezell, 190–8.

144–5   Howe's antigambling edict: *General Sir William Howe's Orderly Book* (Port Washington, New York: Kennikat Press, 1970), 37.

145   Gambling in the British armies: Chafetz, 30.

145   Washington's gambling: Marvin Kitman, *The Making of the Prefident 1789* (New York: Harper and Row, 1989), 39–42.

145   Washington's antigambling edict: Chafetz, 29.

146   The United States Lottery: Daniels, 182; John Samuel Ezell, *Fortune's Merry Wheel: The Lottery in America* (Cambridge: Harvard University Press, 1960), 61–3.

145–6   The First Continental Congress's statement against gambling: First Continental Congress, "The Articles of Association; October 20, 1774" (New Haven: Avalon Project, Yale University). Accessed at: *http://www.yale.edu/lawweb/avalon/contcong/10-20-74.htm.*

146   Betting on Yellow Fever: Chafetz, 37.

148   1793 federal lottery: Chafetz, 41.

148   Plymouth Beach lottery: Herbert Asbury, *Sucker's Progress: An Informal History of Gambling in America from the Colonies to Canfield* (Montclair, N.J.: Patterson Smith, 1969), 79.

148–9   Early United States lotteries: Asbury, 76–80.

149   Thomas Jefferson's aborted lottery: Asbury, 73–6.

150   Denmark Vesey's lottery win and its consequences: Asbury, 82; "People of Faith: Denmark Vesey," accessed at: *http://www.pbs.org/thisfarbyfaith/people/denmark_vesey.html.*

150   Decline of legal American lotteries in the 1820s and 1830s: Asbury, 82.

151–2   American policy: Asbury, 90–5.

152   Frontier gambling: Chafetz, 44–6.

152–3   Henry Clay's gambling: Chafetz, 48.

153   Andrew Jackson's gambling: Chafetz, 45.

153   American Faro: Asbury, 7–9, 15.

154–5   Elijah Skaggs and the spread of professional faro dealers: Chafetz, 51–4.

155–6   Gambling in Washington, D.C.: Asbury, 134; Chafetz, 180.

156   Scandal over John Adams's White House billiards table: Edwin A. Miles, "President Adams' Billiard Table," *The New England Quarterly*, vol. 45, no. 1 (March 1972), 31, 36–42.

156   All presidents from Van Buren to Cleveland (minus Hayes) as poker players: J. F. B. Lillard, *Poker Stories* (New York: Francis Harper, 1896), 17–18.

157   Hall of the Bleeding Heart: Asbury, 141–2, 144–6.

Chapter Eight: Baiting John Bull

158–9   Early eighteenth-century London gaming houses: Ashton, 22–4, 58–9.

159   Coffeehouses: Nevill, 2–3; A. L. Humphreys, *Crockford's: or The Goddess of Chance in St. James's Street, 1828–1844* (London: Hutchinson, 1953), 13, 20.

159   Growth of gambling clubs: Nevill, 182–184. Ashton, 90.

159–60   The earl of Sandwich: H. T. Waddy, *The Devonshire Club—And Crockford's* (London: Eveleigh, Nash, and Company, 1919), 137.

160   Linda Stradley, "What's Cooking America: The History of Sandwiches." Accessed at: *http://whatscookingamerica.net/History/SandwichHistory.htm*; N.A.M. Rodger. *The Insatiable Earl: A Life of John Montagu*, Fourth Earl of Sandwich, 1718–1792. (London: HarperCollins, 1993), 76–79.

160   The rules of Almack's: Ashton, 90–91.

160   Public outcry against clubs: Ashton, 83.

160–1   Low hells: Ashton, 133–136.

161   Sharpers: Steinmetz, vol. 2, 193–4.

161   Lord Chesterfield's playing with sharpers: Barnhart, 27–28.

161   Sharpers as vegetarians: Steinmetz, 32.

161   "For this end they studied . . ." Steinmetz, 32.

162   Lady Archer and Lady Buckinghamshire: Ashton, 76–82.

162   Increased police harassment of gambling houses: Steinmetz, 200–202.

162   Continued prevalence of social gambling: Ashton, 83.

162   The game of Macao: Steinmetz, 185–186.

162–3   William Crockford: Humphreys, 39–48; Nevill 190–191.

163–4   Description of Crockford's club: Waddy, 120–136, 147; Nevill, 191; E. Beresford Chancellor, *Memorials of St. James's Street, Together with the Annals of Almack's* (New York: Brentano's 1922), 164–6.

164–5   Crockford's retirement and death: Waddy, 137, 143–4; Ashton, 148.

165   "Come and once more let us greet . . ." Humphreys, 13.

165–6   Whist's evolution: William Pole, *The Evolution of Whist: A Study of the Progressive Changes which the Game Has Passed Through from Its Origin to*

the *Present Time* (London: Longmans, Green, and Company, 1897),
10–19, 26, 35–6; An Amateur, *Whist: Its History of Practice* (London: Bell
and Wood, 1843), 18, 27, 29.

166–7   Early British gaming guides: Parlett, 55–8.

167   Hoyle and his rules: Pole, 41–2, 46, 48–9; Amateur, 41; Parlett,
59–60.

168   Whist becomes intellectual: Pole, 73–83.

169–71   Cockfighting in Britain: Cotton, 102–111; Strutt 224–6; "Cockfighting."
In *Encyclopaedia Britannica*, Eleventh Edition. Accessed at:
http://14.1911encyclopedia.org/C/CO/COCK_FIGHTING.htm; Iris M.
Middleton. "Cockfighting in Yorkshire during the Early Eighteenth
Century, *Northern History*, vol. 40, no. 1 (March 2003), 135.

171   Cockfighting outlawed in 1835 and its consequences: Middleton, 133–5.

171   Throwing at cocks: Strutt, 227.

171–2   Bear- and bullbaiting: "Bear-baiting and Bull-baiting," in *Encyclopaedia
Britannica*, Eleventh Edition.

172   "You see the virtue of a wager . . ." Hartmann, xii.

173   Elizabethan wagers: Ashton, 154–153.

173–4   Siege betting: John Childs, "Fortune of War," *History Today*, vol. 53, no.
10 (October 2003), 50–6.

174   "Than if he had carried . . .": Ashton, 153.

174   Walpole's wager: Ashton, 155–6.

174–5   Outrageous bets and pedestrianism: Ashton, 158, 161–5.

175   Bookmaker etymology: *http://www.etymonline.com/index.php?l=b&p=14*

175   Medieval horse racing: Strutt, 32–33.

175–6   Early British horse racing: Roger Mortimer, *The Jockey Club* (London:
Cassell, 1958), 2–3.

176   Northbrooke on racing: Strutt, 35–36.

176   James I and racing: Mortimer, 3.

176   Importance of horses and racing to British society: Wray Vamplew, *The
Turf: A Social and Economic History of Horse Racing* (London: Allen Lane,
1976), 18.

176   "So noble an animal . . .": Ashton, 171.

176–7   Early racing at Newmarket: Mortimer, 3.

177   Charles I and racing: Ashton, 178.

177   Cromwell and racing: Mortimer, 4.

177   Professionalization of racing: Mark Clapson, "A Bit of a Flutter," *History
Today*, vol. 41, no. 10 (October 1991), 37; Mortimer, 5–6.

177   Tregonwell Frampton: Mortimer, 7.

177–8	Racing becomes popular: Mortimer, 8; Vamplew, 22.
178–9	Origin of the Jockey Club: Mortimer, 10–12.
179	Gambling booths at racecourses: Vamplew, 18–19.
179	Parliamentary testimony about gaming booths: Ashton, 198.
179	Early oddsmaking: Ashton, 211–212.
179	Early tout sheets: Ashton, 209.
180	Growing popularity of race betting: Clapson, 39.
180	Development of modern racing: Vamplew, 39–48.
180	Edward's view of horse racing: Russell T. Barnhart, "Edward the Seventh: An Edwardian Gambler," in Russell T. Barnhart Papers, University of Nevada Reno Special Collections. Box 7.

Part IV: Europeans Gamble at Home and Abroad
Chapter Nine: Seeking the Cure

186	Spa's sixteenth-century emergence: Russell T. Barnhart, *Gamblers of Yesteryear* (Las Vegas: GBC Press, 1983), 53–4.
186	Early attractions at Spa: Barnhart, 58–61.
186	Early gambling at Spa: Barnhart, 79.
186–7	Opening of the Redoute: Barnhart, 79–80.
187	Horseracing at Spa: Barnhart, 71.
187	Velbruck's resolution of intercasino tensions: Barnhart, 80–1.
187	The English Club: Barnhart, 81.
187	Fire at the Redoute: Barnhart, 79–80.
188	Scandal at the Redoute: Barnhart, 83.
188	Trente-et-quarante: Barnhart, 80; Parlett, 78.
188–9	The French Revolution's impact at Spa: Barnhart, 88–90.
190	The decline of Spa: Barnhart, 90–3.
190	"the ball spins more slowly . . .": Andrew Steinmetz, *The Gaming Table: Its Votaries and Victims, in All Times and Countries, Especially in England and in France,* vol. 1. Originally published 1870. Reprint published in Montclair, New Jersey: Patterson Smith, 1969. 171–2.
190	Railroads bypass Spa: Barnhart, 90–3.
190–1	Early years of Baden-Baden: Klaus Fischer, *Faites Votre Jeu: History of the Casino Baden-Baden* (Baden-Baden: Hans Werner Kelch, 1975), 7, 22.
191	The Promenade House opens: Barnhart, 100.
191	Other gambling operations: Fischer, 25.
191	Johann Peter Hebel's praise of Baden-Baden: Fischer, 16.
192	Growing popularity of Baden-Baden: Fischer, 17.

192   Chabert: Barnhart, 100.

192   Jacques Bénazet: Barnhart, 100–1.

192   End of Parisian gambling (1837): Barnhart, 101–2.

193   Bénazet moves to Baden-Baden: Barnhart, 114.

193   Bénazet's success at Baden-Baden: Fischer, 44.

193–4   Old Father Martin: Barnhart, 111–3.

194   Edward Bénazet's continued success: Barnhart, 115–6.

194   "all bearing the semblance of gentility . . . ," description of Baden-Baden: Steinmetz, 159–60.

195   Léonie Leblanc: Steinmetz, 168–9.

195–6   "If the public were not such simpletons . . .": Barnhart, 108.

196–8   Hesse Homburg, mercenaries, and the dissolution of the principality's fortune by Wilhelm: "Hessians," *Wikipedia*. Accessed at: *http://en.wikipedia.org/wiki/Hessians*; Barnhart, 125–132; "Prince-elector," *Wikipedia*. Accessed at: *http://en.wikipedia.org/wiki/Prince-elector*.

198   Brahms at Baden-Baden: Barnhart, 106–8; Leon Botstein, ed., *The Compleat Brahms: A Guide to the Musical Works of Johannes Brahms* (New York: W. W. Norton and Company, 1999), 144; Malcolm McDonald, *Brahms* (New York: Schirmer Books, 1990), 132.

199   Offenbach and Strauss at Baden-Baden: Barnhart, 106–8.

199   Last years of Baden-Baden as a gambling resort: Fischer, 60–1.

199   Countess Kissileff: Barnhart, 145–8.

199   Gogol at Baden-Baden: Barnhart, 104–5.

200   Tolstoy at Baden-Baden: Barnhart, 110.

200   Turgenev and Tolstoy: Ivan Turgenev, "Dying Plea to Tolstoy," in John Cournos, ed. *A Treasury of Classic Russian Literature* (New York: Capricorn Books, 1961), 75.

200   Dostoyevsky writes *The Gambler*: Count Corti, *The Wizard of Homburg and Monte Carlo* (London: Thornton Butterworth, Ltd., 1934), 210–11.

200–1   Dostoyevsky's July 1867 trip to Baden-Baden: Barnhart, 121.

201   "Apart from my own gains . . .": Fyodor Dostoyevsky, "Meeting with Turgenev," in John Cournos, ed., *A Treasury of Classic Russian Literature* (New York: Capricorn Books, 1961), 48.

201   Dostoyevsky's growing desperation: Cournos, 48.

201–2   Existing tensions between Dostoyevsky and Turgenev: Barnhart, 121–2.

202   Dostoyevsky/Turgenev confrontation: Cournos, 49–50.

202   Dostoyevsky stops gambling: Barnhart, 124.

202   Closing of Rhine spa gambling resorts: Fischer, 22.

203   Aachen and its gambling: "Aachen," *Wikipedia*. Accessed at:
      http://en.wikipedia.org/wiki/Aachen; Steinmetz, 202–6.

203   Development of Wiesbaden: "One of Europe's Most Attractive Casinos."
      Informational brochure in Promotional and Publicity Material: Spielbank
      Casino, Wiesbaden, Germany. UNLV Special Collections.

203   Wiesbaden in 1868: Steinmetz, 207–13.

204   "ghastly creatures . . .": Steinmetz, 213–5.

204   "An edifying sight is this venerable dame . . .": Steinmetz, 215–7.

205   The Blanc brothers' early years: Corti, 17–26, 30–3.

205–6 Landgrave Ludwig negotiates with the Blancs: Corti, 38–41.

206   Casino dedication ceremony: Corti, 45–6.

207   Blanc strikes a deal with Landgrave Philip: Corti, 42–4.

207   Blanc's efforts to lure visitors to Homburg: Corti, 45, 47–9.

207–8 Opening of the permanent casino at Bad Homburg: Corti, 50.

208   Description of Bad Homburg casino: Barnhart, 139; Steinmetz, 180–1.

208   Suicide at Bad Homburg and dealers' nonchalant response: Steinmetz,
      188–9.

208–9 Nongaming amenities at Bad Homburg: Barnhart, 140.

209   George Augustus Sala's description of Bad Homburg: Barnhart, 153–4.

209   "We are throwing sprats . . .": Corti, 104–5.

209   Cheating at Bad Homburg and Blanc's countermeasures: Corti, 90–2.

209–10 The prince of Canino comes to Bad Homburg: Barnhart, 141–2; Corti,
      93–9.

210   "Red sometimes wins . . .": Charles Kingston, *The Romance of Monte
      Carlo* (London: John Lane, 1925), 36.

211   Blanc's marriage and prosperity: Corti, 100–2.

211–2 Thomas Garcia's wins and Blanc's countermeasures: Corti, 113–4,
      118–26.

212   The German National Assembly's antigambling edict and Blanc's maneu-
      vering: Corti, 63–74.

212   Dostoyevsky on the press's favorable coverage of gambling resorts:
      Cournos, 27.

212–3 Prussian consolidation of Rhine states and the end of gambling: Corti,
      200–1, 203–4.

213   The end of German gambling: Corti, 204, 248–9; Barnhart, 168.

214   Blanc transitions to Monaco: Corti, 249.

Chapter Ten: Flight of the Sparrow

216   Aurangzeb and the Moghul stance on gambling: *The Xenophile Historian: A Concise History of India.* Accessed at: *http://xenohistorian.faithweb.com/india/in04.html.*

216   Indian horse racing: Anil Mukhi, "Evolution of Racing in India." Accessed at: *http://www.indiarace.com/Archives/RacingEvolution/history.htm.*

217   Gandhi on gambling: Mohandas Karamchand Gandhi, *Drink, Drugs, and Gambling* (Ahmedabad: Navajivan Publishing House, 1961), 8–9, 145.

217   The Republic of India legalizes gambling: Mukhi.

217–8   The walled city of Kowloon: Seth Harter, "Hong Kong's Dirty Little Secret: Clearing the Walled City of Kowloon," *Journal of Urban History,* vol. 27, no. 1 (November 2001), 97.

217–8   The Hong Kong Jockey Club's founding and early years: Peter Moss, *The Race Goes On: A Millennium Retrospect of Racing in Hong Kong* (Hong Kong: The Hong Kong Jockey Club, 2000), 4, 6–13.

219   Betting at Happy Valley: Moss, 13–4.

219   The Derby Day Massacre: Moss, 18–22.

219   Chinese involvement in the Hong Kong Jockey Club: Moss, 29–32.

219–20 World War II and the Jockey Club: Moss, 32–3.

220   HKJC and philanthropy: Moss, 38–9.

220   Postwar growth of the HKJC: Moss, 41–5.

220–21 The HKJC under Chinese rule: Moss, 41.

221–22 The Portuguese settlement of Macau: Geoffrey C. Gunn, *Encountering Macau: A Portuguese City-State on the Periphery of China, 1557–1999* (Boulder, Colorado: Westview Press, 1996), 8–9.

222   Macau legalizes gambling: Gunn, 6–7, 88–9; A. Pinho, "Gambling in Macau," in R. D. Cremer, ed., *Macau: City of Commerce and Culture* (Hong Kong: UEA Press LTD, 1987), 157.

222   Games of Macau: Pinho, 155–156; *Macau's Journey* (Macau: Sociedade de Jogos de Macau, S.A., 2004), unpaginated.

223   "The flotsam of the sea . . ." Jonathan Porter, *Macau: The Imaginary City: Culture and Society, 1557 to the Present* (Boulder, Colorado: Westview Press, 1996), 94.

224   Mahjong's philosophy and origin: Li Yu Sang, *Sparrow: The Chinese Game Called Ma-Ch'iau: A Descriptive and Explanatory Story* (New York: The Lent and Graff Company, 1923), 3–4, 9–11, 19–20.

224   Playing mahjong: Sang, 41–50.

224   Babcock and mahjong's American popularity: Frederick Lewis Allen, *Only Yesterday: An Informal History of the 1920s* (New York: Harper & Row Perennial Library, 1959), 68, 158.

226   "The ancient, beautiful, beneficial Chinese game . . .": Sang, 24–5.

226–7   The *pakapoo* lottery: Stewart Culin, *The Gambling Games of the Chinese in America* (Philadelphia: University of Pennsylvania Press, 1891), 6–12; C. T. Dobree. *Gambling Games of Malaya* (Kuala Lumpur: Caxton Press, 1955), 48–9.

227   Other Chinese "lottery" games: Dobree, 14–6, 39.

228   Early gambling in Australia: Peter Charlton, *Two Flies Up a Wall: The Australian Passion for Gambling* (North Ryde, Australia: Methuen Haynes, 1987), 9–15, 38; John O'Hara, *A Mug's Game: A History of Gaming and Betting in Australia* (New South Wales University Press, 1988), 10–11.

229   William Francis King and Joe Hilton: Charlton, 34–5.

229   Australian horse racing: O'Hara, 13–19, 32–3.

230   Australian coursing: O'Hara, 73.

230   The Melbourne Cup: O'Hara, 71; Charlton, 280–1.

230–1   Tote betting: Charlton, 124–131, 156–170.

231   Betting with cards and dice: O'Hara, 31–2; Charlton, 22–3.

231   Gambling during the Australian gold rush: Charlton, 73–7, 81–5.

232   Chinese gambling in Australia: Charlton, 87–8, 93–4.

232   "Striking factor in the development . . .": Charlton, 159.

233   The development of sweeps: O'Hara, 78–9, 99; Charlton 174–7, 181–96.

234   Two-up: Charlton, 257–8.

234–5   Early New Zealand gambling: David Grant, *On a Roll: A History of Gaming and Lotteries in New Zealand* (Wellington: Victoria University Press, 1994), 18–20, 30, 38, 42–3.

235–6   Games of New Zealand: Grant, 26, 28; Parlett, 188–9. "Bagatelle Games." *http://gamesmuseum.uwaterloo.ca/vexhibit/bagatel/baga.html*

236   Prevalence of New Zealand gambling: Grant, 23–5.

236–7   New Zealand horse racing: Grant, 48–50.

237   Ekberg and the tote: John C. Schmidt. *Win, Place, Show: A Biography of Harry Straus, the Man Who Gave America the Tote* (Baltimore: Johns Hopkins University, 1989), 43.

237   Chinese gambling in New Zealand: Grant, 36–7.

237–8   Gaming and Lotteries Act: Grant, 55–8.

238   New Zealand's gambling prohibitions: Grant, 54–5, 89–92.

238–9   Native American gambling in Canada: Culin, 267, 527.

239 Playing cards as currency: Herbert Heaton, "The Playing Card Currency of French Canada," *The American Economic Review,* vol. 18, no. 4 (December 1928), 652, 654–60.

240 Canadian laws against gambling: Ronald G. Robinson, "The History of the Law of Gaming in Canada" (Edmonton, Alberta: Gaming Specialist Field Understudy Program, Royal Canadian Mounted Police, 1983), 43.

240 Canadian horse racing: Glen Mikkelson, "The Sport of Kings in \Victorian Canada," *Beaver* (August/September 1996), vol. 76, no. 4, 18–9.

240 Exceptions to Canada's gambling ban: Robinson, 59.

240 Chinese gambling in Canada: David Chuenyan Lai, *Chinatowns: Towns within Cities in Canada* (Vancouver: University of British Columbia Press, 1988), 229–30.

240 The Klondike gold rush and gambling: Charlene Porsild, *Gamblers and Dreamers: Women, Men, and Community in the Klondike* (Vancouver: UBC Press, 1998), 101–5.

Part V: The United States Bets Big
245 U. S. Grant interrupts a poker game: Lillard, 159–60.

Chapter Eleven: Wild Cards
246 "Those who live in the midst of democratic fluctuations . . .": Alexis de Tocqueville, *Democracy in America,* Book 2, Chapter 19.

246 Louisiana's legal gambling: Asbury, 110–2.

248–9 John Davis's gambling house: Asbury, 114–5.

249–50 The genesis of poker: David Parlett, "The History of Poker." Accessed at: *http://www.pagat.com/vying/pokerhistory.html.*

250 The evolution of craps: Barnhart, 23–4, 27–8; Asbury, 46–7; John Scarne, *Scarne on Dice. Eighth Revised Edition* (New York: Crown Publishers, 1980), 19–21.

251 The shell game and bunco: Asbury, 52–6.

251 Gambling in southern river towns: Chafetz, 55.

251–2 The Vicksburg vigilante hangings: Asbury, 219–24; Chafetz, 56–7.

253 New Orleans continuing gambling: Asbury, 122.

253–4 Riverboat regulation: Kermit L. Hall. *The Magic Mirror: Law in American History* (New York: Oxford University Press, 1989), 93.

254 Riverboat gamblers: Asbury, 201–2; Chafetz, 74.

254 Blacklegs: Asbury, 204–5.

255–6   George Devol's career and recollections: George M. Devol. *Forty Years a Gambler on the Mississippi* (Cincinnati: Devol & Haines, 1887), 129–30, 148.

256   General Benjamin Butler in New Orleans: Devol, 119–120.

256   Gambling among Union troops: Bell Irvin Wiley, *The Life of Billy Yank: The Common Soldier of the Union* (Baton Rouge: Louisiana State University Press, 2001), 149–50, 250–1.

257   Gambling among Confederate troops: Bell Irvin Wiley, *The Life of Johnny Reb: The Common Soldier of the Confederacy* (Baton Rouge: Louisiana State University Press, 1996), 36–40.

258   Gambling across the lines: Wiley, 318–9.

258   "The first orders we would receive . . .": Devol, 117–8.

260   Gambling en route to the goldfields: J. S. Holliday, *The World Rushed In: The California Gold Rush Experience* (New York: Touchstone, 1981), 76, 94, 96, 412.

260   Gambling at the goldfields: Holliday, 355, 364.

260   "Where men are congregated . . .": Roger D. McGrath, *Gunfighters, Highwaymen, and Vigilantes: Violence on the Frontier* (Berkeley: University of California Press, 1984), 11–2.

262   Typical Western saloon: McGrath, 111.

261   Animal sports and betting: Rodman Wilson Paul and Elliott West, *Mining Frontiers of the Far West, 1848–1880* (Albuquerque: University of New Mexico Press, 2001), 214–5.

261   San Francisco gambling halls: Asbury, 53, 312–5.

262   Chinese gambling in San Francisco: John Philip Quinn, *Fools of Fortune, or, Gambling and Gamblers* (Chicago: G. L. Howe & Co., 1890), 449–50.

262   Revenue of San Francisco gambling houses: Asbury, 317.

262–3   California gambling prohibitions: Roger Dunstan, *History of Gambling in California.* (Sacramento: California State Library, 1997). Accessed at: *http://www.library.ca.gov/CRB/97/03/crb97003.html#toc.*

263   Gambling in Western cities: Asbury, 328–33, 335, 341.

263   Gambling in Santa Fe and Kansas City: Asbury, 340.

263   Gambling in cowtowns: Chafetz, 146.

264   "He was too much of a gambler . . .": Bret Harte, "The Outcasts of Poker Flat," in *9 Sketches* (West Virginia: West Virginia Pulp and Paper Company, 1967), 36.

264   Wild Bill Hickok: Robert K. DeArment, *Knights of the Green Cloth: The Saga of the Frontier Gamblers* (Norman: University of Oklahoma Press,

1982), 333–6; Chafetz, 156; Bill Kelly, *Gamblers of the Old West: Gambling Men and Women of the 1800s, How They Lived—How They Died* (Las Vegas: B & F Enterprises, 1995), 18–20.

264–5   Doc Holliday: Kelly, 80–1, 84–5.

265–6   Bat Masterson: Kelly, 113–8.

266   Doña María Gertrudis Barceló (La Tules): DeArment, 229–237.

266–7   Belle Siddons (Lurline Monte Verde): Kelly, 31–6.

267   Eleanor DuMont: DeArment, 240–1, Chafetz, 172–5.

268   Poker Alice: DeArment, 269–76.

Chapter Twelve: Fools of Fortune

269   Early New York gambling: Asbury, 156–7.

270   Wolf traps: Asbury, 185–7, 272–4.

271   Second-class houses: Asbury, 176–7.

271–2   Brace rooms: Asbury, 181–4.

272   "At these dens . . .": Asbury, 175–6.

272   Horace Greeley's estimates of New York gambling losses: Asbury, 162.

272–3   New York's first-class houses: Asbury, 160–1.

273   New York Association for the Suppression of Gambling statistics on gambling: Asbury, 163.

273–4   Reuben Parsons: Asbury, 167–8.

274   Henry Colton: Henry Chafetz, *Play the Devil: A History of Gambling in the United States from 1492 to 1955* (New York: Bonanza Books, 1960), 236.

274–5   Pat Herne: Chafetz, 231–4.

275   Other noted New York gambling operators: Chafetz, 233–9.

275   John Morrissey's early years: Asbury, 360–2.

276–7   Morrissey's later career: Asbury, 367–88.

278–9   Rondo: Edmund Hoyle, *Hoyle's Games: Autograph Edition. Revised, Enlarged, and Brought up to Date* (New York: A. L. Burt Company, 1907), 334.

279   Keno: Hoyle, 247–8.

279   Cincinnati gambling: Chafetz, 209–10.

279   Midwestern gambling: Chafetz, 205.

280   Professional gamblers in the Midwest: Chafetz, 206.

280   Milwaukee gambling: Asbury, 264–6.

281–2   Early Chicago gambling: Asbury, 286–91.

282   Wat Cameron: Asbury, 291.

283   George Trussell: Asbury, 293–5.

283   Louis Cohn and the Chicago fire: Chafetz, 417.

284   Mike MacDonald: Asbury, 295–7.

284   "The town was literally handed over . . .": John Philip Quinn, *Fools of For-tune* (Chicago: G. I. Howe and Company, 1890), 402.

284   The store: Asbury, 298–9.

285   MacDonald's decline: Asbury, 300–5.

285   "They wore every variety of dress . . .": Edgar Allan Poe, "The Man of the Crowd," in *The Annotated Tales of Edgar Allan Poe* (Garden City, NY: Doubleday, 1981), 189.

285–7   Fakirs and their games: Quinn, 284–891.

287   Wheel-of-fortune odds: Robert C. Hannum and Anthony N. Cabot, *Practical Casino Math*, Second Edition (Reno: Institute for the Study of Gambling and Commercial Gaming, 2005), 117.

287–9   Honest John Kelly's life: Julien J. Prosauker, *Suckers All! The Life of Honest John Kelly as Told from His Diaries* (New York: The Macaulay Company, 1934), 23–53; 93–179; 182–199, 200–91; 317–8.

289   John Philip Quinn: John Philip Quinn, *Gambling and Gambling Devices* (Las Vegas: GBC Press [facsimile of original 1912 edition] 27–8.

289–90 Gambling devices: Quinn (1912), 136, 145–6.

290–1   Punchboards: Quinn (1912), 226–30.

Part VI: Gambling for Fun and Profit

295–6   The captain visits Monte Carlo: " 'Breaking the Bank' Costly to Tourists," *New York Times* (September 2, 1923), XX4.

Chapter Thirteen: A Sunny Place for Shady People

297   Early history of Monaco: Count Corti, *The Wizard of Homburg and Monte Carlo* (London: Thornton Butterworth, Ltd. 1934), 130–2, 137–8; "Monaco: History," accessed at:
        http://www.monaco.mc/monaco/info/history1.html.

298   Eynaud's investigation: Corti, 139.

298–9   Blanc's doubts about Monaco: Corti, 85, 141.

299   Langlois and Aubert's attempts to run a "bathing establishment": Corti, 142–9.

299–308 Daval tries his hand at Monaco: Corti, 155–9.

300   Duc de Valmy's company strikes out: Corti, 159–168, 179.

300–1   François Blanc signs a contract with Charles III: Corti, 177–180.

301   Blanc's successes at Monaco: Corti, 182–7, 193–9, 218–9, 225–6; Charles Kingston, *The Romance of Monte Carlo* (London: John Lane, 1925), 16.

301–2   Blanc's entrance card system's genesis: Corti, 252–3.

302   London *Times* article on Monaco: "Monaco," *New York Times* (April 23, 1873), 4.

302   Blanc's largesse toward the French government: Corti, 259.

303   Blanc's death: "Gambling at Monte Carlo," *New York Times* (September 17, 1877), 2; Corti, 266.

303   Monaco at Blanc's death: Stanley Jackson, *Inside Monte Carlo* (New York: Stein and Day, 1975), 45.

304   Monte Carlo and casino chips: Barnhart, 181; Dale Seymour, *Antique Gambling Chips: Revised Edition* (Palo Alto, Calif.: Past Pleasures, 1998), 7–14, 66–72, 109–120.

304–5   Marie Blanc's death: Jackson, 48–9.

305   Camille Blanc's improvements at Monte Carlo: Jackson, 49; Charles Graves, *The Big Gamble: The Story of Monte Carlo* (London; New York: Hutchinson, 1951), (1951), 112.

305–6   Monte Carlo's dealer school: Graves (1951), 113.

306   Expansion of the casino: Barnhart, 183–4.

306   *New York Times* criticism of Monte Carlo: "An Italian Gambling Hell," *New York Times* (April 7, 1878), 2.

307   Misadventures of a railroad scion, 1882: "An American at Monte Carlo," *New York Times* (December 18, 1882), 3.

307   Queen Victoria and Prince Edward at Monte Carlo: Barnhart, 185–6; Jackson, 53.

307   The lucky churchman's hymns: Adolphe Smith, *Monaco and Monte Carlo* (London: Grant Richards, Ltd., 1912), 449–455.

307   Monte Carlo suspicions: Smith, 456–662.

308   Monte Carlo during and after World War I: Smith, 345, 440–4; Graves, 1951, 95, 145.

309–10   Martingale and Grand Martingale: Darwin Ortiz, *Darwin Ortiz on Casino Gambling: The Complete Guide to Playing and Winning* (New York: Lyle Stuart, 1992), 73, 175–6.

310   Labouchere system: Ortiz, 177–8.

310   The d'Alembert system: Ortiz, 179–80.

311   Patience system: Ortiz, 181.

311   Gagnante Marche system: Ortiz, 182.

311   François Blanc on systems: Graves (1951), 61.

312   "Breaking the bank" ritual: Graves (1951), 90.

312–3   Pair of Parisian swindlers: "Their System Didn't Work," *New York Times* (June 26, 1887), 11.

313   Jaggers's "system": Graves (1951), 76–7; Mordaunt Hall, " 'Breaking the Bank' Costly to Tourists," *New York Times* (September 2, 1923), XX4.

314   Charles Deville Wells: Jackson, 72; Graves (1951), 90–1.

314–5   Lord Rosslyn versus Sir Maxim: Barnhart, 191–4; "Rosslyn Ahead in Gambling Test," *New York Times* (September 28, 1908), C1; "Rosslyn's Defeat Easy," *New York Times* (October 8, 1908), C1. For Maxim's book-length exposition of the falsity of systems, see Hiram S. Maxim, *Monte Carlo: Facts and Fallacies* (London: Grant Richards, 1904).

317   Chemin-de-fer's spread: Charles Graves, *None But the Rich: The Life and Times of the Greek Syndicate* (London: Cassell, 1963), 1–2.

318   French gambling clubs: Eugène Villiod, *The Stealing Machine*, Russell Barnhart, trans. (Las Vegas: Gambler's Book Club, 1906), 24, 27, 31, 35, 46.

319   Taxes on French casinos: Charles Graves, *The Price of Pleasure* (London: Ivor, Nicholson, and Watson, Ltd., 1935), 1–2.

319–20   The Greek Syndicate: Graves (1963), 11–21, 29, 40; Graves 1951, 27–8.

320   "Never bet on a race horse . . .": "Famed Gambler Dies in Switzerland at 68," *New York Times* (April 23, 1953), 6.

320–1   The Deauville casino: Graves (1963), 56–7.

321   Zographos's death and the survival of the Greek Syndicate: Graves (1963), 61–4, 101, 165.

321   Camille Blanc's ouster and death: Jackson, 12, 123–4, 130–1; "Blanc, Who Grew Rich in Monaco, Dies at 81," *New York Times* (December 23, 1927), 19.

322   René Léon's career at Monte Carlo: Jackson, 132, 140; Clair Price, "A Roulette Battle Resounds in Europe," *New York Times* (March 4, 1934), SM5.

322–3   San Remo: Price, 5.

323   France legalizes baccarat: Price, 19.

323   Léon leaves Monte Carlo: Jackson, 163.

323   Monte Carlo in the late 1930s and early 1940s: Graves (1935), 4–6.

323–4   Postwar Monte Carlo: Jackson, 183–4.

324   Aristotle Onassis buys, sells, controlling interest in SBM: Jackson, 228, 244–6.

324   Monte Carlo in the 1970s: Jackson, 252.

324   Monaco gaming revenues: Rachel Billington, "A Promenade in Monte Carlo," *New York Times* (March 13, 1988), SMA24.

Chapter Fourteen: Wise Guys and One-Armed Bandits

325 Early Saratoga: Jon Sterngass, *First Resorts: Pursuing Pleasure at Saratoga Springs, Newport, and Coney Island* (Baltimore: Johns Hopkins Press, 2001), 150.

325–6 Saratoga racetrack and the Travers Stakes: Sterngass, 148.

326 Morrissey's role in Saratoga race betting: Sterngass, 149.

326 Morrissey's clubhouse: Asbury, 383–4.

326 Morrissey successful at Saratoga: Asbury, 387.

326–7 Johnny Chamberlain, Long Branch, and Monmouth Park: Asbury, 393–6.

327 Canfield's early years: Asbury, 419–27.

328 Canfield's style: Asbury, 420–1.

328 Canfield at Saratoga: Asbury, 439–40.

329 Canfield's administration of his gambling clubs: Asbury, 444–5.

329 Canfield and high-end play: Asbury, 445.

329 "Bet-a-Million" Gates: Asbury, 448–50.

329–30 Canfield's death and legacy: Asbury, 466–8.

330 Gambling machines: Quinn (1913), 188–197, 219.

330 Early slot machines: Marshall Fey, *Slot Machines: A Pictorial History of the First 100 Years*, Fourth Edition (Reno: Liberty Belle Books, 1994), 13–21.

331 Charles Fey and the Liberty Bell: Fey, 40–2, 53–4.

331 Slot machines dispensing gum: Fey, 106.

331 Frank Costello's slot empire: Fey, 104–5.

332 Peytona beats Fashion: Roger Longrigg, *The History of Horse Racing* (New York: Stein and Day, 1972), 207–13.

333 The Triple Crown: Longrigg, 224, 227–8; "Belmont Stakes." *http://en.wikipedia.org/wiki/Belmont_Stakes.*

333 New York racing: Longrigg, 227–8.

334 Arrival of bookmaking in the United States: Longrigg, 229.

334 Bookmaking's deleterious effect on racing: Longrigg, 230.

335 "Men and women, boys and girls . . .": Harry Brolaski, *Easy Money: Being the Experiences of a Reformed Gambler* (Cleveland: Searchlight Press, 1911), 116.

336 Western Union and the race wire: Mark H. Haller, "Bootleggers and American Gambling 1920–1950," in *Gambling in America*, Appendix 1 (Washington, D.C.: U.S. Government Printing Office, 1976), 107.

336–7 Mont Tennes: John Landesco, *Organized Crime in Chicago. Part III of the Illinois Crime Survey, 1929* (Chicago: University of Chicago Press, 1968), 45, 53, 58–70, 80–1; Brolaski, 192.

337   Matt Winn and the pari-mutuel: Arthur Daley, "The Passing of a Legend," *New York Times* (October 19, 1949), 43; Chafetz, 384.

337–8   Daniel O'Leary: J. C. McCormick, "Old Time Pedestrians," *Los Angeles Times* (February 10, 1896), 3.

338   "If I succeed in making San Francisco . . .": "A Cowboy's Tramp," *Los Angeles Times* (September 4, 1888), 5.

338   Baseball, betting, and corruption: Richard O. Davies and Richard G. Abram, *Betting the Line: Sports Wagering in American Life* (Columbus: The Ohio State University Press, 2001), 20–2, 39–40.

339   Arnold Rothstein: Davies and Abram, 23–4;

339   The Black Sox scandal: Davies and Abram, 25–7.

339–40   Betting on football and other sports: Davies and Abram, 47–8.

340   Boxing and betting: John Sugden, *Boxing and Society: An International Analysis* (Manchester: Manchester University Press, 1996), 29–32. See also Elliott J. Gorn, *The Manly Art: Bare-Knuckle Prize-Fighting in America* (Ithaca: Cornell University Press, 1986).

340–1   Gambling syndicates: Haller, 107.

341–2   New York Gambling Commission: "This City's Crying Shame," *New York Times* (March 9, 1900), 1.

342   Chicago gambling syndicate: John Philip Quinn, *Fools of Fortune, or, Gambling and Gamblers* (Chicago: G. L. Howe & Co., 1890), 405.

342   Minneapolis gambling syndicate: Asbury, 270.

342   Creation of the Louisiana Lottery: Chafetz, 297; Quinn (1890), 462.

343   Louisana experiments with legal gaming houses, 1869: Chafetz, 299–300.

343–4   Louisiana Lottery's extent: "Louisiana," *New York Times* (October 21, 1874), 3.

344   Decline and death of the Louisiana Lottery: Chafetz, 306–8; "To Kill the Lottery." *New York Times* (March 3, 1895), 4.

345   Policy shops in New York and Chicago: Asbury, 95–7.

345   Zachariah Simmons: Asbury, 98–101.

346   Albert J. Adams: Asbury, 101–6; "Failure of the New Anti-Policy Law," *New York Times* (June 15, 1902), 28.

Part VII: The Legitimization of American Gambling
Chapter Fifteen: Hard to Resist

351   "Of all the seductive vices extant . . .": John B. Reid and Ronald M. James, eds. *Uncovering Nevada's Past: A Primary Source History of the Silver State* (Reno: University of Nevada Press, 2004), 66.

351 Early Nevada tolerance, prohibition of gambling: Barbara and Myrick Land, *A Short History of Reno* (Reno: University of Nevada Press, 1995), 33; Eric Moody, *The Early Years of Gambling in Nevada, 1931–1945* (Reno: Doctoral dissertation, University of Nevada, 1997), 10–11.

352 1869 legalization of gambling: Moody, 11–2.

352 1871, 1875 amendments to gaming law: Moody, 14–5.

352 1877, 1903, and 1905 amendments to gaming law: Moody, 16–9.

353 1909 prohibition of gambling: Moody, 20–1.

353 Permitted gambling after 1909: Moody, 22–31.

353–4 Boxing in early twentieth-century Nevada: Phillip I. Earl, *This Was Nevada* (Reno: Nevada Historical Society, 1986), 178–9.

354 McKay and Graham: Moody, 180–1.

354 Failure of gambling decriminalization in the 1920s: Moody, 32–4, 51–2.

355 Graham and McKay take advantage of legal gaming: Moody, 174.

356 The game of pan: Murray M. Sheldon, *Pan (Pangingue): Rules of Play and How to Win* (Miami Beach: Pan Book Publishers, 1969), 15–6.

356 Graham and McKay's legal struggles and imprisonment: Moody, 184.

357 The Palace Club: Moody, 186–8.

357 African-American and Asian casino entrepreneurs in 1930s Reno: Moody, 234–7.

357 Bingo (tango): Moody, 188.

358 Keno: Moody, 189–90.

358–9 Harolds club: Barbara and Myrtle Land, *A Short History of Reno* (Reno: University of Nevada Press), 87–91; Moody, 191, 193, 195.

359 Harrah's early history: Land and Land, 94–6; Moody, 215–217; Mando Rueda Oral History Interview.

361 Other Reno casinos: Moody, 197–9, 204–6.

361 Slot routes: Moody, 113–5.

361 Reno redline: Land and Land, 100–2.

361–2 The Cal-Neva: Moody, 272–4.

362 The Commercial Hotel: Moody, 280, 420.

364 Las Vegas gambling hall licenses: Las Vegas City Commission Minutes. 156–7, 162–3, 183.

364 J. Kell Houssels: Moody, 258.

364–5 Women in early Las Vegas gambling: Moody, 105, 126–7, 140–1; Thomas "Taj" Ainlay and Judy Dixon Gabaldon, *Las Vegas: The Fabulous First Century* (Charleston: Arcadia Publishing, 2003), 49–51; Moody, 105, 126–7.

365 Las Vegas keno: Moody, 129–31.

365 African-Americans and early Las Vegas gambling: Moody, 269.

366   Nevada legalizes poolrooms: Moody, 293.

367   Former illegal gambling operators in Las Vegas: Moody, 263–5, 296–9.

Chapter Sixteen: The Salvation of Sin

369–71   Harry Straus and the tote: John C. Schmidt, *Win-Place-Show: A Biography of Harry Straus, The Man Who Gave American the Tote* (Baltimore: The G. W. C. Whiting School of Engineering, The Johns Hopkins University, 1989), 41–50, 95–6.

371   Statistics on racing's resurgence: *The 2004 Original Thoroughbred Times Racing Almanac* (Lexington: Thoroughbred Times Books, 2004), 37–8.

371   For more on Seabiscuit, see Laura Hillenbrand, *Seabiscuit: An American Legend* (New York: Ballantine Books, 2001).

372   *2004 Racing Almanac,* 39–40.

372   Professional sports bookmaking: David G. Schwartz. *Cutting the Wire: Gambling Prohibition and the Internet* (Reno: University of Nevada Press, 2005), 169–75.

373   Charles McNeil: William Barry Furlong, "Of Lines, Point Spreads, and Middles," *New York Times* (January 2, 1977), 142.

373   Bill Hecht and Leo Hirschfeld: Paul Gardner and Allan Gould, "Brain of the Bookies," *Collier's* (October 25, 1947).

373–4   New York Off-Track Betting: Weinstein and Deitch, 95–96; *2004 Racing Almanac,* 40–1.

374   American greyhound racing: *Gambling in America: Final Report of the Commission on the Review of the National Policy on Gambling* (Washington, D.C.: Government Printing Office, 1976), 105–7; William E. McBride, *The Gambling Times Guide to Greyhound Racing* (Secaucus: Lyle Stewart, 1984), 5.

375   Jai Alai: William R. Keevers, *Gambling Times on Jai Alai* (Hollywood: Gambling Times, 1980), 3–9.

375   Success of OTB: Jockey Club Fact Book at *http://home.jockeyclub.com/FACTBOOK/handle.html.*

376   2002 "Volponi" betting scandal: *2004 Racing Almanac,* 42–3.

376–8   Bingo: Roger Snowden, *Gaming Times Guide to Bingo* (Hollywood: Gambling Times, 1986), 11–4.

378–9   Typical church bingo: John C. Devlin, "Housewives' Dreary Chores Bow to Excitement and Prizes of Bingo," *New York Times* (September 10, 1954), 17; *Gambling in America,* 160.

379   Bingo in Moscow: "U.S. Center is Hotbed of 'Beengo,'" *New York Times* (October 10, 1954), 56.

380 Origin and spread of the numbers: *Development of the Law of Gambling* (Washington, D.C.: United States Government Printing Office, 1977), 118, 748–9; Howard McGrath, address at *The Attorney General's Conference on Organized Crime, February 15, 1950.* (Washington, D.C.: Department of Justice, 1950), 6.

381 For a complete analysis of the numbers, see Lawrence J. Kaplan and James M. Maher, "The Economics of the Numbers Game," *The American Journal of Economics and Sociology* (1970) 391–407. Reprinted in Lawrence J. Kaplan and Dennis Kessler, *An Economic Analysis of Crime* (Springfield, Ill.: Charles C. Thomas, Publisher, 1976), 104–23. For an explanation of how numbers bankers determine the winning number, see "Computation of the Winning Number," reprinted in Kaplan and Kessler, 124–125. For a quick description of policy, see Haller, 105.

381 Numbers' profitability: *Gambling in America,* 172–3.

381 Numbers in Harlem: Thomas A. Johnson, "Numbers Called Harlem's Balm," *New York Times* (March 1, 1971), 1.

381 Bolita: "Florida's Jobless turn to Gambling," *New York Times* (August 14, 1932), E8; Harris G. Simms, "Tampa in War on Gambling," *New York Times* (July 24, 1938), 58; Selwyn Raab, "Longtime Numbers King Goes Public to Clear His Name," *New York Times* (July 6, 1997), 13.

382 San Bernardino: Noah Sarlat, ed., *America's Cities of Sin* (New York: Lion Books, 1950), 63–4.

382 Bergen County resorts: Noah Sarlat, ed., *Sintown USA* (New York: Lion Books, 1952), 123–7.

382–3 Atlantic City's illegal gambling: Jonathan Van Meter, *The Last Good Time: Skinny D'Amato, the Notorious 500 Club, and the Rise and Fall of Atlantic City* (New York: Crown Publishers, 2003), 40, 50, 60–1, 109–10.

383 Palm Beach: Chafetz, 409–14.

384 Biloxi: Deanne Nuwer and Greg O'Brien, "Gambling: Mississippi's Oldest Pastime," in Denise Von Hermann, ed., *Resorting to Casinos: How the Mississippi Casino Resort Industry Was Made* (Jackson: University of Mississippi Press, 2005), 14–32.

385 Hot Springs, Arkansas: Hank Messick and Burt Goldblatt, *The Only Game in Town: An Illustrated History of Gambling* (New York: Thomas Y. Crowell Company, 1976), 68, 70.

385 Newport, Kentucky: David Wecker, "Before There Was Vegas, There Was Newport," *Cincinnati Post* (September 9, 2004).

385   "A never-to-be-forgotten chapter . . .": Advertisement, *New York Times* (April 15, 1951), P 4XX.

385   Cuban revolution and the closure of casinos: "Batista and Regime Flee Cuba; Castro Moving to Take Power; Mobs Riot and Loot in Havana," *New York Times* (January 1959), 1; "Havana's Last Casino Closed," *New York Times* (September 30, 1961), 13.

385–6   Agua Caliente (Mexico) casino: Messick and Goldblatt, 115–6.

386   Montreal gambling: Sarlat (1950), 107.

387   Alaska's ice "lottery": "Nenana Ice Classic." Arctic Science Journeys Radio Script. *http://www.uaf.edu/seagrant/NewsMedia/97ASJ/ 04.29.97_IceClassic.html*

387–8   New Hampshire's lottery: Ann E. Weiss, *Lotteries: Who Wins, Who Loses?* (Hillside, New Jersey: Enslow, 1991), 37–40; *Gambling in America*, 145–6.

388   Lottery expansion in the 1970s: David Weinstein and Lillian Deitch, *The Impact of Legalized Gambling: The Socioeconomic Consequences of Lotteries and Off-Track Betting* (New York: Praeger Publishers, 1974), 15–6.

389   Daily lottery games: *Gambling in America*, 147.

388–9   Lottery expansion through 2003: Don Catlin, *The Lottery Book: The Truth Behind the Numbers* (Chicago: Bonus Books, 2003), 19–21.

389   Scratchers (instant lottery tickets): Teresa La Fleur, *La Fleur's 2004 World Lottery Almanac* (Boyds, Maryland: TLF Publications, 2004), 103.

389   Lotto: La Fleur, 139.

389–90   Lottery variations and escalating jackpots: La Fleur, 6.

390   Multistate lotteries: Catlin, 21–3.

390   2002 Big Game Jackpot: Kim Masters Evans, *Gambling: What's at Stake?* (Farmington Hills, Michigan: Gale, 2003), 99.; *http://www.world-bank.org/data/databytopic/GNI.pdf*

390   For more about lottery winners, see H. Roy Kaplan, *Lottery Winners: How They Won and How Winning Changed Their Lives* (New York: Harper and Row), 1978.

Chapter Seventeen: A Place in the Sun

392   Early evolution of casino resorts: David G. Schwartz, *Suburban Xanadu: The Casino Resort on the Las Vegas Strip and Beyond* (New York: Routledge, 2003), particularly Chapter 2.

393   Nevada Biltmore: Moody, 389–90.

394   The Last Frontier: William Moore, *Oral History*. Elizabeth Nelson Patrick, interviewer. (Reno: University of Nevada Oral History Project, 1981), 5, 13.

394–5   Billy Wilkerson and the Flamingo: W. R. Wilkerson III, *The Man Who Invented Las Vegas* (Los Angeles: Ciro's Books, 2000), 98, 104, 110–1, 166–7, 225–6.

396   The Mayfield Road Gang: Wallace Turner, *Gamblers' Money: The New Force in American Life* (Boston: Houghton Mifflin Company, 1965), 288.

399   Commercial gaming overtaking mining as Nevada's leading revenue source: Moody, 459.

399   Tax Commission role in collecting gaming taxes: Moody, 446–8.

400   Nevada's gaming regulatory system: A. L. Higgenbotham, *Legalized Gambling in Nevada: Its History, Economics, and Control* (Carson City: Nevada Gaming Commission, 1971), 11.

401   "Money moves the world . . .": Robert Thomas King, *Fighting Back: A Life in the Struggle for Civil Rights*. From oral history interviews with Dr. James B. McMillan; conducted by Gary E. Elliott; a narrative interpretation by R. T. King. (Reno: University of Nevada Oral History Program, 1977), 98.

402–3   John Scarne's early years: John Scarne, *The Odds Against Me* (New York: Simon and Schuster, 1966), 9.

403   Scarne during World War II: John Desmond, "Help for G.I. Suckers," *New York Times* (October 10, 1943), SM14.

403   Scarne's later years: Joan Cook, "John Scarne, Gambling Expert," *New York Times* (July 9, 1985), B6.

403–4   Nick Dandolos: "Nick the Greek Arrested," *New York Times* (June 2, 1929), 22; Gladwin Hill, "Why They Gamble: A Las Vegas Survey," *New York Times* (August 25, 1957), 60; "Nick the Greek Is Dead on Coast," *New York Times* (December 27, 1966), 35.

405   Edward Thorp and card counting: Edward O. Thorp, *Beat the Dealer: A Winning Strategy for the Game of Twenty-One* (New York: Blaisdell Publishing, 1962), 5–6, 15–7, 78.

406   Ken Uston and team play: Ken Uston with Roger Rapoport, *The Big Player: How a Team of Blackjack Players Made a Million Dollars* (New York: Holt, Rhinehart, and Watson, 1977), 10, 76.

406   The MIT team: Ben Mezrich. *Bringing Down the House: The Inside Story of Six M.I.T. Students Who Took Vegas for Millions* (New York: Free Press, 2002).

407   Jay Sarno and Caesars Palace: Jack Sheehan, *Players: The Men Who Made Las Vegas* (Reno: University of Nevada Press, 1997), 92–5; George Stamos, Jr., "Caesars Palace," *Las Vegas Sun Magazine* (October 14, 1979), 92–6.

408   Tanya the Elephant and Circus Circus employees: Interview with Joyce Marshall.

409   Sarno's personal habits: Sheehan, 97–8.

409   Circus Circus after Sarno, his plans for the Grandissimo: Sheehan, 99–100.

410   Howard Hughes in Las Vegas: Omar V. Garrison, *Howard Hughes in Las Vegas* (New York: Lyle Stuart, 1970), 47–50; "Mark on Nevada by Hughes Staggering," *Las Vegas Review-Journal* (April 6, 1976); Robert Maheu and Richard Hack, *Next to Hughes: Behind the Power and Tragic Downfall of Howard Hughes by his Closest Advisor* (New York: HarperCollins, 1992), 198–9.

410   "A freak, or amusement-park category . . .": Michael Drosnin, *Citizen Hughes,* (New York: Holt, Rinehart, and Winston, 1985), 107.

411–2   Benny Binion: A. D. Hopkins, "Benny Binion: He Who Has the Gold Makes the Rules," in *Players: The Men Who Made Las Vegas* (Reno: University of Nevada Press, 1997), 55–6.

412   William Lee Bergstrom: *Weekly Variety,* February 20, 1985.

412   Binion's legal troubles: Hopkins, 54–60.

412–3   Though in his memoirs Moss claimed the contest took place at the Horseshoe, Binion did not open that casino until 1951. Either the game was at the Westerner, which Binion owned at the time, or Moss misremembered the year.

413   "Mr. Moss, I have to let you go . . .": A. Alvarez, *The Biggest Game in Town* (Boston: Houghton Mifflin, 1983), 17–24.

413   Origins of the World Series of Poker: Crandell Addington, "The History of No-Limit Texas hold 'em," in Doyle Brunson, ed. *Super System 2: A Course in Power Poker* (New York: Cardoza Publishing, 2005), 78–80.

413   Origins of Texas hold 'em: Personal communication with Crandell Addington, April 4, 2006. ·

413   Texas hold 'em: Oswald Jacoby. *Oswald Jacoby on Poker* (Garden City, New York: Dolphin Books, 1981), 73–77; Hopkins, 61–2.

413   Some believe: Edwin Silberstrang, *Playboy's Book of Games* (Chicago: Playboy Press, 1972), 9–82.

415   Steve Wynn and the Golden Nugget: Mark Seal, "Steve Wynn: King of Wow!" in *Players: The Men Who Made Las Vegas* (Reno: University of Nevada Press, 1997), 174–7.

415   Jackie Gaughan: Bill Moody with A. D. Hopkins, "Jackie Gaughan:
       Keeping the Faith on Fremont Street," in *Players: The Men Who Made
       Las Vegas* (Reno: University of Nevada Press, 1997), 123–6, 129–31.

415–6 Sam Boyd and Boyd Gaming: Jack Sheehan, "Sam Boyd's Quiet Legacy,"
       in *Players: The Men Who Made Las Vegas* (Reno: University of Nevada
       Press, 1997), 104–18.

417   Ernest Primm: Land and Land, 113.

417   Del E. Webb and corporate ownership of Nevada casinos: Schwartz
       (2003), 105–6; Lionel Sawyer & Collins, *Nevada Gaming Law* (Las Ve-
       gas: Lionel Sawyer & Collins, 1991), 81–3.

419   Alex Shoofey and the Flamingo: Alex Shoofey, *Oral History Interview*
       (Las Vegas: University of Nevada–Las Vegas Oral History Program,
       2003), 35–8.

419–20 The International: Full-page advertisement. *Las Vegas Now* (July 1970);
       Schwartz (2003), 152.

Part VIII: Gambling's New Prominence
Chapter Eighteen: Runaway American Dream

428   Early casino lobbying efforts in Atlantic City: Ed Davis, *Atlantic
       City Diary: A Century of Memories, 1880–1985* (McKee City, New Jer-
       sey: Atlantic Sunrise Publishing Company, 1980), 113.; Jonathan Van
       Meter, *The Last Good Time: Skinny D'Amato, the Notorious 500 Club, and
       the Rise and Fall of Atlantic City* (New York: Crown Publishers, 2003),
       230–1.

429   Failure of 1974 New Jersey casino referendum: John Alcamo, *Atlantic
       City: Behind the Tables* (Grand Rapids, Michigan: Gollehon, 1991), 12–13.

429   Success of 1976 casino referendum: Alcamo, 17–9.

429   "Keep your filthy hands off Atlantic City . . .": Alcamo, 35.

431   Resorts International opens: Alcamo, 40.

431   The Marlborough Blenheim/Bally's Park Place: David G. Schwartz,
       "Castle in the Sand: The Marlborough-Blenheim and Its Place in Atlantic
       City History, *Casino Connection*, vol. 2, no. 2 (February 2005).

432   New Jersey casino regulations: New Jersey Casino Control Commission,
       1979 Annual Report (Trenton: Casino Control Commission,1979), 8.

432   1984 Atlantic City statistics: New Jersey Casino Control Commission, *1984
       Annual Report* (Trenton: Casino Control Commission, 1984), 17.

433   1924 Bureau of Indian Affairs recognition of tribal gaming: S. Rep No.
       99-493, 3.

434 "It's more than beads . . .": Jennings Parrott, "Bingo Name of the Game in Indian War," *Los Angeles Times* (July 14, 1981), OC2.

434 Yaqui high-stakes bingo: William E. Schmidt, "Bingo Boom Brings Tribes Profit and Conflict," *New York Times* (March 29, 1983), A1.

435 Indian high-stakes bingo: "Cherokee Bingo Session Attracts Thousands," *New York Times* (July 3, 1983), 14; "Big-Stakes Bingo Brings Them into Oklahoma by the Busload," *New York Times* (December 27, 1984), A1.

435 *Cabazon* decision: U.S. Supreme Court, *California v. Cabazon Band of Mission Indians,* 480 U.S. 202 (1987). Accessed online at *http://caselaw.lp.findlaw.com.*

435 Reagan Administration encouragement of Indian gaming: S. Rep No. 99–493, 5.

436 Congressional legislation on Indian gaming: Senate Report 100–446; "Indian Gaming Regulatory Act." Cited in *The Indian Gaming Regulatory Act, Annotated* (Washington, D.C.: Hobbs Straus, Dean, and Wilder), 1989, A-3. Hereafter cited as *IGRA Annotated.*

437 The first Indian casino: Howard Blum, "In Garage Casino, Sky Is a $5 Limit," *New York Times* (February 26, 1984), 24.

437 Mashantucket Pequot struggle for recognition and gaming enterprises: Eisler, 51–60, 106–7; Richard D. Lyons, "Pequots Adding New Venture to Enterprises," *New York Times* (January 26, 1986), CN1; Dirk Johnson, "Tribe's Latest Enterprise: Bingo," *New York Times* (July 12, 1986), 29.

438 The opening of Foxwoods: Mark H. Spevack, "A User's Guide to Foxwoods Casino," *New York Times* (June 21, 1992), CN10.

438 Foxwoods statistics: Peter Passells, "Foxwoods, a Casino Success Story," *New York Times* (August 8, 1994), D1.

438 Spread of Indian gaming: Nina Munk. "Two-Armed Bandits," *Forbes* (May 22, 1995), 151–4.

439 Proposition 5 and California Indians: David J. Valley with Diana Lindsay, *Jackpot Trail: Indian Gaming in Southern California* (San Diego: Sunbelt Publications, 2003), 26–7.

440 Efforts to legalize Iowa riverboats: Bernard Goldstein with William Petre, *Navigating the Century: A Personal Account of Alter Company's First Hundred Years* (Chantilly, Virginia: The History Factory, 1998), 131–5.

441 Riverboat gambling begins in Iowa: Goldstein, 140.

441 Iowa riverboats move to Mississippi: Goldstein, 153–4.

441 Success of riverboat casinos: Ronald Smothers, "With Casino, the Poor See a Change in Luck." *New York Times* (December 22, 1992), A18.

442 "With a live boy or a dead girl.":
http://www.cnn.com/2000/ALLPOLITICS/stories/05/10/edwards5_10.a.tm/; for a book-length treatment of the Louisiana scandals see Tyler Bridges, *Bad Bet on the Bayou: The Rise of Gaming in Louisiana and the Fall of Governor Edwin Edwards* (New York: Farrar, Straus and Giroux, 2001).

442–3 Edwin Edwards convicted of casino corruption: George Loper, "Louisiana Politics: Is Edwin Edwards Running out of Luck?" (January 2000). Accessed online at: *http://www.loper.org/~george/archives/2000/Jan/60.html*

443 Deadwood, South Dakota casinos: Geoffrey Perret, "The Town That Took a Chance," *American Heritage*, vol. 56, no. 2 (May 2005), 54.

Chapter Nineteen: All In

447–8 Hobiki: Tsutomu Hayama, "Pachinko: The Lonely Casino," in Atsushi Ueda, ed., *The Electric Geisha: Exploring Japan's Popular Culture* (Tokyo: Kodansha International, 1994), 41–2.

448 Corinthian game: Hayama, 37; Elizabeth Kiritani, "Pachinko, Japan's National Pastime," in John A Lent, ed., *Asian Popular Culture* (Boulder: Westview Press, 1995), 203.

448 Postwar and current popularity of pachinko: Hayama, 38–9.

448 Professional pachinko players: Kiritani, 206–8.

448–9 Pachinko balls exchanged for cash: Eric Prideaux, "The Trickle-Down Effect: Pachinko Is a National Obsession—but Who's Winning?" *Japan Times* (April 7, 2002).

449 American gaming revenues: *http://www.americangaming.org/Industry/ factsheets/statistics_detail.cfv?id=7*

448–9 Japanese horse racing: "Organization and Operation of Horseracing in Japan," *http://www.jair.jrao.ne.jp/guide/org/main.html*; Captain Japan and Eric Prideaux, "Japan's Horse Racing: Changing with the Times," *http://www.bigempire.com/sake/horse.html*.

449 Bicycle racing: Peter Power, "An Evening at the Keirin, Ikimasu Yo!" *http://www.cyclingnews.com/features/?id=hakodatekeirin*; Japan Keirin Assoiaiton, "Keirin," *http://www.excite.co.jp/world/english/web/?wb_url= http://www.keirin.go.jp/land/foreign_site/f_index.html&wb_lp=JAEN&wb_ dis=2&wb_co=excitejapan*

449 Motorboat racing in Japan: Captain Japan and Eric Prideaux, "Japan's Motorboat Races: Peace Through Propeller." *http://www.bigempire.com/sake/boat.html*.

449–50   Japanese lotteries: Bryan Elwood and Hal Tennant, *The Whole World Lottery Guide,* Second Edition (Toronto: A Million$ Publication, 1981), 177.

450   Other Asian lotteries: Phillip R. Green, *The Whole World Lottery Guide,* Fourth Edition (Toronto: World Media Brokers, 1991), 199, 201; Elwood and Tennant, 170–87.

451   Macau creates casinos in the 1930s: Geoffrey C. Gunn. *Encountering Macau: A Portuguese City-State on the Periphery of China, 1557–1999* (Boulder, Colorado: Westview Press, 1996), 88–9.

451   Laorong Fu: A. Pinho, "Gambling in Macau," in R. D. Cremer, *Macau: City of Commerce and Culture* (Hong Kong: OUEA Press LTD., 1987), 157.

451   Tak Iam Fu: Gunn, 135; Pinho, 135.

452   Career of Stanley Ho: Jason Zhicheng Gao, *An Overview of Macau Gaming Industry* (Lecture presentation. University of Macau, 2004); *Stanley Ho* (Beijing: Xinhua News Agency, 1999), 62, 156–8; Gunn, 124.

451–2   STDM: Pinho, 158.

453   Macau racing: Jonathan Porter, *Macau, the Imaginary City: Culture and Society, 1557 to the Present* (Boulder, Colorado: Westrip Press, 1996), 147; *Macau's Journey.*

453   Prosperity of STDM: Pinho, 162.

453   Widespread business operations of STDM and Stanley Ho: *Macau's Journey*; *Stanley Ho,* 198–199.

456   Cotai Strip: Gilberto Lopes, "Gaming Rouses Macao" (*Macau Magazine,* September 2004).

456   South Korean Casinos: Anthony N. Cabot, William N. Thompson, Andrew Tottenham, and Carl Braunlich, eds., *International Casino Law,* Second Edition (Reno: Institute for the Study of Gambling and Commercial Gaming, 1993), 435.

456   South Korean casino opened to Koreans: "Booming Locals Casino in Korea Selling Stock," *Las Vegas Sun* (October 25, 2001).

456   PAGCOR: Cabot et al., (1993), 529–31.

456–7   North Korean casino: "Odds Against North Korean Casino as China Stops Flow of Dirty Cash," *Casino City Times.* *http://www.casinocitytimes.com/news/article.cfm?contentId=148872*

457   Lim Goh Tong and Genting Highlands: Lim Goh Tong, "My Dream." *http://www.genting.com.my/en/mydream/mydream12.htm*

458   Beirut's casino: Anthony N. Cabot, William N. Thompson, Andrew Tottenham, and Carl Braunlich, eds., *International Casino Law,* Third Edition (Reno: Institute for the Study of Gambling and Commercial Gaming, 1999), 493–4.

458   Egypt's casinos: Cabot (1999), 493.

458   The Jericho casino: Edward B. Miller, "An Oasis or Just a Mirage: The Jericho Casino and the Israeli-Palestinian Peace Process," *Richmond Journal of Global Law and Business*, vol. 2, no.1 (winter/spring 2001), 33–60.

459   Australian lotteries: John O'Hara, *A Mug's Game: A History of Gaming and Betting in Australia* (New South Wales University Press, 1988), 171–5.

459   Australian TABs: O'Hara,194.

459   Australian bingo: O'Hara, 196–8.

460   Pokie machines: O'Hara, 198–200; Terri C. Walker, *The 2005 Casino and Gaming Market Research Handbook* (Atlanta: Terri C. Walker Consulting, 2005), 354–5.

460   Australian casinos: Walker, 352–4.

460   Kerry Packer barred from Las Vegas casinos (allegedly): "For Las Vegas Gamblers, Getting the Heave-Ho," *New York Times* (November 15, 1998), A1.

460–1   New Zealand horse racing: David Grant, *On a Roll: A History of Gaming and Lotteries in New Zealand* (Wellington: Victoria University Press, 1994), 99–100, 124–31, 135.

461   Other New Zealand gambling: Grant, 137–40.

461–2   Canadian gambling: Suzanne Morton, *At Odds: Gambling and Canadians, 1919–1969* (Toronto: University of Toronto Press, 2003), 10–11; Cabot et al., (1999) 170–1.

463   Canadian VLTs: National Council of Welfare, 6.

463   Mexican gambling prohibition: Walker, 399.

463   Brazilian gambling: "The Godfather is Gone," *Brazzil Magazine*. *http://www.brazzil.com/rpdmay97.htm*; Walker, 339.

463–4   Argentine casinos: Cabot et al. (1999), 207, 277–280; Walker 337.

464   Puerto Rican casinos: Clement McQuade, ed., *Gambler's Digest* (Northfield, Illinois: DBI books, 1971), 267.

464–5   South African Gambling: Lotteries and Gambling Board, *Main Report on Gambling in the Republic of South Africa* (Pretoria: Lotteries and Gambling Board, 1995), 29–33.

465   Sol Kerzner and Sun City: Joseph Lelyveld, "Bringing a Bit of Vegas to South Africa's 'Homelands,'" *New York Times* (July 19, 1981), F7; Bill Keller, "Resort (Not Too African) for Rich Tourists," *New York Times* (December 3, 1992), A1.

466 Sun (Kerzner) International: Larry Rohter, "Waterscape in the Bahamas," *New York Times* (May 28, 1995), A1; Seth Lubove, "Atlantis Rising," *Forbes* (November 11, 2004); Cabot et al. (1999), 495–8.

466–7 Postapartheid South African casinos: Cabot et al. (1999), 495–8; Walker, 348.

467–8 European gambling (lotto, racing, and toto): *The Smart Gambler's Guide of Europe* (1988), 19–21, appendix 13; *http://www.intertoto-cup.com/*.

468 Twentieth century European casino resurgence: Clair Price, "A Roulette Battle Resounds in Europe," *New York Times* (March 4, 1934), SM5; *http://www.lucienbarriere.com/localized/en/portail/ casinos/mythes_realites/index.asp?art_id=4121*.

469 Baden-Baden reopens under the Nazis: Klaus Fischer, *Faites Votre Jeu: History of the Casino Baden-Baden* (Baden-Baden: Hans Werner Kelch, 1975), 80–3.

469 Postwar German casinos: Cabot et al. (1993), 287–8.

469–70 Casinos Austria: Cabot et al. (1993), 253–54; Casinos Austria. *Essentials.* *http://www.casinosaustria.com/downloadDocument.aspx?id=131*.

470 Belgian casinos: Cabot et al. (1993), 259–61; Walker, 361–2.

471 British casinos: Cabot et al. (1993), 302–12.

471 Moscow casinos: Peter Finn, "Gambling Proves a Tough Hand to Beat in Russia," *Houston Chronicle* (July 9, 2005).

472 Monte Carlo in recent years: Richard Bos, "Monte Carlo on the Mend," *International Gaming and Wagering Business* (March 1998), 22–8.

472 Italian lotteries: Elwood and Tennant, 124; Seville, 19.

472 French lotteries: Elwood and Tennant, 104–6.

472 Belgian lotteries: "Our Story in Words and Pictures," Loterie Nationale Web site. URL: *http://www.loterie-nationale.be/pages/show.aspx? Culture=en&pageid=lln/histo/histo4&cache=d787505c*

473 The Irish Sweepstakes: Ewen, 346–50; Elwood and Tennant, 120.

473 British lotteries: "The Lottery's Winners and Losers," *BBC News*, (November 3, 2004). Accessed at: *http://news.bbc.co.uk/1/hi/magazine/3975517.stm*.

473–4 Soviet Union lotteries: Green, 181.

Part IX: Into the Twenty-First Century
Chapter Twenty: A Clockwork Volcano

480–1 Bally Manufacturing: Robert N. Geddes, *Slot Machines on Parade* (Long Beach: The Mead Company, 1980), 167, 190–1; Basil Nestor, "The 10 Most Influential People in the History of Slots," *Casino Journal*.

481   Raven Electronics: Richard M. Bueschel, *Lemons, Cherries, and Bell-Fruit-Gum* (Denver: Royal Bell Books, 1995), 280–2.

481–2   Steve Wynn's first plans on the Strip: Robert Metz, "Marketplace," *New York Times* (February 3, 1981), D8.

482   1987 plans for Mirage: "Golden Nugget's Leader Hailed for Sale Move," *New York Times* (January 20, 1987), D2.

482   Success of the Mirage: Mark Seal, "Steve Wynn: King of Wow!" in *Players: The Men Who Made Las Vegas* (Reno: University of Nevada Press, 1997), 170; Anne Raver, "Fooling with Nature," *New York Times* (July 11, 1993), V5.

484   "Granddaddy of all miniature golf castles": Alan Hess, *Viva Las Vegas: After Hours Architecture* (San Francisco: Chronicle Books, 1993), 105–7.

484   Glenn Schaeffer and Mandalay Resort Group: Dave Berns, "The Ringmaster," *Las Vegas Review-Journal* (February 28, 1999).

486   Steve Wynn's sale of Mirage Resorts: David Strow, "Casino Observers Speculate on Wynn's Future," *Las Vegas Sun* (March 7, 2000).

488   High rollers in Vegas: Brett Pulley, "Casinos Paying Top Dollar to Coddle Elite Players, *New York Times* (January 12, 1998), A1.

488   Casino design: Bill Friedman, *Designing Casinos to Dominate the Competition: The Friedman International Standards of Casino Design* (Reno: Institute for the Study of Gambling and Commercial Gaming, 2000), 89, 136, 139–40.

488–9   Early Internet casinos: Joshua Quittner, "Betting on Virtual Vegas," *Time* (June 12, 1995), 63–4.

489   Antiguan sports books: Brett Pulley, "With Technology, Island Bookies Skirt U.S. Law," *New York Times* (January 31, 1998), A1.

489   Early online sports books: Personal interview with Jay Cohen, December 15, 2003. Federal Prison Camp, Nellis, Las Vegas, Nevada.

489   Capital OTB: David Rohde, "Upstate OTB Wants to Put Horse Wagering on Internet," *New York Times* (December 26, 1996), B4; David Kushner, "Racing's Brains: Handling the Bets at Tracks and Elsewhere," *New York Times* (January 28, 1999), G5.

489   Coeur d'Alene online lottery: "Tribe Starts New Business: Gambling Site on Internet," *New York Times* (July 5, 1997), 8; Peter H. Lewis, "On the Net: Lawmakers Gear Up to Try to Control the Surging Online Gaming Industry," *New York Times* (September 2, 1997), D4.

490   World Sports Exchange: Jack Boulware, "Online Pirates of the Caribbean," *SF Weekly* (December 15, 1999).

490   1998 online gaming: Brett Pulley, "With Technology, Island Bookies Skirt U.S. Law," *New York Times* (January 31, 1998), A1.

490   Statistics on number of gaming sites: Sue Schneider. "The Market— An Introduction," in Mark Balestra, ed., *Internet Gambling Report*, Sixth Edition (St. Charles, Missouri: The River City Group, 2003), 56.

491   Australian Internet gaming: Jamie Nettleton, "Australia," in Mark Balestra, ed., *Internet Gambling Report*, Fifth Edition (St. Charles, Missouri: The River City Group, 2002), 431–43, 449.

491   Terrestrial operators go online: "Aspinalls Online to Outsource Casino Operations to Golden Palace," *Rolling Good Times Online* (April 3, 2002) Accessed at: *http://www.rgtonline.com/ Article.cfm?ArticleId=34558&CategoryName=News&SubCategoryName= Featured*; Liz Bentsen, "Station Casinos Shelves Net Gambling Plans," *Las Vegas Sun* (August 26, 2002); Liz Bentsen, "Kerzner Drops Internet Gambling Operation," *Las Vegas Sun* January 3, 2003).

491–2   Philippine online betting: "PAGCOR Okays Philweb's Online Cock-fight Betting System," *The Philippine Star* (March 3, 2005). *http://www.philwebinc.com/template.asp?target=news/2005/P_mar03_ism*

492   "March Madness" charges: "Online Sports Books Charged," *Las Vegas Review-Journal* (March 5, 1998).

492   Antigua vs. United States, WTO case: World Trade Organization, *United States—Measures Affecting the Cross-Border Supply of Gaming and Betting Services: Report of the Panel*. WT/DS285/R10. (November 2004). Accessed at: *http://www.wto.org/english/tratop_e/dispu_e/285r_e.pdf*. Cited hereafter as WTO. Page 5; Liz Benston, "WTO Net Gambling Details Remain Secret," *Las Vegas Sun* (March 25, 2004); WTO, 272.

493   Party Poker: Michael Friedman, "The Poker Party is Just Beginning," *Poker News* (July 15, 2005). *http://www.pokernews.com/news/2005/07/ poker-party-just-beginning.htm*.

PHOTO CREDITS

◆ ◆ ◆

7   Stewart Culin, *Chess and Playing-Cards. Catalog of Games and Implements for Divination Exhibited by the United States National Museum in Connection with the Department of Archaeology and Paleontology of the University of Pennsylvania at the Cotton States and International Exposition, Atlanta, Georgia, 1895.* (Washington, D.C.: U.S. Government Printing Office, 1898), 828.

18   Stewart Culin, *Chess and Playing-Cards. Catalog of Games and Implements for Divination Exhibited by the United States National Museum in Connection with the Department of Archaeology and Paleontology of the University of Pennsylvania at the Cotton States and International Exposition, Atlanta, Georgia,* 1895. (Washington, D.C.: U.S. Government Printing Office, 1898), 761.

39   historicgames.com

43   Mrs. John King Van Rensselaer, *The Devil's Picture Books: A History of Playing Cards* (New York: Dodd, Mead, and Company, 1893), 65.

45   Mrs. John King Van Rensselaer, *The Devil's Picture Books: A History of Playing Cards* (New York: Dodd, Mead, and Company, 1893), 73.

48   Mrs. John King Van Rensselaer, *The Devil's Picture Books: A History of Playing Cards* (New York: Dodd, Mead, and Company, 1893), 81.

59   Mrs. John King Van Rensselaer, *The Devil's Picture Books: A History of Playing Cards* (New York: Dodd, Mead, and Company, 1893), 105.

75   William George Waters. *Jerome Cardan: A Biographical Study* (London: Lawrence & Bullen, 1898).

87   Reproduction in UNLV Special Collections.

113 ch6_01_compleat.tiff
     Reproduced in *Games and Gamesters of the Restoration* (London: George Routledge and Sons, 1930), xx.

132 Oliver Goldsmith, *Beau Nash* (London: Grolier, c. 1900).

147   Library of Congress, Rare Book and Special Collections Division, Conti-
       nental Congress & Constitutional Convention Broadsides Collection,
       Cont Cong no. 16, pt. 3

154   John Nevil Maskelyne, *Sharps and Flats: A Complete Revelation of Cheating
       at Games of Chance and Skill* (New York: Longmans, Green, and Co.,
       1894), 190.

164   Ralph Nevill, *London Clubs* (New York: Frederick A. Stokes Company,
       1911), 228

168   *Whist* "Cavendish." The Whist Table. London, John Hogg, 1895?

172   William B. Boulton, *The Amusements of Old London* (London: John C.
       Nimmo, 1901), xvi.

178   ch08_3_horses.tif
       Ralph Nevill, *The Sport of Kings* (London: Methuen, 1925), 125.

189   Ralph Nevill, *Light Come, Light Go* (London: MacMillan and Company,
       1909), fr.

195   Harvey's Collection, UNLV Special Collections

206   *Monte Carlo: Its Sin and Splendor* (New York: Richard K. Fox, 1893), 93.

220   Photograph by author

223   *Frank Leslie's Illustrated Newspaper,* December 17, 1887. In UNLV Special
       Collections.

225   *Babcock's Rules for Mah-Johngg*

227   Stewart Culin, *Chess and Playing-Cards. Catalog of Games and Implements
       for Divination Exhibited by the United States National Museum in Connec-
       tion with the Department of Archaeology and Paleontology of the University
       of Pennsylvania at the Cotton States and International Exposition, Atlanta,
       Georgia, 1895* (Washington, D.C.: U.S. Government Printing Office,
       1898), 903.

255   George H. Devol, *Forty Years a Gambler on the Mississippi* (Cincinnati:
       Devol and Haines, 1887), 193.

261   *Harper's Weekly* (April 24, 1869), 288. UNLV Special Collections

278   George W. Walling, *Recollections of a New York Chief of Police* (New York:
       Caxton Book Concern, 1887), 376.

290   Evan D. Rangeloff Collection, UNLV Special Collections

303   Harvey's Collection, UNLV Special Collections

309   Harvey's Collection, UNLV Special Collections

332   Mills Automatic Money Makers catalog in Harvey's Collection, UNLV
       Special Collections

335   *Harper's Weekly,* April 2, 1892, in UNLV Special Collections

360   Harrah's Entertainment Collection, UNLV Special Collections

365	Manis Collection, UNLV Special Collections
371	Historic American Buildings Survey (Library of Congress), Survey number HABS KY-210
379	Library of Congress, Prints & Photographs Division, FSA-OWI Collection
392	Manis Collection, UNLV Special Collections
408	Las Vegas News Bureau Collection, UNLV Special Collections
414	Binion's Horseshoe Collection, UNLV Special Collections
430	Source: Resorts International Annual Report 1976, in UNLV Special Collections
444	Harrah's Entertainment Collection, UNLV Special Collections
454	Photograph by author
483	Mirage Promotional and Publicity File, UNLV Special Collections

Following page 250

Frank Leslie's Illustrated Newspaper, Feb. 8, 1873 p. 345 v. 35, no. 906. Western History/Genealogy Department, Denver Public Library, X-33693.

David A. Curtis, *Stand Pat, or Poker Stories from the Mississippi* (Boston: L.C. Page and Company), 1906.

Harper's Weekly, July 15, 1865, in UNLV Special Collections

Harper's Weekly, February 23, 1867, in UNLV Special Collections

Monte Carlo: Its Sin and Splendor (New York: Richard K. Fox), 1893.

Binion's Horseshoe Collection, UNLV Special Collections

Sands Collection, UNLV Special Collections

Harrah's Collection, UNLV Special Collections

Harrah's Collection, UNLV Special Collections

Las Vegas News Bureau Collection, UNLV Special Collections

Sands Hotel Collection, UNLV Special Collections

Dunes Hotel Collection, UNLV Special Collections

Dunes Hotel Collection, UNLV Special Collections

Photograph by author

Nevada State Museum and Historical Society

New Jersey Casino Control Commission Annual Report, 1986, in UNLV Special Collections

MGM Mirage Collection, UNLV Special Collections

Wynn Las Vegas Promotional and Publicity File, UNLV Special Collections

INDEX

◆ ◆ ◆

Note: Page numbers in *italics* refer to illustrations.